W9-ADA-552

# COMMUNITY CHEST

## A Case Study in Philanthropy

JOHN R. SEELEY

BUFORD H. JUNKER

R. WALLACE JONES, JR.

AND

N. C. JENKINS    M. T. HAUGH    I. MILLER

OF

## Community Surveys, Inc., Indianapolis

UNIVERSITY OF TORONTO PRESS

1957

LIBRARY
College of St. Francis
JOLIET, ILLINOIS

Copyright, 1957, by
University of Toronto Press
under the Canadian Copyright Act, 1921,
including all Berne Convention countries
Printed in Canada

1989

University of St. Francis
GEN 361.76 S450

Community Chest;

3 0301 00067852 0

# COMMUNITY CHEST

## A Case Study in Philanthropy

"I deem it the duty of every man to devote a certain portion of his income for charitable purposes; and that it is his further duty to see it so applied as to do the most good."

Thomas Jefferson

361.76
S450

# Foreword

VOLUNTARY CONTRIBUTIONS by private citizens and corporations in amounts ranging from a few coins to millions of dollars are a major factor in the maintenance of the American way of life. It is difficult even to imagine the adverse changes that would come about if this source of support for the work of religious bodies, health and welfare agencies, and educational and research institutions were to be materially reduced. Fortunately, there seems to be no likelihood that the flow of philanthropic dollars will be diminished in the foreseeable future, since giving for the benefit of others, to use Frederick Keppel's felicitous phrase, is an integral part of the American way of life.

The word "giving," however, tends to convey a one-sided impression of what actually takes place when a contribution is made for a philanthropic purpose. The contributor in fact always buys something with his gift, not for himself in any immediate material sense, but some tangible goods or service for someone else. Acceptance of a philanthropic dollar promises something of value in exchange. Emphasis on the buying and selling aspects of philanthropy is not intended as a mere play on words. Its purpose is to focus attention on the problem that faces potential voluntary contributors in deciding between the multitude of philanthropic opportunities. There is a responsibility on the contributor to have a reasonable basis for his decisions as well as on the recipient to live up to the promise of his wares. Social benefit from philanthropic giving depends on the understanding and acceptance of the nature of this relationship.

Philanthropy can take credit without argument for benefits to mankind beyond enumeration, and holds unquestioned promise for the future. Nevertheless, there are handicaps limiting its effectiveness in the United States which are unusual, in that they are without close parallel in other aspects of American life. One of these is the widespread traditional feeling, if not conviction, that benevolent intentions are not subject to public question. Good deeds, it is held by many, acquire additional merit if done in secret, and are best if they come from the heart. The role of rational judgment based on knowledge is minimized in esteem for the donor. What a man does with his own money is generally regarded as his own business as long as it is not clearly contrary to the prevailing concept of the public

133,320

interest. The philanthropist is praised for his intent, and need not be concerned about the possibility of criticism should his expenditures fall short of their purpose. Even the recipient agency, because of benevolent intent, is judged in its performance by exceptionally lenient standards more relevant to purpose than to achievement.

The lack of an adequate body of organized knowledge about past philanthropic experience and current activities is also a major handicap in the development of improved philanthropic practice. Much has been written about the substantive fields in which advances have been appreciably dependent on philanthropy, but the subject of philanthropy as such has received comparatively little attention except in books and brochures intended to aid in fund-raising or in uncritical and usually laudatory expositions. The small number of objective studies of voluntary giving is of course in large measure a consequence of the uncritical spirit with which good works are regarded in the United States. There is some indication, however, of a still slight but growing concern about the facts and role of philanthropy in our society.

This growing concern can be attributed to a variety of factors, including the recent increase in the number of private foundations and the value of their holdings, the rapid development of corporation foundations, the multiplicity of fund-raising campaigns with their mass-appeal marketing techniques, the two congressional investigations of foundations within the past decade, and the considerable publicity which has been given charity rackets. Whatever the reasons, there is no question that the use to which philanthropic money is put is less and less regarded as a private matter between donor and recipient. The principle of public accountability in the raising and expenditure of philanthropic funds may no longer be ignored.

The generous tax exemptions given both to philanthropists and to the recipients of their benefactions are convincing evidence of the high regard on the part of the public for the American pattern of voluntary support of needed work in social welfare, health, education, religion, and scientific research. This same tax exemption, federal, state, and local, is by itself sufficient justification for requiring some degree of reporting by those who benefit thereby. It may be noted in passing, however, that legislated duty to account for tax-exempt contributions and expenditures does not imply any right of legislative control of lawful purposes and programs.

Accountability for philanthropic activities is not just a matter of tax exemption. The privilege of raising and using private funds for public benefit presumes a privilege on the part of the public to know how they are being used. Furthermore, it is important that such knowledge be available to the public for guidance and encouragement in further giving. Operating agencies and their professional personnel also need to know as much as possible about philanthropic experience beyond their own immediate view for guidance in their activities and aid in securing funds to accomplish their purpose. Possible short-run gains from a policy of philanthropic secrecy are without question far outweighed by the advantages of pooled knowledge.

The book for which this foreword is written is a contribution to the pool of philanthropic knowledge and deserves special recognition because it is a report of a study of mass fundraising and giving without precedent in design, scope, and detail. Its scope is exceptionally broad inasmuch as the authors were forced to reach out for relevant material which in practically any other field would have been available in the reports of previous studies, to which the reader could be referred. The historical background in the United States as a whole, in the state of Indiana, and in the city of Indianapolis had to be reviewed to provide a setting for the analysis of current giving. The record of mass fundraising in other cities as well required investigation for comparative purposes. A variety of possible financial and social standards by which to judge the record of voluntary contributions in Indianapolis and to aid the setting of goals in the future required review and evaluation. The assembling and analysis of such ancillary material was a large task in itself; the gathering, ordering, and interpretation of the details of the Indianapolis experience was a work of staggering proportions.

Let us consider just a few of the questions on which data were required. How does one estimate the need for philanthropic dollars in a given community? What may one reasonably expect in contributions from business and industrial firms, from the wealthier citizens, from members of the various professions, from executives, and other salaried workers or hourly wage-earners? What effect does a federated campaign have on the fundraising success of agencies which conduct independent campaigns? What are the relative merits of the multitude of fundraising techniques and gadgets commonly in use? What do we know about fundraising organization and campaigns that may be helpful in guarding the interests of both the ultimate recipients of assistance and the general public, including the donors? In short, what are the elements crucial to the success or failure in financing the voluntary agencies of a community, not merely in terms of dollars but with full regard for the needs and potentialities of all the citizenry and the community as a whole?

The reader who expects definitive answers to such questions will be disappointed. The answers must of course be subjective and in terms of alternative costs and gains balanced on the scales of subjective values and goals. He will, however, find in this book an extraordinary amount of material, both factual and interpretive, which should be helpful in reaching informed judgments on the perplexing problems of community fundraising. The study it reports demonstrates the urgent need for much more research on the intricate problems of philanthropy which require resolution in the transition from inadequately informed "giving" to rational collection and expenditure of voluntary contributions for the benefit of others.

DONALD YOUNG
*Russell Sage Foundation*

# Preface

THIS IS a study of giving, perhaps the most characteristically North American gesture. A segment of giving, it is true, in one section of America, focused on one city, and indeed one particular institution, at one particular time: the Community Chest of Indianapolis in the early 1950's. Limited as such a study must be, the hope precedes and the reality, with fortune, follows that the universal is somehow caught up and illumined in the particular. The importance of the topic, its relative neglect as a subject of scientific study, and the current uneasiness and struggles as to how giving is to be organized, seemed to give the matter peculiar timeliness.

There has been much study of "getting"—in one sense, the whole of Economics is such a study—but of giving, very little. And yet, for many—the true philanthropists—giving is very nearly the object of getting. Like mercy, doubtless, "it blesseth him that gives and him that takes"—but only under the right circumstances. Hence, giving—particularly sensible giving—is important, and the study of it urgent, since sense in giving does not always come by the light of nature. Under the wrong circumstances, there can be but "suckers" on one side and "crooks" on the other. Americans, generally, seem to wish to avoid becoming the one as urgently as they wish to suppress the other. We have studied neither.

What follows represents a serious, indeed a critical, look. We hope it is only the first of many like it. For what it is worth, as a beginning, we dedicate it to generous givers, ardent seekers, the intended beneficiaries of both—and to students of all three.

THE AUTHORS

# Contents

# I. INTRODUCTION

# 1. The Study

WELL-WORN CUSTOM has it, for good reason, that a study such as this should begin with an account of its own nature, object, scope, and method. Since a study changes and develops also as it proceeds, and since some of the changes in it reveal obliquely something about its subject-matter, the history of the study should also be of interest. Finally, it is usual to acknowledge formally the major debts which the study has accumulated as it has gone along. These tasks must be briefly performed in this chapter.

Before the history of the study can be told perhaps a word should be said of the organization making the study: Community Surveys, Inc. of Indianapolis. Community Surveys was born as an idea about 1952 and came into effective operation in 1954, as an independent, non-profit, local organization to carry out such research in the fields of Health, Education, Recreation, and Welfare as its Board of Directors might deem wise. The need for such an organization was locally felt to arise from the difficulty many laymen experienced in getting facts in these fields, presented fully and without systematic bias, or at least authenticated by an organization essentially neutral with regard to the actual or latent disputes and differences of opinion which intermittently or continuously rive any local "welfare community." In its first three years of active operation, Community Surveys was to do a number of minor studies, and one other major one (*Redevelopment: Some Human Gains and Losses*) besides the study here under report.

## HISTORY

In its narrowest definition, this study is a report upon the Community Chest in Indianapolis. The "presenting problem" was that the Community Chest had for a long time been "failing." This "failure" was almost universally defined as "failure to meet its goal," i.e., inability in each of many campaigns to produce the sum of money which the Chest itself had named as its objective.[1] This definition of the problem took the reasonableness of the goal for granted and inquired only as to the reasons for failure to achieve it, but many people—and many of these the same people—had doubts as to the reasonableness of the goals set. Most people saw the locus of failure in the fundraising process; some saw it in the goal-setting process;

and a few felt it lay in both. Yet all felt that the *fact* of failure was unquestionable; and this view of the situation seemed common both to the concerned and worried laymen and to the concerned and frustrated staff.

Initial interviewing of staff and prominent local laymen revealed early that many of these thought that a brief study would serve to locate the "reason for the failure" and to identify rapidly the indicated remedy. Most of these interviewees had a single-factor explanation which they expected the research could "easily show" to be the true underlying difficulty. The only hindrance was that these single-factor explanations—usually preceded by "Now, you know the *real trouble* over there is . . ."—ran in the first few weeks to as many as thirteen major hypotheses, most of them mutually incompatible. The "real trouble" was thought to lie variously with the public-relations program, the publicity materials, the underlying philosophy of the paid staff generally, the character of this or that staff member or one of his named acts, too much or too little "hoop-la," the presence or absence of this or that campaign gimmick, the "rotation off the Board" of Directors of the Chest of the town's leading citizens, the premature withdrawal of those same citizens because they were "old and tired before their time," the nature of the social participation of the manager ("Not seen often enough in the right places with the right people"), the seizure of power by junior leaders ("They've got a lot of corporals over there trying to do the generals' job"), and so on to "There's nothing *seriously* wrong, you know."

On both the lay and professional sides the belief or hope existed that a brief study—six weeks to three months—would suffice to show either that the trouble was just what the layman interviewee said it was, or that "essentially we're on the right track," as one senior staff member deeply believed. On both sides were those who believed that the difficulty, if any, could be located and the remedy applied in time for the next campaign, i.e., that a research staff could be built, the research done, recommendations drawn, and action thereupon taken in a six-month period. One professional believed that a six-week observation period by one man would be sufficient to "give us a clean bill of health," and that a further six weeks to report so (with the aid of a part-time secretary) would be a generous allowance.

Fortunately, not all professionals or laymen thought so; nor did many of those who thought so initially prove inflexible when confronted with some of the difficulties.[2] In fact, greatly to the credit of all parties concerned, it was possible to move from a conception of research essentially superficial, technically naïve, and often in purpose investigatory or punitive on one side and defensive on the other, to an attitude of honest inquiry with some intellectual curiosity and some enjoyment of the process, in addition to the original problem-solving concern.[3]

For this reason, within a few months of the initiation of the project we had agreement from the Board of Community Surveys, from our financial sponsors, and from the Chest staff and Board on a study-plan based upon more adequate standards of attention to fact, absence of bias, and fitness of methods of inquiry and reporting. Under this agreement, the eye had been lifted from preoccupation with the Chest problem as a matter of looking for obvious petty defects, to an examination of the whole "philanthropic" activity in Indianapolis (as exemplified in selected charities) in the context of philanthropic behavior elsewhere and of other behavior there.

## NATURE

To put the operation of the Chest into some meaningful context requires, then, comparison with other philanthropic activities in Indianapolis and elsewhere; so that, on a somewhat wider definition, this is a study of, or at least an exploration into, philanthropy in North America.

The word "philanthropy" because of its root-meaning (the love of man) may be somewhat misleading. We did not wholly choose our focus. We did not, for instance, study motives—such as love—which lead to "gifts." What we were actually *given* as an object of study was a set of organizations, all of which assume that, for their purposes, one cannot wait for gifts to be given, particularly spontaneous or impulse gifts, based upon personal motives. The professionals and laymen in each of these organizations are very much aware of the necessity to organize a vast variety of human motives (from love, perhaps, through cupidity, to fear) into behavior that issues not so much in a *gift*—in any psychologically meaningful sense—as in a *yielding up* of a sum demanded.[4]

If we are, however, to retain part of the meaning of the word "gift"—i.e., the notion that there is some discretion in yielding to demand—without carrying along the erroneous notion of any great freedom or spontaneity, we shall have to say that what we have studied is *the organization of gift-yielding* (from the giver's side) *or gift-extraction* (from the fundraiser's side) rather than a system merely of giving or receiving, as such.

For obvious reasons, then, it has seemed desirable to study the social organization for this purpose, its stated or inferred logic, and its public and visible consequences—all of which would tend to be common to most such mass fundraising—rather than to study motives for giving, which are relatively private and difficult of access, and which patently occupy a vast spectrum from the meanest to the noblest. Motive is now, in any case, treated as largely irrelevant by the fundraisers and has little to do with the setting of fundraising policy.[5]

## OBJECTS

Broadly speaking, the study had two major objects, each represented dominantly by the two major parties thereto. The parties from the local community—donors, Community Surveys' Board of Directors, the Chest

Board and staff—had, naturally enough, as their primary interest the solution of a local problem. The parties from outside Indianapolis—the researchers themselves and their colleagues, as well as social workers and fundraisers elsewhere—had, equally naturally, as a paramount interest some addition to general knowledge that would, hopefully, also be useful elsewhere— useful for both social theory and philanthropic practice. Neither set of parties underestimated the importance of the other's concern, and the resultant agreed program was intended to do the study in such a way as to help with the local problem while, as far as possible, making a contribution to the general one. Actually, these objectives were not in conflict: it is doubtful if the study would have been of much local help if we had not examined local problems in a general perspective first; and it is even more dubious whether any significant general statements could have been made if we had not first been deeply caught up in a local problem.

These twin objects—the solution of a problem and the addition to knowledge—had, moreover, themselves, twin children or sub-objectives. The community problem turned out to be partly a problem in self-evaluation— "How does Indianapolis rate [as a Chest city]?"—and partly a problem in spelling out possible lines of action—"What can be done to 'improve' things?" The general problem similarly turned out to be partly a problem in social-work practice—"How do Chests operate?"—and partly a problem in sociology —"How do people in a modern United States city organize their 'voluntary' gift-giving?"

## SCOPE

The objects of the study in one sense already define its scope, but that scope had again to be limited by practical considerations.

We would certainly have liked to study in some detail all United States cities in all respects that might have any bearing on philanthropy, in order to answer the question "How does Indianapolis rate?" Within Indianapolis, we would have wished to study all important aspects of at least all major agencies receiving voluntary gifts, in order to answer the question "How does the Indianapolis Chest rate in relation to other agencies benefiting similarly from voluntary gifts?"

Under the best of circumstances, such an undertaking would have been too vast. But upon this study, more than most with which the authors were familiar, fell unusually onerous burdens. In addition to the usual restrictions inherent in time and money, we found as we embarked upon the study that the literature was scant, the believed-in theories mostly vague and often wrong, and the data, both local and national, by which any theory might be tested, in an almost incredible state of defect, disarray, or error. Sometimes lack of curiosity, often want of funds or know-how, most frequently a view of data as only counters in an argument (usually for greater effort or more money) confronted us with a morass at virtually every point at which a firm beginning point of fact from which to branch out in exploration was sought. Thus despite the generosity of our sponsors and supporters, necessity was forced to curtail ambition.

It speedily became evident that it would be impossible to bring so disorderly a domain under orderly survey in any short interval. We would have to count ourselves lucky if we were able to establish a few bench-- marks and trace a few paths with sufficient force and clarity that they might serve for our successors as the beginning-points for what will some day, we hope, be an ordered system of sound knowledge and apt practice.[6] This, we hope, is what we have done.

Accordingly, the scope of the study had to be somewhat restricted, primarily to a limited number of cities (the forty-one most nearly relevant[7]), to a limited number of Indianapolis beneficiaries (the Indianapolis Community Chest, Inc.; the Indianapolis Chapter, American Red Cross—a national corporation; and the Indianapolis Hospital Development Association, Inc.), and to certain limited aspects of each. In the upshot, as the present volume will show, we concentrated[8] on selected problems of *mass, operational, periodic, secular* fundraising (to be referred to as MOPS fundraising) as exemplified in the Chest and Red Cross and contrasted[9] with those of the Hospital Association.

## METHODS

The methods of the study were essentially those of the social anthropologist (or sociologist), those of the economic analyst, and those of the observing citizen or participant-observer.

A staff of nine people[10]—some new to the community, some long-time inhabitants—lived in the city for approximately three years, followed events, read its papers, noted its activities (especially those of its prominent citizens), its preoccupations, its expressed anxieties and manifest prides. All this while inevitably, informally, participating in the life of the city like other citizens—but continuously with a special eye to what was or might be relevant to any aspect of the study.

Similarly and simultaneously we worked in—virtually dwelt in—another "community." Our offices were located in a new building,[11] the headquarters of some thirty social agencies, including two of the organizations (the Chest and the Hospital Association) under study. Here for three years we shared washrooms, meal-tables, coffee-hours, chit-chat, ideas, and discussion with the executive personnel, the staffs, and, frequently, the visiting laymen. Such laymen form the entourage of the agency, furnish whatever rule or government it has, and manifest the ideology which the agency stands for or "educates" about or embodies in its acts.

Such long exposure (sometimes deepened by extramural activities as well) is in a sense analogical to that of an anthropologist living for some time with "his" tribe or primitive community. Whether we were defined as potential allies to be enlisted, or curious people (in both senses of that term) we were made party to a continuous outpouring of "explanation" or "information," anecdote, joke, gesture, and behavior.

In addition to all this, we had ourselves (Community Surveys, Inc.) the experience of being (or being defined as) "an agency." The goal of Community Surveys was, of course, unlike that of any agency, and its staff unlike in background, goal, and orientation; but its structure was similar, and some of its problems, the same. At the very least, this aspect of our situation sensitized us in observation and focused some of our questions, and permitted, sometimes, introspection to supply leads for further inquiry.

We read with some care what little literature of any utility exists in the field, and we interviewed informally such of the national figures within it as opportunity gave us access to.

All the foregoing, somewhat "informal" knowledge, exchanged among ourselves, compared, recorded, sorted, and analysed, is part of the background for the study, as is also such literature as we were able to compass in our search for some understanding or appreciation of the "Hoosier" cult, culture, and character. In most of this participant-observation the emphasis was more on participation, and the resulting knowledge is of the nature of deep "acquaintance with" rather than precise "knowledge about."

Beyond this more informal activity was one more formal, in which the emphasis fell on observation and the element of participation was minimized.[12] Members of the staff attended, noted, and reported at length upon literally hundreds of campaign events, innumerable meetings of the Chest Board of Directors, the Executive Committee of that Board, and the Budget Committees, and a vast variety of other meetings of other social agencies. Extended formal reports of these activities, examined and re-examined, analysed, re-analysed and cross-compared, furnish one body of data upon which is based what follows in this report.

Because of practical limitations—largely imposed by the necessity of hunting up "unavailable" data, and cleaning up what was available—we had to forego very frequently the advantages of interviewing laymen[13] systematically and at length. Because of unforeseen opportunity—in so far as people came to us in greater numbers than we had any right to expect to tell us of experiences and to give us information which we would otherwise have had to get by long, probing interviews—we were driven to abandon such interviewing and to conclude finally that the loss in breadth was compensated for very nearly by gain in depth. Any weakness arising therefrom, moreover, was very largely offset by what we gained from detailed observation of behavior in campaign and committee, and by less formal (frequently telephonic) interviewing of key figures subsequent to critical events.

More formal, again, than any of these activities, and yielding a different and, we hope, complementary kind of knowledge are the statistical analyses of actual results in money gifts. These analyses were embodied in some hundred or more sub-studies,[14] which furnish foundations for several of the chapters to follow (in particular chapters 6, 8, 9).

Thus, in an adaptation of means to circumstances, it might be said that the study employed methods from the most formal statistical analysis to the most subjective, introspective, or empathetic inquiries—to test hypotheses or to seek clues, respectively, as to the nature of what was going on before us in the strange new world of philanthropy.

## ACKNOWLEDGMENTS

We are indebted to many people in many ways. There remains now the pleasure of thanking such of them as space and discretion will permit.

Among those to whom our thanks are most chiefly due are members of the Indianapolis community, members of both the fundraising and social-work organizations we studied and those we didn't, our scientific colleagues, and other persons and organizations.[15]

Within the community we are indebted severally: to our own Board of Directors[16] (and membership) for direction, advice, and social and moral support; to our sources of financial support,[17] particularly the Lilly Endowment, Inc., for money and freedom to use it without undue restriction; and to the Bureau of Governmental Research of the Indianapolis Chamber of Commerce[18] who helped us with advice when apt, and information when they had it.

Our thanks in very great measure must go to the Boards of Directors, the entire staffs, and particularly the chief executive officers of the three principal organizations we studied: the Chest,[19] the Hospital Association,[20] the Red Cross.[21] We are perhaps twice indebted to the Board of the Chest because, after the study was defined and initiated, it gave Community Surveys, Inc. a string-free gift of $12,000 as a token of interest in the study; but we are also twice indebted to the other two Boards because they permitted their organizations to be studied with very much less prospect of direct benefit than had the Chest.

From friends in the field of social work and from colleagues in universities we received generous aid of many kinds. For sociological and anthropological advice, we had direct access, among others, to Professors E. C. Hughes and David Riesman of the University of Chicago; we also had help from Dr. David L. Sills of the Bureau of Applied Social Research of Columbia University, and Mr. B. R. Blishen, Chief of Institutions Section, Bureau of Statistics, Government of Canada. Aid in thinking about social work came largely from Professor C. E. Hendry, Director, School of Social Work of the University of Toronto, and Professor Murray G. Ross of the same school, now Executive Assistant to the University's President. Generous mathematical aid was freely made available by Professors H. S. M. Coxeter of the University of Toronto, Stuart C. Dodd of the University of Washington, Herbert A. Simon of the Carnegie Institute of Technology, and members of the Statistical Laboratory of Purdue University.

We are also happy to have had help and advice from the Community Chests and Councils of America (now United Community Funds and Councils of America, Inc.), particularly from Mr. Kenneth Wood and Mrs. Esther M. Moore of the Department of Research and Statistics; from the Canadian Welfare Council and Dr. R. E. G. Davis, its Executive Director; from the American City Bureau, particularly from Messrs. James E. Almond, Bart Brammer, F. Glenn Wood, Maynard Hammond and H. Theodore Foley; from the National Social Welfare Assembly and Mr. George W. Rabinoff, its Assistant Director; and from Community Chests and Community Chest managers and staffs, too numerous to mention. All of these are responsible for any success the report may have; none is responsible for its undoubted shortcomings.

Finally, we owe perhaps most to those who are here anonymous: our interviewees and informants in the community where the study was done—people who had little directly to gain and much in time and comfort to sacrifice in submitting themselves to our observations and inquiries. On their own initiative, or upon our solicitation, they gave freely and generously of both their time and their capacity for difficult, penetrating, and honest analysis. Without them the study could not have been done, and the sole return we may make for their aid is this record of our enduring gratitude.

# II. THE CONTEXT

# 2. Philanthropy in North America

THE HISTORY OF PHILANTHROPY in America—especially in its contemporary phase—has only recently drawn the attention of social scientists and other scholars. To take a single topic, one pioneer, studying the work of the Foundations, though he began his book, published as late as 1938, by noting that "The Philanthropic foundation is a social institution important enough to be ranked with the school, the press, and the church," could also note that, as of 1930, "there was not available a single book on any phase of the work of philanthropic foundations."[1] Still applicable today is a comment made in 1897: "I have learned that philanthropy is still one of those disorganized branches of human knowledge in which he who takes anything for granted is lost."[2]

Since the present study is devoted chiefly to that phase of contemporary philanthropy in America which is exemplified by Community Chests and United Funds, the brief history which follows is intended only to sketch an appropriate background for it. The true background for the history of philanthropy is, of course, the history of America, and we have attempted here to interleave the one with the other.

Philanthropy in America has flourished in a political system favorable to its growth. In two centuries this country has grown from a number of small colonies of European countries to a mature nation which has experienced wars, depressions, vast shifts in population, technological development, and economic changes unmatched in world history. A brief glance at the history of the past two hundred years gives some idea of the reason for the amazing growth and for the changes of philosophy in regard to philanthropy and social welfare.

## BEGINNINGS

*Colonial America had a long time-span: the period from the founding of Jamestown in 1607 to the Declaration of Independence in 1776 encompasses as many years as the period from the Declaration to the end of World War II in 1945. France, Holland, Spain left their marks on the colonies, but it was Britain that played the predominant role. Her influence continued in the use of the English language and of English ideas on government and politics, on religion and morality, on literature and art, on business and education.*

The early history of American philanthropy is, for obvious reasons, especially meager. Busy pioneers kept few records of the significant events in that field.

Colonial America, and the new state governments, adopted the principles of the English Poor Laws, including the use of tax funds for the relief of the poor. Private health and welfare activities were unorganized. Neighborly help was usually available in time of need, and various private philanthropies of a more formal nature sprang up later to meet what were thought to be the needs of the day as they were recognized. The churches and church societies ministered largely to their own. Nationality groups formed benevolent organizations for their people. Among the earliest of these was the Scots Charitable Society, organized in Boston in 1657,[3] a half-century after Jamestown was founded; similar in aim were the St. Andrews Society (1756) for the English, and the German Society (1784).

## DEMOCRACY DEVELOPS

*The leaders entrusted with the working of the new Constitution were exceptionally competent men and set precedents of far-reaching consequence. Two parties vied for control of the government: the Federalists, spokesmen of wealth and privilege, who wanted centralization of power in the hands of the national government, and the Republicans, (known today as Democrats) who advocated "the welfare of the common man" and "the less government the better." When the Republicans, with Jefferson as their presidential candidate, won the election of 1800, control was taken from the Federalists and the process of liberalizing the Constitution began; this process has continued, with only occasional reverses, ever since. The election of 1800 might be said to symbolize the rise of the common man to a much higher level in thought, culture, and self-expression.*

*The War of 1812 much affected American thinking, creating a wave of national fervor. Legislation exhibited a strongly nationalistic tinge, the Supreme Court exalted the nation above the individual state, the necessary increase in manufacturing freed the country from great dependence on Europe. The war introduced an era of party evolution, developing democracy, cultural growth, major changes in transportation, humanitarian reform. The industrial revolution forced recognition of labor problems. A group of reformers appeared who overhauled the nation's educational system; demanded equal rights for women; sponsored movements for temperance, prison reform, and peace; and, most significant of all, embarked upon an abolitionist crusade.*

As the country grew and the population multiplied, local governments were forced to increase their previously meager welfare efforts. Money and voluntary time for charitable purposes were made available, generally by religious groups. When Thomas Jefferson proclaimed it to be "the duty of every man to devote a certain portion of his income for charitable purposes, and . . . his further duty to see it so applied as to do the most good," he was stating a philosophy held by most Americans of his time.

Dissatisfaction with the duplication of voluntary effort, in many instances, and the failure of church-centered groups to meet needs, in many more,

stimulated the organization of secular voluntary agencies. This movement is
now about a century old. "An excellent example of the new type of agency
was the New York Association for the Improvement of the Conditions of
the Poor. It was organized in 1843 and immediately became a very useful
organization. It endeavored not only to relieve poverty but to prevent
dependency as well."[4] Soon, similar non-sectarian associations in other cities
made strides in assisting the needy.

An interesting sign of the times was the gift of James Smithson, a British
chemist, who, in 1829, bequeathed about $500,000 to the United States to
found "an Establishment for the increase and diffusion of knowledge among
men." Congress debated from 1835 to 1846 on what to do with the money—
and finally decided to establish the Smithsonian Institution.[5]

## SECTIONAL CONTROVERSY—ITS AFTERMATH

*The Civil War, the worst conflict the United States had yet known, settled the
question of slavery, but it also had other important economic results. It accelerated
the changes taking place in the manufacturing industries. It marked the emergence
of the northeast as the major site of the industries of the nation, and as the leader
among the sections of the country. Business on a local scale now began to give
way to business on a national scale; big business began to force little business
out. The new business world operated at first without much restraint from government, but inevitably government action became necessary: the Granger Laws,
the Interstate Commerce Act, and state and national antitrust legislation. Even
so, the leadership of business in the United States was not seriously threatened
during the nineteenth century. In the 1870's and the 1880's, however, the cause
of union labor was advanced. This was also a period of great immigration.*

*The country was just recovering from the effects of the Civil War when it was
greatly shaken by the depression that began in 1873 and lasted until almost 1880.
Social problems also came to light through the effort to right the evils of Recon-
struction and to check fraud in government and business; the pre-war interest in
humanitarian reform was revived.*

*The years from 1850 to 1900 marked the great shift in the laboring population
from rural to urban occupations, with the consequent phenomenal growth of
cities. This rapid transfer of people from an older way of life to a new one caused
problems in social adjustment of immense range and complexity. The attempts
to solve these problems, through the advance of education and the application
of scientific methods, formed the background for the development of many
present-day social welfare services and philanthropies.*

In these years of conflict and change, specialized voluntary associations
were being formed in different parts of the country. An organized service,
the Travelers Aid, was instituted in 1851 when Judge Bryan Mullanphy,
then Mayor of St. Louis, left a large part of his fortune for the relief of
stranded persons who were arriving in St. Louis in covered wagons and
river packets.[6] In 1853, Charles Loring Brace founded the Children's Aid
Society of New York City, a pioneer organization in child welfare. The International Red Cross had been founded in 1864 in Switzerland, and Clara
Barton succeeded in 1881 in forming the American Red Cross.[7] The Society

for the Prevention of Cruelty to Children began its work in 1874 in New York City.

During the last three decades of the nineteenth century the secular private welfare agencies began to avoid "direct relief" cases, hopeless cases, and those requiring permanent institutional care; these they left for government agencies. The private agencies began rather to specialize in services for families and children; professionally trained personnel were preferred for the charge of casework.

With all this activity, numerous voluntary associations in each city were soon duplicating services in particular cases and in particular divisions of welfare. In an attempt to bring order out of confusion, the Charity Organization Society was introduced from England to America. The first such society was organized in Buffalo, New York, in 1877, and others soon appeared in many American cities. Their prime function was the promotion of "co-operation" among the various agencies and the gradual elimination of duplication of services. "Since there existed at that time few specialized agencies, such as day nurseries, legal aid bureaus, savings societies, the Charity Organization Society undertook many such activities. These when developed, were frequently cut loose by the parent organization and given an independent existence."[8] Following the growth of these specialized agencies, the Charity Organization Societies gradually limited their functions to family welfare, and many of them became the Family Service Associations of today.

Religious groups also undertook responsibility for the support of many agencies. With the growth of numerous agencies, however, the welfare work of church groups was at the same time gradually diminished. Protestantism, representing the majority of the population, accepted the secularization. Jewish and Roman Catholic policies maintained the agencies under the church in the latter case, and with the religious-ethnic label clear in the other, so that there resulted a separate series of Jewish and Roman Catholic agencies within the community.

Concurrent with these several movements in private welfare ran the development of unpaid but official bodies, often called State Boards of Charities and Corrections, which supplemented private or semi-private charity by public supervision and control.

In 1889, five years after it had originated in England, the Settlement House was introduced to America. Its services in recreation, adult education, health, and the restoration of neighborhood life were predecessors of many present-day specialized services.[9]

The financing of much health and welfare service and of education was, in this period, largely the accepted responsibility of a few, wealthy, socially minded men. Giving out of personal income or capital was not impeded by high tax rates, and the role of local philanthropist brought high social and civic prestige.

Co-operative fundraising by American philanthropic groups came to the fore in the latter part of the nineteenth century. One of the earliest instances occurred in New York City, when a committee of citizens organized a Hospital Sunday on December 28, 1879, for the collection of funds for ten hospitals under religious auspices. A little over $25,000 was realized.[10] The forerunner of today's Community Chest was organized in Denver in 1887 as the Associated Charities.[11] Four persons (two ministers, a priest, and a rabbi) brought together a federation of twenty-three agencies, which raised $20,000 in its first campaign. Five years later, when the federation campaigned as the Charity Organization Society, there were fifteen member agencies.

In 1896, Jewish leaders in Boston and Cincinnati federated for mutual support and to represent their agencies in the welfare activities of the community. These federations were an extension of the Hebrew tradition from biblical days.[12] Within a few years, there were Jewish federations in other large cities having substantial Jewish populations.[13]

The first use of the intensive financial campaign, especially in a form enlisting corporate support, is credited to the Young Men's Christian Association. Established in the United States in 1845, the "Y" first organized railroadmen in 1872 in Cleveland. The work went slowly, but progress was made, and "Railroad Associations" were established at railroad terminals and division-point cities across the country. *Association Men* for November, 1903, under the general subject "Christianity and Corporate Interests," says:

The Railroad Companies have in the past 30 years appropriated several million dollars for the railroad YMCA's. Secretaries are generally placed on the payroll of the companies. Companies furnished coal, light and supplies, and contributed about one-third of the expense of the organization. One hundred and thirteen buildings have been erected at a cost of about $1,800,000 of which the railroads paid more than one-half. . . .[14]

At first railroad companies paid a considerable part of expenses, but, later, employee-members were paying the greater portion of operating costs. The success of the "Railroad Y" led to activities for men in other industries.

Industrial development in the United States had by now built many great fortunes. Millions of dollars became available for philanthropy. Much attention was given at first to higher education, individual donations for its benefit eventually exceeding in size those made for any other single beneficent purpose. In 1831, $2,000,000 was willed by Stephen Girard to found a school for boys in Philadelphia; no such gift had previously been heard of. After the Civil War, gifts like this became increasingly common and were sought—and eventually expected—by colleges and universities. In 1865, Ezra Cornell (of the electric telegraph) donated half a million dollars to found Cornell University. Cornelius Vanderbilt, the railroad magnate, in 1873 gave a like sum to establish Vanderbilt University. Johns Hopkins

University was founded in 1876 with a $4,500,000 gift from the merchant, banker, and railroad director, Johns Hopkins.

"Foundations" now came into favour as rich men looked about them for appropriate means to put their wealth to philanthropic uses. A typically American institution, the Foundation is defined as "a nongovernmental, nonprofit organization having a principal fund of its own, managed by its own trustees or directors, and established to maintain or aid social, educational, charitable, religious, or other activities serving the common welfare."[15] In 1867, George Peabody set up the Peabody Education Fund, with a principal fund of over $2,000,000 for the advancement of education in the South. In the latter part of the nineteenth century, several similar foundations were established.

Following the Civil War and the emancipation of the slaves, the education of the American Negro, especially in the South, became—as it is today[16] —an object of philanthropy.

### EXPANSION AND REFORM

*In the expansive mood of the first decades of the twentieth century, nationalists showed an interest in the Pacific area and sought a closer relationship with Latin America. American business interests were active in foreign markets. Domestic reform was the main topic at home: the day of the "muckrakers" had arrived.*

*The twentieth century marked the beginning of an era of increasing social awareness for Americans generally. Just at the time when great philanthropists, like Carnegie and Rockefeller, were turning to the establishment of modern foundations and when smaller philanthropists began utilizing the organization of community trusts, the less wealthy engaged in forming voluntary associations for a variety of purposes. The effects can be traced in the social movements and in the tremendous growth and multiplication of various social agencies. In one six-year period, 1906-1912, the Boys' Club Association, the Boy Scouts, the Camp Fire Girls, the Girl Scouts, Goodwill Industries, and the Family Service Association were organized nationally. In the next year, 1913, the American Cancer Society, today one of the "Big Six" independent health organizations, was founded in New York.[17]*

In the year 1900 itself, the Committee on Benevolent Associations of the Cleveland Chamber of Commerce undertook the endorsement of approved agencies which solicited funds in that city, and began an educational program to inform givers as to minimum standards for charitable organizations. The result of this project was the development of a set of sanctions and standards which has since been widely copied.[18] Indeed this was the first of several innovations in community planning and financing of charitable organizations to take place in Cleveland. In 1913, after some years of agency endorsement and study by the Chamber of Commerce, the Federation of Charities and Philanthropy in Cleveland was organized. This represented a conscious attempt to reduce dependency on a few large contributors. Practically all the social welfare organizations, private and public, were almost simultaneously united in the Cleveland Welfare Council. The federation conducted an intensive mail campaign to supplement the incomes of the fifty-five member agencies. Its unique contribution, which has gained for it the recognition of being the first of the modern Community Chests, was the initiation of the principle of budgeting as a method of presenting to "the community" a "picture of total needs and resources."[19]

In the same period as the innovations in Cleveland, Milwaukee was pioneering in organizing a Council of Social Agencies (1909). Other cities soon followed suit.

The first decades of the twentieth century witnessed the birth of other ideas which were to be expanded many times over during the following years. One of these was the sale of "seals," similar to postage stamps, in a philanthropic endeavor. In 1907, Emily Bissell borrowed the then three-year-old Danish plan of selling Christmas stamps to help sick children; she applied the proceeds to helping tuberculosis patients. The goal for that first year was only $300, but $3,000 was raised.[20]

The idea of federating charities was gradually taking hold in cities across the country. In most, the central organization concentrated on budget study, "educational" publicity, and the elimination of competing appeals for funds. The federations were supported by numerous voluntary efforts including charity balls, tag days, and other methods still in use today. They received little support from corporations, essentially because it was felt they lacked universal community appeal and an effective money-raising technique—and perhaps also because the legal fiction that a corporation is a person had not yet been extended into the notion that it was also a "corporate citizen" and therefore also had personal—civic and religious—responsibilities for charity. This extension was not to occur until well on in the century.

### War and Peace

*The Wilson administration marked the climax of the era of reform. During World War I, all subsidiary objectives had to be sacrificed to winning the war. When peace was achieved, Americans convinced themselves they could be a great nation and at the same time enjoy their old isolation. For more than a decade the country was in the firm grip of conservatism. Economically, after a brief period of post-war adjustment, it enjoyed a period af abundant prosperity. Notable gains were made in technological processes. Life was geared to the automobile, movies, radio and mechanical gadgets. Efforts were made to extend the benefits of education to everyone. There were experiments in social welfare. Prohibition was attempted.*

World War I brought a demand for social services at home and abroad. At first, funds for the relief of the European victims of war were needed. After the United States entered the war, the demands from numerous organizations for money became both urgent and confusing. Utilizing the YMCA campaign techniques—a short, intensive campaign with a definite goal, under the leadership of well-known financiers, industrialists, and merchants—appeals on behalf of War Services were made to the whole community, treating it as if it were a constituency. In 1917 and 1918, "War Chests" were organized in some three or four hundred cities. Some included in their "appeal" the provision of funds for local welfare work as well as war work, and later many of these developed into Community Chests.[21] The national YMCA and Red Cross both conducted war appeals in these same two years, using similar techniques. In November, 1918, the big effort, the United War Work Campaign, repeated them. All these campaigns were successful—in fact were oversubscribed by millions of dollars.[22]

Aside from the establishment of Chests—which lived on successfully later as peacetime Community Chests—other important precedents established by the War Chests were the general policy of corporate giving to philanthropy and definition of the legal right of deduction of charitable contributions from taxable income. Corporate giving was an important factor in the success of the wartime Red Cross and War Chest campaigns. Patriotic spirit and large wartime earnings meant that this type of giving met little opposition from corporate directors or stockholders. For a brief period, some corporations issued special Red Cross dividends to stockholders, with the recommendation that they add them to their Red Cross donations, but this plan was not as successful as had been hoped. A third consequence of the War Chests was the organization in 1918 of the National Investigation Bureau (now the National Information Bureau, Inc.). Meeting in New York, representatives of the twelve leading War Chest cities established the Bureau for the investigation of national appeals and for advice to contributors. (An indication of the present coverage of N.I.B. appears in an appendix to this chapter.)

By the time the last national appeal of World War I (the United War Work Campaign of November, 1918) was made, the local charitable federations had come to be included in the War Chests in a dozen cities. These participating federations received more money through the War Chests than they had ever previously raised by themselves. It has since been thought that it was this inclusion of the regular peacetime federations in the War Chests that resulted in continued corporate contributions to the agencies when the War Chests were replaced by the Community Chests.

A few years before World War I, a new profession, destined to have a significant role in the financing of modern philanthropy, was making an appearance: the professional fundraiser whose business it was to mobilize local manpower, money, and ideas to secure an ever increasing monetary flow. The acceptance of the profession was slow, but gradually "ethical" and successful counselling won recognition and substantial income for the growing number of fundraising firms. Many major campaigns today use the services of professional fundraising counsel.[23]

World War I was a milestone in the history of the American economy.

Entering the war as a debtor nation, the United States emerged a creditor nation and soon entered a tremendous boom era. This boom was very evident in the philanthropic response of the day. Tax returns for the period show that the American public had been trained to give "something," almost irrespective of income, during the war, and that now the habit had been established. Total philanthropic giving advanced (it is estimated) from $1,730,600,000 in 1921 to $2,330,600,000 in 1928, the high point of the 1920's.[24]

This money was distributed to a wide variety of "causes." Educational institutions, for instance, entered a new era of financing. The Harvard Endowment Fund created a precedent in 1919 by setting a goal of $14,000,000 and raising $14,200,000 with the help of professional fund-raisers. Other schools reported similar successes. A study made of New Haven, Connecticut,[25] as a typical American city, showed gifts to *local* philanthropies had increased from $555,000 in 1900 to $2,239,000 in 1925. It is interesting to note where the increases occurred: the receipts of Protestant agencies doubled, as did those of secular agencies for health and for "character-building"; receipts of Jewish agencies multiplied five times; of Catholic, six; hospitals multiplied their philanthropic take eighteen times.

The growth of the Community Chest movement was concurrent with that of other philanthropic endeavors of the decade. By the end of World War I, almost every large city had a Chest. In 1920, Chest campaigns in thirty-nine cities raised about $19,600,000 for local services; by 1930, the amount raised by 353 Chests was almost $76,000,000.[26] (For a picture of the growth of the Chests see Charts 1 and 2.)

Three basic types of fundraising have been differentiated and developed through the years: the intensive campaign, usually recurring on an annual or other periodic calendar, designed to raise funds to meet *operating* budgets or deficits; the specialized appeal, for *capital* projects with predetermined objectives; and the campaign to provide funds for a *development program* as part of long-term institutional planning.

### DEPRESSION AND WAR

*The year 1929 brought the greatest economic and social crisis and the deepest economic depression. It brought want—and humiliating relief—to millions of Americans. Depression relief measures were initiated by the Hoover administration, and succeeded by the Roosevelt policies of the "New Deal." The series of remedies attempted or instituted under the New Deal policy of relief, recovery, and reform was almost revolutionary. Dozens of new agencies were created that had no precedent for their existence in the history of American government.*

*The Great Depression lasted on in varying degrees of intensity until the outbreak of World War II. As the United States came closer to war, unemployment was virtually eliminated. Again, all the resources of the country were mobilized. American production went into high gear. War bond drives, with the help of public figures, raised immense sums to help finance the war effort. Social disloca-*

*tion occurred: war brought the transfer inland of Japanese-Americans from the coast cities; housing for defence workers and the families of military personnel was at a premium. War meant other drastic changes in American life. Civilian production involving war materials was rigidly controlled. Food, fuel oil, and gasoline were rationed, and purchases of luxuries were limited by shortages and taxes.*

Until the 1930's, it was an item of the dominant philosophy in the United States that health, welfare, research, and, to some extent, higher education were chiefly responsibilities of private philanthropy. State and local governmental agencies (rather than federal[27]) were primarily responsible for what government-financed work was performed. During the early years of the depression, 1930-2, private philanthropy tried to carry the suddenly and enormously increased relief load through existing private agencies. Three great emergency employment campaigns were held. The "Mobilization for Human Needs" campaign of 1932 marked an important change in emphasis from pure preoccupation with relief needs to a concern with an all-round social welfare program.[28] As the needs of the unemployed outran the resources of private, local, and state authorities, the national government assumed more and more responsibility for the provision of relief. By 1933, public funds supplied nearly 95 per cent of total relief expenditures, and the pattern of increasing federal responsibility thus clearly set during the early New Deal days, has not yet been reversed regardless of the philosophy of the party in power. Private agencies from this time forward emphasized non-relief programs.[29]

Many of the New Deal measures were temporary and short-run. But among the more important agencies established then, and still operating in the social welfare field, are the Social Security Administration of 1935, the Railroad Retirement Board of 1935, the School Lunch Program, and the Office of Vocational Rehabilitation. The federal programs generally "supplemented" those of the local governments where such existed. Where there was no state department of public welfare (and many states had none), state legislative action had to be taken and machinery set up for the administration of the federal funds. Another significant development at the state level occurred in connection with laws for Workmen's Compensation.

Community Chests, Red Cross Chapters, and other voluntary organizations struggled through the early 1930's. Community Chests fell furthest short of their goals in 1933 and 1934. Nevertheless, the number of Chests grew steadily from 353 in 1930 to 561 in 1940 (See Charts 1, 2).

The number of national voluntary health agencies had meanwhile also been increasing steadily during the twentieth century. However, during the depression years, the only major new entry in the field was the National Foundation for Infantile Paralysis, established with the aid of President Franklin D. Roosevelt, in 1938. Nation-wide publicity and dramatic appeal helped to establish the Foundation, with its new technique of the "March of Dimes," as a leader among health agencies in terms of financial size and also in terms of mobilizing widespread small giving.

With the outbreak of World War II, Americans again answered the appeals of numerous organizations for the relief of suffering due to war. As the United States prepared for war, especially after Pearl Harbor, old-established voluntary organizations and new specially created ones co-operated to "meet needs of servicemen and their families at home and abroad." Services for civilian war workers had to be increased. During the war years, the federal government necessarily added to its social work services, particularly as a means of facilitating war-necessitated adjustments.

It is estimated that by 1942 there were seven hundred war relief agencies in the United States.[30] At the suggestion of the President and his War Relief Control Board, most of them (including the largest), combined appeals and worked together as the "National War Fund" for three years, during which time more than $329,000,000 was raised.

## Post-War

When the war ended in 1945, the American people were not ready to retreat to the isolationist position they maintained after World War I: they had become more internationally minded. The United States became one of the stronger and more active members of the United Nations.

A new policy for veterans was inaugurated in 1944—the "GI Bill of Rights"—under which they were entitled to special unemployment compensation, government-guaranteed loans, on-the-job training, and higher education. College and university enrolments, as a result of the latter, rose to startling figures.

By mid-century, the United States had reached a position almost undreamed of when the country was founded, and one that could hardly have been foreseen in 1900 or 1930. The country's place of might as a world leader was virtually unchallenged. Unrivalled business activity brought unprecedented prosperity. The position and strength of organized labor were secure and immense. Technological advances had hastened the development of many new products. Science was making progress in the treatment of disease.

The business economy was now quite different from what it had been in the days of the great tycoons. Ownership of the powerful corporations was more widely diffused; control consequently shifted generally from a few leading stock-holders to management. The federal government, and sometimes even state and local government, curtailed the old power of the corporations, when it redefined its powers to regulate prices, enforce minimum wages, limit advertising claims, prosecute on anti-trust grounds, and, most significant, collect taxes on earnings and excess profits, taxes for social security, etc. The merging of both large and small corporations was accelerated after the war.[31]

The population of the United States had been steadily increasing throughout its history as a nation. The growth since 1940 has been much larger numerically than in any previous period of equal length, though the percentage gain is comparatively modest. Population changes within the country were also significant: the Pacific Coast and Southwest regions witnessed tremendous population growths; Florida, in the South Atlantic states, was surpassed only by California

*and Arizona. Throughout the country, as earlier, the proportion of city-dwellers
increased, while the rural proportion dropped.*

*The Korean War (1950-3) brought numerous draft calls again. Though the
country was not plunged into total conflict, the Korean War and the "cold war"
in Europe increased tensions. Again emergency agencies were set up or reactivated—on a smaller scale, of course. Congressional committees conducted loyalty
investigations of individuals and organizations.*

*When, after twenty long years, the Republicans regained the Presidency in
1953, the country's system of federal social welfare agencies was already firmly
established. Among President Eisenhower's first acts of reorganization was the
combination of these principal agencies into the Department of Health, Education and Welfare, a major division of the government.[32] Legislation has recently
been proposed which would greatly expand governmental activity in the health,
welfare, and education fields. Social security was liberalized and expanded by the
Eighty-Fourth Congress (1955-6). Government aid to education and health insurance were issues then, and they will undoubtedly come up again.*

*A glance back over the past two hundred years shows significant changes in the
country and its governmental philosophy. Industrialization with the consequent
urbanization, immigration (and Americanization), and specialization stand out as
major developments. The shift from the Jeffersonian ideal of "the less government
the better" to a powerful central government is a concurrent major development.
For the past twenty-five years the nation has been in a period of unusually rapid
transition, accompanied by a great enlargement of government functions.[33]*

The end of World War II marked the beginning of a new era in American
philanthropy. The many military, political, and social events of the years
just sketched all affected its commitments.

The Veterans Administration, one of the major federal agencies in the
social work field, and now the largest single employer of fully trained social
work personnel,[34] was charged with many new tasks. The federal government, financing, by means of the GI Bill, college education for thousands of
veterans, and thus aiding in the unprecedented growth of American colleges
and universities, was also adding strains. The tremendous increase in
student enrolment found the institutions of higher learning lacking buildings, equipment, and personnel. Private philanthropy, as represented by
individual alumni, corporations, and Foundations, was called on to help
finance the expansion. Funds were sought in many ways—from unorganized
solicitation of small gifts to well-organized long-range "development plans"
under the direction of professional fundraisers.

As government increased its activities in health and welfare, a corresponding expansion was occurring in the private field. These expanding functions
of private agencies, however, were working more towards the *prevention* of
social trouble than towards direct relief: aid to the individual and the family
through counselling services and through educational and recreational activities is rapidly becoming the major role of voluntary welfare agencies.

Increasingly, national and state laws facilitated corporate giving. In 1955,
at least twenty-nine states had permissive laws. States without such laws are
largely in non-industrial areas having few corporations ( or Foundations ) of

important size. Decisions in court cases have also been favorable to corporate giving. The A. P. Smith Manufacturing Co. case in New Jersey (1930) was the first court case in thirty years to test the right of a corporation to contribute to higher education in general. More recently, the decision of the New Jersey courts upholding an otherwise undesignated gift for education from the Standard Oil Company of New Jersey to Princeton University is felt to be responsible for a major increase in corporate giving in the field of higher education.[35]

In the second period of Foundation growth, beginning in the 1930's and still under way, individuals and corporations, especially those in the upper income groups, are seeking to dispose of their wealth in such a manner that the least possible amount goes to taxes. In 1930, of the 200 Foundations in the United States, most had been established by a single donor out of a personal fortune. Within the past ten years, a few thousand family Foundations have been established, mostly for receiving, holding, and distributing deductible contributions.[36] The majority of these family Foundations are not concerned with major projects but with helping the annual operating budgets of local or regional organizations and institutions in which the founding family is interested. Since 1950, many corporation Foundations have been established; it is estimated that there are more than 1,500 such Foundations today. These "tax-exempt, non-profit legal entities separate from the parent company but with trustee boards consisting wholly or principally of corporation officers and directors [whose] purpose [is] facilitating corporation giving,"[37] have attracted widespread interest because of the magnitude of their gifts."

It is estimated that there are probably, all told, some 5,000 philanthropic Foundations in the United States today, a high proportion being located in the industrial Middle Atlantic and East North Central states.[38] David Riesman recently remarked: "Today, men of wealth, fearful of making a wrong move, harried not only by taxes but by public relations and their own misgivings, are apt to give over the now-dreaded responsibilities for spending to a foundation, which then on their behalf can collect research projects or artistic works—protected by bureaucratic organization and corporate responsibility from imputations of extravagance."[39] During 1952 and 1953, activities of some of these tax-exempt Foundations were subject to congressional investigations,[40] in relation to their responsibilities as public trusts. "The criticism most frequently made against foundations and . . . the one urged with the greatest vehemence [is], Have foundations supported or assisted persons, organizations, and projects which, if not subversive in the extreme sense of the word, tend to weaken or discredit the capitalistic system as it exists in the United States and to favor Marxist socialism?"[41] The final conclusion of the hearings was that, although mistakes in judgment had been made, the record of the Foundations was good.

The "Community Trust" movement experienced its greatest growth prior

133,3 20

LIBRARY
College of St. Francis
JOLIET, ILLINOIS

to 1930. The idea of co-trusteeship for the administration of endowments created to serve the community was another Cleveland innovation. Its birth-date may be taken as 1914. Such a Trust provides economy of administration of those endowments (especially small ones) where, as a rule, funds are distributed in the local community or area.[42]

A new plan for financing independent higher education was developed in the form of the co-operative approach to industry, used by the independent non-tax-supported colleges. Initiated in Indiana (Associated Colleges of Indiana), in 1948, by President Frank Sparks of Wabash College, the move-ment endeavors to show industry how it can contribute to the support of higher education, with mutual benefit. The idea spread rapidly. By 1956, there were thirty-one state federations and five regional ones, with a total membership of 425 colleges. The interest that corporations are showing in financing higher education is evidenced by their estimated $24 million in corporate gifts in 1948, and an estimated $100 million annually at the pre-sent time (1956).[43]

The interest and support given to health and hospital campaigns is one indication of the degree to which the American public has become health conscious (if not hyper-anxious) in these early days of the Atomic Age. Philanthropically supported non-profit hospitals care for more patients than all government (county, state, and federal) hospitals combined, even though government hospitals have three times as many beds (chiefly for the long-term care of mental, tuberculosis, and veteran patients). Among the ways in which the needs of non-profit hospitals are being met today are federal aid-for-building programs (Hill-Burton Act, 1946) and corporate giving, with the latter becoming a substantial item. Hospitals are, next to welfare causes, the largest recipients of corporate gifts.[44] Corporations have become more interested in voluntary hospitals since these have shifted their emphasis from the needs of the sick poor to "the needs of the community as a whole"—including corporation employees. Hospitalization insurance has accelerated this shift. Labor unions, with their vital interest in health and hos-pital insurance, are usually active participants also in hospital fund drives.[45]

Great medical discoveries, especially during and after World War II, are undoubtedly also major factors in the increased interest in health campaigns. National voluntary health organizations, devoted to attacks on specific diseases, have been in existence for decades, but it has only been within the past ten years that most of them have been expanding on anything like their present scale. More of these health agencies are being successfully organized almost every year. Among those established nationally within the past decade are organizations concerned with cerebral palsy, the common cold, multiple sclerosis, muscular dystrophy, and myasthenia gravis. Their work ranges from direct service to patients and provision of hospital facili-ties, to education, publicity, counselling, and research. Funds for these agencies are obtained in a variety of ways. Some employ a short membership campaign; others, a year-round solicitation. Some appeal primarily to individuals; others, to both individuals and corporations. Among the more recently organized agencies, new methods of fundraising have been used, for example, the "Telethon," "Mothers' March," and "Fire Fighters' March."[46] Charts 3 and 4 give a visual impression both of the relative magnitudes of the sums collected by these national health agencies (Chart 3) and of the estimated prevalence rates[47] of "their" diseases (Chart 4). It is to the discrepancies between the monies collected and the prevalence rates that people point when they state that the health agencies represent "a glaring imbalance." This argument is not to be accepted uncritically; but it does seem as though sentimentality on one side and promotional skill on the other were the principal determinants of the relative sizes of the takes of the health (and, no doubt, other) agencies.

Community Chests continued to flourish in the 1940's and 1950's. The number jumped from 561 in 1940 to 772 in 1945 and 1,318 in 1950.[48]

In 1949, a more complete federation of social agencies was introduced in Detroit, called "The Torch Drive." This "United Fund" (as it is known) collectivizes the Chest with all the national, "unilateral" (i.e., one-cause, such as Cancer, Heart—their term) charities in one immense, annual fundraising campaign. Proponents of the plan claim it attracts top leadership and is economical; they also maintain that the idea has received wide public support from industry and labor unions. The big health crusades have resisted it fiercely. Only one, however, the National Foundation for Infantile Paralysis, has refused nationally to join any United Fund, or to accept money raised by any organized means other than its own March of Dimes. (In a few instances, local groups do participate in United Funds.) Until April, 1955, the American Red Cross was most reluctant to allow its chapters to participate, but at that time it issued a statement permitting any local chapter to join the United Fund if it could preserve certain rights.[49] At this writing, the number of cities having a United Fund is steadily increasing. Chart 5 shows the growth of United Funds.

Opponents of the United Fund argue that philanthropy is a personal thing, not to be modelled on public taxation, and that "an individual has the right to choose his charities." They maintain that unilateral fund campaigns can raise more money, and say they can show their experience in United Funds to prove it. The United Fund idea has, however, spread from large centralized industrial cities like Detroit to smaller towns with more diversified economies. In 1955, the 463 Community Chest campaigns (excluding United Funds) raised $110,916,950, while the 555 United Funds[50] raised $188,527,022.[51] A full discussion of this movement is reserved for chapter 13.

Another form of co-operative giving has developed recently. This is represented by an organization of *donors*[52] such as the Los Angeles Associated In-Group Donors (AID) and the Los Angeles Area Building Funds, Inc. These organizations aim "to channel donations from employees and business to deserving charities at the lowest cost with the least inconvenience to the donors." In selecting charities, AID requires endorsement by the Los Angeles Social Service Commission. Giving standards for employees have been set at one-half of one per cent of pay each week, and collection is effected by means of a payroll deduction system. Corporate donors' gifts are kept confidential. Building Funds, Inc., which solicits only corporations, asks for $1.50 a year per employee plus one-fourth of one per cent of net income. Many local charities are said to be pleased with the co-operative giving because more money is collected; but some of the nation-wide fundraising groups are critical of the plan.[53]

As will be evident from the figures given in the immediately preceding paragraphs, total philanthropic giving in the United States within the last few years has reached unprecedented heights. The Russell Sage Foundation statistics show that giving for religion, education, private health and welfare services, and all other tax-deductible charities on the part of individuals, corporations, or through charitable bequests was over $4 billion in 1949. The total for 1953, a new high, was estimated to be $5.466 billion; in 1954 it declined slightly to $5.401 billion. The Foundation reports that the 1954 philanthropic $1 consisted of 74 cents from individual donors, 6 cents from corporations, 4 cents in grants from Foundations, 4 cents in charitable bequests, and 12 cents in income from capital representing past giving.

The year 1955 was the greatest (money) year in the history of American philanthropy. From January, when John D. Rockefeller, Jr. contributed $20 million to strengthen American Protestant theological education, through December, when the Ford Foundation announced its gift of $500 million to 615 private colleges and universities, to 3,500 privately supported hospitals, and to privately supported medical schools, the year was marked by successful fundraising.[54] The John Price Jones Company estimates the total philanthropic contributions for 1955 to approach, if not exceed, $6 billion.[55]

American philanthropic giving has not been without its limitations. In many instances the giving has been sporadic and the results somewhat chaotic. Efforts have been and are being made to correct abuses and weaknesses, and to "develop a philosophy."[56]

Many local and state governments have enacted laws requiring charity groups to register and file financial statements. Some cities (including Indianapolis[57]) require solicitors for voluntary philanthropic organizations to be licensed.[58] In many places the local Chamber of Commerce (or the Better Business Bureau or a Solicitations Committee) "advises" members on charity appeals. As mentioned previously, the National Information Bureau, Inc., issues information to its members on national appeals. Yet with all these safeguards, a New York State Investigating Committee was reliably informed in 1953 that between $100 million and $120 million (or perhaps 2.5 per cent of the total philanthropic giving) was taken every year by "charity rackets."

In April, 1954, the Cleveland Chamber of Commerce and the National Information Bureau sponsored the first National Conference on Solicitations "for the co-operative study of contribution problems, policies and procedures."[59] The growth of the Conference each year (the Second and Third Conferences were held in March, 1955 and 1956) shows that many people are coming to think it desirable to enlighten and protect the public in matters of voluntary giving.

Attempts to use government police powers to control charity solicitations have been made in a few cities, but the determination in American society to preserve the principles of freedom of association and freedom of speech tends to work against such methods. Here and there, we were told, more or less secret committees have attempted to limit the number of charity appeals, but such *sub rosa* methods are not common.[60]

It seems inevitable that in the United States, as it is constituted, there will always be new appeals for all sorts of worthy causes—new associations to promote them and new ways to raise money for them. Along with this encouragement to give effect to "the freedom to give" there remains, for the present at least, some "freedom to say 'No.'"

## TIME AND TITHE

To gain another perspective, it may be helpful to step away from the foregoing history of particulars and to see both the story of philanthropy and at least the recent story of America in broadest outline and in terms of tendencies and trends. Knowing all the risks that attach to history so written and so generalized, we have thought it worth while to attempt to catch in the sketch that follows a theme that might otherwise be lost in detail.

It is obvious that what will be regarded as a fitting, generous, or adequate scale or manner of giving will vary with time and circumstance. Recommendations run from those hoary with antiquity and substantial and religious—"Go and sell that thou hast, and give to the poor . . ." or "All the tithe of the land . . . is the Lord's"[61]—to the latest, more moderate, definitely secular, plea rather than injunction, for anything from "1½ per cent of pretax net" to "four hours' pay per year" (roughly ⅒ of 1 per cent or less of gross income).

Even in the brief sweep of American history important social changes have implied profound changes in the logic of sensible giving, and the latter, no less, have made social operations possible that made for further social change. The private endowment of numerous universities and colleges would be an example.

It may be precisely because these reciprocal changes have been so far-reaching and so rapid, it may be because of the speed of the transition we are in, that much of the confusion of counsel and defeat of intent which we note as endemic, take place. In any case, it is difficult for any donor or fundraiser to see clearly where he is, or whence he has come, and whither his enterprise seems to be tending—unless he sees his present situation in the flow of history, or at least in its most obvious and important historic context.

The relevant changes in America may be separated for convenience of discussion into economic, political, social, technological, religious, and legal changes, although, of course, these are not independent of one another. Much of what can be said under each of these rubrics is commonplace, perhaps, needing only to be recalled to establish the context within which the problems of this study may be viewed.

The economic history of America might almost be told in terms of a single sweeping line (such as that on Chart 6) showing an ever increasing national income—whether measured in terms of nominal dollars or in terms of real income, whether measured by the total national take or by "take-home pay" per family or per capita. The basic economic fact of American life is nothing so conservative as the "ever normal granary"; it is something as radical as the cornucopia of ever accelerating flow.

Within this all-encompassing sweep,[62] seeming all the more relentless for its largely unplanned character, changes in demand and supply, as well as changes in tax policy, have been occurring, all of which are pregnant with meaning as opportunities or conditions of action (or models) for the philanthropic enterprise.

On the side of demand—again part cause, part effect of what is supplied and sold—there is the obvious but potentially dramatic story of the sheer quantity of things consumed. It is but a moment in time from a car as a scientific or mechanical curiosity to a car as a rich man's toy, to Henry Ford's car for every man, to the two-car garage beside every "respectable" house (and more than one chicken in every pot, besides). More striking even to the non-American eye than the sheer volume of standard goods produced is the multiplication, the limitless proliferation (like nothing so much as wild-cell growth) of the kinds or categories of goods available. The story of invention in America is so dramatic and so oft-told that, no longer a novelty in American ears, its retelling would be trite.

What is true of the quantity of goods is true of the quality, so that it is now an expert housewife, probably trained in domestic "science," who can make good use of the range of opportunity presented her on virtually every purchase: from "extra fancy," through "fancy," "extra choice," and "choice" to "Blue Ribbon" or whatever is current merchandisese for the lowest grades.[63]

This transition in quantity and quality, effectively demanded, is also accompanied by a substantial shift from purchases intended very nearly[64] for the satisfaction of need to purchases more nearly intended for the expression or indulgence of taste.

On the side of supply, by definition what is concretely supplied is what is, as described above, demanded. The interesting aspect here is the human and industrial and commercial organization that has emerged to supply, and evoke and "create" or sustain, demand.

The story of the change in America of the typical unit of production from pioneer or pioneer-and-family, through one-man business, to family or "closely held" firm to public corporation (limited stock company) to a vertical or horizontal organization of these into a giant of modern industry is again a well-worn story. The essence of this story of growth, expressing the talent and genius of America, is of course the "production line." The essence of the production line—which includes here the arts of management as well as the artifices of physical production—is the breakdown of a complex job into innumerable simple parts on the planning and physical side, and therewith the differentiation of acts and skills and the specialization of personnel to perform them on the human side. "Functional rationalization,"[65] accompanied by further inventions of machinery to substitute for human intervention,[66] and further inventions of devices for holding these immense organizations together[67]—this is the wonder-story of American production. Organization, differentiation, specialization, merger, reorganization, unification, rationalization, merchandizing, packaging, public relations: in the realities that these words but sketch the surging growth of the American economy is epitomized, acted out, and made simultaneously the labor, the pride, and the principal product of American hands in their everyday employ.

It is against this background of surging material success that philanthropy is continuously viewed. It is from among the leading engineers of this success that the management cadre of MOPS fundraising is drawn, and it is upon the engineers and the rank-and-file producers of this success that MOPS fundraising operates.

But if this daring triumph is the background of philanthropy it is also a part of philanthropy's problem. For philanthropy is variously seen (and sometimes simultaneously) as a *poor copy* of this ideal model; as a *contradiction* of the principle of the major system; as the *complementary system* to the free play of competitive forces; and as the *best defence* the system could have against any alternative system.

Those who see the materially productive economy as the model, tend to be impatient with the management and the production-processes of great parts of the philanthropy-supported enterprise. The indefiniteness of aims, the uncertainty about the product, the difficulty in determining the loci of responsibility and control (and, indeed, the separation of these from one another) are hardly borne with, because they do not fit the businessman's self-image or the professional worker's image of the businessman or the business-system.[68] It is from this source, chiefly, that comes the very proper demand for businesslike methods and scientific research where they are apt; but it is from the same source also that comes the demand for a kind of pseudo-businesslike busyness, for example, in line-by-line budget or monthly cash-position analysis in a situation where no one can define or wants to tackle what the main business of the organization is.

Those who see the whole philanthropic enterprise as essentially a contradictory system to the major or "free enterprise" system, in the sense that it embodies alien, competing, and distasteful principles, react to it in various ways, even though they may intimately "support" it. They may regard it, like inevitable sickness, as a necessary expression of human weakness, to be borne with but not admired or "accepted"; or, more actively, they may regard it, rather like evitable sickness, as something to be combatted and minimized, or, better, stamped out. Expressions of these views range from "If they [the 'social dreamers'] had their way pretty soon everything would be *free!*" to "The main thing is to find some way to cut back" to "If you go on allowing it, *where's it all going to end?*"

Those who regard philanthropy as complementary to the main system, constitute probably the vast majority (though many will hold to other views simultaneously). These tend to see the enterprise either as dealing with those limited few whose misfortune or weakness makes the application of the ordinary rules[69] inhuman or inhumane, or as dealing in commodities not suitable for commercial merchandising at all.[70] The outlook of the first group lends the emphasis to "fundamental education," to self-help and rehabilitation (i.e., apprenticeship to the main system for those who missed it, or restoration to the main system for those temporarily out of the running). The outlook of the second leads to the desire for a clear distinction between what is a marketable commodity and what is not, and within the latter category what it is the business of the state and what the business of the philanthropic system to supply.

Lastly, those who see philanthropy as the major system's best defence may feel that it is such because (a) it is itself an example of free (uncoerced) initiative at work, another businesslike system with its self-evident virtues, or because (b) it is a sign of the vigor of the free enterprise system to be able to sustain easily out of its surplus so vast a subsidiary enterprise (in addition to the state and tax-supported system), or because (c) in supplying what the main system does not, it blunts at least the edge of discontent, and therefore minimizes the likelihood of action to tamper with the free system, or because (d) ideologically and practically it supplies those very things that proponents of other systems claim theirs would supply, if adopted.[71]

In any case, and from whatever viewpoint, philanthropy is seen, evaluated, and operated in the context of the central institution—the market—to which it is in fact, by scale and importance, peripheral. Nothing could, perhaps, be more fundamental than the clarification of what exactly the relationship should be[72] and is.

But the historical context of philanthropy is not only in economic history;

it is also in political history, both domestic and foreign. The emergence on the world scene of major powers based upon non-primitive economic systems that are also non-capitalist (in the sense in which that term refers to the American economy)[73] makes the successful operation of the American system in the "American way" not only or primarily an economic problem but a problem also in world-politics, in prestige and in power. The necessity to demonstrate that the system "works better than any other that the mind of man has conceived" becomes not only a matter of business pride but a matter around which international allies may be won or lost, and the chances in cold war or hot substantially altered. Not that philanthropic decisions on a local basis are largely made in the light of international power considerations, but that those who manage the institutions are able to add to the motivation of business pride (or fear) the motivation of national pride (or fear), and that thus the successful operation of the combined business-and-philanthropy system becomes doubly to be desired, and anything that threatens it doubly to be feared.

What is true for the emergence on the world scene of competing forms of national economy is true on the domestic scene for changes in the power-structure, and, more particularly, for the emergence of new power-groups. While the socialist party in America is not now—and never was—a serious contender for power, and while the Communist party, except in its conspiratory aspect, holds small threat, and has scant chance as an appealing economic program, nevertheless it would not be right to conclude that no spectre stalks business North America. Under a variety of names,[74] the vision of a native form of the highly centralized, highly planned, highly income-equalizing, highly regulated substitute for the present system—characterized by relatively low degrees of each of these—certainly haunts the most vocal of Hoosier businessmen, if not the majority.[75]

The rise of "centralism" to a position of closely latent possibility—so that its embodiment in actuality is partly a fact of recent history and partly a proximate political possibility, if not probability—again cuts both ways as far as philanthropy is concerned. Those who see philanthropy as a defence for or a complement to the free enterprise system, feel driven to perfect the philanthropic enterprise and to enlarge it substantially, if that is necessary to its performance of this function. Those on the other hand who see in the philanthropic system any of the following, are naturally enough, concerned lest it become too satisfactory or, especially, "too large": (a) the model for an alternative system of "everything free," or "handouts," (b) a stage through which various no doubt good causes move before they become part of government program, (c) a place where social workers ("social dreamers" and "planners") are trained, paid, and recruited, later to move into government service to promote their ideology from there, (d) a sort of "third force" in the society, representing an ideology alien to business (and therefore bad) and of growing power as it expands in size, and (e) economically, a growing incubus upon the free enterprise system, that could (like excessive taxation) with sufficient growth reduce the ability of that system to operate successfully, i.e., with a sufficiently high profit-rate and tendency of earners to accumulate savings.

For reasons similar to the foregoing, the social and political transformations that have in the last few decades brought old minorities or relatively powerless groups into positions of greater power, have affected the philanthropy movement and are continuing to face it with problems, perplexities, and uncertainties. The proximate disappearance of the foreign-born both in absolute numbers (see chapter 4) and as a body of philanthropy's beneficiaries, the arrival into positions of status and power of former religious minorities,[76] these have required alike revisions, not yet completed, in the definition of the philanthropic task, in the determination of what is—even from a pragmatic or working viewpoint—adequate "representation" in the government of the philanthropic enterprise, and, more particularly, in the adjustment to one another of philanthropic practices and organizations that grew up with the minorities and that now, as the minorities become relatively assimilated, must find new reasons for their continued existence or independence or semi-independence.

Spectacular among these shifts of power in the last few decades has been that attended by the redefinition of the role and relation to each other of management and labor union. No matter what the political or ideological position from which the trend is evaluated, the inescapable *fact* is a radical shift in the power, respectability (and, perhaps, program) of the unions in America. This shift is attended by necessary alterations in the philanthropy-supported program,[77] by problems again of "representativeness" in philanthropy's government and a possible struggle for power or transfer of responsibility, by misunderstandings or genuine struggles over "credit" for philanthropic performance,[78] and by a need, scarcely yet felt perhaps, but undoubtedly latent, to re-evaluate and re-define the basic philosophy involved, in terms of the new *de facto* situation.

A social history of America, illuminating as it might be for the problem of present-day philanthropy, has for pressing space reasons no place here. Two words that might be caught from such a history, however, point towards well-known sweeping tendencies whose implications for philanthropy have not yet seemingly been fully assimilated by philanthropists. The two words are "secularization" and "urbanization."

In a sense, the story of philanthropy—or of MOPS fundraising, rather—as we tell it, is the story of the secularization of another segment of American life, and the attendant trials and tribulations of such a transition from the largely sacred to the largely secular realm. The problem for many is to find an appropriate and satisfying secular vehicle to embody some large part of the active answer to a sacred question: "Am I my brother's keeper?" In order to provide an operationally adequate scheme in a mass society like the American, the institution must clearly be secular; in order to satisfy many of the leading giver-participants, the institution must satisfy sacred motives and must embody behavior and symbols consonant, at the very least, with sacred beliefs. As the secular institution adapts itself to the facts of the market and the opportunistic needs of successful operation, the temptation merely to exploit sacred symbols for ends which have become autonomous —"success"— brings it into conflict with those who wish it to behave as a true embodiment (if not model) of religiously enjoined or motivated behavior. Appropriate canons of conduct for the officials or other persons so situated is a matter about which there is some unease; but little attention seems to have been given to working them out.[79]

The problems of urbanization have received too much attention and the literature concerning them is too readily available for any extended comment upon this head to seem called for here. Two aspects that have perhaps not received sufficient attention in philanthropic circles for their bearing on philanthropy might, however, be mentioned. The first has to do with the shift in the origins of those flowing into the lowest urban ranks; they are no longer "foreigners," but rather native, rural American folk of many generations' occupancy of the land—largely, though by no means exclusively, "hillbillies" and Negroes.[80] For a nation long accustomed to joining the satisfaction of generosity with the titillation of self-esteem by making "others" (i.e., non-Americans or persons becoming "Americanized") the principal beneficiaries of donation, a situation where those needing help are principally "our own" may pose new problems of motive and perspective.[81]

A second aspect of recent urbanization whose consequences for philanthropy (indeed for the whole welfare community) remain to be examined and engineered for, is the "suburbanization" or "exurbanization"[82] of a great part of the leadership, actual or potential, of the philanthropic organizations of most if not all cities. Even with increasingly rapid instruments[83] of transit, the time-distance between the homes of the leaders and the officers of the organization (or the homes of paid staff) tends with almost every year to increase, and certain kinds of meetings (with their attendant typical informalities of process and relation) tend to disappear or be minimized. These spatial problems may have something to do with the attenuated social relations between laymen and professionals, the great and difficult-to-bridge social distances that we point to, as productive of other problems, in chapter 12.

We cannot cover here, either, the impact of the dramatic technological changes of recent years in America on the operation of philanthropy. Invention follows invention, wonder upon wonder, gadget upon gadget, culminating momentarily in the advent of atomic power (peaceful and bellicose), automation, the Salk vaccine and the "wonder drugs." It requires no detailed history, however, to permit two observations. The first is that this progression of inventions and improvements (whose impact is widely appreciated even when its cause is not understood) is as much part of the context of philanthropy as is the web of production miracles earlier alluded to. It also creates an air of expectancy around the philanthropy-supported enterprises—to the effect that they too should solve[84] their problems with equal drama, promptness, and visibility or tangibility of result. It is perhaps from this source (as much as from anywhere else) that stem the vague pervasive feelings of something like dissatisfaction on the lay side and something like guilt or defensiveness on the professional side, with the results of philanthropy and philanthropy-born (or philanthropy-borne) enterprises.

The second observation on this head is that the technological changes themselves may deeply and directly affect the philanthropic enterprise. Any problem holding out hope of early solution is, to a success-loving people, a saleable package, and therefore one around which it is possible to rally leadership and for which it is easy to raise funds.[85] The ready solubility criterion singles out—in the present state of human knowledge—physical or biological problems, particularly such as have highly visible or palpable consequences. Popular money[86] makes research funds for these rather readily available. The success of such research, in a relatively rapid interval (as in the case of the Salk vaccine), sets the mode so that more money proportionately tends to be poured into this type of enterprise. The final upshot is a seeming justification of the funds expended—i.e., a cycle of self-justifying expectation has been completed.[87]

It is, then, within this context of sweeping social, economic, technological, political, legal, and fiscal changes that philanthropy must needs be seen and evaluated, and to these changes it must adapt and re-form.

But philanthropy is not only the toy of forces in the large society, playing themselves out upon it. For reasons intrinsic to it (as well as those extrinsic) it has undergone and is undergoing change; and for any individual policy-maker at any instant these changes are (or should be) a part of the background of decision. The history of a changing philanthropy has been touched upon in this chapter, and will be touched upon again in chapter 4 (Philanthropy in Indianapolis). A merest outline would have to take count, at least, of all of the following:

1. Changes in the institutional roots of philanthropy: from church to corporation (and to some extent to Foundation) with reference not so much to who gives but who organizes those who do give.

2. Changes in the ethics of giving: from giving as religious duty or aid to salvation to giving as civic duty or aid to good public relations.

3. Psychological changes: from giving on impulse to planned giving,

culminating in the near-total alienation from impulse implied in payroll deduction, i.e., giving by instalment credit.

4. Attitudinal changes: from passivity in the receiver and activity in the giver (the church collection plate, the silent beggar's bowl) to activity in the fundraiser and passivity in the giver (accepting the "standards" of a modern campaign).[88]

5. Changes in the personnel: from laymen to part-time ministerial or other personnel, to specialists such as Chest managers, to super-specialists in fundraising organizations such as the American City Bureau or the Wells Organizations.[89]

6. Changes in the scope and intent of the supported activities: from occasional relief of personal or mass misfortune or disaster to sustained or continuous attempts to secure a "better" or "healthier" or "wiser" or "happier" life for all—i.e., a double transformation from occasionality to regularity, and a transformation from the alleviation of distress to the "improvement of life."

7. Changes in interest proceeding seemingly in two directions at once: (a) from concern with unattached individuals to concern with families, to concern with community organization and planning, to the first whispers of concern to "get back to our interest in social reform"; and (b) from a beginning point in social reform, in the large sense, to a preoccupation not only with the individual, but with the individual in his most idiosyncratic manifestations as viewed in psychoanalytic theory and revealed in psychoanalytic practice.

8. Changes in the type of problem thought to be focal: a shift in preoccupation (no matter whether directed towards relief of distress or improvement of life) from the provision of physical and tangible reliefs and benefits to the supply of psychological and social counsellings, therapies, restructurings, aids and opportunities.

9. A change in beneficiaries: from some (or a few) to all (or nearly all).[90] "Everybody benefits; everybody gives."

10. A change in supporters: on one side from voluntary associations to government (e.g., most "relief"); on the other side, from predominantly an upper-class élite to mass support (the early Chests) to a return to relative dependence on the middle-class semi-élite of the managerial and professional sectors and on the corporation both as donor and as donor-organizer.

These and other changes—including changes in the techniques both of fundraising and of what fundraising supports—represent the flux of circumstance in which the day-to-day operational philanthropic decisions must be made. Small wonder perhaps that counsel is divided and uncertain (or intermittent as to direction), especially where, as in Indianapolis, the piloting of the Chest ship through these troubled and uncharted waters is regarded as the avocation of busy men with little time to give, little of that little continuously (see chapters 10, 11, 12), and hardly any of it for securing secure facts or proved techniques—or the perspective that comes from long immersion in philanthropy's special history.[91]

## APPENDIX

JUNE, 1956, PARTIAL LISTING OF ORGANIZATIONS (NEITHER APPROVED NOR DISAPPROVED) ILLUSTRATIVE OF THE COVERAGE OF NATIONAL INFORMATION BUREAU, INC.

I. NATIONAL HEALTH AGENCIES (including Physically Handicapped)

*Alcoholism*
National Committee on Alcoholism

*Allergic Diseases*
American Foundation for Allergic Diseases

*Arthritis & Rheumatism*
Arthritis & Rheumatism Foundation

*Blindness & Sight*
American Foundation for the Blind
American Printing House for the Blind
Blinded Veterans Association
Braille Institute of America
Christian Record Benevolent Assn.
Eyes Right, Inc.
John Milton Society for the Blind
National Council to Combat Blindness
National Federation of the Blind
National Foundation for Eye Research
National Society for the Prevention of Blindness
New Eyes for the Needy
Ophthalmological Foundation
Recording for the Blind
W. C. Handy Foundation for the Blind

Note: Many single institutions also try to raise money nationally as:
Guide Dog Foundation for the Blind
Guiding Eyes for the Blind
Leader Dogs for the Blind
Seeing Eye, Inc.—etc.

*Brain*
Brain Research Foundation
National Society for the Brain Injured

*Cancer*
American Cancer Society
Babe Didrikson Zaharias Fund
Children's Cancer Fund
Damon Runyon Memorial Fund for Cancer Research

Francis Cancer Research Foundation

*Cerebral Palsy*
United Cerebral Palsy Associations

*Colds*
Common Cold Foundation

*Diabetes*
American Diabetes Association

*Epilepsy*
National Epilepsy League

*Crippled or Handicapped*
American Federation of the Physically Handicapped
International Society for the Welfare of Cripples
National Amputation Foundation
National Association of Handicaps
National Rehabilitation Association
National Society for Crippled Children & Adults

*Hearing*
American Hearing Society

*Heart*
American Heart Association

*Hemophilia*
Hemophilia Foundation

*Leprosy*
American Leprosy Foundation— Leonard Wood Memorial
American Leprosy Missions

*Maternal Welfare*
American Committee on Maternal Welfare
Maternity Center Association
National Committee on Maternal Health

*Mental Health*
American Fund for Psychiatry
League for Emotionally Disturbed Children
National Association for Mental Health
World Federation for Mental Health

*Multiple Sclerosis*
National Multiple Sclerosis Society

*Muscular Dystrophy*
Muscular Dystrophy Assns. of America
National Foundation for Muscular Dystrophy
National Muscular Dystrophy Research Foundation

*Myasthenia Gravis*
Myasthenia Gravis Foundation

*Nephrosis*
National Nephrosis Foundation

*Nursing*
National Assn. for Practical Nurse Education
National League for Nursing

*Paraplegia*
National Paraplegia Foundation

*Parenthood*
Planned Parenthood Federation of America

*Polio*
Sister Elizabeth Kenny Foundation
National Foundation for Infantile Paralysis

*Social Diseases*
American Social Hygiene Association

*Tuberculosis*
National Tuberculosis Association

*Miscellaneous Health*
Alcohol & Addictive Diseases Foundation
American National Red Cross
American Public Health Association
Health Information Foundation
Music Research Foundation
National Assn. for Retarded Children
National Committee on the Aging
National Foundation for Asthmatic Children
National Fund for Medical Education
National Health Council
Society for the Rehabilitation of the Facially Disfigured
Veterans Health Agencies (see Section IV)

II. PROMOTION OF "FREE ENTERPRISE," "AMERICAN WAY OF LIFE," ECONOMICS, ETC.

Advertising Council
American Economic Foundation
American Enterprise Association
American Heritage Foundation
American Museum of Immigration

American Progress Foundation
American Viewpoint
America's Future
Christian Anti-Communist Crusade
Citizens Committee for the Hoover Report
Committee for Constitutional Government
Committee for Economic Development
Committee on Foreign Trade Education
Committee for a National Trade Policy
Congress of Freedom
Constitution and Free Enterprise Foundation
Defenders of the American Constitution
Economists' National Committee on Monetary Policy
Facts Forum, Inc.
Flag Foundation of America
Foremanship Foundation
Foundation for Economic Education
Foundation for the Study of Cycles
Franklyn Library of American Enterprise
Freedom House
Freedoms Foundation
Granite Foundation
Guardians of American Education
Harding College—Dept. of National Education
Horatio Alger Awards Committee of the American Schools & Colleges Assn.
Institute of Fiscal & Political Education
Intercollegiate Society of Individualist
Invest in America Week
Investors League
Joint Council on Economic Education
Junior Achievement
Junior Americans of the U.S.
Lincoln Educational Foundation
Manion Forum of Opinion
National Academy of Economics and Political Science
National Associated Businessmen
National Assn. for Maintenance of Free Enterprise
National Economic Council
National Federation of Independent Business
National Republic Lettergram
National Right to Work Committee
National Tax Equality Association
Patriotic Education

Rice Leaders of the World
Small Business Economic Foundation
Spiritual Mobilization
Tax Foundation
United Shareholders of America
Etc., etc.

III. YOUTH

American Youth Hostels
Big Brothers of America
Boy Scouts of America
Boys' Clubs of America
Boys, Inc.
Child Study Association of America
Child Welfare League of America
Future Scientists of America
  Foundation
Girls Clubs of America
National Child Labor Committee
National Citizens Commission for the
  Public Schools
National 4-H Club Foundation
National Foundation for Under-
  privileged Children
National Kindergarten Association
National Merit Scholarship Corp.
National Midcentury Committee for
  Children and Youth
National Society for the Prevention
  of Juvenile Delinquency
Spokesmen for Children
Thomas Alva Edison Foundation
Young Men's Christian Associations
Young Women's Christian Association

Note: Many single institutions also try
to raise money nationally as:
Boys' Athletic League, N.Y.C.
Boys Town (Father Flanagan's Boys'
  Home)
Boys Town of Missouri
Boystown of Indiana
George Junior Republic
Girls Vacation Fund, N.Y.C.
Girls' Town U.S.A., Florida
Girlstown, U.S.A., Texas
Etc.

IV. VETERANS

*Men, Women, Mothers, and Wives*

American Legion
American War Mothers
Amvets Service Foundation
Blinded Veterans Association
Disabled American Veterans
Gold Star Wives of America
Handicapped War Veterans
  Association
Marine Corps League of U.S.A.

Military Order of the Purple Heart
Military Order of the World Wars
National Assn. of Veterans
  Employment Councils
Paralyzed Veterans Assn. of America
Veterans of Foreign Wars
World Veterans Fund

V. WELFARE—GENERAL & SPECIALIZED

American Civil Liberties Union
American Committee for Cultural
  Freedom
American Council to Improve our
  Neighborhoods
American Federation of International
  Institutes
American Friends Service Committee
American Good Government Society
American Humanics Foundation
American League to Abolish Capital
  Punishment
American National Red Cross
American Public Welfare Association
American Seamen's Friend Society
Carrie Chapman Catt Memorial Fund
Common Council for American Unity
Euthanasia Society of America
Family Service Association
Foundation for Research on Human
  Behavior
Frontier Nursing Service
Keep America Beautiful
International Social Service
League for Industrial Democracy
League of Women Voters of the U.S.
National Association on Service to
  Unmarried Parents
National Conference on Social Work
National Council for Community
  Improvement
National Legal Aid Association
National Municipal League
National Planning Association
National Probation & Parole
  Association
National Publicity Council for Health
  and Welfare Services
National Recreation Association
National Rehabilitation Association
National Sharecroppers Fund
National Shut-in Society
National Social Welfare Assembly
United Community Defense Services
United Defense Fund
United Seamen's Service
United Service Organizations (USO)
U.S. Comm. of the International
  Conference on Social Work
Volunteer Service Photographers

VI. Negro Welfare

Geo. Washington Carver Memorial Institute
Institute of Industrial Race Relations
National Assn. for the Advancement of Colored People
National Assn. of Colored Women
National Council of Negro Women
National Scholarship Service and Fund for Negro Students
National Urban League
Southern Conference Educational Fund
United Negro College Fund
Universal Negro Improvement Assn.

VII. Human & Race Relations

Association on American Indian Affairs
Council against Intolerance in America
National Comm. for the Aaronsburg Story
National Conference of Christians and Jews
National Congress of the American Indian
Panel of Americans

VIII. Conservation

American Forestry Association
Friends of the Forest Preserve
National Conservation Association
National Wildlife Federation
United Conservation Fund

IX. International Relations

American Assn. for the United Nations
American Christian Palestine Committee
American Comm. for Liberation from Bolshevism
American Committee on United Europe
American Council on NATO
American Field Service Scholarships
American Friends of the Middle East
American Friends of Russian Freedom
American Fund for Free Jurists
American Society for Friendship with Switzerland
Americas Foundation
Asia Foundation
Committee for World Development and World Disarmament
Council for International Progress in Management
Crusade for Freedom

English-Speaking Union of the U.S.
Foreign Policy Association
Friendship among Children and Youth around the World
Fund for Asia
China Institute in America
Committee for Cultural Relations with Latin America
Comm. for a Democratic Far Eastern Policy
Comm. for Freedom of North Africa
Committee on Friendly Relations among Foreign Students
Committee of One Million
Council on Foreign Relations
Eisenhower Exchange Fellowships
Hiroshima Peace Center
Institute for International Education
Institute of International Order
International Friendship League
Lafayette Fellowship Foundation
League of Winant Volunteers
National Committee for Free Europe
Netherland America Foundation
Pan-American Society of U.S.
Radio Free Europe
U.S. Committee for the United Nations
United World Federalists
War Resisters' League
Women's International League for Peace & Freedom
World Peace Foundation
Youth of All Nations

X. Foreign Relief, Aid & Rehabilitation

Aid Refugee Chinese Intellectuals
Albert Schweitzer Hospital Fund
American Bureau for Medical Aid to China
American Council for Emigrés in the Professions
American Farm School
American Foundation for Overseas Blind
American Friends Service Committee
American-Korean Foundation
American Middle East Relief
American Women's Hospitals
Bataan Foundation
Boys' Towns of Italy
Christian Children's Fund
East West Children's Aid
Forgotten Generation
Foster Parents' Plan for War Children
Foundation for Orphans in Greece
Free China Fund
Health for the World's Needy

Highland Fund of North America
International Comm. of the Mass
  Education Movement
International Rescue Committee
Japan International Christian
  University Foundation
Kosciuszko Foundation
League for Orphan Victims in Europe
  (LOVE)
Meals for Millions
Medical and Surgical Relief
  Committee
Near East Foundation
Save the Children Federation
Tolstoy Foundation
Unitarian Service Committee
United Friends of Needy and
  Displaced Persons of Yugoslavia
United Lithuanian Relief
U.N. International Children's
  Emergency Fund
World Literacy
World Neighbors
World Rehabilitation Fund
World University Service
World Vision

XI. MISCELLANEOUS

Air Force Aid Society
American Humane Association
American Institute of Management
American Merchant Marine Library
  Assn.
American Ordnance Association

American Science & Historical
  Preservation Society
Benjamin Franklin 250th Anniversary
  Celebration
Care, Inc.
Children to Palestine
Cordell Hull Foundation
Council for Agricultural and
  Chemurgic Research
George Gershwin Memorial
  Foundation
Golden Rule Foundation
International Research Fund
International University Foundation
Italian Charities of America
Junior Police Citizens Corps
Laymen's National Committee
National Arts Foundation
National Comm. on Immigration &
  Citizenship
National Council of Social Studies
National Council against Conscription
National Council of Women of U.S.
National Dog Welfare Guild
National Fire Protection Assn.
National Humane Society
National Plant, Flower & Fruit Guild
Necktie Workers Organization
Newcomen Society
Pestalozzi Foundation
Religion in American Life
Robert A. Taft Memorial Foundation
United National Assn. of Postal Clerks
U.S. Olympic Committee
World Welfare and Peace

# 3. Indiana and Indianapolis:
## "The Hoosier Way"

### INDIANA: HOOSIER STATE

CAPITAL: Indianapolis. AREA: 36,291 sq. mi., rank, 37th. POPULATION: (Census of 1950) 3,934,224, rank, 12th. MOTTO: Cross-roads of America. FLOWER: Zinnia. BIRD: Cardinal. TREE: Tulip. SONG: On the Banks of the Wabash. ADMISSION: 19th.

Indiana, a North Central State. . . .

A great manufacturing state (8,000 industries) . . . has 200 coal mines. . . . Six out of every 10 persons are employed in metal industries . . . ranks 3rd in steel production, provides over 80% of all building limestone used in the U. S., makes 12% of the nation's household furniture, has large brick and tile industry. Rubber processing and prefabricated houses are new industries.

Greatest steel production is in Calumet region. . . . Gary was a sand dune in 1905 . . . now has 133,911 pop. (1950). . . .

. . . 223 airports. . . . Principal railroads. . . . Indianapolis has famous Speedway. . . .

Diversified crops are combined with stock raising, with high-grade dairy farms. . . . Central Indiana is a meat-producing area. . . .

Among 38 institutions of higher education are. . . . It takes high place in literature with Booth Tarkington, George Ade, Gen. Lew Wallace, Meredith Nicholson, Jas. Whitcomb Riley, Maurice Thompson, Theo. Dreiser, Lyman Abbott, George Fitch, Max Eastman, Gene Stratton-Porter, whose Limberlost area is a state park.

. . . 16 state parks . . . 14 state forests . . . 4 well-stocked game preserves and 13 fish hatcheries. . . . Among 14 state memorials are the Vincennes memorial to George Rogers Clark, New Harmony (Rappite) community, Tippecanoe and other Indian battlefields, site of Lincoln's boyhood home, grave of Nancy Hanks Lincoln in Spencer County, World War Memorial, Indianapolis, national office of American Legion.

The famous post-office, Santa Claus, is in Indiana.

The state constitution forbids issuance of state bonds, and all state expenses are met from current income.

*The World Almanac and Book of Facts, 1956*[1]

THE FOREGOING represents one level of factual information about Indianapolis and Indiana; the rest of this chapter, presenting, rather, garnered impression, carefully sifted against what is known, is intended to help make more understandable the special character of Indiana, of mass philanthropic fundraising in Indianapolis, and particularly the problems of federated fundraising as represented in the annual campaigns of that city's Community Chest.

In 1955-6, Indiana could be recognized by a non-resident as the "Crossroads of America," to use its own Motto, but, for many, the name of the state conveyed not much more than that. The cross-country tourist may easily miss Indiana en route north to south; and in going east to west he is likely to cross the state on a main highway so swiftly that he may not stop even to buy gasoline. Scratch most Americans and it may well be found that, among those with any picture of Indianapolis or Indiana at all, the majority have fragmentary bits of knowledge. Only those whose knowledge of history extends back beyond this week's daily news will remember a great deal about Paul McNutt, and the Indiana version of the "New Deal," or note the declining political power of the American Legion, or recall much about Indiana's involvement with the Ku Klux Klan (a story kept alive for Indianans by occasional news reports of D. C. Stephenson's efforts to win parole from the state prison); very few will correctly place as "Hoosiers" such bygone figures as Kenesaw Mountain Landis, Will Hays, or Tom Marshall.

Among all American non-residents of Indiana, perhaps two kinds of closer contacts with this land are the most common: those of visitors to Turkey Run, Brown County, Dunes State Park, etc., and those of businessmen, selling or buying goods or visiting branch factories. Yet a day or two, with little or no intimate interaction with any variety of natives or long-time residents, does not constitute much of an experience of Indiana and its people. What is said of the state is true of its capital city. A one-time visitor remembers the crowds and excitement at the "500 Mile Race" he attended as a youth; another recalls only the Circle and the War Memorial Plaza: "All I know is it's a city of monuments!"; another, who was driven up North Meridian Street but saw almost no other part of town, says, "It's really a charming city!"

There is, also, a remarkable lack of scholarly literature regarding the social life of all but one contemporary Indiana community, despite (or perhaps because of) the Lynds' initial study of *Middletown* (1929) and their later report, *Middletown in Transition* (1937).[2] Some of the most perceptive recent descriptions and interpretations of Indiana we have found were written by "expatriates" who still had some familial ties or roots from formative years in Indiana, just as did Robert S. Lynd, a native of New Albany. One of these is John Bartlow Martin's *Indiana: An Interpretation*, from which we quote later, and the other is Heath Bowman's *Hoosier*.[3] The latter is peculiarly intriguing to the social scientist, and perhaps should be to the general reader interested in social studies, because Heath Bowman's home town was Muncie (Middletown), and in his chapter, "Hoosiers in Transition," he recounts local reactions to the Lynds' book in 1937, particularly after the *Life* magazine article based upon it appeared.

Bowman's sampling of local opinion showed it to be full of anger against the Lynds, mostly due to what was felt to be "unfair" and "untruthful" publicity; and he reports as his conclusion: "I am quite sure that few people in Muncie have read both books from beginning to end."[4]

A public really hostile to social studies might make field work difficult for a social scientist, but at least he might expect his book to be read, and it seems much more likely that a massive indifference to such literature is more important than hostility as an explanation of the Muncie attitude. Actually, the shoe fits both feet: social scientists have neglected Indiana for many years, and one explanation would be that, given Indiana's All-American averageness, its communities, in most cases, never present social problems of wide interest or deal with a problem at hand in a highly original or stimulating way.[5]

As observers of the local scene, albeit for the special purposes of our study of philanthropy in Indianapolis, we have made efforts to learn as much as possible about Indiana and its capital city, guided by our training as social scientists, our native curiosity, and our experience with studies in other communities. In these efforts we naturally felt the lack of a recent or comprehensive social history of the state or the city. Perhaps this lack has another explanation than that already suggested: it seems to be related to a general lack of interest on the part of Hoosiers in any exact record of the past and an antipathy to the tracing of genealogies and "aristocratic" lineages, since they might be used to draw lines between social classes. The omission may be related also to a general tendency to obscure such bench-marks as would permit evaluating "progress" in the present or stating too precisely aspirations for the future. This blurring of reference-points not only helps to make claims confusing and constructive criticism impossible: it gives opportunistic innovation free play, at times with astoundingly favorable results, especially in mechanical inventions, and at times with results in the form of some of the most wrongheaded ideas ever produced on this continent.[6]

## What Makes a "Hoosier"?

Despite the dearth of social-scientific literature about this section of the country, a vast, more "literary," literature exists, which attempts to explain Hoosiers to themselves or to the rest of the country. Many such writers begin by attempting to trace the history of the word "Hoosier," and then proceed to tell of its current use in advertising, editorials and news stories, political speeches, welcoming remarks, and addresses by visitors.

A case evidently can be made out for derivation of the term from the days when Indiana men on the Ohio and Mississippi flatboats (and, later, steamboats) made themselves known as "Hushers," i.e., rough customers in any riverfront brawl, who had learned to "hush" an opponent in wrestling matches at log rollings back home. The earliest appearance of "Hoosier" in print is said to be in a work by John Finley, *The Hoosier's Nest*, back in the 1830's,[7] but a number of writers before and since James Whitcomb Riley—perhaps the most widely known Indiana author—have spread the word and given it many meanings; any one of these which appeals can be used to add antiquity to a still current part-joke. Indeed, "Hoosier" seems to be used at least as often in a humorous as in a serious context, especially by Indiana writers themselves.

The more or less witty anecdote which is often used to portray the Hoosier character, is illustrated in the following one about an early leader in Indiana, O. H. Smith:

. . . In 1836 he was elected senator by the General Assembly. He herded his 500 hogs to Cincinnati, arriving there at night covered with mud; a gentleman in the lobby inquired about the Indiana senatorial election, asking which of the two leading candidates had been chosen. "Neither," said Smith. "Then who?" "I am elected." "You! What is your name?" Smith told them. "You elected as United States Senator! I never heard of you before." "Very likely," said Smith, and next day sold his hogs for $7,000 cash and went home to Indiana (so Smith wrote at least in his memoirs; and George Ade himself never better revealed the Hoosier character, shrewd, dry, smug).[8]

The Hoosier character has also been built up by myth-makers, especially those who originated in Indiana but worked elsewhere.[9] Speaking of Kin Hubbard (creator of "Abe Martin Sez") and of George Ade, James Whitcomb Riley, and John T. McCutcheon, John Bartlow Martin points out that these were all "men whose only pretense was to simplicity and whose stock in trade was derision of pretense."[10]

As a result of both native and non-native attempts to understand Indian-ans—who seem to encourage these attempts by implying somehow that they are more American than anybody else—the pursuit of the term "Hoosier" may lead to a sizable collection of anecdotes, interviews, and news accounts over a period of time. From them the pursuer may gradually be led to believe that the term "Hoosier" truly refers to rusticity of a special kind—that of the "country boy" who is really both shrewd and kindly underneath a sometimes uncouth exterior or awkward manner, and who scores his biggest successes in a kind of confidence game in reverse, a confidence game in which the rustic "takes" the city slicker and turns him into a stupefied yokel. Such rustic characters are common and important in American literature and thought: the Connecticut Yankee, the Southern hillbilly, the Texas cowboy, the Corn-and-Hog-Belt farmer, the resentful natives at a summer resort—all have their legendary versions and living stereotypes. It must be admitted, of course, that the stereotyped and legendary rustic of Indiana seems to be mixed and changeable, not fully captured in any collection of anecdotes or even in the admirable series "Abe Martin Sez."

Nor will this definition hold true on all occasions, unfortunately. For one thing, those who call themselves or are called "Hoosiers" today are people in all walks of life: big city bankers and small town postmasters, industrialists and mechanics, used car salesmen, prosperous modern farmers on the high plains and poor ones in the eroded hills, doctors, lawyers, merchants, and even thieves. In view of this, perhaps the firmest contemporary meaning of the word "Hoosier" is *any person who is or ever was a resident of Indiana*,[11] whether his present newsworthy accomplishment is a heroic achievement, a great world honor, national recognition, criminal notoriety, or just death from old age in Florida. Living in Indianapolis or elsewhere in Indiana (except perhaps in Lake County which is "Gary and Chicago" to many[12]) is sufficient to qualify a person journalistically as a Hoosier of first degree, let us say, regardless of his personal feelings of identity or of his acceptance by "the natives" (those who have been in the state longer than he has).

There is, however, a second degree, called "loyal Hoosier"; and under this variant can be included those who act as if they plan to "live and die" in Indiana (instead of Dixie or anywhere else) or who, if forced to migrate and make good elsewhere, will claim to be Hoosiers in their fame and provide for their own return to a local burying ground—as Paul McNutt did not.[13]

The second degree is succeeded by a number of still higher degrees—up to and including the boiling-point or missionary Hoosier who, having passed the stage of proselytizing for new industry and new settlers within Indiana, instead seeks to make over some other territory into an image of his native land.[14]

## THE "HOOSIER" STANCE

Second and third degree Hoosiers are very conscious of themselves as Hoosiers and very eager to make clear the nature of the distinction to the visitor and potential fellow-Hoosiers. When the authors first came to Indianapolis for the sake of this study, they were repeatedly and insistently told that Indiana and the Hoosiers were and are "different" from other states and their populations. We were made aware that Indianapolis, as the "Hoosier Capital," had, like other places, its own peculiarities—of population composition, of local leadership, of government, and so on—and told that the people would be difficult to get to know and understand. We found it hard to believe in this difficulty, because in many other communities about which the same warnings had been given us as social scientists or persons "making a study of the community," we had soon found easy access to almost any situation in which we could learn what we needed to know. Now, after many months of combined effort, we would say that while Indianans are in most ways no different from Americans anywhere else, there is some truth in the advice we were given at the outset: Hoosiers are difficult to make acquaintance with, partly because so few of them participate very much socially with "newcomers," even when the latter have resided in Indianapolis for twenty years,[15] and partly because *as Hoosiers*, when they adopt that stance, they may indeed be difficult to understand.

Hoosiers are most earnest people, and like all earnest people, they tend to cover that earnestness with jocularity—especially for the stranger. Being a Hoosier is thus in part a career and in part a matter of gentle joke. The joke is carefully preserved. No one who is unwilling to stick around will be let in on that part of it which is available only to initiates.

The stance is especially difficult to recount as a joke: when the attempt is made, as in the following pages, the analysis tends to kill the warming humor, as such analysis usually does. Yet it also reveals something deep down that may well be the hard core of Hoosier distinctiveness on the American stage. Whether or not we state this clearly, fairly, and truthfully the reader must judge; but in any event the attempt must be made, because the Hoosier stance and manner of acting do, we believe, make a difference to the analysis of the problem of the Community Chest and of the larger context of mass fundraising in Indianapolis. There is a cultural factor here, in short, which may account for, among other things, the peculiar history of *federated* fundraising in Indianapolis.

The Hoosier stance is perhaps best revealed as it is most vocally put in the language of the "Aginner." Many Hoosier spokesmen declare themselves possessed of views summarized by the following terms (agin') and illustrated by the bracketed comment on each (for):

(1) *Anti-urbanization* (and nostalgic for Riley's "frost on the pumpkin," "the old swimming hole," farm or small town life as "the best way to raise your children," or the best preparation for rising in the business world: "I'm just a country boy myself . . . ," etc.);

(2) *Anti-secularization* (and favorable towards charity giving to street beggars, for example, as well as special "Christmas funds");

(3) *Anti-specialization* (and favorable towards perpetuating the belief in the omnicompetence of Everyman—as in "Any man can be President" coupled with, "It might as well be you"; or as in the Indiana Constitution's provisions and the workings of Indiana government, which long delayed the raising of standards in the professions of medicine, law, etc.);

(4) *Anti-centralization* (and showing preference for retaining *near* and *small* groups or organizations, except in so far as some centralization is necessary to protect these against still more distant and larger central authorities);

(5) *Anti-"bigness"* (and in favor of the *most local* control that can be maintained: in government, state versus federal, county versus state, township or smallest school district versus county or next larger school unit; in associational life, local group autonomy in preference to the dominance of a federation; and in economic life, home-owned rather than national corporations);

(6) *Anti-"planning"* (and preferring improvisation, especially that which recognizes Hoosier ingenuity; in zoning or annexation matters, preserving the individual's right to seek a "variance" or an exception to the rule, or to make a

"remonstrance" against proposed action by either government or another individual);

(7) *Anti-"continuity"* (and partial to the principle of "rotation" of officers and political parties or other power-holders).

This list could doubtless be extended, but for illustrative purposes perhaps it will suffice. It could be elaborated indefinitely by any good Hoosier, as he adapts himself to one bit of news after another that comes his way. The central theme seems to be "Individualism"; and the outcome, verbally at least, favors "Freedom" over "Order." In actuality, in the long run, and when he gets down to cases, the Hoosier is a *very* practical American; and if "lone wolf" autonomy doesn't produce the results he wants, he will join, or almost as often form, a group—especially one dedicated to preserving individualism! Not since the draft riots of the Civil War have Indianans failed to show the utmost in patriotism: in time of national danger, they are proud to "respond as one man." When we speak of the Hoosier insistence upon the autonomy of the individual, and of Indianans' "readiness to fight," it should be remembered that there is nothing un-American (or, rather, non-American) about this, nowadays at least: patriotism in time of war and local pride in time of peace are generic to American culture, although, perhaps, slightly exaggerated or emphasized in the Hoosier version.

We have already referred to the Hoosier stance as having the appearance of an "in-group joke." A native of Indianapolis whose confidence we came to enjoy told of some business difficulty he was having, and at one point he exploded with exasperated but affectionate "cuss words": "These ——— Hoosiers!!!" This, at first, reminded us of nothing so much as the profanity allowed to one of its members by an "in-group" or "minority."[16] Now it is clear that Indianans are no more a literal "minority" than are the people of any other state; on the contrary, four million Hoosiers are less of a numerical minority than many such aggregates. Why, then, their minority-like behavior? Is their status in doubt anywhere? Are they pushed around as if they were not free American citizens? Are they in fact subordinated, or do they just feel as if they were? Are Hoosiers really discriminated against, or do they simply feel ignored? Is it possible that an originally invidious term has been handed down with the added feeling that to be a Hoosier is to be someone who is loved and wanted, but only "Back Home in Indiana" and nowhere else? Do Indianans prefer being "Hoosiers" to being "dam' Yankees"— or is "Indianan" too close to "Indian"—or just too hard to pronounce?[17]

Every true minority group develops some system of defence against "insults," as well as a recognition-system enabling fellow-sufferers to know and help each other. And out of its interaction with the majority, the "out-group," there comes a kind of social rhetoric which permits scorn or censure to be voiced—half seriously, or half bitterly and half jokingly—by one member of the in-group to another. This semi-private rhetoric effectively reminds each of "what we must look out for" by making use precisely of the hated out-group's derogatory label: "nigger," "poor white," "hick"; historically, it is said, "Yankee Doodle" was such a label. Is "Hoosier" one too? John Bartlow Martin suggests it may be:

. . . Probably "Hoosier" is better known in the United States than any locale nickname save "Yankee." But in Indiana it is used seriously only by editorial writers, 4th of July orators, and chamber of commerce propagandists, and in his private life any of these would shoot like a dog a man who called him a Hoosier. Why does the Hoosier whisper diffidently that he is from Indiana (whereas the Texan bellows that he is from Texas)? . . .[18]

The foregoing partly contradicts our own experience in Indianapolis, and elsewhere. We doubt, for example, that "Hoosier" comes even close to "Yankee" as a nickname in the common knowledge of people outside the locale it describes. Also, in Indianapolis at least, we have heard "Hoosier" used by many kinds of people other than newsmen, orators, or business boosters, without a shooting.[19] In our ken, in the majority of cases, the Hoosier has not been particularly diffident: he has been vocal and assertive, and even boastful at times. He believes he has a pretty good thing, in the Hoosier style of doing business, the spirit of competition, and the drive to win. He wants everybody to know it—at least those fit to keep up with him.

One version of this half-earnest, half-joking self-portrait may be paraphrased, "Now, you see, we Hoosiers are no different from any other good Americans! We just try a little harder to be better than most, that's all!" Another version comes out when one Hoosier has lamented that Indianapolis is "behind the times," for example in not having a zoo, and another rejoins: "Who will pay for the upkeep? Anyway, who wants a smelly old zoo after all!" Or, since the Community Chest is not "leading the country": "Well, we don't want to be on the top, and we don't want to be on the bottom either. What's *wrong* with being average?" Meanwhile, the speaker is confident that in some other departments of life Indianapolis is far ahead of any place else, and isn't it up to a good Hoosier to see that he selects what he wants and gets what he pays for? When the pressure of comparison with other cities becomes too great and action becomes imperative, Hoosiers can nearly always count on one another to divide into factions: one promoting a "great program," the other blocking it or at least trying to do everything possible to keep what will "cost too much" from being carried beyond the planning stage. It is a kind of "block my kick, I'll block yours" teamwork that seems to keep most everybody satisfied. Perhaps caution is at the heart of the matter: "Keep your sights high, but don't waste fuel under the pot until you've brought home the game."

This attempt at paraphrasing a frontier motto reflects our impression that the contemporary expressions of Hoosier individualism do often evoke the images of pioneer days: of "self-help" in the raw (truly a matter of "Root, hog, or die!"); of "neighbors helping neighbors" face to face, and sharing wariness for outsiders or for government beyond the township level; of the struggle to achieve a system of state and local government which would elevate and protect the "ordinary man"; and of the everlasting fight to keep modern industrial civilization—its highways and factories—from "eating up good farm land," thereby destroying the good life associated with McGuffey's Readers, James Whitcomb Riley, and "Back Home in Indiana." These and other ancient battles are still being stoutly fought by good Hoosiers—especially in new situations which elsewhere would be met by planning, careful consideration of the real costs for the long run, firm resolution, and decisive action. In Indianapolis, it sometimes appears that Hoosiers prefer the fight to the victory: in 1955, it was evidently more fun to squabble over the care of the state-owned University Park than to divert energies and small funds to the maintenance of the only oasis of greenery in the downtown area. Certainly, as an introduction to the Hoosier way, such incidents serve their purpose in educating the newcomer.

## What Makes a "Hoosier" Tick?

In seeking an answer to this question, we can hardly begin better than by looking at a statement published by the Indianapolis Chamber of Commerce, which includes in its preamble that very suggestive phrase, "all loyal Hoosiers":

Pictorially and in brief narrative form our record growth is dramatically described in this report, which marks the 64th year of the Indianapolis Chamber of Commerce. The pictures and charts cover the calendar years, 1946 to 1954, inclusive.

The story, which will be pleasant and stimulating to all loyal Hoosiers, and perhaps surprising to a great many, is not the work of any one organization or of a few individuals.

Instead it is the result of the creation of a climate, beneficent to economic growth, in which a great many have had a part. Here on Hoosier soil there is a wholesome belief in the principles that have made our peculiar American economy dynamic and productive, in the supremacy of the individual over a collective, centralized state. Such a climate nurtures economic growth, out of which spring cultural, social and even religious endeavors, each an expansion and improvement over past effort, and all contributing to the conscious design to make a better community for all.

The statement continues with an eloquent proclamation of some of the strongest and most persistent convictions held by many Indianans, especially by those business leaders and rank-and-file who, given an opportunity, would, it is widely boasted, vote "a little to the Right" of the late, great "Mr. Republican," Robert A. Taft:

Far and wide, Hoosiers are known as men and women who believe in the principle of limited government and the importance of individual opportunity, and who conform their deeds to their words by steadfastly resisting the encroach-

ments of the state through federal aids and subsidies. Out of this characteristic
have come a community and a state with a minimum of laws and regulations to
harass and control business. Indiana has not gone to the extreme of many states
in passing radical laws. It perhaps has adopted fewer of the socialist-inclined
ideas than any other state in the Union. Its people are recognized as extraordinarily good workmen, whether at the desk or the bench. Industry has found
Indianapolis and Indiana attractive for its expansion.

This organization [the Indianapolis Chamber of Commerce], of course, has had
an important part in strengthening and nourishing this Hoosier characteristic.
Our program has been to help create and expand widespread understanding of
the economic principles which are fundamental to our economic growth; and
this means, conversely to resist the tendency in this post-war world to revive
socialist ideas and bestow all problems, economic and social, upon the government for solution.[20]

Back of this praise for an individualist philosophy of business is an
economic fact that tells a good deal about what makes a Hoosier "tick":
*money*. There are few states in America, and probably few places in the
world, which offer a truly able business or professional man such an
opportunity to build a personal fortune as does Indiana. For one thing, the
state Gross Income Tax (levying on all personal income, less certain exemptions, a flat rate of 1 per cent) is not payable, we were told, on receipts
from interstate transactions; more than that, this tax is classified as a type
of sales tax,[21] and there is no Indiana tax comparable with the progressive
income tax on personal incomes now levied in about thirty other states and
the District of Columbia. For another, the state constitution forbids the
issuing of state bonds, and hence all state expenses are met from current
income. Other constitutional arrangements make for an absence of "Home
Rule" (substantial autonomy for the local authority, especially in money
matters) for the growing cities and tend to impose restrictions on fundraising; this provision also functions to keep local taxes low.

Indianapolis, as the only "Class One City" in the state, is said to be
peculiarly "handicapped" in this respect. In another city, the home-owner
of equivalent property may pay a real property tax twice or more the
amount collected in Indianapolis, and will also pay state income tax, as
well as a direct sales tax. Those who have lived in cities in other states
sometimes point out that "where people pay more, they expect more"—more
in the form of all kinds of modern metropolitan services and physical
facilities, especially streets, sewers, and sanitation. Judging from the
reported efforts to "keep taxes down," the Indianapolis way of thinking is
just the opposite: where people are not led to expect too much, they will
not have to pay too much. Although this principle has not operated to
prevent Indianapolis from having a good public school system (supported
by separate funds administered by the "school city"), it has been reinforced
in other attempts to improve conditions by the operation of the state
constitution in limiting, chiefly by delaying actions, the leadership of the
civil city—especially when those attempts, if successful, would either entail
costly capital expenditure or require expensive upkeep.

There has been no lack of planning in Indianapolis history. In fact, it is occasionally asserted that Indianapolis is a "planned city" because the system of streets, radiating out from the Circle that now contains the Soldiers and Sailors Monument, was designed by an associate of the French architects who planned Washington, D.C. But the planning is evidently not of such a kind as to provide against periodic serious crises in reference to streets, sewers, transport, lighting, alleys, sidewalks, etc.[22]

All these complicated political and economic affairs seem examples of the interrelationships that underlie local behavior in response to almost every civic problem and many another problem that comes up in Indianapolis; they may be observed again in the long-delayed full functioning of the Metropolitan Planning Commission (authorized by the Legislature of 1955), the talk for many decades about a Civic Auditorium, the abortive, long-drawn-out efforts to secure a zoo, the difficulties of slum clearance[23] and "urban renewal," and perhaps some of the problems of federated fundraising.

The hospital situation in Indianapolis illustrates, in a serious way, the pattern of the Hoosier approach to a problem affecting the public interest and the general welfare. By 1950, the demand for hospital facilities had so far outstripped local provisions that a real crisis could be recognized, and even the Medical Society was sponsoring a petition-movement to secure a county hospital. In the sequel, after a group of outside experts had made a survey and recommended a long-range plan for a co-ordinated development of public and private facilities, a relatively small part of the larger, planned program was undertaken. With a very considerable amount of local effort, and national as well as local publicity, a great fundraising campaign succeeded in making a goal of $12,000,000 by December, 1953 (with collections on pledges continuing in 1956); this was enough to construct the new Community Hospital and to begin or purchase some additions to certain other private voluntary hospitals. So well "sold" was this campaign as a "one-shot, once-in-a-lifetime" affair, that many people say they are "going to wait and see" if any more facilities, public or private, will be needed, despite the original acceptance of a survey which clearly spelled out a long-range and much more costly program, and which contemplated a program on the present scale as making sense only as a "first step."[24]

When civil troubles assert themselves, they must, it would appear, develop to a serious crisis before action can be thought of; a long-range plan may be glanced at, but the immediate part of the task is by far the more appealing; and then, with a tremendous amount of energy and often much ingenuity, the clear and present danger is overcome—leaving later generations to have just as much fun going through another crisis, and paying for the extra cost that lack of foresight charges. This certainly *appears* to be a costly way of doing things, but perhaps, if all the economics were known, it might turn out that the Hoosier way really does "save money." At any one point in time, at least, the present residents are not having to pay out as much as they would be if they were "building for the future." "Besides," this view has it, "who knows for sure what the future will be?"[25]

What makes this way of "doing business" (at least the business of the commonwealth) so much preferred by Indianans? It is very much an oversimplification to say, "It's money!" For one thing, Indianapolis is probably about as wealthy a community, both in economic resources and in private fortunes, as a city can be—and it rates highly, as we shall show later, in terms of production or average income. The record of philanthropy alone justifies the claim that, with respect at least to many causes, "the people of Indianapolis are generous."

Nor can the Hoosier stance regarding government, which is adopted by a good many, if not all, completely satisfy us as an explanation. Even though, in a discussion about reapportionment in Indiana (to effect a modernized system of representation in the legislature, etc.), the audience could laugh when it was suggested that the federal Census be the basis for revision every decade and another could say, "There'd be no objection [to such federal aid] if it didn't cost any money!" and even though, in the daily press, a recurrent issue is any matter involving "accepting federal funds," the vast majority of Indianans today are becoming accustomed, if reluctantly, to non-local controls of all kinds, in government as well as in private enterprise.

There *is* a residuum of the early pioneer distrust of bigness, remoteness, and expertness, but it is becoming smaller. One example may be given in some detail. The Indiana Constitution of 1851 originally provided no power for the Supreme Court or the legislature to establish a system for admission to the bar or to prescribe qualifications for attorneys other than those it itself set up in the following brief statement, Section 21, Article 7: "Every person of good moral character, being a voter, shall be entitled to admission to practice law in all Courts of justice."[26] According to one commentator, "This was the Indiana system, the American system, the stubborn refusal to yield to central authority, however capable."[27] But by July, 1931, authorized by the General Assembly,[28] the Indiana Supreme Court *had* adopted rules regulating admission to the practice of law in Indiana, and had appointed the first Board of Law Examiners, which henceforth administered regular examinations for new candidates to determine their professional fitness. To ease the transition, a "grandfather clause" exempted those who had been admitted previously to the practice of law, since the earlier procedure often amounted merely to an appearance with sponsors and affidavits in a circuit court in the applicant's county of residence.

The Indianapolis Bar Association had been established in 1878, and the state Bar Association earlier, and it was the latter that was represented by *amici curiae* when the Supreme Court heard the case *In re Todd* (and refused rehearing, April 12, 1935).[29] The Court dismissed the petition of

Lemuel S. Todd for admission to practise law in Indiana[30] on the ground that Section 21, Article 7, had been abrogated by virtue of its submission to the voters at the general election of November 8, 1932.[31] In this election the voters had approved an amendment to repeal Section 21, Article 7, the vote being 439,949 for adoption and 236,613 against, out of all those who chose to vote on the amendment; however, "the number of voters favoring adoption of the amendment was much less than half the number of voters who voted for political candidates at the general election."[32]

We may consider 1935 as a significant date, for it points to one fairly recent example of what is still to be found in Indiana and Indianapolis: the frequently long struggle between "progressive" and "laggard" parts of the governmental (or even the social) system to bring Indiana standards and performance in such fields of specialization as the law "up" to the level attained much earlier elsewhere in the nation. That is, until only two decades ago, in this specialized but rather important respect, Indiana exhibited a kind of "culture lag,"[33] a clinging to frontier individualism in the modern day: not merely "every man his own lawyer" but, by virtue of freedom to practise, "every man his neighbor's lawyer"—and, potentially, somebody else's too.

On the other hand, this recent example illustrates the fact that Indiana *is* changing. This has been especially true since World War II, and the change is certainly more rapid than the myth-makers realize; and, we should like to say, with luck and much foresight on the part of Indianans, there is hope that the changes will not result in making the state a mere carbon copy of more eastern and northern industrial agglomerations, but in making "Hoosierland" as pleasant to look upon as it is and will be prosperous.

## THE LEADERS AND THE LED

If we reject either or both "it's money" and "it's rugged individualism" as fully satisfactory explanations for the Hoosier way, what else is there? A very great deal, no doubt. But let us follow one more track through the maze: what are the preoccupations of the available civic leaders and what are the characteristics of those to be led?

For some decades, Indianapolis has been a center for the introduction to city life of large numbers of migrants from rural and small-town back-grounds in the South as well as in Indiana itself. Without adopting a local prejudice that sometimes says these people bring in "low standards," one can fairly state that their expectations of what a metropolis should be are rather different from the dreams of the European immigrants to our other great cities, who brought with them notions, so it is said, of "streets paved with gold," and who, even if it is true that some kept coal in the bath-tub, made a great leap in migrating at all and tended to continue to strive upward, once they had planted roots in America. The Indianapolis "in-migrants," however, include quite a few whose dream is to "make a bundle" and go back to the farm, and many who do indeed migrate back and forth in their lifetimes, perhaps trying Detroit or Chicago after graduating from the Indianapolis experience. Yet many stay, to raise families here, so that for them educational level and even level of urban sophistication is raised in succeeding generations.

In very recent years, there have been other changes in population, aside from those incident to World War II alone. Indianapolis has received many in-migrants from other cities, some even larger. It is these people, concerned with trade, finance, publicity and advertising, and a considerable variety of new manufacturing enterprises, who are the "newcomers," and they are most conspicuous in such civic affairs as they are admitted to, for example the Community Chest campaign. It is not known if any natives complain that these bring in high—or too high—standards, but it is known that the "newcomers" from larger cities have a good deal to say about Indianapolis. One hears such comments as:

"You get used to that relaxed manner, after you've been here awhile."
"I wouldn't mind paying higher taxes to get some of these things taken care of [sewers, streets, sanitation, etc.]."
"These Hoosiers make the finest friends a man could want, after you get to know them."
"Now that I've been here six years I can go downtown and say to myself, 'Why it's quite a pretty town after all!' "
"Why do they need all those sirens [on ambulances, and on police and fire vehicles]?"
"It's so dusty and treeless downtown!"
"These discontinuous streets—how would they ever get the people out of town in case of an air raid?"
"One thing! Most of the drivers are so relaxed and polite, and the pedestrian really gets a break in this town."

Perhaps one phrase to synthesize all these is: "Now I know what these people mean when they say, 'It's just a small town after all!' "

What the preoccupations of the civic leaders are, it is more difficult to say. But they seem to be more continuously busy with industrial and commercial concerns, and with politics beyond the local level, than they are with what are more strictly the possible civic concerns of Indianapolis people. One explanation often extended has it that, owing to the lack of "Home Rule," the present local leadership hasn't had much practice at the social engineering necessary to securing even the basic physical facilities needed by a metropolis of half a million or more. Because making the ancient machinery work at all is such a struggle, there is little time or energy left to promote "the better things" locally. This interpretation is suggested by thoughtful persons ranging from high-status managers to taxi-drivers. Another explanation relates to the previously mentioned missionary zeal of Hoosiers of the higher degrees: they are too busy telling people of other cities about the Hoosier way to pursue the tasks requiring co-operation, except for sporadic efforts to keep up what they want to talk about to citizens elsewhere. Still other possibilities are that Indianapolis loses, by "leadership export," able men who go away to "make good"; and that it also exports "experts," professional men and women attracted else-where by higher salaries and different working conditions. We shall discuss this question later. As in every community, there are some who feel that "they"—meaning the top owners and controllers of "everything in town"—are "not doing their share," and are probably off enjoying life in Florida or somewhere.

There is another possibility to be mentioned: it is the traditional American, especially Midwestern, and perhaps peculiarly Hoosier, attitude about *local* leaders. The feeling is that connected with a rejection of the very idea of "aristocracy," and with saying, firmly, "There are no classes here." The logic is that "everybody is equal," even if "some are more equal than others"; and the aspiration is to maintain, and personally to succeed in, a ladder of equal opportunity. The setting or social context is that of the small town newspaper and small town gossip, such as in "Home Town Boy Makes Good," but also in, "Well, now, we knew him when . . . ," and the consequence is that the would-be local leader often finds himself to be a prophet without honor, one who "stuck his neck out and got it chopped off."

Indianapolis is, of course, *not* a small town in a population sense, and yet, how are we to understand the prevalence of small-town attitudes? Perhaps one explanation is that the people who express them are psychologically still living "back home" in whatever home town they came from. And even natives of Indianapolis often have family ties to rural places in Indiana and elsewhere. Perhaps this ultimately accounts not only for alleged public apathy but also for alleged lack of leadership: who would want to "rock the boat"?

General allegations such as these have been made, from time to time, about practically every city in the United States. Louisville was once called "An American Museum Piece," and Birmingham, "The City of Perpetual Promise," for example; and what has been said about Philadelphia or Chicago—"Time for Another Fire"—is not being said, herein at least, about Indianapolis! John Gunther's comment about Indianapolis—"the dirtiest city in the United States"—is being forgotten, but it is useful as a goad in a campaign to win for this city the national title of "Cleanest."[34]

The "Cleanest City" campaign, of course, is another example of what we have called the Hoosier approach. A very large amount of publicity has been given to this campaign and it has been linked up, in an interesting way, with the "Self-Help" or "Keep Taxes Down" themes in connection with the "Yard Parks" campaign: "Make Your Yard Like a Park." The latter is the contemporary slogan of an older movement in Indianapolis that seems to have grown out of the long-established tradition and still largely true fact that "Indianapolis is a city of homes" rather than of apartments and tenements. In 1929, even, there was some attempt to start a movement with the slogan "Home Play Week," and it was said, "Indianapolis still has many back yards but only small numbers of them are equipped with simple play facilities for children. . . ."[35] Apart from the "Yard Parks" campaign, the Hoosier approach in the clean-up mission has been to turn what the Dutch would regard as a civic duty into a prize-seeking contest, with an attempt even to introduce this theme into the 1956 Democratic campaign platform, as part of a "Make America Beautiful" program. At times it appears that the Hoosier approach is to make it possible for everybody, at one time or another, to get into the "Winner's Circle," as at the 500 Mile Race, or to be the "Champ" in the "Hoosier Madness" of the state basketball finals, or to win a ribbon at the Fair. Competition, and winning, count for a great deal in this culture, and provide one of the many ways in which the ladder of opportunity is offered to all, at least symbolically.

At the same time, behind the carnival trimmings, it is often possible for serious work to take place: as for example, in the efforts to control air pollution that are part of the "Cleanest City" campaign. It is sometimes difficult to remember that tax money is spent, year in and year out, for such things, partly because less publicity is given to the undramatic and essential than is given to the hearings and charges and counter-blasts that go on in connection with local government. After all, the services that preserve the public safety and the public health do continue, the parks system and recreation services are in business to stay—even if it took Indianapolis until about 1899 to get a Park Law that was "constitutional"[36]—and much work is planned and under way to provide improvements in the basic governmental machinery and physical equipment one expects in a modern city. "Desegregation" in the public schools has been a fact for some years now, and in this and other matters Indianapolis is quietly going about the tasks of keeping up with social change. The Hoosier way of speaking perhaps obscures the picture rather than impedes fulfilment of program, but the situation in Indianapolis in 1955-6 was sufficiently confusing to make it difficult to see beyond the possible joke as it applied in each incident we observed or heard or read about in the local press.[37]

In 1955-6, Indianapolis gave every sign of being a city in transition—a civil unit that in some ways had "grown like Topsy" and that comprised a congeries of ancient neighborhoods and disappearing villages along with brash new real estate developments; a collection of individuals who had little "sense of community" and very little recognition of the local internal social structure; a diversity of persons who were living psychologically in many different small towns and close to kith and kin, but who were also performing tasks in an almost miraculous modern industrial civilization; and a community which was moving from "Small Town" to "Big City" almost without direction, and almost with reluctance, with much nostalgia for the simpler life, and with waning remembrance of this city's "Golden Age" (1880 to 1910 or so). Thus, in 1955-6, it seemed that change dominated the landscape, and that the bits of Hoosier character we encountered from time to time were vestigial, perhaps atavistic, and possibly non-adaptive in the modern world.

Yet as we read newspaper clippings or consulted earlier reports on Indianapolis affairs, we began to wonder if the times were unusually out of joint, or if, perhaps, Indianapolis has a habit of being in transition. Could it be that, despite its lack of "Boom and Bust" in the past fifty years, despite its lack of a large European immigrant population to assimilate, despite the steady predominance of something very close to a 70 per cent native white Protestant majority year after year, despite the city's difficulties in trying to expand physical facilities to match its growth in population and area, despite everything that has made the city so "typically American"—and, hence, so lacking in tough, challenging problems—could it be, to repeat, that Indianapolis has had, for decades perhaps, an underlying "dynamic" that really is a peculiar one in this day and age?

Our highly tentative answer must be "Yes," and at the risk of events eventually confounding prophecy we have labelled this dynamic "Change without Progress." For many reasons, it even seems possible that this dynamic will permit Indianapolis soon to cover double its present area— with a population of over 750,000, and perhaps a total of one million in the county, including the city—*without* fundamental change in the characteristics of the masses of the people ("replacements" being continually born back in the hills somewhere), without basic disruption to the neighborhood system, especially those parts which facilitate urbanization of rural in-migrants, and without improvement in the relations between old families and newcomers. As an urban community, Indianapolis has an admirable social organization to prevent the development in most people of any strong sense of belonging to the rest of the city, and to perpetuate the sense of belonging instead to the land, the state, as a Hoosier of some degree. And the new great industries developing on the fringes will draw more and more workers who will continue to commute from smaller settlements for miles and miles around. "Greater Indianapolis" is more than a slogan: it is rapidly coming into existence. But its underlying social organization is much more likely than not to reproduce a large number of its present outcropping manifestations.

Elsewhere (chapters 11 and 12) we discuss social class stratification in detail, and it is sufficient perhaps in so preliminary a sketch of Indianapolis merely to indicate the seemingly unusual obstacles to its social integration. These might well be symbolized as in the accompanying diagram, where the usual pyramidal social class hierarchy is shown as intersected by a horizontal barrier dividing the "top top leaders" from those "down the line"—

for communication and mobility—and where a further vertical barrier divides the "old timers" from the "new people" at every social level. Such a community emphasizes discontinuity (both in time—i.e., history and tradition—and in social organization) and prizes invention and innovation; it achieves "Change without Progress"; it tends to reject the "aristocratic" or "noble" individual, but it gives recognition to individualism by applying the Principle of Rotation ("spinning one's wheels" in the vernacular, or "kicking

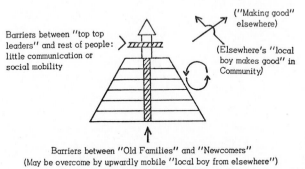

Barriers between "top top leaders" and rest of people: little communication or social mobility

("Making good" elsewhere)

(Elsewhere's "local boy makes good" in Community)

Barriers between "Old Families" and "Newcomers"
(May be overcome by upwardly mobile "local boy from elsewhere")
(Layers indicate social status)

COMMUNITY OF TRANSITIONAL TYPE

the rascals out" in political and associational affairs, or providing in advance that an elected officer cannot succeed himself) and the Principle of Variance (the extension from the real estate field of the notion that every individual is entitled to try to obtain a release from the rules or forces making for compliance, while, on the other hand, those who wish to maintain a *status quo* are entitled to appear as remonstrators against any change). In the Indiana case, such a community thus tends to preserve "the Hoosier way."

"Greater Indianapolis" is called "an overgrown country town" by some, especially natives, who remark, "I can say that because I was born and raised here, but people resent an outsider saying it!" If anyone feels that this description is implausible when speaking of a city of half a million, then let him try the description "metropolitan cultural center." As observers, we are inclined to neither extreme; and though we would say Indianapolis is in transition to the latter, we think the theory worth considering that Indianapolis has been in this condition for at least forty years. It may even well be true that it was more purely a metropolis, and a cultural center relative to its hinterland, from about 1880 to 1910 than ever before or since. The "Golden Age" involved much that is lacking in Indianapolis today, especially a greater degree of local control in commerce and industry, and greater effort to sustain civic pride and to make Indianapolis the cultural as well as the political capital of the Hoosier state.

The local lack of interest in vistas (as evidenced in the discontinuous street patterns), the monuments to the past, the preoccupation with the

"Winner" (a temporary record-breaker), and on the whole, the "aristocratic" interest in the completed product rather than a "democratic" concern for the process of making it: all these may well enter into an assessment of "What's Hoosier about Indianapolis?" It comes close to a *dynamic nostalgia* that keeps most people in appropriate ruts and avoids contact with anything new and strange which might put fundamental changes in motion—such as a constitutional convention to rewrite the Indiana Constitution of 1851. From this viewpoint, Indianapolis might be said to be "less American" than New York City or Chicago or Cleveland or even, perhaps, Gary, Indiana.

So "dim" a view may be easily challenged, of course, and it ought to be. A staff member reading a draft of this chapter reacted as follows, especially with regard to the suggested possibility of "Change without Progress" as the city reaches 750,000 population:

I don't think the city can continue as suggested. If such expansion takes place, more and more national firms will be introduced with resulting influx of managerial people unaccustomed to the Hoosier outlook. What we are very probably seeing now is the impact of these people on contact with "We can out-slick the city slicker"; and the more cosmopolitan view appears to be coming into ascendancy. Since we see no evidence of anyone coming up to replace . . . [one of the leading families in Indianapolis] it seems improbable that, as they pass from the scene (having been long preceded by other families controlling local enterprise), the "Hoosier" cult can long maintain itself.

This statement pinpoints the problem: *Is* the "more cosmopolitan view coming into ascendancy"? If it had been strongly ascendant in 1950 to 1956, what evidence can be pointed to that is either tangible (a visible physical structure or changed conditions in the city) or intangible (a new governmental development or an innovation in private organization)?

Our "dim view" can be opposed by a less radical view than that the "new managers" will replace the older leadership; modern corporations usually encourage their executives instead to "fit in." Another possibility is that the old families will make a concerted effort to hold together and to re-assert an aristocratic type of social leadership, providing positive sanctions for civic concerns and making good use of the "new managers" to do the necessary jobs—thus incidentally putting themselves into closer relationships with the newcomers. After all, not all the newcomers are transients, oriented only to the structures of the national corporations which send them here, with expectations of moving onward and upward by means of transfers and promotions. This re-assertion might do all that would be necessary to accelerate the "Hoosierization" of newcomers all the way down the line, and thus secure "Change with a Little Progress." It is likely that this is what we are seeing and hearing now, in 1956.

More evidence than we have at hand would be needed to choose between these views of the future of Indianapolis, but remembering the history of other cities with deep-rooted cultures, and recognizing that the Hoosier case has endured for a relatively long time (in terms of American history), it is a safe bet that no massive change will occur overnight, and that the larger this city grows, the more costly will be the necessary revision of its physical facilities and neighborly ways of life. When Indianapolis had only half its present population, there were, no doubt, persons who said it could not possibly accommodate half a million with such an outmoded physical plant, or without improvements much too costly to contemplate. But who would now say (in 1955-6) that the old City Market is done for? Much of the old, and not too much of the new, makes it possible for a city as large as this to go on growing for a long, long time. And perhaps, when the inevitable crisis arrives, the once-new managers, or their sons, will join in the Hoosier fun of first drawing up a grand design for a New City, and then building instead only that needed bridge or sewer addition or whatever is most urgently wanted in 1975!

Meanwhile the voices of protest are scarcely to be heard at all in Hoosierland. A minor, and much ignored one in Indianapolis is that of "The Citizens Committee of Greater Indianapolis" which publishes to a small circulation a mimeographed sheet called *The Tattler*. Its July, 1956, issue dealing with the gubernatorial election to be held in November, commented, in part:

. . . So Indiana will stumble into an election between individuals we cannot help but feel will not represent what Indiana deserves. The economic life in Indiana is far outdistancing Indiana's political leadership. The stresses and strains caused by our rapid industrial expansion and increase of population are going to catch up with each tax payer, and very soon. These very problems will then make possible a political resolve lacking in the confused, topsy-turvy picture today. Then Indiana voters will be made pointedly aware of their plight by whosoever is forthright to state his position and program of action. We will continue to doubletalk ourselves from roads to schools, schools to municipal self-government, municipal self-government to taxing powers, taxing powers to reapportionment, reapportionment to political machines, and back to roads again. But each problem in its way becomes annually a little bit worse. Eventually, we must bury our dead.[38]

## America's "Classless Society" and the Hoosier Social System

American society, it seems generally agreed, is organized around the fundamental dynamic of an "open class system,"[39] and if Indiana and Indianapolis are "different" from the rest of America, what part does this open class dynamic play in Hoosier society? Is the Hoosier subdivision of the general American society "the same only more so"? Or does the Hoosier way involve: (1) A fundamentally different social class system? or (2) an extra freedom of social mobility ("social climbing" or "declining")? or (3) a markedly different aggregate of people, as a consequence of a special mixture of frontier and other culture strains brought by in-migrants?

Speaking only of Indianapolis, and then only from observations and impressions, we would guess that a thoroughgoing community study of this metropolitan city[40] would show that Indianapolis, Marion County, and the relevant contiguous parts of central Indiana *are* somewhat unique, not only in the United States generally, but even within Indiana. Apart from the fact that Indianapolis is "the largest city in Indiana, and second largest State Capital, [and] the largest city in the world not located on a navigable waterway,"[41] it is, more significantly from a sociological point of view, the "hub city" of the high plains of central Indiana and belongs much less to the northern third of the state and somewhat less to the southern portion than it does to the middle tier of counties. It is obviously more Hoosier than Gary, or perhaps Fort Wayne; and it is less "Southern" than Evansville or Madison. Thus, when we speak of social classes, vertical mobility, or the in-migrants, in connection with Indianapolis, we are not referring to Indiana as a whole, even though the state is sometimes regarded as "Hoosierland." If a phrase is wanted, we are speaking about the "Heart of Hoosierland."

### 1. *The social class system*

There are at least six social classes[42] in the Indianapolis community (comprising certainly the city and the county, even if some rural residents speak resentfully of Indianapolis as "Big Brother"). These social levels are broadly differentiated by local behavior and local evaluations of such behavior in ways that are very similar to those found generally all through the Midwest. For example, in Indianapolis (as elsewhere) the several professions and occupations, as well as the various positions in business organizations, etc., are accorded varying degrees of social prestige, and tend to be associated with varying amounts of power in economic, social, and political affairs. Sources of income, as well as amounts, are differentially evaluated: inherited or earned wealth rates "high" and dependency upon public welfare rates "low," with a "good salary" and "honest wages" somewhere in between. The family's choice or achievement of neighborhood as well as its elected or accepted type of dwelling—from an estate with a large house to a shack near the dump—also makes some difference to its social participation.

A person of very high status in Indianapolis also has peers with similar incomes, styles of life, interests, backgrounds, and viewpoints in other American cities. A middle-class businessman in Indianapolis may be transferred by his company to any one of hundreds of other American cities and find there a niche much like that he has just left. A laboring man similarly could find work and a way of life elsewhere much like that he had in Indianapolis.[43]

Before World War I, when practically everybody who belonged in the Indianapolis community lived "in town" (although the well-to-do and wealthy owned farms and summer places, as many do nowadays), it was doubtless possible to explore the important streets and the side-streets and even the alleys and see with one's own eyes the outward appearance of varying life styles from "high" to "low" class, if only in the architecture of the dwellings. The mansions of the "top top leaders" of the community were well known, and the unsanitary dwellings of the "lowest" class were not yet so concentrated and isolated in vast slums as they had been in many northern industrial cities.[44] The present preference for home ownership was just as strong then; and then, as now, Indianapolis was "a city of homes"— detached houses being preferred. The city's arrangement into neighborhoods which had gained or lost in reputation made it possible, upon hearing a home address, to make a pretty close guess as to the occupation, income, and probable life style of the family that dwelt there. To a much greater extent, probably, than is true today, "everybody knew everybody else"—or, at least, "everybody who mattered." The "top top leaders" of the community were active in civic affairs—more so than they are today, so far as we can judge from behavior in the fundraising and related organizations we studied.

It is our impression that, as the "top top leaders" withdrew more and more from comprehensive, direct control of local affairs, they simultaneously moved out from the showplaces that had been their dwellings, especially from along the city's famed and highly visible North Meridian Street. This flight to the suburbs did not, as in older American cities, where it occurred earlier, take the form of following the most rapid transportation lines then available—the railroads (as in Philadelphia's Main Line, New York's West-chester County, Boston's and Chicago's North Shores, etc.) Perhaps the Indianapolis flight coincided with increasing availability of the automobile. At any rate, no very large wealthy suburbs developed, and today one finds the homes of the Indianapolis élite scattered widely, in a number of tiny clusters (which may or may not be incorporated), with five or ten families on big estates. It is as if the "top top leaders" fled from well-known show-places to ill-known hideaways—or at any rate, to locations off the beaten track of the busy highways.[45]

If there is anything peculiar about the American social class system as it is organized locally in Indianapolis, it seems to be that the social distance between the "top top leaders" and those nearest them has been growing. And it may be that hideaways symbolize, if they do not actually cause or facilitate, this withdrawal of the "upper crust" from active participation and direction of Indianapolis affairs.[46]

## 2. *Extra freedom of mobility*

Hoosier claims certainly emphasize the Indianapolis climate of "oppor-tunity for all," but we have no firm evidence that Indianapolis people actually score or do not score more individual rises in the world than do those of any other Midwestern city.

The single relevant study of Indianapolis itself that we know of does not bear directly upon this point, but does clearly establish great year-to-year steadiness in the amount of *occupational mobility,* comparing 1910 with 1940. "For the population as a whole [Indianapolis], the average mobility rate did not change over the thirty year time span. During both time periods, occupational moves were made, on the average by about four-fifths as many men as expected on a . . . basis of no relation between fathers' and sons' occupational class. If we use these mean mobility rates as a single measure of the openness or rigidity of the occupational structure they indicate that no change took place during the past three decades."[47]

Studies of business leaders for 1928 and 1952 show that Indiana has evidently declined as a site of concentration in comparison with the rest of the United States; other states in the East North Central region have, however, scored relative gains, as shown in Table I.[48]

TABLE I

DISTRIBUTION BY STATE OF RESIDENCE OF 1928 BUSINESS LEADERS AND BY
STATE OF PRESENT BUSINESS OF 1952 BUSINESS LEADERS

| State | State of residence of 1928 leaders (percentage[a]) | State of present business of 1952 leaders (percentage[a]) | Percentage[b] gain or loss |
|---|---|---|---|
| Illinois | 5.1 | 11.2 | 119 |
| Indiana | 1.3 | 1.2 | − 8 |
| Michigan | 2.9 | 3.9 | 37 |
| Ohio | 4.5 | 6.4 | 43 |
| Wisconsin | 1.1 | 2.0 | 78 |
| TOTAL (Region) | 14.9 | 24.7 | 66 |

[a]Percentage of U.S. sample.  [b]Percentage gain or loss relative to 1928 figure.

Indeed, the picture regarding Indiana leadership, whether it is compared with other states in the region or whether it is compared with other regions must appear black even to many well-wishers.

Let us turn first to the *production* of leaders. The average age of top business leaders in the nation is about fifty to sixty years, and one would therefore expect that the number of such leaders in any state would be roughly proportionate to the adult population of that state in 1900 (i.e., to the potential parents who could have produced them then). Table II A shows for the East North Central region the proportions of just such a national sample of business leaders now to be found in the constituent states, and compares these proportions with proportions of adults in the 1900 population. The last column shows the "productivity ratio," which is the ratio between the number of leaders actually produced and those one might reasonably have expected on the basis of population. It is obvious that Indiana is at the bottom of the list, and produces fewer leaders by far than its presence in the region would lead one to expect. If Indiana's production of leaders is now put in national instead of in regional perspective, the picture is in many ways clearer, and in some ways, worse. It may be read off from Table II B, where the observation is virtually forced upon one that only Indiana and the South failed to produce at least their expected

TABLE II A

DISTRIBUTION OF 1952 BUSINESS LEADERS BORN IN EAST NORTH CENTRAL REGION
BY STATE OF BIRTH AND 1900 ADULT<sup>a</sup> POPULATION BY STATE OF RESIDENCE

| State | Percentage of leaders born in region who were born in state | Percentage of region adult population who were residing in state in 1900 | Productivity ratio of state relative to region |
|---|---|---|---|
| Illinois | 39.55 | 30.16 | 1.31 |
| Indiana | 11.14 | 15.74 | .71 |
| Michigan | 13.37 | 15.14 | .88 |
| Ohio | 23.79 | 26.01 | .91 |
| Wisconsin | 12.14 | 12.94 | .94 |
| TOTAL (Region) | 100.0 % | 100.0 % | 1.00 |

<sup>a</sup>Adult = 20 years of age or more.

TABLE II B

DISTRIBUTION OF 1952 BUSINESS LEADERS BORN IN THE UNITED STATES BY REGION OR
STATE OF BIRTH, AND 1900 ADULT<sup>a</sup> POPULATION BY REGION OR STATE OF RESIDENCE

| Region or state | Percentage of leaders born there | Percentage of 1900 U.S. population living there | Productivity ratio relative to U.S. |
|---|---|---|---|
| New England | 9.999 | 7.358 | 1.36 |
| Middle Atlantic | 28.091 | 20.337 | 1.38 |
| East North Central | 25.713 | 21.036 | 1.22 |
| Illinois | 10.170 | 6.345 | 1.60 |
| Indiana | 2.865 | 3.311 | .87 |
| Michigan | 3.438 | 3.186 | 1.08 |
| Ohio | 6.117 | 5.471 | 1.12 |
| Wisconsin | 3.123 | 2.723 | 1.15 |
| West North Central | 13.909 | 13.616 | 1.02 |
| South Atlantic | 8.337 | 13.742 | .61 |
| East South Central | 3.653 | 9.932 | .37 |
| West South Central | 3.610 | 8.596 | .42 |
| Mountain | 2.206 | 2.204 | 1.00 |
| Pacific | 4.484 | 3.180 | 1.41 |
| TOTAL (U.S.A.) | 100.0 % | 100.0 % | 1.00 |

<sup>a</sup>Adult = 20 years of age or more.

quota of top business leaders. This gives, perhaps, fresh force to the often-heard characterization of Indiana as "the most Southern of Northern States."

Another comparison, equally illuminating, is possible. This comparison has to do, not with the production of present leaders, but with their present place of business as compared with the present distribution of adult, male population. This gives us a "residence ratio." If the ratio exceeds 1, it is an indication that there are more top leaders in the state than the present number of adult males would lead one to expect by chance; if the ratio is less than 1, there are fewer resident leaders than one would expect on this basis. Table III A shows the data within the East North Central region, and it clearly indicates that Indiana has less than half the leaders one would expect, on this basis, to be doing business here. Within its region, and on

TABLE III A

DISTRIBUTION BY STATE OF PRESENT BUSINESS (WITHIN EAST NORTH CENTRAL REGION)
OF 1952 BUSINESS LEADERS AND 1950 ADULT[a] MALE POPULATION

| State | Percentage of region's 1952 business leaders | Percentage of region's adult male population 1950 | Residence ratio |
|---|---|---|---|
| Illinois | 45.53 | 30.27 | 1.50 |
| Indiana | 5.00 | 12.65 | .40 |
| Michigan | 15.74 | 19.64 | .80 |
| Ohio | 26.25 | 25.81 | 1.02 |
| Wisconsin | 7.48 | 11.63 | .64 |
| TOTAL (Region) | 100.0 % | 100.0 % | 1.00 |

[a]Adult = 20 years of age or more.

TABLE III B

DISTRIBUTION OF 1952 BUSINESS LEADERS BY REGION OR STATE OF PRESENT
BUSINESS AND OF ADULT[a] MALE 1950 POPULATION

| Region or state | Percentage of U.S. business leaders resident | Percentage of adult males | Residence ratio |
|---|---|---|---|
| New England | 7.118 | 6.511 | 1.09 |
| Middle Atlantic | 38.370 | 21.790 | 1.76 |
| East North Central | 25.480 | 21.059 | 1.21 |
| Illinois | 11.601 | 6.374 | 1.82 |
| Indiana | 1.275 | 2.665 | .48 |
| Michigan | 4.010 | 4.135 | .97 |
| Ohio | 6.689 | 5.436 | 1.23 |
| Wisconsin | 1.905 | 2.449 | .78 |
| West North Central | 8.551 | 10.429 | .82 |
| South Atlantic | 6.803 | 12.319 | .55 |
| East South Central | 1.833 | 7.218 | .25 |
| West South Central | 3.208 | 9.233 | .35 |
| Mountain | .888 | 3.127 | .28 |
| Pacific | 7.748 | 8.315 | .93 |
| TOTAL (U.S.A.) | 100.0 % | 100.0 % | 1.00 |

[a]Adult = 20 years of age or more.

this basis, Indiana appears more barren of top leaders even than Wisconsin. Similarly, within the perspective of the whole nation (Table III B), only Indiana, among the states in the region, resembles the South Central and Mountain states in having less than half the number of leaders expected on the basis of its present proportion of all adult males.

We may turn to another series of measures for further illumination on the problem of Indiana leadership. One such measure would neglect the question of production of leaders and simply ask: "Of the number of leaders (however few or many) born in the state, how many are still there?" This would give us a measure of what Warner and Abegglen call "stability" with respect to leadership. In Table IV it is visible, first, that less than a fifth of the top leaders born in Indiana stayed there; and, second, that of all the states in the region, and all other regions in the country, only the Mountain region has greater instability in its native leadership.

## TABLE IV

LEADERSHIP STABILITY BY STATES AND REGIONS

| Region or state | Leadership stability[a] |
|---|---|
| New England | 43.3% |
| Middle Atlantic | 75.1 |
| East North Central | 60.6 |
| Illinois | 49.9 |
| Indiana | 19.0 |
| Michigan | 48.3 |
| Ohio | 48.0 |
| Wisconsin | 24.3 |
| West North Central | 35.6 |
| South Atlantic | 46.9 |
| East South Central | 29.0 |
| West South Central | 42.1 |
| Mountain | 17.5 |
| Pacific | 68.1 |

[a]Leadership stability is the percentage of leaders who were born in the state or region who are still there.

Another way to look at the same problem, taking count of gain as well as loss, is simply to compare the number of leaders now in the state or region with the number born there, and to compute the percentage gain or loss. This has been done in Table V, and again it is evident that only the Mountain states have suffered a *net* loss of top leadership comparable with Indiana. So large a percentage loss out of an already low production of leaders is even more significant socially than the figure by itself suggests.

## TABLE V

STATE OR REGIONAL NET GAIN OR LOSS OF LEADERS SHOWN AS
PERCENTAGE OF LEADERS BORN IN EACH STATE OR REGION

| Region or state | Percentage increase or decrease over number of leaders born in region | |
|---|---|---|
| New England | | −28.8 |
| Middle Atlantic | +36.6 | |
| East North Central | | − 0.9 |
| Illinois | +14.1 | |
| Indiana | | −55.5 |
| Michigan | +16.7 | |
| Ohio | + 9.4 | |
| Wisconsin | | −39.0 |
| West North Central | | −38.5 |
| South Atlantic | | −18.4 |
| East South Central | | −49.8 |
| West South Central | | −11.1 |
| Mountain | | −59.7 |
| Pacific | +72.8 | |

Lastly, a composite measure of loss (for details of its computation see Warner and Abegglen) is embodied in what is called an "Average Ratio of Mobility out of the State or Region." Essentially it consists in comparing actual movements of leaders out with the movements that would be expected if chance alone were operating. On this basis we get the picture in Table VI.

TABLE VI

| Region or state | Average ratio of mobility out of state or region |
|---|---|
| New England | .41 |
| Middle Atlantic | .39 |
| East North Central | .48 |
| Illinois | .66 |
| Indiana | .87 |
| Michigan | .72 |
| Ohio | .50 |
| Wisconsin | .76 |
| West North Central | 71 |
| South Atlantic | .54 |
| East South Central | .95 |
| West South Central | .60 |
| Mountain | .77 |
| Pacific | .42 |
| Average | .64 |

Where the Indianapolis leaders go to create this unusually high average ratio of mobility out of the region is not a strictly relevant question, but the answer may be a matter of interest. They go disproportionately to Michigan, Illinois, Ohio, the West North Central states, Wisconsin, and the Pacific states—in that order of disproportionate frequency. Of course, what is important is not *where* they go, but that they *do* go in such numbers and from so small an initial pool. When we talk of "top top leadership" in Indianapolis we must, hence, be aware that we speak of what is at the top of this radically reduced pool.

The evidence of decline in the whole state therefore suggests that—inasmuch as other cities in Indiana have developed industrially and commercially between 1928 and 1952—Indianapolis could not have been notable as a city providing opportunities for big business leaders in the last quarter century. On the contrary, it has doubtless exported more upwardly mobile men than it has provided places for at home.

Yet Indianapolis is continually bringing in new people at all social levels, and one may assume that the opportunities which attract them must in many cases lead to further personal advancement than that possible in other centres. Elsewhere, we have mentioned the favorable tax opportunities Indiana offers to industrialists and able men in all professions and lines of business, which enable the successful to acquire fortunes there. Although much more research would be needed to establish all the facts, we would expect that it would show that Indianapolis, if it does not offer many positions for the very biggest business leaders, does offer considerable freedom of mobility to lower-class and lower middle-class persons.

At the same time, Indianapolis and the Hoosier way make it easy for relatively non-mobile persons to find a niche in the city and still preserve the ties they cherish to rural and small town backgrounds. It seems highly probable that the vast majority of the people of Indianapolis are more persons of this type than they are "strainers" or "strivers." They may account for the rather low level of expectations regarding the physical conditions of urban life as well as regarding the serious cultural offerings and the lighter amenities of the "Big Town." They would provide a following for local conservatism in relation to government and taxes, and would create difficulties for leaders seeking to stir people to make "grass roots" demands for anything new that might prove to be an expensive drain on either tax funds or philanthropic resources. A native of Indianapolis, induced to join one of the writers on the roof of the newest, tallest, fully air-conditioned apartment building in the downtown area, was able to point out all the main streets and to identify all the landmarks and neighborhoods for some miles around. He concluded with satisfied surprise, "Why, it's a small town after all!"

Indeed, in Indianapolis, the widespread satisfaction with things as they are (or at least, things as they seem to be) makes for a placid pace not only in public affairs but in little details too: the genuinely "relaxed sell" approach of clerks in stores and of business people generally; and the lack of "pressure" in minor details of life—the rare occurrence of impatient horn-honking in traffic, for instance.

For some temperaments, and evidently even for phlegmatic types in the long run, life can get a bit dull in Indianapolis—which is odd because a metropolitan city usually offers an immense variety of activities—and it may be this that accounts for the occasional outbursts of crowd excitement over some novelty that comes to town or originates there. Indianans, like most Americans, "love a parade," but in Indianapolis a "great turn-out" can confidently be expected. For examples, in the mass fundraising field, in peacetime at that, observers might recall the first Telethon in 1953, or the peak of the Hospital drive in 1952 and early 1953, which according to all accounts aroused widespread interest in the community. Of course, much of this endemic energy finds its outlet in regulated, periodic ways, as, for example, during the basketball season, when what is affectionately called the "Hoosier Madness" is permitted to rage.

Nevertheless, in a city of half a million, a big parade or a "500 Mile Race" viewed by thousands will still leave many more who stay home or go fishing. "Staying put" helps to keep levels of aspiration for metropolitan conditions and cosmopolitan enjoyments fairly low, in favor of serving the goals of another definition of a "good life": home, family, church, and the simpler, less expensive pleasures of quiet picnics and the like. For many people, Indianapolis and Indiana offer about as much "civilization" as they are ready to absorb at this stage of their careers, and they can easily avoid exposing themselves to influences from newcomers at home or from involvement when abroad. A kind of self-perpetuating cultural isolationism prevails, at least for the many who never attend the Symphony or the relatively high-level performances of Broadway hits brought by road companies to the Murat Theatre, or other events of that character.

The consequences for the leaders in community affairs seem to be (a) that their appeals for support from such a possible following must be couched in "grass roots" terms—and for this, the Hoosier approach supplies the style and the language, and (b) that rapid or large-scale change is easier to resist than to win support for—especially if the project is to be costly. In the resulting debate, if any, the Hoosier tradition supplies the conservative side with more than enough ammunition to ensure victory, most of the time. For one thing, the competence of experts is not only easily challenged in such a climate, but there is a widespread belief that local experience has repeatedly proved that "planning always calls for greater expenditures" than expected or desired. "Besides," the thought continues, "why spend all that money on just 'talk'?"

Ultimately this state of affairs may be due to the "successful" interaction between the Hoosier tradition and the peculiar population aggregate that occupies Marion County. We turn now to an effort to characterize the people as in-migrants.

### 3. The Indianapolis "mix" of frontier and other cultural strains

As a central hub in the "Cross-roads of America," Indianapolis has received migrants for over a hundred years. These came along three main pathways: from the east and north via the Erie Canal and Great Lakes; from the east and south via the Cumberland Gap and the Ohio River; and from the modern South, overland, via Kentucky and Tennessee. It is beyond our resources to trace this long history, but for our immediate purposes it seems useful to set forth our impressions of three features, particularly:

(a) Indianapolis has never had anything like the influx of Europeans from southern and central Europe which made "Americanization" programs so important in many eastern and northern cities. Even settlement houses in Indianapolis seem to have had a quite different history (and now have a different role) from their prototypes elsewhere; they still exist here, in a larger number than in other cities of similar size, and with a different role, which may testify to the continued feeling of need for agencies helpful in "urbanizing" American in-migrants from more rural environments. In Indianapolis only the Germans ever formed a large European immigrant group; although the "second wave" of this migration, after 1848, included socialists, etc., who shocked and therefore stood out from the earlier arrivals, and although the German-speaking families maintained a group solidarity here even longer than did their peers in Milwaukee, for example, they are now apparently merged with the general population, and German patronyms are found at all social levels.

(b) The Yankee influence in Indianapolis was probably greater before

1900 than it has been since, whereas the movement from the Border States has continued to reinforce the Southern influence traceable to the earliest migrations. It is this earlier migration, made by slow stages through the Cumberland Gap and Ohio River valley, that gives many Hoosiers genealogies leading proudly back to Virginia. The contemporary Southern influence is reflected in the quip, "Indianapolis is the most Southern town in the Northern states," or the local saying that "Southern Indiana begins just south of Washington Street [U.S. Route 40]." Southern "aggressiveness" or "readiness to fight"—as well as Southern courtesy and gentleness—seem to be more strongly woven into the Hoosier tradition in Indianapolis than is the Puritan conscience; though the latter, in making a virtue of hard work, continues to be so strong that "retirement" for many a man is felt to be best accomplished by strenuous efforts to continue some *productive* hobby.

(*c*) The Hoosier values and virtues of self-sufficiency, self-help, individualism, and local independence from higher, remote authority, seem, today, to be an expedient blend of what survives from the actualities of the pioneer days (brought to political expression in the Constitution of 1851); they are embellished by the notion that they were somehow hammered out by man's unique experience in Indiana and that there is something peculiar about the "Hoosier soil" which nurtures them. The historical truth, even if we could establish it either way, would not matter to those who make this claim, and in any case, for our purposes, it is enough to recognize what exists in this society today: a tendency to very vocal insistence upon the Hoosier way as a reality in Indianapolis and as a model for the world. The reality, at least, is the persistence of a community about which it continues to be said that the people are "over 70 per cent native white Protestants"— and which in fact has had a steadily declining proportion of foreign-born ever since 1870.[49]

### HOOSIER CULTURE AND FEDERATED FUNDRAISING

Does the cultural factor help to explain the dilemma of the Indianapolis Community Chest? We believe it does.

The Chest is first of all a "federation" for fundraising, originated after World War I to "reduce the multiplicity of appeals" and to centralize budgeting for local social welfare agencies. In Indianapolis, as we shall see (especially in chapters 10 and 11) it has operated as a rather loose *confederation* more than as a strong centralizing organization.

We suggest that the Indianapolis community, not suffering seriously from deep social cleavages due to religion or ethnic background, is so *homogeneous*—especially when rallied around the Hoosier way—that it is a wonder, not that the Community Chest has been a "failure," but that it has survived at all and done as well as it has. In other cities, *heterogeneity* in the business and social worlds gives a fundraising federation at least the significant mission of carrying out rituals and pecuniary functions that express and help to organize the important differences in a grand ceremonial declaring the integration of the various elements into a larger social whole: *this* community or "Our Fair City."

There are, however, two cleavages in the Indianapolis community which the Hoosier viewpoint refuses to perceive and deal with. The cleavages, far from being used, so far, in the service of the Community Chest—or, contrariwise, far from being accepted as "social conflicts" which can be expressed and resolved by proper ceremonial use of the Chest's campaigns— are these: (1) the cleavage caused by the withdrawal of "top top leaders" from active personal direction of civic affairs and the subsequent gaps in communication "down the line" which, in chain reaction, create uncertainty and maladjustment in the ranks—we may call this a *stratification cleavage*;[50] (2) the cleavage between the old timers and the newcomers—between the new Hoosiers and Hoosiers of the higher degrees—this may be called a *segmental cleavage*.[51] It is very significant that a clinging to Hoosier manners operates to maintain *both* these cleavages; and, at least in the realm of *federated* fundraising, these cleavages persist despite occasional efforts to introduce the urbaneness, the metropolitan viewpoint, the cosmopolitan or "sophisticated" preferences, which bridge such cleavages wherever people really desire to close them. As we shall see, this division need not and does not affect *all* MOPS fundraising in Indianapolis, for the Indianapolis Chapter of the American Red Cross "succeeds" financially just because it makes good use of the motives and desires produced or reinforced by the two cleavages referred to.[52]

The heart of the matter seems to lie in the Hoosier stance regarding the strong federation—or the necessary centralization and more remote controls—which really large-scale fundraising requires. The Indianapolis solution to the Hoosier dilemma[53] seems to be to turn the federation[54] into a confederation, and then to let it "fail" in order to prove that centralization and remote controls (even of this degree) don't work anyway—at least in civic affairs such as private philanthropy has tended to become in America. Nothing like this would be tolerated in business administration, of course, whether in the successful home-owned firms or in the great national corporations represented in Indianapolis.

In conclusion, it should be remembered that the cultural factor, stubbornly resistant to change though it is, is, after all, *man-made*. Indianans, at least as far as we have seen them in Indianapolis, have chosen the "Hoosier way" in preference to any other version of the "American way." This they are free to do. But they cannot fairly ask technicians to make any part of their social organization work as if it belonged in some other region of America. Specifically, they will have to make a decision between a Chest as a strong federation and a Chest as a loose and incomplete "confederacy," and one of the choices may entail some modification in or compromise about what we have taken to be the Hoosier way.

# 4. Philanthropy in Indianapolis

To SEE IN PROPER PERSPECTIVE the present-day organization and status of welfare in Indianapolis, and to appreciate the attitude of the civic leaders towards philanthropy and philanthropic problems, it is necessary not only to know something of the history of the national (and international) welfare agencies and movements, but also to have some knowledge of the history of welfare services in Indianapolis and the unique features in their development. In order to present this development we might tell the story by periods—in horizontal layers, as it were—recounting the telling events of each one. Or we might tell the story of each organization from its origin to its end—cutting time, as it were, into vertical slices. In either case something would be lost: the continuity of organizations in one case, the coherence of a period in the other. Wishing to minimize both losses, we have compromised, telling the story substantially by periods, but allowing ourselves the liberty of flashing forward to a later date, before the main chronological sequence is resumed.

## THE BEGINNINGS

Indianapolis became known as "benevolent" during its emergence as one of the "large"[1] cities of the United States; in fact, organized philanthropy was so prominent in its story almost from the beginning, that it was said "the very foundations of the city were . . . laid on charity."[2]

Even before the founding of the city of Indianapolis, public provision for the care of the poor of the area had been made: the Territorial laws of 1790 provided for the appointment of "township overseers of the poor." The State of Indiana was admitted to the Union in 1816,[3] and its Constitution of that date, effective until 1851, mandated: "indoor relief"—asylums or farms for the poor; a "contract system"—the poor as a group placed with a private individual who was paid by the county; a "farming-out system"—individuals placed with private citizens who were paid by the county; an apprentice system—"binding out" minor children; and "outdoor relief"—families given relief in their own homes.[4]

Indianapolis was a "planned" city in the sense that its site, centrally located in the state, was selected, by a committee specially appointed for that purpose, at a time when, the records show, only one family was living on it.[5] In 1820, several families settled there, and by 1822 county commissioners had been elected and local government put in operation.

The commissioners from the hills of southern Indiana selected the site for Indianapolis because "It's as level as a barn floor." They could only reply to the question put to them by a young Boston mechanic about provision for drainage: "Well, I'll be d...d. Nobody but a Yankee would ever have thought of that." The early settlers, however, soon found out the troubles which the terrain could cause them.[6]

The plain on which the city stands has an average elevation of about 720 feet above sea level, and is quite flat, with somewhat higher ground on all sides. It has been conjectured by geologists that it was in some past age the bed of a lake. Across it runs the valley of Pogue's Run, which has lost much of its original breadth by filling, and which was formerly rather swampy in character.

Northeast of the city . . . was an extensive swamp, later known as Fletcher's Swamp, which in wet seasons discharged its overflow through the site of the city in what were called "the ravines"; and in time of floods Fall Creek also discharged much of its surplus water through this swamp and the same channels. . . .

In these ravines there were a number of deep places where the water stood most of the year; and outside of them, scattered through the dense forest, were many low places where the water stood for weeks, especially in wet seasons. Southwest of Greenlawn Cemetery was a body of stagnant water known as "Graveyard Pond," of which it was said: "In the summer it is covered with a green, filthy scum, and is the habitation of various kinds of reptiles and bullfrogs. . . ." These conditions made a natural field for malarial diseases.

The summer of 1821 was especially wet, with "storms occurring every day in June, July and August"; and it was distinguished also by the great amount of sickness resulting (so it was believed) from the excessive rains. In late August "the community was prostrated." The same account continues: "Though so general, the disease [malaria?] was not deadly,[7] about twenty-five cases only, mostly children who had been too much exposed, dying out of several hundred cases." Presumably the growth of the town was greatly retarded since "New comers were disheartened . . . and some left the country, circulating extravagant reports about the health of the town."

There were at least three doctors living in Indianapolis that summer, but two of them "were prostrated with ague." However, anybody who was well enough to get about ministered to the sick, even taking them into his own home if necessary. Although not glamorized by the label, "philanthropy," such acts of kindness accomplished much the same purpose as organized welfare work—providing for the needs of the sick and destitute—with an added personal touch born out of common necessity. "Their mutual suffering . . . bound the early settlers together in after life, and none recur to this period without emotion." Thus the town had early shown two characteristically Hoosier ways of dealing with a community problem: bad planning followed by determined and loyal improvisation of "remedies."

Of interest in the study of philanthropy is an item on the first tax-rate list, approved on May 13, 1822:

> On each male person over the age of twenty-one years . . . . $0.50
>> Provided that persons over the age of fifty years and not free holders, and such as are not able from bodily disability to follow any useful occupation, and all idiots and paupers shall be exempt from said last named tax.[8]

This and other reports indicate that there were, among the settlers who came to Indianapolis, many who were very poor, even by the standards of that day. To help them, clothing, food, and medicines were collected, and lodging was provided by various individuals and later by church groups. "Men and women thought not of themselves but of others," says a later pamphlet on the charities of the city.[9]

In 1825, the government offices were moved from Corydon to Indianapolis, which was now a thriving town of 762 inhabitants. And it continued to grow slowly, with settlement gradually succeeding the wilderness and its life and ways. The Delaware Indians, under their treaty of 1818, had been allowed to occupy their lands for three years; after their removal they still hunted in the forests of Indiana; however, by this time, they caused little if any annoyance to the settlers. Wild game was abundant—deer, bears, wolves, and an occasional panther roamed the forests. Wild turkeys were commonly seen even within "the mile square," the sections of land originally plotted as the city of Indianapolis, and bounded by East, West, North, and South Streets. Trapping and fishing were profitable occupations.[10]

There were also obstacles to this early growth. One of the worst was said to be the lack of "mills." But in 1823, so reports the *Censor* in its first issue,[11] "The town now contains . . . mechanics of almost every description, and men of all professions."[12] By then, four saw mills and two grist mills were in operation within a mile and a half of Indianapolis, and several others were being built. An "attraction" of the town was implied in a report of a census taken in 1824: ". . . 100 families, with 172 voters and 45 unmarried women between the ages of fifteen and forty-five years."[13]

The disadvantages of bad roads and poor mail service were multiplied when Indianapolis became the state capital. A Lawrenceburg newspaper complained, in 1825, that "owing to the present arrangement of the mail . . . it will be impossible to have any information from the legislature before . . . nine days from the commencement of the session"; and it would be nearly the close of the session before the second mail would arrive from Indianapolis.[14] The road laws provided that "each male between 21 and 50 years of age . . . do three days of road work annually."[15] But road-building consisted in little more than clearing the trees; and the more the roads were used, the worse they became. Such conditions tended to make Indianapolis necessarily a self-sustaining community, and must have hampered its growth, which was reported to have been "very slow" up to 1835. Hugh McCulloch described conditions in Indianapolis in 1833 thus:

As a director of the State Bank, I was under the necessity for many years of making quarterly trips on horseback from Fort Wayne to Indianapolis through a country almost impassable by carriages of any kind, and yet I never encountered mud deeper or more tenacious than in the streets of the capital of the state. I have seen many of the incipient towns of the West, but none so utterly forlorn as Indianapolis appeared to me in the spring of 1833. It had no local advantages except the fact that it was surrounded by a very fertile country; nothing to recommend it but its being the metropolis of the state.[16]

By 1835, work on the "National Highway" had begun, the Canal[17] was being built, and the first capitol in Indianapolis was completed—all public works which attracted workmen to the city and made for a rapid increase in population. From 1,683 persons in 1835 the population had grown by 1838 to an estimated 4,000.[18] It was during this time that a need was felt for systematic "charity," and this resulted in the organization of the Indianapolis Benevolent Society.

### THE BEGINNINGS OF ORGANIZED CHARITY

In 1835 (when Andrew Jackson was still President of the United States) the Indianapolis Benevolent Society was founded—the first "family agency" in the United States organized "to meet the needs of individuals and families on a community-wide basis and without regard to race or creed."[19] Colonel James Blake, who had come to Indianapolis with the first settlers in 1821, was the leader of this organization from 1835 until his death in 1870;[20] it was manned entirely by volunteers until its reorganization in 1879.[21] Looking back over a span of fifty years, a speaker at an anniversary meeting of the Society described the conditions in Indianapolis under which it began its work: "Fifty years ago, when this society was formed, there were no railroads, no telegraphs, no free schools, no daily mails, no cities, in the State of Indiana. There was no pauper class in Indiana. . . . Each man, each inhabitant, knew all the other inhabitants [of Indianapolis]. . . . Under such circumstances but little machinery was necessary to carry on the operations of the Benevolent Society. The poor were here; . . . but the causes that induced poverty were well known and instantly recognized."[22]

The Benevolent Society was, then, "a purely relief society that aimed to give temporary aid to those who were in distress from poverty."[23] Its organization with respect to fundraising and social service, as reported in the same account, seems well enough adapted to conditions at that time:

The town was divided into districts and to each was "appointed a gentleman and a lady whose business it was to visit every family in their ward, to solicit donations in clothing, wood and money. After the donations were obtained the money was paid to the treasurer and the clothing placed in the depository." It was, further, the duty of these collectors to attend to the wants of the poor in their respective districts: the cold and hungry were relieved and the sick visited . . . prominent in its [the Benevolent Society's] membership were those fathers of the city whose names[24] are now most honored in its early history for the part they took in its general upbuilding.

Immigrants from Europe began to arrive in numbers about 1848. It is doubtless significant for the social structure and culture of Indianapolis that in 1920 over 90 per cent of the city's population of foreign extraction—i.e., foreign-born whites, native whites of foreign parents, and native whites of mixed (foreign and native) parentage—had roots in northern Europe.[25]

In 1849, the Benevolent Society proposed the formation of a society to take care of "certain classes of persons in distress which the Benevolent Society was unable to reach."[26] The Widows' and Orphans' Friends Society was organized, and the following year the Widows' and Orphans' Asylum was established. However, there was no physical plant until 1855, when the first home was built at a cost of $1,200. In the interim, boarding-home care was provided for the children, and relief grants were made for widows. An attempt was made to finance this project by house-to-house solicitations conducted by "inexperienced" women; the money raised by this method was insufficient, so by 1855 the program was reduced to the care of children, since assistance to widows had proved to be both "unsatisfactory and too expensive." Membership fees in the Friends Society were set at "$3.00 for males, and $1.00 for females."[27] The city fathers showed their interest in the Orphans' Asylum by appropriating, in 1869, $1,000 for an addition to the home which increased its capacity to seventy-five children. In 1875, the Indiana General Assembly changed the name of the institution to the Indianapolis Orphan Asylum; in that same year, it took over buildings abandoned by Butler University when the latter moved to Irvington.

The Orphan Asylum was governed by a Board of sixteen members, who visited the institution regularly. They were responsible for the health of the children, their education and their "moral outlook," but "according to the records, the most time-consuming Board responsibilities were those of housekeeping, staffing and financing the institutional program."[28]

The minutes of those years seem to report more troubles than joys and my own recollection of the Board meetings from 1915 until we gave up the institution, is largely of changing cooks and laundresses, defective plumbing, leaking roofs, heating problems, etc. As one member remarked, the buying of a sauce pan was made a matter of prayer. . . . Much was recorded about the physical property and practically nothing about the children.[29]

The final home of the Orphan Asylum was built in 1903. During one year (1915) 175 to 200 children[30] were committed to the agency by Marion County Juvenile Court and other district courts. Twenty-five cents per day was allowed from public funds for the care of each child. However, reports show that 66 per cent of the children taken in (1886-1940) were placed in homes.

Fundraising for the Orphan Asylum was the responsibility of the Board until 1921. Because it was difficult to secure sufficient funds, the Board several times in the history of the institution considered giving it up or "turning it over to the public." In 1922, when the Asylum joined the Community Fund, $1,800 was received from the Fund out of a total budget for the agency of $62,000. "At every meeting of the Board of Managers [Orphan Asylum] the feeling grew that a better job could be done." In 1927, the Board sought advice from the Child Welfare League of America. As a result of an investigation of the institution by the League and the suggestions it made, the interest and support of the Indianapolis Foundation were gained in setting up a demonstration program in the Asylum and in continuing financial aid; professional social workers and a skilled child psychiatrist were obtained to advise and educate the staff and the Board in the proper handling of children; and the first social service department of the agency was established. Emphasis on placement in homes, and establishment of the county public child care program (1936) resulted in a drastically reduced population in the Orphan Asylum; by 1941, children still needing "institutional care" were referred to the General Protestant Orphans Home.

It would seem that up to 1927 the "untrained" staff of the Orphan Asylum had focused its attention on providing the "essentials"—food, clothing, and shelter—for the children under its care, and very little was received in the way of "character-building" and "personality development" except for what the children absorbed in their attendance at Sunday School and public school. In the developments of 1927 and the following years we see the change from "charity" work by untrained but well-meaning citizens to welfare work by "trained personnel." The "personal touch" often used as an argument in favor of the former was decidedly lacking in the administration of the orphanage under the old regime—preoccupation with "material things," inadequate funds, as well as the prevalent attitudes towards children[31] and the large numbers often crowded into the Orphanage were not conducive to a "home-like" atmosphere or personal contacts with the children.

Within a few years of the founding of the Asylum in the 1850's we hear of new agencies dealing with new needs. The Young Men's Christian Association appeared in 1854,[32] with Benjamin Harrison (later President of the United States) as its leader until 1860. The early history of the Indianapolis "Y" was one of constant growth in membership, diversification of the services offered, and expansion of facilities. In 1887, it moved into a new building; twenty years later, when the building proved inadequate, it was sold and a new site purchased for $125,000. Despite the recession of 1907, the Y.M.C.A. building fund campaign aimed at raising the largest sum ever sought in Indianapolis previously for charitable purposes,[33] and the ten-day appeal actually resulted in $273,838 pledged—$24,000 over goal. J. K. Lilly, chairman of the drive, gave the largest gift—$10,000. In 1909, the building was dedicated. Local report has it that the Indianapolis Y.M.C.A. was considered at that time as one of the outstanding "Y" organizations in the nation: in the same year, it won the national Y.M.C.A. trophy for night school attendance; in 1909-1910 it was selected as the best of the "Y" night schools in the country. The offerings included "a wide range of studies, literary, technical and manual, with special classes for boys."[34]

Over the years its aims have been variously described. A pamphlet of 1938 states: "It strives to prevent delinquency among boys and young men through educational classes, vocational training, handicraft, gymnasium, camp and swimming pool facilities. The 'Y' is non-sectarian, non-political and non-exclusive."[35] By 1939, a change in its organization to take account of its expansion was necessary: Parker P. Jordan came to Indianapolis as general secretary of the Y.M.C.A. with a program of decentralization. As of 1955, there were seven branches[36] and a summer camp aiming "to develop Christian personality and a Christian society. [The Y.M.C.A.] offers youth and adult club and recreation activities, physical education and sports, informal education, resident rooms and food services for members."[37] A comparison of the last two statements of purpose reveals a radical change from service for the "needy"—in this case potential delinquents—to activities for everyone, as well as from a restricted clientele of "boys and young men" to one all-inclusive, "youth and adult." (*Family*-night programs at the Central Y.M.C.A. were popular during the winter of 1955-6.)

As we have seen, before the Civil War, philanthropy in Indianapolis was almost entirely in the form of "charity"—dedicated to caring for the destitute and needy. As time went on, the term "needy" was to receive an ever wider definition.

While Indianapolis was a small town and every man knew his neighbors, the simple plan of "lending a helping hand in time of need" was successful and adequate. In Indianapolis then, as in Middletown later, the "chronic inability of a certain number of the group to operate under the existing system requiring the proffering of money at every turn is taken for granted; indeed some . . . persons point to the statement, 'For the poor ye have always with you' in support of this attitude."[38] However, as Indianapolis developed, there came "the ever-multiplying stranger, whose deserts everybody did not know; then the vagrant deadbeat or 'foreign pauper,' and by 1851 we find the [Indianapolis Benevolent] society resolving 'that it be recommended to the citizens to refuse their assistance to foreign paupers soliciting money at their door or in the street.' "[39]

The need for "supervised discrimination" was recognized; the benevolent-minded began to realize that food and shelter alone were not sufficient to rehabilitate the mendicants; the conscientious could not condone certain "inhuman practices," "such as selling the service of the county poor to the highest bidder, thus maintaining a sort of chattel slavery." "In a word, the public conscience was acquiring that sensitiveness that has brought about the great modern movement in philanthropy."[40]

The close of the Civil War brought its own particular problems. The Home for Friendless Women, to take one example, was an outgrowth of conditions at this time. It was established in 1866 "for the aid and improvement of abandoned women,"[41] and financed with funds raised by canvassing the city. A new home was built in 1870 with $7,500 from the City of Indianapolis, $7,500 from Marion County, and gifts from individual donors. A unique source of support, until 1881, was "fines and penalties assessed and collected for breach of certain classes of penal ordinance of the City."[42] From 1881 until about 1900, the City of Indianapolis and the County Commissioners each contributed $600 annually to the support of the Home. The residents themselves—organized as the Stitch and Chatter Club—helped provide for their own care by selling handiwork in "bazaars." Another common means of raising money for charity in the early 1900's is illustrated by the activities of a card club: instead of spending money for prizes, its members gave fruit, street-car tickets, clothing, etc. to the women in the Home in answer to specific requests. In 1913, the organization's object was stated to be the "care and support of aged females who cannot support themselves," and its name was changed to the Indianapolis Home for Aged Women. Beginning in 1935, the scope was widened to include men as well as women and the new name, Indianapolis Home for the Aged, again reflected the change of function. Twenty years later, the function of the home had altered once more, and also the economic level served. In 1955, it was open to women over 65 years of age; "admission by application only." A $1,000 entrance fee was required; other funds for expenses were provided by endowments, contr'butions, gifts, and membership fees.

The economic  pheavals of the Civil War[43] and the following "hard times"—the "difficult decade" of 1870-9—were doubtless contributing factors to a changing attitude with regard to philanthropy which became obvious about then in Indianapolis as elsewhere. By 1879, conditions in the city had reached a crisis: one-fifth of the total population were on relief rolls and word had got around, so at least it was reported, that "Indianapolis was such a benevolent city."[44] The Benevolent Society was discouraged and ready to disband, when Rev. Oscar C. McCulloch, the pastor of the Plymouth Congregational Church, assumed its leadership and almost single-handed reanimated the membership so that both the Township Trustee (who by this time was administering a large portion of the "relief") and the Benevolent Society felt impelled to act effectively. A full-time executive was employed by the Benevolent Society; a confidential exchange of information (later the Social Service Exchange) was established; and "The Friendly Inn" was opened, to furnish meals and lodgings to transients in exchange for work. Even more co-operation seemed imperative, however. In 1879, in the law office of General Benjamin Harrison, the Charity Organization Society came into being—"a citizens' association of business men and charitable societies for the purpose of united effort in dealing with the problems of poor relief."[45] The evolution from personal "charity" to organized "social service" seemed well on its way.

## REORGANIZATION AND EXPANSION

Specifically, the Rev. Oscar McCulloch called a meeting in 1879 of the Flower Mission, the South Side Aid Society, and the Benevolent Society (of which he was president) to discuss ways and means of avoiding duplication of effort. He hoped to get these three organizations to send their statistics in regard to every case to a central file which could be referred to by all of them. As was fitting, he was elected first president of the Charity Organization Society, whose objects were "to distinguish between poverty and pauperism; to relieve the one and to refuse the other; to reintroduce the personal element in charity; to keep careful records of the cases, and to do what it could to substitute work for alms."[46] Mr. McCulloch's vision and foresight are thus praised in an account of 1952: "What we now know as the Indianapolis Community Fund is an organization such as was sincerely desired by our subject, who hoped to avoid duplication and waste of effort. Having assembled the charities of the city for the most part under one roof, his own church, he hoped for and advocated a *united treasury* set up on the basis of proved need by the affiliated groups."[47]

The agencies which co-operated in 1879 were the Benevolent Society and the Township Trustee for "cases of destitution," and the Flower Mission which "did its work of mercy among the indigent sick." The Charity Organization Society and the Indianapolis Benevolent Society operated as supplementary organizations, but they employed a single executive and agency staff. The Benevolent Society continued to function mainly as a "relief agency," receiving its financial support from the Charity Organization Society. The Charity Organization Society was the vehicle for co-operative effort, both operational and fundraising, among the social agencies. Serving as a referral, research, and general administrative organization, it could be characterized as a "charity clearing house."

During the 1870's a number of other welfare agencies were organized, most of which ministered to a select group of people. (The Appendix to this chapter lists the dates of organization of selected Indianapolis welfare and social service agencies.)

The Congregation of the Little Sisters of the Poor was established in Indianapolis on Christmas day in 1873, part of a world-wide Order devoted to the care of the aged poor, regardless of color or creed.[48] Another Roman Catholic charitable organization, the Convent of the Sisters of the Good Shepherd, established the House of the Good Shepherd in Indianapolis in the same year to care for "young girls who might easily cross the borderline of delinquency or worse." In the vivid verbal currency of the newspaper:

Forlorn as rain-drenched sparrows, young girls, most of them 12 to 16 years old, seek shelter under the protection of the nuns. They come from all over Indiana. Some of them are sent by the courts, some of them by welfare organizations because of broken homes, poverty or indifference on the part of their parents.[49]

Non-Catholic as well as Catholic girls are cared for; in fact, it was reported in 1948 that two-thirds of the girls came from non-Catholic homes.

The Flower Mission has, since 1876, been one of the most active of the welfare organizations in Indianapolis. Again as reflected in journalistic appreciation:

Back in the early days of Indianapolis when Washington Street knew neither skyscraper nor semaphore, when horseless carriages and airships were but flights of fanatics' fancies, when spanking bays had the right of way and the hitch rack held no overtime parking terrors, a group of young girls met one bright day in the stately old home of General George Wright, and pledged themselves to a mission of carrying cheer to the homes of the sick and needy.[50]

In 1879, the young women of the Mission carried on a week's solicitation for funds—$1,068 was pledged—with which they opened a Newsboys' Home for "the young waifs of the street" (a forerunner of the present Boys' Club). In 1883, Mr. McCulloch, still the center of philanthropic activities, pointed out to the young ladies of the Flower Mission "things far more useful than simply carrying flowers to sick and discouraged people." As a result of his influence and aggressiveness, the Mission, in co-operation with the City Hospital, established the Training School for Nurses, the first in Indianapolis.[51] Funds for this and many other projects of the Mission were raised by elaborate fairs and bazaars, and elegant balls and garden fêtes;[52] after World War I, endowments and Community Fund allotments took care of the expenses. "Another dream of the organization was realized when the Eleanor Home, a hospital for children, was made possible by the generosity of Mr. and Mrs. Eli Lilly (1895)."[53] Still another interest of the mission was the "Summer Fresh Air Mission"—cottages at Fairview Park, where "tired mothers and wan babies were restored to health."[54] A culminating event in the productive history of this organization was the dedication, on May 12, 1937, of the Flower Mission Hospital, a modern medical unit for tuberculosis patients. The original fifty-bed hospital, dating from 1866, was purchased by the city, and torn down; the money realized from its sale was used as a nucleus for financing the new hospital.

The list of agencies of which we have knowledge that were founded during the decade 1870-9 is completed by the Maternity Society (1878-1948) which, furnishing clothing for infants in needy families, received its support from the Congregational Church, and by the Employment Bureau of the Indianapolis Benevolent Society.

The next decade saw further change. The adaptation of organized philanthropy to the needs of the rapidly expanding community seemed to be a continuous and often critical problem. The dilemma appears clearly in a statement made in 1886:

County, neighborhood and village charity will not do for cities, unless we deliberately intend and propose to increase and perpetuate permanent pauperism. The curse of unearned bread and ill-advised or careless alms-giving is almost as great, and often far greater than the course of want that it is intended to relieve. The problem before us is, how to deal with want and wretchedness in thickly populated cities.[55]

Several of the new agencies of this decade reflect the poverty and "dire need" of those most affected by the "hard times" following the Civil War. But, rather than dispensing charity outright, they, in line with what was coming to be Indianapolis tradition (see chapters 3, 12, etc.), encouraged "self-help" activities. Officials of the Charity Organization Society and the Benevolent Society continued to warn generous persons against "indiscriminate giving"; even the beggars on the city streets were, at one time, offered jobs whereby they could make an "honest" living.[56]

The Friendly Inn, previously alluded to, was very actively utilized in the eighties. It was primarily a haven for transients, and supported to a large extent by its "Wood Yard," where destitute men could earn meals and lodging. The daughter of the Rev. Charles C. Bogert, who took the superintendency of the Inn in 1880 shortly after it was founded, reported that "meals were 10 cents, and 50 cents a cord was paid the woodcutters in meals. The cords were divided up into one-fifth cords, however, so that a meal at a time could be split or sawed."[57] In the *Indianapolis Journal* of April 10, 1884, the Friendly Inn offered for sale "several hundred cords of dry, seasoned, and partially seasoned hard wood . . . of the best quality . . . at $6 a cord, for block, and $6.50 for split, delivered." This wood was prepared by the men who had obtained food and lodging at the Inn during the previous winter. The report continued: "The number at the Inn has been larger than ever before. There have been registered 848 men, 58 women, and 29 children, and there have been furnished 4,663 meals and 3,530 lodgings."[58] Friends of the Benevolent Society were urged to order from the Yard the wood they might need "for immediate or future use."[59]

Another product of the eighties was the free kindergarten movement which started in 1881. In Indianapolis, again at the instigation of McCulloch, the Free Kindergarten Society was organized, and a kindergarten opened the next year. For twenty years, the kindergarten was maintained by individual donations and afternoon teas; thereafter, it was supported by the state, eventually becoming a part of the public school system of Indianapolis.

The Dime Savings and Loan Association, established in 1887 by the Charity Organization Society (and liquidated in 1935), encouraged the poor "to attain self-respect and a higher standard of living" by putting aside small amounts of money regularly for general living needs when they arose and as an "insurance against emergencies."[60] At the beginning, four collectors made weekly visits to homes, receiving the deposits and banking them. Within five years, transactions totalled almost $50,000 annually. In 1910, there were about 1,500 depositors; the collectors then made their rounds every two weeks.[61]

Another "first" in the history of philanthropy was a home for "aged colored women": Alpha Home, opened in Indianapolis in 1883. The resources on which it was founded were a three-room house, several acres of ground, and a promised $100 per year for at least fifteen years. Voluntary subscriptions, contributions from churches, and proceeds from an annual picnic helped out with the expenses. The receipt of a $5,000 legacy in 1918 enabled the Home to purchase a double house, and to admit men.[62]

The civil government, although giving financial support since 1845 to social service and charitable organizations, began in this same decade to take a more active part in their administration and operation. The change was reflected, for instance, in the establishment of the County Workhouse, the Board of State Charities, and the Board of Children's Guardians.[63] (These were, in 1936, combined in the Department of Public Welfare.) But, since this is primarily a report of private philanthropy, the history of public institutions—even though of great importance from the very beginning of organized charity—must be omitted except where the two types of welfare work—one supported by taxes, the other by voluntary donations— become so intertwined as to make it impossible to describe them adequately in separation (see, for example, chapter 12).

At the close of this decade (1880's) the organization of philanthropic effort in Indianapolis was evidently attracting national attention: "By this time [1888-9] the Associated Charities of Indianapolis had become an organization of national repute, and at the National Conference of Charities and Corrections at Baltimore, in 1890, Mr. McCulloch was made its president, and the annual meeting for 1891 was fixed at Indianapolis. It convened in May, and was a great success in every way, especially as an inspiration to organized charity throughout the state."[64] Further evidence of the position of leadership held by Indianapolis was the fact that in 1890 the first training courses for social workers in the United States were offered in Indianapolis: a series of ten lectures was given that year at the agency office of the Benevolent Society and Charity Organization Society to train paid workers and volunteers.[65]

An enlightening comment regarding the Indianapolis of the 1890's, as seen through professional eyes, appears in a contemporary Salvation Army statement:

. . . There were two or three efforts to establish a station [of the Salvation Army] here in the next decade, but none succeeded until 1892. Possibly the reason was that there were no slums in Indianapolis, but the army has found plenty of material to work on since that time.[66]

However true it may be "that there were no slums in Indianapolis" at that time,[67] benevolent citizens saw the need or felt the desire—or both—to establish more agencies for the benefit of the "underprivileged": the Summer Mission for Sick Children,[68] Home Libraries (which made reading materials available to those living in congested areas), the Wheeler Mission (material rescue and spiritual salvation),[69] the Young Women's Christian Association, Volunteers of America,[70] Flanner House, and the Day Nursery, all begun in the 1890's have offered continuous service, in one form or another, to the community up to the present time (1956).[71]

Flanner House has received national publicity for the special work it undertakes. It began in 1898 as a mission house for Negroes—"a learning center, an employment center, an educational center, a health center"— and its effectiveness has since been commented upon many times. For instance, a group of recreation specialists defined its work in 1929:

Flanner House is touching at vital points the helpless, the baffled, the inefficient among the colored people. It helps them to find themselves and their place in normal community life. It shields them from cruel buffetings but on the other hand, guides them into the ways of dignified self-respect. It holds up standard of achievement and braces courage. And in all these ways who will say that it is not, in the last analysis, making a noble contribution to interracial understanding and good will?[72]

Two elements of its program have attracted especial attention: Flanner House Homes and "Fundamental Education." The first is essentially a housing co-operative, carried out with unusual boldness, skill and imagination, which supplies the organization, direction, and supervision, and provides a channel for handling construction and costs of homes being built by selected Negro families in specific areas.[73] The second is really a generalization of the first—into other activities as well as housing and into preoccupation with other disadvantaged populations as well as Negroes; since it is still largely in the planning stage we may let description rest with its leaders who refer to it as "basic training in everything that makes a productive American," and as "fuller production, wider use of skills, better use of the land, better housing, *better people*."[74]

The question of "public and neighborhood baths"[75] was one of the problems considered by philanthropic-minded citizens in the 1890's; apparently, at least as far as the records are concerned, no action resulted from their deliberations.

Although, after 1880, the proportion of foreign-born in Indianapolis was never as great as that for the United States as a whole (see Chart 9), the European immigrants of earlier years were finding their places in the social structure of Indianapolis. The Jewish population was especially active in providing for the needs of Jews through the Jewish Welfare Federation (organized in 1904): the Shelter Houses, Borinstein Home for Jewish Aged, the Kirshbaum Community Center (1926) are among the better known Jewish agencies. The Germans established their Altenheim, "Home for the Aged," and various centers ministered to the needs of the Slavic groups.[76]

The Guild movement started in the early 1900's. It was made up of groups of women, usually church-related, who provided "extras" for the needy in hospitals and carried out other charitable projects, generally in connection with an established welfare organization. In Indianapolis, it produced, among others, St. Margaret's Guild, St. Mary's Guild, St. Vincent's Guild, and the Needlework Guild.

"Christmas Seals," to raise funds for the fight against tuberculosis, first made their appearance in Delaware in 1907 (see chapter 2). That same year civic pride and enthusiasm were running high in Indianapolis. One historian tells us that "the year 1907 was memorable as a year of donations."

It began early by raising $95,000 by public subscription for Butler University. The Y.M.C.A. and the Y.W.C.A. were both desirous of new quarters, and also appealed to the public, in organized campaigns. The Y.M.C.A. began first, and in a whirlwind campaign of 17 days, closing March 1, obtained pledges of $273,000. General enthusiasm was aroused, and dozens of business men, some of them having no connection with the Y.M.C.A., gave their time and effort to the work. As soon as this was finished most of them volunteered to help the Y.W.C.A., which began work on March 2, and completed a ten days campaign on March 11, with pledges of $140,000. This made a total of over half-a-million dollars raised for public purposes in Indianapolis in less than three months.[77]

During the years immediately preceding World War I, "social work" or "social service" began to gain prestige, and "professional" groups were increasingly seen in the philanthropy field and in activities supported by philanthropy: medical social service was instituted at the Indianapolis City Dispensary, the Indiana University Division of Social Service was organized, and the Legal Aid Bureau[78] provided free legal advice for the needy. Many well-known social-service organizations were formed, or established branches, in Indianapolis during this period before World War I: Red Cross, Camp Fire Girls, Girl Scouts, Boy Scouts, Tuberculosis Association, Travelers' Aid Society, Indianapolis Federation of Churches, and the Christmas Clearing House.[79]

The multiplicity of philanthropic institutions which had sprung up in Indianapolis resulted, it was said then—as it is being said today—in overlapping, inefficiency, and lack of co-operation in many cases. Thus "factional feeling, frequent appeals and increasing demands" led many citizens "to withhold their support from worthy causes." At a meeting of the Allied Charities in 1911 the situation was discussed and a committee of eleven appointed to "canvass the local field, study the methods in other cities and submit a report including recommendations for the future welfare of the charities of Indianapolis."[80]

After a painstaking survey of charities in Indianapolis and other cities, the committee reported that "Indianapolis is abreast of the leaders when we consider the resources and needs." Its specific recommendations and suggestions can be briefly summarized as follows:

(*a*) That a representative body be organized and designated the Indianapolis Council of Charities.

(*b*) That the "headquarters of the various charitable, relief and philanthropic and correctional societies of Indianapolis be located in the same building or group of buildings."

(*c*) That the "generous business man" and "generous public" be made aware of the need for such a building.

(*d*) That no new organizations be formed if the proposed service can be effectively carried on by an existing organization; and that "mushroom, unworthy or unnecessary charities be restricted."

(*e*) That the Charity Organization Society conduct and maintain a central registration and confidential exchange for the co-operating charities.

(*f*) That "we socialize our Charities." "What we seem to need most is some broad common ground upon which all may meet, and in frankness and forbearance consider the greatest good for the greatest number."

(*g*) That the Indianapolis Council of Charities publish an annual report.

(*h*) That an Indianapolis School of Social Service be organized offering courses to volunteer and professional workers.

Exactly what were the *immediate* effects of this investigation and the resulting recommendations is not known; but history shows that in the succeeding forty-five years there was evidence of effort and that all of the recommendations have by now been carried out to some extent. The English Foundation Building now houses the central offices of many of the philanthropic agencies; a Health and Welfare Council, successor to a Council of Social Agencies, "co-ordinates" the work of some one hundred social service organizations;[81] a central registration service is maintained;[82] an annual report is published by the Council; "educational lectures" have been given for volunteer and professional personnel; and attempts are continuously made to foster a spirit of understanding and co-operation among the various component agencies. It should be added, however, that some strong feeling against the financial federation exists in many powerful agencies, and considerable anti-Council feelings even in agencies that are "members" of the Council.

## WORLD WAR I

### The Red Cross

In July, 1916, the Indianapolis Chapter of the American Red Cross was organized amidst growing war tensions—United States troops were on the Mexican border, war was raging in Europe, the *Lusitania* had been sunk; and "military preparedness was fast becoming a must."[83]

When the United States entered the War, the Red Cross immediately went into action. A conference of representatives from every one of the Red Cross Chapters (of forty cities) met in Washington, in May, 1917, to discuss plans for raising money. William Fortune and Frank D. Stalnaker represented the Indianapolis Chapter. They returned full of enthusiasm, and immediately set about perfecting plans for probably the most spectacular fundraising campaign up to that point in the history of Indianapolis. Of the $100,000,000 national goal, $300,000 (⅓ of 1 per cent) was accepted as the Indianapolis quota.[84] Two-thirds of this amount was subscribed in less than an hour, and at that before the opening of the campaign. The goal was first voluntarily raised to $400,000 and then to $500,000, which was "topped" in a campaign lasting for one week.

Evidence that Indianapolis was "first with the most" in this emergency, is given in the following quotations:

. . . the vigorous way in which she began and carried on the drive, stiffened the backbone of more than one community. She was given the credit of having made the finest start of the drive—and her enthusiasm never flagged.

The fact that Indianapolis had taken the lead of all the cities of the country in starting the drive for the fund of $100,000,000 had been much commented upon in New York.

"Big news stories of Indianapolis spirit going out to the country at large. Indiana sending in wonderful reports. Using your reports to inspire others to emulate your example. Middle west leads all the rest."

Approximately $600,000 has been raised by Indianapolis Chapter, a larger amount than has been raised by any city of its size in America, greater in proportion to wealth and population than that of any city, great or small, in the entire land.[85]

Red Cross activities along other lines were equally impressive.[86] At the close of its membership drive on Christmas Eve, 1917, the Indianapolis Chapter numbered 100,000 members. Fifteen thousand volunteer workers were active in wartime projects. The universality of the patriotic spirit was expressed by: "You either join the army or the Red Cross."[87]

## The War Chest

The "inescapable overhead expense" in small-scale fundraising was one of the prime motivating factors in the creation of the War Chest. "James K. Lilly, chairman of the Chamber of Commerce committee on charities, estimated that the city raised about $600,000 each year for about sixty incorporated charities, and that it had been costing in the neighborhood of $100,000 a year to collect that amount."[88] This experience contrasted with that of the Red Cross: ". . . the cost of the [Red Cross] campaign in which subscriptions amounting to $500,000 were secured was $4,578.35, or less than one per cent."[89]

In April, 1918, executives in business and industry, leaders in civic and service organizations, labor and community leaders[90] met and formed a central organization. ". . . it is the sense of this board that we shall endeavor to provide for all war and benevolent needs in Indianapolis, heretofore supported by donations, according to the judgment of the War Chest Board as to their merits."[91] The War Chest Board raised $2,793,070 from 100,000 subscribers[92] in May, 1918. In addition to donations for war activities, large sums were appropriated by the Board to the Red Cross; to Italian, Jewish, Armenian, and Syrian relief; and to local charity and philanthropic organizations. The Indianapolis Chest was one of the participants in a conference of twelve of the leading War Chests (instigated by a leader of the Cleveland Chest) which resulted in the organization of the National Information Bureau (see chapters 2 and 13)—a sort of "Better Business Bureau" in the field of philanthropy.

The Indianapolis Foundation (to be discussed below), which was another product of the "merger movement" in philanthropy, also came to birth in the war period.

A survey of charities and philanthropies in Marion County was authorized by the War Chest Board, and attempts were made to secure the co-operation of the agencies in implementing the "three fundamental principles that the community and the War Chest Board were interested in having made effective, namely: first, that sound philanthropic and economic principles should be applied to the work of all charity organizations; second, that duplication and waste should be eliminated; third, that good business methods should be applied in the expenditure of money by charity organizations."[93] The president of the War Chest Board believed it was "quite hopeless" to expect the representatives of organized charities to "agree upon new constructive plans."[94] A concerted effort, almost to the point of threatening to withhold support,[95] was made to consolidate the Charity Organization Society, the Mothers' Aid Society, and the Children's Aid Association, but such efforts finally ceased without accomplishing their purpose. These strong decisions to take action, followed by no outcome, seem to be frequently repeated in the philanthropic history of Indianapolis, as though dissatisfaction could readily be organized but no resolution enforced. Attempts to organize a United Fund in the last decade continue the pattern.

By 1920, the war emergency had passed; plans for the future, as they related to philanthropy in Indianapolis, were discussed by representatives of the agencies,[96] and the "Community Chest plan" was approved. The Community Chest and War Chest Boards met jointly for some time, and several names appear on both Board lists.[97] On May 1, 1922, the Board dissolved the War Chest, transferring all of its assets to the Community Chest.

## CO-OPERATIVE FUNDRAISING AND SOCIAL SERVICES

### The Community Chest

In 1920, the Community Chest was organized, a "federation of agencies—of, by and for the agencies."[98] Plans to hold a joint campaign in November were approved by delegates from forty organizations. The goal was set at $1,000,000;[99] but "people failed to respond as volunteer workers" and the first campaign obtained only $313,194. It was decided to "continue the campaign" in the Spring, in the hope of raising an additional $200,000. A fundraising company was retained at "$6,000 and additional expenses allowed of $12,000,"[100] but again the Chest was faced with failure ($88,266 was raised in this second attempt) and the agencies were forced to reduce their budgets. The first Chest achievement was thus some 40 per cent of "goal"—even with "top leadership."[101] It was subsequently to do better in terms of goal achievement, but "success" in these terms never did become a characteristic of the Indianapolis Chest.

After this first campaign, the Community Chest Board faced the problem of deciding whether to disband or continue. It was maintained that "even in failure, the agencies would receive more money than they had been able to raise individually prior to the Community Chest campaign";[102] so, at a meeting in October 1921, the Board voted to continue the Community Chest and to secure a full-time secretary.

A second professional fundraising firm was retained, at a fee of $10,000, for the 1921-2 campaign. Again receipts did not reach the goal set and solicitation for funds continued after the campaign dates. (Subsequent goals, amounts raised and other information concerning the fundraising campaigns are given in Tables IX and X.)

In the summer of 1922, the Board subscribed to the following policies:

(a) One campaign a year.
(b) Analysis of budgets before setting the campaign quota.
(c) Careful supervision of finances of member organizations.
(d) Co-ordination of social service activities of member organizations.
(e) Elimination of duplicated or obsolete services.
(f) Information about social service to be made public all through the year.[103]

That fall, two additional organizations were included: the Red Cross (which had been holding its own "membership drives" since 1916)[104] and the Girl Scouts. After another unsuccessful campaign, as far as reaching the financial goal was concerned, the Board "concluded that in order to have a successful Fund, the organization would need to be more than a Federation of agencies; that it must be an organization of contributors and workers as well as agencies."[105]

*The Community Fund*

In April, 1923, the name of the organization was changed from "Community Chest" to "Community Fund," a new constitution was adopted, and the basis of membership broadened. A plan for a Council of Social Agencies was adopted. The following statement of claims purports to summarize the record from 1920 to 1924 of the new Fund:

1. More adequate financial support.
2. More contributors.
3. One campaign each year instead of thirty-eight.

4. Elimination of tag days, benefits, special appeals, etc. by member organizations, except for capital expense, such as building funds.
5. Formation of the Family Welfare Society by the consolidation of three member organizations previously working in related fields, with the later amalgamation of two additional agencies.
6. Establishment of the American Settlement through the union of two adjacent neighborhood houses.
7. Detailed study of budgets of member organizations.
8. Financial administration of the Community Fund kept below 8 per cent.
9. Central auditing service supplied to member organizations.
10. Establishment of the Indianapolis Council of Social Agencies.[106]

### The Indianapolis Council of Social Agencies

As we have seen, the major impetus to co-operation among social agencies came during the First World War period. One phase of this national co-operative movement has already been described in Indianapolis: the development of the Community Chest to "conserve the efforts of the solicitor group and to insure that all people were solicited once for all major needs."[107] The co-operative money-raising appeal, however, did not include public agencies and many others which contributed towards "a community goal of better opportunity and better standards of living for all . . . citizens." In order to bring together the approximately eighty agencies of all types (including public bodies) "for a better mutual understanding, and coordination of services," the Council of Social Agencies was formed.[108]

The resultant organizational relationship of the Council of Social Agencies and the Community Fund is shown in the accompanying diagram.[109]

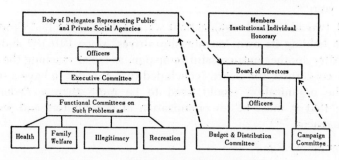

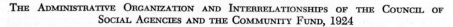

(Dashed lines indicate privilege of nomination)

THE ADMINISTRATIVE ORGANIZATION AND INTERRELATIONSHIPS OF THE COUNCIL OF SOCIAL AGENCIES AND THE COMMUNITY FUND, 1924

### Changes in the 1920's

Many new agencies were formed in the period after 1920. Some of these are shown in the appendix to this chapter (in general, tax-supported agencies have been omitted from the list given there); financial changes are indicated by the increase in the total amount raised as shown in Table IX.

In 1925, the Board of Directors of the Community Fund contributed prizes of $50, $30, and $20 for a "progress plan" contest. The "first-prize plan," submitted by a committee of five persons from the Indianapolis Chapter of the American Association of Social Workers, was briefly as follows:

I. Improvement of Service
   1. The creation of a continuous research bureau . . .
      (a) To gather facts regarding the functions and standards of the individual agencies. . . .
      (b) To promote various undertakings looking forward to improvement of service rendered by the agencies. . . .
      (c) To work . . . with . . . the Council of Social Agencies in securing and evaluating facts.
   2. Joint housing of social agencies maintaining downtown headquarters. . . .
   3. Transferring of the social service exchange to the Council of Social Agencies and arranging some more satisfactory method for the reception and direction of social service inquiries.

II. Co-operation with Governmental Social Agencies. Recognition of the following principles:
   1. That services initiated through voluntary support should be shifted to bodies supported by taxation as rapidly as practicable. . . .
   2. That public relief administration should be developed and stabilized through a plan which will safeguard performance from political changes, and develop the recognition of established standards of service and relief in the public department.
   3. The mutual responsibility of both governmental and private agencies in the . . . social service program. . . .

III. Enlisting and Sustaining the Interest of the Giving Public. Recognition of the following principles:
   1. The desirability of wide participation in policy making and support. . . .
   2. The intensification of the education of the general public through continuous presentation . . . of facts concerning the major lines of social endeavor within the community. . . .
   3. The responsibility of the well-to-do members of the community, in proportion to their ability, both in the leadership of the movement, and as financial supporters. . . .[110]

This outline dates from over thirty years ago. Present evaluation would show I 2 (joint housing) accomplished, and the first part of I 3; proposal II 1 would probably shock many laymen and professionals as a principle; all of III probably stands today where it stood then. The pattern of high resolve and little action is repeated again.

"Good times" economically are reflected in the report for 1926[111] which describes outstanding expansion with respect to buildings and equipment. Also reflecting the prosperity of the times is the comment that "a survey of those habitually begging on the streets revealed they are all professionals, some collecting as much as $15 a day."

In 1927, President Fred Hoke, in his annual report, likened the progress of the Community Fund during the past seven years to "stepping around in a pair of seven-league boots"[112]—even though the Chest had "succeeded" only once in that period, it had improved over its first "failure" by about 62 per cent. The expansion in physical facilities continued; but progress was also reported along other lines, for instance, at least to the point of "studying" recreation—and probation.[113]

In 1928, with new and added facilities, many organizations in every field of endeavor were "studying their services" and looking towards or actively engaged in the revision and expansion of their programs.

## THE DEPRESSION

By 1932—and even before—the picture had changed completely. The "crash" had occurred, and the nation had plunged to the depths of the Great Depression with its widespread unemployment and physical suffering. The welfare agencies were shifting their emphasis back again from "character-building" to "relief"[114]—81.7 per cent of the Community Fund distributions in Indianapolis were for the latter purpose in 1932.[115] The Red Cross joined in with efficient work in this time of crisis.

"Made-work" programs of the national government—NYA, WPA, CCC, and others[116]—and of local agencies helped relieve the situation. Community Fund disbursements for local "made-work" programs in Indianapolis were reported to be over $40,000 in 1931.[117]

The Community Fund's campaign materials for these years had a particularly strong emotional appeal. Its pamphlet, *How 70,230 Citizens Saved a City*, presented its message in words aimed at arousing awareness of the need for morale as well as money.

The program of RELIEF AND HUMAN SERVICE rendered by the Community Fund's 40 agencies . . . saved Indianapolis from suffering a major disaster last year. . . .

Many cities experienced serious outbreaks of violence with resultant loss of life and property. Many cities lost human values which it had taken long years to build. Due to the intelligent generosity of 70,000 Community Fund contributors, Indianapolis was, in the main, more fortunate.

As we face the fourth winter of this depression it is apparent that the need will reach an unprecedented peak. . . . The privileged person today is the job-holder. It is his privilege not only to contribute money, but by so doing to GIVE COURAGE to the increasing thousands in Indianapolis who, through no fault of their own, are at the point of despair.[118]

The increase in the "need" from "last year to this year" showed, among other items: 76 per cent increase in rent paid for individual families; 33 per cent increase in lodging and meals for homeless men; 56 per cent increase in clothing for the needy; 304 per cent increase in quarts of milk for children and the sick.

In January, 1933, "conforming with the request of the American Red Cross that Indianapolis should conduct thereafter an independent Roll Call,"[119] the Indianapolis Chapter severed its relationship with the Community Chest;[120] it had been at that time a participating agency for eleven years.

The gradual return to "normal times" brought a similarly gradual change in welfare-agency policies from "relief" back again to "service" and "character-building." In 1940 and 1941, approximately equal proportions of Chest funds were allocated to these two types of activity.[121]

## World War II

Soon after Pearl Harbor, "Eli Lilly succeeded in coordinating all the *approved* patriotic and war relief activities, except the American Red Cross, into the United War and Community Fund—commonly known as the United War Fund."[122] In 1942, the quota of $1,500,000 (more than double that of the Community Fund for the previous year) was over-subscribed by more than $300,000. In the following two years, over $2,000,000 was raised annually for the United War Fund activities.

The United War Fund Campaign budget for the first year included, in addition to those agencies "on the home front" regularly included in the Community Fund budget, five agencies providing for "our own service men," and nine agencies giving relief to war victims of countries other than the United States.[123] The proportion of the $1,500,000 United War Fund budget allocated to each item shows that by far the largest part was to be spent for the established activities in Indianapolis, which had been supported—at least in part—by the Community Fund.[124]

## Post-War Changes

As a symbol of the growing emphasis on service and "character-building," in 1945 the name of the Family *Welfare* Association was changed to the Family *Service* Association.[125] Its program was reportedly "changed from one of serving only the economically disadvantaged to one of providing casework service to any person in the community regardless of economic or social status," and there is no doubt that it has moved in that direction.[126]

Perhaps the most noticeable trend in the field of philanthropy since World War II has been the organization of agencies—or Foundations—to disseminate knowledge concerning specific diseases and physical deformities and to carry on research dealing with them: the Heart Foundation, Speech and Hearing Clinic, Cancer Society, Multiple Sclerosis Society, Infantile Paralysis, Cerebral Palsy are but a few of the organizations represented in Indianapolis.

Two important organizations whose names have been repeated in this account, were to undergo at least one more transformation. In March of 1950, the present (1956) Indianapolis Community Chest resulted from a reorganization of the Community Fund. At the same time, the Council of Social Agencies, which had been part of the Fund organization, became the present-day Health and Welfare Council.

The Hospital Fund Drive, 1952-3, should perhaps be mentioned again (as it will be later) as an outstanding example of a successful "once-and-for-all" campaign—the type of fundraising which history shows usually succeeds in Indianapolis.

Generally, in this period, "opportunities for giving" are truly legion (see Chart 10) in spite of repeated efforts, since 1879, to reduce the "multiplicity" of appeals for welfare funds. The proportion of the income of the Community Chest agencies acquired through the co-operative fundraising campaign has been decreasing since 1936[127] (actually from more than 80 per cent in 1936 to less than 40 per cent in 1954; see Table VII), which means that even Chest agencies are seeking separate support for increasing amounts.

## TABLE VII

PROPORTION OF AGENCIES' TOTAL OPERATING BUDGET PAID BY THE
COMMUNITY CHEST IN SELECTED YEARS

| Year for which money was raised | Chest payment to member agencies | Agencies' total operating budget | Percentage of agencies' total operating budget covered by Community Chest contribution | |
|---|---|---|---|---|
| 1936 | $  587,731 | $  720,593 | 81.6% | |
| 1937 | 602,091 | 748,482 | 80.4 | 80.7% |
| 1938 | 613,694 | 766,394 | 80.1 | |
| 1949 | $1,087,979 | $2,547,628 | 42.7% | |
| 1950 | 1,113,899 | 2,630,865 | 42.3 | |
| 1951 | 1,172,068 | 2,865,003 | 40.9 | |
| 1952 | 1,261,886 | 3,039,619 | 41.5 | 40.7% |
| 1953 | 1,313,427 | 3,383,545 | 38.8 | |
| 1954 | 1,333,654 | 3,417,929 | 39.0 | |

Source: Indianapolis Community Chest Records.

### FINANCING THE WELFARE AGENCIES

It is seldom that an agency receives its financial support from only one source; the more usual situation is for many sources to contribute to the support of any one agency. The accompanying diagram depicts some of the variety of sources of income involved.

### 1. The People of Indianapolis: Fundraising Campaigns

In the early days in Indianapolis, most of the support for charity came directly from individual citizens: house-to-house solicitations by volunteers provided money, food, clothing, and other necessities to be distributed to the poor. The "house-to-house"—or "office-to-office"—method of collecting money has persisted in Indianapolis to the present time, although these collections now represent only a small fraction of the total amount spent for philanthropy.

Before 1918—except for occasional co-operative efforts—the solicitations were made for, or by, each welfare organization separately. At that time there were approximately forty organizations dependent in whole or in part on the "welfare dollar" in Indianapolis. The object of "eliminating

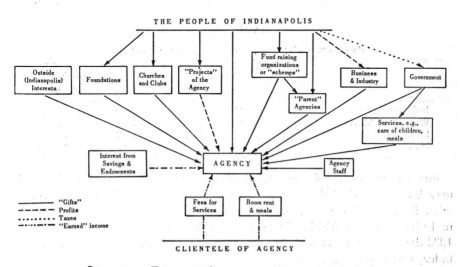

SOURCES OF FINANCIAL SUPPORT OF WELFARE AGENCIES

the multiplicity of appeals" was and is a strong point in favor of "co-operation" in fundraising. Yet the Community Chest has, of course, not by any means united all appeals. The Heart Foundation and the Red Cross— to name two of the largest organizations—carry on their own campaign; the National Tuberculosis Association has its Christmas Seals; the Girl Scouts, their Cookie Sale; and Polio has its March of Dimes.

Fundraising campaigns may be classified into two broad categories: those which are periodic, occurring at stated intervals (usually annually), and those designed to raise money in time of crisis or for one specific object— the "once-in-a-lifetime" type in which widespread public enthusiasm is often engendered and spirits run high. The ability of Indianapolis citizens to "come through" in times of crisis is quite evident: the "Year of Donations" (1907) is referred to earlier in this chapter. At the time of the flood disaster in 1913, almost $105,000 was raised for relief. The "Judge Ross plan"—individuals giving $100 each for the re-establishment of a family— was noteworthy. In 1918, approximately $2,767,000 was contributed for the War Chest by over 100,000 persons (about half the adult population of

Indianapolis); but after the First World War, forty welfare organizations in a co-operative effort (1920) were unable to reach $402,000 in a united campaign for $1,000,000. After twenty-one campaigns of the Community Fund in which goal was attained only four times, the United War Fund was organized in 1942, and "made goal" every year, even though quotas were doubled and almost tripled.

An inter-city comparison of the per capita giving for the Ohio-Mississippi Valley flood disaster in 1937[128] and the per capita giving to "all private social work" the following year[129] shows a complete reversal in the standing of Indianapolis among the four cities[130] common to the two campaigns:

TABLE VIII

PER CAPITA GIVING IN EMERGENCY AND AS ROUTINE

|  | 1937 Disaster | | 1938 Social work | |
|---|---|---|---|---|
|  | Percapita | Rank | Percapita | Rank |
| Indianapolis | $0.67 | 1 | 1.89 | 4 |
| Worcester, Mass. | .39 | 2 | 3.01 | 2 |
| Minneapolis | .33 | 3 | 3.87 | 1 |
| New Orleans | .23 | 4 | 2.00 | 3 |

For a summary of relevant information on fundraising, Tables IX and X may be consulted. Table IX gives the amount raised—along with several other items—during each of the thirty-five years of co-operative fundraising in Indianapolis. In Table X the increase in the amount raised, based on 1930 data, is compared with increases in disposable income, consumer price index, and population.

## 2. Projects

From the time when Indianapolis became large enough to support such projects, dinners, teas, bazaars, dances, and many other forms of entertainment helped fill the coffers of the agencies while entertaining the donors and giving them "something for their money." About the time of World War I, interest in this type of fundraising diminished somewhat, although even at the present time entertainments of various kinds (e.g., the "Christamore Follies") draw large crowds, and produce appreciable amounts for "favorite charities." Compared with the total effort, this method of securing income is seen to be generally restricted to small "upper-class" (and a few quite lower-class) groups and to specific objectives or agencies.

## 3. Government

As early as 1845, government gave financial aid to welfare work. From about 1881 to 1900 both the City of Indianapolis and Marion County were giving $600 each, annually, for the support of the Home for the Aged.

## TABLE IX

INDIANAPOLIS COMMUNITY FUND (AND CHEST), FUNDRAISING DATA

| Year 1 | Goal 2 | Amount raised[a] 3 | Percentage of goal 4 | Amount paid to Chest agencies 5 | Percentage paid to Chest agencies 6 |
|---|---|---|---|---|---|
| 1920–21 | 1,000,000 | 406,261 | 40.6% | — | — |
| 1921–22 | 605,412 | 447,569 | 73.9 | — | — |
| 1922–23 | 644,047 | 546,078 | 84.8 | 509,602 | 93.3% |
| 1923–24 | 650,000 | 606,385 | 93.3 | 548,143 | 90.4 |
| 1924–25 | 700,215 | 632,912 | 90.4 | 518,561 | 81.9 |
| 1925–26 | 650,662 | 651,042 | 100.1 | 572,652 | 88.0 |
| 1926–27 | 683,000 | 657,646 | 96.3 | 575,415 | 87.5 |
| 1927–28 | 722,800 | 726,154 | 100.5 | 651,731 | 89.8 |
| 1928–29 | 781,800 | 753,768 | 96.4 | 657,450 | 87.2 |
| 1929–30 | 786,853 | 771,297 | 98.0 | 701,721 | 91.0 |
| 1930–31 | 865,000 | 898,443 | 103.9 | 797,003 | 88.7 |
| 1931–32 | 1,043,686 | 1,043,348 | 100.0 | 846,023 | 81.1 |
| 1932–33 | 1,052,632 | 817,078 | 77.6 | 656,510 | 80.3 |
| 1933–34 | 824,462 | 701,745 | 85.1 | 555,226 | 79.1 |
| 1934–35 | 727,217 | 674,360 | 92.7 | 575,812 | 85.4 |
| 1935–36 | 724,360 | 693,779 | 95.8 | 587,731 | 84.7 |
| 1936–37 | 745,742 | 700,081 | 93.9 | 602,091 | 86.0 |
| 1937–38 | 721,287 | 700,941 | 97.2 | 613,694 | 87.6 |
| 1938–39 | 711,633 | 657,003 | 92.3 | 577,232 | 87.9 |
| 1939–40 | 683,710 | 680,538 | 99.5 | 586,201 | 86.1 |
| 1940–41 | 688,500 | 692,185 | 100.5 | 591,332 | 85.4 |
| 1941–42 | 688,500 | 701,445 | 101.9 | 677,455 | 96.6 |
| 1942–43 | 1,500,000 | 1,809,320 | 120.6 | 635,375[b] | 35.1 |
| 1943–44 | 1,975,000 | 2,043,519 | 103.5 | 658,274[b] | 32.2 |
| 1944–45 | 1,975,000 | 2,007,760 | 101.7 | 808,844[b] | 40.3 |
| 1945–46 | 1,821,000 | 1,600,315 | 87.9 | 923,545[b] | 57.7 |
| 1946–47 | 1,328,000 | 1,229,560 | 92.6 | 1,015,934 | 82.6 |
| 1947–48 | 1,279,200 | 1,196,250 | 93.5 | 1,081,665 | 90.4 |
| 1948–49 | 1,504,772 | 1,257,196 | 83.5 | 1,087,823 | 86.5 |
| 1949–50 | 1,280,000 | 1,282,629 | 100.2 | 1,113,899 | 86.8 |
| 1950–51 | 1,472,760 | 1,402,552 | 95.2 | 1,172,068 | 83.6 |
| 1951–52 | 1,697,302 | 1,565,228 | 92.2 | 1,261,886 | 80.6 |
| 1952–53 | 1,643,856 | 1,579,018 | 96.1 | 1,313,427 | 83.2 |
| 1953–54 | (1,743,856)[c] | 1,589,046 | (91.1) | 1,333,654 | 83.9 |
| 1954–55 | (1,843,856)[c] | 1,561,820 | (71.5) | 1,364,952 | 87.4 |

[a]Various figures published; these are from the Chest's records.
[b]"Regular less War Activities."
[c]Goal $300,000 increase in three years. Assumed, therefore, $100,000 per year.

Prior to that time, a considerable sum was derived from "fines and penalties assessed and collected for breach of certain classes of penal ordinance of the City."[131] Aid also came indirectly to those agencies caring for public wards because of government payments for their board and room.

## TABLE X

COMPARISON OF INCREASE IN NATIONAL INCOME AND IN THE POPULATION OF
INDIANAPOLIS WITH THE INCREASE IN THE AMOUNT RAISED BY THE
COMMUNITY CHEST (COMMUNITY FUND)

| Year of campaign | National per capita disposable personal income[a] (% of 1930) | Population of Indianapolis (% of 1930) | Amount raised by Community Fund in given year (% of 1930) | Consumer Price Index[b] (% of 1930) |
|---|---|---|---|---|
| 1930 | 100.0% | 100% | 100.0% | 100.0% |
| 1931 | 95.0 | | 116.1 | |
| 1932 | 81.3 | | 90.9 | |
| 1933 | 80.0 | | 78.1 | |
| 1934 | 86.0 | | 75.1 | |
| 1935 | 93.8 | | 77.2 | 82.2 |
| 1936 | 105.3 | | 77.9 | |
| 1937 | 108.7 | | 78.0 | |
| 1938 | 101.7 | | 73.1 | |
| 1939 | 109.2 | | 75.7 | |
| 1940 | 115.7 | 106 | 77.0 | 83.9 |
| 1941 | 131.4 | | 78.1 | |
| 1942 | 146.7 | | 201.4 | |
| 1943 | 150.4 | | 227.5 | |
| 1944 | 157.3 | | 223.5 | |
| 1945 | 154.3 | | 178.1 | 107.7 |
| 1946 | 149.5 | | 136.9 | |
| 1947 | 142.5 | | 133.1 | |
| 1948 | 147.6 | | 139.9 | |
| 1949 | 145.8 | | 142.8 | |
| 1950 | 154.5 | 117 | 156.1 | 144.0 |
| 1951 | 154.3 | | 174.2 | |
| 1952 | 155.3 | | 175.8 | |
| 1953 | 159.0 | | 176.9 | 160.2 |
| 1954 | | | 173.8 | |

[a]From Bureau of the Census, *Statistical Abstract of the United States 1954*, Table 333.
[b]*Ibid.*, Table 367.

The governments—national, state, county, and city—spend each year for charity and social service many times the amount raised by the Community Chest. In 1940, considerably over $12,500,000[132] was spent in Indianapolis for health and welfare services; during that same year the Indianapolis Community Fund paid to the various agencies $586,000. The corresponding 1950 figures were probably of the order of $20 million and $1 million respectively.[133]

### 4. Outside Interests

An example of "outside interests" which give support are the Metropolitan Life Insurance Company and the John Hancock Life Insurance

Company which supported the Public Health Nurses (now the Visiting Nurses Association) from 1913 to 1951. Prior to that time, these companies had had nurses in the field doing work similar to that of the Public Health Nurses. In 1913, the companies decided to support the Nurses Association and to turn over to them the work they had themselves been doing.

### 5. *Foundations*

The income of the Indianapolis Foundation, created in 1916, has since that time been disbursed to many of the agencies for use in "the relief of the needy poor and the improvement of living conditions . . . the care of the sick or aged . . . educational and philanthropic research in Indianapolis."[134] In 1955, the income of the Indianapolis Foundation available for philanthropic purposes for the first time exceeded one-quarter of a million dollars. Twenty-two community service organizations shared in gifts from the Foundation totalling almost $215,000.

The first disbursement of the Lilly Endowment, Inc., a Foundation organized in 1937, was a gift to the Indianapolis Community Chest. Since that time, the Endowment has made substantial grants in the fields of what it classifies as: social science and humanities, including religion; education; cultural projects; community services; and public health. In 1955, out of total grants amounting to $1,881,343, over $900,000 was given to agencies in Indianapolis.[135]

The Baxter Foundation and the Arthur Jordan Foundation also give substantial assistance to social service organizations in Indianapolis.

### 6. *Fees and Service Charges*

The old people's homes generally have fixed entrance fees and/or monthly charges. Other homes and agencies catering primarily to the poor and destitute charge fees based on ability to pay. The Visiting Nurses, for example, follow this policy. Service organizations, such as the Family Service Association, also regulate fees to correspond to the financial status of the client.

### 7. *Membership Dues*

"Membership dues" refers to dues paid, not by the clients of a welfare agency, but by the "members" of a sponsoring organization. There are many organizations (e.g., Guilds, Junior League, etc.) in which members pay dues and which sponsor welfare or social service projects; and there are other organizations (e.g., Red Cross and the Indianapolis Hospital Association) in which "paying membership dues" is merely the name attached to their method of fundraising. In the former case, to put it bluntly, the organization is primarily interested in the "members," and in the latter, the organization is interested primarily in the "dues."

## 8. *Unique Money-Raising Schemes*

The Tuberculosis Association's Christmas Seal sale has been an annual event since 1907. The "March of Dimes," which was inaugurated for polio research during F. D. Roosevelt's presidency, netted the National Foundation for Infantile Paralysis in Indianapolis almost $5,000 in December, 1941. The "Clothe-a-Child" campaign of the *Indianapolis Times* each year arouses the "Christmas spirit" among both the "givers" and the "underprivileged." The "Telethon" when first used proved to be a successful method of raising money in Indianapolis: a continuous television program lasting (generally) for sixteen to twenty-four hours on which appeals are made for funds, and there is provision for receiving them at the site of the broadcast.[136]

Some of the innumerable "opportunities to give" in Indianapolis are illustrated in Chart 10 (1955), together with the approximate dates of the fundraising campaign or "project." Of the seventy agencies (exclusive of the Community Chest) listed in this chart, eleven receive grants from the Indianapolis Community Chest.[137] The list does not purport to be complete —the names are those called to our attention through direct solicitation, mail requests for contributions, or newspaper notices and/or advertising. The organizations and campaigns listed appeal (as far as we are able to ascertain) to the general public; there are many other appeals to "friends" of agencies and other selected or restricted groups. During this year—1955— there was not a day when a potential donor did not have at least four "causes" from which to select a recipient for his philanthropic contribution.

## APPENDIX

### SELECTED SOCIAL AGENCIES AND THEIR DATES OF FOUNDING

1835: Indianapolis Benevolent Society
1850: Widows and Orphans Friends Society
1851: Widows and Orphans Asylum of Indianapolis
St. Vincent's School (Catholic orphanage)
1854: YMCA
1863: Young Men's Library Association
1864: American Red Cross
1866: Home for Aged and Friendless Women
1870: Indianapolis Board of Public Health and Charities
1872: Sisters of the Good Shepherd (Marydale School)
1873: Little Sisters of the Poor
Public Library
1876: Flower Mission
1877: Social Service Exchange
1878: Maternity Society
1879: Charity Organization Society

Employment Bureau of Benevolent Society
Newsboys' Lodging House
1880: Friendly Inn Wood Yard
Salvation Army
1881: Free Kindergarten;
Children's Aid Society
Reforms in Asylum for Poor
1883: Alpha Home (for aged and infirm Negroes)
Evangelical Lutheran Orphans Home
1887: Dime Savings and Loan Association
County Workhouse
1888: Associated Charities
1889: Board of State Charities
Board of Children's Guardians
1890: Summer Mission for Sick Children
1891: Board of Public Health and Charities
Home Libraries

1892: Boy's Club Association
1893: Wheeler Mission Wood Yard
1895: YWCA
      Eleanor Home
1896: Volunteers of America
1898: Flanner Guild
      Flanner House
      Day Nursery
      Stern Memorial Hospital
1899: Indianapolis Industrial Home for
      Blind Men
1900: YMCA, Senate Ave. Branch
1901: Indianapolis Truancy Department
      Indianapolis Day Nursery
1902: Shelter House (Jewish relief)
1903: Marion County Juvenile Home
      Juvenile Court
1904: Mutual Service Association
      Jewish Welfare Federation
1905: Children's Aid Association
      Christamore House
      Humane Society
1906: Marion County Juvenile Detention
      Home
      St. Mary's Hospital Guild
      (Episcopal)
      St. Margaret's Guild
      Fairview Settlement
1907: Mother's Aid Society
      St. Margaret's Hospital Guild
1908: Foreigners Help Office
1909: Old Folks Home
1910: Zetathea Club
      Altenheim
      Catholic Womens Association
1911: Medical social service begun,
          Indianapolis City Dispensary
      I.U. Division of Social Service
      Southwest Social Centre
1912: Legal Aid Bureau
      Christmas Clearing House
      Indianapolis Church Federation
      Camp Fire Girls
1913: Public Health Nursing Association
      Florence Crittenton Home
1914: Marion County TB Association
      Central Indiana Council of Boy
          Scouts of America
1915: Boy Scouts
      Travelers Aid Society
1916: Red Cross Chapter
1920: Community Fund organized
      Travelers Aid
      Catholic Charities Bureau
      Catholic Community Center
1921: St. Elizabeth's Home
1922: Family Welfare Society
      Indianapolis Council of Social
      Agencies

1923: American Association of Social
          Workers (Indianapolis
          Chapter)
      Indianapolis Council of Social
          Agencies
      YWCA (Phyllis Wheatley Branch)
      Hassler Philanthropic and Non-
          Sectarian Society
      Hawthorne Social Service
          Association
1924: Christamore Women's Club
1925: Jewish Welfare Fund
      Indianapolis Employment Bureau
      Christmas Sisters Fund of Family
          Welfare Society
      YWCA, South Side Branch
      American Legion—Child Welfare
1926: Kirshbaum Community Center
1929: Goodwill Industries
      Catholic Daughters of America
1930: *Indianapolis Times* "Clothe-a-
          Child" campaign
1931: "Individual Gifts Fellowship"
          organized
      "Made work" programs
      Relief Kitchen
      Children's Bureau of Indianapolis
          Orphan Asylum
1932: Maternal Health League
      Auxiliary to Indianapolis Orphan
          Asylum
1933: St. Vincent's Hospital Guild
      Planned Parenthood Association
1934: Volunteer Committee of Indiana-
          polis Council of Social
          Agencies
1935: Suemma Coleman Home of
          Indianapolis
      Transient Referral Bureau
      NYA
1936: County Welfare Board
1937: Flower Mission Hospital
1938: Salvation Army Men's Lodge
      National Foundation for Infantile
          Paralysis, local Chapter
1939: Indiana Rehabilitation League
      Catholic Youth Organization
1941: Legal Aid Society
      U.S.O.
1942: Esther Hall Deaconess Home
      Speech and Hearing Society
      Legal Aid Society
      General Protestant Orphans Home
      Marion County Cancer Society
      "War Fund" Campaign
1943: Social Hygiene Association
1944: Norways Foundation
1945: Family Service Association
      Mayer Neighborhood House

1948: Indiana Heart Foundation
1949: Marion County Mental Health
       Association
1950: Community Chest, from reorganiza-
       tion of Community Fund
1952: Muscular Dystrophy

1953: Commission on Alcoholism
       Noble School for Retarded
       Children
       Cerebral Palsy
1954: Multiple Sclerosis
1956: Myasthenia Gravis

# III. THE COMMUNITY CHEST

# 5. Aims and Purposes

EVERY SOCIAL ORGANIZATION has more or less explicit aims and purposes. These purposes, if they are effective, serve to guide policy and action in the short run; and, over the long run, they are in a sense what organizes the organization and gives meaning to membership in it. One "belongs" to an organization to the degree that one shares in its purposes; and the organization "belongs to" its membership (in a different sense) in so far as that membership determines or controls policy, or shares in its determination or control. Thus purpose acts both as the test of fitness in action and as the felt basis for the social or moral solidarity which is the measure, objectively, of the organization's strength, and, subjectively, of its value.

It is patently not necessary for the survival of some organizations that they have only one purpose at a given time—nor that every member make any particular one of its purposes his own. The purpose of an army may be to defeat the enemy, the purpose of a sergeant within it may be to "buck for promotion" by making his the best platoon in the company, and the purpose of a private may be more simply to minimize his discomforts under stated conditions. These things may and do occur without detracting sensibly from the effectiveness of the army: the command organization, with its relatively unbounded control of rewards and punishments, ensures that disparity of purpose among members does not result in unconcerted, disconcerted, or otherwise self-defeating action.

But a "voluntary" fundraising organization is not an army. It is true, as will appear later (chapters 10 and 11), that it wields considerable powers of punishment and holds out considerable possibilities of reward to the "volunteers" and to the "voluntary" givers. These powers, however, compared with those operating in an army, are somewhat attenuated, and a great deal of reliance must be placed on relatively free consent, or, at least, on minimizing active resistance. Under these circumstances, it is of considerable importance that participants of all kinds should have the feeling of sharing in a common purpose (as against, say, feeling either that the program and procedure are meaningless—have no purpose—or that the purposes they have are opposed to the participants' wishes). In the absence of such a consensus about aims, actions are likely to be stultified or mutually self-cancelling; and, even where parallel action is "engineered," it is likely to be emptied, for many participants, of satisfaction, let alone the glow of enthusiasm. In so far as an organization like the Chest is a "voluntary" movement, therefore, it must rely for unity and effectiveness in action, to a considerable degree, on the attractiveness of its purposes—as expressed in word, ceremony, and businesslike action—for those whom it needs to motivate and enthuse.

But the Chest—together with similar organizations—is not merely a *voluntary* fundraising organization. It is a *mass* voluntary fundraising organization; it views as in its potential donorship everyone living within a given area,[1] or, indeed, everyone whom it could bring under suasion, whether living in the area or not.[2] The statement that it is a *mass* fundraising organization does not quite mean that it is a mass movement, and the distinction is rather important. It is a mass organization only in the sense that it needs contributions of money from everyone—the masses—not that it needs the enthusiastic moral commitment of everyone.[3] On the contrary, as we shall see later (chapters 10 and 11), "success" in money-raising will turn largely on (1) the enthusiasm of a few leaders, (2) the "positive support" of a larger number of power-figures, (3) the willingness to give (as directed or suggested by the power-figures) of the greater part of the employee population, (4) some small similar willingness in part of the residentially organized "public" and, probably, (5) no strong, organized or vocal opposition anywhere.[4]

If the structure of the Chest (or a similar organization) is seen as something like that in the accompanying diagram,[5] then the relevance of purpose to effectiveness increases as we work from the upper right corner (the "outside") in, decreases as we work from the lower left corner (the "inside") out. At the outside, about all that is really needed is the absence of effective opposition or veto. In the inner shells, something only a little short of total commitment is probably necessary and certainly desirable. Disagreement or confusion on any matters felt fundamental will have progressively greater repercussions on the outside, the nearer the center that confusion or disagreement occurs or persists.

It will be the contention of this chapter (1) that the Chest seems plagued by a number of conflicts and confusions about its basic role or mission or purpose, (2) that these confusions and conflicts are rarely made explicit, (3) that they can be seen as sources of irritation and mutual frustration between people in the Chest organization, (4) that concerted action is difficult and inefficient as a consequence of these frustrations, among other things, and (5) that the removal of these frustrations depends on setting up appropriate procedures and machinery to deal with them (see chapters 12 and 13). The confusions and contradictions are found not only in opinions regarding what are the primary *objectives* of the organization (a "value" problem) but also in opinions as to what are the *facts* of life in this field (a "fact" problem) and what are and are not acceptable modes of arguing about or *discussing* them (a "logical" problem).

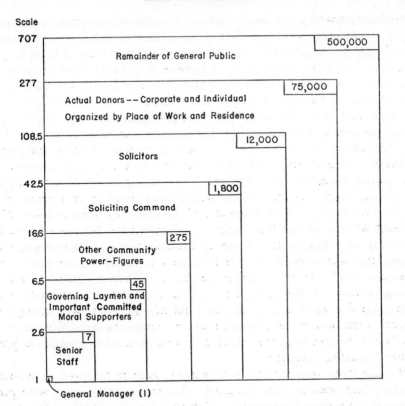

APPROXIMATE "STRUCTURE OF INTIMACY" OF INDIANAPOLIS COMMUNITY CHEST
(Scale: The numbers in each square correspond to the area—on a logarithmic scale)

## CENTRAL VALUE-CONFLICTS

### Business Success versus Community Organization

In a recent campaign a very prominent layman shocked some part, at least, of the Chest's staff by referring to the Chest as essentially a "collecting agency" (for the social agencies). What was shocking to the staff people was not so much the possibility of a public-relations error in referring to the Chest's function so baldly and unemotionally. Rather they received a genuine moral shock—a sudden feeling of social distance and alienation between those who regard the Chest primarily as a semi-sacred movement in the realm of "community organization" (for which money is, incidentally, needed) and those who regard money-raising as the commonsense and natural heart of the enterprise (for which some community organization is, incidentally, necessary). Persons may be found, probably, in every intermediate position from those who consider the money-raising function nearly all-important to those who consider the community organization nearly all-important. For some, the Chest represents almost a venture in brotherhood in which money-raising occurs; for others, it is almost an adventure in otherhood, in which the emotional focus is on the money-extracting process.[6]

These alternate views as to the paramount or primary interest to be served do not represent merely matters of interpretation of what is going on, or more or less devotion to or interest in different elements of a total program. They may not represent purely opposed alternatives, such as, say, the alternative between driving north or driving south; but they do represent substantial opposition, such as, say, driving northeast or driving southeast—one gets east in either case, but not at the same point or near it.

The conflict has a bearing on practical matters. Should the primary criterion of the Chest's success, for instance, be a campaign measure such as "participation," or "gift per donor," or "per capita gift,"[7] or should it be a non-campaign measure such as would be reflected in an estimate of the proportion of people that "knew about" the Chest[8] or "were in favor of" the Chest,[9] whether or not they could or did contribute. No one perhaps took seriously any attempt to set one of these as having exclusive priority or value; this was particularly true of those who thought some non-financial measure "really" most important—i.e., no one could be found to say that the education of the community or its organization sentimentally was justifiable if it yielded no money or a net loss. But those who thought that participation was more important as an immediate issue than percapita really felt divided from the others, and were inclined to promote or pursue other policies in practice.[10]

Among those who thought first priority ought to be given to increasing participation were people convinced either that existing givers were giving "enough" (an ethical judgment) or "about as much as they're going to give, anyway" (a judgment of fact or of practicality). On this view, since either no increase should be demanded of the givers or no such demand would be effective, the only possible source of increase is the non-giver, the successful persuasion of whom would then increase participation.

Others among the participation-emphasizers, however, had different practical and ethical reasons to adduce for their preferences. One of the practical arguments, quite credible on its face, ran to the effect that in any giving unit (such as the employees in a factory department) the acts of giving are more interdependent when it comes to the question of *whether* to give at all (which is frequently known to everyone in the unit) than they are when it comes to the alternative question as to *how much* to give (which is frequently not known to most of them). On this view, it is "easier" to use social interaction to increase participation than it is to use interaction to increase percapita. And what is easiest ought to be done first. Another practical argument rests on an "intuitive" conviction that the ease of getting another giver out of any particular group is in some way related to the number one already has got[11]—so that great attention to participation is justified from the viewpoint of economizing persuasive resources.

In any case, the gulf between the percapita-minded and the participation-minded is less often founded on such practical arguments, and much more frequently on an important difference in general orientation, value-system, or ethical set. For those oriented to participation, the question of the relative ease or difficulty of securing increased participation as against increased percapita is largely irrelevant, since their question is not "What is easy?" but "What is *right*?" or "What is *good*?"

The participation-minded and the percapita-minded are found among both the laymen and the professionals, although their reasons for occupying these positions are somewhat different.

The percapita-minded professionals tend to pay attention to the "under-giving" of those who do give; they feel (comparing their city with other cities, or comparing different classes of givers, or contrasting actuality with wish) that (1) the givers give too little, (2) that this is "wrong" and should be "righted," and (3) that the fact that these givers give at all shows recognition of an obligation, which it would take relatively little effort to get discharged on a more appropriate scale. The percapita-minded laymen, on the other hand, tend towards the same conclusion on one of two very different urgings: (1) a sense of *noblesse oblige* (or, more exactly, *argent oblige*)—a feeling that they and their peers are not giving enough in proportion to their "potential," or (2) a feeling of "injustice" or unfairness in that, while they give enough, the givers among their peers do not, and that this is urgent for correction.[12]

The lay and professional participation-minded differ similarly. This layman feels that low participation is "bad" either because it is "poor public relations" or because, without the check of "saleability," he considers he has, himself, little or no basis for judging value. It is "poor public relations" because it is "risky to get too far out ahead of the crowd." The second reason means that, probably, "if the crowd won't buy it, it shouldn't be sold," i.e., the unpopular isn't worthy of support. The high premium put on participation is in the first case a measure of safety; in the second a check by the market, as it were, on selling enthusiasm.

The professional, on the other hand, is less likely to feel that his enthusiasm needs check, or that the value of his product needs proof or supporting evidence. He is likely to take his stand on a feeling, a mystique almost,[13] that flows from his high valuation of, and his interpretation of what is involved in, "democracy."[14] The general feeling that, in all matters that concern them, as many people as possible should be "involved"—ideally "all the people"—runs like a thread thick and strong through much of the social-work fabric, and participation in money-giving on a wide scale is just one particular expression of the desire to "get everybody in" so it will be "democratic," i.e., from this viewpoint, right.

## Democratic versus Aristocratic Orientation

The discussion of the "business success" versus "community organization" (and percapita versus participation) orientation has brought us to the edge of another distinction or division of view as to aims and purposes:

what might be called an "aristocratic" view of the organization as against what might be called a "democratic" view.[15]

The "aristocratic" view takes it for granted that the Chest is inevitably, or "ought" to be, an organization of the "best" people for the sake of "those not so favored." If this is the case, or if it ought to be, then the Chest's principal advantage is (or would be) just precisely that it is able to indulge the aristocratic virtues—nobility, generosity, a certain ability to deal largely and openhandedly and to make quick decisions on large events without being unduly sensitive to public relations and general opinion.

The "democratic" view maintains that, on the contrary, an organization like the Chest "ought to be"[16] essentially an organization of "all the people" or, at the very least, an organization that "represents"[17] all the people.

Again, the differences in view have considerable practical consequences; some effort will be made by the democratic-minded to secure the involvement of "more people" or the "representation" of "more groups," or at least the semblance of the latter. The "aristocratic-minded" may, and some do, feel that the representation of fewer interests would lead to a firmer and more certain policy and one that would involve the relevant few (relevant in terms of power in the community and ability to give or cause giving) more deeply and enthusiastically. They may well feel that too many people are already engaged in decision-making for resultant decisions to be really bold and commanding of effective support.[18]

Some compromise clearly characterizes the Indianapolis Chest as it probably does most Chests. The typical compromise is to extend the nominal governorship of the institution, while effectively concentrating power in "committees" on which the élite or community power-group is disproportionately represented.[19]

The greatest loss in connection with this unresolved, and largely unconfronted, issue comes, however, not so much, we suspect, from actual struggles to concentrate or disperse power in line with the respective views as it does from a vague uneasiness or distress or feeling of "bad conscience," stemming from the discrepancy between what many feel to be "proper" or ideal and what is actually the case or what may be the only possibility. There is little or no open—as against "off the record"—discussion of what is involved, and particularly little facing of the possibility that for an organization like the Chest an élite or power-group control might be not only inevitable but appropriate. For some others, distress arises less because of the discrepancy in this respect between what the Chest is and what it ought to be and much more because of a felt discrepancy between what it is and what it makes itself out to be. What it makes itself out to be is very various, depending at least on the particular audience addressed and the purpose of the "message." But with sometimes one emphasis, sometimes the other, and, most often, both, it makes itself out either as an organization of the very best people, the leaders of the leaders, or as a "representative" group "no different from you or me," almost in the sense of a random sample of the community population. That the latter version has always or nearly always to be emphasized indicates the feeling either that it ought to be the true one, or that it must be made to appear so.[20]

The preceding discussion brings us face to face with another perennial issue: appearance versus substance.

## Appearance versus Substance

A famous recommendation to effective government may be found in Machiavelli's *Discourses*: the Prince, to be "successful," should seem to be honest. A more long-standing recommendation, also embedded in Judeo-Christian culture, is found in the unconditional "Thou shalt not lie."

The choice between (relative) honesty as a goal and the mere appearance of it is not, of course, peculiar to any one human organization. For some, it hardly appears as a problem at all. A vendor in the more high, wide, and handsome days of selling, when even the legal maxim bade the buyer beware, could scarcely feel himself enjoined to any more honesty than made for effective selling (in the short run), which was often not a very great deal. In more recent days, while honesty is said to be the best policy, some allowance is commonly made in practice for something less than "full, frank and free disclosure." The amount of what may be called "permissible dishonesty" will vary from enterprise to enterprise[21] and business to business, though all will permit themselves some leeway.

In many, if not most, human enterprises that fall clearly within *either* the secular field or the sacred field, the weight to be given to honesty as against its semblance is determined with relative ease by the definition of the field within which each falls. When, moreover, many years of operation have permitted what was once contrived and conscious to become habitual and largely unconscious, tradition acts as a buffer to unease; indeed, for most people, the standard of honesty is probably the standard of what is customary.[22]

But, when, on the contrary, a movement is both sufficiently new, so that no tradition has had opportunity to crystallize (see chapter 2), and also, for some, on the border between sacred and secular, for others an admixture of both, for still others a secular expression of sacred motives and for yet others a secular substitute for sacred functions (see chapter 2), it is likely that there will be marked differences of opinion as to what constitutes proper behavior, and marked conflict within and between people as a consequence. Such conflict might be expected to be peculiarly acute in an organization that aims to be at one and the same time the epitome of business—money-getting—and a major focus for the American secular religion of "service."[23]

Unfortunately for simplicity, we cannot attribute the differential concern with honesty (as against enough appearance of it to "get by") to one party or the other, either layman or professional. One cannot, even for the same person, count upon consistent differential concern, one way or the other, as he shifts about from role to role. A layman sitting temporarily on a budget committee,[24] or critically examining an internal financial statement, will have standards of accuracy very different from those he will have as a campaign chairman.[25] Similarly, the same professional, acting now as general manager now as campaign director, will also have different standards on different occasions, and will feel some strain and consequently exhibit some cynicism.

Each will, generally, also allow himself much greater leeway with the facts when he is addressing a large audience than when he is addressing a small one. The addressees may otherwise be the same, but large numbers reduce intimacy and therewith, simultaneously, the felt mandate to honesty and the possibility of cross-examination, i.e., the internal and external checks on wish and imagination.

Again, these are matters of immense consequence for policy: some people experience an acute "internal" problem of wear and tear because they feel either that they are driven to act in terms of an ethic they cannot approve, or that they are hampered in their effectiveness by over-scrupulous and unrealistic "social dreamers." But there are also "external" problems arising out of this evidently unresolved conflict between the substance and the seeming of truth. We have seen laymen and professionals, disaffected, alienated, or in some degree demoralized because of the conflict as to standards; we have also heard expression of a cynical "how could it be otherwise?" Thus while there is considerable individual uneasiness, there is no collective policy, explicit in words or implicit from practice.

But this may not be the most important practical problem—though it is not trivial. Another practical problem that arises inescapably when a deception-system is to be adopted is the protection of that system so that the organization does not too patently appear to contradict itself when it speaks at the same time through different members, or at successive times through the same member. This requires superior communication and record-keeping, as every propaganda director knows. It also requires clear distinction between the in-group to whom relative access to truth is permitted and the out-group to whom it is not. Some devices are also needed to prevent detection—an analogue to counter-intelligence in military or political affairs. In the absence of such machinery, experience would indicate some difficulty in maintaining elaborate deceptions (i.e., in effectively deceiving those who are to be deceived) *in the long run*.

## Long-Run and Short-Run Emphasis

But this brings us to another type of division within and between people as we have encountered them. And this difference also characterizes laymen and professionals.

The difference is essentially between those with predominantly short-run preoccupations and those with predominantly long-run ones. If a simile can be permitted that treats the population of potential givers as a "field," the difference lies between those who would "farm the land" and those who would "mine the land," between the "cultivators" and the "exploiters," the "conservators" and the "harvesters." One group tends to think in terms of maximum yield now; the other, in terms of greatest total yield over an indefinitely long life, perhaps extending beyond the present generation.

It is a well-known fact that most[26] of the "leading citizens" associated with a movement such as the Chest will ordinarily regard themselves as more permanent members of the community, while many if not most professionals will recognize that, willing or not,[27] they are relatively transient through it. It is widely believed, upon this ground, that the laymen will incline to the long-run view and the professionals to the short. Again, unfortunately for simplicity, this appears simply not to be the case.

In the first place, the laymen, even the town's "leading citizens," are no longer, in these days of large national firms, so predominantly people whose past is that of their present community or whose future—if they are "successful"—is bound up with the future of any one city. They were born elsewhere, and they expect and frequently hope to be yet elsewhere soon. They are therefore, even though otherwise conservative, under some necessity to follow the mandate "That thou doest, do quickly."

For many other leading laymen, moreover, time presses in the sense that their "period of service" in such organizations as the Chest has to fit into increasingly stringent career requirements. If the "service" is to be useful to the career it must not come too early in it or too late, and this means that whatever is to be done must be done fast; it also means that what is done fast should be "successful," for little credit, relatively, accrues to the businessman in the business world from service in a "failing" organization. For both of these reasons there is considerable pressure on laymen to produce notable results immediately. One would have to add to these complications a third: that under some circumstances[28] leaders who are in one or many senses marginal to the "top top leadership" will be called into positions of most active direction precisely *because* their marginality will permit or encourage them to take steps that are, to say the least, not traditional and therefore, while potentially "successful," not open to the "top top leadership." Such steps are almost inevitably in the direction of improvising relatively startling schemes for relatively short-run ends, with reduced regard for long-run consequences.

On the other side, for the professional, is the erroneous guess that his transience would invariably give him a short-run view. Three factors in his situation, and perhaps a fourth, incline him, however, in the opposite direction: (1) his professional past and (2) his professional future, (3) his immediate social relations, and (4) his (somewhat remoter) relations to other fundraisers. His past experience and his expectation of a permanent career in fundraising somewhere, give his knowledge some extension by way of information as to what has succeeded and failed elsewhere, and put him under some pressure to develop a personal ethic and a relatively long-run policy for himself. His relative social distance from businessmen and his relative social closeness to social workers incline him perhaps to take a "professional" view of what is involved, and therefore to view it in a longer time-perspective. His association with other fundraisers works probably ambiguously, since the ethics of stewardship seem no more dominantly represented in their gatherings than the ethics of exploit.[29]

In any case, and for whatever reasons, it seems unambiguously clear that both laymen and professionals can be found who have long-run and short-run orientations.

And again it seems clear that no simple resolution of the conflicting claims of present and future can be made—in general, or at any one time— as a permanent solution. What is remarkable, perhaps, is the relative lack of awareness of the problem despite disputes actually based upon it, the absence of a working policy (which nearly every good business has explicitly, and nearly every good farmer implicitly), and the resultant tendency for "policy" in the long run to become, therefore, a succession of short-run adaptations to successive emergencies or crises.[30]

## Volunteer and Conscript: Suasion and Pressure

One might suppose that the ideal situation for a MOPS fundraising outfit would be one in which enough people would spontaneously (preferably for the "right" reasons) send in enough money, often enough and with enough promptness, to make any large effort unnecessary and, therefore, any large organization superfluous.

Since people do not in general so act, it appears that they must be "sold," and in order to sell them, a vast organization of salesmen—"volunteers"— must be recruited, trained, motivated, controlled, and maintained. Ideally, again—even if spontaneous money-giving on a wide scale cannot be had— it would be desirable that the army of "volunteer" salesmen or persuaders should be genuinely a volunteer army. It seems obvious that, in practice, this cannot be had either, and there must therefore be a prior process to "persuade" the army of workers who are to "persuade" the much larger population of "givers." "Voluntary gifts" which are not wholly voluntary must thus be collected by "volunteer solicitors" who are not wholly volunteers.[31]

Every voluntary organization, no doubt, would wish to appear to be as voluntary as possible, while desire for "efficiency" tempts it constantly to mobilize all the sanctions—rewards or penalties—it can muster to ensure that "free" choice shall have a foregone outcome.[32] But for every organization this poses at least three problems: where shall the actuality be located (how much "pressure" is actually to be used—or is it "proper" to use); where shall the public image be located ("What is our pitch, here?"); and how is the discrepancy between the two to be accounted for and thus rendered harmless or even palatable?[33] For an organization like the Chest (or probably for any MOPS fundraising organization) these problems are peculiarly acute

since the need to *seem* ethical—for the sake of efficiency—referred to earlier
is conjoined with the need (for many) to *be* ethical—which stems from
the Chest's origins and from the meaning the whole operation has for many
laymen and professionals involved in it.

The tendency, in practice, is to locate the public representation close
to the "voluntary" pole, so that, with rare exceptions, the public image
fostered or the private image cherished is very largely one of free men
willingly banded together to achieve an object that most or all actively
desire. The main difficulties and conflicts, therefore, occur chiefly around
where to locate the actual level of coercion; and, to a less degree, how to
deal with the gap between appearance and reality. Both difficulties have to
do with pressuring the pressurers ("recruitment"), and the pressurers'
pressuring the givers ("soliciting").

There are really two problems in connection with "pressure" that are
often sharply felt but only dimly distinguished; these have to do, severally,
with the amount of pressure applied and with its nature or character.
Pressure may be much or little, high or low as to amount; it may also, in
its nature, be relevant to the issue at hand or largely irrelevant.[34] Relevant
pressure means pressure that really addresses itself to the issues at hand;
irrelevant pressure makes use of rewards or sanctions that have little or
nothing to do with any natural consequence of the choice, for example, a
threat to cease trading with a given individual unless a gift is forthcoming.
The accompanying schema may make the various kinds of pressure clear.
Among both laymen and professionals can be found those who are willing
or eager to use each of these types of pressure, some of them or all of
them, according to need or circumstance. A few laymen think that none
should be used, and many people "wish" none need be.

| Kind of pressure | Degree of pressure | | |
|---|---|---|---|
| | Relatively low | | Relatively high |
| Largely relevant | Type I | ⫷⟶ | Type III |
| | ⇑ ↓ | | ⇑ ↓ |
| Largely irrelevant | Type II | ⫷⟶ | Type IV |

Suggestions as to how best to secure results range through all these types
of pressure: from gently (by printed matter and mail) "telling people about
the need" (Type I) to trying to involve them in games and stunts and
mild competition which "people don't like to miss" (Type II) to earnest,
forceful, face-to-face and heart-to heart talk about the facts and the moral
issues involved (Type III) to the idea of publishing a "blacklist" of non-

donors or "inadequate" donors, which, hopefully, would "bring a man around" under pressure of threat to his business or livelihood.[35] The major conflict is, however, between those who would wish to see only Type I pressure employed ("just give people the opportunity to give") and those who favor fairly widespread use of Type IV ("There are always some . . .'s that are hard to get in").

The division of opinion as to what is legitimate and proper, here, is of course highly correlated with the division between those who think dominantly in financial terms and those who think dominantly in human terms. But the coincidence is not exact, for among those who do think predominantly in terms of human values, many are so deeply impressed with the need of the ultimate beneficiaries (whom they see largely as the poor or disadvantaged) that the end of serving them adequately justifies the use of almost any means; and among some who do think primarily in financial terms there is a realization that, except in the very short run, some bounds on pressure may actually yield more money.

For obvious reasons, there is also some correlation between those who divide on the issue of pressure and those who divide on short-run versus long-run perspective. But again the coincidence is not perfect since more considerations than these enter into a decision as to what kinds of pressure to apply.

Except under rare circumstances, it is probably difficult to find a campaign or an element of a campaign where only Type I pressure is actually used, though there are some situations where indifference to the Chest's "cause," or delicate relations with labor, or ethical principle[36] has maintained such an island or islands. But, in general, pressure both to man the machine and to secure "gifts" tends to be of Type II or III. As fortune fails to smile or, for whatever reason, failures cumulate, there is great temptation to resort to Type IV—especially perhaps, though not exclusively, against those who are neither so big as to be identified with the policy-making group ("one of us") nor so small as to be thought worthy of special protection ("the little giver"). The tendency to and direction of breakdown to higher and more irrelevant pressure are indicated by the arrows in the chart.

There is reason to believe, perhaps, that the cycle of failure could be reversed by a few successes, and that this might make for less pressure, so that those who believe in the present use of high and irrelevant pressures may be neither short-sighted nor unprincipled. Some of these people believe, in fact, that present high pressure will lead to "success," success will permit a lowering of pressure, and with lower pressure a spiral could occur, which would make for greater success, leading to still less pressure—and so on.

Nobody knows, of course, whether this could occur. Everybody, however, is working on some implicit model of "how it works" and on some implicit assumptions of "what is right." With different people, these models of reality and demands for ideality are different, and the policy recommendations that all of them put forth, often with considerable force, are correspondingly incompatible but vested with deep feeling. It is difficult to believe that clarification of what is at issue and subsequent discussion would not eventuate in fruitful, if temporary, compromise and some diminution in intrapersonal and interpersonal tensions.

### Charity and Service

One more continuous latent conflict (probably less important than the foregoing) lies between those who think the Chest is or ought to be primarily a "charity" organization and those who think of it primarily as a "community service" organization.

For some, mostly laymen, the whole meaning of the enterprise is that it represents or makes possible the discharge of the impulse or deep desire to help the less fortunate. On humane or religious grounds or both, it is deemed desirable or necessary to give aid, in suitable form and under suitable safeguards, to the disadvantaged; the Chest is intended as the major vehicle for the performance of this privilege or duty.

For others, this is almost the exact antithesis of what they would wish to think of the Chest as being, or what they would wish it to become, in so far as they can at all affect policy. The discharge of the obligation to "clothe the naked, feed the hungry, visit the sick, and comfort the fatherless" they would regard as being sufficiently met by government at various levels: "For that, we pay taxes." The object of a *Community* Chest should be, they feel, the provision of a better life for all, but most particularly the provision of "services," not for the unfortunate, but for those most worthy or promising, the solid, substantial "backbone of the community" or "promise of America's future."

Few see this as an all-or-none choice between sharply defined alternatives, but many would wish to reduce in fact or play down in publicity the one element or the other in what the Chest "supports." Indeed there are four related sets of preferences, presented in the accompanying diagram, upon which individuals will express preferences, sometimes very strong ones. Those who are attracted to one end of any one scale are usually

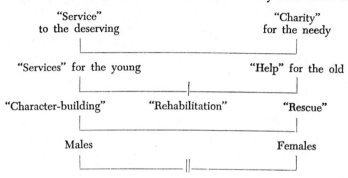

similarly attracted to the same end of the other scales: indeed one could work out combinations showing polar opposite preferences such as: a character-building agency giving service to young and not-needy boys *versus* a charity agency relieving the needs of old women.

For those who have strong preferences, the Chest is in the perhaps unfortunate position that it and a great many of "its" agencies do not represent in anything like pure form either one type of program or the other. Many agencies incorporated in the Chest's appeal have both a "charitable" function and a "service" one;[37] some agencies incline more heavily one way or the other (e.g., the . . . Mission as against, say, the Boy Scouts), but few, if any, represent pure cases, and the Chest cannot successfully represent itself as fulfilling either the one or the other function.[38]

The solution the Chest finds in practice to the problem of self-representation in this respect is a not very successful attempt to emphasize or mention exclusively now its one aspect, now the other, for different audiences or on different occasions, But at campaign time it is particularly difficult to limit the appropriately biased message to its intended audience; and, on occasion, it is hard to escape appearing to say to one and the same audience that the Chest benefits primarily or exclusively "people like you," and that it is really, primarily, or exclusively intended to care for the "less fortunate."

This problem of representation makes for enough difficulty, but the really tough problems are those of action: what agencies are to be admitted or kept out of the Chest? And, for those admitted, what is to be budget policy towards agencies differentially emphasizing opposite ends of these various dimensions of possibility?

Again in practice this problem tends to be dealt with by a polite sort of log-rolling, which poses this particular agency's budget request presented by these particular laymen or power-groups against that one, for this particular year. Compromises are thus effectively arrived at, but hardly enduring ones, and very often unsatisfactory ones with some residue of bitterness. Complaint is frequently made that laymen are "agency-minded" (i.e., they tend to fight against the whole for the interest of "their particular agency"). The observation is, no doubt, well founded, but the possibility that, underlying these choices of favored agencies, are perhaps deep-seated preferences for different segments of the population or types of work or social relations seems never to have been explored. Perhaps exploration of such differences might make for better, clearer, and more enduring, or, at least, better understood, resolutions or compromises.

## Human Relations and Beliefs

These unresolved, continuous, latent value-conflicts have direct consequences of the kind suggested in connection with each of them. But, taken as a whole, the situation of unresolved conflict is intimately bound up (both as cause and as consequence) with the prevailing interpersonal relations, with the state of belief as to what the key facts in the field are, and even with some peculiarities in the forms of "logic" employed (and accepted) as convincing argument. One might say that all these are reciprocally related in the following fashion, without implying any opinion as to which is the cause of which.[39]

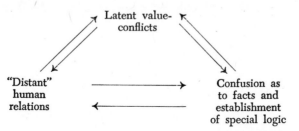

This is not the place to undertake a detailed documentation of these statements. They will be expanded upon later. It will perhaps suffice to say here that our observation indicates that the latent conflicts are both causes and symptoms of what seems a lack of intimacy between the protagonists of various views, especially perhaps, but by no means exclusively, between professionals and laymen.

The lack of "intimacy" *expresses* also markedly different opinions as to what the facts are. But it also *causes* great difficulty in discovering what is fact, since it is often characteristic in situations of low intimacy for each party to treat information as a pawn or counter in the implicit struggle or competition. Thus "a certain amount of selling" or "making the best of the figures" or "putting things in their best light" goes on on all sides, but in different directions. When this goes on long enough, all parties run the risk of being taken in by their own propaganda, and being therefore unable any longer to determine even relatively elementary facts, whether for "home consumption" or the enlightenment of relatively neutral and benign researchers. Lastly, under these circumstances, there tend to develop (and we have observed them in action and document) some peculiar, though evidently accepted, logical forms[40] that still further confuse views of the facts and tend to perpetuate the conflicts about purposes.

The questions that confront any organization like the Chest can, we believe, be put in purely social engineering terms, if it is preferred to avoid discussion in openly ethical ones. The first question is as to the nature or character of the human relations that must obtain if such an organization is (a) to be financially successful, (b) to endure, without, presumably, intolerable strains, and (c) to retain some acceptable level of "voluntariness," sufficient, for example, to distinguish it from fraud on one side or formal government on the other.

If this question can be settled, at least in terms of working approximations, the level or levels of intimacy required will become obvious, the requirements for the machinery of operation evident, and procedures for getting true and relevant facts, and for solving or resolving value-problems by discussion or compromise, manifest.

There are other and "technical" questions for any MOPS fundraising organization. But solving the technical problems in the absence of solutions for these major non-technical problems is not likely, we think, to lead towards what any party to such an enterprise would regard as full success.

# 6. "Success" by Financial Standards

THE LAST CHAPTER will have abundantly made clear that there is no unanimity between laymen and professionals, taken as groups,[1] as to how "success" is to be measured or appraised. It is even hard to decide whether financial success—no matter how that financial success is measured—is, for many, the overriding consideration, or indeed what its place in the evaluation of Chest (or other MOPS) fundraising is.[2]

Assuming, however, that financial success is of some considerable importance, and neglecting for the moment the price at which it may be "bought,"[3] we wish to examine in this chapter two questions: (1) Which of many possible criteria of financial "success" does it seem wisest to adopt? and (2) Having selected one criterion, how are sensible measures of it to be developed?

## CRITERIA FOR FINANCIAL SUCCESS

Just as, for a commercial organization, volume of sales, total net profit, rate of net profit, or share of the existent market might variously, and for various purposes, be thought of as appropriate measures of financial success, so a variety of measures might be thought, and have been thought, appropriate to MOPS fundraising organizations. Among the many put forward by various people[4] or employed in various situations, those tabulated in Table XI seem to be the principal[5] contenders.[6] These claimants merit separate discussion.

### Need (Type I)

The argument that the financial success of a Chest (or other MOPS fundraising organization) ought to be assessed in terms of the ratio of what is raised to what is "needed" is indeed intriguing.[7] How much is done out of what must be done to complete a task, represents a measure close to everyday, commonsense habit: the correct completion of fifteen arithmetic problems out of twenty required by the teacher[8] might be rated 75 per cent efficient, and might allow us to compare one child with another. The idea is attractive. But—alas for attractiveness!—the whole notion turns out to be "void for vagueness," and has to be rejected on this, if no other ground.

TABLE XI

MEASURES SUGGESTED FOR EVALUATING MOPS FINANCIAL PERFORMANCE

| Type | Basis of measure | Description of suggested measure |
|------|------------------|----------------------------------|
| I | "Need" | Proportion of total, local, relevant "need" met |
| II | Gross performance | Total amount of money raised |
| III | Intent | A. Achievement or non-achievement of "goal"<br>B. Proportion of "goal" achieved |
| IV | "Progress" | Consistent, substantial, annual increases in "take" |
| V | Share | A. Share of national income<br>B. Share of income of all Chests |
| VI | "Equity" | An internal measure of the amount of "disequality" as between gifts |
| VII | Opportunity or market | A. Amount raised per capita<br>B. Amount raised per household<br>C. Amount raised per household in proportion to average family income<br>D. Amount raised in relation to "effective buying power"<br>E. Deviation of percapita from "expected" value |

Perhaps no word in the whole lexicon of social work ( or psychology) has quite the attractive force and fatal emptiness of meaning as has the word "need." The word has a dual appeal: if anyone knew what the "needs" were, it would be relatively easy to state what resources were required to "meet the need"; if the "needs"—particularly the "unmet needs"—of the population (or a segment of the population) could be stated, probably few could be found hard-hearted enough that they would not wish to see these "needs" "met." If there were not such desperate persistence in the usage, including elaborate attempts to construct lists of "needs," or to demonstrate that the program a certain agency happens to have is what the community or a part of it happens to "need," it would hardly be necessary to demonstrate its emptiness here. But the word is widely used, and it goes some considerable way to confuse discourse and to confound action.

A "need"—if the term must be used at all—is something in the absence of which something the speaker doesn't like will occur, or something he does like, won't. Generally, if a man is to eat (and stay off relief in kind) he "needs" an income; and, if he has an income of sufficient size and if he is to stay out of prison he "needs" to pay taxes. But this tells no one else anything about community "needs," unless these others wish him to eat and stay out of prison—*and* regard this as a community responsibility. The word "needs" simply confuses the statement that "if you want *this* (e.g., to lower the delinquency rate) *that* (e.g., recreation) must be provided."[9] The threefold advantage of talking, nevertheless, about "needs" is: ($a$) that it does provide a sort of shorthand, or seeming economy of expression, ($b$) that it puts beyond examination the usually dubious[10] propositions in social engineering that are implied, and ($c$) that it permits an easy transition, almost unnoticeable, from "If you want $X$, $Y$ is required" to "If you want $X$, *you* must provide $Y$."

The use of "need" also permits the blurring of a distinction that has been of considerable importance in the history of the Western World, that is still of considerable importance to many Americans, and that may be of quite decisive importance in the formation of social policy: this is the distinction between rendering aid (especially in cases of acute and obvious distress and especially on such aid being requested) and striving to make people better or happier.[11] The word "need" is associated with such words as "the needy" and "necessitous" which have historic association with the most deprived and disadvantaged elements in any community at a given time and place. When the word is extended in meaning so that the children whose parents are in the top half of the community's income pyramid "need" a camp, the community "needs" a symphony orchestra, and the town's leadership "needs" to be made to understand about poliomyelitis or coronary occlusions, quite obviously there is some hoped-for carryover of meaning from one usage to the other, and some serious attendant confusion.

It should be obvious that, once the distinction between the relief of distress and the creation of happiness has been sufficiently obscured, the theoretical measure of "need" is literally infinity,[12] and the practical limit is the community's entire income.[13]

In order to avoid being thrown on this horn of the dilemma, the users of the "need" vocabulary frequently seek refuge in a shift from the "needs" of the ultimate beneficiaries to the "needs of the agencies."[14] But every objection so far urged against the use of "need" as a concept—or slogan— must be redoubled in the case of the "needs of the agencies." The "needs of the agencies" (from the MOPS fundraising point of view) are the sum of their wants (given their idea of the "needs" of "their" clientele) less their fee or other income,[15] less such prunings or reductions as their lay governments deem prudent or right in principle.[16] The concept is as vague as to meaning (although it is easier to attach a money figure to it) as the concept of "community need" or the "needs" of the population or some segment of it.

It would seem best, then, for the reasons given, to abandon the attempt to measure Chest success in relation to "need."[17]

## Gross Performance (Type II)

It is perhaps uncommon to find Chests being compared or evaluated on the basis merely of their total money income, since nearly everyone seems to realize intuitively that a meaningful measure of performance must be related to a meaningful measure of *possible* performance.

The tendency is thus to restrict comparisons, when they are to be made in terms of total take, to Chests that are presumed to be "alike," i.e., properly comparable. The problem of finding what is a comparable Chest (or other MOPS fundraising organization) will be dealt with later in this chapter, but the usual first approximation in practice is to take for comparison those cities that raised "similar" amounts of money.[18] The ranking of a given city compared with all cities raising like amounts, is commonly used as an evaluative or propaganda tool.

This measure has certain obvious disadvantages in its crudity[19] and the arbitrariness in the setting of classification boundaries.[20] There are other disadvantages. It is difficult to understand, for instance, how—unless mere self-improvement is the criterion—one can logically measure this year's adequacy by making the basis of the comparison simply last year's performance.[21] Again, we have assumed that the object of measurement is to permit proper authority, lay and professional, to evaluate actual performance in relation to possible performance or probable performance, i.e., to measure something closely related to efficiency or effectiveness of effort. If this *is* what is intended, the measure under discussion is largely irrelevant.[22]

These defects, taken severally or together, incline us to reject the measure as having little utility for the purposes of this study.

### Intent: Achievement or Non-Achievement of Goal (Type III A)

This is perhaps the most commonly used measure of Chest "success" or "failure": indeed, if no other definition is explicitly given, a Chest that has "failed" or "is failing" generally means a Chest that has not made or is not making its goal. The measure recommends itself as being obvious,[23] unambiguous (every Chest that announces its goal before campaign can be classified), and already in the Chest folklore—and indeed in common speech. These are strong recommendation to its use, if possible.

If one could assume that the "goals" themselves were set upon some basis that made sense (i.e., in relation to "opportunity"), and if one could further assume that there was little or no tendency to make a Chest successful by selecting a particularly easy goal, there might, at least at first blush, seem to be little objection to the use of this measure.

So attractive, in its simplicity, did this possibility seem, initially, that we carried out some eleven studies that bore in whole or in part on the correlates of "success" and "failure."[24] We were driven, nevertheless, to abandon the measure owing to the following considerations:

(1) It has an all-or-nothing character, which makes perhaps for simplicity, but contravenes the widespread desire for a measure that will reflect successive steps in a *movement* towards success, or successive increments of effective effort.

(2) While we had demonstrated that in general the goals set in the Chests across the country bore a close relation to selected measures of community potentiality[25] and that it was not, in general, true that successful Chests had unexpectedly low goals—these two *general* facts were of little aid in the evaluation of any one Chest. The nagging question would still remain if a given Chest was "successful" whether this occurred because it had set a low goal or, if it was "failing," whether this occurred because it had set its goal "too high." And if, in each particular case, we must assess potentiality in some way in order to estimate the reasonableness of goal so as to evaluate success or failure, why not eliminate the intermediate step and assess performance directly against potentiality?

(3) The "success" or "failure" rate does not correlate well with many of the city characteristics known to affect giving—perhaps because of the elements of judgment involved in setting the goal in the first place.

(4) In the analysis of a compound "Welfare Index," one of whose elements was a "success-factor," we had already discovered that the index without the success-factor correlated at least as well with certain city characteristics as it did when the success-factor was in.[26] The inference from the study was that since such an estimate of success added little to the sensitivity to city characteristics of the "Welfare Index," it might as well or had better be dropped.

On these grounds, but especially in the face of objections (1), (2), and (3) we abandoned Type III A.[27] For interest's sake only, then, is Chart 11, showing take and goal for Indianapolis, published.

### Intent: Proportion of Goal Achieved (Type III B)

This measure also has much to recommend it, although its use is not as widespread as that of the all-or-nothing "success" or "failure." It has the advantage over the black-or-white, success-failure scheme, that it *does* provide for reflection of every step towards (or away from) "success."

But it has all the other disadvantages of the all-or-nothing measure; and objection (4) which had less relevance to the earlier (Type III A) proposal is more cogent here, i.e., the measure seems to permit little that can be "explained" in terms of opportunity, presumably because one of its elements, the denominator or goal, already reflects somebody's estimate of local opportunity.[28] Moreover (as reported in the appendix to the chapter) this is a most unstable measure.

### Progress (Type IV)

Consistent, substantial periodic increases from year to year or otherwise over a time period have been represented to us as constituting perhaps a better independent measure of Chest financial "success"—or, at least, as a measure that ought to be used to supplement other measures.[29] One authority in the field puts the case thus:

The degree to which a community consistently shows substantial increases over a period of time in the amounts raised in the federated campaign might be a third important factor in this kind of analysis. It would seem that we could almost assume for practical purposes that increased amounts available for voluntary services should be regarded as an indication of a sound and healthy situation. The rising costs of operating services during recent years would almost be sufficient justification for this assumption. In addition, there is the fact that public understanding of the value of services, and demand for facilities and services, is greatly increasing; also improved technical knowledge of how to deal with certain problems tends to create more demand. At the present writing there certainly is no norm as to absolute need, and it would be difficult to set a "ceiling" on the amounts which profitably could be spent for such activities, for example, as health research. All of these considerations seem to validate the use of the relative increase in campaign returns as a factor in analysis of campaign success.[30]

The argument—and it has rarely been put to us better—left us in some doubt, partly because we could not bring ourselves to accept as a premise that "demand" for the services financed was rising; or—even granted that it was rising—that a rise in demand necessarily implied a rise in that portion of the resultant costs that a Community Chest ought to incorporate in its collections from the donor-aggregate.[31] We simply did not feel that we had—or indeed that anyone had—sufficient knowledge about the relationship between rising demand[32] and an appropriate consequent expectation from the Chest, to warrant our adopting the social philosophy underlying the proposed measure.

There is a further weakness in the proposed measure, which is similar to the weakness objected to in connection with the Type II measure, i.e., that it really constitutes "handicapping" and may, at best, measure gain relative to previous performance, good or poor. Such gains are interesting, no doubt, but difficult to evaluate without a measure for the "previous performance"—which puts the question back where we started from.

For the reasons given, we abandoned this measure also. For those interested, however, a graphic view of local Chest performance (from 1920 to 1955) in current dollars and (from 1925 to 1954) in "standard" (1947-9) dollars appears in Chart 12. Whether either line (and the standard-dollar line should, we agree, be regarded as more relevant) shows "consistent, substantial" periodic progress must be left to the reader, as must also the question of whether it "ought to" do so. If payments to agencies, however, are taken as the measure of consistent, substantial progress, between 1924 and 1954 the Indianapolis Chest averaged gains of less than 1 per cent per annum (in standard dollars), as Chart 13 shows.

*Share of National Income* (Type V A);
*Share of Income of All Chests* (Type V B)

It is not often put forward explicitly, but it is implicit in much discussion that one might well expect a given local Chest to get a fixed share of the national income from year to year, or a corresponding share of the income of all Chests combined. ·

Since most contributions are in fact made out of current income (rather than savings or reserves or other accumulated capital) the fixed share of the national income might seem a reasonable expectation. Certainly, if an equal-share-of-the-pie is a minimum demand (as it is in some other bargaining), then the take of all Chests combined might be expected to bear a fairly constant relation to the national income. As Chart 14 shows, this is indeed the case, and the result is similar to the return to be expected if the combined Chests were able to impose a one-mill income tax, i.e., to tax income at the rate of 0.1 per cent.

If, however, an attempt is made to apply the argument to a particular local Chest, to make it equally cogent one would have to know the *local* total income—and this unfortunately is unavailable. Similarly, to make the comparison with the total income of all Chests appropriate, one would have to assume that Indianapolis (in this case) should still represent the same fraction of the income of all Chest cities as it has done in other years. In view of the known considerable redistributions of dominance between United States cities from year to year, we feel we cannot safely make such an assumption,[33] and while we publish Charts 15 and 16 as "interesting," we feel they should be interpreted with care. We could only say from them that *unless* Indianapolis has diminished in importance in the scale of national income and in its relative wealth as compared with all Chest cities it is true that the local Chest's early years were on the whole better than its later ones.

Given these difficulties, we made no further use of this measure either.

## *Equity* (Type VI)

Many people do regard "equity" or fairness in what we have come to call "distribution of the gift-load" as a partial measure of the "goodness" of a Chest. Some regard the determination of it as a moral issue; and, of those who do not, most regard it as a means to financial success rather than directly as a measure of it. Since—morals apart—we believe we can show that such measures of equity are correlated with appropriate measures of the take, we shall reserve this matter for discussion below, after we have considered measures of opportunity, and we shall have to examine the matter in still more detail in chapter 8.

## *"Opportunity" or "Market" Measures: Amount raised per capita* (Type VII A)

Despite the foregoing lengthy discussion devoted to other measures, the one which is most commonly employed and most commonly talked about is the "Amount raised per capita," i.e., ideally, the amount raised divided by the population of the solicitation area.[34] To provide a short form for convenience in discussion, we shall simply call this index "the percapita."

The percapita certainly constitutes a measure in relation to opportunity, since at least it refers to a figure, the total population, which is in its turn related to the number of potential donors. It is still by no means satisfactory, for our purposes, even as a first measure. What is needed is, surely, the number of potential donors. Presumably infants, who are included in the population figures, are not "potential donors" (except, perhaps, by proxy); and, presumably also, the corporations, which are not included in the population count, *are* "potential donors." The corporations can be "argued away," if it is assumed that (within tolerable limits of accuracy) they "give for" their wage-earners, who in turn "represent" their families, and thus practically everybody is represented in the total corporate gift. This does not, however, dispose of the difficulty about counting children. Perhaps a better measure, then, than percapita—for evaluating both corporate and non-corporate total gifts—would be gift divided by the number of persons in the labor force (instead of the total population.) It might well be worth while in a later study to test whether this measure is not a better measure in terms, at least, of sensitivity to local conditions and characteristics.

Unless, however, it can safely be assumed (*a*) that the only important factor affecting the total gift is the population of potential donors, and also (*b*) that the total gift "should" or does grow proportionally (i.e., that percapitas for all cities should be equal), the assessment of Chests by comparing their percapitas does not take us far enough. Indeed, if the percapita is taken as a first measure of Chest success, the problem might still be stated in following form: "Under what conditions may a percapita of a given size be expected?"[35] This is the problem that will need attention in the second half of this chapter.

### Amount Raised per Household (Type VII B)

In an attempt to cope with the difficulty of a per capita measure, some students[36] have used a measure of "giving per household," i.e., the total gift divided by the total number of households counted by the census for the solicitation area. Such a measure goes some way towards meeting the objection raised to the percapita, but in a day when an increasing number of "households" incorporate two or more wage-earners it seemed to us to "drop" too much; that is, in effect, it properly "drops" children out of the count of "potential donors," but improperly drops all wage-earners but one from the many households where there is more than one. This constitutes so small a gain that it appeared idle merely for the sake of it to oppose settled practice in speaking of percapitas.

### Household Gift related to Family Income (Type VII C)

This suggested measure seems not only open to the stricture made in the last paragraph, but also (as explained in note 13) to mean nothing more, in effect, than an expression of the Chest's take as a fraction of the community's income. Since, however, mean incomes (which would be required to make the index meaningful) are not published by the Census Bureau, but only median incomes (which, if used, would make the index hard to interpret)[37] we decided, valuable as such an index might be, to try the use of other measures first.

### Amount Raised in relation to Effective Buying Power (Type VII D)

A most attractive index of performance in relation to opportunity is that secured when the take is divided by the income of the potential donors, or, better still, by their "disposable personal income," i.e., that portion of their income which is, legally or otherwise, a "free" fund from which gifts could presumably be made. There are difficulties, however (as noted in note 37), in getting estimates of such disposable personal income. One available statistic is the index of "Effective Buying Income," published for selected cities by *Sales Management*.[38] We dropped our interest in this potential measure, however, when we discovered that the preparation of the index was a "trade secret,"[39] and that we had, therefore, no way of checking its relation to the figure we were seeking, and no way of assessing our own confidence in a measure developed from it.

### Actual Percapita in relation to Expected Percapita (Type VII E)

If, despite the weaknesses of a per capita measure (referred to above), we could develop a way of estimating what kinds of percapita (how much money per head of population) could reasonably be raised under what constellations of opportunity, we felt we would have something close to the measure we were looking for. If, in particular, for a given city we could say "Its percapita is so many dollars and cents, but a reasonable expectation for a city like this is this many dollars and cents per capita" then the difference between the two figures might well be a satisfactory measure of the "success," or satisfactoriness in financial performance, of the Chest, or other MOPS fundraising organization, concerned. From the fundraiser's viewpoint,[40] if the actual percapita is greater than the "reasonably expectable" percapita, the Chest is doing well; if the converse is true, the Chest is, from the same viewpoint, doing ill.

This vital "difference" is what we shall refer to henceforward as the "deviation"; we shall always mean by it the *actual less the "expected"* value —so that if the actual value is greater the deviation will be positive (e.g., actual percapita $5, "expected" percapita $4; deviation: $1), and if the "expected" percapita is higher, the deviation will be negative (e.g., actual percapita $5, expected percapita $6.50; deviation: —$1.50).

We said in the next-to-last paragraph that, if we could compare actual percapitas with those to be expected, we would be in a better position to assess the Chest's results or performance. Such expected values must be developed on the basis of theory or by trial-and-error. The point has already been sufficiently made, perhaps, that no such body of theory[41] exists in reference to philanthropy—indeed that it is difficult to get at even the most primitive facts or to have confidence that alleged facts are indeed facts.

There being no such body of theory, the researchers were thrown back upon an essentially trial-and-error examination of those characteristics which might be thought to affect Chest (or other MOPS fundraising) performance. We were not wholly without guidance in our choice of variables to examine, since, despite or because of the lack of theory, there exists a mass of folklore and untested but firmly held opinion, both among professionals and laymen; and to this mass we had access. We also had access to our own conjectures derived from more general sociological theories or, in a few cases, from some limited work already done by a few sociologists.[42] This folklore, these conjectures, and this work gave us a list of some thirty-odd variables[43] that might be worth testing for the degree to which they seemed to have an impact on MOPS fundraising percapitas. The list of leading characteristics that we assembled, ranging from such obvious ones as population to such relatively remote or esoteric possibilities as mean (or highest) annual temperature, has been summarized in Table XII.

The object of the tests was not merely to see whether any or all of these are correlated with giving in some statistically significant way,[44] but to find an *economical* list of characteristics from which it would be easy to predict the most probable percapita of a city having those characteristics. The economical consideration is a practical one, not a theoretical one. It might be theoretically interesting to predict the percapita very closely from a list of a hundred or half-hundred city characteristics. But to be useful to fundraisers and laymen, any formula should, likely, be limited to no more than half a dozen variables—especially if, as is usually the case, after the first few variables have been used, the remainder add very little to the "explained variance."[45]

We wanted, then, to find (1) *a small number of* (2) *readily accessible,* (3) largely *independent*[46] *social characteristics that would* (4) *explain* a relatively *large proportion of the variation* in Chest (or other MOPS) fundraising percapitas. Having done this, we should want to test to make sure that no other obvious variable will explain much of the variation not already explained.

Space and time will not permit the incorporation in this chapter of a full account of the various ways in which all these variables were tested. The interested reader will find a full account in the relevant C.S.I. studies.[47] We are forced to limit ourselves here to the main line of positive findings that leads from our first inquiries to our final conclusions, and to neglect the variety of interesting side-roads necessarily (and usefully) explored. To this "main-line" account a few remarks will be added, at the end of the chapter, on several intriguing if subordinate points.

## TABLE XII

CITY CHARACTERISTICS INITIALLY TESTED FOR RELATIONS TO CHEST PERCAPITAS

I. Indicators of potential in general
   A. City size or population
   B. Population growth
   C. Population mobility
      1. In-migration
      2. Out-migration

II. Indicators of economic potential
   A. Income
      1. Level
      2. Distribution
   B. Productivity
   C. Savings
   D. Wealth
   E. Local corporate organization
      1. Firm size (typical)
      2. Locus of control of firm
      3. Firm distribution by size

III. Indicators of group or community "responsibility"
   A. Community giving levels
      1. Religious (Church giving)
      2. Secular
         (a) Red Cross
         (b) T.B.
   B. Community service levels
      1. Religious
         (a) Number of clergymen per capita
         (b) Number of religious workers per capita
      2. Secular
         (a) Number of social workers per capita
         (b) School expenditures per child

IV. Indicators of social control, or "goodness of life" or level of
civilization or community "integration"
   A. Population composition
      1. Percentage non-white
      2. Percentage foreign-born white
   B. Crime level
   C. Housing
      1. Type
      2. Occupancy
      3. Value

V. Indicators of Chest policy
   A. Type of organization
   B. Participation or "coverage"
   C. Campaign expenses
   D. Equity—or equality—in gift-load distribution

VI. Miscellaneous indicators
   A. Region
   B. Latitude
   C. Temperature

## The Selected Variables

### The Region

The first point to be established refers to the variable listed in Table XII as VI A, "Region." We have no way of knowing whether the various regions into which the United States may be divided differ in their giving-patterns *because* the regions differ in climate, style of life, preponderant social outlook and value-system, ways of organizing, level of "needs" (in the jargon of social workers), expense of meeting those needs, or other characteristics. But we had learned with reasonable certainty early in our inquiries[48] that "the South"[49] differed in important and, for the study of philanthropy, significant ways from the rest of the country, and that, therefore, giving in Southern cities should probably not be compared with giving elsewhere.[50]

Sensitized by these early studies (which, however, were not directly addressed to the same problem) we raised the question of regional differences in other early studies,[51] and concluded that for any detailed analysis it was generally important to distinguish at least four major regions, and to avoid for most purposes comparison across regional boundaries.

Having concluded that it was necessary to divide the United States into regions for purposes of analysis, and having also concluded that too many such divisions would leave too few comparable cities for reliable analysis in each, we decided to pursue further analysis only in terms of the four regions defined by the Census: West, North Central, Northeast, and South.[52] Since Indianapolis is in the North Central Region, most of our subsequent analysis was limited to this area (Illinois, Indiana, Iowa, Kansas, Michigan, Minnesota, Missouri, Nebraska, North Dakota, Ohio, South Dakota, Wisconsin).

### The Population

Concurrently with our analysis of regionality and other factors, we had been exploring the effect of population on percapita. As stated earlier, a widespread belief existed that, in general, "the bigger the city, the bigger the percapita." This belief—though vaguely put—turned out both to be capable of precise statement and to be well founded.

Neglecting for the moment all other complicating factors, we were able to demonstrate that the per capita gift to a Chest, for the United States as a whole, was likely to be a relatively "simple function" of the size of the city in which the Chest had its headquarters. Moreover, it could be safely said that the larger the city, the larger the percapita (by a known amount) —and hence that as population increases, the gift to the average Chest increases much more rapidly.

In order to keep the text of this chapter free of technicalities for the general reader, we shall not state the precise relationship here,[53] but the relations between (1) population, (2) percapita, and (3) total gift, in simplified but substantially accurate form, are shown in Table XIII, and the relationships between the first two are shown on Chart 17. It can be stated here that, to a very close approximation, the percapita to be expected in any city is a simple function (of the logarithm) of its population.

TABLE XIII

POPULATION, EXPECTED PERCAPITA FOR CHEST, AND EXPECTED TOTAL GIFT, 1951

| Population | Approximate percapita | Approximate gift |
|---|---|---|
| 1,000 | $1.36 | $ 1,364 |
| 2,000 | 1.61 | 3,229 |
| 5,000 | 1.95 | 9,728 |
| 10,000 | 2.20 | 21,961 |
| 20,000 | 2.45 | 48,932 |
| 50,000 | 2.78 | 138,890 |
| 100,000 | 3.03 | 302,830 |
| 200,000 | 3.28 | 655,760 |
| 500,000 | 3.61 | 1,805,000 |
| 1,000,000 | 3.86 | 3,860,500 |
| 2,000,000 | 4.11 | 8,222,000 |

The importance of this general finding can hardly be overemphasized. Whether the percapitas actually achieved in United States cities are taken to represent some summary of "needs" (or, at least, of unresisted local agency demands) or whether they are taken to represent the local resources available to the fundraiser ("potential" is the fundraisers' term), the following statements are true:

1. *The more people* in one place *the greater the "need" per person* for social services—or, the more generous the amount made available.

2. The *"need"* (or resource) *per person increases logarithmically as the numbers increase arithmetically,* in something like the following scale:

$$10 \text{ persons} - \$1.00 \text{ each}$$
$$100 \text{ persons} - 2.00 \text{ each}$$
$$1,000 \text{ persons} - 3.00 \text{ each}$$
$$10,000 \text{ persons} - 4.00 \text{ each}$$

3. The *total need* (or resource) therefore *increases more rapidly than the size of the population.* Thus, to illustrate from Table XIII, with a given ratio of increase in population, we would expect a larger increase in gift, something very like that shown in Table XIV.

4. To *secure,* therefore, *a given percentage increase in percapita one would* expect (all other things being equal) *a very much larger population increase* (or corresponding increase in "effort"). Thus, again, from Table XIII, places of the sizes shown in Table XV might expect to grow by the percentages shown before they could "normally" expect, say, a 25 per cent increase in percapita.

TABLE XIV

POPULATION INCREASE AND RELATED INCREASE IN EXPECTED GIFT

| A<br>Postulated increase<br>in population<br>(in thousands) | | B<br>Expected increase<br>in total gift | | C<br>Postulated<br>percentage<br>increase in<br>population | D<br>Expected<br>percentage<br>increase<br>in gift |
|---|---|---|---|---|---|
| From | To | From | To | | |
| 50 | 100 | $ 138,890 | $ 302,830 | 100% | 118% |
| 100 | 200 | 302,830 | 655,760 | 100% | 117% |
| 500 | 1,000 | 1,805,000 | 3,860,500 | 100% | 114% |
| 1,000 | 2,000 | 3,860,500 | 8,222,000 | 100% | 113% |

TABLE XV

POSTULATED PERCAPITA INCREASE AND REQUISITE POPULATION INCREASE

| A<br>Postulated<br>place<br>size<br>now | B<br>Present<br>percapita<br>expected<br>(approximate) | C<br>Present<br>percapita<br>plus<br>25% | D<br>Approximate<br>population<br>normally<br>required<br>for C | E<br>Percentage<br>population<br>increase normally<br>needed for 25%<br>percapita increase |
|---|---|---|---|---|
| 10,000 | $2.20 | $2.75 | 45,680 | 357% |
| 100,000 | 3.03 | 3.79 | 813,500 | 714% |
| 500,000 | 3.61 | 4.51 | 6,075,000 | 1,115% |

The meaning of this important point should, perhaps, be further clarified. For each line of Table XV, the figure in column B represents the percapita to be expected "on the average" (without unusual effort, let us say). Because of special "need," or because of ambition or for other reasons, it is desired to get on the average 25 per cent more per capita, i.e., the percapita shown (approximately) in column C. The figure aspired to (column C) then represents what one would expect "without unusual effort" in a city of the size shown in column D. The figures in column E are probably suggestive of the relative amounts of extra effort that would need to be put forth to secure the per capita increase aspired to at each level; *the larger the city and the larger the existing percapita,* probably *the greater the difficulty in raising it by a further given percentage* (25 per cent in the illustration).

## Population and Region

Having already established the importance of regionality and the basic form of the relationship between population and percapita, it is time to bring them together and to establish the proper relationship for each geographic region separately.[54] For the region in which we are most interested, the North Central region, a picture of the "average" relationship (for 1953) may be deduced from Chart 18 or from the equation given in the note.[55] The *total* expected gift may be easily computed.

On a regional basis, this one factor alone—population or place size—accounts for 37.5 per cent of all the variation in giving that there is to account for.[56] We wished, however, to improve upon this predictive power if possible.

In order to do so, we first sought to improve upon the population estimates which were initially used as the base for the equation.[57] After considerable labor we established that, in most cases, it was true that (a) the "Standard Metropolitan Area" (SMA)[58] was nearer to the Chest's actual solicitation area, whereas many Chests consider the Central City population a proper one to report, and (b) the use of the appropriate population figure—usually that of the SMA—made prediction of percapita considerably better.[59]

We also experimented with other forms of relationship between population and gift, but returned after these tests to the first-discovered formulation of the relation between percapita and "log of population."[60]

Lastly, because of our particular interest and because we had reason to think that very small and very large cities might differ in other ways from middle-range cities, we dropped from further consideration Chests in SMA's with populations much greater than one million or smaller than one hundred thousand. From here on, then, we concentrated on Chests in the North Central region, whose SMA populations lay between one hundred thousand and one million. There are forty-one such cities in the North Central region.

| ILLINOIS | Peoria | MINNESOTA | Duluth |
|---|---|---|---|
| | Rockford | | Minneapolis |
| | Springfield | | St. Paul |
| INDIANA | Evansville | MISSOURI | Kansas City |
| | Fort Wayne | | St. Louis[61] |
| | Indianapolis | | Springfield |
| | South Bend | NEBRASKA | Lincoln |
| | Terre Haute | | Omaha |
| IOWA | Cedar Rapids[61] | OHIO | Akron |
| | Des Moines | | Canton |
| | Sioux City | | Cincinnati |
| | Waterloo[61] | | Cleveland[61] |
| KANSAS | Kansas City | | Columbus |
| | Topeka | | Dayton |
| | Wichita | | Springfield |
| MICHIGAN | Flint | | Toledo |
| | Grand Rapids | | Youngstown |
| | Jackson | WISCONSIN | Madison |
| | Kalamazoo | | Milwaukee |
| | Lansing | | Racine |
| | Saginaw | | |

We now wished to refine our "prediction equation" by adding a limited number of variables, and for this purpose we tested a number of those listed in Table XII, especially:

(1) Possible indicators of community integration
    (a) Percentage non-white, 1950
    (b) Percentage foreign-born white, 1950
    (c) "Migration" per 100 population
    (d) Percentage growth, 1940-1950
    (e) Percentage growth, 1920-1940

(2) Possible indicators of sense of responsibility to community
    (a) Percentage of dwelling units in one-dwelling-unit detached structures, 1950
    (b) Percentage of dwelling units occupied by owners, 1950
    (c) School expenditures per pupil (1949-1950; city data)

(3) Possible indicators of community ability to give
    (a) Percentage of 1950 families with $5,000 or more income during 1949
    (b) Percentage of 1950 families and unrelated individuals with $10,000 or more income during 1949
    (c) Per capita wholesale and retail trade (dollar amount of trade, 1948; population, 1950)
    (d) E-Bond sales per capita, 1950
    (e) Median family income (1950 families, 1949 income)
    (f) Median value of one-dwelling-unit structures, owner-occupied, 1950
    (g) Per capita value added by manufacture (dollar amount of value, 1947; population, 1950)

(4) Possible indicator of ease of organizing a fundraising campaign
    (a) Percentage of manufacturing establishments with 250 or more employees, first quarter 1950 (data from OASI program)

By a process of testing,[62] we finally arrived at a set of four variables which, between them, accounted for—or explained—74 per cent of all the variation in percapitas.[63] The four variables chosen to account so economically for so much of the variance were: *Population Size,*[64] *Productivity,*[65] *Population Composition* (actually "Percentage non-white")[66] and *Savings.*[67] The relative importance—for "prediction" of performance—of the variables is in the order shown.[68] The first variable—Population Size[69]—is overwhelmingly the most important. By itself, it accounts for 55 per cent of the variation—so that the other three variables between them only account for a further 20 per cent.

The effect[70] of increasing population, productivity, and savings is to *increase* Chest percapitas; the effect of an increasing percentage of non-whites in the population is to *decrease* Chest percapitas.

Table XVI shows the forty-one cities, their "scores" on the four variables, their actual Chest percapitas in the 1950 campaign (column 1), the percapitas one would expect, given these four city characteristics (column 6), and the differences (or deviations) between these actual and "expected" values.[71]

The Indianapolis reader may be principally interested in the conclusion that in 1950, Indianapolis was getting about 53 cents less per capita (about $300,000 less in total) than might reasonably ("on the average") be expected from a city with its potentialities, in terms of the four characteristics considered. The increase, then, required to meet expectation would have been of the order of 20 per cent, i.e., the total expected "should be" something more like $1.7 millions than the $1.4 odd millions actually raised.

The estimate may be brought up to date in a way that is probably sufficiently accurate for any purpose for which it is likely to be used (e.g., as one consideration in goal-setting, or as one major element in self-evaluation). It would, of course, be preferable if new estimates, up to date for the four variables employed, could be had from year to year. These are, however, not available. Failing this, one way to estimate the total gift to be "expected" in the campaign *for* 1955 (i.e., the campaign carried on in late 1954) is to multiply the total gift already estimated for 1950 by the ratio:

$$\frac{1955 \text{ national Chest take}}{1950 \text{ national Chest take}}$$

This ratio turns out to be 1.418, that is, a 42 per cent increase in the four-year period. On this basis, the "expected" total gift for Indianapolis for the 1954 campaign should be in the neighborhood of: 1.418 × $1.6935 millions = $2,402,000. This may be compared with the $1,560,000 actually raised.

Further prediction might be based on the average annual rate of growth (in dollars) of the whole Chest movement from 1925 to 1955—5.65 per cent per annum[72]; or, more reasonably, with an eye to recent history, on the Chests' average rate of growth in the last fifteen years—i.e., 8.71 per cent per annum. These two "guesstimates" suggest an "expected" gift to the Indianapolis Chest for 1956 (i.e., in the 1955 campaign) of either $2,538,000 or $2,611,000. The actual take was in the neighborhood of $2.03 million. A look ahead would suggest then an "expectable"[73] total of $2,681,000 or $2,838,000, for the campaign to be held in 1956.[73a]

This year-to-year and "practical" use of the new knowledge, important as it is, may, however, be less important than the recognition of the general facts established and the further exploration that knowledge of these Chest "deviations" makes possible.

The important and central fact to be recognized lies in the general statement that, without reference to the nature of the organization (e.g., how many agencies included, how many supposedly "competitive" drives), without any evaluation of Board performance or the various characters, philosophies, skills, or views of the various general managers, without regard to the publicity media employed or how they are utilized, without reference to gimmicks, public relations, program, or campaign expenditure —on the basis of four city characteristics alone, as much as three-quarters of all the variation in "giving" behavior (as between cities; not, as between individuals, of course) can be accounted for. Evidence suggests, moreover, that some part of the remaining (26 per cent) variation could also be accounted for merely by knowing the city rather than knowing the Chest

## TABLE XVI

### Variables, Chest Percapitas Computed from Regression Equation, and Deviations

| State | City | $Y_1$ Chest percapita, campaign for 1951 | $Y_2$ Logarithm of population in thousands | $Y_3$ E-Bond sales per capita 1950 | $Y_4$ Index of per capita business volume[a] | $Y_6$[b] Percentage Non-white 1950 | Chest percapita computed from regression equation | Deviation, i.e., actual minus computed percapita |
|---|---|---|---|---|---|---|---|---|
| | | (1) | (2) | (3) | (4) | (5) | (6) | (7) |
| ILL. | Peoria | $2.158 | 2.3988 | $27.61 | 18.60 | 2.597 | $2.831 | —$ .673* |
| | Rockford | 2.438 | 2.1830 | 31.04 | 18.06 | 2.607 | 2.534 | — .096 |
| | Springfield | 2.226 | 2.1189 | 30.68 | 11.40 | 3.445 | 2.095 | .131 |
| IND. | Evansville | 2.819 | 2.2052 | 23.19 | 15.35 | 5.736 | 2.181 | .638* |
| | Fort Wayne | 2.556 | 2.2641 | 33.19 | 18.24 | 2.922 | 2.689 | — .133 |
| | Indianapolis | 2.542 | 2.7418 | 30.32 | 19.85 | 11.830 | 3.069 | — .527* |
| | South Bend | 2.326 | 2.2333 | 43.88 | 16.88 | 4.307 | 2.703 | — .377 |
| | Terre Haute | 1.879 | 2.0220 | 26.41 | 11.38 | 4.224 | 1.840 | .039 |
| IOWA | Cedar Rapids | 2.164 | 1.9926 | 42.57 | 15.04 | 0.792 | 2.378 | — .214 |
| | Des Moines | 3.092 | 2.3541 | 43.18 | 14.74 | 3.777 | 2.802 | .290 |
| | Sioux City | 3.032 | 2.0166 | 46.49 | 28.62 | 1.156 | 3.077 | .045 |
| | Waterloo | 2.179 | 1.9315 | 29.46 | 11.65 | 2.690 | 1.830 | .349 |
| KANS. | Kansas City | 1.322 | 2.3581 | 22.02 | 10.65 | 13.242 | 1.868 | — .546* |
| | Topeka | 1.475 | 2.0228 | 38.74 | 7.75 | 7.363 | 1.754 | — .279 |
| | Wichita | 2.238 | 2.3469 | 28.67 | 12.12 | 4.564 | 2.395 | — .157 |
| MICH. | Flint | 2.639 | 2.4330 | 46.20 | 16.02 | 5.269 | 2.969 | — .330 |
| | Grand Rapids | 2.713 | 2.4598 | 26.58 | 15.37 | 2.506 | 2.766 | — .053 |
| | Jackson | 1.818 | 2.0330 | 23.13 | 12.75 | 4.699 | 1.843 | — .025 |
| | Kalamazoo | 2.004 | 2.1028 | 17.42 | 16.76 | 2.205 | 2.139 | — .135 |
| | Lansing | 2.556 | 2.2378 | 35.75 | 14.42 | 1.986 | 2.560 | — .004 |
| | Saginaw | 2.512 | 2.1861 | 24.38 | 12.44 | 5.982 | 2.031 | .481* |
| MINN. | Duluth | 2.403 | 2.1934 | 33.60 | 9.82 | 0.660 | 2.305 | .098 |
| | Minneapolis | 3.502 | 2.8303 | 31.34 | 19.74 | 1.296 | 3.662 | — .160 |
| | St. Paul | 4.166 | 2.5506 | 36.01 | 16.76 | 1.790 | 3.157 | 1.009** |

|  |  | (1) | (2) | (3) | (4) | (5) | (6) | (7) |
|---|---|---|---|---|---|---|---|---|
| Mo. | Kansas City | $3.501 | 2.7681 | $43.58 | 24.82 | 9.864 | $3.640 | −$ .139 |
|  | St. Louis | 4.080 | 3.1014 | 35.72 | 17.69 | 13.320 | 3.551 | — .529* |
|  | Springfield | 1.118 | 2.0204 | 21.98 | 8.83 | 2.102 | 1.788 | — .620** |
| Nebr. | Lincoln | 2.520 | 2.0781 | 44.49 | 8.31 | 1.389 | 2.213 | .307 |
|  | Omaha | 3.580 | 2.4487 | 52.28 | 24.08 | 6.080 | 3.424 | .156 |
| Ohio | Akron | 2.652 | 2.5740 | 42.60 | 16.46 | 6.470 | 3.093 | — .441* |
|  | Canton | 2.039 | 2.3506 | 22.62 | 14.49 | 4.475 | 2.409 | — .370 |
|  | Cincinnati | 3.708 | 2.8597 | 31.83 | 22.19 | 12.522 | 3.351 | .357 |
|  | Cleveland | 4.271 | 3.1355 | 42.68 | 21.03 | 11.022 | 3.968 | .303 |
|  | Columbus | 2.753 | 2.7019 | 26.71 | 12.58 | 10.369 | 2.682 | .071 |
|  | Dayton | 3.367 | 2.6003 | 45.39 | 18.08 | 9.463 | 3.127 | .240 |
|  | Springfield | 1.903 | 2.0481 | 19.48 | 14.35 | 9.007 | 1.695 | .208 |
|  | Toledo | 2.698 | 2.6034 | 34.72 | 16.96 | 6.798 | 3.014 | — .316 |
|  | Youngstown | 2.559 | 2.3666 | 43.54 | 14.24 | 9.488 | 2.564 | — .005 |
| Wisc. | Madison | 2.223 | 2.2159 | 22.23 | 8.44 | 0.625 | 2.086 | .137 |
|  | Milwaukee | 3.506 | 2.9400 | 41.92 | 19.25 | 2.668 | 3.928 | — .422* |
|  | Racine | 2.865 | 2.0195 | 25.74 | 16.00 | 1.716 | 2.139 | .726** |
|  | AVERAGE | $2.637 | 2.3670 | $33.40 | 15.66 | 5.245 | $2.637 | .000 |

* and **: these deviations are at least one and two standard errors in magnitude, respectively. There were no deviations as large as three standard errors. The standard error was $.397 and was computed as follows: the square root of the variation around the regression equation, divided by 36. Actually, this figure cannot be used to construct exact prediction intervals for Chest percapita for given values of the independent variables, and given probability levels. Such exact prediction intervals would vary in width for different values of the independent variables. Using $.397 would give prediction intervals that are too short. However, it was felt that this figure could be used, as it was here, for indicative purposes.

*Multiple Regression Equations:* $Y_1 = -\$2.037 + 1.532\ Y_2 + .017\ Y_3 + .045\ Y_4 - .042\ Y_6$. If the population is not stated in thousands, but units, we have: Expected percapita $= 1.532$ (log population) $+ .017$ (E-bond per capita) $+ .045$ (Business per capita) $- .042$ (percentage non-white) $- \$6.63$.

[a] .28954 of dollar volume of wholesale and retail trade during 1948, plus dollar value added by manufactures in 1947, divided by 1950 population, and divided by 100. In brief, this is a per capita index expressed in hundreds of dollars.

[b] "$Y_6$" rather than "$Y_5$" because it was the sixth variable in the original study, and it is desired to make comparison with that study easy.

—and that the obstacles to adding further variables are only the economic ones involved in computation costs.

What this would seem to mean, at first glance, is that city characteristics within the region in which the fundraiser's city is located—which are a datum for him, something he cannot hope to change in the short run or at all—will determine to a very large degree what he can hope to achieve; indeed, that the characteristics of the city he goes to are at least three times as important as anything he can hope to do there or persuade his laymen and public to try.[74]

Safe interpretation would say, so far, that the greater portion of the variation between cities in giving behavior is associated with certain city characteristics, and is substantially independent of the behavior of the Chests. This, of course, makes the "policy" of the Chests appear less important, but by no means unimportant, since the portion that *may* be determined by their behavior may mean for the agencies the difference between affluence and penury, and, possibly, for the agencies' clients the difference between modern and *passé*, or even "adequate" and "inadequate" services—if we could define these terms,[75] and if money were sufficient[76] to ensure their corresponding realities. What the recognition of the general fact ought perhaps chiefly to achieve is some diminution in the widespread belief in the omnipotence of any particular detail of organization or fundraising method or aspiration, and some realistic appreciation of the limits set at any one moment by the realities external to the life of the Chests (or any MOPS fundraising organization). If this, in turn, should operate to diminish the frequently very high sense of pressure—because great outcomes are believed to turn on small acts—so much gain might by itself reward sufficiently the establishment of the foregoing or similar generalizations.

But, as indicated, we may also go beyond the *general* fact established, and now that we have, in the "deviations," more appropriate measures of Chest "success" or "failure," we can go on to examine what, independently of the variables already considered,[77] seems to be associated with these deviations.

Possible further items[78] associated with the "deviation" measures of Chest success or failure might be of three kinds:

(1) additional city characteristics
(2) measures of giving behavior to organizations other than the Chest; and measures of "services" supplied
(3) measures relating to the behavior of the Chest itself.

## FURTHER CITY CHARACTERISTICS

Population mobility or migration (I C, I C 1, and I C 2 of Table XII) had been tested earlier[79] and found to be a significant factor; but, brought under review, in context with the four variables already employed, it did not seem to add much by way of further explanation.

Population growth[80] (variable I B), no matter whether 1920 to 1940 or 1940 to 1950 is taken as the unit, suffers similarly from non-independence.

Measures of income level and distribution (variables II A 1 and 2) suffered a similar fate, although percapitas are very highly related[81] to such a measure of income as the percentage of families earning $10,000 or more.

A measure of wealth such as the median value of owner-occupied one-dwelling-unit structures (variable II D) was, for similar reasons, rejected.

Interest at times turned to the matter of the local corporate or commercial-industrial organization. The percentage of large-sized (250 or more employees) firms (variable II E 1) had been considered in Study 68 as a possible indicator of relative ease of organization, but had been rejected as seemingly not clearly related to Chest performance.

The view had frequently and forcibly been put to us also that Chest percapita depended largely on the distribution in any city of the proportions of "home" and "national" firms within it (variable II E 2). The belief ran that somehow the local patriotism of the "home" firms would cause them to give much higher corporate gifts per employee than would the relatively "non-involved" "national" firms. We have no intercity comparisons on this basis, but we do have refutation of the principle for Indianapolis. Since we already knew that the size of the firm affects the firm's giving per employee,[82] we simply matched the total list of national firms (as far as we could) firm by firm for size with an otherwise random sample of "home" firms. So matched, there was no difference between the corporate gifts per employee of the two groups.[83] So "locus of control" (home or absentee) appears to have little relevance for Chest percapita as far as the corporate gift is concerned; it also does not appear that the giving of employees of national firms is adversely affected, since the national firms tend to organize this giving to an unusually efficient extent.

We had also been told that the distribution of firms by size (variable II E 3) in a given city was very significant for percapita, both because of its bearing on the ease of organizing the donor-aggregate and because of its economic implications. Again we have no intercity data, but we did test for Indianapolis the distribution of firms by size in terms of what might be expected in a mature and stable urban economy.[84] The data suggest that Indianapolis has to an unusual degree the characteristic sizes and numbers of firms to be expected in a mature and stable system. At least, we feel any Chest deviation in this city cannot be ascribed to an unusually inimical distribution of firms by size.

Housing values, types of houses, and occupancy patterns (variables IV C, 1, 2 and 3) had been tested in Study 68, and thought to provide little additional explanatory value.

This brings us to the last[85] "additional community characteristic" to be considered here: the crime rate (variable IV B). This variable entered into the analysis in many studies.[86] We knew that—for whatever reason—

crime rate and an index of "welfare effort"[87] had been negatively correlated[88] in 1940. We also knew that, in 1940, Indianapolis had a crime
rate that was unusually high[89]—so high indeed that, at that time, if her
crime rate had been taken into consideration in estimating her "welfare
effort," she would have to be considered as doing above average. By 1950,
she had moved down to the eighth highest place in terms of crime rate
among the same twenty-eight cities, but again if this crime rate (and whatever it connotes or indicates) is taken into account, she was doing as well
on this "welfare index" as could be, on the average, expected.

To test more rigorously the significance of this crime rate,[90] its bearing
on per capita giving was re-examined, but now in context with the other
variables.[91] It correlates so highly,[92] however, with population composition,
that its capacity to contribute any explanation independently is limited.[93]
In any case (although new equations to estimate its effect were not computed so late in the study) the net effect of the high crime rate (and
whatever it connotes) would be slightly to depress the "expected" percapita shown in Table XVI, i.e., to make the performance of the Indianapolis
Chest look slightly "better" although still "bad."

So much for city characteristics.

## MEASURES OF OTHER GIVING AND SERVICES

### Other Giving

It had been many times put to us that "what probably accounts for the
poor Chest showing in Indianapolis" is that Indianapolis people "favor"
other organizations more. Indeed, what was put to us in many variations
was what might be called an "it-all-comes-out-of-one-pocket" or "limited-
pool-of-resources" or competitive theory of fundraising, whose fundamental
assumption is that what one fundraiser or fundgetter gets, another doesn't.
In strict literalness, such a theory can hardly be doubted. The dollar given
to A cannot properly and may not legally be also given to B. But this is
not to say that the act of giving A a dollar may not increase the likelihood of
a donor's giving B a dollar also: it may well be (as, perhaps, with parental
gifts to children in a family) that this is normally the case. And it obviously
can continue to be the case as long as donors are still willing to remove
dollars from other uses and employ them for gifts, i.e., as long as the
gift-pool is not truly, or yet, a strictly limited resource-pool. The question
then is, "Which is generally true: the view based on 'you can't give the
same dollar twice,' or the view that 'giving one dollar loosens another'?"

In an attempt to test these important hypotheses we secured intercity
data on giving to churches (per member),[94] to Red Cross (per capita),[95]
and to each local unit of the National Tuberculosis Association, via "sales"
of seals (per capita).[96]

At first glance, the results seem unequivocal enough, and in favor of
the "one dollar loosens up another" side of the argument. In the analysis

of church giving, we examined the per member gifts of two major Protestant denominations, city by city, in relation to each other—and each (and both together) in relation to Chest percapitas for the same cities. The relations are significant and "positive," i.e., the higher the gift to any one of these, the higher, in general, the gift to the others.[97] Not only is this true, but the gift-giving in one denomination is only about as closely related to the gift-giving in the other, as either is to the gift-giving in each city to the Community Chest. It looks as if a common factor underlies both "religious" and "secular" giving,[98] and as if one kind of religious giving is no more closely related to another religious kind than either is to secular giving. Such a factor could be liberality or generosity, thought of as differentially embodied or expressed in the cultures of the several cities; but later analysis has caused us to doubt this interpretation (see below in this chapter).

A similar analysis was made of giving to the Red Cross and to the Chest for each of two years, with essentially the same results: a significantly high and positive relation between the two.[99] Lastly, a similar comparison for TB seal-sale data and Chest percapitas, while it yielded a very low and probably insignificant relation, nevertheless showed a positive sign.[100]

Hence, at this first level of analysis, the "competitive" theory of inter-organization take is clearly *not* supported.

But, it will be recalled, in order to add to our explanatory or understanding powers new variables must be independent of those already employed. And in order to show non-competitiveness in fundraising, we have to make allowance, in the case of the other organizations also, for the city characteristics that influence giving to the Chest—*if* they are relevant to other giving.

We have, therefore, first to establish which of our variables are relevant for the other forms of giving. For the church, it seems that city size is significant for gift size.[101] While the other variables tested are also related, none of them is significantly so, and none adds anything significant to what may be explained on the basis of city size alone.[102]

Similarly with Red Cross: city size is significant,[103] but the other variables add little to the explanatory power of population by itself. For the T.B. Association, perhaps understandably, none of the city characteristics used for explaining Chest percapitas seems to have any great relevance.[104] Population, in particular, so important for the larger percapitas, seems to have little weight in determining the relatively very small T.B. seal "sale" per capita.[105] We shall, therefore, omit these sales from the following comparison.

It is interesting to speculate whether the Red Cross is genuinely less dependent even on city size than is the Chest: we cannot answer unequivocally since a difference of the order found would arise by sampling chances about once in every seventeen trials in the absence of a "true" difference. It is, however, a reasonable guess that it *is* less dependent. This would be consistent with expectation based upon interpretation of the earlier finding: that the Red Cross is not significantly dependent for its percapita on the other city characteristics either. What all this suggests strongly is a hypothesis of rather important consequence, i.e., that *only* in a campaign as large as that of the Chest is the amount required sufficiently large to press really seriously on city resources and therefore to be highly correlated with many city characteristics. (Other campaigns, then, in this sense, are relatively "easy.") This general view is further made plausible by the relatively still greater independence of the seal-sale figures of these gross city characteristics—and by the closer dependence on city characteristics of percapita for United Funds, as compared with "Other Extended Federations" and non-extended Community Chests.[106] One might be tempted to generalize to the following: "As unification proceeds toward greater and greater incorporation of voluntary association deficits into one budget, the more clearly is seen the dependence of the total on the characteristics of the city and the more certainly can the sum raised be predicted."

The critical question about other giving in relation to giving to the Chest may now be put: After Chest percapitas have been freed of the influence of their relevant city characteristics (population size and composition, productivity and savings) and Red Cross percapitas of theirs (population) and gifts to the church per member of theirs (population), do the remaining figures ("deviations") suggest the "competitive" view, the "one dollar loosens another" view, or neither, i.e., "independence"? The answer seems to be, clearly enough, that freed of their common dependence on common city characteristics (population size, in particular) gifts to the Chest, gifts to the Red Cross, and gifts to the church per member are independent on an intercity comparative basis, i.e., these organizations neither compete with one another nor sensibly aid one another in fundraising. Their seeming positive relation is due to their common situation in each city and not to any influence, competitive or co-operative, that they have directly on each other, or indirectly, because "dollars can only be spent once."[107]

We have thus settled a more or less general and very important point, in passing—a point bearing on the widely held view that "after all, there's only so much money to go round." But we have also settled a point more central to our present inquiry: the point that knowledge of cognate or allied or parallel giving will not add much to our present power to predict Chest percapitas from a knowledge of city characteristics alone.

## Cognate Services

It had similarly been suggested that some measures of the richness or lavishness of the resources employed in cognate or "related" spheres (social work, school, church) might be related to liberality or generosity, and might therefore function also as indexes of Chest percapitas to be expected.

School expenditures per pupil, a notoriously "tricky" index, had been explored (in Study 68) and found to have little explanatory value.

The number of clergymen per capita was first, naïvely perhaps, thought of as a potential measure of liberality. The forty-one cities ranged in terms of provision in this respect from about a half clergyman per thousand people (.7) to about three times this number (1.7) or over one and a half clergymen per thousand; on the average, about one such functionary (1.1) per thousand potential flock seems to characterize the cities under study in this region.

Strangely, relative to the anticipations we had begun with, both Chest percapitas and church gifts are related to this clerical provision, but negatively so, i.e., the more clergymen per capita the lower the giving per capita, especially to the Chest.[108] This might suggest a return to the alternative-uses-of-money theory, i.e., the dollar that supports a clergyman can't be given to the Chest. But, obviously, this will not hold either, since church gift (which includes the clergyman's salary) also goes down (per member) as the number of clergymen goes up. One may well conclude, on further reflection, that the presence in a city of many clergymen probably implies many congregations, and that this in turn implies in many places many *small* congregations—which may in turn point to low urbanization and a widespread habit of doing things in a small way.[109]

Unfortunately, again, for better prediction of gifts to the Chest, the number of clergymen per capita correlates highly enough with the other city characteristics that it cannot add significantly to the variation already explained.

The same is true for the number of "religious workers" per capita and the number of social workers[110] per capita, although the correlation of both of these with Chest gift per capita (and with one another) is positive.[111]

So much for cognate giving and cognate services. They are clearly related to Chest percapitas, but they do not add in statistically significant amounts to the variation we can already explain on the basis of the four city characteristics. This leaves us free to examine those phenomena lying more clearly perhaps within the domain where Chest policy is determinative: type of campaign ("United Fund," "Other Extended Federation" or "other"), participation or household coverage, expenditure for campaign and administration, and equity or "distribution of gift-load."

## CHARACTERISTICS OF CHEST POLICY

### Form of Campaign

We shall not discuss in any detail here the various forms of organization and their consequences, since these have a more direct bearing on the material of chapter 13. We have already made the point, above, that a United Fund percapita is more readily predictable from city characteristics than are the percapitas of "less United Funds," and we have suggested that this may well be because a United Fund necessarily presses more heavily on community resources than does any one of its components.[112]

It may be particularly worth noting that the United Fund form of organization is not by itself a guarantor of "success" in the sense of achieving goal.[113] Though we have rejected achievement of goal as a satisfactory measure for general purposes, the failure rates[114] in Table XVII may drive home the last-made point:

TABLE XVII

FORM OF CAMPAIGN ORGANIZATION AND FAILURE RATE, 1953

| Form of campaign | Failure rate |
|---|---|
| United Fund | 49.6% |
| "Other Extended Federation" | 52.7% |
| "Other Community Chest" | 62.7% |

Beyond this, we do not feel we can go at this point, since the effect of unification requires further careful analysis apart from problems of prediction.

*Participation*

There would seem to be little doubt that "participation"—defined at this point as number of pledges divided by population—would be significantly related to Chest percapita.[115] In context with our previously used variables,[116] our data suggest a positive relationship of participation to percapita, which might add, if included in our prediction equation, another three or four percentage points to the "amount of explained variation." This seemed "uneconomical," and hence we did not adopt participation as a separate variable.[117]

It is striking and seems worth reporting that Indianapolis ranked eighth highest on the "index of participation" in a list comprising thirty-eight of our forty-one cities.[118] With a range, for the list, from 47 per cent to 93 per cent, Indianapolis stood at 78 per cent.[119] For this reason it seems safe to conclude that whatever "the trouble is" in Indianapolis it is not primarily with participation, as defined.

*Expenses*

We now come to a question whose handling is, perhaps more than in any other case, under Chest control: "What proportion of the Chest budget shall be spent on 'campaign and administration expense'?"

Before we had "standardized" on our forty-one cities, and before we had shifted our preoccupation from raw percapitas to the more illuminating "deviation from expected percapita" we had done a study of the relation between "Administrative and Campaign Expense Per Capita" and Per Capita

Gift (for 1954 and for all cities raising $1 million or more for which we could obtain the information).[120] The relationships were positive and very high,[121] which led us initially to suppose either that cities that spend high per capita get high returns per capita as a consequence, or that cities that get high percapitas spend high per capita as a consequence. However, city population and Administrative and Campaign expense per capita are themselves so closely correlated[122] that we are almost driven again to ascribe the seeming relation between money expense and money result to the common factor of population.[123]

But perhaps not quite. For those eight cities which are common to our standard forty-one and the list of twenty-five of Study 47, there is a suggestion of a positive relation between the deviation per capita and either the Administration and Campaign expense per capita or this expense stated as a fraction of total take.[124] We are left, in this matter, only with a suggestion that the proper allocation of money to Administration and Campaign expense may quite likely influence the Chest's deviation from expectancy, i.e., its disappointing performance or otherwise, given the opportunities of the city in which it is located.

### Equity

The problem of "equity" has become, understandably, so important a matter for the Chests in terms of social engineering, and so difficult, evidently, for them in a technical sense that we have thought fit to devote the whole of chapter 8 to an elucidation of the problem. We shall not, accordingly, deal in detailed fashion with it here. In order, however, to complete the treatment of percapitas we must do so, at least in a preliminary way.

The notion of equity or fairness comes very close, in Chest usage, to the thesis "from each according to his capacity"[125]—the principle also, presumably, of a "fair" or equitable tax system. Since, in most cases, data on income are not available on which to base judgments of capacity to pay —the Chests cannot demand tax returns—the tendency is to shift from a demand for equity based on known capacity to pay, to a demand for equality of payment per "productive unit."[126]

At a very gross level, the "productive unit" is the pledging unit—the individual or corporation making the gift. We cannot suppose that each of these should make equal gifts, but for every city we can develop crude measures, for all or part of its gift-distribution, which will reflect in rough fashion the amount of concentration or disequality[127] in its giving behavior.

One of these measures—a very rough one—is the percentage of the total gift to the Chest represented by the ten largest gifts. This "measure of concentration" correlates negatively with the deviations we have been discussing throughout,[128] i.e., the greater the concentration or the greater the amount of dependency on a few large givers the more "disappointing" is a Chest performance-in-relation-to-opportunity likely to be.[129]

This measure of concentration, moreover, appears to be sufficiently independent of population size or productivity factors (as measured by the index we used) for each city that we have reason to think it would add to the variation already explained by the chosen four city characteristics.

On this index of concentration, or dependency on leading gifts, Indianapolis finds itself in fifth highest place (tied with Dayton, among the thirty-one cities out of our original list of forty-one on which we could get data). This position—in the "worst" sixth of the concentration distribution—is suggestively linked with Indianapolis's position in terms of her failure to meet "expected" percapita—i.e., her being also in the "worst" sixth of the performance distribution.

If we wished to summarize the leading positive and seemingly definite contentions of the second half of this chapter we might say that:
1. It is valid *within a region* to found Chest percapita expectations on:
   (a) Population size: *the greater the population, the higher the expectation*;
   (b) Productivity: *the greater the productivity, the higher the expectation*;
   (c) Population composition: *the higher the percentage white, the higher the expectation*;
   (d) Savings: *the higher the savings rate, the higher the expectation.*
2. The greater the independence of the Chest from a small number of large givers, the greater the likelihood of meeting or exceeding these statistical expectations.
3. Crime rates seem also to be sensitive indicators of poor Chest performance, for reasons which are not immediately evident. Rates of participation in Chest giving seem also good indicators of good Chest performance per capita.
4. Within cities, it seems that the per capita takes of the various philanthropies are independent of each other (once allowance for city characteristics has been made) or perhaps weakly related positively. In any case, there appears to be no foundation for the view that they are competitively related. This has an important bearing on the United Fund problem to be discussed in chapter 13.

It also seems safe to say on the basis of this chapter that Indianapolis was (and is) performing disappointingly in relation to expectation.

## APPENDIX

### Some Observations on Chest "Success" and "Failure"

If Chest "success" is defined as meaning what occurs when the sum raised (or, rather, pledged) equals or exceeds the sum announced before the campaign as the campaign "goal," and if "failure" is defined as the absence of such "success," then the following propositions hold true (for the regions and years studied):

1. Members and non-members of the Community Chests and Councils of America in 1953 succeeded or failed in "making their goal" in like proportions. Of 836 members reporting, 40.9 per cent were "successful"; of 146 non-members, 42.5 per cent made their goal.

2. "Failure" to reach goal is more common than "success." For the United States (members and non-members), 41 per cent report themselves as having made (or bettered) their goal—"succeeded"—and 59 per cent as having failed to do so.

3. The regions of *relative* high success are the North Central (49 per cent) and the South (46 per cent); the regions of relative low success are the Northeast (34 per cent) and the West (22 per cent).

4. The divisions within the regions are essentially like the regions as wholes. Success rates range from 18 per cent (Pacific states) to 53 per cent (East South Central).

5. Rates of success for the states range from 0 to 100 per cent, with a median of 39 per cent successes.

6. *Income.* By divisions within the United States, and by states within the United States, the tendency is for the failure rate to rise as median income rises.

7. *Population size.* For the United States as a whole, successes tend to be more frequent in the small (1 to 9,000) and large (250,000 and over) centers.

8. *Population and income.* In low-income states, the larger centers (over 100,000) tend to succeed disproportionately; in high-income states, the smaller centers succeed rather better.

9. *Goal.* There is no evidence that failure in the larger Chest campaigns is the result of over-aspiration in the crude sense of conducting too large a campaign for a small community. In the small campaigns, the opposite may well be the case: failure may be associated rather with crude under-aspiration.

10. With respect to differential failure rates for United Fund campaigns, (UF), Other Extended Federation (OEF), and Other Community Chests: in general, failure rates increase in the order: UF, OEF, CC; but there are notable exceptions, for very small and very large places. Moreover United Funds tend to have higher failure rates than do Chests in the "poor" states, and lower failure rates than Chests only in the rich ones.

11. There is no consistent relationship between success-failure and in-migration in fifty-six large cities; but percentage growth (1940 to 1950) of these same cities indicates that a low increase in population is clearly related to a high failure rate. In the South, particularly, a high growth rate is related to success.

12. Related to the all-or-nothing succeed-or-fail concept, is the ratio of the amount raised to goal of Community Chest campaigns—a measure of "degree of success." Any ratio less than 1.00 would classify a campaign as a "failure"; a ratio of 1.00 or more would indicate "success." With "degree of success" expressed in terms of this ratio, the following statement may be made with regard to consistency for the same Chest from year to year: the ratios of amount raised to goal in 1950 bear practically no relationship to the same ratio for the same city in 1940. That is, if a city subscribed well over its goal in 1940, that fact was no indication that it would do so again; and, furthermore, failure to reach goal in 1940 was no indication of failure to do so in 1950.

# 7. "Success" by Social Standards

IN CHAPTER 5 we saw that a Chest's aims and purposes are, in the minds even of those lay leaders and paid workers who are in or closest to the permanent central organization, subject to a number of conflicts and confusions, not only at the level of ideals but also in the realm of facts. We also saw, in chapter 6, how carefully one must go about measuring the "success" of MOPS fundraising organizations, even when the criteria are relatively simple money units that can be counted.

While we saw, finally, that a Chest's financial "success" can be assessed in terms of how well the per capita amount it raises matches what can be reasonably expected, given the city's comparative characteristics among cities in its region, we warned the reader, at the outset of chapter 6, that "there is no unanimity" among persons actively or even professionally interested in these matters as to how such "success" can in turn be related to criteria for evaluating a Chest in non-financial or social terms.

Nevertheless, we may ask: Does a satisfactory method exist, or can we devise any, for assessing Community Chests by social standards, which would be analogous to financial standards, such as per capita amount raised? Social standards depend upon point of view, of course, and for our purposes we shall attempt only to review what "success" of a Chest may mean in the eyes of (a) those who view the community as a whole as something of a problem of *social control,* (b) those who view the Chest or any other institution as a possible *civic asset* (or liability), (c) those interested in the *"goodness"* of the people of a community, and (d) those whose standards of "success" for the Chest derive from their involvement in *"welfare"* enterprises, especially in agencies that are members of the federation or are members of the Health and Welfare Council. These are not, of course, necessarily mutually exclusive categories of people, although in general they do serve to distinguish different people with different pre-eminent interests.

If any adequate and accepted standard for measuring the social success of the Community Chest exists, we do not know of it.[1] Most attempts to measure this social performance begin with rather sweeping, and often unstated, assumptions about the nature of "community organization," and the role and influence of a voluntary fundraising enterprise therein. The aura of the whole American heritage lends an almost sacred sanction to voluntary welfare activities. The American people's capacities for "doing good works," especially in and through associations, are celebrated and have been since the days of de Tocqueville, and their tolerance for almost any kind of welfare effort is so very generous that various checks on "charity rackets" have had to be devised.[2] Since, in protecting the public, it is desired also to preserve certain Constitutional freedoms, these devices of prevention seem to many less satisfactory than the process of endorsing only "worthy" appeals, made by organizations which meet certain standards. Community Chests and similar federations are one of the means used to establish some social control, at least, in the welter of philanthropic activities into which so many Americans so enthusiastically throw themselves.

## Social Control

The sheer persistence of the idea of federated fundraising is perhaps in itself some indication of the social success of the Chest movement in many American communities. But we know of no systematic effort to compare Chests in various communities in terms of something like "effectiveness of social control." Such a study would need to measure the extent to which these federations:

(a) "reduce the confusion of a multiplicity of drives," either initially or over the long pull;

(b) reduce giving to "charity rackets" by providing an established channel for philanthropy through a federation of approved agencies;

(c) increase the roles of reason and wisdom in planning for, and acting to maintain or raise, the general welfare, so far as it is affected by the voluntary agencies included in the federation; or

(d) maintain or increase the interest and active participation of "the best people," or at least avoid the social, and perhaps eventually the financial, consequences of their withdrawal, by abdication or deposition, as the case may be.

The four areas listed are a few of those in which fundraising federations may have more or less measurable influences or results that are of more or less interest according to different points of view.

Historically, so far as reducing multiplicity of drives is concerned, the Chest movement scored initial successes which had the effect of winning support for the idea of federation all across the country—even Boston succumbing in the mid-1930's. But the United Fund movement of the 1950's shows that federation of the earlier degree and kind is no longer enough, in the eyes of the leaders in many cities, at least in prosperous years. The idea of "more federation" will undoubtedly be put forward again and again as a "dynamic" or "progressive" concept: when the United Funds find themselves outflanked by a new "multiplicity of drives" the scope will again have to be enlarged, if it is to bring this larger area under *this* form of social control.

So far as control of rackets is concerned, a federation that merely survives, regardless of whether it is financially successful by other standards, may well, by that very survival, be doing much to discourage charity rackets, particularly if it stands well in the eyes of a Chamber of Commerce "Contributions Committee" (or its equivalent in a Better Business Bureau), and if other forms of social control, especially appropriate local publicity, are functioning effectively.

In the matter of rationalizing the local welfare enterprise, the fundraising federation may go far to help,[3] through a budgeting and allocation process, to give the leading donors and others in the donor-aggregate a feeling that they have (or, at least, "could get") a clearer "picture of total needs and resources" in the local setting. As we have seen, in chapter 6 especially, the whole question of "needs" is, however, one in which reason may well bog down; in this respect the means for wise social control are least well developed.

It is reported that, before the Chest movement of the 1920's, the earlier financial federations "were in many instances contributors' protective associations," and that they "provided only a portion of the contributions support of the co-operating agencies," which in turn included only a "small proportion of the total number of social work organizations in the community"; and, further, that they "exercised no budgetary controls."[4] In Indianapolis in 1955 (and before) the Chest's condition was not nearly so feeble as that of the earlier federations elsewhere. But to the degree that its agencies were collectively weak,[5] and to the degree that their closest supporters were not yet well organized,[6] to that degree it seemed entirely possible that a "contributors' protective association" was just what some donors and leaders would have welcomed—either operating the Chest itself, as such, or perhaps operating as a separate body.[7]

Since we have seen neither solution in actual practice, we can only speculate as to whether either design for strengthening social control would succeed any better than would a more hard-headed (as well as wholehearted) application of energies within the existing arrangements. Leading donors, of all people, should have the least difficulty in making sure they are well informed if they really want to strengthen their share in exerting social control. Their comparative absence from the direction of Chest affairs in Indianapolis, and the inability of others "down the line" even to communicate with them, has had far-reaching effects, in terms of both social control by donors and the morale of those "left."

It is in its relation to social structure that we come to what seems to us to be the heart of the matter of social control in the realm of contemporary mass philanthropy—of which Community Chests are only major instances, of course, and not the sole forms. The fundamental structure of social control, certainly in voluntary philanthropic enterprises, is determined largely by what is often called "community leadership," in so far as that leadership affects the relations of the higher and lower social classes found in the community.[8] In one common downward spiral, as a fundraising federation becomes a middle-class *enterprise* and loses almost all its character as an upper-class *concern*, it "slips" socially as an institution in the community, and its adherents suffer from shaken morale and loss of confidence. Consequently, its program becomes more subject (and subjected) to the scorn or indifference of people of higher positions, its moral code becomes less principled and more opportunistic—and finally "failure" in the financial sense may occur in its campaigns. This, in turn, leads often to further opportunism, and to more deterioration in principle and morale. As the campaigns fail, the institution can be kept alive only by "transfusions": especially help at the last minute from those elements in the business community who are least willing to see the federation—a familiar symbol of civic virtue, if no longer an object of strong civic pride—collapse. If persons in high positions act at all in such crises, their usual behavior is to "assign" the actual tasks to their subordinates in the business system (usually, also, to their subordinates in the community's class system) thus perpetuating the federation's standing as a merely middle-class enterprise. Whether the "community leadership" has abdicated or been deposed really does not, after a short time, matter greatly, in effect, any more.

Such a downward spiral may be part of a larger and more general philanthropic revolution. It may be that a division of labor in philanthropic activities is coming about, such that people of highest status find their energies and resources—of time even more than of money—taken up with different concerns: higher education, the fine arts, world affairs, anything but the perhaps more parochial-seeming kind of thing associated with "the Red Feather Services." Chest failure may be a transitional cost attached to emerging cosmopolitan interests at the top of the social structure.

Welfare federations, seemingly now becoming less and less involved with "charity,"[9] are, at the same time, more and more involved with "services" attuned to middle-class value-systems, for example, the Family (meaning the immediate family) and the Child (meaning a problem for guidance and counselling); Group Work, Informal Education or "Character-Building"; Rehabilitation and "Self-Help"; certain health services; inter-denominational work or the services given by church-linked agencies.

The consequence of all this—especially if Community Chests are indeed becoming even more middle-class than they were in the 1920's—would be that what was once thought of as *the* common effort to provide for the general welfare on a voluntary basis, with "community leadership" from "the top" down, must now be viewed as a "class-bound" and ethically rather limited "free enterprise,"[10] conducting but one among the many "drives" which occur each year in a highly differentiated community (not to say a disorganized one, for it is not).[11]

Later,[12] our comparisons of the Chest with the Red Cross will make it possible to see in more detail what happens to a federation that loses "community leadership," but without fear of anticipating the wealth of detail to follow, we may here contrast the current Chest and Red Cross "etiquette" in recruiting volunteer leaders for their fundraising campaigns. For this purpose, two anecdotes (names fictitious, of course) make the point:

*Incident in a Chest campaign:* Mr. Smith said, "The Chest asked me to help out in this campaign. What gets me down is that they had someone on the Staff phone my office and leave a message, because I was out. I called back and found out what it was all about. Of course I'll do the *job*, but! . . . I would like to have someone I *respect* ask me to do it. . . . Now the Red Cross is different: the Chairman of the whole campaign, or else at least the head of the section they want you in, will call you personally. . . . Some people are just snobs! I could talk about snobs all afternoon!"

*Incident in a Red Cross campaign:* At a Chest meeting Mr. Wilson said to Mr. Everest, "I hear that Joe - - - - and Mark - - - - had a nice visitation with you the other day." (That is, two men of high status had called upon Mr. Everest to ask if he would accept a leadership position in the next Red Cross campaign.) Mr. Everest smiled and replied, "Yes. I was very flattered that they came to see me. But I won't be able to do it this year. . . . I was very sorry but until we finish the re-organization out at the plant I'll be out of town and tied up too much to do a good job [in the campaign]."

As later materials will show,[13] although the Chest has lost the "top top leaders" who can get action with the judicious use of "the pat on the back" (or "the cold shoulder"), the Red Cross has kept those social skills in use, so far at least. It is the absence of these skills, perhaps, that has caused the Chest to let the logics of "business efficiency" make it possible for staff persons (paid workers) to be charged with volunteers' functions. The "correct" behavior in the professional-lay relation is not maintained, and this reflects and reinforces the kinds of relations that develop among volunteers when "community leadership" is lacking, when "top top leaders" are not setting an example in interpersonal relations throughout the campaign organization.

Suppose we now attempt to view the federation as part of the larger locally organized cultural system. We may see that the community, which puts a very great emphasis upon "freedom to solicit," at least preserves, as a high value, "freedom to give," and even tolerates some non-giving. This emphasis is consistent with what, in general, turns out to be an extraordinary degree of individuation—a kind of generalized "freedom to differ" —in many areas other than simple philanthropic activity.[14] If it were possible to assess the "success" of the Community Chest in contributing to greater or lesser degrees of individuation, and if (as chapter 3 suggests) Hoosier culture makes "freedom" (to "give" or to be different) a prime value, then one might say that the Indianapolis Chest has by its very lack of success in imposing standards, up to this point, fitted well into the general cultural scheme of things.

## THE CHEST AS A CIVIC ASSET

Presumably no one would want to see a Chest or any other MOPS fund-raising organization become a civic liability in some other way, no matter how successful it was financially. Indeed, the original Chest movement, launched in 1918 by the American Association for Community Organization, was favored by businessmen as a more rational method of raising philanthropic funds because it consolidated currently approved appeals into "one big campaign," and centralized the budgeting and allocations functions. Along with its practicality, the movement inspired many with the idealism of its purpose, which was, as stated in one phrasing, "To encourage and stimulate collective community planning, and the development of better standards of community organization for social work."[15] Along with this, in many cities, this mode of organization and fundraising, albeit secular, carried with it overtones of religious idealism, especially the themes of brotherhood and inter-faith co-operation; and the fact was that in many cities, by 1918, the maintenance of co-operation, in other respects as well, among "Protestants, Catholics and Jews" was of considerable importance to the vitality of the business community.

Industrial expansion, and relocation movements in some trades, helped to bring about changes in the composition of many local business communities, and Catholics and Jews were emerging as leaders in a number of localities where their European origins had either been erased by "Americanization" or were simply no longer factors holding them "down," and where religious differences, as such, had become socially less important. Jews had developed federated fundraising within their own communities in most cities where they were sufficiently numerous; Catholics had their distinctive forms of charitable organizations, especially those church-linked and under diocesan control; and much of Protestant philanthropy was sectarian or "inter-denominational," with some agencies or institutions having more prestige than others, but most having generally higher standing in the eyes of the community than the Jewish or Catholic enterprises. The rise in social status of once lowly religious and ethnic minorities in American cities now began to make it unfitting for them to appeal for general community support and at the same time maintain tight in-group control over the uses of such charitable funds. Besides, they were ready for "recognition" as full-fledged citizens. The Protestants, long secure in their majority position and often long-established "old family" status at each social level, were more and more sharing the economic tasks and rewards of the growing city and nation with Jews and Catholics who were also rising to positions enabling them to "take more responsibility" (were they not now employers themselves?) and to join in the general community's philanthropic activities.

The community-wide campaign for a *federation* of agencies therefore presented, in itself, both the challenge and the means to reduce the potentially divisive forces of religious and ethnic groupings, and, so far as membership-through-contributions could add to this knitting together, it provided both the task and the way to bring large numbers of persons and business organizations together in association in a common enterprise in the name of "The Community" or "Our Fair City."

Such an association was, and still is in many circles, regarded as a civic asset. Indeed, one of the oldest and most persistent ideas about The City is that it requires and provides various means for achieving some unity out of considerable diversity: it fosters differentiation (occupational specialization, for example) and strives to protect all against one, as well as one against all (civil codes, for example). The Chest movement provided one more way—in a voluntary association—to build a city from a mere population aggregate into a larger social unity.

In the United Fund movement of the 1950's, much the same sort of thing is going on; but this time the rise of the modern corporation and the development of management-labor relations on a mass basis have brought the "Corporation as Citizen" and the "Union as Citizen" into active alignment in the contemporary form of the association for federated fundraising. It may be that religious and ethnic cleavages have either almost disappeared or become minor in current importance in many cities and that the deep and possibly serious gulfs between management and labor are relatively more important than they were in the 1920's. The United Fund pattern may be a matter of making good use of community-wide fundraising as an activity in which the larger social unity that encloses both corporations and unions can be experienced and enjoyed, as a satisfying extra-mural interaction in which erstwhile or intermittent opponents in collective bargaining can combine (*and* compete) in "doing something for the good of all."

Since any federation for fundraising must be organized and at times reorganized to adapt to whatever cleavages exist in its local community, if only to maximize its financial chances, the composition of the federation (the ethnic, religious, social class, or other linkages maintained by its agencies) probably reflects, if that federation is effective, what is currently the state of affairs in the power structure of the community. In one city we were told, for example, that "if the [federation] doesn't have [the support of] the Catholics and Jews, it has nothing!" and that therefore a desire for a United Fund, attributed to certain Protestant business leaders alone, would never be fulfilled, in that particular community. In Detroit, it is well known, a United Fund was brought into being by a coalition of top management and top union leadership, thus not only demonstrating the power of Big Business and Big Union, but also, by the enlargement of their participation in the civic philanthropic enterprise, acknowledging the new social standing won by the leaders and the rank and file in the labor camp. If the major cleavage in a growing city like Indianapolis has become that between "Old Families" and "Newcomers," and if there are no other equally important differences demanding recognition and resolution, the fundraising federation may suffer from a lack of mission in the field of "community organization" when, for whatever reasons, the "top top leadership" among the "Old Guard" either do not perceive the need and the means to integrate the "Newcomers" or, seeing the problem and the task, refuse to act. In such circumstances, as long as they persist, the Chest or any other federation is not likely to be viewed so much as a potential "civic asset," but rather as something to be kept from becoming too much of a civic liability.

### THE CHEST AS AN AGENCY FOR PROMOTING THE "GOODNESS OF PEOPLE"

Many people (including, evidently, the social scientists who studied the financial results of Community Chest campaigns as symptoms of "moral integration" or "goodness of life" in American cities[16]) are probably ready to believe that the financial vigor of a Community Chest is itself an index of something "good" about the locality which supports it. They presumably know, or can fairly easily learn (at least in crude terms), what kinds of agencies are kept going with the funds raised, and they feel reasonably sure that, like the ideal physician, these agencies seek to do what good they can, and certainly try to avoid doing any harm.

Most people, then, are more aware of the role of Community Chests as fundraising organizations; few are as well informed about their functions in the fields of budgeting, allocations, and, sometimes, "community planning." Few laymen manage to learn much about all the agencies brought together in any one federation. Most accept the community welfare enterprise on faith, and, perhaps, some hearsay—at least the combination of agencies in a Chest. Indeed, many view the Chest itself as "another agency," and some contribute to its drive on the same basis and in the same money amounts as they do to each of several other community-wide campaigns.

Public awareness of Chest agencies being what it is, rather meager (and at best particularized according to personal experiences or the lack of them) compared with public familiarity with Chest fundraising (which "touches" all, in fundraising theory at least), it seems reasonable to believe that little could be learned about what makes a Chest socially successful from any poll or survey of popular opinion and belief. Such a federation, simply by its continuing to exist, is itself clear evidence that the *idea* behind it has won at least minimal acceptance or has not evoked active and effective opposition. (A Chest or other federation *can* arouse organized opposition—as some have, with resulting threatened or actual withdrawals of member agencies or with refusals to join or to admit.) At worst, minimal acceptance chiefly affects its comparative financial success, and secondarily its social effects.[17] Even if a Chest is not a "success" financially or socially, then, so long as it stays in business, no organized opposition is managing to persuade the community that the federation is not making some contribution at least to "the general welfare."

But even those best informed about MOPS fundraising are usually more preoccupied with financial "success" and the reasons therefor than they are with the social implications of these campaigns, unless it is perceived that a given social consequence or possibility definitely affects the financial side. In Indianapolis, we heard very little discussion about positively desired social consequences that would give us even rough standards for evaluating "success" in terms of human organization, although there was much complaint about undesired social effects.

One standard is suggested by the common notion held by experienced fundraisers: namely, that it is possible for a campaign to "fail" financially, yet prove later to have been a "success" in an "educational" sense. That is, one social consequence, as perceived by some, of a campaign, even or perhaps especially a financially disappointing one, may be that "the constituency" (a church congregation, a body of school alumni, or even the people of a Chest territory) will be better prepared to respond next time, presumably because they have "heard the story" before. The financial result of the second effort is then taken as a measure of the educational effectiveness of the first one. Continued financial "failure" cannot, of course, be so evaluated.

On the other hand, a campaign may "succeed" financially but leave rather long-lasting memories of how painful it was. Or it may leave, in the minds of some, the lasting and mistaken impression that it will "never" have to be duplicated, as did the "once-in-a-lifetime" and highly successful Indianapolis Hospital drive. But we have heard very few references to socially negative *mass* results of MOPS fundraising; most of the complaints we heard had to do with the effect on a given individual. Even the individual who complains about the obligations he incurred in persuading others to work or contribute in a campaign he helped to run, is, in doing so, also actually calling attention to the fact that at least he did enter so far into weaving that part of the social fabric which is important to him as well as to others. This illustrates one of the ways in which fundraising allows people to "brag by complaining." It must not, however, be assumed that the complaints heard were not sufficiently numerous or sincere as to be indicative of real trouble, actual and latent.

In Community Chest and other MOPS fundraising campaigns, the direct local social consequences may be usefully looked at as belonging in three categories:

(a) Those associated with participation in the *campaign organization*:

    (1) at the campaign *leadership* levels, there is the creation (or development and continuation) of social relations which may well combine activities significant both for the business and for the philanthropic careers[18] of the persons involved;

    (2) at the level of campaign *worker* or solicitor one consequence for many will be the creation of new friendships (or customers), the discovery of non-friendships, or the maintenance of old friendships and loyalties; for others, especially newcomers to the community, the most significant consequences may be "getting better acquainted" and becoming known.

(b) Those associated with participation as a person or as a corporation manager in the *aggregate of possible donors*: by becoming a contributor or refusing to give one thereby defines to that extent and in that narrow sense, how one stands or wishes to be esteemed as a person in the community or as a "corporate citizen" in the local setting.

(c) Those associated with *"stewardship,"* or, over a period of time, participation in both fundraising and contributing: the combining and continuing of these activities through time are what produce the contemporary "well-known philanthropic leader," the person about whom it is said early in his career, *"That* campaign made him!" and, later in his career, "He can make or break *this* campaign!"

Such social consequences as these become evident when the attitudes and behavior of people in a community can be carefully studied over a period of time, but we have found no short-cut measures or any easily gathered index of the "successes" or "failures" of Community Chests in these matters; without them we cannot compare cities simultaneously and otherwise fairly, in these respects.

Even harder to assess, and certainly more difficult to measure for comparative purposes, is a community's level of morale, or what might be called its civic *esprit de corps*. Yet it appears to be rather widely believed that a community benefits when its people are "good givers."

Much of the thinking about the moral or social consequences of Chest and other community-wide campaigns is traceable to the ancient dictum that "It is more blessed to give than to receive." In Chest campaigns, which can no longer, given their makeup, stress "charity," and which must instead emphasize that they are "selling services used by all," a common slogan is, "Everybody benefits when everybody gives." The notion is conveyed that not only should each bear a "fair share" of the costs of services which are doing some good for everyone, but that the campaign activity itself, in seeking "100 per cent participation" (gifts from "everybody") has some extra virtue in offering the "opportunity to give"—in helping to "meet the need of the giver to give." Giving time or money or both to the campaign is believed to benefit the individual: it makes him "feel good," it is alleged; it increases his self-respect, or even improves his chances for the after-life. And in turn, it is implied, the community is improved when a maximum number of its people recognize each other as "good givers" and develop a strong shared faith that this is "our way" of promoting some phase of the general welfare.

A kind of democratization of the philanthropic man seems to be proposed, as part of a struggle against the nineteenth-century or Victorian "Great Philanthropist" (a parallel to beating the dead horse of old-fashioned paternalism in industry). Others propose such democratization as a "necessity" in the present day, because "the large givers have disappeared." At the same time, however, Chest campaigns have acquired a new kind of "large giver," the great corporation; and a Community Chest may become just as "dependent" upon large corporate gifts as any charitable agency might have been on a small number of individuals in the days of the "Great Philanthropists."[19] But the significant difference is that the modern corporation wants (and has means to secure) more giving by individuals—not merely to spread the load, but also to assure management and stockholders that the amount of "popular support" *shows* how important supporting the cause is to the public relations of the "Corporation as a Citizen." The curious thing about this is the circularity of the process: in seeking to reassure themselves that "the cause is just" (something worthy of the support of the "Corporate Citizen"), managements get trapped into "advertising" it to employees and executives (including themselves) in order to increase the "demand" (measured by money contributions). They then find, over and over again, that they have created a perennial obligation with a tendency to grow—that they have, in short, placed upon themselves (and others, as well as the corporations) a requirement to "increase giving," if not each year, at least with great frequency.[20] The president of such a modern corporation will say, "We want our people to be good givers," and will justify "some pressure" to secure this result. When management and labor join forces, as in some United Fund cities, with the declared intent to "increase participation" (i.e., raise the percentage of those who are givers, often by a payroll deduction for contributions), the "voluntary" factor seems to become much less important, and it is difficult to believe that one could apply the same scale or measure of "community morale" to that kind of situation as one might use in the situation permitting maximum "freedom to give."

That is, we may conceive of community situations with regard to fund-raising as varying, from one place to another (or through time in the same locality), along a scale from "minimal voluntarism" (and maximum "pressure") to "maximum voluntarism" (and minimal "pressure"). Now one might, mistakenly, assume that high community morale would invariably appear at the "maximum voluntarism" end of the scale, and that it would become lower and lower in situations nearer the "minimum voluntarism" end. But that this is not necessarily the case is suggested by comparisons of military morale in units that vary in "discipline" all the way from attempts to "command by persuasion" to attempts to secure "absolute obedience" by more or less harsh measures. The latter, in one setting, may well produce an *esprit de corps* and "pride in the outfit" like that of a crack Marine regiment, while it may instead, in a different group, produce "goofing off." In community-wide fundraising, it may be that "pressure" which secures, but does not try to reach much beyond, say "65 per cent participation," will, in a particular community, help to develop "high" morale, whereas in another community "pressure" for "100 per cent," far from being destructive of morale, may be conducive to widely desired money results as well as human satisfactions.[21]

The "goodness of life" in any community, while on the whole brought about by the whole range of human efforts, may be influenced (improved or deteriorated) by the social consequences of Chest or other federated fundraising efforts, taken by themselves, but, as we have indicated, the tangible or measurable results are few. They seem to be limited to: (*a*) the "educational" effects of campaigns—results of the appeals reaching people through the mass media and results of such contacts as they may have with solicitors—which effects, for any one campaign, would have to be assessed in relation to the effects of the great number and variety of "educational" efforts to influence individuals not only as potential contributors but also as consumers of everything from corn-flakes to caskets (an almost insoluble research problem); (*b*) the knitting together of persons in relations in the business world and in the community generally through their participation in the campaign as leaders, workers (solicitors), or donors, and the honorific differentiation of a few through "stewardship"; (*c*) the results, apparent in the formation of attitudes and community morale, of "giving" (or refusing) in situations that vary according to the "pressure" and amount of "voluntarism" allowed—results which we cannot yet measure *in context* (as would be required for comparisons from one city to the other).

Perhaps the difficulties of analysis of this aspect of the social "success" or "failure" of Chest campaigns are not too important: people's lives are probably too complicated and their year-round activities too varied for Community Chest campaigns, whatever their social consequences, to do much harm to too many. Otherwise, surely, they would not have the degree even of passive acceptance that they do have in many American cities.

## THE "WELFARE" OF THE WELFARE COMMUNITY

Agencies deriving all or part of their contributions support from Chest allocations are staffed and directed by persons who of course recognize that the financial "success" of the Chest is vital for agency and professional "growth," if not sheer survival. But there is a kind of division of labor between these persons who compose the leadership of the "Welfare Community"[22] and those who engage in fundraising. The latter are in a kind of philanthropic activity which has its own "professionals," or at least "paid workers," and its own lay "specialists."

Persons whom we identified as in the leadership of welfare enterprises— both lay and professional—were, in 1955, rarely active in the leadership of the financial campaigns of the Chest. Whatever else they did in connection with fundraising was not conspicuous in the federation's campaign at least, though it might be important in securing "outside" contributions when needed or in enlisting volunteers for agency work. Some, of course, on our list may have done their "bit" in fundraising in years past, and have now gravitated to the "program" or fund-spending side of the welfare enterprise.[23]

Those in the fundraising campaign sometimes complain that "The agencies don't help enough with the campaign—they don't get their board members to do a job." When the contention that agency board members might play a larger part in fundraising is looked into, one finds that (a) many of them are women, and the Chest in recent years has very much played down both the residential solicitation and the general participation of women in any part of the fundraising enterprise; and (b) that it is no simple matter to locate the few members who have an influential position within some business firm which is not already "organized" for the Chest campaign through other personnel. For example, a board member of an agency might be quite willing and able to further the campaign from where he sits in the organization of a large enterprise, but the latter already usually has an established program for determining the corporate gift and for conducting in-plant fundraising for the Chest as well as other campaigns. It would be wasteful, and perhaps productive of annoyances and conflicts, for the Chest campaign organization to by-pass the regular channels just to make use of the agency board members scattered here and there in the business community. And, of course, if a board member is really in a "key position" to help with the campaign, the chances are great that this fact is already known to the Chest and that he has been or will be approached *on that ground*, and not just because he happens also to be an interested participant in a particular part of the welfare enterprise that is included within the Chest.

From observation of campaigns it was clear that the Chest's financial and social "success," while potentially contributory to the financial benefit of the agencies (as well as to the improvement of their repute) was not of sufficient concern to most of the welfare leaders to bring them actively out onto the "battlefield" of fundraising. Their role seemed more analogous to that of the captive maidens in the castle waiting for the knights to bring home the spoils of war. They were "interested in how the campaign is going." They seemed also to share the thinking of professionals in the Chest movement, to the effect that the community's gifts are like a "vote of confidence" in the work of the agencies. But even if they interpreted the amount raised as "not enough," they, as members of a federation, would not count this as a vote of "no confidence" or "less confidence than deserved"; nor would they be inclined clearly to place the blame on any one agency of the group, or even on all. Success, on this view, is a vote of confidence in the agencies; failure is a vote of no confidence in the Chest.[24]

Although the welfare leaders, including the professional social workers, want the Chest to succeed, and therefore must wish it to enjoy a favorable public acceptance as well as the greatest possible support from the donors, it is doubtful if they would welcome the active intervention of businessmen generally in the internal affairs of the agencies (especially if it took the form of "interference" due to "ignorance") or tolerate too close supervision and application of "business efficiency" logics (particularly if this disrupted "good casework practices"), even if these were thought necessary to the Chest's success. What is welcomed, of course, is the participation of business leaders in the vaguer and "larger" affairs of "community planning"—as in the meetings and special study groups of the Health and Welfare Council—or else in the petty detail and minutiae of "the business side." In and through the former—the "planning"—the businessmen and other lay leaders can develop a quite intimate and extensive awareness of the problems of the agencies, as they are seen by the professional welfare leaders, or, at least, of as much as the professionals think it discreet to reveal as the two groups come together at the Council level. Such "involvement" of lay persons undoubtedly means the development of considerable mutual sympathy and understanding between professional social workers and some members of the business community.

But the latter, in getting so involved, develop their roles in the welfare community: they become less and less "representative" of the business world and more and more the ambassadors to the uninvolved of the welfare cause or causes. It is even possible for a man to operate in three "worlds" almost simultaneously: as a leader in fundraising, as a proponent of a particular agency's cause, and as an active donor or even "leading donor" (and perhaps as "donor leader" or influencer of others, as well). What we have said, therefore, should not be interpreted as describing complete cleavages between fundraisers, donors, and welfare leaders, such that no person is found in two or more roles. Some people do have several roles, but this is much less common than "specialization" in one.

Professional social workers, and their warmest supporters among the leaders of the "Welfare Community," tend to view the Chest's financial "success" as a matter of how far it permits "growth." The expansion of program, or provision of valued "services" to many more persons, tends to be a matter of concern to those who "believe in" a given agency, of course. For one thing, it may mean a gain in reputation for the local agency within the profession nationally, which in turn may help attract desirable colleagues to work in that center. An ability to budget for inclusion of the agency in a national body, or for the membership dues and convention expenses of paid workers of the agencies, is thought to be helpful in making for "professional growth" and in contributing to the "improvement of standards" both nationally and locally.

Leaders of the Chest, and perhaps also those in the Health and Welfare Council, sometimes complain that certain people are "too agency-minded" —that they see only the problems and prospects of their own welfare enterprise. But the professional and paid workers of both Chest and Council have their career lines, too, and in the whole collectivity of the "Welfare Community" their aspirations join with those of others in such a way that the observer may well conclude that "growth" in the not-for-profit field has meanings for those in the field just as the corporate business world has meanings for those in that world.

When "planning" to create "the better and better community" proceeds along the lines of current "Welfare Community" thinking, especially in the present economic climate and in the social milieu developed in and through the great growth of modern corporations (perhaps the most generally admired institutions of our time), is it surprising that, in view of the really small part played by the Chest agencies in fundraising, many believe (and some fear) that in this field only "the sky is the limit"? The success of federated fundraising in diverting small percentages but sizeable amounts of the community's disposable income into these channels cannot be denied, even if, in Indianapolis, the Chest has not been "growing" at the same rate as all Chests and federations nationally. The latter fact must cause many dissatisfactions throughout the "Welfare Community," and its leaders have been steadily developing a much improved instrument for its more perfect organization, the Health and Welfare Council. At the same time, as we shall see in chapters 10 and 11, the donors have failed to develop consensus, or a sense of mission and an organization of their own to accomplish it, at least in Indianapolis. In fact, the lack of "success"—both financial and social—that has characterized the Indianapolis Community Chest is probably attributable to lack of organization among the donors, more than anything else. A few donors ask, "Where will it all end?" but the vast majority, judging from the Chest's money results, seem to prefer the uneasy state of affairs which is characterized by little social control, no great possibility so far of claiming the Chest as a civic asset, a great amount of "freedom to give" (or not), and a rather constricted or delayed "growth" of the *federated* welfare enterprise.[25]

# 8. Problems of Mass Fundraising: "Sharing the Burden"

THE MOPS FUNDRAISER, presuming he has a "marketable" cause at all, has two basic problems to which all others are probably subsidiary: (1) How much he can raise as the total gift (or should attempt as a goal), and (2) How he can distribute (or should distribute) this total gift-load or burden[1] over various potential donors. These are, in fact not independent judgments although they are commonly thought of in isolation from each other, and have here been separately treated initially. The fact that they are not independent—that the distribution of the gift-load affects the level of giving—is a discovery of first-order importance and one that would seem to have important implications for policy. Such considerations are the main object of this chapter.

The bearing of various easily ascertainable city characteristics on the percapita to be expected, and hence, of course, on the total gift, was the subject of chapter 6, and will not be re-examined here. That chapter suggested a method of arriving, for a given size-range of cities in a given region for a given year, at an estimate of what on the average might be expected. One of the variations, we hypothesized, that might make a difference from such an "on the average" performance, would be the manner of "distributing the gift-load."

## DISTRIBUTION OF LOAD

The fundraiser's problem would be complex or difficult enough if he had a situation of the following kind: (a) a known and agreed or accepted goal (say, $5,000); (b) a small group (say, five or six) (c) of people (d) of equal basic capacity to give or equal disposable income[2] and (e) under equal obligation to share equitably the known and agreed total gift-load. He might then ask himself or them (or both) an ethical question —"How *should* the load be shared?"—or a practical one—"What will changes in the 'sharing' method do to subsequent willingness to give?" He may find the answers that have an ethical recommendation in conflict with what seems practically desirable; or, on the contrary, he may find that what is recommended as good on one ground seems wise on the other—so that equity like honesty turns out to be the best policy.

But he does not have this simple situation. He has, on the contrary: (a) a goal that has not been discussed with, let alone agreed upon or actively accepted by, the great majority of the donors; (b) a vast mass, neither small in number nor in any sense a group: the potential donor-aggregate or public, which is (c) not composed solely of people, but is a mixed bag of institutions (corporations, partnerships, Foundations, etc.) and persons ("individual donors") who are (d) of unequal capacity to give, and (e) except by gratuitous assumption, under no known or arguable equality of obligation to do so.

If any policy[3] of gift-load distribution—except trial-and-error exploitation of every opportunity—is to be arrived at, these several differences between the relatively simple ideal problem and the complex reality have to be dealt with in some way, one at a time.

Every MOPS fundraising organization, no matter what its particular formula of internal distribution (i.e., between its contributors) tends to assume moral equality of obligation of all to share, according to their "capacity," in the gift-load. All men are evidently created equal not only before the law but before the collection-box or the "solicitor"—just as they are before the tax-collector.

This assumption would perhaps meet with no great difficulty, as far as social philosophy is concerned, if (or to the degree that) the collecting agency—the MOPS fundraising organization—could justifiably assume a position of being able to speak for all charitable enterprises, local, state, or national, taken together.[4] Under such circumstances, this super-united fund might confront corporation or individual with a single bill, like the bill for government expenditure; it would then be easier to argue that all citizens should share in this bill within their capacity.[5]

But when a number of MOPS fundraising organizations (as well as organizations that are non-mass, non-operational, non-periodic and/or non-secular) confront the potential givers unequally with their claims, the resultant schemes are indeed dubiously founded. If, for instance, an unusually modest[6] Chest were to set before the executives in its donor-aggregate the "reasonable" request that they provide it with 1 per cent of their gross income, and if, further, a variety of other organizations made, as they would be similarly entitled to do, similar flat-rate claims, and if, further —as seems to be the case—the number of organizations making claims on any potential donor, whether person or corporation, is roughly proportional to the income of that donor, then we might have a set of situations like that of Table XVIII. The actual effective rates for total charitable giving, for this hypothesized group of donors and donees, are shown in the last column. We are not suggesting that the rates shown in that column are "too high" in some absolute sense. Nor are we suggesting that the rates ought

TABLE XVIII

HYPOTHETICAL SCHEMA OF PHILANTHROPIC DEMANDS BY INCOME

| Donor | Income of donor | Chest 1% | Organization B ½ of 1% | Organization C 1% | Organization D ¼ of 1% | Total "claims" | Total rate |
|-------|----------------|----------|------------------------|-------------------|------------------------|----------------|-----------|
| A | $25,000 | $250 | $125 | $250 | $62.50 | $687.50 | 2.75% |
| B | 20,000 | 200 | 100 | 200 | — | 500.00 | 2.50 |
| C | 10,000 | 100 | 50 | — | — | 150.00 | 1.50 |
| D | 5,000 | 50 | — | — | — | 50.00 | 1.00 |

or ought not to be steeply "progressive"[7] as are the ones shown. We are only demonstrating the obvious possibility—and the probable actual tendency—i.e., that, even in a situation where all the fundraisers are agreed that a flat rate on income represents equity, their separate operations may, nevertheless, secure a quite different result.[8]

As unification of voluntary fundraising proceeds towards totality,[9] this objection loses its force. Meanwhile, we can only note but not deal with the specious, albeit "natural," methods by which each organization manages the difficulty. One way is by maintaining that its claims have an ethically prior status over those of all other organizations; the other is to take the position that it can at one and the same time declare to the donor what is right and equitable, speaking for "the community," and also count on his "protecting himself" as he would and should against any other suspect claim or argument. The latter position eventuates in some practical as well as ethical contradictions, but evidently not enough of them to make it widely untenable.

Further argument will have to disregard this difficulty and to proceed—as everyone, regardless of consistency, does in practice—as though the organization being discussed held in each case a monopoly of rightful fundraising claims.

### Distribution Problem One: The Division between Corporate and Non-Corporate Shares

Turning now to a problem that does have to be faced—in contrast to the one just discussed which can perhaps be blinked away—the MOPS fundraiser must come to terms with what may be called the "primary heterogeneity" of his donor-aggregate: the fact that it consists not only of individuals, but also of such "associations" or entities as corporations, partnerships, and Foundations.[10] A decision must be made as to how the total load is to be distributed between these two primary divisions. After we have examined what may be done about this primary division, we shall have to go on to examine alternatives for the divisions logically subsequent to it.

The facts of division are relatively simple. With those basic 41 cities (see chapter 6) for which we have data for 1954 and 1955, the picture is as shown in Table XIX.

TABLE XIX

CORPORATE DEPENDENCY, 1954 AND 1955

| Statistic | Year | | | |
|---|---|---|---|---|
| | 1954[a] | | 1955[b] | |
| | % of Total corporate | % of Total other | % of Total corporate | % of Total other |
| City most dependent on corporate gift | 54% | 46% | 54% | 46% |
| City least dependent on corporate gift | 30 | 70 | 29 | 71 |
| Range of dependency | 24 | 24 | 25 | 25 |
| Average dependency | 42 | 58 | 41 | 59 |
| Indianapolis | 48.6% | 51.4% | 51.0% | 49.0% |

[a]Number of cities: 19. Data on others not available.
[b]Number of cities: 16. Data on others not available.

The process by which these actualities are arrived at appears to be simple trial and error. No city known to us has a reasoned policy towards this basic division, either in terms of what ought to be the case or in terms of the consequences of various types of divisions.

Indeed it is difficult to see how a reasonable policy-in-principle could be arrived at, since it is by no means clear who really pays the corporate share in any case. It is obvious—indeed it is part of the "appeal"[11]—that a sizeable part of what is called the "corporate gift" (like a sizeable part of most large individual gifts) actually comes out of the general tax fund.[12]

If no policy-in-principle can be evolved for this primary division between the corporate and the non-corporate (or firm and non-firm) share of the gift on the ground that the ultimate payer cannot be located, we may be left with the purely practical or pragmatic problem as to what happens to giving generally under various degrees of "corporate dependency."[13] Unfortunately the evidence is not as clear as we would wish, partly because we came to the problem late and could not push analysis as far as we wanted, and partly because the data we needed for recent years were not readily available. What evidence we had, however, suggests that, on the average, there is a positive relation between degree of corporate dependency and degree of disappointingness of Chest performance,[14] i.e., the more dependent a city is on corporate gifts, the more likely it is, in general, to be a city performing below expectation, given the characteristics of that city.[15] Since this dependency may not be wholly independent of city size it may be worthwhile to examine Table XX showing average Chest performance in 1951 and corporate dependency in 1954. (The evidence should be taken as suggestive only, in view of the small number of cases.) When A is

## TABLE XX

CHEST PERFORMANCE BY SIZE OF PLACE AND CORPORATE DEPENDENCY

| Size of place | Chest Performance | | Difference in favor of low-dependency cities |
| --- | --- | --- | --- |
| | Corporate dependency *Low* for place size | Corporate dependency *High* for place size | |
| Under 175,000 | A (N=5) 18¢ per capita *above* expected value | B (N=4) 5¢ per capita *above* expected value | (N=9) 13¢ more per capita (above expectation) |
| 175,000 or over | C (N=5) 1¢ per capita *below* expected value | D (N=5) 6¢ per capita *below* expected value | (N=10) 5¢ more per capita |

compared with B, and C is compared with D, we have an indication, even after the interrelation of dependency and size of place has been allowed for, that *within these limits* high-dependency Chests tend to be more "disappointing" ones. Most crudely, for 1955, the relations shown in Table XXI obtain:

## TABLE XXI

CHEST PERFORMANCE AND CORPORATE DEPENDENCY (1951)

| Chest performance | Number of cases | Average corporate dependency, 1955 |
| --- | --- | --- |
| Up to or above par | 10 | 39.8% |
| Below par | 9 | 42.7% |

Certainly the evidence is inconclusive—though in the expected direction[16] —but it might well serve to call into question the wisdom of the announced policy of at least one[17] major corporation. Its self-adopted standard, now being widely promoted for general use, states essentially that the corporation will match in a given year (on a per employee or per employee's family basis) the area percapita for the previous year. If this became general policy for corporations—as is widely hoped—the long-run tendency would be for the corporate gift to become one-half of the total gift. In context with this suggestion, it should be noted that all the cities (except one that had a 45 per cent rate) that had dependency rates of 45 per cent or over in 1955 were "disappointing" (negatively deviant) cities in 1951.[18] The four cities that had dependency rates of 50 per cent or higher had an average deficiency from expectation of 31½¢ per capita, implying, of course, five-figure dollar deficiencies in total gift in each case.

As far as the evidence goes, then, it would suggest great caution in attempting to solve the Chest's problem by an effort to increase the corporate share of the yield—at least to any great extent beyond the present

41 to 42 per cent level and under present circumstances. It might well be, however, that the subject of the corporate share could become a matter for rational negotiation between management and other parties to the enterprise, and that, *if* it seemed desirable on political, ethical, or public-relations grounds, this share could be increased without the percapita actually falling below expectation. At present, however, no machinery for such rational negotiation is in sight.

*Distribution Problem Two: The Corporate Gift and "Trade Groups"*

Assuming that the goal is known and that the respective shares of the corporate and the non-corporate donorship are determined, the next problem is essentially that of sorting all corporations into homogeneous groups —homogeneous, that is, with regard to capacity or obligation to pay, or both.

If we also assume that there is adequate reason for any payment at all by corporations out of corporate funds,[19] and that all are equally obligated to pay according to "capacity," and further that any payment actually does come out of the potential profit-pool and hence out of the stockholders' pocket,[20] it might be thought that some simple function of corporate income would be a valid and acceptable standard. If this were the case, no further subclassification of corporations into "trade groups" would be necessary, since a simple demand for a fixed[21] fraction of income would apply to all alike.

But it is obvious to any business tyro that gross income has—from the stockholders' viewpoint, at least—no relation to capacity to pay. Two firms with identical gross incomes may have very different net incomes.

The next position has been historically to attempt to key the standard to "pre-tax net," i.e., net income before taxes.[22] But this standard—in a situation where the tax of one corporation may be 25 per cent of net and that of another may be virtually 47 per cent of net—seems to have no close relation to capacity-to-pay as measured by "disposable income" of the corporation; the simple example of Table XXII shows this. It is inherent in the suggested principle that one corporation should be paying at a higher rate than the

TABLE XXII

Hypothetical Example: Gift and Disposable Income

|  | Corporation 1 | Corporation 2 |
|---|---|---|
| Pre-tax net income | $20,000 | $200,000 |
| Gift asked | 300 | 3,000 |
| Post-gift net | $19,700 | $197,000 |
| Corporation tax (at relevant rates) | 4,925 | 87,090 |
| Disposable income after tax and gift | $14,775 | $109,910 |
| Gift as percentage of disposable income | 2.03% | 2.73% |

other on its post-gift, post-tax income—in the case of the illustration, at a rate 34 per cent higher.

Common sense might next suggest a retreat to a fraction of post-tax income,[23] and this would certainly remove whatever inequity is pointed to in the last paragraph. But here we run into a difficulty of another kind which tends to force discussion away from any measure that requires knowledge of any privately held firm's gross or pre-tax net or post-tax net income —let alone net-profit rate. The difficulty is (and it is enough to make impractical or impossible the operation of such a system) that in many cases these figures for individual firms are a secret whose protection is of considerable competitive consequence. Hence many firms (of those not compelled) would be unwilling either to disclose their income figures to the Chest (for checking conformity to "standard") or, *a fortiori,* to disclose these figures to general and public inspection, as a plain inference from their gift for anyone who wants to make one or two shrewd assumptions[24] and a single brief calculation.

Under these circumstances, the would-be standard-setter or load-distributor is driven back upon treating firms in groups, and then making suitable assumptions as to what constitutes an index of *relative* profit (and, hence, capacity to pay) within each group. For example, he may group all banks together, and decide or be advised that the number of dollars on deposit at each is a suitable rough index of the profit-share of that bank.

While this type of index may do well enough for a single trade group, it does not deal with the problem of equity among trade groups. To treat this problem still on rational principles the fundraiser would at least have to know the total net income or total profit of each group, in order to allocate the load equitably among them. This information is in general not available to him, either, and hence he is forced to the arbitrary assumption that what the various trade groups *have been* giving is an adequate index of what they should be giving. If he is willing to make this leap[25] he next has (1) the problem of grouping his firms, then (2) the problem of selecting a unit-of-comparative-profitability for each group, and then (3) that of determining standards for these units.

Given his orientation—that classification must be in conformity with ability-to-pay-per-unit—all that he has to do is to divide his firms into groups within each of which relative profits are roughly keyed to certain units, for example, number of employees in a factory, number of rooms in a hotel, etc. This division might result in like-sized firms being put together in broad classes, or in wholesale firms being grouped regardless of business by volume-of-business categories, or in any one of a number of other classifications.

But experience shows that the fundraiser here encounters another desire: he wishes firms that are classified together to be "naturally" in a competitive relation to one another so that this "competitiveness" can be suitably exploited in the campaign—to the believed advantage of the MOPS fund-raising organization.[26] At this point, there is a tendency to confuse economic realities with social and psychological ones. It is probably, and up to a point, an economic reality that firms with a common or like product are in economic competition with one another, and hence may be somewhat more likely to have the similar-profit-per-unit characteristic. So in attempting classification by capacity-to-pay, classification into trade groups has something to be said for it.[27] But if it is hoped to make use either of competitive relations in good works or of a common desire to preserve shared repute, the appropriate or most effective unit of classification is by no means necessarily the trade group. A given firm—say, a large publishing house—may think that it is "like" and, justly, therefore, only comparable with ( $a$ ) other, similar top-drawer publishers elsewhere, or ( $b$ ) other firms in the same city with a Dun and Bradstreet rating of AA A1, or ( $c$ ) other major companies in the same city with all stock privately held, or ( $d$ ) all companies in the same city, regardless of product or size, whose active executives are and have been "old family" (birth élite) for generations. The group, whichever it is, with which it thus "*identifies*" (in sociological terms, its "reference group")[28] is the psychologically and socially relevant group as far as competitive or co-operative (mutually reinforcing) behavior is concerned, and the only one upon which the fundraiser can hope to implement his ambitions to use social relations to secure his fundraising aims. Since, however, the distinction between trade group and group of identification has historically escaped him, since he generally lacks the research machinery to discover what these reference groups are, since he wants the capacity-to-pay-by-unit to be a credible message,[29] and since, moreover, he wishes simultaneously to standardize for obligation-to-pay, he is driven back upon trade groups[30] as the "homogeneous" groups and, generally, upon employees as the unit-of-accountability.

## Distribution Problem Three: The Unit of Accountability

The last point is perhaps peculiarly important, though, as usual, it is somewhat obscured by a host of "practical" compromises to take into account competing considerations. If, for a given trade group, a suitable measure of the capacity-to-pay of any one corporation is the number of employees it has (relative to the whole trade group's employment figure), then it is probably also reasonable to assume that the same figure is a measure of "obligation to pay." It needs only a limited number of assumptions,[31] none of them too incredible, to conclude that a firm's "fair share" of the cost of "voluntary services" for its employees is roughly proportionate to the number of those employees. If so, the per employee measure is doubly suitable.

This happy issue—the conjunction of a measure of capacity to pay with a measure of obligation to pay in a single unit of measurement, the employee

—is somewhat clouded when the argument is extended beyond the boundary of any one trade group. If the obligation-to-pay aspect is kept focal, it is probably a reasonable inference that all trade groups should then have equal standards per employee. If the capacity-to-pay view is carefully maintained, one might expect, since it is obvious that different trades (e.g., banking versus small-machine assembly) have different profit-rates per employee, that different standards of giving per employee would be applicable.

As usual, an attempt is made to avoid the dilemma by arguing both ways at once, hopefully separately to different groups.[32] For some, especially firms with a low ratio of profits to employees, the argument runs: *your fair share is based on utilization of services* which is roughly proportionate to number of employees, so give on this basis if you wish to carry your share. For others, especially those with a high ratio of profits to employees (and, moreover, frequently, a low utilization of services per employee) the argument runs: *your fair share is based on capacity to pay,* so give on this basis if you wish to carry your share. If the argument were baldly stated it would have to say: *each firm's "fair share" is whichever is the greater of (a) a charge per employee* for services presumptively consumed, *or (b) a charge per dollar* of profits regardless of consumption.[33] The argument cannot, of course, be so baldly put, and the tendency is to abandon the obligation-to-pay-because-of-utilization part of it, except where it is especially convenient or convincing, and to use the employee as a simple unit-of-profitability index within trade groups. If employees are to be the "accounting unit" but equal shares of profits are the intended real aim, we should simply expect different trade groups to have radically different per-employee standards.[34]

But again this simplicity is abandoned, in practice, partly on public-relations, partly on technical grounds. On public-relations grounds it evidently seems unwise to publish radically different per-employee standards: it is felt that to do so would serve to call into question and severely shake the equality-of-obligation-because-of-utilization argument, which is still used as public campaign plea in certain quarters, even after it has been abandoned as a suitable basis for private or in-group thought. Technically, moreover, there are cases where it can be argued that relative earnings are more nearly keyed to some other unit than to number of employees, for example, to amount of deposits, in the case of banks.[35]

The upshot is that for most purposes the fundraiser chooses employees as the unit of accountability; and, for others, such miscellania as volume of bank deposits, number of hotel rooms, volume of sales.

He now has the problems of setting standards per unit, and—if it is not a wholly new campaign—of deciding how to get from present practices of giving via a moving standard to the standard he wants finally to achieve. Discussion of these two problems will entail some reporting on present practices of giving, and of efforts to set "standards." We must leave these two matters, however, until we have discussed the other crucial decisions in the non-corporate segment of the donor-aggregate.

### Distribution Problem Four: Division of Non-Corporate Share between Corporately Organized and "Other"

What is not to be secured from the corporation must be secured from "individuals," and the appeal for their subscription may be made to them: (a) at their place of work, and in virtue of their membership as workers[36] (i) in a firm, and (ii) where relevant, in a labor union, or (b) at their place of residence, in virtue of their location in a neighborhood, and in appeal to them directly in their capacity as citizens.[37]

Either form of appeal—except for those rare citizens who have no one in the immediate family who has a job or place of work—would exhaust the universe of potential non-corporate givers, if the convention is accepted as valid that workers give or ought to give on behalf of their entire family. Logically, then, these seem to provide for alternative forms of social organization for a campaign.

But, again, no clear resolution is made between these forms of organization, and both are employed, the vast bulk of the non-corporate gift coming from the corporately organized sector[38] as Charts 20 and 21 show. A number of arguments—mostly of considerable dubiety—support the retention of some form of Residential soliciting organization, although many professionals and laymen in the Chest movement[39] wish to see it dropped altogether. The arguments in its favor aver that it is good public relations;[40] that it is "not too costly";[41] that it suitably employs "the women";[42] that it is good for a mop-up operation, i.e., it "catches" those who escape the place-of-work dragnet;[43] and that it is a source of additional money.[44]

In any case, the problem of dividing the load between the corporately organized and the "other" sector does not furnish any real theoretical difficulty for the fundraiser, since, for the Chest at least, the "other," the Residential, is a residual or "velvet" or "gravy" or "so much extra" operation. The problem is really only the practical one of how to reach people, but it should be recognized that giving at work on behalf of the whole family and giving at home for the same purpose on the same behalf are mutually exclusive principles.[45] Whatever small practical advantage Residential solicitation may have, for the Chest, is certainly bought at the price of considerable blurring of its main message.

### Distribution Problem Five: Non-Corporate Gift; Corporately Organized Sector; Division between Executives and Employees

A division in load that seems to have grown up historically within the corporately organized, personal giving sector is based on a distinction between "executives" and "employees."

We have not been able to discover the origin or object or utility of the distinction, although we know its meaning and the kind of differential treatment it permits—which may or may not be (or have been) its purpose. In the first place, as to meaning, an "executive" is not, for this purpose, someone who occupies a given position in industry or business, or one who discharges a given function: it is simply someone who earns a salary in excess of some stated amount,[46] in some regular employment other than self-employment. This term thus brings together under one rubric those who earn alike rather than those who necessarily live alike, think alike, or identify with one another.[47] Whatever might be gained in classifying together persons who think of themselves as alike in some vital and distinctive way is thus probably and for the most part, lost in an essentially arbitrary, socially irrelevant, and merely economic distinction.[48]

What the distinction makes possible is differential treatment, with regard to type of pressure and to standards, of those who make a given salary —$6,000 or more—and those who make less. As we shall see in the discussion of standards—to follow below—it simply divides all wage- and salary-earners into those who are invited to tax themselves on their earnings at a flat rate and those who are invited to tax themselves at a progressive one.[49]

Since there seems to be no good reason for establishing such a distinction —or, rather, since the distinction is primarily economic and related to the strategy of pressure—and since it would seem logically clearer to treat together all wage- and salary-earners (with a subsequent determination of their share by income-categories) we shall treat no further of the executive-employee distinction as a theoretical problem here.

We are left now with two problems: (1) The discussion, with regard to the corporate gift, of standards for firms within trade groups, and (2) The discussion of standards for persons, corporately organized, who are in receipt of salaries or wages. To these problems we shall return after an examination of the existing state of affairs, a way of analysing those affairs, and the currently suggested standards for corporations and persons.

## The Existing State of Affairs

A "gift list"—a list of all the gifts received in any campaign, or any subdivision of a campaign—may be looked upon as a *report* upon a segment of human behavior: a response to the provocative (or, hopefully, evocative) behavior of the MOPS fundraisers. It may, moreover, be looked upon as a kind of "natural" behavior, in so far as deliberate systematic thought has not been given to its control or alteration.[50]

The first question that arises is, what can we learn from such a gift list? Do different gift lists have anything in common, besides their necessary reference to money? How may one gift list be compared with another so as to bring out their likenesses and differences? What are the consequences of the differences?

It is obvious, of course, that every gift list has a stated number of gifts, and it has or can be made to have a total, and therefore an "average," gift. For reasons which will appear later, this average is not a very meaningful statistic.[51]

One obvious way of attempting to make sense of a gift list is to arrange the gifts in order of size, commonly with the largest first. The gifts may now be numbered in order from the largest down.[52] What can we do with such a ranked gift list that could not be done with an unranked one? We have the number of givers and the total as before, and the "average" if we still wish to use it. But we can also see, or compute, another statistic of importance—the median;[53] and we can also readily see what is the leading (or largest) and the trailing (or lowest) gift. An imaginary example (Table

TABLE XXIII

Hypothetical Example A:
Ordered Gift List

| Rank of gift | Amount of gift |
| --- | --- |
| 1 | $25,000 |
| 2 | 12,000 |
| 3 | 8,000 |
| 4 | 6,000 |
| 5 | 5,000 |
| 6 | 4,000 |
| 7 | 3,500 |
| 8 | 3,000 |
| 9 | 2,500 |
| Total | $69,000 |

XXIII) may illustrate. The number of givers is nine; the total gift $69,000; the "average" gift is $7,667; the lead-gift is $25,000; the trail-gift is $2,500; the median gift is $5,000. It will be noted that the median gift differs from the "average" by $2,667, i.e., the average is over 50 per cent greater than the median. This last fact draws attention to the *disequality*[54] which we always find, in point of fact, in any gift list. Here is one reason why it is so difficult to compare one gift list with another: even with identical average gifts, their impact on the donor—and their security or precariousness from the fundraiser's point of view—may be very different. As an illustration, consider Table XXIV with the same average gift (and total) as the last example. This list has the same number of givers (9) as the preceding example, the same total ($69,000) and average ($7,667); but a different lead-gift ($9,667), trail-gift ($5,667) and median ($7,667). Moreover, the median is the same as the average.

But it is not enough to know the median gift and how it differs from the average. We need, if possible, something that will tell us more about the whole list. Is there any regularity in such lists? Fortunately, the answer appears to be "Yes."

TABLE XXIV

Hypothetical Example B:
Ordered Gift List

| Rank of gift | Amount of gift |
|:---:|:---:|
| 1 | $ 9,667 |
| 2 | 9,166 |
| 3 | 8,667 |
| 4 | 8,166 |
| 5 | 7,667 |
| 6 | 7,166 |
| 7 | 6,667 |
| 8 | 6,167 |
| 9 | 5,667 |
| Total | $69,000 |

Let us take some gift lists we actually found on our arrival in Indianapolis, arrange them in order of size, and then—to visualize what they are like—transfer the results to graph paper. Some such lists are pictorialized on Charts 22-32. In every graph, each successive column of squares represents a gift (or a percapita) and the height of the column represents the dollar value of the gift. It is obvious that every one of the graphs presents, when slightly smoothed, a peculiar "J" shape,[55] like that of the accompanying diagram.

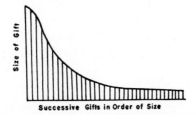

Size of Gift

Successive  Gifts in Order of Size

It does not seem to matter[56] what list we graph—any one of several Chest lists (firms with CIO unions, firms with AFL unions, corporate gifts or executive gifts, total gifts or gifts per employee); or whether we turn from the Chest altogether (say, to the Jewish Welfare Federation);[57] or whether we graph gifts of individuals, or mixed lists of companies, individuals, and partnerships. Every curve is characterized by a similar "steep" fall on the left, indicating great proportionate disequality between the leading givers, and a similar gently sloping "tail" on the right, indicating a large number of trailing givers with relatively small differences between them.

Not all the curves have the same average "slope" (representing the amount of disequality between gifts)—and these differences in disequality, as we shall later discover, have other important consequences for giving. Before we can demonstrate what these relations are, we must find some way of characterizing the disequality in a curve or a gift list. We shall attempt to do this in the next section, and if the description, made as simple as we know how, taxes the reader's patience, at least, in this case, he is being taxed with his knowledge and, hopefully, for his information.

### More Precise Tools for Analysis of the Gift-Curve

In order to get adequate analytic tools to deal with disequality in gift-giving we shall have to refine and render more precise some intuitive notions.[58]

It may help to take, first, another simple hypothetical situation: a situation, let us say, in which five people want to get together to raise some small sum for some good cause. It is clear that they must first settle how much is to be raised, and next how much each is going to put in to make up the agreed sum. Let us imagine four different possibilities in which the goal is either $5,000 or $10,000 and there are two ways to share in raising either share. Four of the possibilities are laid out in Table XXV. It

TABLE XXV

HYPOTHETICAL EXAMPLE:
RAISING TWO DIFFERENT GOALS BY TWO DIFFERENT METHODS

| Donor[a] | Rank by gift size | Goal A: $5,000 | | Goal B: $10,000 | |
|---|---|---|---|---|---|
| | | Method 1 | Method 2 | Method 1 | Method 2 |
| a | b | c | d | e | f |
| Brown | 1 | $2,200 | $3,400 | $4,400 | $6,800 |
| Smith | 2 | 1,100 | 860 | 2,200 | 1,720 |
| Jones | 3 | 720 | 380 | 1,440 | 760 |
| Robinson | 4 | 540 | 220 | 1,080 | 440 |
| Johnson | 5 | 440 | 140 | 880 | 280 |
| Total | — | $5,000 | $5,000 | $10,000 | $10,000 |

[a]Any resemblance in name to any real donor is purely coincidental: the figures do, however, resemble actual giving behavior.

will be seen at once when the gifts are laid out in order of size that they are by no means equal.[59] It will also be seen that the gifts in column e (Goal B, Method 1) are just twice those in column c (Goal A, Method 1); and the gifts in column f are just twice those in column d—in both cases because Goal B is twice Goal A.

The gifts may look as though they were otherwise quite unsystematic, but this is not the case, as Chart 33 indicates. Along the bottom of the chart are the "ranks"[60] of the gifts. Up the side are the sizes of the gifts under each scheme. The gifts that belong together in any one scheme have been joined by a line so that they may easily be seen together. Line A 1 corresponds to Goal A ($5,000) and Method 1 in the table, and so for the other three lines.

From the chart a number of interesting things may be read off: (1) The four gift-schemes are almost perfectly systematic, else they would not appear as straight lines on any paper; (2) schemes A 1 and A 2 are at a lower level (as judged, in this example, by where they cross the left-hand margin) than B 1 or B 2—corresponding to the lower goal for A than for B; (3) Lines A 1 and B 1 are parallel (have the same slope), reflecting the same amount of disequality, i.e., Method 1 of distributing the gift-load which is common to both. Lines A 2 and B 2 are also parallel to each other, reflecting the disequality that they have in common.

Since Chart 33 shows that the gift-schemes are systematic, we ought to be able to discover what the system is in each case. Either from the chart (or from foreknowledge, since we made up this illustration) we can say that if we let $R$ stand for the rank of any given gift, and let $G$ stand for the gift itself, the following formulae will give us (to a very close approximation) all the gifts in each system:

$$A\ 1 \qquad G_R = \$2200\ R^{-1} \text{ or } \frac{\$2200}{R}$$

$$A\ 2 \qquad G_R = \$3400\ R^{-2} \text{ or } \frac{\$3400}{R^2}$$

$$B\ 1 \qquad G_R = \$4400\ R^{-1} \text{ or } \frac{\$4400}{R}$$

$$B\ 2 \qquad G_R = \$6800\ R^{-2} \text{ or } \frac{\$6800}{R^2}$$

It will be seen that schemes A 1 and B 1, which have the same disequality, have the same index (or exponent) following $R$ (i.e., $-1$). And the same is true for schemes A 2 and B 2. These indexes (or exponents) correspond to the slopes of the lines on the chart. It will also be seen that schemes A 1 and A 2, which have a lower goal, have lower multipliers ($2200 and $3400) than have schemes B 1 and B 2 ($4400 and $6800) with their higher goals. These multipliers correspond (in this example) to the height of the lines on the chart or to the "level of giving."

There is still one thing wrong with the formulae as written: while they show that both of the B lines are higher than either of the A lines, they do not show that the A lines represent campaigns of the same size, and that the B lines do likewise. In order to show this vital information we may rewrite the formulae, the "descriptions," of the four campaigns in the following "standardized" form:

| A 1 | $G_R =$ | $5,000 $R^{-1}$ (.44) |
| A 2 | $G_R =$ | $5,000 $R^{-2}$ (.68) |
| B 1 | $G_R =$ | $10,000 $R^{-1}$ (.44) |
| B 2 | $G_R =$ | $10,000 $R^{-2}$ (.68) |

We have now reduced each gift list to a formula that has three vital elements:[61]

Item 1: The "scope" of the campaign, or the goal, or the level of giving—the "$5,000" of scheme A 1, for instance;

Item 2: A measure of disequality in sharing the gift-load: the "index" following the R (the $^{-1}$ of scheme A 1)—the higher the index,[62] the greater the disequality;

Item 3: The "lead-load" (the ".44" of scheme A 1): a measure of the proportion of the gift given (or to be given) by the leading giver.

It will now be evident that what may have looked like playing mathematical games has a definite purpose. What can be done with the four imaginary situations we have created here can be profitably[63] done with every gift list we have so far examined, or indeed, with such "subsections" as "the list of 'individual' total gifts to the Indianapolis Community Chest in 1953" or the list of "per employee corporate gifts from Banks to the 'Blanksburg' Red Cross for 1952."

This means that without much loss of information a long list of gifts (say 500 or 1,000) can be reduced to a formula (of the form $G_R = a'R'c$ with three variables:

$a'$: a measure of the "scope" of the list or the "level of giving"—or, as in the illustration, size of campaign;

$b$: a measure of disequality;

$c$: a measure of lead-load—or concentration on one giver.

We are thus in a position to reduce lists of gifts from different cities, or lists for different parts of a single campaign, or lists for a variety of organizations in one city to an economical form that permits proper comparison in three important respects.[64] What is thus presented also permits fund-raising policy to be founded in terms of three important determinations: the amount to be secured, the disequality to be aimed at or tolerated,[65] and the amount to be asked of the leading giver.[66]

To go back, for instance, to our previous hypothetical illustration (Table XXV); suppose it is wished to raise 20 per cent more than the total of scheme A 1 (i.e., to raise $6,000) but that the policy-making givers are only willing to "go along" if disequality can be reduced "substantially" (say, to about half its present level). Let us call the new scheme C 3, and compare it with scheme A 1. The comparison (Table XXVI) shows obviously

## TABLE XXVI

### Hypothetical Example:
### Scheme to Increase Total Gift While Reducing Disequality

| Donor number | Scheme A 1 | Scheme C 3 | Percentage increase required |
|---|---|---|---|
| 1 | $2,200 | $1,860 | — 15% |
| 2 | 1,100 | 1,315 | + 20% |
| 3 | 720 | 1,070 | + 49% |
| 4 | 540 | 925 | + 71% |
| 5 | 440 | 830 | + 89% |
| Total | $5,000 | $6,000 | 20% |

that A 1 and C 3 are very different schemes, and their differences may be summed up in their formulae:

$$\text{A 1} \qquad G_R = \$5000 \ R^{-1} \ (.44)$$
$$\text{C 3} \qquad G_R = \$6000 \ R^{-\frac{1}{2}} \ (.31)$$

It is clear that:

(1) Scheme C 3 has the higher level of "giving" ($6,000 vs. $5,000);

(2) Scheme C 3 has lower disequality or greater equality (½ vs. 1);

(3) Scheme C 3 is less dependent on the leading giver (31 per cent vs. 44 per cent).[67]

To sum up this section, we have here, then, both a tool for the scientific analysis of existing gift-systems and a tool that, *before a campaign,* would permit one to know the actual sizes of gifts required if the campaign were to meet a given goal and if a known or agreed level of disequality only were to be tolerated.[68]

### Disequality and "Equity"

Few people, however, take the position that "disequality" in raw gifts is of itself a good or a bad thing. What they are concerned about—if they are concerned—is the existence of undesired or undesirable disequality-in-relation-to-capacity-to-pay (and/or disequality-in-relation-to-obligation), i.e., with what they feel to be "inequity."

Disequality must therefore be treated in context with some measure of capacity or potential, and this may be done in either or both of two ways: (1) by applying the kind of measure of disequality[69] we have developed only to homogeneous groups having about the same capacity (and obligation)[70] to pay; (2) by applying these same measures of disequality not to the raw gifts but to the gifts-per-unit-of-capacity-to-pay, e.g., the gifts-per-thousand-dollars-of-income, or the gifts-per-thousand-dollars-of-profit, or the gifts-per-employee (if each employee in an industry represent a rough measure of paying capacity and/or obligation). In some cases, one method of making the gifts morally comparable will recommend itself, in other cases the other method, sometimes both.

To illustrate the first method (sorting people into homogeneous groups and then analysing), we may turn again to our hypothetical example (Scheme A 1 from Table XXV).

(1) If the five donors all had equal incomes (and equal obligation to pay in proportion to income) then the gifts, as listed, show not only disequality but inequity.

(2) If, on the other hand, we suppose that for some reason (e.g., that one group represents family men with other heavy obligations and the other group represents bachelors with none) Brown and Smith as a group are not comparable with Jones, Robinson, and Johnson as a group, then we ought to analyse these two groups[71] separately, with the following results:

For Brown and Smith:            $G_R = \$3300\ R^{-1}$   (.67)
For Jones, Robinson and Johnson: $G_R = \$1700\ R^{-.45}$ (.42)

If we also suppose that Brown and Smith as a group have twice the capacity and obligation to pay (because they have no families) that Jones, Robinson, and Johnson have, and if moreover the capacity of each (within his group) is equal, then we could safely say, perhaps, that *as groups* they were performing about right ($3300 *vs.* $1700) but that in distributing the shares to individuals within the groups the sharing was about twice as inequitable among the non-family men as compared with the family men.

If, however, we know the facts, we may use the second method, and try to take income directly into account. Let us develop the example further by supplying each (imaginary) donor with an (imaginary) income, as shown in Table XXVII.

### TABLE XXVII

HYPOTHETICAL GIFT-PATTERNS FOR TWO GOALS AND
TWO METHODS: BY DONOR'S INCOME

| Donor | Income | Gift under scheme | | | |
| | | A 1 | A 2 | B 1 | B 2 |
|---|---|---|---|---|---|
| Brown | $46,900 | $2,200 | $3,400 | $4,400 | $6,800 |
| Smith | 33,200 | 1,100 | 860 | 2,200 | 1,720 |
| Jones | 26,800 | 720 | 380 | 1,440 | 760 |
| Robinson | 23,200 | 540 | 220 | 1,080 | 440 |
| Johnson | 21,000 | 440 | 140 | 880 | 280 |
| Total | $151,100 | $5,000 | $5,000 | $10,000 | $10,000 |

If we express the four gift-schemes in relation to the incomes of the donors,[72] we get the following four very simple formulae (where $I'$ is the income in tens of thousands of dollars).

$$
\begin{aligned}
\text{A 1} \quad & G = \$5,000\ (I')^2 \quad (.02) \\
\text{A 2} \quad & G = \$5,000\ (I')^4 \quad (.0014) \\
\text{B 1} \quad & G = \$10,000\ (I')^2 \quad (.02) \\
\text{B 2} \quad & G = \$10,000\ (I')^4 \quad (.0014)
\end{aligned}
$$

The formula, like that for ranks, is in three parts which may be written:

$$G = a(I')^b c$$

where

G is the gift from a person of a given income;

$a$ is an index of level of giving, i.e., it is the amount raised in the campaign;

$I'$ is the income in suitable units, say, thousands or tens of thousands;

$b$ is a measure of disequality, as before;

$c$ is a measure of "unit load," i.e., the fraction or proportion of the total goal to be expected from a person having unit income (e.g., $10,000 in our illustration).

It will be clear from the formulae that:

(1) Scheme A 2 shows much more disequality than scheme A 1; and similarly with scheme B 2 as compared with scheme B 1. Scheme A 2 also shows a much lower percentage of total take (0.14 per cent) to be expected from a $10,000-a-year man, than does scheme A 1 (2.00 per cent).

(2) Scheme A 1 differs from Scheme B 1 only in level and not in disequality; and so also for Schemes A 2 and B 2.

(3) If "equity" is represented by a gift proportional to income[73]

(a) All four schemes are grossly inequitable,[74]

(b) Schemes A 2 and B 2 are fantastically so.

We now have the tools to deal with the problems at hand, and it is time to return to concrete Chest problems. We can, by their means, with a sufficient degree of accuracy for most practical purposes,[75] resolve any set of gifts or any set of "standards" (i.e., goals for gifts) into three[76] components: (1) an index of gift-total or goal, i.e., *level* of giving; (2) an index of disequality or, if fairness is measured by equality (under appropriate circumstances), a measure of inequity, and (3) a measure of *dependence* on the leading giver or on the "standard" giver (the giver who has "unit" income).

The critical question for consideration now is the *effect* of disequality in giving on level of giving.

### Disequality and Evaluated Level of Giving

The reader will have been adequately forewarned that we cannot use crude level of giving (the first figure in the preceding formulae) as an index of satisfactoriness of performance: as the preceding chapter has shown, the criterion adopted in this study for judging level of performance is percapita-in-relation-to-opportunity, i.e., deviation from the predicted percapita based on city characteristics for each city. We have called this deviation, if negative, the "degree of disappointingness."

We, therefore, now wish to assess disequality in relation to disappointingness of Chest performance. It would be desirable to reduce comparable gift lists for different cities, or for different organizations in the same city, to formula terms and then compare in detail the disappointingness or otherwise of the results. This we have not been able to do.[77] We have evidence enough, however, we believe, to render plausible the general hypothesis that the greater the disequality (or, if appropriate, the inequity) the lower is likely to be the level of giving in relation to potentiality—i.e., the greater the disequality, the greater the disappointingness. The evidence, though not as conclusive as we could wish, shows that a disappointing Chest performance is related to (a) dependence on the corporate gift; (b) disequality in the total gift list; and (c) disequality of executive gifts. We shall treat each of these briefly, in turn.

*Dependence on corporate gift.* The most fundamental disequality,[78] perhaps, lies in the division of the total load between the corporate and noncorporate gift. We have already established the point, earlier in the chapter, that the greater this dependence on the corporate gift is, the greater in general the disappointingness of the corresponding Chest.

*Disequality in the total gift list.* Data on the gift-systems of the various Community Chests are available only in the crudest form,[79] indeed in so crude a form that, for the most part, refined tools of analysis, as developed, are inapplicable to them. Even so, however, the evidence here—for the city's whole gift-structure—seems to confirm the hypothesis that the greater the disequality or "concentration" the more disappointing the performance.

For this purpose, we compared the deviation from expected performance (the disappointingness) of the Chest in each city[80] with each of two measures:[81] (i) An *index of disequality* (or concentration) based upon the exponent (b) developed in the section on analysis by ranks; (ii) An *index of concentration* (or disequality) based upon the percentage of the total take contributed by the ten leading givers.[82] The correlation between the *index of disequality* and the measure of disappointingness turns out to be .38, which points to an underlying positive relationship;[83] and the correlation between the *index of concentration* and the measure of disappointingness turns out to be .55, which is also significant.[84] The data support the view that concentration and disappointingness go together.

*Giving by executives.* Except in the case of Indianapolis,[85] we did not have detailed reports on giving by executives. But for a number of cities we had the next best thing, a record of "standards" of such giving. These standards all (except in the case of Boston and Indianapolis)[86] bear a systematic relation to the actual behavior. The relation is guaranteed by the process by which the standards are established. The process is the following. The data, from co-operating firms, are assembled and sorted by income categories. The gifts within each income category are then ordered by rank. From the ordered pile in each city, the "most generous fifth" and the "second most generous fifth" of the givers are separated. The mean gift of this "most generous fifth" (and of the "second most generous fifth") is then computed for each income category. With or without a little "smoothing," these averages or means are then published as a "standard"—to which it is recommended that executives adhere, and for which senior executives are encouraged to press junior ones.

It is not difficult to demonstrate[87] that the disequality in the standards will parallel the disequality in the actual giving, although the giving will, of course, be well *below* the level of (but not more unequal than) the former. So the standards may be used as indexes to disequality in the actual giving.

With this in mind, the standards may be represented as in Chart 34: in a series of lines drawn at various degrees of steepness (all steeper, i.e., more "progressive" than the income tax structure) and at different "levels" on the paper, i.e., reflecting different degrees of generosity. The important question is, "What is the relation between the different degrees of progressiveness (or disequality in rate) and the different degrees of 'generosity'?" In order to examine this question we had to convert the formulae for the several cities to a standardized form,[88] as shown in Table XXVIII. The

TABLE XXVIII

ACTUAL EXECUTIVE GIVING "STANDARDS" FOR SELECTED CITIES:
FORMULAE IN STANDARDIZED FORM

| Executive giving plan | Formula | | |
|---|---|---|---|
| | a | b | c |
| Chicago | $G = .0085$ | $I^{1.98}$ | $(\$14,450)^{-.98}$ |
| Cincinnati | $G = .0125$ | $I^{1.72}$ | $(\$14,450)^{-.72}$ |
| Cleveland | $G = .0156$ | $I^{1.54}$ | $(\$14,450)^{-.54}$ |
| Indianapolis | $G = .0105$ | $I^{1.78}$ | $(\$14,450)^{-.78}$ |
| Lowell, Mass. | $G = .0147$ | $I^{1.83}$ | $(\$14,450)^{-.83}$ |
| Milwaukee | $G = .0113$ | $I^{1.80}$ | $(\$14,450)^{-.80}$ |
| Philadelphia | $G = .0144$ | $I^{1.94}$ | $(\$14,450)^{-.94}$ |

general reader may neglect the element of the equation under *c*, and concentrate his attention on the elements under *a* and *b*. The first element, *a*, is a standardized measure of the "generosity" implied in the scheme; the element under *b* is a measure of "progressiveness" or disequality, or (if gift *should* be a fixed or decreasing fraction of income) of inequity.

The evidence suggests clearly the greater the progressiveness the lower the generosity.[89]

As far as the relation between the index of disequality (*b*) and the measure of disappointingness is concerned, our data are still more limited, since only four of the cities whose standards for executives are available are also in our list of forty-one. Slight as it is, however, the evidence (see Table XXIX) points in the same direction—disappointingness and disequality go hand in hand.

### TABLE XXIX

DISEQUALITY AND DISAPPOINTINGNESS FOR FOUR CHESTS

| Direction of deviation | City | Deviation (per capita) | Disequality index |
|---|---|---|---|
| Positive | Cincinnati | + 36¢ | 1.72 |
| | Cleveland | + 30¢ | 1.54 |
| Negative | Milwaukee | −.42¢ | 1.80 |
| | Indianapolis | −.53¢ | 1.78 |

The conclusion of this sub-section must be that, as far as the evidence goes, disequality in the giving of executives and both disappointingness[90] of the city and lack of generosity among the executives themselves tend to go hand in hand.

The conclusion of the whole section must be to the effect that disequality in general, as far as the evidence goes, makes for disappointingness in general. The implication would seem to be that what may readily recommend itself on ethical grounds—the search for adequate and equitable standards of giving—seems demonstrably to recommend itself on pragmatic ones, i.e., it makes for "better" (higher) giving in relation to resource.[91] To the degree that this is so, it becomes important to bring under critical review the proposed standards, and, where possible, to suggest for consideration "better" ones if the existing ones seem as inadequate to the policy-makers as they do to the researchers.

### THE STANDARDS CURRENTLY SUGGESTED

The standards most often suggested (and more or less widely employed) currently are of the two kinds previously discussed: for corporate and non-corporate giving. The standards for the latter, the non-corporate sector, are usually subdivided into separate standards for "executive," "professional," and "employee" giving.[92] We shall deal briefly, in order, with the corporate and then with the non-corporate sector.

### Standards for Corporations

As has already been suggested, there are, in connection with these standards, two basic problems—assuming that direct access to information regarding post-tax earnings by firms cannot be had,[93] and that ability to pay rather than desire to pay or obligation to pay is the decisive criterion.[94] The subsequent discussion also waives the question as to whether corporations should be regarded as potential donors at all. This last question may be "academic" in the sense that no fundraiser is now likely to "let the corporations escape their obligations," and perhaps no corporation really wishes to forego the public-relations benefits of participation (if such benefits exist) even if all firms withdrew together. But the question is not academically put. It is the authors' view that the object, meaning, and consequence of various degrees of corporate involvement from zero to total responsibility need most careful examination and reappraisal.

The first problem asks how the corporate share of the load, once decided upon, is to be distributed between the various trade groups (if there are to be such). It has received but little attention, and certainly no satisfactory solution. Both the United Community Funds and Councils of America and the Cleveland Chest[95] (which has been noted for development of standards) and the corresponding bodies in New York and Los Angeles regard this as an urgent item of unfinished business, but seem to have made relatively little progress in solving it.

As of February, 1956,[96] only one MOPS fundraising organization that we know of (not, in this case, a "Chest"), the Greater New York Fund, had made much evident progress at this level. Its procedure for setting standards for the several trade groups might be described briefly as follows. For those firms for whom the scheme is relevant (in the present New York scheme, only publicly owned corporations):

   (i) On a national basis, determine the earnings of a given industry;
  (ii) Similarly, determine its annual average total employment;
 (iii) Compute an average-earnings-per-employee figure by dividing (i) by (ii);
  (iv) Determine the number of employees of that industry in the local area;
   (v) Multiply (iii) by (iv): this gives an estimate of local earnings for that industry, and
  (vi) Allocate goals among industries locally in proportion to these presumptive local earnings.

Provided earnings are not directly available, and provided that earnings are the agreed basis, and provided that a proper determination of the total corporate share has been made, some such scheme as this is undoubtedly required. It cannot approximate equity, of course, until virtually all industries, trades, and other relevant groupings of corporations have been included; and it needs initial and periodic readjustment to allow for differences between national and local average-earnings-per-employee.[97] But with such a process of continuous adjustment the scheme seems fundamentally sound, and would undoubtedly serve.[98]

This is not, however, necessarily the only method to achieve the intended end, and there is actually implicit, in another scheme, a whole system that would dispense with the trade-group problem and the year-to-year decision on the corporate *vs.* non-corporate proportion altogether. It also obviates entirely the problem of explicitly determining earnings. We have already referred without naming it to the now widely discussed "Shell Formula" (see page 171). In essence, the corporate gift of the firm is set as follows:

$$\frac{\text{Last year's total Chest take}}{\text{Last year's area population}} \times \frac{\text{Corporation's present}}{\text{number of employees}} \times \frac{\text{Average family}}{\text{size for area.}}$$

This actually reduces to:

Chest's per-family take $\times$ Corporation's number of employees.

If most families living in the area had one (and only one) employee in the area, general adoption of this scheme would have the following long-run effects:

(i) The "corporate share" for the community would stabilize at 50 per cent of the total take.
(ii) *All* gifts of corporations would be equal on a per-employee basis.
(iii) Corporation policy would, in effect, *follow* "community" policy in so far as community policy is reflected in personal giving ("individual," "professional," "executive" and "employee"), i.e., the individuals' decisions would be decisive.
(iv) All the problems of "standards" would reduce to one problem: the setting of "fair shares" for individuals according to income (either at a flat rate or a "progressive" rate). The total result (the corporate gift being thus "automatically" set) would then indeed reflect what the Chests say they aim at: the vote of confidence, expressed in money, of the persons in the local community, each acting as a deciding unit, as they do when balloting.[99]

Assuming now that the total corporate gift for the solicitation area, and its subdivision among trade groups, have been agreed upon—the next question is how these loads are to be suballocated among the constituent firms in each trade group.

The recommended,[100] the most widely adopted, and, except for certain peculiarities, perhaps the most sensible scheme—given all the assumptions previously outlined—is the plan developed in Cleveland, Ohio, and known, naturally enough, as "the Cleveland Plan."[101] To quote one of our own studies, the fundamental assumptions of the plan are:

(a) That corporations can be classified into trade groups that have, with reference to some common denominator, essentially uniform profits per unit of common denominator.
(b) That these essentially uniform profits per unit of common denominator constitute therefore essentially uniform giving potentials (and obligations) per unit of common denominator.
(c) That the "Standard Industrial Classification" prepared by the Community Chests and Councils of America constitutes a classification with the characteristics demanded by (a).
(d) That within such classifications—("trade groups")—firms should in successive campaigns be urged towards equality of per unit giving, while simultaneously none should be allowed to reduce its total gift.
(e) That this can be done.
(f) That the Cleveland Plan as set forth below effects this transition from inequitable to equitable giving—"equitable" meaning here effectively equal giving per unit of common denominator.

Again, to quote or paraphrase the study, the Cleveland Plan can be reduced to the following three rules:

(1) First, for the total campaign, compute

$$r_{01} = \frac{G_1}{G_0},$$

the ratio between the campaign goals of the base year and the year in which the yardstick is to be first applied.

(2) Separate the firms on the trade-group list into two classes—"above average" and "below average"—according to the following scheme:[102]

    (a) An *above-average firm* is one whose employment this year multiplied by the average per-employee gift of the trade group last year would be less than (or equal to) that firm's last year's gift.

    (b) A *below-average firm* is one whose present employment multiplied by the trade-group average last year is greater than last year's gift from that firm.

    (Thus *classification* depends on last year's gift and this year's employment.)

(3) Assess standards against the various firms as follows:

    (a) For above-average firms: last year's total gift multiplied by $r_{01}$ regardless of changes in employment, i.e., regardless of per capita result.

    (b) For below-average firms: last year's trade-group average per capita, multiplied by this year's firm employment, multiplied by $r_{01}$.

Since it may be less than immediately obvious what these rules do to a firm's per-employee "assessment,"[103] let us examine, first, the assessment under this scheme of three hypothetical firms who gave above average, at average, and below average (per employee) in the base year, and then the fate of these three firms under various employment conditions. Table XXX shows the assessments that result under the Cleveland Plan. It is perhaps

### TABLE XXX

Per-Employee Gifts Assessed against Three Hypothetical Firms under Selected Employment Conditions by Cleveland Plan

(Assuming campaign requires a 30% over-all increase)[a]

| Type of firm by logical classification[b] | Base-year employment | Base-year gift per employee | Per-employee assessment, given the employment indicated in the campaign year | | | | | |
|---|---|---|---|---|---|---|---|---|
| | | | 1500 | 1200 | 1100 | 1000 | 900 | 500 |
| Above average | 1000 | $2.40 | $2.60 | $2.60 | $2.84 | $3.12 | $3.47 | $6.24 |
| Average | 1000 | 2.00 | 2.60 | 2.60 | 2.60 | 2.60 | 2.89 | 5.20 |
| Below average | 1000 | 1.60 | 2.60 | 2.60 | 2.60 | 2.60 | 2.60 | 4.16 |
| Total | 3000 | $2.00 | $2.60 | $2.60 | $2.68 | $2.77 | $2.99 | $5.20 |

[a]Since the proportion of increase required is assessed against all gifts, its amount affects none of the relations between assessments, i.e., the relations would have been the same even had we chosen a 5 per cent increase for the illustration.

[b]This classification—"average," "above average," etc.—means what it says. It is not to be confused with the Cleveland special meanings.

obvious from the table that what is demanded depends on the exigencies of employment, and that therefore both the total gift secured by the method from the three firms combined, and the amount of per-employee disequality between givers depends on these chances. If, to take an extreme (and perhaps unlikely) instance, the "above average"[104] firm fell on evil times and lost half its employees, while the other two either held or increased their employment, the situation shown in Table XXXI would result. It is

TABLE XXXI

HYPOTHETICAL EXAMPLE:
RESULTS OF SELECTED EMPLOYMENT CHANGES UNDER CLEVELAND PLAN

| Type of firm by logical classification | Assessed percapita | New ratio of percapitas to one another | Old ratio of percapitas to one another | Percentage increase in percapita demanded |
|---|---|---|---|---|
| Above average | $6.24 | $2.40 | $1.50 | 160 % |
| Average | 2.60 | 1.00 | 1.25 | 30 |
| Below average | 2.60 | 1.00 | 1.00 | 62.5 |

clear that the disequality between the percapitas would under these circumstances be increased.

It is perhaps only a little less obvious (given the possibilities of variation in per-employee gifts) that the total gift yielded by the whole trade group, if it follows the "standard," will vary enormously also. It will be recalled that the reason for setting the standard was (a) to introduce equity, and (b) to secure the "needed" $7,800 from the group. We have dealt with the first aim. As to the second, any of the totals shown in Table XXXII could result, depending on mere accidents of employment, such as those of Table XXX. Thus the scheme, if the Chest were successful in getting a trade group to adopt it, would always yield *at least* what was said to be needed

TABLE XXXII

HYPOTHETICAL EXAMPLE: CLEVELAND PLAN, TRADE-GROUP TOTAL GIFT AND
PERCENTAGE OF AMOUNT AIMED AT (DEPENDING ON EMPLOYMENT
CONDITIONS) COMPUTED FROM PERCAPITAS IN TABLE XXX

| Possible total | Percentage raised (under stated conditions) of amount needed |
|---|---|
| $11,700 | 150% |
| 10,920 | 140 |
| 10,660 | 137 |
| 10,400 | 133 |
| 10,140 | 130 |
| 9,880 | 127 |
| 9,620 | 123 |
| 9,360 | 120 |
| 9,100 | 117 |
| 8,840 | 113 |
| 8,580 | 110 |
| 8,320 | 107 |
| 8,060 | 103 |
| 7,800 | 100 |

from that trade group, and, except in the rarest of instances, considerably more than was "needed."

Another not too obvious property of the scheme (if adopted by a trade group) is that what the total gift would be, and therefore that year's "trade-group average," and therefore the next year's minimum "assessment" is partly independent of employment conditions in the industry or trade group as a whole. Thus in our hypothetical illustration, with the following employment levels, any one of the "trade-group averages" shown in Table XXXIII might be found (see Table XXX), depending on which particular firms

TABLE XXXIII

HYPOTHETICAL EXAMPLE: CLEVELAND PLAN, POSTULATED EMPLOYMENT LEVEL IN AN INDUSTRY OR TRADE GROUP AND RESULTING NEW TRADE-GROUP AVERAGE DEPENDING ON EMPLOYMENT VARIATION BETWEEN FIRMS IN THE INDUSTRY

| Percentage change in employment level of trade group | Employment level of trade group | Possible trade-group averages depending on which firms have what employment changes[a] | | | | | | |
|---|---|---|---|---|---|---|---|---|
| + 50% | 4500 | $2.60 | | | | | | |
| + 40 | 4200 | 2.60 | | | | | | |
| + 37 | 4100 | 2.60, | 2.66 | | | | | |
| + 33 | 4000 | 2.60, | 2.73 | | | | | |
| + 30 | 3900 | 2.60, | 2.67, | 2.80 | | | | |
| + 27 | 3800 | 2.60, | 2.67 | | | | | |
| + 23 | 3700 | 2.60, | 2.67, | 2.74 | | | | |
| + 20 | 3600 | 2.60, | 2.67, | 2.74, | 2.82 | | | |
| + 17 | 3500 | 2.60, | 2.67, | 2.75, | 2.82, | 2.97, | 3.12 | |
| + 13 | 3400 | 2.60, | 2.68, | 2.75, | 2.83 | | | |
| + 10 | 3300 | 2.60, | 2.68, | 2.76, | 2.84, | 2.92 | | |
| + 7 | 3200 | 2.60, | 2.68, | 2.76, | 2.84, | 3.01, | 3.17 | |
| + 3 | 3100 | 2.60, | 2.68, | 2.77, | 2.85, | 2.94, | 3.02, | 3.10, 3.19 |
| 0 | 3000 | 2.69, | 2.77, | 2.86, | 2.95, | 3.03, | 3.21 | |
| − 3 | 2900 | 2.78, | 2.87, | 2.96, | 3.05, | 3.17, | 3.23, | 3.32 |
| − 6 | 2800 | 2.88, | 2.97, | 3.06, | 3.16, | 3.25 | | |
| − 10 | 2700 | 2.89, | 2.99, | 3.08, | 3.18, | 3.27, | 3.28 | |
| − 13 | 2600 | 3.00, | 3.10, | 3.20, | 3.30, | 3.40 | | |
| − 17 | 2500 | 3.12, | 3.22, | 3.33, | 3.43, | 3.64, | 3.85 | |
| − 20 | 2400 | 3.25, | 3.36, | 3.47 | | | | |
| − 23 | 2300 | 3.39, | 3.50 | | | | | |
| − 27 | 2200 | 3.55, | 3.78, | 4.02 | | | | |
| − 30 | 2100 | 3.71, | 3.84, | 4.09 | | | | |
| − 33 | 2000 | 3.90, | 4.16 | | | | | |
| − 37 | 1900 | 4.11, | 4.24 | | | | | |
| − 50 | 1500 | 5.20 | | | | | | |

[a]Assuming, as in Table XXX, that no firm suffers more than a 50 per cent gain or loss in employment, i.e., the figures represent the permutations among the possibilities in that table. The actual scatter of possibilities is greater.

suffered what employment changes. The significance of this scatter of possibilities may perhaps be better appreciated from Chart 35. With identical conditions for the industry as a whole (for each employment level) it implies quite a variety of future assessments. Within a wide range there is, therefore, great arbitrariness in the assessments that will be put upon an industry's "giving potentiality" from year to year.

But, further, in so far as there is order in the data, it runs in the contrary direction to what one would expect on any reasonable economic assumptions, i.e., the more employment in the industry falls (the "sicker" the industry) the more will be demanded of it per employee; and the more its employment increases the less will it be asked for per employee. This shows clearly in Table XXXIII and Chart 35. If employment in the industry increases by 50 per cent, the expected gift per employee will be *half* of what would be demanded if employment fell by 50 per cent.

The last point has clear implications for the distribution of burden among industries. Since the sum to be raised in any one year is determined independently, and the corporate share of that sum is also independently fixed, the scheme must operate from year to year to shift the relative weight of giving (per capita) onto declining industries and to lighten the weight (per capita) on vigorous or growing ones. A shift in employment from one industry to another would result in increased load per employee in the industry shifted from, and decreased load in the one shifted to. The sense in which this is "equitable" is difficult to determine. Equity apart, the economic possibility even of long-term operation of such a scheme would seem to be questionable.

If the Cleveland Plan is to be judged on the basis of one stated intent, i.e., that it "aims primarily at achieving equitable giving *within* trade groups," and if by "equitable" is meant approximately equal percapitas, it seems clear that, except under very stable employment conditions in firms and industries, such "equity" is unlikely to be approximated.

If, on the other hand, it is aimed primarily to "provide conscientious solicitors with persuasive ammunition for a business-like interview with businessmen,"[105] then, apart from reservations about the meaning of "conscientious," the test would have to be an empirical one: will businessmen in the long run indeed regard such argument as foundation for a "business-like interview"? Whether it *is* believed in, is a matter for further research. Whether it is to be believed in (i.e., is credible) is a matter for further logical analysis along the foregoing lines. That analysis so far raises grave doubts. (A formal proof of these contentions appears in the Appendix to this chapter.)

What gives the Cleveland Plan these surprising effects is the peculiar method of allocating firms to "below-average" and "above-average" categories, and the implicit rule that no matter what happens to employment, the total corporate gift of any corporation cannot be allowed to decrease under any circumstances. Both peculiarities reflect the usual attempt to "have it both ways," i.e., to introduce equity not only without sacrificing present gift-levels both in total and in any particular[106] but also without sacrificing (and, if necessary, by adding to) any present inequity.[107]

We are not called upon to make recommendations, here, but a much simpler scheme, and one less patently inequitable, would be, once the total "needed" from a trade group was determined, to divide that total by the total current employment in the group. This would give the average sum per employee needed. The figure might be published as the ideal figure (the standard) aimed at. All firms already giving more than this per employee might be asked to maintain the same rate of per-employee giving[108] as previously—though even this is a concession to cupidity or lag; while those giving less would be asked gradually to catch up over an agreed period, say five years. Any resultant deficit from the trade group's agreed share could be carried forward to next year's trade-group "load"; any resultant surplus could be used to reduce it. No donor need feel, at least under such circumstances, that as a result of previous generosity he was being singled out for further accelerated differential victimization.

### Personal Standards

Enough has been said, perhaps, earlier, to give an idea of the nature of existing standards for personal giving. Mostly, they arbitrarily segregate "professionals," and then "individuals," with the remainder being divided into "employees" and "executives." To the "employees" (meaning wage-earners or people earning less than $4,000 or $6,000 or some such figure in salary) a flat-rate standard (4, 6 or 8 hours' pay per annum) is applied; to those earning more, a "progressive" rate.

We have already made the point that no viable argument has been put forward, in our hearing, for treating "individuals" (presumably neither "employees" nor "executives," i.e., retired or unemployed) differently from other income-earners. But even if this dubious practice were abandoned, and all individuals contributing as individuals were treated indiscriminately as persons of a certain income, we should in most cities, including Indianapolis, according to present practice have the structure shown in the accompanying diagram. The right-hand segment (corporation giving) we

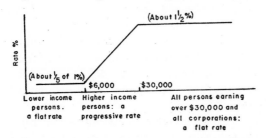

have already discussed. The middle segment is worth further examination.[109]

Chart 36, in addition to showing the (implied) Chest standards for executives in Cleveland, Cincinnati, Chicago, Columbus, Indianapolis, and Philadelphia, shows also a set of standards developed by one church in

Indianapolis and the (implied) income tax standard for the United States. It is obvious from the chart that the tax *level* is higher than the church gift level and that the latter is higher, in turn, than any Community Chest level. It may also be obvious, though the chart does not emphasize it, that the income tax is least "progressive," the church scheme somewhat more progressive, and the Chest schemes most progressive of all.[110]

We have already made the point in general that cities having more "progressive" standards for executives have in general lower levels of executive giving, and greater tendency for the campaign results to be "disappointing." We suggest that the whole question of progressive rates is worth re-examination, particularly rates that are more progressive than, it seems, legislators dare, or think wise, to impose as taxes, or that the sense of the country or the logic of the economy would permit. The problem might be even further sharpened if the logic of the gift as a charge on post-tax net were examined,[111] since, after all, the net gift must really come out of post-tax income, if a donor is not to be generous with the Treasury's money and indifferent to his legal fate. Viewed in this perspective, the standards appear to recommend as equitable a more severely progressive "tax" than the income tax, to weigh with increasing force (proportionally) on those who have the smallest *proportion* of their incomes left after tax. If progressive gift standards are applied to gross (in the face of existent progressive income taxes), then the net costs to giver (after claiming exemption for his gift) as a fraction of his net net (after tax and gift) are still higher than the original gift standards,[112] and moreover, more progressive.[113]

Beyond this, it seems entirely arbitrary to divide the giving curve into a flat-rate segment, a progressive segment, and another flat-rate segment. At least, the question of consistency might be faced, in asking whether it is not preferable to maintain one or other principle throughout, i.e., either the view that the gift standard should be some fixed fraction of income or that the gift rate should increase with income. Since it seems unlikely that labor support could be secured for a series of progressive rates at the bottom of the income pyramid,[114] and since it also seems unlikely that corporations would hold still for the equivalent of another progressive tax, the alternative to evident inconsistency of treatment seems to be the rapid restoration of the gift rate for executives to a flat rate also. On the logic of note 89, such a change *might* be effected over five annual steps as shown in Table XXXIV A.

The present Indianapolis standards, the suggested "midway[115] standard" (the first-year change), and the possible ultimate standard (flat rate) are depicted on Chart 37, from which the gifts under the three standards can be approximately gauged. If, however, the successive standards were to be employed, the exact figures would be needed as computed and shown in Table XXXIV B.

### TABLE XXXIV A

POSSIBLE TRANSFORMATION STAGES FROM PRESENT PROGRESSIVE STANDARDS
FOR EXECUTIVES TO FLAT-RATE STANDARDS

| Stage | Formula | Description |
|---|---|---|
| Present stage | $G = .000008\ I^{1.78}$ | |
| 1st year change | $G = .0001\quad I^{1.5}$ | Equivalent to *least progressive* present Chest standard |
| 2nd year change | $G = .0006\quad I^{1.3}$ | Progressiveness of present income tax |
| 3rd year change | $G = .0016\quad I^{1.2}$ | |
| 4th year change | $G = .004\quad I^{1.1}$ | |
| 5th year change | $G = .01\quad I$ | A flat 1% rate |

### TABLE XXXIV B

STANDARDS FOR EXECUTIVES COMPUTED FROM TABLE XXXIV A

| Income in thousands | Present actual Indianapolis standard | Suggested changes | | | | |
|---|---|---|---|---|---|---|
| | | First year | Second year | Third year | Fourth year | Fifth year |
| $ 1 | | 3 | 5 | 6 | 8 | 10 |
| 2 | | 9 | 12 | 14 | 17 | 20 |
| 3 | | 16 | 21 | 24 | 27 | 30 |
| 4 | | 25 | 30 | 33 | 37 | 40 |
| 5 | | 35 | 41 | 43 | 47 | 50 |
| 6 | 33 | 47 | 51 | 54 | 57 | 60 |
| 7 | 41 | 59 | 63 | 65 | 68 | 70 |
| 8 | 54 | 72 | 75 | 77 | 78 | 80 |
| 9 | 61 | 85 | 87 | 88 | 89 | 90 |
| 10 | 88 | 100 | 100 | 100 | 100 | 100 |
| 11 | 101 | 115 | 113 | 112 | 111 | 110 |
| 12 | 125 | 131 | 127 | 124 | 122 | 120 |
| 13 | 131 | 148 | 141 | 137 | 133 | 130 |
| 14 | 141 | 166 | 155 | 150 | 145 | 140 |
| 15 | 163 | 184 | 169 | 163 | 156 | 150 |
| 16 | 174 | 202 | 184 | 176 | 168 | 160 |
| 17 | 184 | 222 | 199 | 189 | 179 | 170 |
| 18 | 221 | 242 | 215 | 202 | 191 | 180 |
| 19 | 254 | 262 | 230 | 216 | 203 | 190 |
| 20 | 284 | 283 | 246 | 230 | 214 | 200 |
| 21 | 317 | 304 | 262 | 244 | 226 | 210 |
| 22 | 346 | 326 | 279 | 258 | 238 | 220 |
| 23 | 362 | 349 | 295 | 272 | 256 | 230 |
| 24 | 386 | 372 | 312 | 286 | 262 | 240 |
| 25 | 409 | 395 | 329 | 300 | 274 | 250 |
| 26 | 424 | 419 | 346 | 315 | 286 | 260 |
| 27 | 443 | 444 | 364 | 329 | 298 | 270 |
| 28 | 453 | 469 | 382 | 344 | 310 | 280 |
| 29 | 478 | 494 | 399 | 359 | 323 | 290 |
| 30 | 450 | 520° | 417 | 374 | 335 | 300 |
| 35 | 525 | 655° | 510 | 450 | 397 | 350 |
| 40 | 600 | 800° | 606 | 528 | 460 | 400 |
| 45 | 675 | 955° | 707° | 608 | 523 | 450 |
| 50 | 750 | 1118° | 811° | 690 | 587 | 500 |
| 100 | 1500 | 3162° | 1996° | 1585° | 1259 | 1000 |

°These figures, though systematically consistent, may be strategically contraindicated.

## Standards in General

We have already detailed the evidence that would lead us to believe that standards are of consequence to levels of giving (as well as to integrity, good human relations, and morale). In the setting of standards, technical proficiency and good sense have a great value. But even more important, if possible, than technical accuracy—or at least as indispensable in the long run to the result sought—is the method by which they are set and the intent in their use.

There is reason—from general knowledge about social organization (especially the theory of small groups) as well as from observation in this field for this study—to believe that the most valuable by-product, if not the principal product itself, of standard-setting is in the consensus and morale of the small groups of donors (in each trade or sub-trade, or more appropriate reference group, if such exists) who agree in genuine discussion on the standards.[116] If this is so, then provision would need to be made for the bringing together of groups small enough to come to grips with the issues in an atmosphere free of desire to (or potentiality to) "sell" or mislead or manipulate or coerce opinion. Any consensus so arrived at is likely to be more binding—as well as more intelligently appropriate—than a decision arrived at by fiat or on the basis of meeting a crisis that allows no time for thought or discussion.

But if standards are to be so set, it seems likely that the quantity and quality of the Chest staff work will need considerable change, and a decision will have to be made between standards as tools of rationality and equity and standards as patter under which a process essentially of sleight-of-hand is to go forward.[117]

### APPENDIX

#### FORMAL ANALYSIS OF CLEVELAND PLAN FOR CORPORATE YARDSTICKS

A. *Symbols*:

For any one trade group, define:

$e$   as employment (number of employees)

$e_0$   as the employment in the base year

$e_1$   as employment in the next year, and so on

$e_{01}$   as the employment of a given firm ("firm number 1," arbitrarily) in the base year, etc.

Define, similarly:

$g$, $g_0$, $g_{10}$   as the corresponding total gifts

$p$, $p_0$, $p_{01}$   as the corresponding gift-per-employee (or other "common denominator unit")

$T_0$, $T_1$   as the corresponding campaign total (the actual total for the base year; the intended total, or goal, for the next year)

B. *Division into "above-average" firms and "below-average" firms*

1. An above average firm is, then, a firm for which

$$g_{01} \geqslant e_{11}p_0,$$

i.e., for which

$$e_{01}p_{01} \geqslant p_0,$$

i.e., for which

$$\frac{p_{01}}{p_0} \geqslant \frac{e_{11}}{e_{01}},$$

i.e., for which the ratio of its base-year "percapita" to the trade-group percapita is at least equal to its inter-year employment ratio.

2. A below-average firm is one for which

$$g_{01} < e_{11}p_0$$

and therefore

$$\frac{p_{01}}{p_0} < \frac{e_{11}}{e_{01}}.$$

For any given firm, then, for which $p_{01}$ is fixed by its last year's gift, and $p_0$ is fixed for the trade group, its *classification as above or below average depends on its employment level* (relative to the base year). Note that the percapita of the firm in relation to that of the trade group does *not* determine the classification.

C. *Assessment of percapitas*

The following rules define what is demanded of each class of company ("above average" and "below average"):

1. First define $r_{01}$, the inter-year increase factor required to reach the expected year 1 total goal,

$$\text{i.e., } r_{01} = \frac{T_1}{T_0}.$$

2. For "above-average" firms, demand from each:

$$g_{11} = r_{01} \, g_{01}$$
$$= r_{01} \, e_{01} \, p_{01}.$$

Note that this is wholly independent of this year's employment. On a per capita basis this is

$$p_{11} = r_{01} \, p_{01} \, \frac{e_{01}}{e_{11}}$$

so that the load per capita depends here on the inter-year changes in employment.

3. For "below-average" firms, demand from each:

$$g_{11} = r_{01} \, e_{11} \, p_0.$$

Note that this is wholly dependent on this year's employment and wholly independent of this firm's last year's gift. On a per capita basis, this is:

$$p_{11} = r_{01} \, p_0$$

and the percapita here expected is independent of employment in either year.

4. For both together, whether this procedure leads towards or away from equalization of percapitas depends on the accidents of employment.

D. *Total gift from trade group*

The total gift required $(G_{1R})$ from the trade group is, by definition,

$$G_{1R} = r_{01} \sum_{i=1}^{n} g_{0i}$$

where there are $n$ firms in the trade group.

Suppose there are $k$ above-average firms in the trade group, and further suppose, for simplicity, that in no case does $g_{01} = e_{11} p_0$—an unlikely coincidence anyway.

Let $G_{1A}$ = the actual total gift in the year 1 of a trade group that adopts the scheme.

Then

$$G_{1A} = \sum_{i=1}^{n} g_{1i}$$

$$= r_{01} \sum_{i=1}^{k} g_{0i} + r_{01} \sum_{i=k+1}^{n} e_{1i} p_0$$

$$= r_{01} \left( \sum_{i=1}^{k} g_{0i} + \sum_{i=k+1}^{n} e_{1i} p_0 \right).$$

But since, for every below-average firm,

$$e_{1i} p_0 > g_{0i},$$

then:

$$\sum_{i=k+1}^{n} e_{11} p_0 > \sum_{i=k+1}^{n} g_{0i}$$

and therefore

$$G_{1A} > r_{01} \sum_{i=1}^{n} g_{0i}$$

i.e., $G_{1A} > G_{1R}$

i.e., the actual trade-group gift, if the scheme is adopted, is greater than required, on the supposition of the scheme itself.

E. *New trade-group average*

Since no simple statement about the trade-group total gift can be made—except that it will be higher than required—it is equally difficult to make any statement about the new trade-group average:

$$p_1 = \frac{r_{01} \left( \sum_{i=1}^{k} g_{0i} + \sum_{i=k+1}^{n} e_{1i} p_0 \right)}{\sum_{i=1}^{n} e_{1i}},$$

except that $p_1 \geqslant r_{01} p_0$, i.e., that the new trade-group average must be at least at the equitable figure and will most frequently be above it.

# 9. Results in Indianapolis: Money

AFTER THE GENERAL examination of money problems in the last chapter, we turn now to a specific observation of how money is obtained in Indianapolis. Money, as we are now well aware, is not the only test by which a fund-seeking organization is to be judged, but it is *one* test, perhaps the most frequently applied; and certainly failure to obtain it, if long-sustained, spells continuing weakness and probably eventual death to the organization. We may properly ask three kinds of questions related to money results in Indianapolis: (1) How does money-raising in Indianapolis for either the Chest or the Red Cross compare with money-raising for the Chest or the Red Cross elsewhere? (2) How does money-raising for the Indianapolis Chest compare with money-raising for the Indianapolis Red Cross or Hospital Association? (3) How does one campaign division within the Chest or the Red Cross compare with another?" or "What groups are carrying what shares of the gift-load?" We have dealt with the first question[1] in earlier chapters, and have seen how Indianapolis rates as a money-giving city. We proceed here to examine the second and third. The answers should indicate, respectively, whether or not Indianapolis is a fertile field for one organization or appeal and not for another, and whether some portions of the field are better tilled, cultivated, or "reaped" by the Chest than others, or better or worse by the Chest than they are by others.

## A. INTER-ORGANIZATION COMPARISON

In our attempt to find out how the Chest does in comparison with other fundraising campaigns in Indianapolis, we would have examined, ideally, all other fundraising enterprises in the city. Of course this is too vast a task, and limitations had to be imposed. For a variety of reasons, but mainly because of the contrast presented by the types of campaign and the size of goals, the Red Cross campaign and the Hospital Development Association campaign were chosen for attention.[2]

The selection of the campaigns for comparison brought us face to face with a set of problems which in some respects we have not solved in a thoroughly satisfactory way. So that the reader may assess the accuracy and reliability of the findings, our search for solid ground upon which to build the analysis is briefly reviewed.

Although most fundraising campaigns similar in size[3] to these three follow a common general pattern in the organizational scheme for soliciting and publishing results, there are, as with most groups and organizations, individual variations in the pattern. These differences may be due to special circumstances surrounding a particular campaign, but more often they appear to be the result of historical accident. The Red Cross, Community Chest, and Hospital campaigns of Indianapolis are no exception. Within the general pattern, each organization has a different way of handling some particular parts of the solicitation and reporting. For the Hospital campaign, these differences seem to be associated mainly with the particular problems of a single ("once in a lifetime") building fund campaign. The Red Cross has a long-established "way of doing things," while the Chest often varies from year to year. At the same time, the method of book-keeping of both Chest and Red Cross has remained almost unchanged over a period of years. This lack of reflection in the permanent records of actual campaign changes results in great difficulty in comparing published reports of "results" with the accounts which are the sole reliable material.

The Chest and Red Cross use identical names for the "divisions"[4] of their campaigns, but the reported results by divisions seldom include exactly the same sources of gifts. Indeed, the reporting system of no one of the three organizations studied is directly comparable with that of any other.[5] It therefore seemed to us necessary to develop new reporting units which would be identical in all cases, and which would thus permit meaningful comparison between organizations. But this could not be carried far enough to allow consistent application to the records of all three organizations: to set up such a system would have required examination and classification of each and every record of a gift[6] in their files. We turned then to attempts to obtain a broad picture of giving from the records as they exist, without undue sacrifice of the accuracy we also sought.

Over-all reports of both the Red Cross and the Community Chest showed plainly that the greater part of the money raised came from contributions by firms and their employees. While these represented only some two thousand of the records of gifts in both the Chest and the Red Cross, they seemed the most accurately and carefully kept among all the records of both organizations. Consequently, we devised a reporting unit which initially included all firms in the Commerce and Industry division of the Community Chest and in the Industrial, Commercial and Public Service division of the Red Cross. We called this group "Industrial and Commercial Organizations"—"ICO"—and shall refer to it as a new reporting unit by this term.[7] This gave us one peg upon which to hang the analysis, and we can state, in properly comparable fashion, what the giving behavior for these firms and their employees (as a group) is over the period of years covered (1950-5 for the Chest, 1952-4 for the Red Cross).[8]

This solution was not, however, completely suitable for the examination of the Hospital campaign records. For the most part, the number of employees that the firms had at the time of the campaign and the number of these who contributed were not available. But this was the smallest problem for comparative purposes. Actually, not all of the employees of a particular company were reported as giving through the company, even though they may have actually given. For example, if some of the executives or other employees of a company chose to pay their pledges directly to the Association (rather than through payroll deduction at their place of work) the present records would not be easily accessible for compiling a record similar to that constructed for the Chest and Red Cross.[9]

A number of other problems had to be dealt with, moreover, before the material could be put into comparative form. Inaccuracy of data proved very troublesome;[10] and, in addition to coping with inaccuracy, we had the problem of changes occurring continually over the period in question. Problems arising from changes in the several firms in ICO were relatively simple to handle. The main concern here was with firms which had changed names or ownership, or which had merged or gone out of business. There seemed to be no general rule possible for handling each such situation; we solved each problem as it came up in the context of all the previous decisions on the same type of problem. A more difficult problem was what to do with firms which have subsidiary plants or organizations in Indianapolis. The firm gift is often given in the name of the parent organization. It is the practice of the Chest and Red Cross to assign the full amount of this gift to the largest of the subsidiary firms.[11] Since an important part of the analysis lies in the area of the firm gift, we felt that it would be better to prorate this gift, in proportion to number of employees, among the several subsidiary firms of the same company.

Yet another problem arose in determining what campaigns could be compared. All three organizations keep their records by calendar years. On the other hand, the question arose: Is the fall campaign of the Chest (for funds for the following year) to be compared with the spring campaign of the Red Cross which has already taken place in the same year, or should it be compared with the Red Cross campaign of the following year? The rhythm of philanthropic campaigns seems to be accentuated from September through June, cutting across calendar years. The tempo begins to rise in late September, reaching crescendo in October, December, and March, then gradually subsiding, all but disappearing, during the summer months. Only the dull throb of long campaigns and faint noises from the "planning" for the fall campaigns are heard in June, July, and August. The period from September to June might, therefore, be called the basic campaign year. In some respects, then, the campaign of the Red Cross in the spring following is more properly compared with the Chest campaign of a given year than is the one which occurs in the same year. We resolved (though we did not solve) this problem by making comparisons in both ways. The differences between the two kinds of comparisons are minor, however.[12]

## WHERE THE MONEY COMES FROM

Having described how we tried to meet the problem of varying reporting systems by "inventing" new categories, we can now proceed to more detailed comment on the results of the campaigns.

The usual campaign in Indianapolis combines into "divisions" the "reporting units,"[13] whose members obtain gifts both from institutions and from individuals. One useful way to group gifts, however, is by distinguishing whether they are given by persons or by organizations. In so doing, we are focusing on decision-making, i.e., on whether the decision to give and how much to give is made by individuals, as such and for themselves, or by "organizations."[14] The categories resulting from looking at the matter in this way may be called "Personal" (individual decision) and "Impersonal" (organization decision).

Another approach, which we also use later, is to examine results in terms of the way solicitation is organized, i.e., the way in which the "selling" job is carried out. The grouping of both the firm and the employee giving of any corporation into a unit by the campaign organizations has a realistic basis in the solicitation or selling pattern in Indianapolis and most other cities. The major portion (about 80 per cent) of giving in Indianapolis is organized around place of work; the resultant unit of reporting, therefore, includes the gift of a firm, its "executives" and its "employees."[15] The two categories that result from this way of looking at things are "Firm Organized Giving" and "Non-Firm Organized Giving." The latter includes the contributions of persons, solicited as individuals, usually at their residence. We have also included here the contributions of Foundations (and a few other organizations).[16] The distinction here is based on more than just the place of solicitation: the type of campaign waged to produce giving among "Firm Organized" donors and that waged to produce giving among "Non-Firm Organized" donors is quite different.[17]

It is necessary before proceeding further to identify several terms we shall be regularly using.

We shall refer to "Sources" of giving, by which we mean the various aggregates[18] from which the contributions are received. Only four will be dealt with here, and their gifts are labelled as follows: (1) "Firms": the total of all contributions made in the name of a firm; (2) "Employees": the total of all sums reported as contributed by any employee of a firm; (3) "Foundations and Organizations" (sometimes shortened to "Foundations"): the total of all gifts made in the name of Foundations, churches, clubs, veterans' organizations, fraternities, sororities and similar associations; (4) "Individuals": the total of all other giving—composed mainly of contributions from individuals solicited at home and of contributions by professional persons.

A second term which we shall use regularly is "Sector," by which we mean groupings of "Sources." Thus we shall refer to the "Personal Sector" (which is composed of Individual and Employee sources), and to the "Impersonal Sector" (which is composed of Firm and Foundation or Association sources).

Table XXXV shows the distribution of pledges from the Personal sector and from the Impersonal sector, by source, for the Hospital, Chest, and Red Cross campaigns. Charts 38, 39, and 40 show the same data in graphic

TABLE XXXV

PLEDGES FOR THE HOSPITAL, COMMUNITY CHEST, AND RED CROSS FOR
SPECIFIED PERIODS BY SECTOR AND SOURCE

| Sector and source | Hospital (July, 1952-June, 1953) | | Community Chest (1952) | | Red Cross (1953) | |
|---|---|---|---|---|---|---|
| | Amount[a] | Percentage of total | Amount[a] | Percentage of total | Amount[a] | Percentage of total |
| TOTAL | $11,435,700 | 100.0% | $1,579,000 | 100.0% | $511,900 | 100.0% |
| IMPERSONAL | 6,868,800 | 60.1 | 864,400 | 54.7 | 212,400 | 41.5 |
| Foundations[b] | 1,218,600 | 10.7 | 139,400[d] | 8.8 | 15,300 | 3.0 |
| Firms | 5,650,200 | 49.4 | 725,000 | 45.9 | 197,100 | 38.5 |
| PERSONAL | 4,566,900 | 39.9 | 714,600 | 45.3 | 299,500 | 58.5 |
| Employees | 3,611,300 | 31.6 | 541,300 | 34.3 | 226,000 | 44.1 |
| Individuals[c] | 955,600 | 8.3 | 173,300 | 11.0 | 73,500 | 14.4 |

[a]To the nearest $100.
[b]Includes Organizations, such as clubs, churches, fraternities, sororities, veterans' organizations.
[c]Includes Medical, which amounted to 4.3, 0.8 and 1.8 per cent for the respective organizations.
[d]Organizations not included, since the data were not easily accessible. However, for both Hospital and Red Cross, this amounted to less than 10 per cent of the total for Foundations and Organizations. Even though there may be gifts from Organizations included in Individuals for the Chest, changing them to the proper category would have little effect (i.e., 1 per cent or less change in the figures shown).

form. The largest campaign in dollar volume—the Hospital campaign—is most dependent on the Impersonal sector for support (60.1 per cent); the smallest—the Red Cross—is least dependent (41.5 per cent); and the intermediate campaign in size—the Chest—is intermediate in its dependence (54.7 per cent). This suggests that, within a city, there is a direct relationship between the size of the campaign and its dependence on pledges from the Impersonal sector: the larger the campaign, the greater is its dependence on Impersonal pledging.

This relationship also holds true for each part of the Impersonal sector. The Red Cross is least dependent on Firms or Foundations, the Hospital campaign is the most dependent on both, and the Chest is in the middle.

The larger the campaign, then, the more dependent is the campaign on the pledges of Firms—and also on those of Foundations.

It follows logically, of course, that the reverse must hold for the Personal sector, in general, i.e., that the Red Cross is most dependent on personal pledging, the Hospital is the least dependent, and the Chest is again intermediate in dependence. But, more than this, the dependence *both* on Employee and on Individual pledging is in this same order. It would seem from the Indianapolis data, that, within a city, then, the larger the campaign, the less the dependence not only on the Personal sector generally, but also on each of its components: Employee and Individual pledges.

Pledging by Doctors and Dentists[19] is also of interest because it represents a particular segment of Individual giving which is on the borderline of Impersonal giving, since the professional man gives partly in response to business pressures or obligations and partly in response to his personal feelings or sense of obligation.[20] A pattern related to the program of the organizations emerges. None of the campaigns was greatly dependent on Medical pledging, even though in the Hospital campaign about half of its Individual contributions came from that source. This difference in the Hospital campaign is probably attributable to differential pressure applied consciously by its campaigners upon doctors, to the self-interest of medical practitioners in the Hospital development program, and the nearness of the "cause" to the physician's high valuation of health. Similarly, when we compare only Chest and Red Cross, the relatively greater support of the Red Cross by physicians might be elicited because the interests of the healing and life-serving professions, especially those of the physicians, are more closely related to the Red Cross program, which has a great deal to do with "health matters" (e.g., "first aid," life-saving and physical care), generally. Whether difference in interest accounts for it or not, the fact is that the Chest receives from medical sources less than half percentagewise what the Red Cross does.

We may now rearrange the data by unit of organization rather than by decision-making unit. Table XXXVI summarizes the pledges from the Firm Organized and the Non-Firm Organized sectors for the Hospital, Chest, and Red Cross campaigns. Charts 41, 42, and 43 show these same data in graphic form. With this rearrangement of the data of Table XXXV into the form shown in Table XXXVI, a surprising degree of similarity between the three campaigns emerges. All three organizations are almost equally dependent (81.0, 80.2, and 82.7 per cent, respectively) on Firm Organized pledges. This result seems to be related to the similarities in the type of solicitation which all three campaigns use.

Table XXXVII gives the order of dependence of the Hospital, Chest, and Red Cross on the four sources. It indicates that the Chest and Red Cross are identical in order of dependence on Foundation and Individual sources, while the Hospital and Chest are identical in order of dependence

TABLE XXXVI

FIRM AND NON-FIRM ORGANIZED SOURCES OF PLEDGES FOR THE HOSPITAL,
COMMUNITY CHEST, AND RED CROSS

| Sector and source | Hospital (July, 1952-June, 1953) | | Community Chest (1952) | | Red Cross (1953) | |
|---|---|---|---|---|---|---|
| | Amount[a] | Percentage of total | Amount[a] | Percentage of total | Amount[a] | Percentage of total |
| TOTAL | $11,435,700 | 100.0% | $1,579,000 | 100.0% | $511,900 | 100.0% |
| FIRM ORGANIZED | 9,261,500 | 81.0 | 1,266,300 | 80.2 | 423,100 | 82.7 |
| Firms | 5,650,200 | 49.4 | 725,000 | 45.9 | 197,100 | 38.5 |
| Employees | 3,611,300 | 31.6 | 541,300 | 34.3 | 226,000 | 44.1 |
| NON-FIRM ORGANIZED | 2,174,200 | 19.0 | 312,700 | 19.8 | 88,800 | 17.3 |
| Foundations[b] | 1,218,600 | 10.7 | 139,400[d] | 8.8 | 15,300 | 3.0 |
| Individuals[c] | 955,600 | 8.3 | 173,300 | 11.0 | 73,500 | 14.4 |

[a]To the nearest $100.
[b]Includes Organizations, such as clubs, churches, fraternities, sororities, veterans' organizations.
[c]Includes Medical.
[d]Organizations *not* included, since the data were not easily accessible. However, for both Hospital and Red Cross, this amounted to less than 10 per cent of the total for Foundations and Organizations. Even though there may be gifts from Organizations included in Individuals for the Chest, changing them to the proper category would have little effect (i.e., 1 per cent or less change in the figures shown).

TABLE XXXVII

ORDER OF DEPENDENCE[a] OF HOSPITAL, COMMUNITY CHEST, AND RED CROSS
ON SOURCES OF PLEDGES

| Source | Hospital (July, 1952-June, 1953) | Community Chest (1952) | Red Cross (1953) |
|---|---|---|---|
| Firms | 1 | 1 | 2 |
| Employees | 2 | 2 | 1 |
| Foundations | 3 | 4 | 4 |
| Individuals | 4 | 3 | 3 |

[a]From Tables XXXV and XXXVI. Dependence is equated with the proportion the source represents of total amount raised: the higher the proportion, the greater the dependence.

on Firm and Employee sources. The Hospital and Red Cross show no identity in their order of dependence on sources but—along with the Chest —are quite similar in their dependence on the Firm Organized sector. This is true not only for the sector as a whole, but curiously, it holds regardless of the proportions contributed by Firms and Employees, respectively, within the sector. Which contributes more seems to have little effect; both together produce about the same results in all three campaigns.[21]

Table XXXVIII shows the percentage of the Firm Organized sector represented respectively by Firm and Employee sources, for each of the three recipients. It emphasizes the similarity of the Hospital and Chest in

TABLE XXXVIII

FIRM AND EMPLOYEE SOURCES AS PERCENTAGE OF FIRM ORGANIZED SECTOR[a]
FOR HOSPITAL, CHEST, AND RED CROSS

| Sources | Hospital (July, 1952-June, 1953) | Community Chest (1952) | Red Cross (1953) |
|---|---|---|---|
| Firm | 61.0% | 57.4% | 46.6% |
| Employee | 39.0% | 42.6% | 53.4% |
| TOTAL | 100.0% | 100.0% | 100.0% |

[a]Data the same as in Table XXXVI.

being more dependent on Firm source (as between Firm and Employee gifts) than the Red Cross. It might be said that Hospital and Chest are more dependent on "management," while the Red Cross is more dependent on "labor."[22]

In summary, the Impersonal sector is of greater importance to the Hospital campaign and the Chest than to the Red Cross. For both, more than 50 per cent of the pledges come from Firms and Foundations and Organizations. The Red Cross, on the other hand, relies on the Personal sector for more than 50 per cent of its pledges, and Employee and Individual pledges are more important for it. When, however, we look at dependence from the organizing unit basis, all three seem to be about equally dependent on the Firm Organized sector (over 80 per cent of total pledges). Within this sector, for Chest and Hospital the greatest dependence is on Firm pledges, while for the Red Cross the greatest dependence is on Employee pledges, i.e., the two larger campaigns rely more on Firm gift than on Employee gift.

## LEADING GIFTS

There are many other ways to examine the giving or pledging patterns of fundraising campaigns, as we have seen in connection with intercity comparisons.[23] For the intra-city comparison now being made, three seem sufficiently useful to report in detail. These deal with "leading gifts," i.e., the largest dollar gifts in the campaign.[24]

### Ten Leading Gifts

One division under this heading marks off the ten largest gifts (from any source) made in the campaign. Table XXXIX shows the total amount of the ten largest gifts and the percentage they comprise of the total campaign for the Hospital (November, 1950 through December, 1953),[25] the Community Chest (1952), and the Red Cross (1953). The pattern here

TABLE XXXIX

TEN LEADING GIFTS AS PERCENTAGE OF TOTAL AMOUNT RAISED FROM ALL SOURCES FOR
THE HOSPITAL, COMMUNITY CHEST, AND RED CROSS

| Organization | Total amount raised[a] | Total of Ten Leading Gifts[a] | Ten Leading Gifts as percentage of total amount raised |
|---|---|---|---|
| Hospital | $12,139,000 | $3,356,000 | 27.6% |
| Community Chest | 1,579,000 | 364,000 | 23.1 |
| Red Cross | 512,000 | 62,000 | 12.1 |

[a]To nearest $1,000.

is quite clear. The Ten Leading Gifts in the Hospital campaign account for
a large portion of the total amount raised; to the Chest they furnish a
smaller, but very similar proportion; to the Red Cross, they furnish a
relatively small and quite dissimilar part. It seems that, within a city,
the larger the campaign, the greater is the percentage raised from the
ten leading donors.

## One Hundred Leading Firm Gifts

It may be of interest to pass from the Ten Leading Gifts (regardless of
source) to the Hundred Leading Firm Gifts, particularly since Firm giving
is so important to all three organizations. Table XL shows the amount
contributed by the one hundred[26] leading firm donors as a percentage of
the total amount raised for the three organizations for the same periods
as previously reported. Again, we see a similar pattern: the Hospital cam-

TABLE XL

TOTAL OF 100 LEADING FIRM GIFTS AS PERCENTAGE OF TOTAL AMOUNT RAISED FROM
ALL SOURCES FOR THE HOSPITAL, COMMUNITY CHEST, AND RED CROSS

| Organization | Total amount raised[a] | Total of 100 Largest Firm Gifts[a] | 100 Largest Firm Gifts as percentage of total amount raised |
|---|---|---|---|
| Hospital | $12,139,000 | $4,318,000 | 35.6% |
| Community Chest | 1,579,000 | 536,000 | 33.9 |
| Red Cross | 512,000 | 126,000 | 24.6 |

[a]To nearest $1,000.

paign obtains a very large percentage of its total from a small group of
donors, the Chest gets a smaller but similar proportion from the small
group, and the Red Cross relies least on these big contributions. It looks
as though, generally, within a city, the larger the campaign, the greater
percentage of the total that is raised from a given number of leading gifts.[27]
It might be possible that what we have observed can be partly explained
by the fact that each organization has a different total number of Firm

givers. Perhaps we should take for comparison instead some fixed fraction of each one's total number of Firm givers. Table XLI, accordingly, shows the percentage of the total amount raised from all sources represented by the gifts of the top 20 per cent of all Firm contributors (employing 25 or more persons)[28] to the Red Cross and Chest,[29] for the same periods as previously. Evidently, even when we take a fixed fraction of each gift

TABLE XLI

TOTAL OF LEADING 20 PER CENT OF FIRM GIFTS AS PERCENTAGE OF
TOTAL AMOUNT RAISED FROM ALL DONORS FOR RED CROSS AND CHEST

| Organization | Total amount raised[a] | Total of 20% Leading Firm Gifts[a] | 20% Leading Firm Gifts as percentage of total amount raised | Number of firms |
|---|---|---|---|---|
| Community Chest | $1,579,000 | $530,000 | 33.6% | 94 |
| Red Cross | 512,000 | 131,000 | 25.6 | 117 |

[a]To nearest $1,000.

list[30] (instead of a fixed number of givers), we get similar results: of the two campaigns, the Chest gets a greater fraction of its "take" from leading donors.

Again, a final generalization is tempting. It looks as though the larger the campaign within a city the greater the concentration, relatively and absolutely, on a few large givers. Such a hypothesis might some day be well worth testing for more fundraising campaigns than we have here and for more cities than one.[31]

## THE HOSPITAL CAMPAIGN VS. CHEST AND RED CROSS

Before we turn from such broad-scale comparisons as we have been making to comparisons in detail between the Red Cross and the Chest, it may be best to deal with the theory often presented to us that the Chest had recently suffered financial "failure" because the huge Hospital campaign ($12,000,000) had "taken so much out of people's pockets."

The Hospital campaign received pledges of $9,560,000[32] in the year from July 1, 1952, through June 30, 1953. This represents 78.8 per cent of the total pledges received—$12,139,000[33]—by December 31, 1953, the official termination date of the campaign.[34] It is possible to compare the Red Cross campaign of 1953 and the Community Chest campaign of 1952 with that Hospital campaign period in which the Hospital Association received slightly more than three-fourths of its total pledges. The Red Cross raised $512,244,[35] and the Community Chest, $1,562,284[36] in these campaigns. Compared with the previous campaign of each organization, this represents a decrease of 2.3 per cent for the Red Cross and an increase of 1.4 per cent for the Community Chest. Taking both together, there is a slight increase. Table XLII summarizes these data.

TABLE XLII

AMOUNT RAISED DURING THE PEAK OF THE HOSPITAL CAMPAIGN BY RED CROSS AND COMMUNITY CHEST—COMPARED WITH AMOUNT RAISED BY EACH IN PRECEDING CAMPAIGN

| Organization | Year | Amount raised[a] | Percentage increase or decrease |
|---|---|---|---|
| Red Cross | 1952 | $ 524,504 | |
| | 1953 | 512,244 | —2.3% |
| Community Chest | 1951 | 1,540,572 | |
| | 1952 | 1,562,284 | 1.4 |

[a]See notes 35 and 36 for detailed explanation.

One's first impression might well be that the Hospital campaign had little, if any, effect on the net money-raising results of the Red Cross and the Community Chest, i.e., that the Hospital campaign was *not* in competition for the dollars which the Red Cross and the Chest get; and this would be in line with the general picture, developed earlier, of non-competition between fund-getters.

But even though the total raised by the two organizations taken together was practically unchanged, the Hospital campaign might have had the effect of "preventing" the Red Cross and the Chest from securing increases in the amount raised. Table XLIII presents some data in the light of which this question might be considered: it shows the total amount raised by the Red Cross and Chest for each year since 1947, and compares the several amounts with those raised in each preceding year by each organi-

TABLE XLIII

AMOUNT RAISED BY COMMUNITY CHEST AND RED CROSS CAMPAIGNS COMPARED WITH AMOUNT RAISED IN EACH PRECEDING CAMPAIGN, 1947-1955

| Year | Community Chest | | Red Cross | |
|---|---|---|---|---|
| | Amount raised | Percentage increase or decrease | Amount raised | Percentage increase or decrease |
| 1947 | $1,199,572 | | $457,299 | |
| 1948 | 1,246,689 | 3.9% | 426,896 | —6.6% |
| 1949 | 1,270,142 | 1.9 | 426,274 | —0.1 |
| 1950 | 1,389,258 | 8.6 | 394,882 | —7.4 |
| 1951 | 1,540,572 | 10.9 | 493,979 | 25.1 |
| 1952 | 1,562,284 | 1.4 | 524,504 | 6.2 |
| 1953 | 1,559,181 | —0.2 | 512,244 | —2.3 |
| 1954 | 1,555,313[a] | —0.2 | 508,561 | —0.7 |
| 1955 | NA[b] | | 515,373 | 1.3 |

[a]Through April 30, 1956. The final figure will not be known until December 31, 1956, and may show an increase over 1953.

[b]Not available. The final figure will not be known until December 31, 1957.

zation. In the four campaigns preceding the start[37] of the Hospital campaign, the Chest showed increases; two of these increases were substantial and two were relatively small. In the three campaigns following the start of the Hospital campaign, the Chest shows a very small net decrease twice and a small net increase once.[38]

At a first glance, the fact that there are decreases for the Chest following the Hospital campaign may appear to be significant. However, if we test merely the *direction* of change (i.e., whether the amount raised increases or decreases) we find that the chances of getting one increase and two consecutive decreases, as is the case—or even of getting three decreases—are about one in six.[39] This means that a succession of three campaigns showing decreases for at least two consecutive years could be expected by chance about once in five or once in seven times in the "normal" course of events. The location in time of the decreases is therefore not very convincingly to be attributed to the Hospital campaign as far as the Community Chest is concerned.

When we carried the examination a step further, and dealt with the amount of decrease rather than the mere fact of decrease, we found that a change as large as that shown by the Chest in the years during and after the Hospital campaign as compared with the earlier four years would occur more often than once in twenty times by chance.[40]

The two tests, taken together, make it difficult to return an unambiguous answer to the question whether the amounts raised by the Chest were affected by the Hospital campaign. Certainly, we cannot say with confidence that the Hospital campaign hurt the Chest.

If, however, we assume that the Hospital campaign did have an effect, we must ask whether it more likely *delayed* than *reduced* the Chest take. Although we do not have the net results for the 1955 campaign—and this would give us somewhat more conclusive evidence—we do know the increase in amount pledged for 1955 over amount pledged for 1954. This was about 30 per cent; and, if the collection of pledges continues at the same rate as over the past few years, the increase in amount raised will also be about 30 per cent. This suggests that the Chest has not only returned to the tendency of annual increases, but that it has made up most, if not all, of the increases which it may have "missed" during the Hospital campaign. If the four-year period "during and after" is compared as a whole with the four-year period "before," the later period has the larger average increase, although this also could be a chance effect.[41] Thus it seems that, if the Hospital campaign affected the Chest, it was by delaying rather than reducing the total income.

For the Red Cross, the data show about the same relations. In the five campaigns prior to the start of the Hospital campaign, the Red Cross showed decreases in three and increases in two, with a net increase for the five years of 14.7 per cent.[42] In the three campaigns following the start of the Hospital campaign, the Red Cross had decreases in two and an increase in one, with a net decrease for the three years of 1.7 per cent. Applying to the Red Cross material the same tests regarding probability as we used for Chest data, we find that the chances of obtaining by chance the distribution actually found, are even greater than for the Community Chest, i.e., there is no clear evidence of any effect by the Hospital campaign. If we compare actual percentage changes for the five years preceding the Hospital campaign with those for the three years following, we get a pretty clear indication of no significant change in the rates of increase for the two periods.[43] Apparently, the Hospital campaign had little, if any, effect on the Red Cross campaign.

There is another way of looking at the matter that again suggests the view that rather than depriving the Chest of funds, the Hospital campaign might have merely deferred the receipt of money by the Chest. If the 1955 campaign eventually shows the increase which it appears to have made, the average annual increase for the eight-year period through 1955 will be about 6.5 per cent.[44] The average annual rate of increase for the four years after the Hospital campaign is 6.9 per cent; and the average annual increase for the years before is 6.4 per cent. This again suggests that the major effect, *if any*, which the Hospital campaign may have had on the net money-raising results of the Chest was to delay the time when the Chest got its money.

In spite of care in treating the data we have, we should warn the reader that much of what we have said is speculative and subject to considerable reasonable doubt, if only because economic and other factors, including the end of the Korean War, were acting at about the same time as the Hospital campaign was at its peak. These could have had as much effect on all performances as did the Hospital campaign, if not more. Moreover, the Chest was seeking to meet a higher goal annually,[45] while the Red Cross had about the same goal (with one exception, when it was lower) throughout the period of the Hospital campaign.

It is also widely believed in Indianapolis that the Hospital campaign served as a stimulus to giving, i.e., that rather than being competitive with the other philanthropies for the "donor's dollar," it may have served to raise the level of giving in Indianapolis generally. This hypothesis cannot be adequately tested until several more years have elapsed, but, in the meantime, it could be said that results, so far, do not contradict this view.


COMMUNITY CHEST—RED CROSS

It might be well to begin our comparison of money-results for the Chest and the Red Cross by looking at a longer time period than we have been using.[46] Chart 44 shows the amount raised by the Chest and Red Cross for the years 1934 to 1956, inclusive.[47]

Through 1932, the Chest and Red Cross conducted a single campaign in the autumn. Beginning in 1933, and each year since, however, the Chest and Red Cross have conducted separate fundraising campaigns. In the autumn of 1942, the first United War Fund campaign was held in Indianapolis, and the Red Cross campaign was deferred until March, 1943. Since then, the Chest campaign has been held in the fall, and the Red Cross campaign in the following spring. As the chart shows, giving to the Community Chest remained at about the same level from the time of the separation until the United States entered World War II. In response to that crisis, the amount raised by the Chest[48] rose dramatically, and remained at the higher level through the campaign for 1945.[49] Following the peak war campaign, the amount raised took a sharp drop in two consecutive campaigns, but even this sharp decline left the Chest well above its pre-war level, in current dollars.[50] Although the campaign for 1948 showed a further slight decline, in the other years following the War, the Chest had small but regular increases—except for the campaigns for 1954 and 1955, which resulted in very small decreases. The campaign for 1956 produced a marked —almost "revolutionary"—increase.

The first Red Cross campaign results after the separation were at a rising but fairly low level until the 1940 campaign, at which time the amount raised showed a tremendous jump. Perhaps this was associated with the beginning of the military draft.[51] The 1941 results registered a decline, but another tremendous jump occurred in 1942, the first campaign following the entrance of the United States into World War II. The next three campaigns also resulted in further large increases. By 1945, the Red Cross was raising more than half as much as the whole United War Fund. However, with the end of the war, Red Cross results dropped considerably for two years, and then, but only slightly, for three more years. The curve turned up again in 1951, and since then the Red Cross has continued at about the same level.

In summary, as Chart 44 shows clearly, after the separation in 1933, the Chest continued at about the same level until the United States entry into World War II, while the Red Cross started at a very low level and made slow gains until 1940, after which, with but one setback (1941), its results boomed. The postwar period shows, after the decline, a levelling out for both organizations, followed by a slight increase. Before the levelling out process, the Red Cross dropped relatively more than the Chest, so that, since the war, the total amount raised for the Red Cross represents about one-fourth to one-third as much as the total amount raised for the Chest, whereas, as already pointed out, during the war period campaigns the Red Cross total was more than half of even the United War Fund total.[52]

### Reports by Campaign Divisions

Earlier we discussed the difficulties in comparing according to the campaign divisions used by the Red Cross and the Chest. However, since many persons we talked to in Indianapolis do make just such comparisons between organizations we shall examine reports of the Red Cross and Chest campaign divisions, asking the reader to bear the risks of non-comparability in mind.

The Red Cross campaign reports money-results by eight divisions, labelled as follows: Residential; Towns; Downtown; Professional; Government and Education; Public Service; Commercial; Industrial. The over-all pattern has been much the same since 1952, the first year to be examined.[53]

The Community Chest campaign has thoroughly revised its reporting system during the same time period, 1952 to 1955. In 1952, the Chest had twelve reporting divisions,[54] as follows: Special Gifts; Residential; Townships; Downtown; Medical; Legal; Public; Commercial; Industrial; Mercantile; Utilities; Railroads. The major emphasis in soliciting was then on an "Advanced Gifts" program, in which the gifts of the larger firms and their executives, as well as other large gifts, were solicited in the Special Gifts Division.[55] A rough comparison can be made between the Red Cross and Chest reports by combining some of the divisions. Table XLIV shows how we first matched divisions of the two organizations in 1952 which were approximately the same, and then how, for the purposes of this report, we applied new names to combinations of the divisions to make the latter reasonably comparable.[56]

TABLE XLIV

COMPARISON OF REPORTING DIVISIONS OF RED CROSS AND COMMUNITY CHEST, 1952, AND METHOD OF RECOMBINING THEM FOR COMPARABILITY

| Red Cross | Community Chest | Combination or division for comparative purposes |
|---|---|---|
| Residential<br>Towns | Residential<br>Townships | *Residential & Towns* |
| Downtown | Downtown | *Downtown* |
| Professional | Medical[a]<br>Legal | *Professional* |
| Government & Education | Public | *Public* |
| Public Service[c]<br>Commercial<br>Industrial | Special Gifts[b]<br>Industrial<br>Mercantile<br>Commercial<br>Utilities<br>Railroads | *Commerce & Industry[d]* |

[a]Includes gifts of Dentists. These are *not* included in the Red Cross's Professional division, but are distributed, instead, over their Downtown, Residential, and Towns divisions.

[b]Includes some gifts which the Red Cross reports in Residential, Towns, and Downtown.

[c]Includes some gifts, particularly of smaller firms and their employees (firms employing 10-24 persons), which the Community Chest reports in Residential, Townships, and Downtown.

[d]Not to be confused with "Industrial & Commercial Organizations" (ICO)—a classification employed earlier.

In 1953, the Chest eliminated the Special Gifts division. The gifts which had been reported in this division were assigned mainly to Downtown, Industrial, Mercantile, Commercial, Utilities, and Railroads divisions, with smaller amounts going to Residental. At the same time, Residential and Townships divisions were combined into one. The major effect of these changes was to put an unusually large amount—both in percentage and in dollars—into the Downtown division. Then, in 1954, the Chest took all firms employing fifteen or more persons out of the Downtown and Residential-and-Towns divisions and reported them instead in Commerce-and-Industry. At the same time, a number of subdivisions were established within Public and Residential.[57] Finally, in 1955, the Chest reshuffled the entire system. In that campaign, only four divisions were used, though all had large subdivisions. Still, with only a minimum of difficulty, we were able to regroup the data to fit our analytical scheme. The Community Chest reporting units for the 1955 campaign appear, then, as listed:

> I "Division A"
>    A. Corporate Gifts
>       1. Firms (about 600 of largest potential givers)
>       2. Foundations
>    B. Professional
>       1. Doctors
>       2. Dentists
>       3. Attorneys
> II Commerce and Industry
>    A. Employees
>    B. Executives
>    C. Firms (all other firms—about 1,000—employing 15 or more persons)
> III Metropolitan
>    A. Downtown
>    B. Real Estate
>    C. Neighborhood Business
>    D. Residential
> IV Public
>    A. Government
>    B. Education
>    C. Non-Profit

Thus, each campaign report required some adjustments[58] in order to make possible any meaningful comparisons between organizations and between years. However, bearing in mind the qualifications suggested, it seems reasonable to use the new combinations of divisions to suggest some of the similarities and differences between the results of Chest and Red Cross campaigns. Table XLV gives the money-results for the divisions of the Red Cross and Community Chest as percentages of the total amount raised for the years 1952 through 1955, using the adjusted divisions and combinations of Table XLIV.

TABLE XLV

DIVISIONAL RESULTS AS PERCENTAGE OF TOTAL AMOUNT RAISED
FOR CHEST AND RED CROSS, 1952-5

| Division | 1952 | | 1953 | | 1954 | | 1955 | |
|---|---|---|---|---|---|---|---|---|
| | Chest | Red Cross | Chest | Red Cross | Chest | Red Cross | Chest | Red Cross |
| Total | 100.0% | 100.0% | 100.0% | 100.0% | 100.0% | 100.0% | 100.0% | 100.0% |
| Commerce & Industry | 79.2 | 73.7 | 76.5 | 71.6 | 77.2 | 71.5 | 81.5 | 72.1 |
| Residential & Towns | 10.4 | 14.0 | 9.7 | 15.4 | 10.8 | 15.1 | 8.2 | 14.3 |
| Public | 5.4 | 6.1 | 5.8 | 6.7 | 6.0 | 7.2 | 5.4 | 7.2 |
| Downtown | 2.8 | 3.7 | 5.7 | 3.6 | 3.4 | 3.5 | 2.6 | 3.7 |
| Professional | 2.2 | 2.5 | 2.3 | 2.7 | 2.6 | 2.7 | 2.3 | 2.7 |

In all four years, each of the Professional, Public, and Residential-and-Towns divisions produces a greater percentage of the total amount raised for the Red Cross than it does for the Chest. Except for 1953, the same is true for the Downtown division.[59] Necessarily, then, the Chest percentage from Commerce-and-Industry is higher in each of the four years than is the percentage from this division for the Red Cross, although for both organizations this division is far and away the most important—providing better than 70 per cent of the total amount raised in each case. Chart 45 shows the data of Table XLV very clearly. It also shows that the Red Cross percentage results for all divisions are much more uniform from year to year than those for the Chest.[60]

*Industrial and Commercial Organizations—ICO*

We mentioned earlier in this chapter how we had set up ICO for comparing the money-results of the Chest and the Red Cross. Now we shall use this method of classification for another look at these results in detail. We shall use Red Cross data for campaigns in 1952 to 1955, and compare with Chest data for campaigns in 1951 to 1955. Thus we are able to examine these campaigns both on a "calendar year" basis and a "campaign year" basis. In 1953, the Chest shifted to a "Unit Account"[61] solicitation system for all firms employing fifteen or more persons; this system had previously also been used by the Red Cross for firms employing ten or more persons. It is these unit accounts which give information for the ICO analysis.[62]

Table XLVI shows the ICO total as a percentage of the total amount pledged for the specified years. Comparing the two campaigns *in* any given year, the Chest is more dependent than the Red Cross on ICO pledging for three out of the four campaigns; and the same is true if the comparison is made between campaigns *for* identical years. In the calendar year 1955, the difference is, for the first time, large enough to be quite noticeable.

## TABLE XLVI

ICO PLEDGING AS PERCENTAGE OF TOTAL AMOUNT PLEDGED,
CHEST AND RED CROSS[a]

| Year | Chest | Red Cross |
|------|-------|-----------|
| 1951 | 68.3% | — |
| 1952 | 68.3% | 69.3% |
| 1953 | 70.6% | 68.2% |
| 1954 | 70.6% | 69.0% |
| 1955 | 75.7% | 69.6% |

[a]Arrows indicate the figures to be compared on the "campaign for" basis. Calendar year comparisons—i.e., "campaign in"—may, of course, be made across each line.

We may now look *within* the ICO totals and compare Firm pledges with Employee (including Executive) pledges. Table XLVII shows separately the percentage of total amount pledged in ICO by Firms and Employees for Chest and Red Cross for the specified years. Here again we find an

## TABLE XLVII

PERCENTAGE OF TOTAL AMOUNT PLEDGED IN ICO BY FIRMS AND EMPLOYEES[a]
RESPECTIVELY FOR CHEST AND RED CROSS[b]

| Year | Firm Chest | Firm Red Cross | Employee[a] Chest | Employee[a] Red Cross |
|------|-------|-----------|-------|-----------|
| 1951 | 58.5% | — | 41.5% | — |
| 1952 | 59.8% | 49.1% | 40.2% | 50.9% |
| 1953 | 59.1% | 49.6% | 40.9% | 50.4% |
| 1954 | 58.4% | 46.6% | 41.6% | 53.4% |
| 1955 | 59.9% | 45.7% | 40.1% | 54.3% |

[a]Including executives.
[b]Arrows indicate figures to be compared on "campaign for" a given year basis. Calendar year comparisons may, of course, be made across each line.

important difference: within ICO, the Chest is relatively much more dependent on Firm pledges, and the Red Cross, on Employee pledges, whether we use campaign years for comparison or calendar years. Thus, within ICO, as we found more generally earlier, the larger campaign in Indianapolis is more dependent on Firm pledging, and the smaller campaign is more dependent on Employee pledging.

In further examination of ICO pledging, it may be of interest to see if there are similarities and differences when we use actual average per-employee pledges in place of percentages of total pledged. Table XLVIII shows the average per-employee pledges of Firms and Employees in ICO for Chest and Red Cross for the specified years. As would be expected on the basis of campaign size, the Chest receives larger per-employee pledges from both Firms and Employees in ICO than does the Red Cross for all years compared. But what is striking is that the Red Cross receives larger

## TABLE XLVIII

PER-EMPLOYEE PLEDGES OF FIRMS AND EMPLOYEES[a] IN ICO FOR CHEST AND RED CROSS[b]

| Year | Firm | | Employee[a] | |
|------|------|------|------|------|
| | Chest | Red Cross | Chest | Red Cross |
| 1951 | $3.91 | — | $2.77 | — |
| 1952 | $4.08 | → $1.03 | $2.74 | → $1.08 |
| 1953 | $3.90 | $1.05 | $2.69 | $1.06 |
| 1954 | $3.99 | $0.99 | $2.84 | $1.13 |
| 1955 | $5.50 | $0.99 | $3.68 | $1.18 |

[a]Includes executives.

[b]Arrows indicate figures to be compared on campaign year basis. Calendar year comparisons may, of course, be made across each line.

Employee pledges per employee than Firm pledges per employee (though they are nearly equal) while the Chest receives much larger per-employee pledges from the Firm itself than it does from the Employees themselves. One could thus say—for ICO—that the Red Cross appears to be equally supported by labor and management, but that the Chest seems predominantly supported by management.

Interestingly, also, in the Red Cross, despite the changes in Firm pledges per employee and Employee pledges per employee, the sum of these two pledges is the same for 1952 and 1953 ($2.11), only one cent greater in 1954 ($2.12), and only six cents greater in 1955 ($2.17): although the total amount pledged to Red Cross from ICO was changing in the three-year period, the per-employee rate of pledging by the units (Firm plus Employee) was thus almost unchanged. The unit account solicitation attained practically the same rate of pledging in all four years.

In contrast, for the Chest, the differences in per-employee pledges between the Firm and the Employee shares are quite large, ranging from $1.14 to $1.82; and, similarly, by way of contrast, in the Chest the sum of Employee and Firm pledges per employee increased, rising unsteadily by 37 per cent over the period. Firms increased their giving per employee by about 42 per cent; Employees increased theirs by about a third. Thus, the per-employee rate of pledging in ICO seems to change considerably more for the Chest than for the Red Cross.[63]

We may next turn from examining ICO as a unit to comparisons of different groupings within ICO.

*Size of firm.* One way to examine giving by firms is in terms of their size[64] (as measured by the number of employees reported to the fund-raising organization[65]). Again we had data available for Red Cross for campaigns in 1952 to 1955 and we used Chest data for campaigns in 1951 to 1955.

Table XLIX summarizes the results in ICO, by size of firm, for Chest and Red Cross for the specified years; they are shown in full in Table L.

## TABLE XLIX

PERCENTAGE OF TOTAL PLEDGES IN ICO BY SIZE GROUPS (FOR FIRMS EMPLOYING 25 OR MORE PERSONS[a]), CHEST AND RED CROSS

| Size groups: number of employees | Community Chest | | | | | Red Cross | | | |
|---|---|---|---|---|---|---|---|---|---|
| | 1951 | 1952 | 1953 | 1954 | 1955 | 1952 | 1953 | 1954 | 1955 |
| | % | % | % | % | % | % | % | % | % |
| TOTAL | 100.0 | 100.0 | 100.0 | 100.0 | 100.0 | 100.0 | 100.0 | 100.0 | 100.0 |
| 5000 & over | 24.8 | 25.5 | 23.1 | 24.6 | 26.5 | 21.0 | 20.8 | 19.6 | 20.1 |
| 1000 — 4999 | 31.0 | 28.8 | 28.8 | 26.9 | 24.5 | 27.2 | 26.0 | 27.4 | 26.3 |
| 500 — 999 | 6.8 | 8.3 | 7.8 | 9.6 | 11.7 | 6.0 | 9.7 | 9.5 | 12.1 |
| 100 — 499 | 26.6 | 26.0 | 27.7 | 26.7 | 26.3 | 28.8 | 25.9 | 27.1 | 25.5 |
| 50 — 99 | 6.5 | 7.1 | 7.9 | 7.6 | 6.5 | 9.2 | 10.0 | 8.2 | 8.5 |
| 25 — 49 | 4.3 | 4.3 | 4.7 | 4.6 | 4.5 | 7.8 | 7.6 | 8.2 | 7.5 |

[a]So that comparison could be made between roughly equivalent numbers of firms, firms employing less than 25 persons were dropped.

No matter whether we compare on a campaign or on a calendar year basis, the Chest receives a greater proportion of the total amount pledged from the largest firms (those employing five thousand and more employees) than does the Red Cross. The Red Cross, in contrast, receives a greater proportion from the smallest firms (employing less than one hundred employees) than does the Chest. For the intermediate size groups (100-4999) the two organizations receive about the same proportion, just under two-thirds, of the total amount accounted for by the table.

We may now break Table XLIX into two—one referring to Firm gifts, and the other to Employee gifts. Table LI A shows Firm pledges per employee by size groups for Chest and Red Cross for firms employing twenty-five or more persons for the specified years. The evidence is not unambiguous, but for the Red Cross there is a fairly consistent pattern of *increasing* Firm pledges per employee from the largest size group to the smallest size

## TABLE LI A

FIRM PLEDGES PER EMPLOYEE IN ICO BY SIZE GROUPS (FOR FIRMS EMPLOYING 25 OR MORE PERSONS), CHEST AND RED CROSS

| Size groups: number of employees | Community Chest | | | | | Red Cross | | | |
|---|---|---|---|---|---|---|---|---|---|
| | 1951 | 1952 | 1953 | 1954 | 1955 | 1952 | 1953 | 1954 | 1955 |
| TOTAL | $3.89 | $4.05 | $3.88 | $3.97 | $5.45 | $1.00 | $1.01 | $ .96 | $ .95 |
| 5000 & over | 3.85 | 4.09 | 4.00 | 4.33 | 5.41 | .70 | .73 | .58 | .58 |
| 1000 — 4999 | 3.67 | 4.08 | 3.90 | 4.25 | 4.92 | .87 | .89 | .85 | .80 |
| 500 — 999 | 3.36 | 3.33 | 3.37 | 3.86 | 7.10 | .80 | .87 | 1.13 | 1.31 |
| 100 — 499 | 4.36 | 4.45 | 4.22 | 3.96 | 6.07 | 1.26 | 1.23 | 1.10 | 1.12 |
| 50 — 99 | 3.79 | 3.28 | 3.40 | 3.06 | 4.15 | 1.17 | 1.44 | 1.07 | 1.06 |
| 25 — 49 | 4.52 | 4.65 | 3.38 | 3.14 | 4.14 | 1.70 | 1.42 | 1.70 | 1.50 |

group, i.e., in general, the smaller the firm the larger the Firm gift per employee. For the Chest, the pattern is more complicated. In 1951 and 1952, the Chest shows the same pattern as does the Red Cross. But in 1953, 1954, and 1955, the Chest shows the reverse pattern—i.e., *decreasing* Firm pledges per employee from the "five thousand and over" group down. Thus, the Chest appears to be in the process of change from the pattern of the Red Cross to one of direct relation between size and Firm pledge per employee; i.e., to one where the larger the firm, the larger the Firm pledge per employee.[66]

Table LI B shows, correspondingly, Employee pledges per employee, by size groups, for Chest and Red Cross for firms employing twenty-five or more persons for the specified years. One very striking fact shows up imme-

TABLE LI B

EMPLOYEE PLEDGES PER EMPLOYEE IN ICO BY SIZE GROUPS FOR FIRMS EMPLOYING 25 OR MORE PERSONS, CHEST AND RED CROSS

| Size groups: number of employees | Community Chest | | | | | Red Cross | | | |
|---|---|---|---|---|---|---|---|---|---|
| | 1951 | 1952 | 1953 | 1954 | 1955 | 1952 | 1953 | 1954 | 1955 |
| TOTAL | $2.76 | $2.72 | $2.70 | $2.86 | $3.71 | $1.07 | $1.05 | $1.13 | $1.17 |
| 5000 & over | 3.89 | 3.86 | 3.60 | 3.79 | 4.83 | 1.41 | 1.37 | 1.48 | 1.50 |
| 1000 — 4999 | 2.35 | 2.38 | 2.71 | 2.98 | 3.73 | .89 | .91 | 1.05 | 1.07 |
| 500 — 999 | 1.82 | 1.79 | 2.03 | 2.76 | 3.25 | .74 | .93 | .83 | 1.10 |
| 100 — 499 | 2.66 | 2.38 | 2.43 | 2.32 | 3.20 | 1.05 | .95 | 1.08 | 1.06 |
| 50 — 99 | 2.63 | 3.17 | 2.55 | 2.75 | 2.95 | 1.12 | 1.12 | .99 | 1.01 |
| 25 — 49 | 3.05 | 3.09 | 2.19 | 2.37 | 3.22 | 1.19 | 1.19 | 1.20 | 1.33 |

diately: in all years, for both Red Cross and Chest, the group of largest firms (5000 and over) has the highest Employee pledge per employee of all the size groups. This suggests that solicitation among employees of the very large firms is "effectively" organized,[67] and it also suggests that solicitation among the companies employing less than five thousand employees has not been nearly as effective as it has been in the companies employing five thousand or more persons.[68]

Neglecting momentarily the fact that the "5000 & over" group consistently produces the largest per-employee pledges, and examining only the remaining size groups, an interesting pattern emerges: there is an inverse relation between Employee pledge per employee and size of Firm for the Chest in 1951 and 1952 and for the Red Cross generally, i.e., there is a tendency for the smaller firms to show the larger Employee gifts per employee. However, for the Chest in 1953, 1954, and 1955 this relation is reversed; so that we see here a tendency for the Employee pledge per employee to increase with firm size. Moreover, the inverse relationship in the Red Cross appears to be attenuating. Combining Chest performance in

## TABLE L

FIRM GIFT, EMPLOYEE GIFT, TOTAL GIFT, NUMBER OF EMPLOYEES, FIRM PLEDGE PER EMPLOYEE, EMPLOYEE PLEDGE PER EMPLOYEE, TOTAL PLEDGE PER EMPLOYEE AND TOTAL GIFT OF SIZE GROUP AS PERCENTAGE OF TOTAL GIFT BY SIZE GROUPS IN ICO FOR CHEST AND RED CROSS

RED CROSS

| Size Group (1) | Firm gift (2) | Employee gift (3) | Total gift (4) | Number of employees (5) | Firm pledge per employee (6) | Employee pledge per employee (7) | Total pledge per employee (8) | Total gift of size group as percentage of total gift (9) |
|---|---|---|---|---|---|---|---|---|
| **1952** | | | | | | | | |
| TOTAL | $164,770 | $175,321 | $340,091 | 164,610 | $ 1.00 | $ 1.07 | $ 2.07 | 100.00% |
| 5000 & over | 23,533 | 47,811 | 71,344 | 33,800 | .70 | 1.41 | 2.11 | 20.98 |
| 1000 – 4999 | 45,682 | 46,770 | 92,452 | 52,293 | .87 | .89 | 1.77 | 27.18 |
| 500 – 999 | 10,645 | 9,886 | 20,531 | 13,294 | .80 | .74 | 1.54 | 6.04 |
| 100 – 499 | 53,239 | 44,560 | 97,799 | 42,313 | 1.26 | 1.05 | 2.31 | 28.75 |
| 50 – 99 | 16,007 | 15,306 | 31,313 | 13,706 | 1.17 | 1.12 | 2.28 | 9.21 |
| 25 – 49 | 15,664 | 10,988 | 26,652 | 9,204 | 1.70 | 1.19 | 2.90 | 7.84 |
| **1953** | | | | | | | | |
| TOTAL | 162,746 | 168,510 | 331,256 | 160,347 | 1.01 | 1.05 | 2.07 | 100.00 |
| 5000 & over | 23,978 | 44,781 | 68,759 | 32,667 | .73 | 1.37 | 2.10 | 20.76 |
| 1000 – 4999 | 42,490 | 43,696 | 86,186 | 47,977 | .89 | .91 | 1.80 | 26.02 |
| 500 – 999 | 15,615 | 16,640 | 32,255 | 17,923 | .87 | .93 | 1.80 | 9.74 |
| 100 – 499 | 48,293 | 37,398 | 85,691 | 39,161 | 1.23 | .95 | 2.19 | 25.87 |
| 50 – 99 | 18,684 | 14,451 | 33,135 | 12,952 | 1.44 | 1.12 | 2.56 | 10.00 |
| 25 – 49 | 13,686 | 11,544 | 25,230 | 9,667 | 1.42 | 1.19 | 2.61 | 7.61 |
| **1954** | | | | | | | | |
| TOTAL | 153,595 | 180,558 | 334,153 | 160,489 | .96 | 1.13 | 2.08 | 100.00 |
| 5000 & over | 18,540 | 47,040 | 65,580 | 31,720 | .58 | 1.48 | 2.07 | 19.63 |
| 1000 – 4999 | 40,857 | 50,846 | 91,703 | 48,337 | .85 | 1.05 | 1.90 | 27.44 |
| 500 – 999 | 18,231 | 13,436 | 31,667 | 16,133 | 1.13 | .83 | 1.96 | 9.48 |
| 100 – 499 | 45,715 | 44,722 | 90,437 | 41,570 | 1.10 | 1.08 | 2.18 | 27.06 |
| 50 – 99 | 14,143 | 13,099 | 27,242 | 13,227 | 1.07 | .99 | 2.06 | 8.15 |
| 25 – 49 | 16,109 | 11,415 | 27,524 | 9,502 | 1.70 | 1.20 | 2.90 | 8.24 |

COMMUNITY CHEST

| | | | | | | | | |
|---|---|---|---|---|---|---|---|---|
| **1951** | | | | | | | | |
| TOTAL | $617,535 | $436,952 | $1,054,487 | 158,556 | $3.89 | $2.76 | $6.65 | 100.00% |
| 5000 & over | 130,035 | 131,266 | 261,301 | 33,732 | 3.85 | 3.89 | 7.75 | 24.78 |
| 1000 — 4999 | 199,142 | 127,906 | 327,048 | 54,336 | 3.67 | 2.35 | 6.02 | 31.01 |
| 500 — 999 | 46,475 | 25,129 | 71,604 | 13,828 | 3.36 | 1.82 | 5.18 | 6.79 |
| 100 — 499 | 174,410 | 106,370 | 280,780 | 40,016 | 4.36 | 2.66 | 7.02 | 26.63 |
| 50 — 99 | 40,629 | 28,205 | 68,834 | 10,710 | 3.79 | 2.63 | 6.43 | 6.53 |
| 25 — 49 | 26,844 | 18,076 | 44,920 | 5,934 | 4.52 | 3.05 | 7.57 | 4.26 |
| **1952** | | | | | | | | |
| TOTAL | 633,502 | 425,330 | 1,058,832 | 156,229 | 4.05 | 2.72 | 6.78 | 100.00 |
| 5000 & over | 138,790 | 131,085 | 269,875 | 33,972 | 4.09 | 3.86 | 7.94 | 25.49 |
| 1000 — 4999 | 192,432 | 112,339 | 304,771 | 47,201 | 4.08 | 2.38 | 6.46 | 28.78 |
| 500 — 999 | 56,962 | 30,580 | 87,542 | 17,101 | 3.33 | 1.79 | 5.12 | 8.27 |
| 100 — 499 | 179,623 | 96,081 | 275,704 | 40,384 | 4.45 | 2.38 | 6.83 | 26.04 |
| 50 — 99 | 38,382 | 37,055 | 75,437 | 11,692 | 3.28 | 3.17 | 6.45 | 7.12 |
| 25 — 49 | 27,313 | 18,190 | 45,503 | 5,879 | 4.65 | 3.09 | 7.74 | 4.30 |
| **1953** | | | | | | | | |
| TOTAL | 645,444 | 449,060 | 1,094,504 | 166,188 | 3.88 | 2.70 | 6.59 | 100.00 |
| 5000 & over | 132,997 | 119,671 | 252,668 | 33,256 | 4.00 | 3.60 | 7.60 | 23.09 |
| 1000 — 4999 | 186,164 | 129,305 | 315,469 | 47,766 | 3.90 | 2.71 | 6.60 | 28.82 |
| 500 — 999 | 52,844 | 31,784 | 84,628 | 15,683 | 3.37 | 2.03 | 5.40 | 7.73 |
| 100 — 499 | 192,562 | 110,858 | 303,420 | 45,612 | 4.22 | 2.43 | 6.65 | 27.72 |
| 50 — 99 | 49,542 | 37,139 | 86,681 | 14,588 | 3.40 | 2.55 | 5.94 | 7.92 |
| 25 — 49 | 31,335 | 20,303 | 51,638 | 9,283 | 3.38 | 2.19 | 5.56 | 4.72 |
| **1954** | | | | | | | | |
| TOTAL | 623,946 | 449,274 | 1,073,220 | 157,055 | 3.97 | 2.86 | 6.83 | 100.00 |
| 5000 & over | 140,850 | 123,196 | 264,046 | 32,530 | 4.33 | 3.79 | 8.12 | 24.60 |
| 1000 — 4999 | 169,665 | 118,684 | 288,349 | 39,886 | 4.25 | 2.98 | 7.23 | 26.87 |
| 500 — 999 | 61,274 | 41,579 | 102,853 | 15,863 | 3.86 | 2.76 | 6.48 | 9.58 |
| 100 — 499 | 180,588 | 105,654 | 286,242 | 45,620 | 3.96 | 2.32 | 6.27 | 26.67 |
| 50 — 99 | 43,100 | 38,718 | 81,818 | 14,094 | 3.06 | 2.75 | 5.81 | 7.62 |
| 25 — 49 | 28,469 | 21,443 | 49,912 | 9,062 | 3.14 | 2.37 | 5.51 | 4.65 |

1953, 1954, and 1955 with the weakening relation for Red Cross in 1954 and 1955, it seems possible that a pattern in which the employees of the smallest firms are making the highest pledges per employee is shifting to a pattern in which the employees of the largest firms are making the highest pledges per employee.[69] (If this is true, the behavior of the "5000 & over" group is not anomalous.)

*Industry groups.* Another way to compare pledging is by "industry groups."[70] All firms in ICO (including those employing fewer than 25 persons) were classified into fifteen major[71] industrial classifications. Table LII lists these groups and indicates, out of all firms which had a unit (Firm and/or Employee) pledge in any year, the percentage which each group represents of the total number of firms pledging. For the most part, the

TABLE LII

NUMBER OF FIRMS SHOWN AS PERCENTAGE OF ALL PLEDGING FIRMS
IN 15 MAJOR INDUSTRIAL CLASSIFICATIONS FOR CHEST AND RED CROSS

| Industrial group | Community Chest (1951-1954) | Red Cross (1952-1954)[a] |
|---|---|---|
| TOTAL | 100.0% | 100.0% |
| Automotive | 7.2 | 6.3 |
| Banks | 2.7 | 3.4 |
| Hotels | 1.6 | 1.9 |
| Manufacturing | 33.5 | 30.1 |
| Insurance | 6.9 | 7.2 |
| Retail | 15.2 | 18.8 |
| Transportation | 9.1 | 6.8 |
| Utilities | 1.7 | 1.3 |
| Real Estate | 1.1 | 1.2 |
| Wholesale | 12.6 | 13.1 |
| Construction | 3.9 | 3.6 |
| Laundries | 2.3 | 2.5 |
| Amusement | 1.3 | 2.1 |
| Miscellaneous | .5 | 1.1 |
| Unknown | .4 | .6 |

[a]Since we are looking at broad averages rather than examining precise relations, the inclusion of data for 1955 would hardly affect the averages shown.

proportionate number of firms pledging from each industry group was about the same for Chest and Red Cross.[72] But the Chest has a somewhat greater proportion from Manufacturing and Transportation than the Red Cross, while the Red Cross has a somewhat greater proportion from Retail than the Chest.[73]

But the proportion of *amount* pledged by the units (Firms plus Employees) in the industry groups bears little relation to the proportion of the *number* of firms represented in each industry group. Table LIII shows the percentage each industry group represents of the total amount pledged in ICO. Comparison with Table LII shows that only Retail has roughly the same proportion for number of firms as for amount pledged. The most striking contrast is for Manufacturing: while this industry group represents about one-third of the number of firms, it produces better than half of the total amount pledged in ICO. It might well be expected that proportion of firms and proportion of amount raised among industry groups should not be the same,[74] but the magnitude of the discrepancy is worth noting.

TABLE LIII

PERCENTAGE OF TOTAL AMOUNT PLEDGED IN ICO BY 15 MAJOR INDUSTRIAL GROUPS, CHEST AND RED CROSS

| Industry group | Community Chest | | | | | Red Cross | | | |
|---|---|---|---|---|---|---|---|---|---|
| | 1951 | 1952 | 1953 | 1954 | 1955 | 1952 | 1953 | 1954 | 1955 |
| | % | % | % | % | % | % | % | % | % |
| TOTAL | 100.0 | 100.0 | 100.0 | 100.0 | 100.0 | 100.0 | 100.0 | 100.0 | 100.0 |
| Automotive | 2.5 | 2.4 | 2.3 | 2.0 | 1.7 | 2.5 | 2.6 | 2.3 | 2.3 |
| Banks | 5.3 | 5.5 | 5.8 | 6.0 | 8.0 | 4.9 | 5.2 | 5.4 | 5.4 |
| Hotels | .3 | .4 | .4 | .3 | .3 | .7 | .6 | .7 | .7 |
| Manufacturing | 53.8 | 53.8 | 52.7 | 53.5 | 51.7 | 51.9 | 51.7 | 51.4 | 52.6 |
| Insurance | 3.0 | 3.2 | 4.0 | 4.1 | 5.2 | 3.9 | 4.1 | 4.6 | 4.4 |
| Retail | 16.2 | 16.0 | 15.0 | 14.8 | 13.1 | 16.4 | 15.7 | 15.1 | 15.0 |
| Transportation | 1.8 | 1.8 | 1.9 | 1.4 | 1.4 | 2.4 | 2.5 | 2.2 | 2.0 |
| Utilities | 9.8 | 9.9 | 9.8 | 9.8 | 10.0 | 7.2 | 7.5 | 8.1 | 8.1 |
| Real Estate | .5 | .5 | .5 | .5 | .5 | .3 | .3 | .4 | .3 |
| Wholesale | 5.0 | 4.8 | 5.4 | 5.2 | 5.8 | 6.2 | 6.1 | 6.1 | 5.7 |
| Construction | .4 | .4 | .8 | .9 | 1.0 | 1.0 | 1.1 | 1.0 | .9 |
| Laundries | .5 | .4 | .4 | .4 | .3 | .7 | .7 | .7 | .6 |
| Amusement | —[a] | —[a] | .2 | .2 | .1 | .4 | .3 | .4 | .3 |
| Miscellaneous | .9 | .9 | .8 | .9 | .8 | 1.4 | 1.5 | 1.5 | 1.6 |
| Unknown | .0[b] | .0[b] | —[a] | .0[b] | .1 | .1 | .1 | .1 | .1 |

[a]Dash (−) indicates no gifts in the industry group.
[b]Point zero (.0) indicates the figure is less than 0.05 per cent.

Table LIII additionally reveals great similarity in pattern between Red Cross and Chest in the proportion pledged by each industry group. The greatest difference found is 2.1 per cent in Manufacturing (1952 Chest compared with 1953 Red Cross on campaign year basis, or 1954 Chest compared with 1954 Red Cross on calendar year basis),[75] which is not a large difference for this distribution. The similarity in proportion raised by each industry group suggests that—despite differences in the type of campaign carried out, or the kinds of pressure and gimmicks tried, or any of the many variations in campaigns—each industry group contributes to Chest and Red Cross in about the same proportion; and it may also be noted that there is very little change as between years, for each organization separately. Even for the year 1955, where many other things in the Chest campaign changed, the proportions received from the several industry groups remained relatively constant. The effect is similar to what one would expect if there were a concerted effort on the part of firms in Indianapolis to maintain a consistent pattern, although, of course, there is no such concert.[76] It appears, then, that each industry group tends to behave, relative to other industry groups, as though it had a pledging potential which, within fairly narrow limits, remains stable. (Certainly, comparison of proportions of total received from each industry group by the Red Cross and the Chest respectively does not suggest any reason for their respective differential degrees of "success" in the total.)

It will be recalled that we had found earlier that Firm pledging per employee and Employee pledging per employee in ICO changed independently. This leads us to examine separately the Firm pledges in each industry group as a percentage of the total Firm pledges, and the Employee pledges in each industry group as a percentage of the total Employee pledges in ICO for Chest and Red Cross. The results appear in Table LIV.

Over all industry groups, both Firm pledges and Employee pledges show a very stable proportion of their respective totals in ICO, both as between organizations for the same year or as between years for the same organization. Although there is somewhat more variation than we found for the total pledges, the magnitude of the differences is only slightly greater. The fact that Firms in their Firm giving and Employees in their Employee giving behave alike towards each organization in any given year, and alike to the same organization from year to year—when they are taken in large industrial groups, and when we have an eye to the *proportion* of the whole contributed—makes doubly intriguing speculation as to the cause; and it also renders doubly doubtful schemes founded on the belief that almost anything can be done by changing campaign appeals. Such remarkable stabilities must have their roots deep in the relatively inflexible structure of business and philanthropic life.

## SUMMARY

We have now covered the main points in inter-organization comparisons. We have shown, within the limitations of the data we could get and treat, that there are many patterns of relations between the campaigns compared. In summary, these are:

A. For Hospital, Chest and Red Cross

1. Whether or not the Hospital campaign had any effect on the Red Cross and Chest campaigns, cannot be unambiguously determined. If there was an effect, the Hospital campaign probably *delayed* the time when the money was received rather than *deprived* the Chest of any income. But there is even a possibility that the Hospital campaign stimulated giving to all philanthropies in Indianapolis.

## TABLE LIV

### Industry Firm Pledges as Percentage of Total Firm Pledges, and Employee Pledges as Percentage of Total Employee Pledges, for Chest and Red Cross

| Industry group* | Community Chest | | | | | | | | | | Red Cross | | | | | | | |
|---|---|---|---|---|---|---|---|---|---|---|---|---|---|---|---|---|---|---|
| | 1951 | | 1952 | | 1953 | | 1954 | | 1955 | | 1952 | | 1953 | | 1954 | | 1955 | |
| | Firm[a] | Emp.[a] | Firm | Emp. | Firm | Emp. | Firm | Emp. | Firm | Emp. | Firm | Emp. | Firm | Emp. | Firm | Emp. | Firm | Emp. |
| | % | % | % | % | % | % | % | % | % | % | % | % | % | % | % | % | % | % |
| Total | 100.0 | 100.0 | 100.0 | 100.0 | 100.0 | 100.0 | 100.0 | 100.0 | 100.0 | 100.0 | 100.0 | 100.0 | 100.0 | 100.0 | 100.0 | 100.0 | 100.0 | 100.0 |
| A | 2.5 | 2.5 | 2.4 | 2.4 | 2.4 | 2.2 | 1.9 | 2.1 | 1.7 | 1.6 | 2.7 | 2.3 | 2.8 | 2.3 | 2.6 | 2.1 | 2.6 | 2.0 |
| B | 6.8 | 3.2 | 6.9 | 3.3 | 7.0 | 4.0 | 7.2 | 4.2 | 10.1 | 4.9 | 6.6 | 3.2 | 7.2 | 3.2 | 7.7 | 3.4 | 7.7 | 3.5 |
| C | .4 | .3 | .4 | .3 | .4 | .2 | .4 | .2 | .3 | .3 | .8 | .7 | .8 | .5 | .8 | .6 | .8 | .6 |
| D | 46.4 | 64.2 | 46.4 | 64.9 | 45.9 | 62.5 | 46.7 | 62.9 | 45.5 | 60.9 | 44.0 | 59.5 | 44.7 | 58.6 | 43.1 | 58.6 | 43.7 | 60.0 |
| E | 2.6 | 3.6 | 2.7 | 3.9 | 3.4 | 4.9 | 3.5 | 4.9 | 5.2 | 5.2 | 3.5 | 4.2 | 3.3 | 4.8 | 3.6 | 5.5 | 3.7 | 5.0 |
| F | 20.5 | 10.0 | 20.3 | 9.7 | 18.8 | 9.4 | 18.5 | 9.7 | 15.6 | 9.4 | 20.3 | 12.7 | 19.4 | 12.1 | 18.8 | 11.9 | 19.3 | 11.5 |
| G | 1.0 | 2.9 | 1.1 | 3.0 | 1.3 | 2.8 | 1.0 | 2.1 | 1.1 | 1.9 | 1.2 | 3.5 | 1.5 | 3.4 | 1.6 | 2.8 | 1.4 | 2.5 |
| H | 11.7 | 7.2 | 12.0 | 6.9 | 11.1 | 7.9 | 11.4 | 7.7 | 11.1 | 8.3 | 8.6 | 5.9 | 8.8 | 6.3 | 9.3 | 7.2 | 9.3 | 7.1 |
| I | .5 | .5 | .5 | .5 | .5 | .5 | .5 | .4 | .7 | .3 | .2 | .4 | .2 | .4 | .2 | .5 | .2 | .4 |
| J | 5.3 | 4.6 | 5.2 | 4.2 | 6.1 | 4.6 | 5.6 | 4.7 | 5.8 | 5.8 | 7.2 | 5.4 | 6.3 | 5.9 | 6.8 | 5.4 | 6.7 | 4.8 |
| K | .6 | .2 | .5 | .3 | 1.1 | .4 | 1.2 | .4 | 1.3 | .5 | 1.1 | 1.0 | 1.1 | 1.1 | 1.4 | .6 | 1.3 | .6 |
| L | .4 | .5 | .4 | .4 | .5 | .3 | .5 | .3 | .3 | .3 | .9 | .5 | .8 | .6 | .8 | .6 | .8 | .4 |
| M | –[b] | –[b] | –[b] | –[b] | .3 | .0[c] | .3 | .1 | .1 | .1 | .5 | .2 | .5 | .2 | .5 | .2 | .5 | .2 |
| N | 1.3 | .3 | 1.2 | .2 | 1.2 | .3 | 1.3 | .3 | 1.1 | .4 | 2.3 | .5 | 2.5 | .5 | 2.6 | .5 | 1.9 | 1.3 |
| O | .0[c] | .0[c] | .0[c] | .0[c] | –[b] | –[b] | .0[c] | –[b] | .1 | .1 | .1 | .0[c] | .1 | .1 | .2 | .1 | .1 | .1 |

*A, Automotive; B, Banks; C, Hotels; D, Manufacturing; E, Insurance; F, Retail; G, Transportation; H, Utilities; I, Real Estate; J, Wholesale; K, Construction; L, Laundries; M, Amusement; N, Miscellaneous; O, Unknown.

[a]"Firm" means Firm Gift; "Emp." means Employee Gift.

[b]Dash (–) indicates no gift.

[c]Point zero (.0) indicates the figure is less than 0.05 per cent.

2. The order of dependence on the Impersonal sector is the order of the dollar size of the campaign; i.e., Hospital, Chest, and Red Cross. Further, within the Impersonal sector, the order of dependence on each of the components (Firms and Foundations) is the same as for the whole sector.

3. The order of dependence on the Personal sector is, necessarily then, the reverse of the order of size of campaign; i.e., Red Cross, Chest, and Hospital. However, further, within the Personal sector, the order of dependence on each of the components (Employees and Individuals) is the same as for the whole sector.

4. All three campaigns are almost equally dependent (about 80 per cent) on the Firm Organized sector (and then, necessarily, on the Non-Firm Organized sector). (a) But, within the Firm Organized sector, the dependence on Firm pledges is in the order of the size of the campaign, while the dependence on Employee pledges is in the reverse order of size of campaign. (b) Similarly, within the Non-Firm Organized sector, the dependence on Foundations is in the order of the size of the campaign, while dependence on Individuals is in the reverse order of the size of campaign.

5. The order of dependence on leading gifts is the same as the order of size of campaign for (a) the Ten Leading Gifts and (b) the One Hundred Leading Firm Gifts.

B. For Chest and Red Cross

1. The Chest is more dependent on the Twenty Per Cent Leading Firm Gifts than is Red Cross.

2. Since 1933 (except for the war years) Chest campaigns have changed their totals relatively less than Red Cross.

3. In giving by Divisions, the Red Cross relies more on Downtown, Residential-and-Towns, Professional, and Public than does the Chest; the Chest depends more on Commerce-and-Industry than does Red Cross.

4. The Chest and Red Cross appear to be about equally dependent on pledging in ICO. But within ICO, the Chest is more dependent on Firm pledges than the Red Cross; and necessarily, therefore, the Red Cross is more dependent on Employee pledges than the Chest.

5. When we examine per-employee and Firm pledging in ICO, these same relations hold true, although the Chest receives much more than Red Cross in both Employee and Firm pledges per employee. Moreover, the difference between per-employee pledges of Firms and Employees to the Red Cross is small, and these same differences are large in the Chest campaign (the Firms, of course, giving much more per employee than do the Employees themselves).

6. By size of firm, Chest receives a somewhat greater proportion of support from Firms employing five thousand or more persons than does Red Cross. In contrast, the Red Cross receives a greater proportion from Firms employing twenty-five to ninety-nine persons than does the Chest. For the intermediate size groups, the proportions for Chest and Red Cross are about the same. (a) For Firm pledges only, Red Cross shows generally an increasing per-employee pledge from the largest size group to the smallest. It looks as if the Chest were changing from the Red Cross pattern to the reverse relation; i.e., the larger the size of the group, the larger the per-employee pledge. (b) For Employee pledges only, both organizations receive the largest Employee pledge per employee from firms employing five thousand or more persons.

7. Red Cross and Chest are strikingly similar in proportion of amount pledged in ICO in major industry groups. And the same pattern is found in Employee and Firm pledges separately.

## B. INTRA-CAMPAIGN ANALYSIS: THE COMMUNITY CHEST

This section will assess the performance of the Indianapolis Community Chest in several different ways. First, we shall look at its money-results from 1920 to 1955 in comparison with the results of all Chests and with the national income. Then we shall examine in detail the money-results in Indianapolis. The detailed analysis covers various time periods depending on the availability of comparable material, but the major emphasis will be on the period 1950 to 1955. We shall concentrate on the gifts of ICO (Industrial and Commercial Organizations) and of Foundations, since they comprise such a large percentage of the total amount raised.

### The Long-Range Picture

The Indianapolis Chest has been reporting money-results since 1920. To put these results in a perspective which would provide some benchmarks for comparison, we looked again at the performance of all Chests and at national income for about the same period as reported in chapter 6. Chart 14 shows in current dollars[77] the income of all Community Chests in millions of dollars, and the national income in billions. Except for two crisis periods (the Depression and World War II) the curves are very similar. As we pointed out there, the Community Chests in the United States receive between them about one-thousandth of the national income, i.e., in effect, they get about the equivalent in yield of a "One Mill tax."

Given the relative constancy of the income of all Chests relative to national income, we next compared, as discussed in chapter 6, money-results of the Indianapolis Chest with the money-results of all Chests. Chart 16 shows the giving to the Indianapolis Chest (1920-55) and to all Chests (1924-54). With the exception of about five years, the Chest in Indianapolis shows until World War II much the same pattern of growth as do all Chests. After the war, however, the Indianapolis Chest fails to keep up with the rate of growth of all Chests. In the early period, and until recently, the relation between the two sets of figures is roughly one to a hundred, so that the Indianapolis Chest was getting about one cent in every dollar raised by all Chests taken together.[78]

Combining the last two items of information, one might therefore say, as a good first approximation, that the Chest in Indianapolis gets about one cent in every thousand dollars of national income.[79]

We have perhaps sufficiently discussed in chapter 6 the limited value of using goal-attainment as the test of success. But we had been so frequently told that while the Chest in Indianapolis was now in bad shape—". . . in the old days the Chest didn't have any troubles," or "It used to be *really* successful"—that we feel it wise to redirect attention to the facts described in chapter 6, and portrayed in Chart 11. From this chart, it is visible that the Indianapolis Chest has succeeded in attaining or surpassing goal only about a third of the time: ten times in thirty-four campaigns with goals, including four war-time campaigns. It appears that about the only time the Chest makes or exceeds goal is in crisis periods. Moreover, the greatest differences between goal and performance occurred in the earliest campaigns. If consistent attainment of goal is taken as the test of success, then there never has been a successful period in the history of the Indianapolis Chest—and certainly the period of least success by this standard was the first few years of the Chest's existence. Perhaps people look through rose-colored glasses when they view the Chest as having been "successful in the old days."

INDUSTRIAL AND COMMERCIAL ORGANIZATIONS (ICO) AND THE CHEST

To assess the changing importance of ICO to the Chest, we compared amount pledged in ICO with the total amount pledged, in the campaigns from 1950 through 1955. Table LV summarizes this material. Since 1950,

TABLE LV

AMOUNT PLEDGED IN ICO AS PERCENTAGE OF TOTAL AMOUNT PLEDGED IN CAMPAIGN, COMMUNITY CHEST, 1950-5

| Year | Total amount pledged in campaign | Amount pledged in ICO | ICO as percentage of total |
|------|----------------------------------|------------------------|-----------------------------|
| 1950 | $1,402,852 | $ 931,353 | 66.4% |
| 1951 | 1,569,180 | 1,071,818 | 68.3% |
| 1952 | 1,579,018 | 1,078,151 | 68.3% |
| 1953 | 1,588,502 | 1,121,382 | 70.6% |
| 1954 | 1,561,938 | 1,102,105 | 70.6% |
| 1955 | 2,032,584[a] | 1,538,330[a] | 75.7% |

[a]As of January 7, 1956.

ICO has increased its proportion of the total amount pledged from about two-thirds to three-fourths: a very considerable proportion of the total amount raised in either case. Pledging in ICO is indeed increasing as a percentage of the total amount raised at a remarkable rate.[80] While the total amount raised by the Chest has increased 44.9 per cent since 1950, ICO pledging has increased 65.2 per cent. So, not only has ICO been very important to the Chest campaign in the period we are discussing, but its importance has been increasing at a rapid rate.

This may, perhaps, be put in a more dramatic way by showing what proportion of each inter-campaign increase (or decrease) was contributed by ICO. The picture would appear as in Table LVI. The conclusion is that virtually all change (96.4 per cent of it) in the period is attributable to ICO, i.e., that the Chest is growing almost exclusively in virtue of the

### TABLE LVI

CHANGES[a] IN TOTAL AMOUNT PLEDGED TO COMMUNITY CHEST, ICO AND OTHER

| Year of change | Amount of change in total | Amount of change in ICO | Amount of all other changes | Percentage of total change contributed by ICO | Percentage of total change contributed otherwise | Total |
|---|---|---|---|---|---|---|
| 1950-51 | $166,328 | $140,465 | $ 25,863 | 84.4% | 15.6% | 100.0% |
| 1951-52 | 9,838 | 6,333 | 3,505 | 64.4 | 35.6 | 100.0 |
| 1952-53 | 9,484 | 43,231[b] | −33,747[b] | N.A. | N.A. | 100.0 |
| 1953-54 | −26,564 | −19,277 | −7,287 | 72.6 | 27.4 | 100.0 |
| 1954-55 | 470,646 | 436,225 | 34,421 | 92.7 | 7.3 | 100.0 |
| Total, five changes | $629,734 | $606,977 | $ 22,755 | 96.4% | 3.6% | 100.0% |
| Average per year | 125,946 | 121,395 | 4,551 | 96.4 | 3.6 | 100.0 |

[a]Negative signs show decreases.
[b]Part of this change is attributable to inclusion in ICO of firms formerly solicited in other divisions. See note 80.

increase in its ICO take. If we add the gifts of Foundations to those of ICO—thus grouping the large givers together—we get the picture shown in Table LVII. Thus, by adding only two large gifts to ICO, three-fourths (1950) to four-fifths (1955) of the total amount raised is brought under examination. However, in further discussion, we shall not include the Foundation pledges; we simply wished to establish here, parenthetically, that these pledges combined with ICO pledges now produce more than four-fifths of the total amount, and that this proportion seems to be increasing by about 1 per cent per annum.

### TABLE LVII

PERCENTAGE OF CHEST TOTAL TAKE PLEDGED
BY ICO AND FOUNDATIONS

| Year | Percentage |
|---|---|
| 1950 | 74.5% |
| 1951 | 75.6 |
| 1952 | 75.5 |
| 1953 | 77.2 |
| 1954 | 77.5 |
| 1955 | 81.5 |
| Total | 77.1% |

Neglecting now the Foundations, the ICO pledges may be separated into Employee and Firm pledges, as in Table LVIII, in order to examine what is happening within ICO, as between Firms and their Employees. The table shows the percentage of the ICO total pledged by Firms and Employees respectively, and the ratio of Employee pledging to Firm pledging.

## TABLE LVIII

EMPLOYEE AND FIRM PLEDGES AS PERCENTAGE OF TOTAL AMOUNT PLEDGED IN ICO
AND RATIO OF EMPLOYEE PLEDGES TO FIRM PLEDGES, COMMUNITY CHEST, 1950-5

|                              | 1950   | 1951   | 1952   | 1953   | 1954   | 1955   |
|------------------------------|--------|--------|--------|--------|--------|--------|
| Total pledged in ICO         | 100.0% | 100.0% | 100.0% | 100.0% | 100.0% | 100.0% |
| Firm pledges                 | 59.9   | 58.5   | 59.8   | 59.1   | 58.4   | 59.9   |
| Employee pledges             | 40.1   | 41.5   | 40.2   | 40.9   | 41.6   | 40.1   |
| Ratio: Employee pledges to Firm pledges | 67.0% | 70.9 | 67.2 | 69.1 | 71.3 | 67.0 |

Throughout the period covered, there is little variation, within ICO, in the proportions pledged by Firms and Employees: a total range of 1½ per cent, and a net change over the period of just zero. These findings may be surprising; the Chest was attempting, especially in 1953 and 1954, to concentrate on Employee giving in its campaigns, but the changes achieved are trifling. The emphasis in the 1955 campaign on Firm giving seems to have changed the ratio back again to the same level as 1950. The net effect of shifting policy in this respect, over the whole interval, seems close to nil.

We may turn from this examination of Firm versus Employee sharing of the ICO total to an examination of the per-employee contributions of each. Table LIX gives the per employee pledges in ICO for the total, for Firms, and for Employees. Each year (with the exception of 1953) the Chest

## TABLE LIX

PER-EMPLOYEE PLEDGES OF FIRMS AND EMPLOYEES IN ICO, COMMUNITY CHEST, 1950-5

| Per-employee pledges         | 1950   | 1951   | 1952   | 1953   | 1954   | 1955   |
|------------------------------|--------|--------|--------|--------|--------|--------|
| Total                        | $6.26  | $6.68  | $6.82  | $6.59  | $6.83  | $9.18  |
| Firms                        | 3.75   | 3.91   | 4.08   | 3.90   | 3.99   | 5.50   |
| Employees                    | 2.51   | 2.77   | 2.74   | 2.69   | 2.84   | 3.68   |
| Ratio: Employee pledge to Firm pledge[a] | 67.0% | 70.9% | 67.2% | 69.1% | 71.3% | 67.0% |

[a] These ratios are, of course, identical with those of Table LVIII.

shows increased total per employee pledging in ICO. This is true both for Firm pledges per employee and (except for 1952 and 1953) for Employee pledges per employee as well.[81]

Another way to look at Firm pledging is to examine pledging per employee for two successive years. We correlated Firm pledges per employee for 1954 with those for 1955 using only those firms (708 in number) which had made a Firm pledge in both years.[82] Excluding non-givers in either year (or both), the correlation showed that the Firm pledge per employee made in one year is closely and positively related to the same pledge in the other year.[83] Close as the inter-year relation is, however, some large part of the variation (44 per cent) must, then, be due to factors other than merely the size of the pledge in the other year; perhaps the size of the previous pledge tends to limit the range of change rather than to determine the new gift altogether.[84]

### COMPARISON WITH 1920's

It has been shown that Firm pledges form a fairly large proportion of ICO and consequently of the total amount raised. A study, published in 1930,[85] gives the percentage of total contributions (from all sources) to the Indianapolis Chest that was received from corporations. Although our

### TABLE LX

RATIO OF FIRM OR CORPORATE GIFT TO TOTAL GIFT, INDIANAPOLIS COMMUNITY CHEST, 1923-1928 AND 1950-1955

| Year | Corporate gift ratio[a] | Year | Firm gift ratio |
|------|------------------------|------|-----------------|
| 1923 | 41.5% | 1950 | 39.7% |
| 1924 | 43.5 | 1951 | 40.0 |
| 1925 | 42.9 | 1952 | 40.8 |
| 1926 | 43.0 | 1953 | 41.8 |
| 1927 | 44.5 | 1954 | 41.2 |
| 1928 | 42.1 | 1955 | 45.3 |
| Total range | 41.5% to 44.5% | Total range | 39.7% to 45.3% |

[a]See the table for note 85.

category "Firm" is not identical with the study's category "Corporations," the two categories are close enough to make comparison meaningful—as in Table LX. Thus, in so far as "Firm" and "Corporation" are comparable, the percentage of total amount raised contributed by corporations then and firms now is just about the same today as it was in the twenties.[86]

### MINOR INDUSTRY GROUPS

In comparing Chest and Red Cross money-results for 1951 to 1955, we discovered that the percentages received from major industry groups were remarkably stable. The only sizeable one of these is "Manufacturing," and the interesting question arises as to whether subdivisions of this great indus-

### TABLE LXI

PROPORTION OF TOTAL AMOUNT PLEDGED IN MANUFACTURING BY ITS SEVENTEEN CONSTITUENT MINOR INDUSTRY GROUPS, COMMUNITY CHEST, 1950-5

| Minor industry groups[a] | 1950 | 1951 | 1952 | 1953 | 1954 | 1955 |
|---|---|---|---|---|---|---|
| TOTAL | 100.0% | 100.0% | 100.0% | 100.0% | 100.0% | 100.0% |
| A | 14.0 | 19.6 | 20.0 | 18.9 | 20.8 | 22.3 |
| B | 7.4 | 7.2 | 6.3 | 5.8 | 6.1 | 5.7 |
| C | 3.5 | 3.0 | 3.1 | 3.2 | 3.2 | 2.9 |
| D | 4.3 | 4.0 | 4.1 | 4.1 | 4.3 | 4.3 |
| E | 27.8 | 25.0 | 25.0 | 22.0 | 22.1 | 20.6 |
| F | 2.4 | 2.0 | 1.8 | 2.2 | 2.6 | 2.6 |
| G | 4.5 | 4.5 | 4.5 | 4.7 | 4.0 | 4.6 |
| H | 18.6 | 17.9 | 18.0 | 21.7 | 21.8 | 20.7 |
| I | 9.3 | 8.7 | 10.6 | 10.2 | 8.9 | 10.3 |
| J | 3.2 | 2.8 | 2.0 | 1.5 | 1.3 | .7 |
| K | 1.3 | 1.4 | 1.0 | 1.6 | 1.3 | 1.1 |
| L | .4 | .7 | .8 | .8 | .8 | .9 |
| M | .4 | .5 | .6 | .8 | .7 | .7 |
| N | 1.0 | 1.2 | 1.2 | 1.2 | .9 | 1.6 |
| O | .0 | .0 | .0 | .0 | .0 | .0 |
| P | .4 | .3 | .3 | .3 | .3 | .3 |
| Q | 1.5 | 1.2 | 1.1 | 1.0 | .9 | .7 |

[a]Not identified by name because it was necessary to preserve a degree of anonymity for individual givers, who, in a few cases, are publicly known almost to dominate a given subdivision.

try group also behave with stability. Table LXI presents the relevant data for the Chest for the six years from 1950 to 1955. Although the consistent proportion of total amount pledged is not so well maintained when we break Manufacturing into minor industry groups, there is still a fairly stable relation.[87] The major differences in proportion among the minor industry groups are in A and E. The change in A seems to be related to a very large increase in number of employees in a single firm,[88] and the changes in E are accounted for mainly by the changes in pledging of one large firm. Given these facts, the stability in proportion contributed is quite remarkable.

Since proportions do not give a complete picture, we have shown in Table LXII the corresponding total gifts per employee for the seventeen minor industry groups in Manufacturing. Although it may be difficult to see it from the table, there is a moderately consistent pattern in the total pledge per employee of the minor industry groups in Manufacturing.[89] In the six-year period most of the groups show a net increase and the nine largest groups *all* show a net increase. But most groups arrive at the net increase by a series of rather sharp increases and decreases, instead of by anything that suggests an explicit or implicit steady policy.[90] When we break the per-employee pledges for the subdivisions in Manufacturing into their Firm pledge and Employee pledge elements, we still get some stability of year-to-year performance, but less than for the larger units of reporting— and this is true whether we look at percentages contributed or actual per-employee data.[91]

TABLE LXII

TOTAL PLEDGES PER EMPLOYEE IN MANUFACTURING OF ITS SEVENTEEN CONSTITUENT MINOR INDUSTRY GROUPS FOR COMMUNITY CHEST, 1950-5

| Minor industry groups | 1950 | 1951 | 1952 | 1953 | 1954 | 1955 |
|---|---|---|---|---|---|---|
| TOTAL | $ 5.28 | $ 5.78 | $ 5.94 | $ 6.03 | $ 6.43 | $ 8.25 |
| A | 4.45 | 4.69 | 4.53 | 5.38 | 5.90 | 8.15 |
| B | 4.61 | 4.78 | 4.21 | 4.51 | 4.76 | 6.40 |
| C | 6.85 | 6.76 | 7.69 | 7.75 | 7.65 | 9.33 |
| D | 5.36 | 6.15 | 5.99 | 5.49 | 5.62 | 7.19 |
| E | 13.29 | 14.40 | 15.73 | 12.46 | 14.39 | 17.96 |
| F | 3.85 | 4.07 | 3.79 | 5.23 | 5.94 | 7.81 |
| G | 3.53 | 4.34 | 5.30 | 5.04 | 5.01 | 6.44 |
| H | 4.02 | 4.53 | 4.91 | 5.15 | 6.17 | 7.36 |
| I | 3.48 | 4.65 | 5.45 | 5.42 | 4.81 | 6.84 |
| J | 6.65 | 7.79 | 6.65 | 8.13 | 6.81 | 4.67 |
| K | 5.28 | 6.49 | 4.94 | 7.83 | 6.59 | 7.06 |
| L | 5.54 | 10.85 | 21.63 | 10.19 | 8.54 | 15.71 |
| M | 2.03 | 2.32 | 3.22 | 3.79 | 3.41 | 4.11 |
| N | 2.57 | 2.72 | 2.31 | 2.22 | 1.80 | 3.99 |
| O | 3.00 | 3.77 | 4.00 | 5.00 | 5.23 | 2.28 |
| P | 7.58 | 4.26 | 4.97 | 5.38 | 4.92 | 6.39 |
| Q | 12.71 | 12.27 | 10.53 | 8.04 | 6.59 | 6.96 |

It seems, in summary then, that the consistent proportions pledged by each major industry group in ICO are not confined solely to major industry groups. The minor industry groups in Manufacturing also show considerable consistency in proportions pledged—though not as great stability as do the major industry groups.

## UNION ORGANIZATION

According to many people we talked to, the co-operation (or lack of same) of labor unions is a factor in Chest money-results in Indianapolis. We were asked, "What effect do unions have on giving?"

We took a look at the results in firms organized by different unions, and also compared their performance with those of firms without unions. We noted no appreciable differences which did not seem at least as much related to size of firm as to type of union or to presence or absence of union. Because of the nature of the data we could not factor out or separate these correlated influences, and hence we did not pursue this phase of the analysis further.[92]

## Summary

1. ICO accounts for an overwhelming proportion of the total amount pledged in campaigns, and this proportion has been increasing since 1950, roughly from two-thirds of the total in 1950 to three-fourths in 1955. (The addition of Foundation pledges would raise these proportions to three-fourths in 1950 and to four-fifths in 1955.) Thus, great dependence on a small number of units is again shown. Indeed, almost all (96 per cent) of the increase in total amount pledged in the Chest campaign in the six-year period is accounted for by the increases in ICO.

2. Within ICO, in 1950 through 1955, the proportions pledged respectively by Firms and by Employees change little from year to year, and there is no net change between 1950 and 1955.

3. Although the per-employee pledging of Firms and Employees increases and decreases in the six-year period, the ratio of Firm pledging to Employee pledging remains extremely stable. What small variation there was, seems to be in the direction which would be suggested by year to year changes in campaign effort.

4. Comparison of 1950 to 1955 data with data from the period 1923 to 1928 indicates that the proportion of the total raised by the Indianapolis Chest which comes from corporations in the early period and "firms" in the recent one is about the same today as it was in the 1920's.

5. Within ICO, analysis of 1950 data shows very stable proportions pledged by the several "major industry groups."

6. Examination of the "minor industry groups," or subdivisions of Manufacturing, as to proportion of amount pledged, shows a pattern slightly less stable than the one found for major industry groups, but still very stable. Total pledges per employee even within these smaller subdivisions are moderately stable from year to year. When we analyse Firm and Employee pledges separately, their relative proportions show some stability, but not as much as does the unit total.

7. Proportions of the total pledged in ICO by firms classified in size groups also show considerable consistency over the years. Per-employee pledges of groups of units classified according to firm size are also closely similar in consecutive years, but over the whole period, the pattern seems to be in process of reversal, i.e., while in 1950 the smaller size groups tended to have the larger per-employee pledges, in 1955 the larger size groups tended to have the larger per-employee pledges.

We have now looked at money-results in Indianapolis in terms of three questions: (1) How do results in Indianapolis compare with results in other cities? (2) How do results of three MOPS fundraising campaigns in Indianapolis compare with each other? and (3) What patterns are found in Chest money-results?

Certainly in the answers to the second and third questions, the similarities between organizations and the stabilities within them seem more striking than the differences and changes. If these invariances are in turn related—as they probably are—to relatively slow-changing economic forces outside and beyond philanthropy altogether, then fundraising policy to be sensible and economical would do well to take due note of them in guiding its own action and aspiration.

# 10. Problems of Mass Fundraising: Manpower

As we turn from the endless detail of money-results to the broad sweep of how they are to be secured, as we turn from money to men, two words from our object of study—mass, operational, periodic, secular fundraising—must especially preoccupy us, since they have peculiar implications for problems of manning. The two words are "mass" and "secular." These two characteristics are not, of course, independent, since in a society religiously fragmented as is the American, mass and religious appeals are virtually mutually exclusive.

A *mass* campaign makes its "Appeal" to "everybody," not just a special group, such as an alumni association. It employs mass media, and even in its "tailored" approach to individuals and firms, which are not regarded as belonging to the masses, it will take some account of judgments as to its popular support and its possible value for public relations in matters of civic pride, "corporate citizenship," and community leadership.

Similarly, a *secular* campaign makes its "Appeal" to people not as members of a religious constituency but as "citizens" of a community "without regard to race, creed, or color." Indeed, for this very reason, the secular campaign can and does make an appeal in quasi-religious terms: terms that celebrate corporate pride, such attenuated bonds of brotherhood as are involved in the notion of a common citizenship, high moral endeavor (a "crusade"), and a whole set of ideas paralleling in general the Christian notion of the fight against evil—or, in this case, evils.

These characteristics, as we shall see, affect the opportunities for manning the campaign, the nature of the manpower pool from which the organization is recruited, and some of the difficulties that occur in maintenance and retention of the philanthropic "labor force."

In the following pages we shall first examine the social context within which MOPS fundraising campaigns operate and gain their significance, a context which must include the American scene generally and also the minds and hearts particularly of those who participate or are touched in any way by these activities. Then we shall look more closely into the problems peculiar to the campaign itself, especially certain matters of its technical design that affect its human organization. Mops fundraising is, of course, an elaborately organized effort; some of its activities, especially soliciting, may be carried on by volunteers without special training and experience, but many of them must be performed by specialists, whether or not they are paid workers, professionals, or volunteers. In studying this organization, we shall follow a typical annual campaign, step by step, as problems arise during the year. Finally, we shall point to some of the long-run problems of the general administration of mops fundraising organizations that appear to be central to the questions to be dealt with in chapters 12 and 13: what might be done to make such organizations more "efficient" as well as more "effective"?[1]

## The Social Context

The "cast of characters" involved in any mops fundraising enterprise is a very large one—well over half a million people in the Indianapolis case. It may be helpful to distinguish these into the following major social groups and population aggregates: the general population; the "Welfare Community" and its leaders; the "Campaign Leadership," volunteers and professionals; the Donor-Aggregate and its leaders; the Ultimate Beneficiaries.

### The General Population

Mops fundraising is conducted, of course, within a *territory* occupied by people who are believed to have some important things in common, such as residence, place of work, or business location. From the fundraiser's point of view, this is the "area served" by the agency or agencies on whose behalf the Appeal is made, and therefore the area of solicitation.[2]

The word "community" is often used to describe the "area served." Since the area is usually designated by a place name or some compound of place names (as in "Indianapolis and Marion County," "Greater Cleveland," or "the Bay Area" in the case of the San Francisco United Fund), and the Appeal is addressed to all the people and all the businesses, the assumption is made, for practical purposes, by the fundraisers that all are "members" of, or in some sense "belong" to, the "community" so labelled.

One need only recall some of the differences between life in a village or small town and life in a metropolitan city or larger area, to realize that "community" is a highly relative term, that there are gradations between "more community" and "less community," between membership in a smaller, more intimate village or town, having a moral authority that is closely binding upon all, and membership in large metropolitan cities where what is most striking is the freedom, the anonymity and the virtual absence of any universal bonds. The details of these gradations need not detain us here, so long as we recognize the broad and important differences mentioned.[3]

In Indianapolis, as in most contemporary American cities, we have an example of "less community": no strong sense of belonging to a social unity transcending their differences appears to be shared by the people found in the territory. This is so evident that we feel the fact helps to account for the persistent concern felt by many persons that "what is chiefly needed is more community organization."[4] Such people include those who get together, usually in a formal association such as a Welfare Council (or any of its constituent member groups or agencies), to express this concern, and who seek to work for "the greater well-being of all the people." They work for this objective either by focusing upon particular "community problems" such as juvenile delinquency, job opportunities for the handicapped, recreational facilities, or certain health services—or by promoting broader programs, aiming to engage whole neighborhoods or communities in "self-surveys" and "taking action" with respect to "felt needs."

### The Welfare Community and its Leaders

All of the people who show any interest in purposes and tasks such as the foregoing, and any others in the fields of health, welfare, recreation, and informal education, may be regarded as members of the "Welfare Community." Not all, of course, are active participants in directing or carrying on the work of agencies in the fields mentioned; an unknown but probably very large proportion of the voting population consists of those who are favorably disposed towards the work but who are not regularly active in it. But even a Cub Scout "den mother" is quite a "participant" in the Welfare Community; and there are thousands of tasks such as hers, through which, in various ways, people enter this not inconsiderable company.

The Welfare Community can thus be said to have "members," who form a large but unknown proportion of the total adult population; "active participants," a somewhat smaller aggregate within the total population, but also a considerable enrolment not recorded in any central place; and a still smaller but better-known part: those who may be called its leaders.

During 1955, we collected the names of over 1,800 persons then active in the more prominent positions of lay leader or paid worker in the fields that are of interest to members of the Welfare Community—especially the names of those associated with organizations holding membership in the Health and Welfare Council of Indianapolis and Marion County. This list of the current Welfare Community Leaders thus includes all the officers, Board members, and other volunteer lay leaders in the higher positions of agency work, as well as the professional social workers or other paid workers in the higher positions of all the well-known agencies, both public and private. Although agency heads are included, the list is overwhelmingly one of lay leaders. It is by no means a complete directory of all the people who may or might wish to be identified as "in the Welfare Community," but it does bring together the names of those who were sufficiently active, in a leading position, in the governing or workings of an organization, especially at its headquarters office, to have their names appear in the records of the Health and Welfare Council, or frequently in the daily newspapers in the cases of those in organizations not represented in the Council.[5]

The Welfare Community within a geographic community might remain a kind of fictitious aggregate or bookish collection of separate groups in each of which real people share some specific common concern or activity, such as the provision of public health nursing services, a certain camping facility and its direction, a particular settlement house, or a group work program for boys. What brings the Welfare Community to life, however, is the organization of a common tool such as a Welfare Council; and the latter's activities are usually intended to maintain the Welfare Community in existence, by providing the members with the framework of a voluntary association, to strengthen it from within, by "planning" and co-ordination, and to win for its program more general support throughout the geographic community, by public relations in all senses. A Welfare Council may attempt to go beyond these tasks, and aim to promote co-operative action throughout the geographic community in one selected enterprise after another, to the end that the Welfare Community and the larger community "develop capacity to plan and act together with respect to their common problems." But there are limits; the effort may be spread "too thin," and severe disturbances, if not "chaos," may occur in the Welfare Community if a Council "goes too far."[6] When the Health and Welfare Council of Indianapolis and Marion County claims to be "the citizens" of the larger community, this may be largely an expression of the enthusiasm so contagious in an age of advertising and publicity; but, for the reasons given, to attempt to act upon such claims may not be the wisest course for the long-run development of the Welfare Community.

This study is not focused upon the Council and its workings, but we have had to investigate its current program for evidence that a vigorous Welfare Community Leadership does indeed exist within the larger community because the matter is important to the fundraising processes we have studied.

*The Campaign Leadership: Volunteers and Professionals*

In each of the two fundraising campaigns whose methods and manning we have analysed in detail—Red Cross and Community Chest—and probably in all MOPS fundraising campaigns everywhere, there are various levels of lay leadership; these can, however, be grouped into two general categories: "the Elder Statesmen" and "the Young Campaigners." In both philanthropies, the "Elder Statesmen" comprise, at the top, the governing Board of Directors, and, in the case of the Red Cross, a "Chapter Fund Committee" which has no formal counterpart in the Chest campaign. In addition, there are the leaders of the actual soliciting divisions: all those recognized in the organization chart or in records of "Report meetings" as responsible for recruiting workers and for supervising their work as solicitors, and who therefore have titles analogous to "Team Captain" or who are of higher rank. The latter we call "the Young Campaigners," and, in the case of the Red Cross, they include the members of the Public Information Committee and the Campaign Executive Committee,[7] as well as the rest of the named leaders of the less well-known workers in the soliciting divisions. In the case of the Chest, the Young Campaigners include the members of the Public Relations Committee; but the Chest's equivalent of a Campaign Executive Committee also has members coming from the Elder Statesmen group, rather informally, and "ex officio" so to speak.

In each campaign there are professionals (as well as lay persons or volunteers): the year-round staff of the Chest, and, for the Red Cross, certain staff persons who are aided at campaign time by special fundraising counsel (from the American City Bureau). These, together with the most highly placed lay leaders in each organization, constitute another, less formal but close-knit group which we shall call "the Campaign Directors."[8]

### The Donor-Aggregate and its Leaders

From the point of view of the fundraiser in a MOPS campaign, "everybody"—every firm and individual in the territory—is a possible "donor." Those who contribute the largest gifts might be called "Leading Donors," and all others who contribute to the Community Chest or the Red Cross (or, what is most common, to both) may be added to these to make up what we call the "Donor-Aggregate." From the Leading Donors it is advisable to distinguish the "Donor Leaders": persons or firms who may or may not be also Leading Donors, but who are known to exert some influence, little or great, upon others in the Donor-Aggregate. Fundraisers sometimes refer to certain donors as "bell-wethers" because they are believed to "lead the flock," but this terminology may come too close to that of sheep-shearing to be used outside a small inner circle. In communitywide campaigns, the more complimentary title of "Leading Donor" is preferred, but in such usage the term is ambiguous: (1) it is used in the bookkeeping sense, to recognize a fact, (2) it is used as an honorific term, in public statements or in private conferences, to influence other donors, and (3) it is used within the fundraisers' small group to label those they hope will be "bell-wethers" if their gifts or pledges can be secured sufficiently far in advance. We shall reserve the term "Leading Donors" for the first, or bookkeeping, usage, and the term "Donor Leaders" for the persons or firms with influence.

If one were to list the Leading Donors (say, the firms and individuals responsible for the 100 leading gifts), one might then ask which of these are also Donor Leaders. There are four broad types of situations that may be distinguished:

(I) of the Donor Leaders, almost all are themselves Leading Donors
(II) of the Donor Leaders, a majority are also Leading Donors
(III) of the Donor Leaders, only a minority are also Leading Donors
(IV) of the Donor Leaders few or none are Leading Donors, and, at
the extreme, may even be in opposition to them.

These situations may be made graphic as in the accompanying diagram.

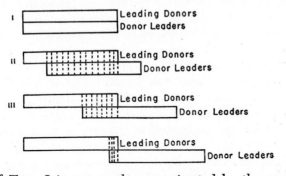

A situation of Type I is apparently approximated by the case of Detroit,
where the "Torch Drive" was virtually instituted by managerial decisions
of the three largest automobile firms acting together with the top leadership of the CIO-UAW. We know of no case of Type IV; such a case might,
however, occur if the Welfare Community Leaders were also the Donor
Leaders, and if they either led an open revolt against the Leading Donors
or covertly organized strongly against them; such situations have been
approximated. Cleveland perhaps best exemplifies a Type II situation: the
Community Chest enlists the support of many Leading Donors who also
act as Donor Leaders in influencing the rest of the Donor-Aggregate.[9] Type
III may include a number of cities, and may be the state of affairs in the
very large ones, such as Chicago—where the Community Fund has not
been replaced by a United Fund, but instead raises only about one-fourth
of all the operating costs of its member agencies; and where the Red Cross
separately raises an amount about equal to one-third of that collected by
the Community Fund. It is our strong impression that Indianapolis is
somewhere between Type II and Type III.

It will be noted that we have chosen terms that distinguish the Donor-
Aggregate from the Welfare Community. The latter has its leadership and
some degree of organization; both leadership and organization are evidenced
in the governing and work of agencies, as well as in their formal association
through the Health and Welfare Council. The Donor-Aggregate in Indianapolis has no such degree of organization, and apparently less leadership:
not enough of its Leading Donors are active as Donor Leaders. There is no
"protective league" for firms or persons in the Donor-Aggregate. Some of
these firms or persons are involved in the Welfare Community (and many
doubtless count themselves among the Ultimate Beneficiaries) but if and
when they act as Donor Leaders, they tend to do so as individuals, and

not sufficiently in concert to constitute anything approximating an organized Donor Leadership group.

Leading Donors acting as individuals seem to have no difficulty in securing some representation in the processes connected with budgeting and goal-setting, but there is some doubt whether the involvement connected with such activity leaves them free to plan and act as truly representative of the interests of Leading Donors or of donors generally. The matter would be quite different if they also helped to compose a leadership group in a "Donor Community" as relatively well organized and as well led as the Welfare Community seems to be. In order to call such a "Donor Community" into existence, independent Leading Donors and Donor Leaders would need to act in concert to organize it. As things are now, basically, the Leading Donors appear to proceed on the assumption that "if a big executive can't take care of himself in the face of a fundraiser's 'Appeal,' he has no kick coming!"—and that therefore the only ones, if any, in the Donor-Aggregate who need protection are the firm's employees.[10]

If the Welfare Community in Indianapolis can be said to have some degree of organization and leadership, in comparison the Donor-Aggregate evidently has only a crowd-like organization, with rather transient leadership. This resemblance to a crowd is shown in an enthusiasm for a "new fashion" in raising money such as a Telethon; the first Telethon in Indianapolis, in 1953, had a success that has not been equalled since. The Donor-Aggregate, otherwise, seems to be "a disordered dust of individuals." But just because the individuals who compose it are, like human beings everywhere, creatures of habit, it has a "potential" to "yield" very considerable sums of money year after year for well-established drives in Indianapolis. Satisfied fundraisers might well, on this basis alone, call the people of the city "a good crowd." But even for the largest, best-established drives—the Chest and the Red Cross—the question is sometimes raised by local people, "Where is the leadership in Indianapolis?" Few have done more than hint that the situation is ripe for the emergence of something like the Donor Leadership that creates a Donor Community in cities such as Cleveland or Detroit. In 1955, at any rate, we found little evidence of this type of leadership in Indianapolis, and instead we found a Donor-Aggregate that has been increasing in size for decades, without a corresponding growth of experienced leaders able to create a Donor Community.[11]

## The Ultimate Beneficiaries

From the point of view of the fundraisers, "everybody" in the population is, hopefully, a potential Ultimate Beneficiary—just as "everybody" is, again hopefully, a possible Donor. An unknown number of people may thus be called the "Ultimate Beneficiaries" of all the activities engaged in by Campaign Leaders, Welfare Community Leaders, and persons in the Donor-Aggregate. Also unknown is the amount of duplication in the membership over all these categories. A given Campaign Leader is also to be found in the Donor-Aggregate; and he may be active as well among the Welfare Community Leaders and may even belong in the category of Ultimate Beneficiaries—as a parent in a family whose members are variously served by the Boy Scouts, the Family Service Association, the Red Cross, Goodwill Industries, or any other combination of services. A citizen may even recognize himself or his firm as one of the Ultimate Beneficiaries by virtue of the advantages of living in a community having the innumerable services listed in the Health and Welfare Council's "Directory of Community Resources for Indianapolis and Marion County."

We have no measures available for differentiating degrees of "benefit" among the Ultimate Recipients, and no data anything like those available for analysing participation in the Donor-Aggregate. We must therefore accept, with some sceptical reservations, the conception of the Ultimate Beneficiaries and the estimates of their number apparently shared by those in the Welfare Community and the Campaign Leadership.

## GENERAL PROBLEMS OF MOPS FUNDRAISING

Within the social context of the whole geographic community, the Welfare Community, the Donor-Aggregate, and others in the "cast of characters," the major problems of campaign organization arise. They begin, logically enough, with matters of design for such a human organization, and these will be discussed first. We shall then turn to the problems of methods and manning, which are more easily described in chronological terms as they are connected with events that regularly occur in the annual calendar of the usual MOPS fundraising campaign.

### Problems of Design

The campaign organization is designed to solve a problem that is simple at a general level, and complicated only at the level of detail. Given a "Goal" and an "Appeal" which are sufficiently accepted in the community to make the campaign effort legitimate and worthwhile to all major parties, the problem is to arrange everything so that, within a limited and more or less publicly defined span of time, the "right person does the asking" in soliciting contributions from every prospective giver in the effort to secure community-wide "coverage." The relation of Solicitor-Donor is the "heart" of or the fundamental structure in such a campaign, and there are several major and not always compatible notions about this relationship in the minds of those who design and conduct these campaigns. Three major definitions might be caught in the terms "equals," "superiors," and "strangers."

*Equals.* Since it is usually believed that the campaign must maintain its "integrity as a volunteer effort to secure voluntary contributions," it is felt to be best if the solicitor "matches" the donor in rank within an industry, status in the business world, or social position in the general community. It is felt to be "bad" if the solicitor out-ranks the donor, since the latter may thereupon be or feel "pressured into giving," and thus be robbed of his "right to voluntary participation in a free society"; and, likewise, it may be "bad" if the donor out-ranks the solicitor, since the former may feel "insulted" and withhold all or part of what he might otherwise give.

Most of the successful and carefully calculated matching takes place only at the higher levels of the economic structures of the community, amongst the comparatively small number of top leaders and higher executives who are likely to be friends or acquaintances. Indeed, since they are *not* strangers, but do maintain other interpersonal relations, the solicitor and donor in such a case may select or create any one of a great variety of possible relationships in the campaign situation. The possible variations are increased by the likelihood that the present donor has once been in the solicitor's shoes, and that the solicitor is elsewhere a donor. When each has previously acted in the other's role, the relation can be an easy-going one, even one of joking or horse-play.

*Superiors.* Since, on the other hand, the campaign must "succeed"—or at least not "fail" or fall too far short of making its Goal—the campaign directors tend to develop an opposite point of view regarding the great mass of donors, and they may say to the solicitor assigned to organize in-plant solicitation in firms other than his own, "Get the top boss—get him to *tell* the employees, 'We want you!' " Given, as a fact, moreover, that the mass of donors numbers thousands and thousands of persons in a city like Indianapolis, the vast majority are bound to be anonymous—nameless and faceless—in the eyes of the campaign directors (and they are most often quite anonymous also so far as the campaign records go, since the aggregate of their gifts is usually reported in a lump sum as "the Employee gift" from each firm). Their very anonymity, however, permits the campaign directors to preserve the integrity of the campaign as a volunteer effort in the eyes of many. Anonymity may be reduced and equality in some degree restored by adopting the principle of "matching" solicitor to donor, which may be applied in practice in in-plant solicitation. Some reduction in anonymity also occurs in so far as the community-wide campaign usually has and needs the endorsement of labor unions which interpose a layer of persons who "know" the small giver.[12]

*Strangers.* It is a fact, whether or not it is recognized,[13] that in a large-scale community-wide campaign the solicitor and the donor are very frequently strangers to each other. The frequency with which they are strangers to each other, however, encourages the development and use of a "sales approach" throughout the design and operation of the campaign. In effect, this tends to define the relation of solicitor to donor as one patterned on the relation of salesman to customer; and "the prospect" then becomes more free to adopt the attitude of *caveat emptor* which he adheres to in the market place. Conversely, the solicitor comes to see his task as one of "selling" intangible benefits in exchange for a pledge of money. Building upon such experiences, the campaign directors—representing as they do the thinking of the business community—find a familiar pattern for the design and conduct of the campaign: the "sales campaign" with all the appropriate trappings of public relations, advertising, "peppy sales meetings," and the encouragement of "aggressive solicitation." In this way, they can overcome the inertia of many "volunteers"; and even though the directors cannot "hire and fire" the campaign leaders and workers, they can use all the standards of judgment of "performance" and all the incentives of "promotion" and other rewards, except pecuniary ones, that are familiar in the business world.[14]

There is a strong tendency in many cities to make "winning recognition" in a fundraising campaign of value to a man's career in the business community, and therefore pecuniary rewards may also flow his way, although indirectly. The modern corporation characteristically encourages its young executives to take an active part in civic enterprises, including fundraising, in the belief that both the firm's reputation as a "corporate citizen" and the man's own development are benefited. Absentee-owned corporations often show a great interest in these aspects of public relations, and expect their local executives to do their bit; but they also tend to fit into the on-going state of affairs, in preference to taking the initiative away from the older-established local firms. In Indianapolis, the more or less leaderless Donor-Aggregate gives the national firms perhaps too little to "fit into," and asks them for more initiative than they have learned it is wise to supply. In 1955, the community power structure appeared to consist of a collection of separate and loosely related peaks with some corporate pyramids towering over the others, but with barriers to communication between those in the Welfare Community (and in the Donor-Aggregate as well) and those at the summits of ownership and control. We were told that this was not merely a problem of remote decision-making by national firms but also a dilemma due to "absentee-ownership on the premises": the top decision-makers were around "somewhere" but nobody could get to talk to them.

Where the Donor-Aggregate has become a Donor Community with appropriate leadership, a tremendous amount of energy for fundraising can be released within the framework of the business community, since corporations will vie with each other in the civic enterprise arena to secure recognition as "good citizens," and, perhaps even more important, to secure training and community status for their executives. A well-organized "promotion system" in a reputable fundraising organization in which leadership within the organization confers honor also in the local community secures an immediate response and a great deal of co-operation from the public-relations-sensitive modern corporation.

While there are other, subtler variations of the relation of solicitor-donor, these subtleties—and indeed the major distinctions themselves—tend to be overborne as the size of the community increases and considerations of mass appeal lead towards neglect of careful study of the social structure, and appropriate utilization of it. More and more the campaign tends to take the form and tone of "an aggressive sales promotion." This might perhaps be expected on other grounds as well: from the importance of the business community in providing both the largest proportion of the money raised and most of the campaign leaders and workers—many of the latter being "volunteered" or assigned to campaign tasks on "company time." Here, however, we discover yet another aspect of the attempt to solve the general campaign problem referred to earlier.

A restatement of that problem may clarify this particular aspect. Given a legitimate and accepted campaign, the problem is to arrange that every donor (every firm or every individual able to give) is approached by the solicitor who is most likely (given *who* he is and *how* he conducts his approach) to secure the gift (or pledge, as the pledge-card has it, "in consideration of the gifts of others") which is large enough because, together with all the other gifts, it will help make the total amount raised at least equal to a satisfactory percentage of the goal.

The key words in the foregoing for our purposes now are *large enough*. The campaign directors here face the problem of "standards": the determination of answers to questions they phrase in such forms as, "What is a Fair Share for [Mr. So-and-So, or the XYZ Company]?" Part of the answer is found by the steps described in chapter 8: once the scope or goal of a campaign is determined, the "distribution" to be aimed at can be decided from within a range of practical and sense-making solutions to another question, "Where is the money to come from?"

A MOPS fundraising campaign, after it has been conducted for two or more years, accumulates records of previous giving and indications of comparative "generosity" on the part of the regular donors. Even in its first year, such a campaign could be roughly planned on the basis of what is known or supposed about local giving behavior, plus certain rules of thumb with which fundraisers are familiar. By means of something like a census, non-givers can be located and their "potential" estimated. Since the donors and non-givers can be "grouped" in such a way as to secure economy of volunteer effort in solicitation, and are intentionally so grouped in the records and solicitation plans of previous campaigns, the past performance of the campaign organization, as a whole or in terms of its parts (Soliciting Divisions, and units within them such as "Teams," "Committees," etc.), can be studied to learn what methods have achieved what results.[15] For example, non-givers and the "least generous" contributors can be grouped for such special efforts as "education," year-round "cultivation," or even certain kinds of "pressure," when it can be shown, on the basis of adequate records, that changes in the personnel of soliciting units have not hitherto secured the desired changes in giving. The study of past performance also gives the campaign directors guidance in allocating less manpower to the soliciting units which are to approach the "most generous" givers, so that personnel can be reserved to man the more difficult assignments—e.g., the solicitation of the "next most generous"—and so on, down the line to the non-givers.

Now the campaign directors may compare the goal and the total raised last year (and in prior years, if conditions make them comparable) and, having asked and answered the question as to where the money is to come from, they can proceed to sum the gifts that all the planned-for acts of solicitation can reasonably be expected to produce. The total tells them the probable outcome of the campaign if it is as vigorously conducted as it has been in past years. One may pretty well count in MOPS fundraising on the fact that most gifts in a long-established campaign tend to be repeated from one year to the next: a greater number of gifts may be raised in amount than are lowered; but, if there is any reduction, withholding the gift completely is more likely than giving a smaller one this year. Certainly, this was the picture in the Indianapolis Chest's 1953 campaign.[16] The important fact is that change is least to be expected: giving tends to become habitual, and non-giving may become almost as habitual as repeating identical gifts.

All of the foregoing problems, therefore, become more acute when substantial increases in giving are desired. If the campaign directors wish to raise, say, a 20 per cent larger sum (a not unusual self-set goal), they may consider a number of suggestions such as the following:

(1) "Ask for a 20 per cent increase from everybody."

(2) "Ask the most generous givers to hold the line, but solicit the less generous givers for proportional increases (considerably greater than 20 per cent, then) which will bring about the 20 per cent total increase needed."

(3) "Ask the most generous givers, and those nearly as generous, to hold the line, but to secure the 20 per cent increase, concentrate on the newcomers in our growing business community, and also develop new approaches to the long-resident non-givers and least generous old-timers."

(4) "Since 40 per cent of the total amount raised has come from a relatively small number of large corporate donors, ask them to increase 10 per cent and also to lend us manpower ('loaned executives' and campaign solicitors) sufficient to sell other firms on programs for increasing Employee participation; these programs, if successful, will yield 25 per cent more in Employee gifts. Simultaneously, aim to increase participation and giving among the smaller firms enough to make up the rest of the total 20 per cent increase needed to reach our Goal."

The campaign directors may decide against the first alternative on the ground that many donors are giving at top capacity and that it would therefore be inexpedient to ask for the same percentage increase from everybody, lest the campaign alienate the most generous givers, some of whom may really be "rate-busters" already. The idea of asking everybody for the same relative increase may then be converted into a plan simply to announce the increase in the size of the goal and "Ask everybody to do what he can to help," i.e., a plan that takes an extreme *laissez-faire* approach.

If a "more aggressive campaign" than this is felt to be desirable, then the campaign directors must proceed to make a much more careful analysis of the question, "Where is the money to come from?" In effect, they have to ask this question as if they were conducting a fund campaign within a *constituency*.[17]

But in MOPS fundraising, the directors do not have a constituency, although, as already pointed out, they think in terms of a more or less fictitious one called "our community." The greater the number of people, the more diversified their industrial and other activities; and the more recent and rapid the growth of the community, the more fictitious is its nature as a "constituency." Large communities of recent and rapid growth are more realistically, therefore, to be regarded instead as something analogous to a "market." But the closest that any fundraisers we know have come to recognizing overtly this "market-like" unit is when, preserving nevertheless the fictional word "community,"[18] they speak of its "potential," which is a market word. On this more cold-eyed basis they assert that, while "No one really knows the potential of a city as large as this," it is possible to "analyse the potential," and then proceed to do just that. This "analysis" entails establishment of target goals for soliciting units arranged by geographic divisions, size groups for industries (number of employees and size of payroll), groupings by type of industry or trade, or other classifications of donors.

What the campaign directors really engage in, then, is more like a market analysis than the operations of a "Rating Committee." Where their analysis makes it possible, something like Rating Committees may also be set up for trade groups, etc., and within these the per-employee giving of the firms can be ranked, and the "top 20 per cent," "the next highest 20 per cent," etc. can be marked out for appropriate kinds of attention. Such Rating Committees for trade groups may even be asked to conduct their own studies to arrive at some sort of consensus about each firm's "fair share." One notion that persists in this connection is that competitors within the same line of business will know better what is "fair" for each firm, and will extend the spirit of competition from the commercial to the fundraising sphere, with desirable results in the campaign.[19]

A sample of the structure of this kind of analysis is given in the accompanying model without further discussion. The model shows how the groupings of donors may lead to the design of the soliciting divisions and the assignments within them; and how the sub-goals of the various units ("Teams," "Committees," etc.) are arrived at.

SAMPLE OF ANALYSIS USED IN THE DESIGN OF A SOLICITING DIVISION
(Modified Unit Account Basis)

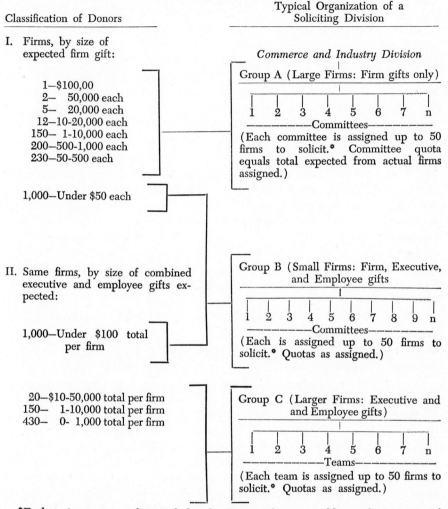

| Classification of Donors | Typical Organization of a Soliciting Division |
|---|---|
| I.  Firms, by size of expected firm gift: | *Commerce and Industry Division* |
|  | Group A (Large Firms: Firm gifts only) |
| 1–$100,00 | 1  2  3  4  5  6  7  n |
| 2–  50,000 each | ————Committees———— |
| 5–  20,000 each | (Each committee is assigned up to 50 firms to solicit.* Committee quota equals total expected from actual firms assigned.) |
| 12–10-20,000 each |  |
| 150–  1-10,000 each |  |
| 200–500-1,000 each |  |
| 230–50-500 each |  |
| 1,000–Under $50 each |  |
| II.  Same firms, by size of combined executive and employee gifts expected: | Group B (Small Firms: Firm, Executive, and Employee gifts |
|  | 1  2  3  4  5  6  7  8  9  n |
|  | ————Committees———— |
| 1,000–Under $100 total per firm | (Each is assigned up to 50 firms to solicit.* Quotas as assigned.) |
| 20–$10-50,000 total per firm | Group C (Larger Firms: Executive and and Employee gifts) |
| 150–  1-10,000 total per firm | 1  2  3  4  5  6  7  n |
| 430–  0- 1,000 total per firm | ————Teams———— |
|  | (Each team is assigned up to 50 firms to solicit.* Quotas as assigned.) |

*Each assignment to solicit includes the Company's name, address, phone, name of executive to call on, and usually the record of last year's gift, gift expected this year, etc.

## Methods and Manning: The Annual Calendar of a Campaign

The Community Chest and the Red Cross campaigns of 1955 are the largest MOPS campaigns in Indianapolis in dollar amounts raised as well as in number of persons engaged in leadership or active as workers in soliciting divisions. They are also the most complex, in respect to technical design and human organization, of any campaigns accessible to our direct observation.[20] The usual Chest or Red Cross campaign has a chronology or annual calendar of events that may be divided into four periods: (1) post-campaign; (2) pre-campaign planning; (3) pre-campaign organizing; (4) the drive itself.[21]

1. *Post-Campaign*. After the close of "last year's campaign," there is a period, of variable duration, between the "Final Report Meeting" of the old campaign and the earliest beginnings of next year's campaign. Where the top responsible lay leaders, as well as the professional or staff persons, feel that the design and conduct of past campaigns are a suitable model for the present and future ones, Period 1 may not be clearly distinguished. The statement made by a professional in one of the Red Cross campaign meetings in 1955 exemplifies such a view: "You might say we started planning this campaign eleven years ago." Similarly confident statements based on past performance could be and were made by lay leaders in the same campaign, comparing last year's results with the sub-division goals for 1955; since they had kept to much the same design for ten years of continued "success," they could assure subordinate leaders that "each one's task can be done." They could even cite dollar results, and show that the current sub-goals were achievable. For the Red Cross, accordingly, Period 1 need not preoccupy the professionals or the lay leaders for more than a few days, and a small permanent staff can later complete the routines begun in it. Quite the opposite has been the case, however, with the Community Chest in recent years: for the 1955 campaign, Period 1 threatened to extend from November, 1954, well into the first half of 1955—a length of time that was quite unsatisfactory to both the professional staff and the top lay leaders.

In any case, and whatever its duration, Period 1 may be divided into phases: (*a*) a time of "post mortem" or "satisfaction" as the case may be, followed by (*b*) a time of "new resolution" or "renewed devotion to the cause." It is also a time for (*c*) "recognition of donors" and "awards to volunteer workers," and (*d*) for review of the past campaign operation to learn what might be done better "next time." For the permanent staff it is also a time for getting in any delayed reports of pledges. Period 1 thus begins a task for those concerned with "collections," while for others it coincides with activities of "cultivation"; it is this overlap that makes campaigning, at least in the case of the Chest, a year-round job.

2. *Pre-Campaign Planning*. Pre-campaign "top level" general planning by the governing body of the organization and its standing committees, assisted by the staff, is also a period of variable duration, but ideally it is one that follows a very short Period 1, and is itself as short as possible, in order to allow ample time for the work of Period 3. The pre-campaign planning period involves consideration of next year's goal and appeal, and attention to the design of the campaign organization, to scheduling, and to the enlisting of next year's General Chairman, other top volunteer

aides (including those needed for public relations) and all the rest of the campaign leadership.

In practice, the duration of Period 2, like that of Period 1, depends largely upon whether or not the past campaign was a "success," and therefore capable of providing the model for next year, at least in its major features. If it was a success, the usual tasks of the period will have become quite routine and can be turned over to the newly selected General Chairman, his top aides, and the staff. The top level planners can henceforth participate in an advisory capacity, remaining in readiness to "help where needed." Specifically, this means "opening doors" or securing introductions to Leading Donors and winning assurances of their continued support; keeping the new campaign leaders informed about business conditions, especially such items of "intelligence" as current profits, tax positions, and forthcoming personnel changes in various firms; and also preparation to make some public appearances as "top leaders" at the small (but otherwise important) or large meetings in Periods 3 and 4. Typical of such activity is "putting in an appearance" at the small meetings of bank presidents, private dinners for selected Captains of Industry, and the larger meetings of campaign workers in Period 4. Clearly, much of this "help where needed" requires great discretion, lest donors become resentful of "pressure" or the use of "inside information."[22]

If all or many components of the campaign design and operation are in question, some of the problems will have had to be explored in Period 1 (in reviews of what happened last time) and some suggested solutions will be available, including appraisals made by the professionals. The top level planners have then to decide whether to extend Period 2 in order to give adequate time and attention to the many important details of campaign design, or whether to delegate the task to the General Chairman, with his top aides, the staff, and an executive committee including leaders of previous drives.

Since the General Chairman is to be in the public eye and the responsible director of all the activities of Periods 3 and 4, and since there may have to be considerable changes in campaign design, the pre-campaign planning period cannot really be completed, or indeed well begun, until after the General Chairman has been selected and has begun to work closely with the lay leaders and the professionals. This is because many interlocking decisions about details are dependent upon his policy choices. Recruiting campaign leaders and workers down the line, for example, which is a task for Periods 3 and 4, depends upon careful scheduling, geared to specific assignments within the organization chart and the plan for solicitation, as well as upon an efficient "service of supply" of "campaign materials" which have to be prepared well in advance.

When this year's campaign follows a "success," the selection of the General Chairman can be made well in advance, even if his identity is not publicly announced until later; the more sought-after is the post, the more likely are the top level planners to have a number of candidates available for future years, so that a system of promotion from the ranks can be developed to provide incentives for volunteers all down the line.[23]

In the event, however, of a campaign's following a previous "failure," the selection of the General Chairman may become such a major problem for the top level planners that the time and energy they must devote to "enlist-ing" (or even "pressuring") a leader to serve, from a list of reluctant prospects, seriously limits their contributions to the redesign of the campaign, which they may well feel is equally urgently needed. Nor, for the same reasons, can they develop a promotion system, or cast much more than a wistful glance at the most desirable candidates. This appears to be the ever-threatening, if not always critical, dilemma of the administration of "failing" fundraising organizations.[24]

One consequence appears to be that, as uncertainties about the campaign lay leadership increase, anxieties abound on all sides and may spread into Periods 3 and 4, there to handicap the recruiting and inspiring of campaign workers, especially if the latter begin to wonder, "Do *they* know what they are doing?" Even the professionals' work on details of campaign design begins to suffer if there are no fixed points, or too few, at the general level, to guide them in doing their jobs. Ideally, the staff executive maintains a customary organizational pattern for the campaign and helps the lay leader-ship in a staff capacity. But if the campaign is in difficulty, the lay leaders feel called upon to take the initiative in redesigning it, and they must therefore frequently initiate action for the staff; this redesign, peremptory and from the outside, not only disrupts the internal authority structure, but also, directly or indirectly, frequently makes mandatory sudden changes in those parts of the campaign organization which *have* had some continuity and record of success. Again, ideally, in an organization that desires to emphasize its "voluntary" character, it is not fitting for conflict to develop over "Who is the boss?" but this seems to be inevitable when replanning without adequate time to think matters through is involved. "Cultivation" or "selling" the organization in personal contacts and public talks also becomes more difficult in an atmosphere of declining confidence in the campaign. Hence it is possible, unfortunately, for more and more of the necessary tasks to get deferred to Period 3, which is itself, by now, shrinking, as the time for "The Drive" (Period 4) approaches. Unresolved problems turn as the days go by into "D-day" anxieties and are felt increasingly to handicap present decision.

3. *Pre-Campaign Organizing.* Detailed planning of the campaign, and even some pre-campaign solicitation, by the staff and lay leaders of the campaign organization ideally begin simultaneously with Period 2. At

first, these tasks may involve only the staff and the top level planners of
the organization's governing body but, again ideally, they should very soon
thereafter involve the next year's General Chairman and his close associates
and staff aides.

The pre-campaign organizing of Period 3 culminates in a number of
meetings arranged for all those in the Campaign Leadership—as well as in
some meetings of major interested supporters and potential donors. The
Campaign Leadership, as we use the term here, includes the General
Chairman and all his volunteer assistants down to "team captains," "group
chairmen," and persons with similar titles whose names appear in the
records of the Final Report Meeting, and especially those whose names
appear in the daily newspapers. Some of these leaders are responsible for
recruiting the workers who will later do various kinds of solicitation (soliciting of firms for firm, executive, and employee gifts; or of individuals by
door-to-door, office-to-office, store-to-store "leg-work"[25]); others will be
assigned to direct solicitation of the larger gifts. While the design of the
Campaign Leadership may assume that most of the leaders merely recruit
actual solicitors and co-ordinate their work, in practice each is expected,
if need be, to step in and complete the solicitation assignments of his
"team" or "group." This kind of "breakdown" in the actual campaign is
regarded as deplorable and avoidable by men with business or military
experience; but if it is not too common, and if morale stays high, it may
be viewed as a test of character, useful not only in the realm of fundraising
but even in the wider business community.[26]

These meetings of leaders, occurring in the final organizing period,
are designed to give them, and perhaps some workers, something akin to
"sales training," i.e., instruction combined with "inspiration." The meetings
are also necessary in order to give them the actual "campaign materials"
or "kits": literature about "the cause," membership cards or receipts, badges
or stickers, lists of prospective givers or prepared pledge cards based on
previous years' giving, report forms and envelopes, etc. The kits may be
used in direct solicitation by the subordinate leaders, or they may in turn
distribute these "campaign supplies" to subordinate volunteers. Messenger-
delivery of the supplies may also be employed, but the "timing" of such
"sales" meetings so that the leaders and their helpers can "go to work" at
once is evidently preferred.

The meetings also serve to establish or reinforce the channels of communication for the campaign. Each worker can meet his sub-group leader,
and so on up the line. Once these channels are securely established, a
small number of phone calls from "headquarters" will ensure the trans-
mission of any emergency message throughout the campaign organization
or to any of its sub-divisions.[27]

Another function of the meetings, related to "building morale," is to induce leaders and workers to perceive each other as if they were salesmen competing for recognition in a serious, business campaign. Still another function is to secure as complete a roster as possible of all those who will ultimately carry the pledge cards or firm-giving records in the actual solicitation of individuals or companies. This is important for the campaign, but also for "security" reasons: unless such records are carefully subdivided and distributed only to those with definite assignments, they might, in any larger compilations, constitute a body of information normally felt to be confidential and certainly not to be allowed to fall into irresponsible hands.[28]

4. *The Drive Itself.* "This year's campaign," although it actually begins much earlier with the first solicitations for the larger gifts (especially from corporations who are also asked to permit, and even carry out, the solicitation of their executives and employees later on), occurs in the period between the first public "kick-off" meeting—luncheon, breakfast, or what not—and the Final Report Meeting. Ideally, Period 4 is that part of the entire annual drama which comes to involve the largest number of active participants in the campaign for funds, although it may not raise the largest proportion of the total amount. Its activities result in the most publicity, which is important for the "educational" values of the campaign. This period also involves the public to the greatest extent, since "everybody" is considered to be a prospective donor; certainly the contacts made by solicitors reach their peak as far as numbers are concerned in Period 4.

During Period 4, following the "kick-off," all the campaign leaders as well as many volunteer workers are invited to "Report Meetings," at which sums of pledges and cash brought in are further totalled by sub-divisions within the campaign organization, and all can see both how far towards Goal the campaign has progressed, and the percentages of sub-goals that have been achieved within each sub-division.

These meetings usually occur weekly through several successive weeks. In the Red Cross campaign, all sub-divisions were brought together in four successive Report Meetings, for each of which a certain ceremonial had been designed or had become traditional. Since past records were available, the people in attendance could be told at each meeting how the campaign was proceeding, relative to past performance. Standard expectation was said to be that at the Second Report Meeting, about 60 per cent of the goal should be reported; at the Third, about 80 per cent; and at the Fourth and Final, something over 100 per cent—which would spell "success" and "victory." Such percentages can be used in exhorting the campaign workers to greater efforts: in the 1955 campaign, "51.1 per cent" of goal was claimed at the Second Report Meeting, and "70.3 per cent" at the Third.[29] Simultaneously, the leaders and workers in the sub-divisions could see how their own percentages compared with the "over-all total," and could feel either rewarded or spurred on. Publicity about the early Report Meetings is also thought to influence some donors to respond more generously or more quickly. However, the newspapers did not give much space to this kind of publicity in 1955 campaigns. Holding back reports of large gifts, as a device to stimulate interest in the early weeks of the campaign, did not appear as a practice in 1955, but such deception is possible, we were told, and effective.

The final stages of Period 4 include some last-minute and urgent actions that quickly become the routines of a new Period 1. A few days, in the case of the Red Cross, and a somewhat longer time in the case of the Chest, are necessary for last-minute "mopping up" operations (getting pledge cards, reports, gift records, and other materials back from the volunteer campaign workers who failed to turn them in at the Final Report Meeting), dismantling the campaign headquarters, turning certain records over to the permanent staff charged with "collections," and in general, bringing Period 4 to such an end that a final audit of results can get under way and permit the new Period 1 to be succeeded by new Periods 2 and 3 as soon as possible.

The Red Cross is usually able to complete its final audit of the amount raised by about thirty days after the Final Report Meeting, and by June 30th, the audit to that date and other materials are ready to be compiled in the Chapter's Annual Report. By December 31st, all the collections on the spring campaign pledges are reported to the American National Red Cross, and any collections in the following year are credited to that year's campaign. Partly because of its larger dollar volume, and partly because more people participate, both in the campaign organization and in the vast aggregate of donors, the Chest has a somewhat longer Period 4 than does the Red Cross, and more collections to carry over into succeeding periods. Although it remains a matter of degree, the Chest campaign is more correctly viewed as a year-round program of "cultivation," solicitation, and collection; the Red Cross, less dependent upon firm gifts and more dependent upon "personal giving," does not receive as much of its total amount raised in the form of payments on pledges over the year, and hence preserves in its campaign more of the character, timing, and symbolic content, of its earlier "Roll Call."[30]

## Problems of a Mops Fundraising Organization

As we have seen, a mops fundraising campaign brings into periodic existence a special organization, manned by a large number of "volunteers for the duration," who are guided by the campaign directors, i.e., the lay leaders and staff of the permanent organization, and perhaps professional consultants from elsewhere. (Since 1945, the American City Bureau has sent a team of professional fundraising consultants to Indianapolis to work with the Red Cross for eight or ten of the weeks included in what we call Periods 3 and 4.) There is also, however, a permanent organization, which is concerned with long-term general problems year in and year out. Its responsible administrators are (1) the officers and (2) the members of the Board of Directors, who are also volunteers and may have entered the permanent organization from the campaign ranks. They are in the positions of top authority both for the permanent organization and for its special expanded form at campaign time; they act for the organization in employing the executive director and other paid personnel, whether these are regular staff members or imported professionals.

As elected leaders of a voluntary organization conducting MOPS fundraising campaigns, each of these administrators nominally "represents" both the voting membership of the permanent organization and any one or several of the various interest groups or aggregates in the community: the various parts of the Welfare Community, the Donor-Aggregate, the Ultimate Beneficiaries, and the General Population.[31] But claims stronger than those on the basis of which they were elected supervene and the leaders tend more strongly to become (a) adherents of the permanent organization and its cause, and (b) advocates for what they believe "the best people" think and desire regarding the organization. Each may also, or alternatively, feel responsible in various degrees to some particular public or publics (one or more of the groups and aggregates mentioned above) which is not necessarily the same as that he was more or less explicitly chosen to "represent."

An elected leadership so composed is obviously not responsible to a single source of authority. It is not like the management of a corporation —which is regarded as being responsible to a voting majority of the stockholders—nor is it like the government of a democratic state, responsible to the electorate.

Diffuse responsibility seems thus initially to characterize the Board of a voluntary organization, and an important consequence of this initial definition is that the Officers and Directors will be, at least on some occasions, confronted with a wide range of choice between trying to be responsible to "all the people" and trying to act responsibly in relation to a particular part of the public.[32] One resolution of possible conflict between "all" and "part," or between one "part" and another, is to seek to act responsibly with regard to the good of the voluntary organization itself: that is, to do whatever promises to ensure its continued existence or improve its well-being. Within this restriction there is still considerable room for alternative choices, and thus an attractive area of freedom in which the Directors can enjoy some delights of creative decision-making that are rather rare in the workaday business world.[33] This consequence of the nature of voluntary associations may well be used to attract successful business executives to long-term service in such organizations.

What are the major problems to be considered by administrators who seek to make the permanent organization, as well as its periodic expanded form, the campaign organization, more "efficient" and more "effective"? These problems center on three outstanding features of any human organization: Purpose, Structure, and Continuity. Every human organization has a *Purpose* that is more or less unifying; it has a *Structure* that defines tasks and behavior in relation to its Purpose; and it has *Continuity,* in so far as it adds new adherents to its Purpose, at least as fast as other members leave its Structure in the course of time. The administrators of such an organization deal with a complex interrelation of these three features or aspects, through the design and development of which they secure results that are measured in dollars (or other *tasks* completed)—"Effectiveness" —and results that are felt as *satisfactions*—"Efficiency."

In seeking to establish these three features, the administrators must take a point of view like that of a captain on the bridge of a ship, who must weave together the perspectives of all hands, from that of the man in the crows-nest to that of the engine room oiler, from that of the purser to that of the cook. He is expected to lead the organization to accomplish something beyond its scheduled tasks: not only to bring the "ship" to "port" with its cargo but to bring it with its personnel sharing such an abiding sense of satisfaction in "a job well done" that most or all wish to "sign on again" for the next voyage (or campaign).

In similar fashion, the administrators of a voluntary organization in American society have a responsibility to "govern" as well as to "rule":[34] if they choose only to govern and not to rule, they will leave their task less than half done. If they rule but do not provide for government, the organization will tend to lose its personnel, and the administrators, turned rulers, will find themselves trying to do all the work.

It appears that a MOPS fundraising organization requires less rule and more government than business organizations, and somewhat more rule and less government than, say, a supervised play-group. In a particular organization the blend that will get the desired results must be sought for. (We are talking here of the primary result—in the case of MOPS fundraising, money. But the "right" blend of rule and government is itself a "desired result," and not only a means to something else.[35]) Regular attendance by responsible laymen at meetings and doing one's "homework" may be enough to perpetuate a smooth-running organization that is already clearly "efficient" as well as "effective"; but a great deal more time and effort than this minimum will be needed if the organization is instead losing the public confidence without which it is difficult to change its campaign record from one of "failure" to one of "success." The task of leadership in the latter situation is made doubly difficult when the officers cannot even count on the attendance of more than half of the Board Members;[36] and, when low morale becomes too pervasive, a process of circular reinforcement of discouragement leading to apathy can only too readily affect the work of all hands and deepen their dissatisfactions.[37]

*Purpose*

It has been said, with business organizations and their employee relations in mind, that "Work without purpose is life without meaning."[38] Many firms make great efforts to engage their employees' interest in the final product and its uses, with the hope that even the small contribution each man makes will thereby be given greater significance in his eyes. Nevertheless, if all their efforts fail to increase the sense of personal worth and pride in the product of their labor of some employees, these workers can feel that their money wages give their jobs at least the kind of significance that is expressed in saying, "Well, it's a living." Firms which aspire to create conditions for higher levels of morale than this usually do so with "sound business reasons" in view: they have learned to anticipate better or less wasteful production, or improved customer relations, or less employee turnover—results that can affect profits.[39]

In mass fundraising the "workers" are, of course, volunteers whose rewards may range from rather minimal satisfactions about "meeting such nice people" (the values of pure sociability) or "becoming better known in the world," to satisfactions, perhaps deeply felt, about "doing the highest civic duty a businessman can perform"—or, more modestly, "doing one's bit to make this a better world"—or, invoking sacred sanctions, "doing the work of the Lord." The rewards may even be material, though indirect, as when "recognition" in the campaign brings a man an offer of a job or a promotion in his firm. Some material rewards may be fairly direct: a salesman sees new prospects in his co-campaigners or in the firms he solicits; a banker finds some "new business"; a politician can grab some of the limelight he needs in his career; public relations experts can display their skills; and almost any businessman with local customers can benefit by learning in conversations with persons he might not otherwise see, "what is going on."[40] Finally, a large-scale campaign does bring together an interesting "cross-section of the community,"[41] and one minor reward for some volunteers may be this part of the drama: an exciting realization of the size and variety of "Our Fair City."

But these heterogeneous individual rewards and satisfactions cannot themselves be summed up into the "Purpose" of the permanent fundraising enterprise. Its administrators have the task of stating that Purpose in the Appeal so that it will be clearly understood, and become something unifying and transcendent—far above individual purposes—something, the leadership's enthusiasm for which can be communicated throughout the ranks of the entire organization at campaign time. If the volunteers add something of this shared "crusading spirit" to their individual concerns, this points to acceptance of the Purpose as stated in the Appeal by the business community most of them come from; and this, in turn, will encourage them to make the necessary efforts in the campaign itself.

As we shall see in more detail in chapter 11, a Purpose which can be translated into an Appeal with more emotionality than rationality is sufficient and appropriate for a "pennies per capita" campaign. But a *federated* campaign (such as a Chest or United Fund) is inevitably, in a city like Inidianapolis, a "dollars per capita" campaign: it depends, for much of its total, upon decisions made at top levels in the business community where rationality is ideally and usually at a premium over emotionality—at least in dealing with large sums of money.

The original Appeal of *federated* fundraising in general was based upon a "rational decision" to attempt thereby "to avoid a multiplicity of drives" (the negative side of its Purpose) and also to ensure continued support for local agencies and to fit them into some "plan" for the general community's well-being (the positive side of its Purpose). Part of the Chest's dilemma, in Indianapolis and elsewhere, has been that faith in the rationality of its positive Purpose has apparently declined along with, but not necessarily in consequence of, the draining away of support for its original negative Purpose, since "multiplicity of drives" rises again to mock at this reason for federation.[42]

A federation cannot, of course, dispense with emotionality. Various forms of emotion seem appropriate in making the Appeal at campaign time; but even then, and more so in the year-round work of the permanent organization, the bedrock of its Purpose is rationality—at least that degree of a rule of reason which corresponds to and reflects the prevailing thinking of "the best people," especially the top business leaders.[43] If their support is lost to the federation because it presents them with a maze of irrationality, then it is difficult to see how the federation can survive, or at least have more than a meager and mostly negative Purpose.

In translating Purpose into Appeal, the administrators of a mass fundraising organization have an opportunity to think through their blend of "rule" and "government" in the interest of the best interrelation of Purpose, Structure, and Continuity. In a voluntary organization it is probably fitting that something like what is called "consultative supervision" in industry be encouraged. The administrators' opportunity at this juncture is to engage the attention of members, volunteers, and persons in the donor-aggregate in discussions or conferences that re-examine, and ceremonies that restate or reaffirm, the main themes and ideals of the organization's Purpose. No real change in the Purpose may be necessary, but it is even then important to leave place for change in the perception of that Purpose as it appears in the minds of the adherents and supporters. In any case, newcomers may receive education to a new idea, and others, a freshening of the vision; while for all there may be a growth in consensus. With such a shared understanding the administrators can bring "rule" and "government" closer together, as all realize that "rule" finally resides in the Purpose which they serve, and not in the person of the leader. The latter may have been a governor-ruler of long service, and now, in ceremonies honoring him, the real point is reaffirmed: that he now most fully embodies the Purpose, that he stands before them, the inside group, and the outer world, as its symbol and defender, and that it is the Purpose, not the man, they must in future serve and guard.

### Structure

While the relationship of Solicitor-Donor is at the heart of the campaign, in the permanent organization, in contrast, the fundamental relationship is that of Leader-Follower. Just how the latter relationship is used to construct a hierarchy, varies from one organization to the other; and, even if the formal structures of two organizations were made from the same blueprint, it is a familiar fact that different persons can use hierarchy wisely or destructively.

The fundraising organization taken as a whole tends, as already stated in this chapter, to have two important levels of leadership: the Elder Statesmen and the Young Campaigners. The former provide "rule" but mostly "govern," while the latter transmit the Purpose through the campaign ranks out into the general population. A "ladder of opportunity" is created, by means of which persons can climb from the bottom to the top, from small Solicitor to big Board member. This makes possible a system of promotion which attracts new adherents, and, in the long run, makes for Continuity.

On establishing their hierarchy, the administrators have two connected sets of problems: (1) to provide rule and to govern the organization—the problems of internal relations; and (2) to design and develop the organization so as to relate it realistically to the structure of the community, with particular attention to the structures of power, influence, prestige, etc. which determine donors' decisions to give more, less, or not at all—the problems of *external relations.* The second problem may be represented as in the accompanying diagram showing the approximate social structure expected respectively for a community, a campaign organization, and what we have called the "permanent organization."

If the structure of the whole organization is correctly designed, the Purpose can be effectively communicated because the organization "fits" into the larger community at the points where the Appeal can be most directly and even sympathetically transmitted. The administrators' choice of a blend of rule and government can be geared to that which is most accepted in the general life of the community, and the latter's concurrence will make all the tasks of administration easier. Even the newcomers, needed for Continuity, will be more easily assimilated, and the future leaders will be the more readily "trained."

ORGANIZATION STRUCTURE                                    STRUCTURE OF THE
    FOR THE CAMPAIGN        COMMUNITY STRUCTURE      PERMANENT ORGANIZATION

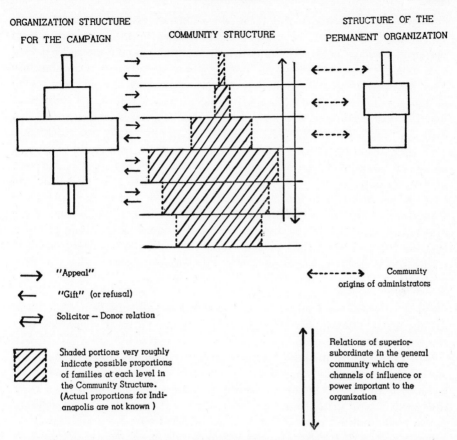

→        "Appeal"                    ←------→    Community
                                                origins of administrators
←        "Gift"  (or refusal)

⇄        Solicitor — Donor relation

░        Shaded portions very roughly           Relations of superior-
         indicate possible proportions          subordinate in the general
         of families at each level in           community which are
         the Community Structure.               channels of influence or
         (Actual proportions for Indi-          power important to the
         anapolis are not known )               organization

RELATIONS BETWEEN THE SOCIAL STRUCTURE OF THE COMMUNITY AND THE
          MOPS FUNDRAISING ORGANIZATION

## Continuity

In planning and acting to assure the Continuity of the organization, one
of the first necessities for administrators is to take the view that "we are
going to be in business for a long time to come," and then to think what
this means for each major decision affecting the design and development
of the organization.

One implication is that new adherents should be won every year, throughout the year. Another is that leadership should be recruited and nurtured
for the years ahead. To do the opposite—to "burn up" or "brown off" the
Young Campaigners, to fail to adjust the structure of the organization,
particularly its ladder of promotion, both to realities in the community and
to the long-run needs of the organization, and to neglect the steady year-
round recruiting process—is to work against the organization's chances to
develop Continuity.

Continuity, as we use the term, does not, of course, imply stubborn resistance to change. Some of our greatest political institutions and modern corporations have achieved Continuity by continuous adaptation, and they can look forward to being "in business" for decades to come because they have systematically brought in personnel as staff for the future. One of the training methods is to rotate new members through the different levels and departments, requiring them to learn, observe, and *report*, often critically and with a mind alert to new ways of improving processes.

An adaptation of industry's methods of training and self-study of departments, etc. might well be suitable for a fundraising organization. Purpose, Structure, and designs for assuring Continuity all need periodic re-examination. Participation in such reviews might offer at one and the same time training for future leaders and newcomers—and revitalization of the interest and enthusiasm of the old hands. Voluntary organizations do not live forever, of course, but mass fundraising organizations seem required to develop a considerable degree of Continuity to survive at all.

## Summary

What has been said about the administrative problems of a mass fundraising organization is merely a general "mapping" of what is actually very complicated social terrain.

Why do some business leaders give so much time and thought and hard work to these matters? Some say, for example, that the business leaders of a modern American city should count on giving at least one-fifth of their time to civic enterprises in order adequately to discharge their responsibility to the community.

Perhaps part of the reason—in addition to all those already adduced—is that there is a tide in American affairs: a reaffirmation of the importance of local controls and of citizens' participation in shaping the institutions by which they live. This goes deeper, for the long run, than a mere reaction to totalitarianism, and is more than just a transient theme in contemporary national and state politics. It probably goes deeper, too—at least for many Americans—than a sentimental nostalgia for "the old days," or a kind of infantile regression in yearning for a simpler, more easily commanded environment. The ones who are truly determined and who hardly measure the time they give to civic affairs are those who know history, who know that human collaboration has never reached high development by chance, and who know that men have had to think and discuss long and hard, and work earnestly together in order to build and maintain successful organizations in any field.

Helping an organization achieve effectiveness and efficiency is, for such a person, rather like building a fine mansion that is also an hospitable home —not just a monument or mausoleum, but a sound structure for living which gives posterity something worth maintaining, remodeling, or even surpassing. A sense of history goes along with this, and like the good engineer who keeps an accurate set of plans recording changes, this person sees that a faithful account is kept of the building process.

For one thing, an organization without a history may be suspected of having a "past," and this hardly helps it attract the most desirable recruits and future leaders needed for its Continuity. By contrast, a history that is persuasive of the organization's past Continuity can enhance the present significance of its Purpose; indeed the first enthusiasts for a cause are often the most eloquent. Finally, by naming the illustrious persons who were earlier volunteers and who held offices in the past, the Structure of the organization is made evident to all, the roles are given prestige, and the service is accorded due respect. All of these measures may provide inspiration for those who serve today, and give the administrators much to live up to.

# 11. Methods in Indianapolis: Manpower

IN OUR DISCUSSION in chapter 10 of methods and manning for MOPS fund-raising, we focused on the design of an annual campaign, on the arrangement of a schedule of some definiteness (the clearer the better), and on the kinds of general problems which have to be acted upon step by step through the year. There we defined the campaign narrowly, by assuming for convenience (and, hopefully, for clearer exposition) that the "Appeal" and the "Goal" are "sufficiently accepted in the community to make the campaign effort legitimate and worthwhile." These terms are intended to point to the *minimal conditions* of "acceptance": if these conditions were not met, the campaign would have to be abandoned. As long as a sufficient number of community leaders[1] continue to act as if abandonment of a certain campaign is unthinkable, and as long as there is no organized opposition, to that extent we may surely say that the campaign meets these minimal conditions for survival.

In this chapter, we move from the abstract to the concrete: from general statements to descriptions of what we observed in the Chest and Red Cross campaigns in Indianapolis in 1955, and what we were able to learn, from documents, interviews, and the data regarding money-results, about their campaigns and others in past years.

Each of these two organizations has clearly met the minimal conditions year after year, even though the Chest's campaign results have been locally evaluated as "failure" in two out of every three years of its whole existence. Replacement of the Chest by a United Fund has been urged by some,[2] and one reason privately suggested was that the Chest is by now unalterably symbolic of "failure" and that a United Fund would, at least, escape this stigma. Apart from these few, however, and in the eyes of most people, the Chest's survival was evidently never in serious doubt after its first year or so. Indeed, the Indianapolis Chest is now so well established (at a level of minimal acceptance at least) that some of its well-wishers see no difficulties in the way of its *enlargement* as a federation with its present form of government (as by "admitting" new agencies) or its incorporation into some kind of United Fund (including the Red Cross and more of the larger "health drives" than the one already included in the Chest). Whether or not there is such development, and whatever its form, it is virtually certain that "federation" in fundraising will continue to receive at least minimal acceptance in Indianapolis: it would take a great deal of hard work to win more than that, but it would take a great deal to destroy local support for the idea altogether.

How does a MOPS fundraising campaign develop more than this minimal acceptance? And what is meant by "more"? In chapter 9, we indicated that, whereas the Indianapolis Chest in 1950 had something very close to minimal acceptance only, the Red Cross Chapter went beyond that to a somewhat higher level of acceptance—both being measured by a comparison of actual per capita gifts with those predicted on the basis of city characteristics. We also saw there that the Indianapolis Chest, compared with all the country's Chests taken together, has lagged behind national growth trends (except for its earliest years and certain years in World War II); even the 1955 campaign, while it raised nearly one-third more than that of 1954, still fell below what the city's "potential" and the national increase in the take of all Chests combined would have made it reasonable to expect.

More than minimal acceptance would clearly characterize the Indianapolis Chest's situation in the 1920's, when it did keep up with the national trend. Only minimal acceptance seems to have been the rule in peacetime years ever since then. (The chances are, if all the facts for 1955 were in, that even in that campaign the Chest was still working close to a "minimal" condition.) "More than minimal acceptance" is what the Indianapolis Red Cross apparently won in World War I, regained in World War II, and has retained in the decade or so since then.[3]

How a campaign develops more than minimal acceptance might perhaps be inferred by comparing the Chest with the Red Cross in some detail, and by partial comparison with the Hospital campaign where relevant.[4]

In making our comparative study of the Chest and the Red Cross, we sought to become as intimately acquainted as possible with every aspect of the whole life of the city, including fundraising and giving behavior in situations other than those of the two major campaigns we observed. We had two reasons for spreading our attention over such a wide field: (1) we wanted to see how people's behavior in each campaign compared with their behavior in other community activities ("Do these people act differently in a fundraising campaign from the way they do in business transactions, in using their incomes, enjoying recreations, etc.?") and (2) we wanted to see whether campaigns differ ("Does fundraising for different kinds of causes involve differences in the style and manner of presenting the Appeal, and therefore relate to the different kinds of people each brings forth as volunteers or moves to become contributors?").

We therefore proceeded to follow the Red Cross campaign from its preparatory stages in January, 1955, through the official period of solicitation (February 16-March 28) and into the post-campaign period, becoming acquainted during the rest of the year with some of the people and activities in the year-round program of the Indianapolis Chapter. When the Chest's 1955 campaign got under way in June, we became more and more deeply engaged in observing every detail and event to which we had access. The official period of that campaign was concentrated in September and October, but the summer was filled with activities, and the post-campaign period continued well into 1956 when we attended the Budget Committee meetings, and also saw what we could of the changes in government, election of officers, etc., the replacement of the staff Manager, and the securing of the new General Chairman for the 1956 campaign. The Budget Committee meetings, particularly the "hearings" conducted by the Review Groups, gave us, in a relatively short time, some acquaintance with the far-reaching and often complex "causes" and "concerns" that preoccupy those in the Welfare Community, and also some idea of the social processes by which convergences and conflicts in these assorted interests are brought into a sort of order by the hard work of the Budget Committee and the staffs of the Chest and the Health and Welfare Council. We obtained a glimpse, at least, into the problems of those who wish to combine, in the single Appeal of a Chest campaign, the varied interests, demands, and pressures that are churning in the Welfare Community.[5]

## SOME COMPARISONS OF RED CROSS AND CHEST CAMPAIGNS

### Planning and Organizing the Campaign

One big difference between Chest and Red Cross lies in the way the two campaigns are planned and organized. The Red Cross campaign follows an established pattern that has been in use for over ten years: procedures are clear and settled, and the human behavior in each role has become almost traditional. Each individual in the Campaign Leadership can learn all the tasks "from the bottom up," "promotions" can be made, and rewards can be evaluated by one's self and others, within an organizational pattern that has been stable long enough to have acquired sentimental value. Such stability, moreover, makes it possible for everyone to recognize readily who's who and what's what in the organization. The steadiness of the pattern means that the success of individuals and teams in furthering the campaign can be reliably compared with the success of other individuals or teams in another campaign, or that of teams or individuals filling the same roles in other years. This makes for a competitive spirit which is highly congenial to those who participate—as perhaps it is to most Americans.[6]

In contrast, the Chest campaign has had a varying pattern, marked by a great deal of improvisation each year; there have been, especially, many changes that make comparison of individual or group effectiveness in the soliciting divisions from one year to the next quite difficult, and often impossible. This robs "sub-goals" of the significance they might have if individuals or groups could compare their results with past performances by others.

The Red Cross campaign is also notable for preserving continuity in its lay leadership. For example, each year's General Chairman becomes next year's Fund Committee chairman; and he often continues thereafter as a member of the Board of Directors, assigned to service on the Fund Committee. Another feature peculiar to this campaign is that it is managed (more or less "behind the scenes," though not, of course, surreptitiously) by professional fundraisers from the American City Bureau who, because they come from "the outside," can, we are credibly told, "say things to the [lay] leaders that a person on the Staff all year round could not say." The Bureau has added further to this quality of continuity by sending the same "team" each year for as many years as possible. Regarding one of these visiting professionals at an organizing meeting, a lay leader could jokingly say, "——— has lived in Indianapolis more years than any of us."

In the Chest campaign, however, and this has a bearing on its characteristic annual improvisation, there has been a history of variable relations between lay leaders and the professional fundraisers, who, in this case, are members of the Chest's own year-round staff. Both in the pre-campaign planning stages and in organizing and carrying on the campaign, the staff can be, and often are, very much subordinated by the lay leaders. The latter, in their enthusiasm, can and do introduce far-reaching innovations or improvisations, either in the campaign organization (the arrangement and naming of soliciting divisions, the grouping of assignments to solicit, etc.) or in the campaign themes, claims, and promises. The latter will, of course, define to a considerable extent the situation which the regular Board members and staff have to "live with" the next year, and thus bind the staff not only in the present, but in the future. Moreover, each change is introduced without an experimental "control group" which would permit testing the effectiveness of an innovation from one year to another.[7] Satisfactory evidence of the effects of any of these frequent changes would require that they be put into effect in such a way that the results could be scientifically assessed; and this would usually add nothing to expense, nor would it cause any appreciable delay, though it might require thought, knowledge, and patience. But in an atmosphere of crisis, even such "cheap" ways of getting vital, secure knowledge are usually felt to take too much thinking time away from action, so that "planning" continues to go forward in a vacuum as to facts, cause-effect relations, or principles.

Since the Chest's innovations of each year tend to be parts of a wholesale

improvisation which is intended to change the campaign result from
"failure" to "success," it has, so long as this policy is pursued, little opportunity for systematic experiment, or, therefore, for the discovery of what a
sound or workable policy would be. A campaign that is steadily successful,
on the other hand, is not likely to be subjected to any major improvisation;
any single innovation might be felt to be of doubtful value, even for the
sake of experiment, although it might be regarded as potentially "lucky" or
as having some chance of stimulating interest.[8]

There is another way in which Red Cross and Chest differ: their use of
manpower, particularly in relation to the size of each goal. In manning the
comparable positions of leadership in their respective campaigns in 1955,
for instance, the Chest used 363 persons, and the Red Cross, 185. This was
a ratio of about two to one, whereas for the goals the ratio was nearly five
to one. This disparity is somewhat redressed when the estimated totals of
all persons—leaders and followers—working in these campaigns are compared. In its Annual Report for 1955, the Community Chest reckoned that
as many as 25,000 volunteer workers participated in the campaign; the Red
Cross has estimated that about 5,000 help each year.

We find no way of determining whether the Chest campaign is "undermanned" or the Red Cross campaign correspondingly "over-staffed."[9] Actually, in neither case can anyone be certain of the total numbers of persons
who "really do a job of soliciting," because such large sums of money come
from business firms, not only in the form of firm gifts, but also in the form
of lump sums representing executive gifts and employee gifts, very often
solicited by persons within the firms whose names are not listed at the
campaign headquarters, and may not be counted in the estimate of number
of volunteer workers. The campaign organization always "moves into battle"
without a really complete and accurate roster of *all* the workers.

To ensure adequate numbers presents practical difficulties. These campaigns are manned by "volunteers" and the leadership's controls over them
are not at all to be compared with those a military commander or a business
executive can employ. Nevertheless, the people we have included in what
we call the "Campaign Leadership" (all those in positions such as "Team
Captain" and above, who are responsible either for recruiting and supervising solicitors or for some major direct solicitation themselves) should be
sufficient in number to achieve "coverage" of all prospective donors,
directly or indirectly. Accordingly, the campaign directors, relying upon
the accumulated experience preserved in the records by professionals, and
supplementing this with the latest available "intelligence" about the
attitudes of donors, available manpower, etc., design the table of organization and fill the roster, right up to the last minute—and beyond—as they see
fit and as best they can.[10]

When we compare Chest and Red Cross manning of campaigns, we find
there is no agreed standard as to what is a desirable number of "leaders per
$100,000 raised" against which the two may be compared. It may be that

the difference in size of goals should not lead one to expect a simple proportionate difference in how many leaders are needed. Since the Chest
apparently, in the raising of its larger goal, relies more heavily than does
the Red Cross on large corporation gifts and less on personal giving (see
chapter 9), the 363 "key" persons engaged in the Chest campaign may be
quite sufficient, given certain conditions. The conditions, doubtless, are that
these key persons include (1) the few who, because they have very high
rank in the business community, can and do secure the largest gifts, in a
limited number of direct contacts, and (2) enough others to recruit solicitors who must conduct the comprehensive coverage of all the smaller
potential donors the campaign has to reach if it is to succeed. Similarly, if
the Red Cross is to rely, as it has in the past, more upon individual giving
than does the Chest, it may be that 185 "key" persons is none too many,
unless they include (1) the few with rank in the business community
sufficient to obtain, as "leading gifts," the somewhat smaller sums from
corporations which help to secure the Red Cross goal; and (2) enough
others who are able to recruit the several thousand women canvassers
needed, as well as the solicitors who will cover business firms. That is, to
raise half a million dollars in Indianapolis, as the Red Cross annually does,
and to obtain a large proportion of that from individuals in direct solicitation, may well require half as many "key" persons in the campaign organization as are needed to raise four times as much money when a large part of
the latter can be obtained by a few campaigners, as in the case of the Chest.
We should, at least, be cautious about concluding that the Chest campaign
is more "economical" in the use of manpower than the smaller Red Cross
campaign.

It should be remembered that even minimal acceptance of the Chest as
a *federation* permits it to ask firms and employees for gifts in proportion
to the size of its goal; and the results, as reported in chapter 9, show that
the donors act more or less accordingly. Therefore, part of the apparently
economical use of manpower in the Chest campaign may be derived from
the donors' readiness, such as it is, to respond to the large-scale federated
drive, and thus help it to produce more money relative to the number of
"key" persons in the campaign organization. A United Fund might gain a
similar advantage. If a really United Fund,[11] which could guarantee that
there would be no "outside" fundraising by member agencies, could be
developed and maintained it would doubtless gain something more than
"minimal acceptance," and it would have many fewer, and less severe,
problems of campaign design and manning than the Indianapolis Community Chest has had for some years; even where it had such problems,
they might be easier of solution. Although a United Fund in Indianapolis
might require more total manpower,[12] since its goal might be double or
more that of the present Chest, it would be easier to obtain that goal in an
atmosphere of greater acceptance.

If the problem of manpower is viewed more strictly in relation to "Size of Goal" certain effects become obvious. If the total amount to be raised is very great—dollars instead of pennies per capita—the money-results must include some relatively very large "leading gifts"[13] and many substantial "sustaining gifts" in order that the burden be not too great on the many less able to contribute. Thus, where dollars per capita are sought, as in the Chest campaign, the organization must be drawn up and manned so as to secure coverage of virtually the entire potential donor-aggregate. This means, in turn, that a relatively large number of persons must be in "key" positions, and must recruit a very considerable number of workers at all levels.

The Red Cross Chapter, on the other hand, benefits because its goal has remained within the range of pennies per capita, so that none of its solicitation, in peacetime at least, has to ask for "sacrificial giving" either from firms or from individuals. The donors who wish to, can "buy respectability" for a fairly low price; and, while the "key" persons in the campaign leadership can get a thrill out of the thousands of dollars totted up in each of their divisions, they can also rest assured that no solicitors have had to exert unpleasant pressures to secure gifts. (This low pressure is almost a necessity for Red Cross; it "retains the right" to conduct extra drives for special disaster relief purposes, and it is hence very desirable that "aggressiveness" in the annual campaign be discouraged, in order to keep the donor-aggregate in a favorable state of mind, in case they should have to be again approached, for such a purpose, between campaigns.)

Another concomitant seems to be that the Red Cross can more easily maintain a *laissez-faire* attitude in fundraising, which is much more in tune with the "voluntary contributions" theme; whereas a Chest, United Fund or large-scale capital funds drive, like that for the Hospital Association, having a much larger goal, must[14] depart, substantially, from any mode of campaigning which leaves too much to voluntary giving and fails to make as many donors as possible yield all they can or will. A different kind of *esprit de corps* may be necessary in any campaign organization that seeks dollars per capita; and it seems likely that *rationality*, pervading every aspect of such a campaign in order to secure well-grounded convictions that the cause is just and the methods fair and honest, is the major requirement for success.[15]

"Size of Goal" can, indeed, have such far-reaching effects on manning a campaign that they will be found in every aspect of MOPS fundraising. The larger the goal, the more likely it is that professionals must be included in the direction of the campaign, that "cultivation" and "collections" must be continued year in and year out, and therefore that fairly complex bookkeeping and office management arrangements must be supported. And since rationality also apparently increases in importance in the eyes of the directors, staff, and donors, as the monies involved increase, a substantial need arises for more research and therefore for much more accurate and complete records than we found in Indianapolis or had reason to believe existed in many other Chest cities.[16] And since the large goal of a federation is itself, presumably, a consequence of applying rationality in selecting the agencies that compose the federation, rationality retains a historic right to question those choices also.

One other, perhaps more minor, difference in the manning of the two campaigns lies in the sex-ratio of each. In the 1955 campaign, over one-third of all the key persons in the Red Cross campaign were females, and in the many meetings observed they were almost always referred to as "the ladies." In the Chest campaign, only about one-fifth of the key participants were females, and they were usually referred to as "the women." The etiquette in each case reflects the status sought after and, as we shall see, evidently obtained—with appropriate consequences.

*Relating the "Goal" to the "Appeal"*

The Red Cross "Appeal" appears to be more unified, compared with that of the Chest, especially because its symbols and themes all revolve around our common experiences of the various ways in which human beings respond in crises. Many symbols appear in the annual Red Cross Appeal: symbols having historic significance in *national* crises, such as the First and Second World Wars; other symbols relating to *community* crises, especially disasters, like floods or tornadoes, but not excluding more limited calamities such as local fires, etc.; still other symbols with closer, more intimate meanings for the *individual*—illness, injury, even the threat of death. All of them can be closely connected by linking them together in one central image: that of some single, great, protecting *Power*.

For the Red Cross, through the years, apparently the two most unifying symbols have been the Cross itself and the Nurse. According to one interpretation, the nurse is merely a surrogate "Mother Figure"; but, regardless of any school's interpretation, the nurse as a unifying symbol remains, safely less sacred than Deity, and more concrete (and more attractive, perhaps) than the Brotherhood of Man or the even more abstract ideal of mercy. The theme of mercy—from its battlefield to its peacetime disaster context—is continuously present in symbolic form in the cross of the Red Cross itself, which appears in badges, arm-patches, banners, and as an identifying insignium on ambulances, field hospitals, equipment, etc. Its color—red—is often associated with both suffering (blood) and compassion (warmth and comfort). The form of the symbol is that of the Greek cross, which differentiates it sufficiently from the Latin cross to avoid too close an association with the Christian sign; but at the same time, it places it in the family of those symbols in the history of Western civilization which have had such great importance in expressing and maintaining group solidarity around ideals of sacrifice, of service, and of devotion to a cause like that of the Crusaders.

This symbolism is effective. At one Red Cross ceremony in Indianapolis, for example, the proceedings were brought to a close with the singing of the "Lord's Prayer" by a young lady while the audience turned to face a large Red Cross banner spot-lighted on the stage; the organization was thus clearly linked with the sacred realm. The symbol, Red Cross, appears in contexts which range all the way from the most sacred to the most secular, and which include the semi-sacred secularity of science—especially medicine, at which point, again, devotion and service are represented by the figure of the nurse. No other fundraising appeal in America has succeeded in developing a unifying symbol with such broad and deep meanings as the Red Cross has acquired over the years.

The Red Cross organization has another advantage. Each year's Appeal can be varied to emphasize, if advantageous, any single one of the major kinds of crisis that may happen to be in the news and public consciousness at the time of the campaign. These include "hot" war, "cold" war, "police action," or—in March, the campaign time—"run-of-the-mill" crises like floods. In the unlikely event that these extremities are not current news, there are always the hazards of recreation, as well as household or Do-It-Yourself accidents, for which first aid and sometimes life-saving—two semi-proprietary themes—come in handy. And should there occur any momentary decline in current large-scale calamities, there remain, for the duration of our civilization, the needs of hospitalized veterans for whom the Red Cross maintains services such as the Gray Ladies, the Motor Corps, and the teaching of arts and skills.

This analysis of symbols and their use should not be thought to imply a critical attitude on our part towards their users or a cynicism regarding their use. Every successful social organization has, and needs, appropriate symbolism, for economy in communication, if for no other reason. Indeed, we are calling attention to these features of the annual Appeal just because they help the Red Cross to operate successful MOPS fundraising campaigns. Emotionality of appeal does not imply that the money raised is spent unwisely or emotionally. In fact, one of the things the American people support, in supporting the Red Cross, is an organization for which other people's "crises" are its "routines."[17] Some informants even liken a Red Cross contribution to a form of hospital insurance: "It's good to have it, but you hope you never need it." Considerations such as this help minimize the expression and force of the otherwise general local attitude that "money should not be sent out of the community." (Perhaps, also, the reputation of the American national Red Cross may explain the fact that we heard very little questioning of the Chapter's sending considerable sums —around 50 per cent of the half million raised annually in Indianapolis— to the national organization.) In contrast, many questions are raised about the desires of member agencies of the Community Chest to send, out of funds collected locally, much smaller sums and proportions to state or national bodies with which they are affiliated. Since "health drives" often follow a "40-20-40" pattern (which means that only 40 per cent of the amount raised is spent locally, while 20 and 40 per cent respectively go to state and national bodies) inclusion of these within the federation is questioned by those who feel more or less strongly that "local contributions should be devoted to local work."[18]

A further advantage accrues to the Red Cross in terms of flexibility. While its Appeal at the level of national coverage can weave all the available symbols into almost equal treatment in posters, publicity, movies, TV and radio broadcasts, and other uses of mass media, it is also possible for a local chapter's campaign simultaneously to give one group of them more prominence than the others, as seems to suit local conditions and events, and the local state of opinion. This ability to combine the universal with the particular, the cosmopolitan with the parochial, the international with the municipal, is no mean advantage.

As pointed out in chapters 3 and 4, Indianapolis people take considerable pride in maintaining the Hoosier tradition. This tradition, in part at least, is a set of attitudes also widespread in America generally, especially in the Great Midwest; but, in Indiana, it is given an added colour from the South in the form of stronger emotional tone than seems common in Ohio, Michigan, Illinois, and other states of the region. In this set of attitudes are combined Midwestern disdain for anything that smacks of "the aristocratic" and a Southern kind of fierce pride in "native sons"; and both are reinforced by insistence upon complete loyalty to "the Old Home Place." As we have already pointed out, one of the consequences of the Hoosier stance seems to be that, in contrast to cities like Cleveland which have a fairly steady output of "strong but quiet" civic pride, Indianapolis achieves community solidarity most readily in the face of disaster, when Hoosiers typically muster pluck and ingenuity in improvising solutions. These improvisations usually occur under temporary leadership which acts and is accepted in a military manner, preferably along the lines of a frontier militia rather than a regular army. We were told over and over again, in discussions of local politics, reform efforts, civic improvements—including the achievement of either a successful Chest or a new United Fund—that "The trouble with this town is that nobody wants to stick his neck out," and that "Every time someone takes the lead he gets his head chopped off—like that!"

It was pointed out (and it can be shown from the records of local history) that a national crisis, such as World War I or II, does bring out "the top top leadership"; and, in such a situation of "clear and present danger," local people in Indianapolis *do* submerge their differences and produce a notably high degree of local community cohesion. This is a truism about human society all over the world, of course, but in the twentieth century the fierce patriotism of the Hoosier capital in time of war or other disaster has repeatedly subsided in quieter times, and the people of Indianapolis have, after each such *tour de force*, happily returned to their old routines. Of course "peacetime" never means any real moratorium on human problems, and since there are those in what we have called the Welfare Community Leadership who wish to carry on and strengthen various humane causes, social agencies continue to exist and new ones to be created; and, ever since World War I, Indianapolis has had a Community Fund or Chest intended to raise funds each year to support these agencies. But the prevalent Hoosier attitude regarding the local Chest has been a wariness, if not a fear, of being "taken for a sucker" in supporting it too enthusiastically —combined with the usual desire to excel in every undertaking. Thus not even civic pride in having a reputation for maintaining a "good" Chest seems to be strong enough in Indianapolis to overcome the difficulties. Comparisons with other cities, when made by local campaign speakers, are likely to be regarded as "propaganda" by some if not all hands—and perhaps that is one reason why such comparisons as we have heard have been rather carefree exaggerations, in one direction or the other.

In contrast, the Red Cross Appeal can and does make a dramatic and unequivocal case for being humane, for giving help in the face of great disasters. Hence, in peacetime, it minimizes Hoosier resistance to "being a sucker" at the same time that it calls to mind the images and evokes the strong feeling of wartime patriotism. The Chest Appeal—and this would be even more the case with a United Fund Appeal—must and can be much less emotional and much more rational in every phase of the campaign: it cannot compete with the Red Cross or the more dramatic "health drives" in presenting a situation of "clear and present danger" or one of "desperate, heart-rending need," for the modern Chest no longer emphasizes "charity" or "relief." The Chest must therefore discover other ways of minimizing Hoosier resistance to "being taken." This again drives it towards the necessity of being unmistakably rational and "businesslike."

The Red Cross Appeal does, then, achieve a large degree of unity and coherence, even though the money raised actually goes for a considerable variety of services. In that connection, the Goal can, however, be presented as meeting budget requirements arrived at under a unified system of accounting and administrative control, since the local Chapter acts as the agent of the national organization, which is a federal corporation, subject to audit by the Department of the Army.[19] Viewed as a whole, the American National Red Cross is a great federation of Chapters that raises funds which can be allocated wherever disaster strikes. Locally, however, the Chapter has considerable autonomy, and budgets for its own program, as well as to meet "the National's quota." But of even more importance, perhaps, in reassuring Indianapolis citizens who might question the Red Cross Goal and hence the Appeal, is the fact that, in the campaign, the leadership can always point to a local budget review made by men of very high position in the business world. In the 1955 campaign, for example, it was emphasized that "Men like ——— have gone over this budget and approved it, and you know when they okay a budget, it's got to be right." Why the Chest has been unable to build similar confidence in its Goal is discussed later in the chapter.

The Community Chest Appeal, in contrast, is diffuse because of the Chest's very nature as a unit which combines a number of agencies, having a great variety of characteristics: the Appeal must therefore be on behalf of a *loose confederation*, an aggregation of more or less autonomous local agencies, plus certain causes that are regarded as rather more national and state-wide than local.[20] The symbols and themes that might be represented in the Chest's Appeal therefore necessarily range over a great hodgepodge of human experiences that are very difficult to weave together or unify. In a sense, the Red Cross "Appeal" is also made on behalf of a "federation,"[21] but a very loose one whose "services" are administratively organized into departments of one organization. This contrast is a fundamental one, and various consequences of it become clearer in discussion of the topics that follow.

## Administration: "Rotation" versus "Continuity"

We had been told, by those in a position to compare the Chest and the Red Cross, that "rotation" of Board members is "mandatory" in the Chest By-Laws and that this has seriously affected continuity of service by persons on the Chest Board of Directors, with a consequent decline in close relations between the Chest as an organization and the leaders of the business community. In contrast, the history of the Red Cross Chapter was described to us as full of cases of community leaders who not only served continuously for many years in the volunteer ranks, but also occupied positions as officers or Board members continuously over long periods. Cases were cited, often resentfully, of civic leaders who were "rotated off the Chest Board," and who found roles in philanthropic leadership elsewhere —on the Red Cross Board, in their churches, in the new "health drives," on the boards of private schools and colleges, or on the boards of local voluntary hospitals.

Some informants said that "rotation" was introduced in the 1930's as a direct consequence of the ascendancy of social workers, who, it was said, achieved their new status and power under the New Deal; others contended that the principle of rotation was intended to "get rid of dead wood" and "bring in new blood." The notion among some businessmen that "social workers" or "social dreamers" have a strong influence in the administration of the Chest may gain a measure of its support from awareness that three of the seven persons on the Nominating Committee for the Chest Board are appointed by the Health and Welfare Council.[22] It is also true that the Health and Welfare Council appoints one more than a majority of the Chest's Budget and Distribution Committee; "failing such action" by the

Council, these appointments are to be made "by the institutional members of this organization in a meeting of their delegates."[23]

A comparison of the Chest and Red Cross By-Laws bearing upon "rotation" shows that the Chest makes no provision for retaining a Board member in continuous service for more than seven years, and one year "must intervene before such member shall become eligible for re-election to the Board." In contrast, the Red Cross By-Laws imply (by not specifying to the contrary) that after two consecutive three-year terms, a Board member is eligible for one of the four one-year terms for which the Board itself "may select" persons. We were told that, in effect, if a Board member were wanted (and willing to serve continuously) the one-year term could be used to intervene between his pairs of three-year terms, so that there is virtually no limit to continuous service, either in the present By-Laws or in practice. Indeed, at the Chapter's celebration of its Fortieth Anniversary (a banquet on May 21, 1956), the "Honored Guests" included six living Charter Members of the first Board of Directors formed in 1916, and one of these is still serving on the Board. Since the Chapter was established, the roster of all the men and women who have served on the Board has reached a total of only 132, indicating that many, if not most of these, must have served many years each. If the Board each year for forty years had been composed of 40 members—the number provided for in the Red Cross By-Laws adopted November 1, 1948—a total of 1,600 membership-years were available over this entire span of time, or an average of 12.1 membership-years per person listed. Applying the same measure to the Chest Board for the eleven years, 1945-55, a total of 133 persons were Board members, yielding an average of only 3.3 membership-years per person, and indicating a much higher rate of turnover.

Both the Chest and the Red Cross Boards seek persons prominent in the business community, of course, so presumably both are affected by the tendency of large national corporations to transfer executives to and away from local branch plants. Each organization must seek to recruit from among the new men enough at each level to replace those who leave town. But this seems to be a less serious problem for either in comparison with the difficulty experienced in retaining the active interest and support of those top leaders who make their life careers in Indianapolis—or at least of enough of them to meet the requirements of continuity for each organization.

Widespread local opinion had it that the Chest has had less success than the Red Cross in retaining such permanent resident leaders. This might be puzzling at first sight, because the Chest Board member who is "rotated off" could conceivably maintain his active interest during an intervening year by serving as a member of the Budget Committee, or in some capacity in connection with the annual campaign. But this is equivalent to expecting an "Elder Statesman" (see chapter 10) to "go back to work," and might be felt to be a "demotion." Structurally, the Chest's permanent organization seems to be lacking in roles for "Elder Statesmen"; and, while its Board is capable of providing such positions, in practice, as we shall see in a later section, a good many Board members find themselves, probably unsuitably, actively engaged in campaign leadership along with the "Young Campaigners." In contrast, if a Red Cross Board member should "retire" for an "intervening" year, there are several positions connected with the year-round volunteer services that he may appropriately take, without loss of dignity, right within the permanent organization and wholly apart from the annual campaign; in these he will usually have an honorary role and a ritual function as an "Elder Statesman."

Members who have left the Board of the Chest may find new roles as leaders in the Welfare Community—for example, as agency board members, or as persons active in the Health and Welfare Council. They thereupon seem to move out of the Chest's "inner circle" for fundraising, often permanently. They may, alternatively, "retire" more completely, and virtually disappear into the donor-aggregate. Because fundraising for the Chest's "dollars per capita" goal is a difficult task, and one hardly crowned with "success" in recent years, the Board members who are continually being "returned to civilian life" are not likely to be very enthusiastic proponents for the present federation, and the principle of "rotation" tends to release them from such commitment as they may have felt during their terms of service.

There is also some evidence that, for considerable periods, membership on the Chest Board has not by any means been eagerly sought after by persons of high status in the business world and in the community generally.[24] Some of them have even stipulated that they be elected for one year only, instead of the usual three-year term. In recent years, some reluctance to serve may, in addition, have been related to a desire to be "available" when and if a new United Fund should be established in Indianapolis, or to a desire to be free to join the leaders of the proposed new federation without having to bear with one the stigma of "failure" attaching to the Chest—or both. Any larger federation than the present Chest would doubtless be well advised to plan carefully for a system of "rotation" that would be less destructive of continuity than the present arrangements, both formal and informal.[25]

## Administration: Budgeting

As already pointed out, Red Cross budgeting is highly unified, with a close "federation" of services under centralized administration. In the case of the Indianapolis Chest, what budget control exists is, as already stated, shared by the Board with the Health and Welfare Council, the latter appointing "one more than half" of the Budget Committee. In some cities, and necessarily if there is to be increasing rationality in Chest campaigns, the requirements of a *strong* Appeal make it important that pre-campaign budgeting and goal-setting be a considered and unified process.[26] If the process can be made to inspire confidence in the ranks of the soliciting divisions, the Goal can presumably be much more easily "sold."

In Indianapolis in 1955, the post-campaign budgeting after the "failure" of the 1954 campaign amounted largely to notifying the member agencies of a "2 per cent cut" in the amount each requested as its Chest allocation. In the 1955 campaign, partly because of the late date by which its General Chairman was secured (early in June), pre-campaign budgeting was very far from a formal procedure carried out well enough in advance so that the Goal set could clearly enter into the pre-campaign planning, recruiting of leadership, and so on. The 1955 Chest Appeal could not, therefore, be strengthened by referring to a well-known and respected budgeting process that clearly made a strong case for the Goal.

In Indianapolis, at least in 1955, it was difficult to define what interests were being represented by whom in the Chest campaign. It was not uncommon for one person to be at once a fundraiser, a Donor Leader (and perhaps even a Leading Donor), *and* a proponent of certain interests in the Welfare Community. Numerous persons with some such combination of interests were interacting with each other in the goal-setting process; and, in the campaign and afterward, they encountered others with still different constellations of interests. Evaluations regarding the announced Goal therefore ranged from "not as much as it *should* be" through "not as much as *could* be raised" to "more" than "should" or "could" be raised. The situation was the antithesis of a structured orderly articulation of donors and Welfare Community leaders.

Indeed, setting the Goal devolved upon the Campaign Leadership (including the General Chairman, once he had been found), and a highly aggressive campaign was built around an alleged "community crisis": it was said that the Chest might not survive another "failure" like that of 1954, and that for the Chest to recoup its past "losses" the Goal should be about 2.3 million dollars. In effect, the underlying "crisis" was converted into a more exciting one in the eyes of the campaigners: that of working to raise the largest sum ever sought by an annual campaign in peacetime in Indianapolis. For this, a "crash program" was rapidly improvised (making considerable use of the basic plans prepared by the Chest staff earlier). One of the key phrases in the Appeal was that the Goal was "really only about equal to what had been raised in 1946," if due allowance was made for inflation, more services, and increased population. In such a context, pre-campaign budgeting related to the agencies' demands became irrelevant: what was held to be central was the big Goal, which was 50 per cent or more greater than the amount raised in recent years, and which meant not only that new donors were to be searched out, but that regular "generous" donors were to be asked to be even more generous. The donor-aggregate eventually yielded about 88 per cent of the amount sought, or about 30 per cent more than the year before, and this result certainly put the Chest in a better position at least to establish orderly budgeting and goal-setting procedures for the future. (In the campaign that succeeded this one there was little clear evidence of such a result.)

In the absence of the more orderly procedures which would accompany more "successful" Chest campaigns, in 1954-55 there was for some time a virtual "gulf" (as far as adequate communication is concerned) between those concerned with the general *government* of the Chest, those concerned with the *budgeting and goal-setting* processes, and those concerned ultimately with the actual planning and execution of the 1955 *campaign*. Only the fact that a few persons acted in all these positions at once made possible such co-ordination as was achieved. One consequence was that the Chest Board (and some "top top leaders" who were not even members of it) "ruled but did not govern": they remained in a position to hand down vetoes, but were not positively active in the government of the Chest.

There seems to be an unbreakable chain of relations between "good" administration of a Chest—an appropriate blend of rule and government— and its "success" in fundraising. The chain includes budgeting—designing the Appeal—setting the Goal—designing and manning the campaign— achieving "success"—and thereby validating the "good" administration which started with budgeting.

*Rank in the Campaign and Social Status in the Community*

Although the Chest's 1955 campaign scored an increase of not quite one-third in amount raised over recent years, the campaigns of the Chest over the years—their ups and downs—make one doubt that Chest methods and manning have reached a state at which they might be stabilized to ensure success in future years. This 1955 achievement (which even so, did not make the announced Goal of $2.3 million) can hardly be regarded as a success in the same sense as the Red Cross Chapter's steady achievement of manifest "success" over the past ten years or more. This Red Cross "success" of recent years had something to do not only with the structure of the campaign organization but also with the people involved. Close observations of the behavior of people in the two organizations and campaigns suggested the desirability of taking a closer look at the possible influence of *social status*. We therefore attempted to see if *social class stratification* in this community—so far as it exists and so far as fundraising campaigns are affected by it—has anything to do with the differences between the campaigns.

The people of this community (Indianapolis and Marion County) like those in other American cities, are obviously ranked by themselves and by others into higher and lower social levels. We needed for our study of fundraising organizations some device to render more precise what people meant when they made such statements as "Top top leadership is needed" (in a certain fundraising campaign) and "The trouble is they have too many 'Corporals' and not enough 'Generals' in this campaign." What people in Indianapolis keep pointing to, in such statements, seems to be a kind of implicit system of rating themselves and each other in terms of prestige, influence, wealth, executive position, occupation, and the like. Various positions on these "scales" in various combinations were evidently felt to be important in the rule and governing of organizations, and in the direction and execution of their fundraising campaigns in the community. Indianapolis people are not unique in using evaluations like these or in making successful use in fundraising of their implicit knowledge of the "social structure." Many told us that such knowledge was put to particularly effective use in the Hospital campaign, where so much money and so many people were involved.

Taking our cues from such evaluations made by those people we interviewed and observed, we found it useful to rate what we called "Estimated Social Status" (or "ESS" for short) along a 7-point scale, from "highest" to "lowest" social positions, position 1 being the highest. The appendix to this chapter gives an exposition of this scale and the uses we intended for it, and shows how Indianapolis may compare with certain other cities with respect to the distribution of the population by social class.

In applying this scale to lists of members of the Board of Directors or rosters of Campaign Leaders, etc., we found that in about half of the cases information was not complete enough for *exact* "placing" of individuals, but that we could, with more hope of accuracy, indicate a narrow range within which such an individual would most probably "rate" if a thorough study of social stratification in Indianapolis were made. We indicate this range (see Table LXIII) by writing the midpoint between the two adjacent points on the scale which appear to bracket this narrow range (for example, 1.5 for the midpoint between 1 and 2; 2.5, for that between 2 and 3; etc.).

TABLE LXIII

SOCIAL CLASS AND ESTIMATED SOCIAL STATUS (ESS) IN INDIANAPOLIS
AS RELATED TO FUNDRAISING

| Equivalent social class | ESS ratings | Percentage of population of Indianapolis (estimated) | Described by fundraisers as including |
|---|---|---|---|
| (1) Upper-upper | 1 | 0.5 | "Top-top leaders"; but "not very active" |
| (2) Lower-upper | 1.5 & 2 | 2.0 | "Top leaders" |
| (3) Upper-middle | 2.5 & 3 | 12.5 | "Key people"; "civic leaders" |
| (4) Lower-middle | 3.5, 4, 4.5 & 5 | 30.0 | "The little fellow" |
| (5) Upper-lower | 5.5 & 6 | 35.0 | "Workingmen" |
| (6) Lower-lower | 7 | 20.0 | "The poor"; "low class people" |

## TABLE LXIV

### Campaign Leadership and Estimated Social Status (ESS)

| Estimated Social Status (ESS) | Elder Statesmen | | Young Campaigners including Elder Statesmen[a] | | | Young Campaigners excluding Elder Statesmen[a] | | | Total (unduplicated names) of persons in both groups | | |
|---|---|---|---|---|---|---|---|---|---|---|---|
| | No. | Per cent | No. | Per cent | Per cent of ranked[b] | No. | Per cent | Per cent of ranked[b] | No. | Per cent of ranked[b] | Percentage[b] |
| **(1) RED CROSS, 1955 CAMPAIGN** | | | | | | | | | | | |
| 1 | 2 | 4.7 | — | — | — | — | — | — | 2 | 1.1 | 1.3 |
| 1.5 | 5 | 11.6 | — | — | — | — | — | — | 5 | 2.7 | 3.1 |
| 2 | 4 | 9.3 | — | — | — | — | — | — | 4 | 2.2 | 2.5 |
| 2.5 | 19 | 44.2 | 9 | 6.1 | 7.3 | 6 | 4.3 | 5.1 | 25 | 13.5 | 15.6 |
| 3 | 10 | 23.3 | 26 | 17.7 | 21.3 | 24 | 16.9 | 20.5 | 34 | 18.4 | 21.3 |
| 3.5 | 3 | 7.0 | 59 | 40.1 | 48.4 | 59 | 41.5 | 50.4 | 62 | 33.5 | 38.8 |
| 4 | — | — | 14 | 9.5 | 11.5 | 14 | 9.9 | 12.0 | 14 | 7.6 | 8.8 |
| 4.5 | — | — | 13 | 8.9 | 10.7 | 13 | 9.1 | 11.1 | 13 | 7.0 | 8.1 |
| 5 | — | — | 1 | 0.7 | 0.8 | 1 | 0.7 | 0.9 | 1 | 0.5 | 0.6 |
| 5.5 or lower | — | — | — | — | — | — | — | — | — | — | — |
| Unknown | — | — | 25 | 17.0 | — | 25 | 17.6 | — | 25 | 13.5 | — |
| TOTAL | 43 | 100.0 | 147 | 100.0 | 100.0 | 142 | 100.0 | 100.0 | 185 | 100.0 | 100.0 |
| **(2) COMMUNITY CHEST, 1955 CAMPAIGN** | | | | | | | | | | | |
| 1 | — | — | 1 | 0.3 | 0.3 | 1 | 0.3 | 0.3 | 1 | 0.3 | 0.3 |
| 1.5 | 4 | 9.5 | 3 | 0.9 | 1.0 | 3 | 0.9 | 1.1 | 7 | 1.9 | 2.1 |
| 2 | 12 | 28.5 | 6 | 1.9 | 2.0 | 5 | 1.6 | 1.8 | 17 | 4.7 | 5.2 |
| 2.5 | 15 | 35.7 | 28 | 8.3 | 9.3 | 20 | 6.2 | 7.0 | 35 | 9.6 | 10.7 |
| 3 | 8 | 19.0 | 59 | 17.6 | 19.7 | 54 | 16.9 | 18.9 | 62 | 17.1 | 19.0 |
| 3.5 | — | — | 148 | 44.0 | 49.3 | 148 | 46.1 | 51.9 | 148 | 40.8 | 45.2 |
| 4 | 2 | 4.8 | 28 | 8.3 | 9.3 | 28 | 8.7 | 9.8 | 30 | 8.2 | 9.2 |
| 4.5 | 1 | 2.4 | 18 | 5.3 | 6.0 | 17 | 5.3 | 6.0 | 18 | 5.0 | 5.5 |
| 5 | — | — | 9 | 2.7 | 3.0 | 9 | 2.8 | 3.2 | 9 | 2.5 | 2.8 |
| 5.5 or lower | — | — | — | — | — | — | — | — | — | — | — |
| Unknown | — | — | 36 | 10.7 | — | 36 | 11.2 | — | 36 | 9.9 | — |
| TOTAL | 42 | 100.0 | 336 | 100.0 | 100.0 | 321 | 100.0 | 100.0 | 363 | 100.0 | 100.0 |

[a] The rosters of Young Campaigners include a few from the Elder Statesmen group who acted at both levels: 5 in the case of the Red Cross and 15 in the case of the Chest. The table allows one to make comparisons including and excluding Elder Statesmen in dual roles.

[b] "Percentage of ranked" is calculated on the basis of omitting "Unknowns."

For our purposes, the "high" end of the scale was most used, and we did not differentiate between individuals as to "race, creed, or color": for example, we rated the status of the relatively few Negro leaders according to occupation, residence, and life-style in general, in just the same way as we used these indicators of status within the white society.[27]

In many of the larger towns and cities of the United States, six levels or social classes may be distinguished by certain methods of community study.[28] If there are six classes in Indianapolis, and we have assumed that more adequate analysis would establish that there are about that number, it will be useful at this point to give them some sociological names and to indicate how the people of each are talked about in fundraising circles. These terms and ratings are given in Table LXIII.

As we have already indicated, campaign leadership in both the Red Cross and the Chest includes (a) the principal leaders of the permanent organization in each case, and (b) the "key persons" in the less permanent campaign organization.[29] These we have called "Elder Statesmen" and "Young Campaigners." Table LXIV shows their estimated social status. From the table one may infer that both organizations have some personnel in the leadership coming from the "top tops" (ESS 1) down through the level of "the little fellows" (ESS 5). When the two organizations are compared, the distribution by status in the community of all personnel is much the same for the Chest as it is for the Red Cross, as Table LXV shows.

TABLE LXV

CAMPAIGN LEADERSHIP[a] AND ESS, RED CROSS AND COMMUNITY CHEST

| ESS | Red Cross | | Community Chest | | Red Cross | Community Chest |
|---|---|---|---|---|---|---|
| | No. | Percentage | No. | Percentage | Percentage, omitting "unknowns" | |
| 1, 1.5 & 2 | 11 | 6.0 | 25 | 6.9 | 6.9 | 7.6 |
| 2.5 & 3 | 59 | 31.9 | 97 | 26.7 | 36.9 | 29.7 |
| 3.5 | 62 | 33.5 | 148 | 40.8 | 38.7 | 45.3 |
| 4, 4.5 & 5 | 28 | 15.1 | 57 | 15.7 | 17.5 | 17.4 |
| Unknown | 25 | 13.5 | 36 | 9.9 | — | — |
| TOTAL | 185 | 100.0 | 363 | 100.0 | 100.0 | 100.0 |

[a]Unduplicated names, Elder Statesmen and Young Campaigners combined.

Both organizations draw Elder Statesmen similarly from the higher social ranks of the community, as Table LXVI shows; but, if it is true, as it is sometimes said, that "The top tops won't work, so it's better to have more of the ambitious new people," then the Red Cross may have the more desirable distribution, even if the Chest has more of the "select" people (except from the very top).

Table LXVII represents an attempt to assess the social class of the two key groups by "averaging" their ratings. One may see that in *both* campaigns

### TABLE LXVI

ELDER STATESMEN AND ESS, RED CROSS AND COMMUNITY CHEST

| | Red Cross | | Community Chest | |
|---|---|---|---|---|
| ESS | No. | Percentage | No. | Percentage |
| 1, 1.5 & 2 | 11 | 25.6 | 16 | 38.1 |
| 2.5 & 3 | 29 | 67.4 | 23 | 54.7 |
| 3.5 | 3 | 7.0 | — | — |
| 4, 4.5 & 5 | — | — | 3 | 7.2 |
| Unknown | — | — | — | — |
| TOTAL | 43 | 100.0 | 42 | 100.0 |

the Elder Statesmen are "on the average" high in the upper-middle class in the community (their mean ESS is about 2.5) and the Young Campaigners are low in the upper-middle class (their mean ESS is about 3.5). To put this in perspective, it might be added that the mean ESS for the Indianapolis population generally (based upon our estimate) is 5.2—the median being 5.7—and thus "on the average" Indianapolis people may be said to be at or near the midpoint between the lower-middle and the upper-lower class.

### TABLE LXVII

CAMPAIGN LEADERSHIP AND AVERAGE ESS, RED CROSS AND COMMUNITY CHEST

| | Mean ESS | | |
|---|---|---|---|
| Campaign Leadership | Red Cross | Community Chest | Total |
| Elder Statesmen | 2.45 | 2.48 | 2.48 |
| Young Campaigners (excluding Elder Statesmen) | 3.53 | 3.44 | 3.46 |
| TOTAL | 3.24 | 3.31 | 3.29 |

The relation of leadership to the sex of the person has already been touched upon. The Community Chest restricts women almost exclusively to the lower echelons in the campaign organization, while the Red Cross shows no significant difference as to the level at which men and women are active (see Table LXVIII).[30]

### TABLE LXVIII

CAMPAIGN LEADERSHIP AND SEX OF LEADER, RED CROSS AND COMMUNITY CHEST

| Category of Campaign Leadership | Red Cross | | | Community Chest | | |
|---|---|---|---|---|---|---|
| | Men | Women | Total | Men | Women | Total |
| Elder Statesmen | 31 | 12 | 43 | 40 | 2 | 42 |
| Young Campaigners (excluding Elder Statesmen) | 87 | 55 | 142 | 249 | 72 | 321 |
| TOTAL | 118 | 67 | 185 | 289 | 74 | 363 |

We have also previously mentioned the problems occasioned by using people in incompatible roles. In the Chest campaign, a larger number of Elder Statesmen were active in positions along with the Young Campaigners than was true of the Red Cross: as many as fifteen in the first case, and as few as five in the second. Moreover, those Red Cross Elder Statesmen who did hold positions in the Young Campaigner group, did *not* act in the soliciting divisions, whereas thirteen of the Chest's Elder Statesmen were prominent in just such positions. Of the five Red Cross Elder Statesmen who also acted at Young Campaigner level, four were on the Public Information Committee and one was the Chapter Chairman, who sat in with the Campaign Executive Committee. The important difference is that the Chest, in order to man its soliciting divisions, apparently had to use nearly one-third of its Elder Statesmen in positions along with the Young Campaigners, while the Red Cross used none of its Elder Statesmen in this way. What the Chest felt driven to do was, in effect, to use Elder Statesmen of higher community status to strengthen the ranks of its Young Campaigners; but, as shown in Table LXIX, the percentage gain in ESS suggests that this use of Elder Statesmen made little difference, on the average, and may even have been wasteful.

TABLE LXIX

SOCIAL STATUS OF YOUNG CAMPAIGNERS (WITH AND WITHOUT ELDER STATESMEN EMPLOYED IN YOUNG CAMPAIGNER ROLES), RED CROSS AND COMMUNITY CHEST

| | Red Cross | | | | Community Chest | | | |
| | Excluding Elder Statesmen | | Including Elder Statesmen | | Excluding Elder Statesmen | | Including Elder Statesmen | |
| ESS | No. | Per cent | No. | Per cent | No. | Per cent | No. | Per cent |
|---|---|---|---|---|---|---|---|---|
| 1, 1.5 & 2 | — | — | — | — | 9 | 2.8 | 10 | 3.0 |
| 2.5 & 3 | 30 | 21.2 | 35 | 23.8 | 74 | 23.1 | 87 | 25.9 |
| 3.5 | 59 | 41.5 | 59 | 40.1 | 148 | 46.1 | 148 | 44.0 |
| 4, 4.5 & 5 | 28 | 19.7 | 28 | 19.1 | 54 | 16.8 | 55 | 16.3 |
| Unknown | 25 | 17.6 | 25 | 17.0 | 36 | 11.2 | 36 | 10.7 |
| TOTALS | 142 | 100.0 | 147 | 100.0 | 321 | 100.0 | 336 | 100.0 |

We must now turn from considering "key people" in general to look at *one* of the people most decisive for success: the General Chairman. In securing a General Chairman, the Community Chest and the Red Cross (or any other MOPS fundraising organization) have a twofold problem. They must, first, obtain the services of a man of such importance and acceptance in the business community that he will (1) attract and stimulate desirable co-workers in the leadership of the soliciting divisions, (2) relate the campaign organization effectively to the Leading Donors in the corporate field, as well as to the community at large, by securing the collaboration of the Donor Leaders, and (3) "succeed" in a way that will enhance the prestige of the office of General Chairman and make it one subsequently sought after by top executives like himself. They must, second, accomplish this both discreetly and expeditiously, especially if it seems hopeful that the next campaign can benefit by a "snowball effect," building upon the momentum of the campaign just completed.

As described earlier in this chapter, the Red Cross provides for the selection and training of campaign General Chairmen through a system of promotion up through the ranks of the soliciting divisions. Those who have served as General Chairmen in years past usually join the "Elder States-men," either as members of the Board of Directors or as members of the Chapter Fund Committee. A man who has served several years in the lower ranks of the soliciting divisions may be promoted to Chairman of a division in the next campaign, and may be selected as General Chairman for the following year. For these and other reasons, the Red Cross has, in recent years at least, been in a very strong position, i.e., able to "select" rather than to "persuade" or coax a man to be General Chairman.

The Chest administration, in contrast, has not been able to develop roles for Elder Statesmen like those of the Red Cross Chapter, nor a similar system of promotion, and this situation makes both parts of this twofold problem particularly difficult for it to solve. But the second part of the problem has been made considerably more difficult in the years since World War II by the failure of its campaign to make an announced goal each year but one[31] in the past eleven years (1945-55 inclusive).[32]

The Chest's difficulties over the years have apparently set up an annual cycle: (1) owing to previous "failures," campaign leaders are slow to come forward; (2) because of delays in "finding the leadership," the campaign must be rapidly improvised, either as a "very aggressive" one or as a "quiet" one—and in either case the professional staff and the lay administrators annually face new problems; (3) with hasty improvisation—and even changes in mid-campaign—errors of omission and commission are more likely to occur, responsibility for which it is difficult to trace, and hence blame may be diffused so as to make many feel unhappy, or concentrated on a "whipping boy" or scapegoat, the choice of whom may lead to some further dissension; (4) owing to a goal set "high," out of regard for "the real needs," or, as it may happen, out of the "enthusiasm" of the lay leader-ship, the campaign "fails" two out of three times. And so on, round and round again.

In each year of the past decade or so, we were told, the General Chair-man was either selected after many others (as many as five, or even "seventeen") had refused, or was "persuaded" to serve by higher executives, perhaps, often primarily in order to "bring him out" in the eyes of the business community. The General Chairman therefore is usually one who is "rising in the world," and not a person long established in the business community or himself of great wealth and social prestige. This selection of up-and-coming people is probably not unusual in Community Chests around the country, and it is not different in the case of the Red Cross in Indianapolis. But what makes the Indianapolis Chest's recent experience different is the context: its General Chairmen usually do not go on to join an Elder Statesmen group and help maintain the system of recruiting and promoting leaders for the future. It is almost as if this General Chairman's job "uses up" a man each year, without reserving enough of his energies to encourage him to continue on in an Elder Statesman role, even if such were available in the Chest.

Instead of enlisting at least an occasional "top top leader" (ESS 1 or 1.5), the Chest has only been able to secure in the past ten years General Chairmen who apparently rated as shown in Table LXX. During major

TABLE LXX

GENERAL CHAIRMEN AND ESS, CHEST CAMPAIGNS, 1946-55

| Estimated Social Status | Number of men |
|---|---|
| 1 | 0 |
| 1.5 | 0 |
| 2 | 2 |
| 2.5 | 4 |
| 3 | 4 |
| 3.5 | 0 |
| 4 or below | 0 |
| TOTAL | 10[a] |

[a]Average ESS: 2.6.

crises, such as the great wars or the Depression, "top top leaders" appear to participate more actively in the governing bodies of federated drives, and are also important in the campaigns. After each crisis has subsided, the larger federation shrinks to one more concerned with local agencies (as did the Community Fund after World War I, and the Community Chest after World War II) and the active leadership devolves upon persons of lower social position, although one or two of "top top" status may remain active. In the years following, those who are left after the departure of the "top tops," in turn evidently find it possible only to secure a General Chairman much like themselves—and that only after very considerable search. On more than one occasion, indeed, when the "survivors" were unable to find any person even remotely suitable they have had to get one of their own group to "step down" and himself serve as General Chairman!

This cyclical regress is evident in the record, and again, since World War II, there has apparently been a downward trend in the status of the General Chairman, and simultaneously in the prestige attaching to the office. As the office loses attractiveness, the recruiting of campaign leaders all the way down the line is affected. But a curious compensatory process may also set in: since many civic leaders would not permit a serious collapse of the Chest, they will work behind the scenes or within their own firms to ensure maintenance in giving, or even to get increases. Thus, even when very few are apparently willing to occupy public positions in the active campaign leadership, many will privately support the effort and guard, in so far as they readily can, against too shameful a "failure," lest it reflect too vividly upon the good name of their "Fair City." Moreover, for those in the business community most interested in having a United Fund, more "success" for each Chest campaign is much to be desired; even those who believe that the Chest should be scrapped, and who would like to launch a wholly new United Fund (on the ground that the Chest is symbolic of "failure") tend to work hard for "success" each year. In 1955, as shown in chapter 9, the Indianapolis Chest made up the gains it might have expected in the prior few years, and henceforth it may reasonably be expected to continue growing, even if the present difficulties in the areas of administration and leadership were permitted to remain. In cities of the size of Indianapolis, complete "collapse" of the Chest almost never occurs; nearly two-thirds of all Chests in a given year "fail" anyway,[33] but they are not allowed to go under completely. Thus, if the Indianapolis Chest were to "fail" only one year (instead of two) out of every three, it would closely approach normal expectations for such federated campaigns. To surpass that expectation, however, it seems evident that solutions to the organizational and leadership problems must be found.

To turn for a moment from differences to likenesses, one outstanding similarity between the Chest and Red Cross 1955 campaign organizations lies in the fact that, in each, the leadership positions were largely occupied by persons who are not found among the Welfare Community Leaders. Less than one-third of the leaders in each campaign were known to us as active in the direction or work of social agencies. More than two-thirds were therefore apparently "specialists" in the fundraising side of philanthropic activities in Indianapolis, and had little to do with "causes" as such, even those for which they help to raise funds.[34] This is apparently a consequence of the manning of such MOPS campaigns: most men from the business community among both the Elder Statesmen and the Young Campaigners are primarily interested in fundraising, and are not, as a rule, interested in becoming active as Welfare Community Leaders.

Even within the Red Cross Chapter organization—where there *are* service as well as fundraising positions of high prestige—those who are volunteers of long standing in the various services were not active in leadership positions in the 1955 campaign. Perhaps they have learned that the two roles call for different types of people, or for similar people at different stages of their careers. In connection with its annual autumn campaign to recruit volunteers for service, for instance, the Red Cross honored 284 persons for their work in the various services, awarding them pins or bars for service of five, ten, fifteen, thirty, or forty years.[35] Of the 284, only 19 (6.6 per cent) had been active as leaders in the 1955 campaign. Although more than these 19 have doubtless been active in fundraising in previous years, and although some of the 284 may have worked as solicitors in the 1955 campaign (below the level of the 185 campaign leaders counted), the great majority of the 284 seem to be persons who have been devoted to "Red Cross work" as active participants in the Chapter's services. Probably they do not act in service roles in other organizations either: only 31 (10.9 per cent) out of the 284 appeared in our list of Welfare Community Leaders.[36] It appears, therefore, that a very large majority (perhaps over 90 per cent) of the deeply interested Red Cross service volunteers were not active in fundraising leadership even in the Red Cross campaign, and were not currently doing much in the Welfare Community outside of Red Cross work.

It cannot, however, be said that there is no relation at all between "Red Cross work" and Red Cross fundraising. The services offer opportunities for self-expression and the exercise of a wide range of interests and skills; but beyond this is a special Red Cross *esprit de corps,* a pride in belonging to the organization that is shared by all hands from top to bottom, from the long-standing Board member to the newest recruit in the canteen. Distinctive uniforms not only identify those in the various services but also connect them symbolically into the larger organization—which, in turn, relates the humblest local person to great personages on the national scene, from the President of the United States on down and from the local élite on up. The volunteers' pride in belonging is like that of members of a crack regiment: it is enhanced by their identifying their work and themselves with "the best," with the élite. The Red Cross organization provides many ways for persons at all social levels to "look up," and its patriotic emphasis makes this attitude palatable to middle-class people especially. Among persons who identify with the lower levels, and who typically and resentfully refer to "the powers that be" as "they," the Red Cross has some of its severest critics. But this merely helps, in the eyes of its supporters, to define the Red Cross as an association of "good people" and to maintain its superior respectability.

The high level of morale among the volunteers in the permanent organization of the Red Cross Chapter seems to carry over into the fundraising organization as well. Apparently this occurs by "contagion," since so few of the "dedicated" volunteers in the services are active in the campaign leadership, and then only those of high rank in the organization and high status in the community. The solidarity of the permanent organization, which evidently is sufficient to secure access to channels of influence in the business community adequate to meet the manpower needs of the Red Cross campaign organization, impresses those newly recruited as campaign solicitors: in Indianapolis they may well hear the most prominent of businessmen declare proudly and in public, "I'm a Red Cross man myself." This kind of statement may also be made in indicating a preference for participation in the Red Cross campaign rather than the Chest campaign— it may even be made by persons who have prominent roles in both.

Such "overlap" occurs, but how important is it? It is widely believed that "the same people do all the work" of fundraising for various causes in Indianapolis. Do the same people take leading positions in both the Chest and the Red Cross campaigns, or is there a special corps of Red Cross adherents?

In 1955, as noted earlier, 185 persons held leadership positions in the Red Cross campaign and 363 persons in the Chest campaign, a total of 548 names. Among these, only twenty-one men appeared in both lists, or less than 4 per cent of the unduplicated total of 527 persons.[37] The statistically unwary reader should beware of misinterpreting this evidence. Whether or not this "overlap" of twenty-one persons means that there is a significant tendency for a man who is in one campaign to be also in the other, depends on an unknown figure: the total "leadership pool." If we assume that that pool—the number of people in Indianapolis who could be "tapped" for such service—is at least five thousand, then this overlap of twenty-one is very significant, and there *is* a tendency to use a man who is working in one campaign in another as well.[38]

Of the twenty-one men active in both campaigns, twelve were Young Campaigners in each, two were Elder Statesmen in each, and seven were Young Campaigners in the Chest campaign but were Elder Statesmen in the Red Cross. Participation in both campaigns, at whatever level, is associated with either very high social status (which makes the man sought after as a leader in these and other fundraising drives) or with occupational role: executives responsible in their business lives for public relations often turn up in more than one fundraising organization (along with employees of lower rank who may be assigned to campaign duty by their firms).

As shown in Table LXXI, the twenty-one men active in both campaigns include larger proportions from the higher statuses in the community than do those who were leaders in one campaign only. The table is further summarized in Table LXXII, to facilitate comparison with the estimated distribution of the total population.

As would be expected, the combined leadership of both the Chest and Red Cross campaigns consists of persons from the middle and upper classes in the community; although an estimated 55 per cent of the total population is lower class, none of these people were represented in the campaign leadership. The 30 per cent of the population estimated as in the lower-middle class (ESS 3.5, 4, 4.5 & 5) provided about 55 per cent of the campaign leadership; the 12.5 per cent who are estimated as upper-middle class provided nearly 28 per cent of the leadership; and the total of 2.5

## TABLE LXXI

PERSONS IN CAMPAIGN LEADERSHIP POSITIONS, BY STATUS IN THE COMMUNITY

| Estimated Social Status (ESS) | Total, unduplicated names, all persons in Chest and Red Cross campaigns combined | | Those active in both campaigns | | Indianapolis population (estimated)[a] |
|---|---|---|---|---|---|
| | No. | Per cent | No. | Per cent | Per cent |
| 1 | 2 | 0.4 | 1 | 4.8 | 0.5 |
| 1.5 | 11 | 2.1 | 1 | 4.8 | 2.0 |
| 2 | 20 | 3.8 | 1 | 4.8 | |
| 2.5 | 55 | 10.4 | 5 | 23.8 | 12.5 |
| 3 | 91 | 17.3 | 5 | 23.8 | |
| 3.5 | 203 | 38.5 | 7 | 33.3 | |
| 4 | 44 | 8.3 | — | — | 30.0 |
| 4.5 | 31 | 5.9 | — | — | |
| 5 | 10 | 1.9 | — | — | |
| 5.5 | — | — | — | — | 35.0 |
| 6 | — | — | — | — | |
| 6.5 | — | — | — | — | |
| 7 | — | — | — | — | 20.0 |
| Unknown | 60 | 11.4 | 1 | 4.8 | — |
| TOTAL | 527 | 100.0 | 21 | 100.0 | 100.0 |

[a]See Appendix, "Estimated Social Status."

per cent estimated for the two upper classes provided over 6 per cent of the campaign leadership. This gives participation ratios[39] of 180 per cent to the lower-middle class, 224 per cent to the upper-middle class and 240 per cent to the upper classes.[40] As far as the "top top" status (ESS 1) is concerned, then, it is over-represented among those who were active in both campaigns, but under-represented in the pooled list of those who were active in either. Similarly, judging from the distribution of all those who participated in either of the two campaigns, the lower classes (ESS 5.5 and lower) are not as well represented in campaign leadership as their estimated proportions in the total population would lead to if selection for these positions were random.

Necessarily, therefore, the upper levels (ESS 3 and above) are more heavily represented than their sheer estimated proportions in the population would suggest: their participation ratio is 227 per cent. This does not mean that persons of high status are as frequently active in the two campaigns as might be desired by those who wish those campaigns greater "success." A close reading of Table LXXII will prove that, if there are as many as 800 male adults at ESS 1 ("birth élite") in the Indianapolis population—as we

TABLE LXXII

LEADERSHIP AND SOCIAL STATUS: SUMMARY

| ESS | Total, unduplicated names, all persons in Chest and Red Cross campaigns combined | | Those active in both campaigns | | Indianapolis population (estimated) |
|-----|------|----------|------|----------|----------|
| | No. | Per cent | No. | Per cent | Per cent |
| 1 | 2 | 0.4 | 1 | 4.8 | 0.5 |
| 1.5 & 2 | 31 | 5.9 | 2 | 9.6 | 2.0 |
| 2.5 & 3 | 146 | 27.7 | 10 | 47.6 | 12.5 |
| 3.5, 4, 4.5 & 5 | 288 | 54.6 | 7 | 33.3 | 30.0 |
| 5.5, 6 & 6.5 | — | — | — | — | 35.0 |
| 7 | — | — | — | — | 20.0 |
| Unknown | 60 | 11.4 | 1 | 4.8 | — |
| TOTAL | 527 | 100.0 | 21 | 100.0 | 100.0 |

would, from our estimates, suppose—only two of these men ( or ¼ of 1 per cent of the pool) appeared as campaign leaders, one of them acting in both campaigns; that, if there are as many as 3,000 male adults at ESS 1.5 or 2 ("mobile élite")[41]—as we would, from our estimates, suppose—only thirty-one persons ( or 1.0 per cent) appeared as leaders, two of them in both campaigns; and finally, if there are as many as 21,000 male adults at ESS 2.5 or 3, only 146 persons (⅔ of 1 per cent) came forth as leaders, ten of them acting in both campaigns. If these estimates are as accurate as we believe they are, it is difficult to accept the contention that the "potential" leadership in Indianapolis has been exhausted when a total of over 25,000 male adults in the higher ranks of the community yielded only 179 persons (¾ of 1 per cent) in actual campaign leadership. If, as is entirely proper, we had taken all adults (instead of adult males) as the leadership pool at each level, the percentages would be half those shown. This, still less, looks like exhaustion.

We may now turn briefly to some comparisons with the Hospital campaign. The public fundraising operations of the Indianapolis Hospital Development Association began with the opening of the headquarters office in January, 1952, and officially ended in December, 1953, with the "final report meeting."

The first date is not of course that of actual initiation. In May and June, 1950, some thousands of signatures were secured on a petition to the Marion County Commissioners urging the issue of bonds up to $5,000,000 for a County Hospital, which had been proposed by the Indianapolis Medical Society.[42] In October, 1950, the Central Indiana Health Council, predecessor of the IHDA, was incorporated by a group of citizens assisted by the Indianapolis Chamber of Commerce. With funds raised by the Council, a survey by outside specialists was made during the period from February to April, 1951, resulting in the recommendation that "an immediate

$12 million program to add 828 patient beds to existing hospitals facilities" be started at once—as part of a long-term construction program to cost about $30 million more during the following twenty-five years. The hospitals' service area[43] was taken as the area for soliciting "individual and corporate potentials of support," and the goal of $12 million was set for the campaign for a new Community Hospital—eventually opened in August, 1956—and for new construction.[44] Since the Victory Dinner, December 17, 1953, the IHDA has continued to receive payments on old pledges and also a considerable number of new pledges; and, as of June, 1956, it still had several hundred thousand dollars to collect to fulfil the $12 million program.

There is no comprehensive history of these activities, and no roster available of all those who worked in this long and strenuous but successful campaign. For our purposes, in comparing it as a human organization with the campaign organizations of the 1955 Chest and Red Cross, we shall therefore have to limit attention to the Board of Directors of the IHDA as of November, 1952, i.e., at about the mid-point of the whole campaign.

The three groups of Elder Statesmen[45] are compared in Table LXXIII, which shows that 71.4 per cent of the Hospital group were ESS 2.5 or higher, compared with 69.8 per cent of the Red Cross Elder Statesmen and 73.7 per cent of the Chest. But the Chest Elder Statesmen included no one of ESS 1, and only four of ESS 1.5, reflecting the comparative absence from the Chest of the "top top leaders," who are found in the two campaigns reputed to be "successful." Perhaps because the Chest also tries to "broaden the base"—not only in giving but also in its attempt to secure "community-wide representation"—its comparatively few Elder Statesmen positions tend to be distributed "down the line" into the middle classes more than is true of either the Red Cross or Hospital group. Table LXXIII further shows that

TABLE LXXIII

ELDER STATESMEN, BY STATUS IN THE COMMUNITY

| Estimated Social Status (ESS) | IHDA Board November, 1952 | | Red Cross 1955 Campaign | | Community Chest 1955 Campaign | |
|---|---|---|---|---|---|---|
| | No. | Per cent | No. | Per cent | No. | Per cent |
| 1 | 4 | 4.1 | 2 | 4.7 | — | — |
| 1.5 | 11 | 11.2 | 5 | 11.6 | 4 | 9.5 |
| 2 | 31 | 31.6 | 4 | 9.3 | 12 | 28.5 |
| 2.5 | 24 | 24.5 | 19 | 44.2 | 15 | 35.7 |
| 3 | 21 | 21.4 | 10 | 23.3 | 8 | 19.0 |
| 3.5 | 3 | 3.1 | 3 | 7.0 | — | — |
| 4 | 3 | 3.1 | — | — | 2 | 4.8 |
| 4.5 | — | — | — | — | 1 | 2.4 |
| 5 & lower | — | — | — | — | — | — |
| Unknown | 1 | 1.0 | — | — | — | — |
| TOTAL | 98 | 100.0 | 43 | 100.0 | 42 | 100.0 |
| Mean ESS | | 2.35 | | 2.45 | | 2.48 |

"on the average" the Hospital Board ranks highest (mean ESS 2.35), the Red Cross next (2.45), and the Chest lowest (2.48). Although the differences are very small, statistically, their significance may be very great, socially, and they may be suggestive when related to reputation for campaign "success."

Although we have no roster of the Young Campaigners in the Hospital drive, it is reasonable to suppose that the pattern of their distribution, by status in the community, was probably similar to that in the Chest 1955 campaign. In absolute numbers, however, the Hospital drive probably involved many more men of high rank in the business and professional world, since it was necessary to secure "coverage" adequate to meet the much larger goal.

### ADMINISTRATION: RULE AND GOVERNMENT OF THE COMMUNITY CHEST

One additional important indicator of the kind of administration given to a voluntary organization is to be found in records of attendance of Board members at regular meetings. It is not unusual for the By-Laws of a Chest or a Red Cross Chapter to require directors to attend at least half of the regular meetings; eligibility for renomination or continuation on the Board may be based on this requirement. We were told that attendance as scant as this minimum requirement is common in many boards, but that, even so, the quality of administration can be maintained, at least in agencies with well-established programs and policies. Since the Indianapolis Chest has had its difficulties as a fundraising organization one might, however, expect that its responsible administrators would not be as casual in attending Board meetings as seems to be possible in very secure organizations.

In order to study the Chest's administration from this particular point of view, we analysed the records of attendance at Board meetings during the past eleven years, as well as for selected years before World War II. As shown in Table LXXIV, over the recent period, only half the members attended half or more of the meetings. The proportion attending at least 50 per cent of the meetings each year has varied from about 60 per cent in 1945, and again in 1953, to only 43 per cent in 1951, and again in 1955. On the basis of this showing, attendance at the Board meetings appears to have been no better than "normal"—or not much worse than what other voluntary organizations have come to expect, judging from what agency executives have told us.

Table LXXV shows that these attendance patterns are not a post-war development, but can be found in years long past (1921, 1925, 1933, and 1940 being chosen for the sake of illustration). As shown in the table, the Chest Board has its "faithful few": about one-third of the members each year account for 50 per cent of the attendance at regular meetings, and about 15 per cent account for 25 per cent of the attendance. In 1921, when the new

## TABLE LXXIV

### ATTENDANCE AT BOARD MEETINGS, INDIANAPOLIS CHEST, 1945-55

| Year | No. of regular meetings | Size of Board | Number of Board members who attended: | | | |
|------|------|------|------|------|------|------|
| | | | Half or more of meetings | | Less than one-half | |
| | | | No. | Per cent | No. | Per cent |
| 1945 | 12 | 36 | 22 | 61% | 14 | 39% |
| 1946 | 16 | 38 | 18 | 47 | 20 | 53 |
| 1947 | 13 | 39 | 18 | 46 | 21 | 54 |
| 1948 | 13 | 39 | 21 | 54 | 18 | 46 |
| 1949 | 9 | 36 | 21 | 58 | 15 | 42 |
| 1950 | 11 | 41 | 18 | 44 | 23 | 56 |
| 1951 | 9 | 42 | 18 | 43 | 24 | 57 |
| 1952 | 9 | 41 | 19 | 46 | 22 | 54 |
| 1953 | 10 | 43 | 26 | 60 | 17 | 40 |
| 1954 | 9 | 40 | 23 | 58 | 17 | 42 |
| 1955 | 7 | 42 | 18 | 43 | 24 | 57 |
| TOTAL | 118 | 437[a] | 222 | 51% | 215 | 49% |

[a]Total equals member-years; actual number of persons involved is 133 (an average of 3.3 years per member).

Community Fund was getting under way, less than one-fourth of the members provided 50 per cent of the attendance at the 33 meetings held.

For many purposes, mere average attendance figures tell us little. For the formation of sound policy, for instance, some *continuity* of attendance is required. How did the Chest fare in this respect? The record shows (see again Table LXXV) that nearly half the members on the average failed to attend any three consecutive meetings, and that one-fifth of the Board did not even attend any two consecutive meetings. "Pairs" or attendances at any two consecutive meetings accounted for only about 27 per cent of all the possible meetings that all the members could have attended. Only about 18 per cent of such possible meetings involved "triples": attendances at three consecutive meetings. Evidently, many Board members did not achieve enough continuity of individual attendance (even if they somehow kept themselves informed about what was going on) to make reasonable the supposition that they could help determine policy, and provide government as well as rule in the affairs of the Chest. Since it seems to be a fairly common practice, then, to attend every other meeting, and thus maintain one's score of 50 per cent attendance, the continuous oversight of the Chest Board's business is apparently exercised by the small number of "the faithful few"—less than one Board member in five.

What kinds of people contributed to this probably serious lack of guidance in the Chest's administration? One answer may be found in Table LXXVI, which cross-classifies attendance for each of the past eleven years by status in the community (ESS). The correlations shown indicate that for every year but the last (1955), the higher the Board member's status the poorer his attendance record. Inspection of the record for each

## TABLE LXXV
### ATTENDANCE AT BOARD MEETINGS, INDIANAPOLIS CHEST, SELECTED YEARS, 1921-40, 1945-55

| Year | Number of regular meetings | *Concentration* Percentage of members who provided of all attendance | | *Discontinuity* Percentage of members who failed to attend consecutively | | *Continuity* Percentage of all attendance opportunities which involved attendance at | |
|---|---|---|---|---|---|---|---|
| | | 25% | 50% | Any two meetings | Any three meetings | Two consecutive meetings | Three consecutive meetings |
| 1921 | 33 | 10.8 | 23.3 | 30 | 35 | 25.5 | 19.7 |
| 1925 | 11 | 13.4 | 28.7 | 35 | 50 | 26.7 | 17.1 |
| 1933 | 9 | 13.0 | 31.0 | 29 | 75 | 25.0 | 11.9 |
| 1940 | 10 | 14.1 | 31.9 | 19 | 47 | 34.3 | 22.6 |
| 1945 | 12 | 15.3 | 34.2 | 14 | 31 | 32.8 | 20.3 |
| 1946 | 16 | 14.9 | 31.3 | 24 | 53 | 21.6 | 10.3 |
| 1947 | 13 | 14.5 | 33.1 | 13 | 38 | 32.0 | 18.1 |
| 1948 | 13 | 15.2 | 33.5 | 15 | 33 | 29.9 | 20.3 |
| 1949 | 9 | 15.8 | 34.9 | 19 | 42 | 33.3 | 20.6 |
| 1950 | 11 | 14.9 | 34.0 | 25 | 54 | 25.2 | 14.0 |
| 1951 | 9 | 12.0 | 27.7 | 42 | 54 | 26.0 | 19.7 |
| 1952 | 9 | 13.3 | 30.7 | 29 | 53 | 30.2 | 21.6 |
| 1953 | 10 | 15.5 | 33.0 | 19 | 52 | 31.2 | 17.9 |
| 1954 | 9 | 15.7 | 35.5 | 15 | 45 | 30.9 | 17.8 |
| 1955 | 7 | 13.7 | 31.9 | 29 | 64 | 25.5 | 12.9 |
| AVERAGES: | | | | | | | |
| All years shown | 12.1 | 14.1 | 31.6 | 23.8 | 48.0 | 28.7 | 17.7 |
| Four pre-War years | 15.8 | 12.8 | 28.7 | 28.3 | 51.8 | 27.9 | 17.8 |
| 1945-49 | 12.6 | 15.1 | 33.4 | 17.0 | 39.0 | 29.9 | 17.9 |
| 1950-55 | 9.2 | 14.2 | 32.1 | 26.5 | 50.5 | 28.2 | 17.3 |
| 1945-55 | 10.7 | 14.6 | 32.7 | 20.4 | 47.0 | 27.0 | 17.6 |

## TABLE LXXVI

ATTENDANCE AT BOARD MEETINGS, COMMUNITY CHEST, 1945-55, AND STATUS
IN THE COMMUNITY (ESS)

| Year | ESS | Attendance | | Total[a] | Correlation between status and attendance (r) |
|------|-----|------------|--------------|-------|------------------------|
|      |     | Half or more | Less than half |       |                        |
| 1945 | 2 or higher | 7 | 7 | 14 | |
|      | 2.5 or lower | 11 | 4 | 15 | |
|      | Total | 18 | 11 | 29 | −.24 |
| 1946 | 2 or higher | 6 | 10 | 16 | |
|      | 2.5 or lower | 9 | 7 | 16 | |
|      | Total | 15 | 17 | 32 | −.19 |
| 1947 | 2 or higher | 6 | 9 | 15 | |
|      | 2.5 or lower | 10 | 8 | 18 | |
|      | Total | 16 | 17 | 33 | −.15 |
| 1948 | 2 or higher | 5 | 8 | 13 | |
|      | 2.5 or lower | 12 | 6 | 18 | |
|      | Total | 17 | 14 | 31 | −.28 |
| 1949 | 2 or higher | 6 | 8 | 14 | |
|      | 2.5 or lower | 14 | 5 | 19 | |
|      | Total | 20 | 13 | 33 | −.31 |
| 1950 | 2 or higher | 6 | 13 | 19 | |
|      | 2.5 or lower | 12 | 9 | 21 | |
|      | Total | 18 | 22 | 40 | −.26 |
| 1951 | 2 or higher | 7 | 14 | 21 | |
|      | 2.5 or lower | 11 | 10 | 21 | |
|      | Total | 18 | 24 | 42 | −.19 |
| 1952 | 2 or higher | 6 | 11 | 17 | |
|      | 2.5 or lower | 13 | 11 | 24 | |
|      | Total | 19 | 22 | 41 | −.19 |
| 1953 | 2 or higher | 6 | 10 | 16 | |
|      | 2.5 or lower | 20 | 7 | 27 | |
|      | Total | 26 | 17 | 43 | −.36 |
| 1954 | 2 or higher | 6 | 6 | 12 | |
|      | 2.5 or lower | 17 | 11 | 28 | |
|      | Total | 23 | 17 | 40 | −.12 |
| 1955 | 2 or higher | 4 | 11 | 15 | |
|      | 2.5 or lower | 14 | 13 | 27 | |
|      | Total | 18 | 24 | 42 | .02 |
| Eleven- | 2 or higher | 65 | 107 | 172 | |
| year | 2.5 or lower | 143 | 91 | 234 | |
| total | Total | 208 | 198 | 406 | −.23[b] |

[a]All figures in this table refer to those for whom we had sufficient information to make ESS ratings: thus total will not always be reconcilable with other tables.

[b]A very significant figure ($P < .000005$). The correlations for each year separately are not, of course, significant, but their cumulative evidence is impressive.

year will make it evident that those Board members whose community status is that of "civic leaders" and "solid citizens" (ESS 2.5, 3, 3.5, and lower) are indeed "the ones who do the work"—at least they attend meetings more regularly than do those of higher status. In 1955, when only seven regular meetings were held, the correlation declined to nearly zero (.02)—not because attendance of high status Board members improved (eleven out of fifteen such persons attended less than half of the meetings) but because lower status Board members did not maintain their better record of attendance established in most prior years (only fourteen out of twenty-seven attended half or more of the meetings).[46]

In short, if a Community Chest, having a record of "failure" to make goal two out of every three years, for thirty-five years, can be said to be in special need of better administration, and if continuity of attendance at Board meetings, especially by members of high social status, is a factor in bolstering government as well as rule, then the Indianapolis Community Chest has had something less than a favorable history of leadership, so far as that can be measured by the attendance records of its Board of Directors. If the record looked any better for the pre-war years (1921, 1925, 1933, and 1940), one might agree that "There were giants in the old days," and that the Chest has perhaps just been "getting old." This is obviously doubtful.

The root of the difficulty seems to be that a mode of administration which may have suited the simpler society of Indianapolis in the 1920's has been continued into the 1950's. When the business community was smaller and more closely knit, when such rivalries and cleavages as existed involved fewer persons, it may well have been possible for a "faithful few" on the Chest Board to provide by their local power and influence an administration sufficient to establish the federation. Now, however, the Indianapolis business community has grown greatly, in size, dollar volume, and diversification of products and services. The scene is filled with examples of the modern corporation, either branch operations of national firms that are wholly new units or the results of mergers, or once purely local concerns grown to national standing. The decisions of leaders in the contemporary business world are no longer the easy agreements of a small fraternity of local merchants, manufacturers, and financiers, but have become increasingly of long-range concern to great corporate managements both local and non-local—they are now interwoven with the larger fabric of the life of the foremost national power in the world.

It seems inescapable that the administration of a fundraising federation will turn out to be just about as effective and efficient as the degree to which its leaders adapt it to the contemporary state of affairs. More and more frequently the major decisions need to be thought out for the long pull, and *ad hoc* approaches, whose only contribution to "continuity" is the necessity for annual improvisation, will then not usually suffice. In effect, and in view of this necessity, it seems that the "top top leadership" of Indianapolis has long since abdicated, so far as providing government, over and beyond rule, for the existing federation for fundraising is concerned.

## THE CHEST'S CAMPAIGN METHODS IN 1955

Perhaps it would be as well—before passing on to possible remedies (in the next chapter)—to pass in review some features of a recent and "aggressive" campaign, so that we may have a dynamic view as well as the benefits of structural analysis.

Like any annual community-wide drive, the 1955 Chest campaign really began with the ending of that in 1954. For the staff and the inner circle of lay leaders, the "faithful few" mentioned in the preceding section, the standard procedure would have followed the annual campaign calendar outlined in chapter 10. But for some reason (perhaps preoccupations with the 1955 biennial session of the state legislature), the usual post-campaign period was unduly prolonged.

The Annual Meeting was not held until March 22, 1955, some time after it had been made known to the member agencies that their allocations for 1955 would be cut 2 per cent. With the stigma of "failure" affecting the morale of both staff and lay leaders, the next campaign could be viewed as "a challenge" only in the grimmest sense.

The staff carried on their usual routines and further elaborated the "1955 Campaign Plan." In the form of a five-page mimeographed document used in the search for a General Chairman for the campaign, this Plan preserved some parts of the organization used in previous years; but, because it appeared that the Chest had been "doing better with employee giving than with corporation gifts or executive gifts"—as the Manager put it—it called for extra emphasis on getting larger corporation gifts[47] and also urged the development and vigorous promotion of "yardsticks" for corporate and executive giving.[48]

The staff could do little, however, to get the 1955 campaign under way until the lay leadership finally located a General Chairman. After prolonged efforts failed to enlist a high-ranking leader from the wider fields of manufacturing and commerce, the banking community at long last prevailed upon a leader in the financial world, though he himself was a member of the Chest Board and one of the "faithful few" who had been seeking a General Chairman. His appointment was announced early in June—rather later than is usually considered desirable from the point of view of allowing time for pre-campaign planning, recruiting of the campaign leadership, preparing graphic materials for the Appeal, etc. It may be surmised from all this that the Chest's "crisis" had become so serious that the banks felt impelled to act, and not a day too soon, in order to save the federation from near collapse. Indeed, Chest Board members had been saying that it was a matter of "a community crisis," and they were highly relieved and gratified when a leader finally took charge.

The Clearing House Association in Indianapolis appears to be one of the outstanding unifying organizations in the civic life of the city. The Chamber of Commerce is even more important, in the number and variety of economic forces it can bring into meaningful co-ordination; but in 1955 at least, its leaders were apparently interested in many affairs other than the Chest's dilemma. The Chamber of Commerce was represented in the administration of the Chest by one of its staff, as a member of the Board of Directors; but, in contradistinction to the situation in other cities or at other times, the "health" or "vigor" of the Chest as a matter of civic concern was evidently not paramount among the interests of the Chamber. The Merchants Association in Indianapolis might be thought to have a concern for the federation, since the Chest movement, ever since 1920, has appealed to retailers especially, but the leading department stores have, of course, other means of supporting the Chest, and presumably the rest of the merchants have been content with the federation as it is, or are at least not in strong opposition to it. Leading Donors, as individuals or management groups, did not, in any direct or co-ordinated way, rally around in the Chest's "crisis" to put forth a leader—an act which may involve more "sacrificial giving" than many people realize—but a few were represented in the inner circle which, in collaboration with the bankers, finally secured someone to take the job. The significant thing seems to be that, at the last ditch in the Chest's "retreat," the banking community was the force that came to the rescue. More knowledge of local history might make some pattern clear in this regard: one year the banks "save" the Chest; another year, the insurance companies; another year, the leading merchants; and so on. Even if this is true, however, it is not sufficiently a matter of public knowledge to have been mentioned to us by anyone concerned with Chest affairs in the entire year and a half of our observations.

The new General Chairman appointed his company's Vice-President as his Co-Chairman, and, for the next few months, he put himself, his business organization, and even his family into a wholehearted, all-out, day-and-night campaign effort.[49] From the point of view of the observer of the permanent organization of the Chest, the 1955 campaign was an extraordinary affair. The past few campaigns had been "quiet" or "low pressure" ones, we were told, and the results, while building towards stability (a fairly well-established "plateau of giving") were disappointing—both to those who felt that the federation "should" raise more and to those who believed that a future United Fund (which, after all, would have to raise perhaps double the Chest's 1954 "take") could hardly be constructed upon the ashes of a dying or quiescent federation.

The new leadership rapidly improvised what can fairly be called a "crash program." A Goal of $2.3 million was proposed, even in the face of doubt such as that vocalized by two businessmen: "There's no new gimmick that will increase giving by half a million dollars in this town!"[50] In sheer dollars, the 1955 Goal was the largest peacetime effort of any annual campaign in the city's history. But this fact was not emphasized: instead, the leaders insisted that in terms of "real dollars," and taking account of population growth, increase in Red Feather services (new agencies and greater volume of beneficiaries), etc., the 1955 Goal was really only about equal to what the Chest had raised in 1946-7.

Possibly no single feature of the 1955 campaign had more impact on the community than this Goal of $2.3 million, especially when corporate managements learned that it implied that many firms would be asked to "double" their 1954 gifts. A variety of "standards for giving" were put forth by the campaigners, including one that asked publicly owned firms to contribute "1.5 per cent of pre-tax net income," a rate at which it was alleged that "many firms" (especially in Cleveland) were supporting the local federation.

During the summer of 1955, the campaigners employed every available means of reaching Leading Donors and all others in the potential Donor-Aggregate. Invitations to "Dutch treat" luncheons; a vast flood of direct mail pieces; telephone and personal contacts; and in the more public period of the campaign (September-October), visits to agencies ("Come and See Tours"), special meetings, newspaper and radio-TV publicity, posters—all the devices of making known the Appeal and the Goal were brought into play.

It seems reasonable to conclude that the combination of the large Goal and the "aggressive" campaign—the plain fact that few of the important donors could avoid "hearing the call"—was responsible for the outcome. As fully reported elsewhere (in chapter 9 especially) the 1955 Chest campaign yielded, or caused to be yielded, slightly over $2 million—about $300,000 short of the Goal, but a very important increase over 1954. The campaign leadership asked permission to conduct "re-solicitation" after the campaign officially ended November 1st, but this was decided against by the Chest Board, whose members felt that a "real," if not a complete, success had been achieved, and that it was best to avoid the loss of goodwill that re-solicitation might well entail.

There was one "innovation" in the 1955 campaign which lends itself to some measurement, even though, as part of a wholesale improvisation, its particular influence is inextricably merged with all the other stimulating features of such a "crash operation." This was the program of "Dutch treat" luncheon meetings held every weekday for three weeks from July 18th through August 5th at the club ranking second in prestige. To them were invited "the 1,600 business leaders": heads or representatives of firms (employing fifteen or more persons) to be solicited in the Commerce and Industry division, as well as, hopefully, representatives of the larger firms assigned to "Division A" (the division set up to solicit corporate gifts from the 600 largest firms). These meetings were the principal means by which the campaign leaders could personally appear before a series of audiences composed of persons widely scattered throughout the business community. The leaders made other appearances, of course—at meetings of bank boards of directors, service clubs, etc.—but in these luncheons, especially, they faced a somewhat more representative cross-section of businessmen. It was in this kind of milieu—seeking pledges of interest in the Chest campaign and faith in the idea of federation—that the leaders developed the "sales approach" of the whole campaign as well as their own skills in presenting the symbolic themes of the Chest Appeal.

The "sales presentation" was made by the four lay leaders most concerned with firm gifts and employee contributions—the General Chairman, his Co-Chairman, the Chairman of Division A, and the Chairman of the Commerce and Industry division (designed to solicit executive and employee gifts in all 1,600 firms, as well as company gifts from the 1,000 smaller firms not covered by Division A). It was felt by the Chest leaders, both lay and professional, that telling the story to the "top executives" would be one way in which companies could be influenced to increase the company gift and to co-operate in the solicitation of their executives and employees. The major emphasis seemed to be on "selling" the corporate "yardsticks," but certainly considerable effort was made to convince the businessmen that the "yardsticks" for executives and employees should also be used in the solicitation within their organization.

Since the stated aim of the Chest was to talk to the "top executives of the 1,600 leading firms" in Indianapolis, we first looked, in attempting to evaluate the effectiveness of the program, to see how well that goal had been attained in attendance. Table LXXVII summarizes the relations of persons attending the luncheons (and the firms they represent) to the various campaign divisions of the Chest. About three-fourths (73.4 per cent) of the persons attending the luncheons represented firms for which the luncheons were specifically designed. But they represented only slightly more than one-fifth (20.8 per cent) of the 1,600 firms invited to send representatives. Thus it is clear that only a small percentage of the firms invited to send representatives to the luncheons did so.

However, this does not tell us whether or not the firms were represented by the "top executives." Table LXXVIII gives the position in their firms of the 426 persons representing firms in Division A and the Commerce and Industry division.[51] Only about half of the representatives of the firms are, evidently, top executives of those firms. This may be but a rough measure of the success of the Community Chest in reaching the top executives, since any officer of the company may well be in the key position as far as the Chest is concerned. In some cases, the personnel manager or the industrial relations manager might be the person most important to reach

## TABLE LXXVII

AFFILIATIONS OF PERSONS ATTENDING FIFTEEN CHEST LUNCHEONS
July 18, 1955—August 8, 1955

| Type of firm or organization | Number of persons attending | Number of firms or organizations represented |
|---|---|---|
| 1. Firms in Commerce & Industry Division and Division A (1600 firms for which luncheons were given) | 426 | 332 |
| 2. Firms in Metropolitan and Professional divisions | 86 | 72 |
| 3. Organizations in Public division | 55 | 21 |
| 4. All other (includes some for whom affiliation was unknown) | 13 | 5 |
| TOTAL | 580[a] | 430 |

[a]Additionally, 32 persons, affiliated with 31 companies, were "briefed" by the campaign General Chairman at meetings of boards of directors of banks. Of these 31 companies, only 10 were represented at the luncheons.

Also, 11 persons who were invited (but who did not attend) had previously attended the Agency Board Members luncheon (in June). Nine are affiliated with companies and 2 are lawyers. Of the 9 companies, 4 were represented at the business leaders' luncheons also. Finally, 4 chief executives of companies did not attend but signed "Pledges of Support"; of these, 3 were represented at the luncheons by their assistants.

It is not possible to give a count of the number of persons attending every luncheon. There is, however, no duplication of count for people who attended more than one luncheon. Some individuals attended many times. Further, staff members of the Community Chest and of Community Surveys are not counted, nor are their organizations.

## TABLE LXXVIII

POSITIONS IN COMPANY OF 426 PERSONS REPRESENTING FIRMS IN DIVISION A
AND COMMERCE AND INDUSTRY DIVISION AT COMMUNITY CHEST BUSINESS
LEADERS' LUNCHEONS

*Top Executives*

| | | |
|---|---|---|
| Members of the company Board (including chairmen) | 6 | |
| Presidents | 98 | |
| Owners, proprietors and partners | 22 | |
| Local managers (top representatives of the company in Indianapolis) | 88 | |
| | | 214 |

*Others*

| | | |
|---|---|---|
| Other officers of the company (VP; Sec.; or Treas.) | 81 | |
| Personnel, Purchasing, Industrial Relations | 57 | |
| Other employees | 46 | |
| Position unknown | 28 | |
| | | 212 |
| TOTAL | | 426 |

in the campaign. But on the basis of the stated purpose of the luncheons, only about one-eighth of the 1,600 firms were represented by their top executive.

It seemed pertinent to find out also whether the people who attended these luncheons were already closely associated with the Chest and its agencies or whether, in essence, this was a "new" audience for the Chest story. Of the 426 persons representing firms in the Commerce and Industry division and Division A, seventy held Board memberships in the Chest or one of its agencies. These seventy held a total of ninety-nine Board memberships. Five of the seventy had wives who held eight Board memberships. And three men who attended but held no Board memberships were married to ladies who were Board members. It would appear, then, that about one-sixth (17.1 per cent) of the persons attending the luncheons as representatives of the 1,600 firms were very closely associated with the Chest or one of its agencies.[52] In addition, 23 persons who were not Chest or Chest agency Board members are in our file of Welfare Community Leaders which means, of course, that they probably have more than the average person's interest in the Chest and its agencies as well as in the agencies in which they are active. Thus, slightly more than one-fifth (22.5 per cent) of the persons representing the 1,600 firms were identifiable as Welfare Community Leaders. It seems, then, that a fairly large proportion (about four-fifths) of those who attended the luncheons were persons who had currently no strong tie to the Chest or the Welfare Community.[53]

To see how the firms in the Commerce and Industry division and Division A which had representatives at the luncheons, *pledged* in comparison with those which did not have representatives at the luncheons, we used data from the campaigns in 1954 and 1955. Of the 332 firms with representatives at the luncheons, 277 had pledges[54] in both years; 27 gave in neither year; 20 gave in 1955 but not in 1954; and 8 gave in 1954 but not in 1955. Table LXXIX shows the results for "attenders" and "non-attenders" for 1954 and 1955.

The "percentage of Total pledged in Commerce and Industry and Division A" by attenders and non-attenders differs only slightly (1.8 per cent) as between the two years. The difference between attenders and non-attenders in percentage increase in the per-employee pledge is also small (4.2 per cent), and, strikingly, the percentage increase for the two groups combined is greater than for either separately.[55] The difference between attenders and non-attenders in percentage increase in the dollar amount of the pledge (14.1 per cent) appears to be large. But we could not be sure that this difference is significant, and even if it were, a number of factors other than attendance might account for the increase. So we tested[56] to see how the attendance at the luncheons and/or the previous generosity[57] of a firm affected the total pledge of these firms.

We analysed the pledges of a sample of one hundred firms[58] to see if

## TABLE LXXIX

PLEDGING OF ATTENDERS[a] AND NON-ATTENDERS: 1600 FIRMS INVITED TO SEND
REPRESENTATIVES TO CHEST LUNCHEONS

| | Attenders | | Non-attenders | | All firms | |
|---|---|---|---|---|---|---|
| | 1954 | 1955 | 1954 | 1955 | 1954 | 1955 |
| Percentage | | | | | | |
| Of C & I total | 77.3% | 79.1% | 22.7% | 20.9% | 100.0% | 100.0% |
| Of total amount raised in campaign | 54.5 | 59.8 | 15.9 | 16.1 | 70.6 | 75.7 |
| Increase in dollar amount, 1954-5 | 42.8% | | 28.7% | | 39.6% | |
| Increase in pledge per employee 1954-5 | 34.1% | | 29.9% | | 34.4% | |

[a]Includes all of the 332 firms represented at the luncheons. If we had used only the 277 firms which pledged in both years, the differences would have been small—ranging from 0.4 to 0.7 per cent.

Attendance, Generosity, and/or the interaction of the two had any effect on the percentage increase in dollars pledged, on the percentage increase in per-employee pledge, or on the dollar increase in the pledge.[59] The results were negative with one exception. Attendance and Generosity, separately, and their interaction have no significant relation to the percentage increase in dollars pledged or to the percentage increase in per-employee pledge. But Previous Generosity is significantly related to the increase in dollar amount.[60] This means that only Previous Generosity seems to have had a significant relation to the increase made by all firms, whether they were represented at the luncheons or not. Attendance, as such, had no measurable effect on the giving of the firms represented at the fifteen luncheons.

However, the cumulative effect of the luncheon meetings along with the many other techniques used in the 1955 campaign has not been, and cannot be, measured. Chest campaigns, unfortunately, are not conducted in such a way as to permit testing of the effectiveness of their many parts. To determine whether there were other results of the luncheons—not measurable in the pledging—would require the setting up of control groups against which changes could be measured. For example, if the Chest wished to find out if the luncheons were useful in campaigning, it would be necessary to exclude a part of the 1,600 firms—say half—from attendance at the luncheons. This has, of course, some limitations as an experimental design—after all, the experimenter could not prevent the executives who had attended from talking to executives who were not invited—but an even more important problem for the fundraiser would be whether or not antipathy would be engendered in persons excluded from attendance by the sampling design.[61] We shall touch again upon such problems in chapter 12.

# APPENDIX

## Estimated Social Status

For our purposes, the ratings of persons according to their relative social status in Indianapolis needed to be somewhat more refined at the "high" end of the scale than towards the "low" end. We were interested in distinguishing the levels of community leadership present in fundraising organizations, so that we could compare these organizations and test what our informants said about the "quality" of each organization's leadership. We might also learn how "rank" in the organization (especially in its campaign leadership) was related to "status" in the business world and in the general community.

The scale for Estimated Social Status is described in the following:

[1]   Persons in families whose names are most frequently given by long-time residents of high status themselves (ESS 3 or above) when they are asked, "What persons would you include in the 'very top top' leadership in this community?" (Because of our interest in fundraising, some such question was usually asked in a discussion of campaigns and their problems—especially the case of the Chest. Informants frequently qualified their answers by saying, "These would be the 'very top top' leadership, if you could get them, but they're not very active." Actually, the families named included many persons who had been active in the past, who were known for their philanthropies, and who had typically been active in fundraising either during wartime or in only the very largest campaigns, such as that of the Hospital Development Association.) Family heads, if not retired, are often Board Chairmen and top executives in the largest firms, in positions to which they have succeeded as members of the "birth élite." Their homes are likely to be large estates or town houses, and they may also have houses at resort places here and even abroad.

[2]   Persons in families otherwise recognized as "top tops" in this community, but not necessarily "Old Family." Family heads are Board chairmen and top executives in large firms, including large branch factories of national corporations, or top leaders in the professions; and most of them are in positions to which they have arrived as members of the "mobile élite"—that is, they were born into lower ranks (ESS 3, 4, 5, and so on). Their homes are often new, large, and luxurious, and their style of life may include a great deal of travel abroad.

[3]   Persons and families who are regarded as "civic leaders," "well-to-do," "solid citizens," and the like. Family heads are executives (vice-presidents in the larger firms, Board Chairmen or top executives in the smaller firms) and professional men of high standing. Their children are more likely than they to become members of the "mobile élite." Their homes are often new, but if so, not so large and luxurious as those of persons in ESS 2. But they may also be found in older houses in older, respectable neighborhoods.

[4]   Persons and families who are also regarded as "solid citizens," but whose occupations or positions in large organizations (or whose firms themselves, even if they hold top positions, or ownership, in them) are not so highly regarded as those of persons in ESS 3. School teachers, social workers, supervisors in offices and factories, accountants, salesmen, and persons in similar occupations are likely to be found in ESS 4. They are sometimes called "middle-middle class," and informants may add that "They don't have much money." Their homes are small modern dwellings, apartments, or "doubles."

[5]   Persons and families who are also "respectable middle class," but whose occupations are not so highly valued as those in ESS 4, 3, etc., even though they may be more highly rewarded financially than many of those in ESS 4. Here are factory foremen, lesser supervisors, workers in the skilled trades, many salesmen, and many "white-collar workers." Their homes, if new, are usually "row houses" in "develop-

ments," or they may be solid older structures in still respectable neighborhoods, or modest doubles or duplexes.

[6] Persons and families who are more definitely "working class," and who make up the great majority of employees and less skilled workers in commerce and industry. (None of the persons known to us as "Campaign Leaders" or "Welfare Community Leaders," even in the lowest ranks, are in ESS 6 or 7.) Their homes, if new, are in the less expensive "developments," but the vast majority of them occupy flats, doubles, or duplexes, or even whole houses in the many side streets and "quiet neighborhoods" which the casual tourist in Indianapolis probably never sees.

[7] Persons and families who are definitely "poor," and, by local judgment, "not respectable," and who make up the bulk of laborers, unskilled workers, and casual workers. Not all on public relief are here, but families in ESS 7 are likely to be composed of those whose financial position is chronically very precarious. Their dwellings are either in long-established slums, or in deteriorating neighborhoods, sometimes even in sections that gain some notoriety for vice and crime.

The use of this 7-point scale, for our purposes, has been simply to take any list of Campaign Leaders or of any sub-group among the Welfare Community Leaders and "rate" each individual to find how the group or aggregate is distributed, or as may happen, is concentrated, in any part of the scale. By using Polk's City Directory, the Indianapolis Chamber of Commerce Blue Book, the local telephone directory, and other information accumulated in our files (including newspaper clippings), we could identify most individuals in any such list as to occupation or profession or executive position. The same process gave us the family's home address, which in turn, with our increasing knowledge of neighborhoods and types of housing in Indianapolis, provided, in addition to occupation as an indicator of income, a rough measure of the kind of "life style" into which this income is being translated. With all these kinds of information, we could "place" almost every individual somewhere on the scale of Estimated Social Status (ESS). For placing an individual in ESS 1, all we had to add was what is well known to many long-time residents of Indianapolis: namely, whether the family head, already known to be of very high position in the business world of Indianapolis, is one whose father was a business leader and one who holds his position in the same firm as that of the father. If this was clearly not the case, we assigned the individual and family to ESS 2 (or even lower, if there were appropriate indications), but if we had any evidence that the case was a doubtful one (e.g., if the founding father, still active, had a son who was becoming well established in the same firm or one related through family investment), we assigned the case to ESS 1.5.

In over half of the cases we encountered two kinds of uncertainty, however: (1) our knowledge of Indianapolis, while growing, was limited inevitably to what our opportunities to learn afforded us in 1955—hence, for example, we had no large scientific sample of the local evaluations of the less conspicuous firms or of the high positions in them, or of the neighborhoods and dwellings throughout the metropolitan area (including the county), and this meant that certainty of distinguishing an ESS 2 from an ESS 3, and so on down the line, was not always very great; and (2) our information in some cases appeared to be contradictory—for example, a family head's occupation might rate "high," but the home address might point to a "life style" that did not coincide. In Indianapolis as elsewhere, people may choose to "live beyond their means" or to "live conservatively." The converse occurred several times: for example, a man listed as "factory worker" (which points to ESS 5 or 6) owned a home in a neighborhood otherwise occupied mostly by persons in ESS 3. In these uncertain cases, we assigned the family to an intermediate standing on the scale (such as ESS 2.5, 3.5, and so on) which of course has the effect of expanding our original 1-point scale. (The "factory worker" with the residence appropriate to ESS 3 was rated ESS 3.5.)

In the scale of Estimated Social Status ratings below, some typical occupations are given, in order to help the reader interpret the text:

[1]  President (of a large manufacturing concern founded by father); vice-president (of a large concern with which the family has long been associated).

[1.5]  President of a large financial institution (in process of identifying with the "birth élite" through children of a "successful marriage"); president of a large bank; realtor; investment broker; surgeon.

[2]  President of a bank; president of a large investment firm; president of a large retail store; vice-president of a large bank; attorney (partner in a prominent firm).

[2.5]  Vice-president (of a large manufacturing firm); officer and part-owner of an old local firm; works manager of a new national firm's branch plant; physician.

[3]  Vice-president of a bank; treasurer and part-owner, large wholesale house; vice-president of an old manufacturing concern recently merged with a national corporation; attorney; dentist.

[3.5]  Auditor (CPA); branch bank manager; local government official; assistant manager of a trade association; personnel department employee in a large factory; head of a social agency.

[4]  Department manager (large retail store); accountant, public utility; teacher; grade school principal; labor union executive.

[4.5]  Toolmaker (large factory); auto repair shop (own business); department manager, railroad; supervisor, public utility.

[5]  Carman, railroad; bricklayer; carpenter, railroad shops; insurance agent; foreman; salesman; office worker.

[5.5]  Operator, factory; route salesman; clerk.

[6]  Majority of employees and less skilled workers in commerce and industry.

[6.5]  Laborers and least skilled workers, but more regularly employed than those in ESS 7.

[7]  Laborers; casual workers; some of those on public relief rolls; those locally judged to be "not respectable" or "shady characters" or "downright criminal."

This expansion of our scale to allow 13 possible "ratings" would be undesirable in a more complete community study, but our study is concerned mainly with problems of leadership, and hence the persons whose status we need to compare are almost all from the higher ranks. Much more research than our time and resources allowed would be required, however, to make our ratings more reliable than the fairly well-informed guess that is applied in each case. But since we are mainly interested in establishing major differences between selected groups, organizations, or categories, each having numbers of people, and since these differences are expressed by the proportions in which the higher ranks of community leadership are present, the comparisons we make are matters of "more" or "less" in broad degrees.

Such comparison is very important if, for example, it helps us to understand how each organization acts in fundraising. It may be that the pattern in one organization is the kind required to secure very large sums of money from the largest potential donors as well as to secure additional large sums from very many smaller donors, in a community-wide campaign. Contrariwise, another organization may have a pattern that may be more effective in securing a modest total from numerous donors within a narrow social class range, i.e., from persons who are also likely to share similar values, interests, preferences, etc.

Studies of American communities enable us to compare Indianapolis with an Eastern city (New Haven), a Midwestern small town ("Midwest"), and a New

England community ("Yankee City"). If Indianapolis is like other cities, as we believe it is, we may hazard an estimate of the distribution of the population by the social classes distinguished in other American cities, as in Table A.

TABLE A

SOCIAL STRATIFICATION—COMPARISON OF INDIANAPOLIS WITH SELECTED CITIES

| Social class[a] | "Yankee City"[b] | Percentage of population | | | Equivalent ESS Ratings |
|---|---|---|---|---|---|
| | | "Midwest"[c] | New Haven, Conn.[d] | Indianapolis, Ind.[e] | |
| 1 | 1.44 ⎱ | 2.72 | 3.1 | ⎰ 0.5 | 1 |
| 2 | 1.56 ⎰ | | | ⎱ 2.0 | 1.5 & 2 |
| 3 | 10.22 | 11.98 | 8.1 | 12.5 | 2.5 & 3 |
| 4 | 28.12 | 32.22 | 22.0 | 30.0 | 3.5, 4, 4.5 & 5 |
| 5 | 32.60 | 41.00 | 46.0 | 35.0 | 5.5, 6 & 6.5 |
| 6 | 25.22 | 12.08 | 17.8 | 20.0 | 7 |
| Unknown | 0.84 | — | 3.0 | — | — |
| TOTAL | 100.00 | 100.00 | 100.0 | 100.0 | |

[a]For the meaning of "social class" and methods of measuring social status, see *Social Class in America* by Warner, Meeker, and Eells (Chicago: Science Research Associates, Inc. 1949). Six classes are distinguished in this table.

[b]W. Lloyd Warner and Paul S. Lunt, *The Social Life of a Modern Community,* vol. I, "Yankee City Series" (New Haven: Yale University Press, 1941).

[c]W. Lloyd Warner, Robert Havighurst, and Martin B. Loeb, *Who Shall Be Educated?* (New York: Harper & Bros., 1944).

[d]August B. Hollingshead and Frederick C. Redlich, "Social Stratification and Psychiatric Disorders," *American Sociological Review,* XVIII (April, 1953), 163-169.

[e]C.S.I. estimates as of 1955-56. In comparison with the older, smaller city (New Haven), Indianapolis apparently has fewer "Old Families" (1), a considerable proportion of "mobile élite" (2), a larger middle class (3 & 4), and a slightly smaller lower class (5 & 6). Indianapolis has a larger proportion of native-born Americans; is a center for government, trade and transportation; and therefore attracts seekers of white-collar jobs. It is in transition, however, from a city of many small industries to a more highly industrialized city with large-scale manufacturing, and its proportion of factory workers may be increasing, so that the class distribution towards the lower end of the scale may be coming closer to that of New Haven (over 63% as compared with the estimated 55% for Indianapolis).

# IV. POLICY AND PROGRESS

# 12. What Might Be Done:
# The Present Chest

THE PROBLEM posed for this study originally was: "Why is the Indianapolis Chest failing, and how can it be made to succeed?" The body of the report (see chapters 5 and 8, especially) will have made clear how ill defined, confused, and ambiguous is the meaning of "success" in this context. Very often, as between laymen on one side and professionals on the other, commonly, as between different laymen (or different professionals) and, often enough, within the same person, criteria for success, many of them incompatible with one another, lie about like so many unrelated scraps of attitude, understanding, wish, or hope. The problem, as we were told about it, was, variously, to raise more money, or to spend less; or to raise less money but spend more wisely what there was. The task, it was also said, was to enable the Chest to get the community "involved" and "participating" so that, in effect, the community would do what the Chest wanted; or, the task was to get the Chest "back under community control" so that it would really be doing "what the community wanted done"; or, the task was to get things going so efficiently that *less* involvement and labor were needed, and the Chest and "the community" could each get out of the other's hair. And so on.

By common consent, however, a Chest—or whatever succeeds to its social role—must do at least three things. It must: (a) raise money; (b) distribute it—"budget"; (c) oversee its expenditure—audit and evaluate. It may delegate all or part of its second and third responsibilities to a "Health and Welfare Council" or similar body, but the public belief that it does all three things ensures that the responsibility for all three belongs to the Chest. Effectiveness or ineffectiveness in discharging any one of the three functions seriously affects, of course, capacity to discharge the other two, so that it is not possible in reality—at least in the long run—to succeed in any one of the functions while failing in either of the others. Anything we can say, therefore, about the conditions for success in fundraising will either simultaneously help in the discharge of the other two functions or will assume that they are being[1] or will be properly attended to.

What we are asking, then, is really the following question: *What might be done in Indianapolis to establish and maintain an effective Chest* (or equivalent mass, operating, periodic, secular fundraising organization)— *from the viewpoint of money-raising—and assuming its other tasks to be well in hand?*

It will be convenient to look at the problem from the inside out—i.e., from the viewpoint of the Chest's Board of Directors, or perhaps the Chest's General Manager—because it is obvious that this is the way the lines of influence flow. Whatever may have been true at some previous period, it is now true that the Chest as an autonomous body fastens itself upon the community and, within tolerated limits, shapes the community to its own logic and purposes. The Chest no more grows out of the community and expresses community-wide wishes than does the local Bureau of Internal Revenue. Both proceed in terms of a general social logic and a national policy; although the local community or power-group may more easily defeat the "voluntary" Chest movement than the mandatory tax movement, the source of that movement and the shape of its intent are formed and re-formed at the national rather than the local level.[2]

Before we can enter upon any extended discussion of these problems, however, we must, in view of one large contingency and of current community talk and action about it, decide to deal separately and in order with:

(*a*) Those things that might be done, assuming that there is to be no significant immediate change in the number of agencies included in the existing federation—i.e., the present Chest.

(*b*) Those things that might be done contingent upon the relatively immediate emergence of some wider federation.

The things that might be done by and in or for a Chest of no wider scope than the existing one, include both those things that the Chest could itself do or bring about, and those things that require action in the community at large (or indeed, perhaps, in other places as well) in which the role to be performed by the Chest is relatively minor. A class of things that might be done by, in, and for the existing Chest but that would also require action elsewhere, would include those steps necessary as a prelude to the institution of a wider federation.[3] We might ask, next, what might be done about the internal organization of the Chest, and about its external organization. By "internal organization" we shall have reference primarily to the paid staff[4] and its organization, and the intimate[5] group of laymen most chiefly affected in its operation. By "external organization" we shall refer to the recruitment of leadership (and its retention and utilization), and the development and communication of an effective message and accepted value-system. Finally, and in the next chapter, we shall discuss the problems connected with the incorporation of other agencies into an expanded Chest or alternative form of federation.

## INTERNAL RELATIONS
### FORMAL RELATIONS

*The Staff of the Chest*

In many respects the operation of the Indianapolis Chest as a business organization exemplifies in sharp perspective some of the problems we have discussed in earlier chapters. While it may be more difficult to see clearly the results of lack of planning or inadequate planning in general Chest policy, at the level of office operation, in contrast, short-sighted approaches to planning are quite obvious.[6]

Although a series of formal organization charts have been prepared over the past years, in practice, as is true of many other businesses, the Chest does not adhere to the patterns of communication suggested by such charts. The actual operational organization of the Chest appears to take the form shown in the accompanying diagram.[7] All formal control of all major phases of office functions is retained by the General Manager. Only subsidiary functions are controlled by any staff member other than the General Manager. In a multi-function organization, this form of control makes internal co-ordination next to impossible, barring the development of informal relations which approximate in operation the functions of formal communications channels.[8]

*General Manager.* The General Manager is directly in charge of the supervision of the two main functions of the Chest—fundraising and budgeting—as well as two other sizeable ones—office administration and personnel management. In practice, the General Manager serves as "Campaign Director," supervising and directing the activities of four Campaign Associates—individually and collectively—and the Publicity Director and the Labor Relations Secretary. In still another role—as "Budget Director"—he collects and analyses agency budgets (lately with the aid of the Health and Welfare Council staff) and, in collaboration with the Council, serves in an advisory capacity to the Budget Committee of the Chest. As "Office Manager," the General Manager directs the routine operation of the office, including IBM processing, bookkeeping (in process of conversion to IBM), and, through his personal secretary, other secretarial and clerical operations. As "Personnel Manager," he selects and assigns all personnel employed by the Chest, and handles the many personnel problems which arise in the normal operation of an office.

The diagram indicates the personnel who are exceptions in so far as they do not come under the Manager's direct control. Three IBM clerk-operators work under the supervision of the IBM Chief. The part-time assistant to the bookkeeper is under the direction of the bookkeeper, solely. But about 45 per cent of the total staff (including sub-staff) are answerable to and receive their direction from the General Manager in person.

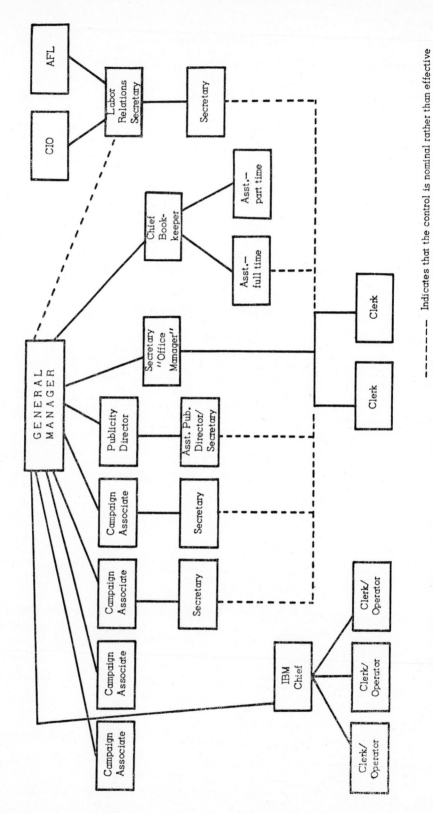

OPERATIONAL ORGANIZATION OF INDIANAPOLIS COMMUNITY CHEST, JUNE THROUGH DECEMBER, 1955

- - - - - - Indicates that the control is nominal rather than effective

In addition, four secretaries who function primarily as assistants to the persons for whom they are nominally secretaries receive major supervision from those persons—two Campaign Associates, the Publicity Director, and the Labor Relations Secretary. But, by some ill-defined arrangement, the four secretaries also receive some supervision from the personal secretary of the General Manager. This latter control seems to occur in the occasional periods when the work of the person to whom they are secretaries is at a minimum and in the frequent periods of "crisis."[9]

There is a very interesting anomaly in the distribution of the assigned secretaries. The General Manager has his secretary; but the other four are assigned, one each to the Campaign Associates for Metropolitan and Public divisions, one to the Publicity Director, and one to the Labor Relations Secretary. However, the Campaign Associates for Division A and for Commerce and Industry division have no secretaries. Yet these two are responsible for solicitation which raises something over three-fourths of the total amount raised. Nominally, they are empowered to give their secretarial work to the secretary of the General Manager for reassignment to one of the other secretaries. But, in practice, more often than not, there is no one to whom she can assign the work, and the Campaign Associate does the secretarial work himself. Clearly, such a situation is very wasteful of what appears to be the most productive manpower, dollar-wise.[10]

*Campaign Associates, Labor Relations, Public Relations.* The Campaign Associates, the Labor Relations Secretary, and the Publicity Director appear to operate somewhat more independently of each other than would seem effective for a co-ordinated campaign. Certainly, to a large extent, each of the people in these positions deals with separate problems of solicitation; but, at the same time, there is but one Community Chest campaign, and the work of each Associate is directed towards the attainment of the total goal. It is, at least, essential that the work of one division not be in opposition to the work of another. Yet, on occasion, this has happened.[11] And the conflicting behavior appears to be the result of lack of formal channels for communication or co-ordination below the Campaign Director level. It is hard to see how efficiency could be achieved when the Campaign Director has so many other duties to perform and, hence, relatively little time to devote to the co-ordination of the work of the various campaign personnel.

Perhaps the most difficult situation to assess is that of the Labor Relations Secretary. Nominally, it is his function to obtain the co-operation and active assistance of labor unions in the solicitation of employees in firms which are unionized. In practice, however, it is far from clear that this is what he is doing.[12] He has refused to carry out Chest campaign policy on the grounds that the unions don't or won't approve.[13] To all intents and purposes, it appears from his own statements, he refuses to do anything without the prior approval of the CIO. Not only does he "take orders" from that group, but he even interprets his job as *representing* the union and union members on the Chest staff.[14] Suggestions that his job is to obtain agreement by the unions to Chest policy are met with his own wholly different definition. The General Manager and the Board seem to have little or no control over his activities, and it is evident that he not only fails to do the task defined for him by Board and administration (assuming he *is* a Chest employee, and not, as he conceives, a union agent) but frequently acts to circumvent the Chest program. Labor Relations secretaries seem to be very effective in Chests in other cities, but in Indianapolis the method of functioning appears to be seriously detrimental to the best interests of the organization—and without visible benefit to the unions, who could readily make their special wishes, if any, effective on policy through regular (i.e., Board) channels.

Another department in the Chest operation appears to be in need of evaluation and, possibly, revision. The Publicity Department seems to operate on a crisis basis. There is much discussion about "long range public relations programs," but very little effort is expended in developing and continuing such programs. Rather, the Chest seems to take up these programs anew for each campaign, and, in the process, one of the more useful aspects of a public relations program—i.e., continuity—is lost.[15]

Perhaps the major weakness in the public relations program is its treatment as essentially a publicity job. Present-day public relations functions include not only "advertising" but the preservation and enhancement of the public reputation of the organization as well. And the public reputation is built of many more bricks than mere publicity—public experience in any contact with the staff and with agencies, solicitation techniques, and creditability or reliability of information releases, to mention only a very few. Public relations programs are sufficiently important to require policy-determination at the topmost level, and subsequently carrying out on a year-round basis rather than on a crisis basis.

It seems to us that one particular aspect of the publicity program of the Chest needs consideration. Much of the talk about and action in publicizing the Chest campaign sounds as though analogies were continuously being drawn from and policy determined on the basis of the selling of a tangible product.[16] However, if the Chest has a product to "sell," it is most definitely an intangible—and sometimes a nearly incomprehensible one when the "dolling up" process is completed. We are not saying that the Chest has no selling job, but that the techniques of advertising tangibles are different from those involved in selling intangibles.[17] The discovery of an appropriate technique to communicate the Chest's particular message or to sell its intangible product—the rationalization of philanthropy—is a matter for continuing thought, experiment, and expert (institutional advertising) advice.

The Chest, moreover, at present, in much of its publicity, plays upon the fears of people (e.g., fears of increased juvenile delinquency, broken homes, disease-racked children, slums, etc.), none of which can be demonstrated to be prevented by the programs of Chest agencies; and the wisdom of the appeal to fear and of founding the message on "facts" so dubious, is very much open to question—both from the viewpoint of the speaker's welfare and the hearer's.

*Campaign Associates.* The same problem—lack of continuity—which plagues the Chest in general, and its public relations program in particular, also plagues its several "divisions." Apparently as a consequence of failing to make goal, the Chest annually adopts the policy of "let's change everything" (virtually). This means that the program in the divisions changes abruptly each year. Occasionally, the campaign methods of one year are diametrically opposed to those of the previous one.[18] Much more frequently, the change is not so dramatic, but is sufficient to destroy any feeling of continuity between the campaigns. One factor which contributes to this effect is the very frequent changing of persons and firms to be solicited from one division or sub-division to another.

Within this picture of annual change, it is difficult to assess the operation of the Campaign Associates who have responsibility for these fluctuating divisions. As pointed out earlier, there is no formal pattern of communication between them, except for staff conferences. In the heat of a campaign, it is frequently not possible to delay decisions until staff conferences are held; yet very often the General Manager is not available, and hence the problem cannot be referred to him for decision, though perhaps it cannot be decided without him. Much of the inefficiency and confusion in the work of the Campaign Associates stems from lack of proper staff organization in the campaign period (as well as from the outside complications, referred to elsewhere).

What we have said thus far indicates some serious—and some not so serious—flaws in the operation of the Chest as a business organization. But as a whole, the Chest staff works fairly well in carrying out the functions of the office. With one exception, perhaps, the staff—both professional and non-professional—seem to be doing adequate and useful jobs, and doing them effectively just as far as they as persons can be effective within the existing structure. Apart then from the effects of lack of planning, of discontinuity, and of inappropriate structure and facilities for communication, the business operation is probably as good as it can be made.

The foregoing suggests strongly the desirability of reorganization along better-defined and more appropriate lines. After careful analysis, examination, and planning by the Chest staff, a scheme similar to one of those in the diagram might be considered. These schemes are, of course, drawn in terms of functions which the staff performs, in contrast to the earlier diagram

General Manager

Research — Budgeting — Campaign — Public Relations — Office Administration and Personnel

Assoc. — Assoc. — Assoc. — Labor Rela. — Asst. Dir. Publicity

Bkp. — IBM — Clerical

OR

General Manager

Assistant General Manager — Operations

Assistant General Manager — Control

Campaign Director

Campaign Associate — Campaign Associate — Campaign Associate — Campaign Associate

Labor Relations Secretary

Public Relations Director

Asst. Pub. Dir.

Research Director — Research Staff

Budgeting Director

Office Mgr. & Personnel Dir.

Bkp'ing Staff — IBM Staff — Clerical Staff

———— Administrative control and responsibility

- - - - - Frequent communication and co-ordination

POSSIBLE REORGANIZATION SCHEMES, INDIANAPOLIS COMMUNITY CHEST which was organized in terms of individual staff members. What is suggested is a separation based on related functions. Thus, the first scheme shows five divisions of the Chest's functions; and it would seem reasonable, if not essential, to map out program for each of these functional divisions separately. But we are not suggesting that each of these functional divisions requires (or does not require) different persons to administer the program. It seems to us that the Campaign Director should be responsible for campaign solely, and that the Publicity Director (Public Relations Director) should control his program only. On the other hand, Office Administration and Personnel, Budgeting, and Research may well be combined in any manner suitable to the capabilities of a staff member,[19] as in the second scheme. All of the above functions of the Chest are at least fully recognized as important now with two exceptions: Public Relations and Research.

The sample schemes show a somewhat different role or function for Public Relations than is currently performed. We have discussed in some detail the view that Public Relations should offer a service at quite a different level than that offered during or before the period of our research. The present activities of the publicity department should not be abandoned, though some modification seems necessary. Rather, the publicity phase of public relations should be, for the most part, tied much more closely to the work of the Campaign Director and his Associates. The Chest might well consider employing a competent public relations firm to establish and direct the public relations program with regard to its policy and planning. We are not suggesting the use of an advertising agency—since the Chest's staff has a fairly sound program in this area—but rather an organization which can advise the Chest, particularly its Board, on the public relations aspects of program and policy.

At present, the Chest has no research program at all. And it seems fantastically wasteful (at least to the writers) that an organization operating in such a relatively new field should continue its social experiments—and that, after all, is what the Chest does—without checking to see what it has and has not done. Of course, the services of the research department of the United Community Funds and Councils of America, Inc., are available to the local Chest, but those facilities are very limited and the orientation of its research is *primarily* towards problems of nation-wide interest.[20] Much of the campaign effort in Indianapolis has not been and cannot be evaluated because the application of program is not controlled in a way which would permit evaluation.[21] Further, no analysis of the cost of program can be made, nor can comparison be made between programs as to their relative costs. It is our belief that an adequate research program would be so valuable to the Chest as to pay for itself fairly soon (two to three years) after its inception. Such a program would encompass the work of the Chest primarily in Campaigning and Budgeting, though it need not be limited to these two functions. To head it, a competent, well-trained research director is necessary and, as with the Public Relations Director, he should be privy to and consulted about all policy and planning decisions.[22]

One essential requisite to an effective (useful and profitable) research program is that the research be freed completely from the necessity of adding pseudo-evidence to the preconceptions of campaign personnel, both lay and professional. Nor should the research program be exposed in any way to influence or pressure from outside the Chest itself, whether that influence be from the Chest's agencies or from firms, citizens, or other organizations.[23] It is our view that what is widely called "research" in these matters in Indianapolis (when it is not "special pleading" as it most frequently is) is more often than not a survey of existing conditions which results in mere and meaningless compilation of data rather than analysis.[24]

What is said above might be regarded as an occasion for re-appraisal and self-examination for the purpose of improving the operation, although three of the items (Public Relations, Research, and Labor Relations) seem to call for fairly drastic action. But changes or modifications here could hardly properly be made without the prior development of a more rational over-all program and policy by the Chest's Board.

### Professional Staff and Lay Leaders: Formal Relations

In MOPS fundraising, the permanent organization (both paid and volunteer) may or may not be closely controlled by the professional or paid head. But in any case, if the annual campaign is to achieve continuity from one year to the next, in the face of turn-over in the lay leadership, the continuity will normally have to be provided by the staff. It is the staff, therefore, that must preserve the basic pattern of the permanent organization; and to do so it must have a strong voice in decisions about the mechanics of the campaign, the assignments to solicit, and the arrangement of soliciting divisions, sub-groups, teams, etc.

In order to discuss the present point, it must be vividly recalled that the General Manager, and through him, all his paid assistants, are employees of the voluntary association on whose behalf the Board of Directors acts. Actually, since a Board of Directors tends to be led by a small group ("the faithful few" who attend meetings and can often secure unanimous approval for actions they propose), the paid staff's real employers may turn out to be a very few persons, or even one person.

Under these circumstances, at least two quite different types of situations can develop in a federation like the Indianapolis Community Chest. Wholly apart from the various contingencies that may arise in the on-going business of the Chest and that may be affected in their outcomes by "personalities" (the interactions of a very few persons), there is one large, perennial contingency in the career and tenure of a General Manager: this is the annual choice of the General Chairman for the "next" campaign. Two types of situations that arise in this connection may be diagrammed:

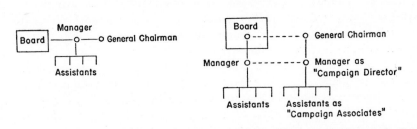

In a situation of Type I (which was approximated in the Red Cross campaign in 1955, although this was not exactly true to type because the campaign director was a visiting paid professional and not one of a year-round staff), the professional is acting in an advisory capacity in relation to a lay leader, the General Chairman, and the latter, together with his lay aides in the top ranks of the volunteer organization, has a clear line of authority to all the volunteer solicitors, as well as a clear responsibility to use the professional staff as experienced advisers and helpers.

In the 1955 Chest campaign, we observed what is described in the diagram as Type II: the General Chairman had been a member of the Board of Directors for some time, and had been a member of the small group which had sought an outsider to take the post of General Chairman. Finally he himself was persuaded to do the job. In this situation, the General Chairman tends to move from one superordinate position to the other, maintaining his roles as Board member and employer in relation to the professional. The latter is in turn taken from his traditional role as staff expert at campaign time, and is put in the subordinate position of employee, almost as if he had taken a job in the General Chairman's factory or office. The professional's proper tasks—those he would have in a staff advisory capacity—tend to get put aside, and he is given assignments of work to get done by himself and with the help of his regular assistants. In the press of accomplishing things in an improvised campaign, the General Chairman may even by-pass the professional Manager and give orders directly to the latter's assistants. *His* mission, and *his* conceptions about how to accomplish it, naturally take precedence in a Type II situation, and the divisive question of "Who is boss around here?" is likely to arise, and does arise, in the minds of the paid staff. The possibilities of confusion, contradictory directives, duplication of effort, and errors of commission and omission are greatly increased. Especially are these risks augmented, if, as was the case in the 1955 Chest campaign, the design of soliciting divisions and sub-groups, the setting of quotas or yardsticks, the making of assignments, and even the development of the appeal, not to mention setting the goal, are all radical changes from what has been done before, and are all parts of a sweeping improvisation aimed to replace "failure" with "success."

A situation of Type II is, of course, avoided by the directors of a fundraising organization if it is at all possible. There is ample recognition of the difficulties to which this structure may give rise: witness the very considerable efforts made to find a prominent outsider to act as General Chairman, and the feeling that it is "wrong" if a Board member "has to step down and take the job of General Chairman himself."[25]

The Chest campaign in 1956 is one which will apparently succeed in avoiding the dilemma of the Type II situation, since the General Chairman is not a Board member and the new General Manager is apparently developing his own role, and those of his top assistants, along the lines of the staff function of the "Campaign Associate"—the paid professional who works with the lay leaders within a specific division of the campaign. Just how this will work out for the year-round routines of the Chest office is not clear at this writing, but it appears that the new Manager has allocated the varied year-round functions (office management, budgeting, "cultivation," etc.) to the several erstwhile "Campaign Associates"—with himself as one of them—he being primarily concerned with Division A: the larger corporation gifts.

## Informal Lay-Professional Relations

It is only to those who have had little contact with the social scientific or business world of the last two decades that any explanation need be made as to the central importance of the informal personal relationships in any organization. Paramount in these important relations are those which develop where the lines of formal authority run; and in any situation, as in the Indianapolis Chest, where the channels of authority are ill defined or muddied, the importance of these informal relations is even greater.

It is difficult, frequently, in this area to define with exactitude what is wrong, to marshal the evidence for one's conclusion, or to sense, let alone establish, what it is that underlies the condition discovered. Such analysis is as subtle as it is important, but while it rests to a greater degree on subjective or judgmental processes, these risks must be accepted or the benefits of analysis must be foregone. The presenting symptoms of "something wrong" not only in the Chest, but in the whole professional side, at least, of the "Welfare Community" in Indianapolis are a feeling, widespread in space and enduring through time, of a malaise, an uneasiness, a feeling of insecurity in job tenure, a felt lack of being "appreciated" in the best sense of that term, i.e., of being known and appropriately evaluated, for better or worse.

In every community known to the authors some such feelings obtain for some part of the Welfare Community at some times: breaches of good feeling arise, misunderstandings occur, issues have to be resolved that sometimes cannot be resolved without the separation of the parties involved. Even a "good" welfare community, like a good marriage, is not always free of strife. But something more than these sporadic strains seems to be involved in the Indianapolis situation, though it goes without saying that this is not true for all professionals or all of the time. There is contrary evidence that some professionals "make the grade" and are warmly accepted, and that something does "turn on personalities." But for whatever reason, and with whatever truth, what is going on in Indianapolis has been going on long enough for the belief to have gained wide ground outside Indianapolis (as well as within it) that Indianapolis is a "bad" or "risky" place for the professional to come to work. We are not speaking now of the social work community alone. Parallel beliefs pass current in such other professional groups as the medical, and this convergence of largely independent accounts lends force to the contentions as evidence of something at issue. Put positively, a professional will say he came here because he regarded it as a "challenge," i.e., a test of his skill in establishing himself and enduring in a difficult situation. The challenge is not like that which drives a golfer to try a tough course for the sake of the fun to be had in mastering it; it perhaps resembles more the one which impels a foolishly bold woman to marry a man in order to reform him: she cannot believe that anything lies beyond her powers.

What is really the nature of this challenge? Rumor has it—widely—that Indianapolis is, for the professional, a cold and lonely place to work, that the years have sifted out and ejected from the professional community many of the gifted, the ambitious, the bold and aggressive, the men of principle in its best sense rather than politics in its worst. Rumor has it—widely again —that Indianapolis is peculiarly a place of peremptory and sudden dismissals, a place where there is no protection for the worker (from his fellow-professionals or sponsoring laymen) if any power-group thinks itself offended by a stand on an issue, a place where "it is foolish to stick your neck out for *anything*," a place where mediocrity and only mediocrity (in the professional world) pays and where distinction is suspect. Rumor has it also—and this conforms with the neglect-and-crisis theme of chapter 3— that "Indianapolis is a great place for bringing in a good man to clean up a mess, and then firing him before he can get it cleaned up." It is likewise said—and this again is comfortable with our own independent analysis of "the leadership"—that the power-structure is so vague to the laymen in it, and so capable of sudden shifts, that they themselves do not know what can and cannot be done within it, and that hence they are broken reeds to lean on in any juncture of forces.

Such generalizations as these are not only explicitly made, but probably underlie such comments as the following:

"Indianapolis, where's *that*?" (an informed, and not generally snobbish social scientist).

"I *warned* him . . ." (a highly placed New York social service administrator).

"I've been here thirteen[26] years and I still don't *know* anybody" (a capable, emotionally outgoing, knowledgeable social worker).

"You might make it if you can stay close to —— [one unusual power-figure], but the rest are pretty weak" (a sponsor speaking to a candidate for an important job in Indianapolis).

"That's Indianapolis!" (of a dramatic and sudden firing from a post other than social work).

"Turnover rates here are fantastic" (a social work executive).

In one sense it does not matter whether there is any substance in the generalizations, or in the bitter comment which often expresses them. Well founded or ill, a reputation—a social definition—is hard to live down, and is just as real in its effects if "untrue" as if "true."[27] It is only when it is desired to do something about it that the question as to what the facts are becomes important, and it is only for this reason that we are driven to inquire as to what the underlying situation may really be.

In the first place, just as it is impossible to "indite a whole people" it is naïve to believe that any high-level generalization will hold for all persons and at all times for an entire community.[28] The question has to do with trend and tendency, recurrent incident rather than continuous performance. It might be phrased as a double question, thus: (a) Is there an unusual degree of uneasiness as between laymen and professionals in the Welfare Community (and elsewhere) in Indianapolis? (b) If so, does Indianapolis have any peculiar characteristics that would account (in part, at least) for what is observed?

In the absence of any systematic inter-city survey of opinion, and in the absence of any precise measures of uneasiness or malaise, we are driven back for guidance, if we want it, on two fallible bodies of information: (1) the experience of the authors in communities elsewhere, and more particularly experience in their welfare communities, and (2) the opinions of "selected informants" whom the authors believed likely to be most capable of informed and detached judgment. These informants would necessarily be mostly non-residents of Indianapolis (though they may have lived here) and they come from many professions, although not all are professionals. Some informed local laymen—indeed some "Elder Statesmen"— in the local Welfare Community had detachment and experience, and willingness to report on that experience.

On this—admittedly slim—basis, one would have to say that such evidence as there is does favor a picture of Indianapolis as a somewhat atypical milieu for the professional, especially, but not exclusively, in the social work and social planning fields. In comparison with communities in the East, or even with others in the Midwest, Indianapolis seems to present an unusual relation between laymen and professionals because of the social distance, the mutual distrust, the felt alienation (active or passive) between them. It does seem true on the basis of our extended experience that "they do not understand each other," that the lack of understanding is engendered by and engenders distrust, and that the distrust has even affected and seriously threatened the very process of communication by which understanding might be reached.

As far as lay-professional communication is concerned, we do have more evidence than mere opinion. On the professional side, there is much discussion[29] of "what you can tell your Board," "how you *can* put things," of the fact that "you have to protect your own position" (with or vis-à-vis your most intimate laymen) and of how this can be done, of the folly of "opposing your Board" (in anything, particularly vital matters) and of the certainty of "getting your head chopped off if you do." One of the technically very best (and, locally, most enduring) agency executives explained that he had learned early from another social worker never to commit himself to a view on a matter his Board was considering. A forthright statement, he said, "could lose you your Board just like that" (snapping his fingers). Another unusually well-informed worker said with admiring glee of the head of his agency: "It's a special skill. W —— never sticks his neck out, never puts his head on the block. Of course he can't lift a finger"—to protest what W —— felt to be a serious wrong done another professional. "But the thing is he *knows* it, and that's where the skill comes in: he *copes* with the community. . . . He'll likely stay." Said another, "Of course, you *can* tell them. It's all a matter of time. But you try and tell them too fast and see what happens to you! You lead them, but, oh, g.r.a.d.u.a.l.l.y." (He was recommending the spreading over years of what another worker wanted to establish quickly as initial working agreements with his Board.)

Such problems of timing, of keeping in-group secrets and manipulating "communication" with the out-group, obtain quite generally on both sides, of course, of every lay-professional relation—and indeed, even, of every inter-professional relation. The secrecy, the defensiveness, the attempted mutual exploitation, and the endured mutual distrust attenuate, it seems, in a "good" structure (clearly defined roles and clear and realistic expectations) and with open two-way communication, and they increase in a "bad" structure (badly defined or conflicting roles and unclear or impossible expectations) or under impeded or one-sided communication. While, therefore, the problems are universal, their capacity to defeat concerted action is a matter of "more" or "less"; but the more or less makes a difference, and the conditions that determine whether more or less *are* subject to some control—and, as business experience has shown, often to very profitable control. Judged by such criteria, Indianapolis probably does fall well towards the low end of the scatter of possibilities, as far as the professions are concerned.[30]

It might be well to state explicitly that the relations we are discussing apply only where the "employers" are generally laymen and their employees members of the "employed professions" or semi-professions: social work (mostly), medicine (some small but vital part in hospital administration, public health, etc.), teaching,[31] etc. Having so limited the universe of discourse, and having established (to the satisfaction of the authors, at least) the existence of an important problem, one might next ask what underlies it.

At the most fundamental level, it might safely be said that the political system of Indiana, as embedded in its constitutional law and surrounding practice,[32] accounts for a great deal both of the problem and of the atmosphere in the non-public (i.e., non-governmental) sector of the Welfare Community.

It will probably come as news to very few that the fate and form of this sector, in a city the size of Indianapolis particularly, are intimately bound up with and dependent upon those of the public (i.e., governmental) sector of the same Welfare Community. In the first place, there is an almost inescapable sense in which the program of the "private" sector is a "residual" one: a program that attempts to provide for those goods or against those ills that the ordinary operations of the economy and the government leave unattended. In a formal sense then, the private sector fills an interstitial role between business and government: its formal program is the "something else" desired or "needed." But, even more important than this formal relation is the informal one in which the private sector adapts itself to shadings of quality in the public sector, so that the former attempts to repair what is ill done in the latter. Thus the formal nature of the public program, and the informal variations in the quality of what it does do, substantially affect the private sector's definition of its task and its actual difficulty in performing that task.

There is also another sense in which the two segments of the Welfare Community are intertwined. The professional fraternity by which they are served knows no emotional boundary differentiating public from private sectors. There is, in this respect, no "them" against which to pose "us"; what happens to a co-professional in the public sector happens to one of "our" profession from the viewpoint also of someone in the private sector; a threat to his status is a threat to the status of the whole profession; and a demonstration that peremptory action by authority against a professional goes undefended is a sign of weakness in which the entire profession is involved. Within the profession, moreover, professional "leadership"—the source of interest and morale—knows no boundaries either; and if adequate or promising people cannot be attracted to, retained in, or saved from ejection from one sector, the whole body suffers and not just the sector directly affected. If a part is weak, the whole is weak; and in a cyclically reinforcing sequence it becomes more difficult to attract into the system at any point the strong personnel called for by its very weakness.

What makes a profession strong—indeed what makes it a profession, as against a mere employment—is its capacity through instruments of its own choosing, sanctioned usually by public law, to control within wide measure its own fate. The generally conceded necessity upon which this "right," if granted, rests is that the "right" (i.e., socially desired) practice of the profession can only be determined by professionals; and that the course of its development must therefore be determined (within limits established by law, of course) by the internal logic of the profession. What differs from this practice is, from the professional's viewpoint, termed "non-professional interference." Such "interference" is, in the common vocabulary, "politics"; the most patent and unabashed form of such politics is "patronage." Between external patronage and professionalism only the uneasiest of co-existences is possible.

Now, it is a rare Hoosier who is not positively proud of his state's brand of freewheeling, hard-hitting, intense, and seriously taken politics. Basketball is "the Hoosier madness" for children; the only non-business activity for adults at all comparable in interest aroused, news-space devoted, or enthusiasm expressed is that of politics: local, county, state, or national. And the symbol of victory as well as the operative motor is patronage. Among those rare Hoosiers[33] who do not "point with pride," few would deny the facts; and in any case, such a one would be hard put to it to convince even a casual reader of three years' newspapers that the facts were much other than described. The hurling of charge and counter-charge, the unexplained serial resignations,[34] the firings without hearings of prominent personnel, the promotions, demotions, and dismissals following every change of political incumbent (and in many offices the incumbent may not lawfully succeed himself) all serve to suggest a style of government not ordinarily thought conducive to the retention of top-notch professionals or to the long-term planning which could stabilize expectations at least in the most important respects.[35]

Given, then, "an exposed right flank" for the Welfare Community in the public sector, it might be thought that some compensatory mechanism could be introduced into the private sector to offset, if only partially, the communicated insecurities from the public sector. This indeed is a thinkable policy.

The mechanisms that might sensibly countervail in this situation are essentially of two kinds—paternal and fraternal—and both are needed if either is to be used, unless new dangers to someone's security are to arise.[36] By "paternal relations" as a source of security we wish to point to the type of relation between local power-figures (Donor Leaders, patrons, sponsors) and the professionals, in which the local laymen are in fact sufficiently informed, sufficiently concerned, and sufficiently powerful in effect to "father" the "cause" and its employed senior professionals. This is not the place to spell out the meaning of a fathering relation, but such terms as protecting, fostering, nurturing, stimulating, providing, promoting, understanding, supporting, and advising come naturally enough to mind.[37] By an effective fraternal relation we have in mind, in the first instance, a relation between like professionals, based both on common interests and on shared sentiments—and embodied in and furthered by an organization sufficiently effective to be able to concert action between members and afford protection for them where this is required.[38]

A third possible relation exists but is noted rather as an "ideal,"[39] since it rarely occurs, is difficult to engineer, and depends on characteristics of "the cause" which are not likely to be routinely found in the welfare field of today. This is the sort of paternal-fraternal relation that obtains, only close to the front line usually, between power-figures (senior officers) and men battling in a common cause (their self-preservation) under unusually adverse circumstances. Such a situation sometimes occurs in some agencies, at least briefly, where the devotion for the cause, whatever it is, common to layman and professional, temporarily bridges differences in power, status, interest, or philosophy.

But to return to the practicalities of today, something short of this ideal would go so far to improve existing relations that perhaps the possibility of that "something short" should be entertained first.

The possibility of an adequate and appropriate fathering relation is sharply limited by several of the "facts of life," some more refractory of change than others, which we have reported as characteristic of life in Indianapolis. The relationship is only possible on the side of the "father-figure" where either (a) the leadership is sufficiently united and strong as a whole so that even a relatively weak layman can nevertheless, because of the unity, adequately discharge his sponsoring, protecting functions for the professional and the agency, or (b) the individual "father-figures" are sufficiently powerful, despite or because of disunity in the leadership, that each can adequately defend and run interference for "his own," both against other leaders and any hostile segment of the general public. The only combination, then, fatal to successful sponsoring or "fathering" would seem to be a disunited leadership together with some weakness in the lay-leaders taken severally.

We have already pointed in one chapter (chapter 11) to the lack of unity or concert or coherence in the Indianapolis leadership—so that one of the fatal conditions seems to be present. We have pointed to the nature and discontinuity of attendance at Board meetings in another part of the same chapter. We have, in addition, we think, observed an unusual degree of attachment to the peace-at-nearly-any-price principle which characterizes the lay group in any community: a preference for avoiding issues between members of the intimate in-group, who are likely to remain in that community for life and who are dependent upon one another for many kinds of "favors"—including the "favor" of giving to one another's causes. We have also noted elsewhere (chapter 3) the tendency for problems to be tackled as a series of crises, and for "marginal" people, rather than people from the core-group of power and prestige, to be thrown into a central position in such crises. Such marginal persons, so employed,[40] are not potential "fathers" in the sense we have defined: indeed, by their own excesses and by their reactions to their own marginality and insecurity they are likely to endanger further or render more insecure the very staff they are aiming to aid and defend. So the second fatal condition may be present in sensible measure too.

This combination of local history and circumstance may not pre-empt any reasonable hope for the establishment of adequate relations of paternality and filiation; but certainly an attempt to establish such relations or to improve notably on present ones, would have to take count of these difficulties. Moreover, by circular reinforcement, the very lack of these relations previously has resulted in such feelings of instability, brevity of duration of personnel, policy, or program, fleetingness of tenure, and uncertainty of career-lines, that it may prove difficult to change over to relations which presuppose relatively long periods of growth and flowering. Perhaps the problems of lengthening time perspective, of establishing adequate and reasonable feelings of security, and of supporting and founding upon these adequate paternal-filial relations[41] all have to be solved together or not at all.

As for the establishment of adequate fraternal relations between professionals, the difficulties that stand in its way appear to be of two kinds: the want of an adequate vehicle to further and carry such relationships, and some feeling that, historically, Indianapolis has been, and probably is, inhospitable to them.

We have been unable to trace to any written or indisputable source[42] the recurring statement that not only has Indianapolis been peculiarly averse to all forms of unionization, but that, further, the very birth of some of the more important of its social agencies marked an attempt to create an alternative to the benefits of unionization or a counterweight to the power of it. The only external evidence bearing at all on the contention would be that labor representatives were welcomed into full Board membership in the Chest only relatively recently.[43]

From this early history, and from a more recent history of conflict between the local chapter of the American Association of Social Workers and "the community"[44] (or, at least, the more powerful and vocal segments of it) as well as from the community's "general reputation," many professionals, if not most, have concluded that any attempt to organize an effective fraternity that could act in their interest, as well as symbolize their sentiment, would be met with such hostility in the community or its leadership as to make the game not worth the candle.[45] Such an organization, it is said, would cause more strain than already exists; and, in any case, the general policy of "not sticking your neck out . . . never put your head on the block" militates against the emergence of an organizer.

In the face of this believed-in local hostility to an effective unifying body for professionals, some expedients have been tried and some hopes nurtured without consequent action. For a while during the life of the study a small group of agency executives met informally, compared notes on minor matters, gentled along hopes for parallel action but avoided plans to act in concert, thought about such things as comparative study of professional wage-scales (of their "workers," not themselves)—but generally circled warily rather than engaged. The professional societies were never heard from, and no one—perhaps following the decisive defeat referred to earlier—seemed to look to them as a locus for sentiment or a protector of interest.

In these circumstances it was somehow vaguely hoped that the Health and Welfare Council could find place for these felt necessities, and means for their supply. But again we encounter the typical conflict about roles: the very definition of itself which the Council would seek most to avoid would be one that defined it as a social workers' interest-group or a protector of agency interests. For reasons parallel to those of the Chest itself, it wishes to be covered by the democratic mantle—seeks as far as possible to be[46] "the citizens of Marion County, planning for their health, welfare and recreation." This definition in terms of "forum democracy" makes it impossible for the Council to recognize, let alone give effect via negotiation, bargain, and compromise, to the divergent, and sometimes conflicting, interests at play. Nothing could be more threatening to the new body than an attempt to have it openly discharge some of the responsibilities of the old "Council of Social Agencies," since this would dispel the fog of spurious amity within which conflict of interests is currently enveloped and obscured.[47]

While weak hope is still reposed, therefore, in the Council by some professionals, it seems unrealistic, on the grounds of its most valued self-definition, to assume that it can function as an organ of fraternity among them. Moreover, whatever it may be nominally, it is from the viewpoint of many agency executives, and, realistically, as far as financing is concerned, itself another agency competing for power, attention, publicity, and money with the other agencies. Indeed, more serious than this, for the possibility of its being an organ of unity among professionals, its most prized function —"planning"—and its attempts connected therewith to have itself cast in an "independent" and quasi-judicial role,[48] rule it out as a possible vehicle for the representation of the common interest.

Any improvement, therefore, in the human relations between the professionals in the Welfare Community would seem to depend on the development of organs specialized for that purpose. And the development of such organs, given the actual history and current beliefs about the state of mind of the lay community, would seem to depend on a clear signal of encouragement from the lay leaders.[49]

If our contention is correct, that in the actual situation the emergence of adequate fraternal relations turns upon the emergence of adequate paternal ones, does the latter, in its turn, have definable conditions, or is it a simple matter of seeing the problem in perspective and acting upon that insight? We do not know the answer, but we suspect strongly that the emergence of adequate fathering does turn upon changes in the business community, and particularly in the "top top leadership" or, rather, in its perspective and policy. Such changes imply costs, but they may well also imply returns.

The business community, more particularly the sector of it represented by the larger corporations, does benefit[50] by the existence of the whole philanthropic structure. It benefits in a diffuse sense, in so far as such enterprises, if sensible and successful, add to the aura of sense and success as a community which is the stock-in-trade of the Chamber of Commerce in attracting into the region new economic units and bodies of workers. But in a much more direct sense the business community gains in so far as the philanthropic structure affords that community a relatively low-cost[51] training and proving ground for executives. It represents a series of operations wherein decisions like those that attach to senior executive positions in the corporation may be made without risk to the corporation, and overseen and reviewed by senior corporate opinion as a means of judging executive adequacy. It is a field particularly in which all those qualities can be tested which are the essence of the new managerial task: "man-management," "opinion making," "human engineering," "public relations," etc. It is a commonplace of Industrial Relations to say that "the major problems of industry are the human problems"; but it is worth adding, perhaps, that these are very nearly the entire content of the field of philanthropy.

This is only to say that it is *possible* to use the philanthropy structure as a training and proving ground for executives. What is additionally necessary, if the corporate community is to get such benefit from its money outlay is, of course, that the philanthropic enterprise be so conducted as to give training in the "right" (desired) methods instead of the wrong ones[52]—and, moreover, that it be sufficiently supervised so that the testing function of discriminating poor executive prospects from good ones can be carried out.[53] This requires that those being "tested" (mostly the "promising" but unproved younger executives) have sufficient time and suport to permit the adequate discharge of their test-responsibilities, and that "top top leadership" be at least sufficiently close to the performance that real effort will be put into it because it is subject to fair evaluation.[54]

It is only, then, when the conditions are fair and the supervision close, that the corporate community is likely to reap the benefits of this low-cost testing, and therefore to recover some portion of what is involved in its money outlay. But this clearly requires a higher rate of expenditure of executive time than is currently being made. It requires perhaps that such expenditure, instead of being viewed purely as costs of public relations and philanthropy, be viewed essentially as part of the personnel training or executive development budget.[55] It is a kind of "off-the-job" training and testing plan which spreads over the whole business community the risks of a particularly risky form of on-the-job training and testing. The alternative seems to be to spend the executive time required to do the job "right" and secure the benefits, or to spend some very large proportion of that same time anyway and reap not merely no benefit, but positive damage (and thus further indirect costs). If this view is correct, the sensible decision seems to lie between spending the additional time and effort which will "save" the existing investment or liquidating the effort and getting out of the field altogether. The continuation of a policy of just-not-sufficient effort seems to imply maximum cost in relation to return.[56]

This analysis seems to lead to the argument that what is necessary to ensure the maximum benefit to corporations is also what is the minimum condition for the improvement of human relations in the philanthropic community. This we believe to be the case. In this limited area at least (assuming, of course, that the corporations are to be committed about as deeply money-wise and time-wise as they are) what would enable management to secure such benefits as are to be secured, would also, it seems, provide the conditions within which good human relations could be developed and good management could have a chance.

## EXTERNAL PROBLEMS
### MANPOWER
#### *"Top Top Leadership"*

No problems can be of greater consequence to the Chest's operation than the inter-related ones involved in the recruitment, training, utilization, and retention of manpower—most particularly for the soliciting team. These general problems seem to turn primarily on the recruitment and retention of the "top top leadership" as a necessary, if not a sufficient condition.[57]

This is a problem not only of quantity but of quality: an army with too many generals is almost as badly off as one with too few; and the same goes for corporals and privates, not to mention all the intermediate ranks.

Nor is it, in the case of the Chest—whatever may be true for an army—simply a matter of having the right number in the right rank on the right occasion: there is the prior problem of defining what is right so that it falls within the realm of possibility, i.e., of so adapting demand to what the community can supply that there is at least some possibility of the demand being met.

Actually, this adaptation of demands for manpower to the locally available human resources is less a problem for the Chest alone than a problem for the Welfare Community as a whole. It is logically obvious—as well as concretely observable—that, in any given state of manpower availability,[58] as long as some "generals" are doing "corporals'" jobs (even if those *are* the senior jobs in some trivial agency) so long is it likely that somewhere else some "corporal" must be attempting a "general's" job. Given the community's leadership resources, therefore, at any one time, the question of allotment is ideally one that relates only to the Welfare Community as a whole. It is a parallel to the question that might be asked by a personnel manager if the whole Welfare Community were "his" firm and the whole leadership potential were "his" staff: how to distribute these persons, regardless of "department" (agency) so as to benefit most the firm as a whole.

But the essence of the problem in the philanthropic community is that that community is not so much one welded unit as a series of divided and competitive sub-communities.[59] Even the two "agencies of the agencies," the Chest and the Council, although they might by administrative logic be thought exempt, are in actuality in competition with each other and with all the others for the available manpower in general and, more particularly, for the élite and power-figures who attract, recruit, and tend to retain and restrain the others.

The best solution for each agency, acting separately, is to get the most of the "best" of this élite pool. The best solution for all of them together is to distribute the élite according to the objective requirements of the job to be done in each agency[60] and the relative importance of that job to the common interest. The present situation—essentially a congeries of otherwise unfederated agencies with one common planning and one common fund-raising arm—ensures virtually that neither of these best solutions can be achieved.

Abstractly, of course, a next-best solution[61] would at least be possible if the several agencies treated their common property—the Chest and the Council—as though its protection and preservation had a priority over theirs, in the event of any clash of interests. But this is probably, practically, too much to hope. The "common arms" are also, in virtue of their police powers (over program and budget), "common adversaries," just as government is to the unreflective citizen—and perhaps to the reflective one as well. It seems too much to hope that any agency would willingly cede (if it had the power to do so) say, to the Chest, any one of those very power-figures upon whose weight the agency relies to pry more money out of the Chest. This would be self-abnegation with a vengeance:[62] the turning over to a potentially hostile power of the very weapons on which survival might depend.[63]

Failing voluntary joint action over the whole Welfare Community with reference to lay leadership, the options would seem to be:

(a) To accept the present state of affairs, and to attempt to improve only the utilization of whatever leadership is available in each agency (e.g., the Chest might take what it has or can, by competition, get from someone else, and "make the best of it").

(b) To force (via concerted or parallel action in the donor community) the rationalization of the distribution of leadership.

(c) So to increase the number of leaders available at each level that, in this condition of superabundance, no serious problem of distribution would really arise.[64]

Although there is much evidence to show that in general and in Indianapolis the leadership pool is larger than is supposed by prominent laymen,[65] there is no reason to think that it is by any means unlimited, or, indeed, sufficiently large to make the question of distribution unimportant—particularly with reference to upper echelon leaders, most particularly "Elder Statesmen." The third possibility listed is therefore a step in mitigation of the problem rather than a solution. The first possibility is also in reality only a step in mitigation and a relatively minor one at that. The major problems of the Welfare Community, or even of its philanthropic subcommunity, cannot be solved or carried any appreciable way towards solution by better (more efficient) utilization of leaders *within* agencies.[66]

This leaves us with suggestion two—the settling of the leadership distribution problem by the Donor Leaders themselves, acting in concert or upon disinterested advice—as the only serious proposal that seems to have practical hope of making any substantial difference. This possibility should be left open for further consideration, at this point, until we have examined other questions that might shed light on the desirability of a donor organization to perform other tasks as well. Such questions will have to be considered in this and the following chapter.

It is time perhaps to return to a hidden assumption underlying the argument that what is desirable (and actually desired, as evidenced in the statements of Donor Leaders) is a best distribution of the whole community's available "top top leadership" over the entire private sector of the Welfare Community's operations. We spoke of the assignment of a "top top leader" to the highest job in some trivial agency as a violation of this principle. The hidden assumption then is that judgments can be made as to which agencies or tasks (and, thereby, agencies) are important or trivial; indeed, that a hierarchy of importance of various welfare jobs, in the private sector we are talking about, can be determined. Many people, both lay and professional, woud be found to dispute this view. They would argue that no one is sufficiently wise to make such decisions for a group, and that attachment to this cause or that, willingness to labor in one agency rather than another, is a private matter, a matter of impulse or taste, and hence best left to the competition of appeals on one side and the individual's own defences and resistances or tendencies to succumb on the other.

This view is difficult to dispute. There is sufficient confusion about what ought to be done, uncertainty about what is being done, and reasonable doubt about the relation between what people are doing and the net social result of all this effort, that lots of room for difference of opinion exists, and the expert is not made who can do much more than favor one set of prejudices (his own or his profession's) as against another.[67] It should merely be noted that if this—very respectable—argument is accepted in reference to the logic of leadership distribution, it must, by the same logic, be accepted for "planning," and "financing," i.e., it not only undercuts the logic on which the Health and Welfare Council "planning" proceeds,[68] but it undercuts the logic upon which the present Chest is founded.[69]

The fact is, of course, that implicit judgments of the value of various agencies or programs are already being made either by individuals acting alone, or, much more important, by small cliques or groups of intimates in the informal setting of club or chance business encounter. Shared opinion is thus being formed anyway, and partial consensuses, ill or well founded, stable or unstable, are being achieved. The practical question, therefore, is less whether or not to have such evaluations of agencies and programs but rather whether to make the procedure open, systematic, representative, and disinterested[70] (as far as unexamined bias in favor of any one agency is concerned). What emerges may well be a "pooling of prejudices," initially, and a pooling of judgments later; but again the practical question is whether or not indeed there can be a better solution, in the present state of knowledge.[71]

In any case, it is obvious that any consensus reached by the Donor Leaders as to the best distribution of leadership would not have the binding effect of law, but only the same type of pressure-to-conform as is involved with the setting of standards (or even of goals) on the financial side. We have pointed out earlier that these pressures are very real, and do operate to a great extent to reduce the voluntary element in giving. We shall not argue here for or against their legitimacy—or desirability—but only, and much more simply, that there is no evident reason for admitting a given degree of quasi-coercion with reference to money-giving and refusing legitimacy to methods of the same kind with reference to the giving of time, skills, and prestige. Indeed, since the effectiveness of the first is bound up in actuality with the second, it seems idle to attempt the setting of money standards without making like provision for the rationalization of the leadership distribution on which the binding effect of the money standards depends.[72]

It should be added that two other opinions bearing on the solution of the leadership problem pass current among the Donor Leaders and Leading Donors in the community. One contention is that the emergence of a "United Fund"[73] would enable such economies in the use of manpower that the problem of distribution of leadership would cease to be serious. This argument will have to be dealt with in its place (chapter 13) but evidence for the contention is lacking; informed persons say whatever economy there is does not apply to the élite group, and hence the argument need not detain us here. The second contention is that the emergence of a "United Fund" would tend to bring back into activity those "top top leaders" whose absence from the current philanthropic scene was noted in chapters 10 and 11. This may be taken, we believe, as a serious argument (and it will have to be dealt with in those terms in chapter 13) but we find it hard to believe that, even with the emergence of a super-federation and the return of some of the quasi-retired leadership, the problem of distributing what is available would be sensibly solved. That problem still requires direct attention, in terms of either the alternatives posed herein or others that might be thought of.

## Middle-Range Leadership

The first condition for the creation and preservation of an adequate middle-range leadership is, of course, the establishment of an attracting and sustaining core in the shape of an adequately selected and enduring "top top leadership."

Beyond this, as we believe, indispensable condition, lie all the problems involved with recruiting, training, rewarding, and retaining which seem to us in only very minor respects peculiar to the philanthropic organization or, indeed, to the broader field of voluntary associations. In so far as these are not peculiar to the field of fundraising—or indeed to the field of the voluntary associations—we deem it best to leave the discussion of these problems to the initiative of the reader, who may learn what he does not already know from any good text on man-management or industrial relations.[74]

We shall touch upon a few of these "peculiarities." But the major ones that are ascribed in common discourse are predicated upon the assumption that things must be very different as between philanthropy and business (or factory) because "philanthropy is *voluntary* and business is not." This exaggeration of the actual differences rests upon a double error. Philanthropy is not nearly so "voluntary" as the layman would wish to think; business and other work organizations are a great deal more "voluntary" than is commonly believed. The first statement is, we hope, amply attested by this book and by other studies.[75] The second statement is attested by the whole Industrial Relations literature of the last decade, which shows how, within a formal structure of authority and a wage-system that supposedly controls incentives, an informal social system based upon the common aims and tastes of the rank and file determines or substantially conditions the productive and counter-productive behavior actually exhibited.

The peculiarities which do appear in the MOPS fundraising field turn, despite the caution enjoined above, on *some* difference between business and philanthropy, more particularly in degree of voluntariness, but most chiefly in the necessity laid upon each to preserve its own myth. It would probably be even more demoralizing, for instance, to recognize fully the play element in business than to acknowledge fully the coercive element in "voluntary" association activity. "Everybody knows" these elements are there, but this is something short of full recognition. Disproof of the supporting facts for a myth rarely destroys the myth as long as it has social utility: one nods—and forgets.

Since MOPS fundraising must operate with some greater degree of "voluntariness," and since, more particularly, an air of great voluntariness must be preserved, the problem of how to associate with this rewards for adequate behavior and sanctions upon improper or inadequate behavior must be given consideration. We do not know as much as we might wish, in detail, as to what the rewards to the middle-range leadership or rank and file for adequate participation are.[76] We must, moreover, distinguish between those rewards which people are likely to be conscious of *and* admit to, on one side, and, on the other, those they may be unaware of or unwilling to admit.

There are doubtless a great many rewards even within the range of those which volunteers have in consciousness and regard as admissible. We know of very little direct evidence on this point, although a study by David Sills[77] suggests something. It reports on the activities singled out by volunteers for the Polio Fund "which gave them the greatest satisfaction." In order of importance he lists these as: making the goal; organizing; "fundraising as fun." It is obvious that his respondents are pointing to *intrinsic* satisfactions, the chief of which lies in the victory itself, the second of which lies in the preparatory part-victory of "organizing," and the last of which is almost purely social—or perhaps sociable—something that in the words of the author comes from "being involved in an activity which has acquired some of the character of a folk festival." Exploit and sociality, then, cover this gamut of satisfactions. The author and the author's informants are quick to contrast, however, the satisfactions possible in this kind of campaign from those possible in a more professionalized, less spontaneous, more planned, "federated" campaign.

Other studies as well as our own would also point for MOPS fundraising, at any rate, to an order of motives *extrinsic* to the campaign itself as furnishing a major if not the principal basis for a system of rewards and sanctions.[78] These extrinsic sanctions mean very simply that (regardless of any intrinsic satisfactions to be had out of "campaigning") success or failure, adequate or inadequate performance in the campaign is (or may be[79]) rewarded or punished with gains or losses in the larger economic or social system.[80] For this reward system to operate effectively (i.e., with adequate coercive power) the social and economic systems must be sufficiently closely meshed with the Welfare Community's own rank system that performance at a given level in either is taken as at least *prima facie* evidence of capacity to perform at a like level in the other.

This possibility of mutual recognition (in the diplomatic sense) seems to imply not only the closeness to the philanthropic operation of the community's power *and* social élites[81] but, in addition, a recognized hierarchy in the Welfare Community parallel to that of the power and social hierarchy of the business community. It requires, moreover, in the philanthropic community sufficient continuity of tradition, sufficient stability in status-definition, sufficient constancy in role-expectation, and sufficient clarity as to promotion-conditions to make it possible for performances in philanthropy to be recognized and rewarded elsewhere, and, conversely, for status elsewhere to be adequately recognized and rewarded in the philanthropic community.

Whatever else these conditions may imply for Chest and community action, it is obvious that they require the clear establishment of long-term policy—perhaps for as far as twenty years ahead—and the abandonment of the freedom to carpenter together every year a new policy to cope with the crisis produced by the last carpentry. This calls, doubtless, for some limitation on the spontaneity or abandon which the crisis-to-crisis form of management permits.

But who can make such changes? And who can secure agreement to and also adequately symbolize the continuity and steadfastness upon which all else depends? Evidently, the most stable element in the community, the representatives of those families who have the power and whose fates are sufficiently bound up with that of Indianapolis, can most easily do what is required: secure the settlement of long-range policy and symbolize the promise of its preservation and protection.

If that leadership (mostly birth élite) is not "available" in Indianapolis, or if it will not join with the leadership representing the newer national corporations (most mobile élite), then, if the fact is known and frankly recognized, perhaps some adaptation, albeit a more precarious one, *might* be achieved. Long-term policy might be settled, and machinery devised to pass on the "tradition"[82] thus born, from incumbent to incumbent, as members of the mobile élite moved through the managerial positions to which they had been assigned. It is difficult to doubt that this would be very much second choice, since the right combination of stable and conservative elements with mobile and experimentally inclined ones probably best provides the continuity in essentials and flexibility in accidentals or particulars that makes for a stable but lively institution. This seems to be the hallmark of several successful Chests.[83]

Another possibility, however, that should not be overlooked rests upon the development of the Donors' Association, touched upon already in this chapter and more fully treated in chapter 13. The belief is widespread in the community that the "top top leadership" has, as well as the virtues of conservatism, one of its vices—timidity—and that it "does not dare to be associated with something that might fail." "It wants to be awfully sure of success—*beforehand*." One of the supporting arguments for the United Fund is based upon this belief, i.e., upon the fact that the Chest is reputed to be "a failing organization," upon the belief in the invincibility of a United Fund, and upon the belief that "the missing leaders" could be attracted back to a failure-proof cause—and only to such a cause. If the assumptions about the attitude of the "top top leadership" are well founded, but if a United Fund should seem to be undesirable on other grounds, or impossible, there remains the possibility that this leadership might be attracted into an assumption of responsibility for a Donors' Association, and that that association, so led, might induce in the Welfare Community the order and stability that it, itself, requires for "success"—by its own definition or that of the Donor Leaders.

The discussion so far may well seem to have been one-sided in so far as it points to requisite changes in leadership, i.e., the lay leadership, if certain changes in the philanthropic community are to be effectuated, without having inquired, as yet, into the corresponding changes[84] required in the professional staff. That such changes would be required is difficult to doubt if a smooth[85] fit of laymen to professionals is to be sought.

The "care and feeding of lay leaders" is just as specialized an art on the professional side as the "care and feeding of professionals" is on the lay side. And, to the degree that it is an art, it is impossible to put rules for its pursuit on paper. It does, however, require for its successful implementation a set of minimum conditions that can, at least, be pointed to. No matter how vague the term may be, one obvious indispensable condition for the smooth fit postulated, is great similarity of "caliber" between the opposite numbers in the lay and professional hierarchies. We are not speaking of an identity of skills, but an identity of felt capacities or of the quality of type-performances. Lay leader and professional at each level must—despite differences in power or, even, of social status—be able sufficiently to respect each other that there is little or no room for the corroding contempt (often mutual) expressed in such phrases as:

"They're just a bunch of social dreamers. . . ."

"I wouldn't want one of them in *my* business. . . ."

"They don't know where they're going or what they're doing. No one over there does."

"Aren't they, likely, people who couldn't earn a living any other way?"

Whatever discrepancies in caliber exist locally—or seem to exist—between lay and professional leaders are by no means, of course, one-sided. Nor can it be assumed, even where the discrepancy seems to run in favor of the layman, that such discrepancies would be general and in the same direction in a comparison between the profession as a whole and the laity as a whole. Indeed the very selection by laymen of lower-caliber professionals—where it occurs—raises questions about the selecting group similar to those raised about a top executive who chooses only "weaker" men to surround him, unless there is no better choice.[86]

Another respect, at least, in which something closer to equality of capacity would be desirable for lay-professional fit, would be in terms of the skills that go into "social engineering," and, most particularly, of the knowledge upon which such engineering must be based. This knowledge is of two kinds: "acquaintance with" and "knowledge about"—the kind of knowledge that accrues to a man as a consequence of living in and being a vital part of a community for an extended period, and the kind of knowledge that accrues from the detached, accurate observation of it and similar communities; knowledge from the inside and knowledge from the outside; the knowledge that is apt to adhere to the fixed and the knowledge that is generally acquired by the mobile; the knowledge of the intimate and the knowledge of the stranger. These two types of knowledge tend to correct and supplement each another, and to provide against, in the layman, limited perspective due to over-involvement, and, in the professional, limited perspective due to superficiality of exposure. In Indianapolis, we were struck by what seemed to us an extraordinarily limited amount of such knowledge on both sides;[87] but particularly on the professional side were we struck by the absence of any great interest in or any systematic methods for assessing who's who and what's what.

Greater equality between layman and professional may also be desirable in the matter of "assurance," at least the assurance each has that "he knows his own business." With due allowance for frequent exceptions,[88] one gets the impression that in general a group of laymen, confident because they know *at least* their own business, confront a group of professionals, less confident because less certain that they know theirs. Part of the difference has some objective foundation in that business is older, more institutionalized, and therefore better prepared to accept its own ignorances and errors than is social work. But part is due to the respective exposures of businessmen and social workers: the former, largely exposed to other "practical" men who confirm certainties; the latter, exposed at least a little to social scientists who heighten doubts. What can be done to dispel this discrepancy in "assurance," where it rests upon illusion, or to cope with it where it rests upon unavoidable uncertainties is not known. But that this is one of the lay-professional differences that increase the sense of alienation between the parties is inferable from a great deal of behavior during meetings and the informal talk that follows. Perhaps mere recognition of the problem and its sources—as against present tendency to ascribe the difference to "personality"—may be of some help.

It would be possible to continue indefinitely listing conditions for the smoother fit—in the sense defined—of layman to professional and professional to layman. Perhaps enough has been said, however, to indicate the desirability of making this problem a matter of continuing study in any well-run philanthropic enterprise.

It is time to turn from the problems of manpower to problems of the message which the manpower is to carry.[88a]

## THE MESSAGE

### The Value Problem

As may be abundantly evident from chapter 5 and other chapters, the "values," or, in another vocabulary, "ideals," that the Chest "stands for," proposes to further, or even aims to move towards, are by no means clear in the first place; nor are they, where clarity spottily appears, consistent, let alone systematic, in the second. This is one problem, and it calls for clarification of values.

As will also be evident from many chapters, especially, perhaps, chapters 8 and 9, the means that are suitable for the securing of given ends have been by no means aptly selected, nor, again, thought through as to consistency, let alone system. This judgment applies with special force, perhaps, to standards, which presumably epitomize whatever it is that the Chest proposes as an alternative to what it claims would otherwise be a fundraising chaos.[89] This is a second problem, and it calls for intellectual or logical clarification.[90]

Having named the problems, it is difficult to say what can be done about them unless or until the Chest has decided upon and defined its own fundamental character—which is a larger problem that has pragmatic as well as ideal dimensions. To put what we have observed as bluntly and as clearly as possible, it is difficult to decide from behavior and speech whether the Chest[91] conceives itself fundamentally as an alien body at covert war with "its" community or as an instrument for the formation, reformation, and expression of "community will" (as it prefers to be defined for public relations purposes).[92]

Bound up with the definition of the Chest as an alien body warring[93] upon the community, are those definitions and behaviors which allow, or rather encourage, the maximization of the warlike advantages of secrecy, deceit, and surprise, and the massing against public opinion of such force, via control, if possible, of the mass media of communication,[94] that not only active opposition but even critical analysis may be overwhelmed. The "overcoming of resistance"[95] is a principal and often clearly stated objective. To it are dedicated a variety of manoeuvres, a planned program of successive assaults upon opposition or apathy or even critical judgment, and, in some quite successful Chests, an intelligence section, ironically called a "research department," using the same methods of discovering and working upon and through "sympathizers" in the enemy stronghold as any practised utilizer of the fifth column principle would recommend.[96]

As against this "otherly" and warlike definition, there occurs and recurs, both in the public relations literature and in the serious discussion of policy, a more "brotherly" and peaceful set of themes, parallel to those which permit the Health and Welfare Council to define itself as nothing more than "the citizens of Marion County, planning. . . ." This thought and action moves in terms of "fair shares," "report to fair shareholders," "partnership in . . ."—in short, in terms of concord, amity, and consent, and of rational, open, and concerted voluntary effort in a common cause.

It would be overly cynical to infer that the talk in the second vocabulary is mere cover for action in terms of the first. What is observable, in many cases, is not mere talk, but dedicated action based now on one set of premises, now on the other, and sometimes both at once.[97]

It would be overly simple, overly "intolerant of ambiguity," and perhaps morally over-demanding to suggest that the Chest must resolve this question of its fundamental definition or its basic relation to the community in either-or, black-or-white terms. All institutions, professions, and groups (and perhaps all individuals) participate in similar ambiguities: they are in one sense in and a part of the society and their fate is reciprocally bound up with that of the whole; and, simultaneously, they are against and in some sense outside it, and their advantage is bound up with some correlative disadvantage for the whole.

The problem for the Chest, once the inevitability of some ambiguity of definition and some consequent variation in behavior is accepted, is partly a matter of deciding more clearly where it stands, and then evolving a philosophy that explains and justifies that stand, and one to which subsequent choices of message and action can be related. When we say that this is the problem for the Chest, we have pragmatic rather than (or, as well as) moral considerations[98] in mind. Whatever definition is arrived at would presumably set limits at least upon "otherhood" in the name of sufficient "brotherhood" to preserve the Chest and the community; and, simultaneously, set bounds to "brotherhood" for the sake of sufficient "otherhood" to get the task accomplished.

If the self-definition finally agreed upon should be well towards the bellicose-exploitative end of the continuum of possibilities,[99] perhaps the Chest's most urgent problem would be to distinguish the "in-group" (or the series of relatively "inner" groups) from the "out-group" (or the series of relatively "outer" groups). To the degree that the warlike element is involved, the definition of friend or enemy, and the principle of discrimination between them, become imperative. Bound up with this, as in any other warlike operation, is the problem of "security." Are there things that only the staff may know if the campaign is to be conducted with maximum effect in terms of "obstacles overcome" and "resistances broken down"? Are there things that only the executive committee of the Board may know? The Board? The soliciting command? The solicitors themselves? Leaving aside the mere withholding of information ("classification" of secret material), who may legitimately be deceived in reference to what? These are practical questions and, if effectiveness is to be achieved and confusion is to be minimized, rules of warfare must be worked out with various degrees of in-ness and out-ness, friendship and enmity, defined as clearly as possible.[100] Warfare on other terms is nearly as hard on one's own troops as on the enemy.

If, on the other hand, self-definition leads to some greater approximation to the pacific-cooperative end of the spectrum, it would seem necessary to forego certain behaviors, certain basic orientations, certain advantages, and to institute others adapted to a more peaceful and civil social state. For example, if consensus is to be aimed at and accepted, rather than submission to a prearranged plan of staff or staff and in-group, then the conference rather than the pep-rally, the exchange of views rather than the propaganda deluge, two-way communication rather than one-way harangue, would seem to be the methods indicated.[101]

Posed in dynamic terms the problem is very like that of moving from war to peace, or of gradually "normalizing" relations[102] in the international sphere. It involves settling "destination," and speed and method of transition.

The mode of settling or resolving the value-conflicts pointed to in chapter 5, and the probable nature of the settlement finally arrived at, turn on what we have been discussing as the primary problem of basic orientation. If the warlike definition is accepted, then the key to success probably lies in the direction of getting rid of personnel, lay and professional, whose ethical system or habitual means of behavior incline them in a more pacific direction.[103] If the more pacific definition is accepted, at least as a real aim, it then becomes necessary, by definition, not to get rid of anyone, but to bring differences of opinion, conflicts of value, questions of philosophy and high policy, as much as possible, as clearly as possible, and as frequently as profitable, into the open for discussion, airing, clarification and, from time to time, dynamic resolution. The commitment is to a process rather than a result, the process of reaching consensus by relatively "democratic" means.

This is not the place to spell out the nature of the process, or the conditions requisite to it. Of course it calls for special lay and staff skills, but not of such a character as are not ordinarily available, or of such a cost as to be prohibitive. The difficulty here, as elsewhere, is rather at the level of commitment to the ends, than implementation or the finding and use of appropriate means. Anyone who has practised any relatively non-directive individual or group therapy, anyone who has learned how to lead a relatively free discussion, any educator—as against indoctrinator—knows what is meant, and what is requisite, and what are the aids and obstacles to such achievement.

It may or may not be warranted to assume that the decision in Indianapolis will go in the direction of "peace." There may be no decision whatever, or the decision may lie in the direction of making better (i.e., more effective) war. In the first case, the study is locally abortive, and further discussion of what might be done is unnecessary, since the skills necessary to the pursuit of a mild war of opportunity seem already well developed and in place. In the second case—the "better war" case—the authors are not sufficiently competent in the strategies of deceit to make their opinions worth recording, but any manual from Machiavelli, through Clausewitz to Dale Carnegie or Hitler, will furnish abundant suggestions.

Assuming, however, that the resolution in the pacific direction will actually be taken, the discussion of intellectual clarification falls into place.

### Intellectual or Logical Clarification

Perhaps enough has been said in chapter 8 on the problems involved in standard-setting, and it remains here chiefly to add a word on the importance of the procedure.

In a sense—as we suggested earlier in this chapter—"standards" epitomize what the Chest (or similar unified fundraising) has to "sell." It is true that the Chest also recommends itself on some economy[104] in fundraising, and on some supervision of expenditures (auditing), and on some allocation procedure in reference to what has been got (budgeting), or is to be got (pre-campaign budgeting). These are, doubtless, gains from the donors' viewpoint, although auditing could easily be supervised by another body (e.g., the Council or a Donors' Association) and budgeting is weak, and, in the absence of either thoughtful planning or genuine free competition, can hardly be very meaningful.

Since unified or federated fundraising divorces the donor still further from the ultimate beneficiary (and, therefore, from one potent source of satisfaction), and since it demands a curb on impulse and the substitution therefor of habit, and since it necessarily confounds in one appeal many appeals that separately would be appealing to many different persons but *en goulash* are appealing to few—it must, to be viable, offer some very definite advantage to offset these disadvantages, some gain to compensate these losses.

Observation suggests that it does offer two notable compensations. One is sheer size alone: given the American love of bigness, this by itself is largely, if not altogether, in favor of the unified fundraising unit as against any of its constituent units. It is impossible to talk to lay fundraisers without being struck by the attraction that such bigness has for them: the very word "millions" preceded by a one- or two-place figure has a magic ring that "thousands" can never recapture; "50 Red Feather agencies" is exciting talk, and 150 would be more so. So the fact of size and the feeling of power and the sense of priviness to large affairs all compensate for the losses of intimacy, detailed control, and relative effortlessness of pre-unification fundraising.

But the ego-expansions which bigness permits are frequently not sufficient sustenance in times of doubt and difficulty. The donors, and lay and professional fundraisers alike, fall back on the belief that the unified fundraising unit permits the introduction of *rationality*, reasonableness or equity, into giving. Once secure in this belief, the "fun" elements in campaigning are felt to be permissible and the introduction of emotionality into subordinate appeals is felt to be justified and legitimized. Shake this belief, however, and the attempted fun is felt to be flat—"It's hard to get the show off the ground"—and the emotionality in the appeal, dangerous.

In an important sense, therefore, rationality *is* what the Chest has to sell, and very nearly all that it has to sell distinctively. Such rationality—reasoning and reasonableness—is what is presumptively embodied in the "standards," and, if clearly defined and sensibly arrived at (in terms of the logic embodied in them and the social processes by which they are reached), they may be the way to the social solidarity that the Chest requires, as well as a symptom or symbol of it. Standards should, then, on the argument advanced so far, be focal in the Chest message; and appropriate social procedures for reaching them and making them effective should be focal in the Chest's operation.[105]

Enough has been said in chapter 8 on the substantive questions involved in standard-setting. Enough has also been said about consensus-seeking procedures in the earlier part of this chapter. The successive steps would seem to be:

(a) The setting of goals by some such rationalized methods as chapter 6 suggests—or, at least, the setting of goals adapted to local circumstances in the context of the kind of knowledge chapter 6 provides.

(b) Some negotiated or otherwise reasonably settled decision as to the proportionate "shares" for the corporate and non-corporate gift.[106]

(c) Some setting of standards for corporate gifts, ideally perhaps on the basis of net cost of gift in relation to post-tax, post-gift net income.[107]

(d) Some similar setting of standards for individual gifts (no matter what the individual's occupation and regardless of place of collection), again, ideally, on the basis of net cost of gift in relation to post-tax, post-gift net income.

Although, as earlier chapters will have suggested, there are some moderately complex technical problems involved in the analysis and setting of standards, they hardly seem to be of such a kind as would be beyond the powers of a decently competent statistician in the employ of the Chest or of a Donors' Association. What seems to be required beyond this technical sufficiency, is a simple, direct, forthright system, free of equivocations and hidden gimmicks, that could not so much be "sold" as agreed to by reasonable and well-disposed men as the least evil of all possible modes of settlement. More than this they ought not, perhaps, to request; and of the unreasonable or ill-disposed nothing can be expected that does not at the same time involve the re-introduction of deceit and disorder into what one asks of one's friends.[108]

## FEEDBACK

Co-ordinate with the problems of value-clarification and logical clarification, and in part a result of those confusions, is the problem of providing systematic information to the Chest as to the consequences of what it *has* done. The pervasive ignorance of the consequences of acts already undertaken not only feeds back into the pre-existing confusion, but renders the new action uncertain in feeling, and spur-of-the-moment in appearance.

At the lowest level of information, a Chest, of course, needs adequate accounting procedures so that, at a minimum, it may know where it is financially, i.e., with respect to current assets and liabilities. As far as we know, the Indianapolis Chest maintains such records so that the information is ultimately, if not promptly, available. Its enviable ratio of money collected to pledges made[109] suggests efficiency in this respect.

With respect to any level above this lowest one, however, and whether for past years or for the current one, it seems exceedingly difficult to get the simplest summary statistics with reliability, consistency, or accuracy. Various documents for the same year name various sums for key statistics, to the point where staff feel "it's really hopeless to try and find out" even such elementary matters as the amount actually pledged in a given division.[110] The reasons for this situation are not fully understood, and some of them may be related to insufficient staff and inadequate equipment. But deeper than this, and harder to cure via more generous budgeting for administration, seems to be a basic attitude bordering on contempt towards facts, data, records, and record-keeping.[111] Viewing themselves as "men of action," dealing in large affairs under high pressure, and with little time for reflection or analysis—except for such little as is necessary further to feed the propaganda machine—they have a tendency to deprecate the procedures necessary to ensure that the action is well founded.[112] There is further reinforcement for this attitude in the belief that the information may not really be "necessary," i.e., that "rough" information will do, or even that, in an organization bent on "making a case," the less exactly known the facts are, the easier conscientious case-building is.

To some extent, the professional staff does seem to be encouraged in this cavalier treatment of data by its laymen: negatively by laymen who do not insist on the same standards of accuracy here as they do in their own business; positively by those who over-emphasize the importance of the ratio of administrative costs to "product."[113] In any case, this uncertainty as to even "second order facts,"[114] while it permits flexibility of argument, adds to the feeling so often expressed by laymen: "You don't know *the facts* over there" or "You can't get to the bottom of anything—it's all up in the air."

While we believe that the primary problem[115] here is the *attitude* towards facts, the questions of familiarity with assemblage of fact, and reporting and competence in the collection of data are also involved. The competence required is of a relatively low order, but does include familiarity with economical, accurate, prompt, and efficient data-processing, some imaginativeness in finding ways to make data "tell their story," and sufficient detachment to make the data tell their actual and legitimate story rather than the story that administrative exigencies require at the moment. Even at this low level of reporting, the employment of a specialist,[116] a person familiar with statistics, may be required.

Beyond this level lies a whole series of neglected possibilities. Taking advantage of them, while not necessary to its day-by-day operation, would nevertheless be of immense benefit to the Chest, even if it merely wishes to employ its resources to best advantage. The level of research indicated here is the level of "market research": the attempt to find out systematically and with sufficient practical accuracy what "customers" (i.e., donors) want or can be brought to "buy." No one in the Chest knows whether "cultivation" "pays,"[117] or who reads what of its propaganda, or what effect on giving the various "lines" adopted have. A great deal of such evidence could have been easily amassed at any point without interfering with the Chest's operational necessities and at no great cost, by any person trained in experimental methods and sufficiently supported morally to ensure that they were adhered to. Indeed in the given state of ignorance and need for information, the Chest's complex operations should afford a field of excitement, interest, and challenge for a market research man or an experimental sociologist for many years to come. Money-raising will always remain an art rather than a science, but so guided and informed it might come eventually to resemble the art of the medical man rather than the medicine man.

We do not think that more abstract research is a function to be located with and to be made a charge upon a Chest (or other MOPS fundraising organization).[118] It is the proper task and inevitable fate of such an organization to be partisan, and the object of its research department is to enable it to be partisan with greater intelligence and effect. The detachment and the long-term view required for basic research in philanthropy are more reasonably to be expected in a university, perhaps in an Institute for Philanthropic Research, specially dedicated, within the university, to that end.[119] But the question of sufficient feedback to allow the Chest to operate, with security for its present position and hope for its future, deserves co-ordinate interest with the other considerations raised in this chapter.

# 13. What Might Be Done:
# Further Unification

ONE OF THE currently suggested remedies for what is widely felt to be the unduly disorderly and disorganized state of fundraising,[1] particularly MOPS fundraising, lies in the direction of further "unification." But unification *of* what? And *for* what? In the clamor of battle and the heat of urgency, neither question seems to have received the attention it deserves.

It is obvious, not only from our own interviews, but from the literature of the whole discussion, and the national movement that seems to bear it along and be borne by it, that unification is sought by the thoughtful not for its own sake, but for the sake either of orderly, intelligent, integrated, inexpensive *fundraising* or of greater order, intelligence, integration, and economy in *giving*—or both.

It is not to be thought—though it widely is—that these amount to the same thing, or that the achievement of the one is likely automatically to call out the other. Quite the contrary. The integration of fundraising as it proceeds could, failing special caution, result in less intelligent, less integrated, eventually more costly giving as a fractionated donor-aggregate confronted a monolithic—but, in its own terms, well-organized—unified soliciting organization.[2] And it may be—though the risks are smaller—that integration of giving could cause disorder among soliciting bodies. The important thing here, in any case, is that we have two problems and not one, and that it does not follow logically, nor seem actually likely, that the solution of one problem would help solve the other. We must ask separate questions regarding the unification of the solicitors and the unification of solicitees. By "solicitors" we mean here any MOPS or similar fundraising organization; by "solicitees," the donor-aggregate. Later, we may be able to bring the two problems together.[3] In the meantime, we shall discuss them separately, looking first at length into the problems of unified fundraising, and then into those of unified giving.

## UNIFICATION AMONG SOLICITORS

### What is Unified Fundraising?

By "unified fundraising" we mean *some joint endeavor by some agencies to raise together, from all or some defined part of the donor-aggregate, some part of the monies they expend.* Before such a definition means very much,[4] unhappily, it is necessary to specify more exactly (once we have defined what an "agency" is): (*a*) what agencies are relevant to the discussion; (*b*) what parts of the agency expenditure are in question; (*c*) what joint endeavors are under consideration; (*d*) what part of the donor-aggregate is to be confronted by unified solicitation. We shall discuss these questions serially.

*What is an agency?* There is probably no point at all in seeking an abstract definition for the term "agency", since there is little agreement on what it means,[5] and the important thing at this juncture is simply to be clear as to what kinds of organizations we are talking about. We have attempted to "point to," rather than define, what is being talked about in the accompanying diagram. If we had to state what an agency "is," *for the purposes of this discussion,* we might specify:

  . . . a formal organization . . .
  . . . not-for-profit (and not in the service of for-profit organizations). . .
  . . . secular . . .
  . . . non-government . . .
  . . . not a formal educational body . . .
  . . . nor one serving primarily the economic, political or sociality interests of its members.

*Which agencies, monies, activities, and persons may be involved?* Any agency not able or willing to support itself wholly by "sales," and therefore in need of "gifts,"[6] is potentially subject to consideration in any scheme of unified fundraising.[7] The shaded area in the accompanying diagram shows what is usually included under this heading. These potentially unifiable agencies include, curiously enough, some "agencies" that are themselves unified fundraising bodies; and, indeed, the finally most inclusive body may represent a unification of a unification of a unification.[8] One of the problems—to which we shall have to return later—that seems to perplex local wisdom in Indianapolis, as elsewhere, is whether or not the highest-level unifying body should consist only of lower-level unifying bodies, or only of agencies excluding these, or of both.

Even this distinction—between pre-existing fundraising unification and "other agencies"—while clear, does not probe to the heart of the matter. What is to be regarded as the one or the other does not depend on size, variety of function, or anything except historic accident and present administrative arrangement. What is presently defined as a unified fundraising unit, for example, the Jewish Welfare Federation, would be simply the fiscal department of an agency, if the underlying Jewish social agencies were to be combined into one agency. What is presently defined as a single agency, for example, the Red Cross, would itself be a unified fundraising body if its several functions such as military service and disaster relief were separated under independent Boards and administrations. When it is recalled, from chapters 2 and 4, that agencies have exhibited both fission and fusion, have

## Total Society

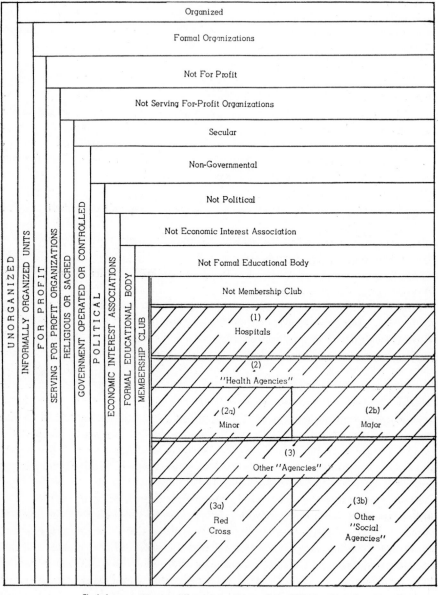

Shaded area is the area of "potential unification" (for MOPS fundraising)

SUBDIVISION OF TOTAL SOCIETY TO LOCATE "AGENCIES" SUBJECT TO
FUNDRAISING UNIFICATION

both spawned new agencies to carry on some separable function and incorporated old agencies, it is clear that the whole problem of fundraising unification depends on the present non-rational, accidental division of functions into arbitrary units called "agencies." It is only on the basis of taking this accidental distribution for granted (at least, for the present) that the necessities for joint "planning" (of operations) and common operational services (e.g., the social service index) arise for solution by a "Council," and the necessities of joint fundraising arise for solution by a Chest or other unified fundraising body. The history of both bodies seems to show that they end, as they begin, with essentially the initial arbitrary collection of agencies, i.e., that little can be done by such means to rationalize the agency structure.[9]

The most frequent solution, then, to the problem of inclusion is to take in a mixed bag of agencies and lower-level "unifications"; thus the organizations commonly thought of as falling within the area of potential fundraising unification are: (1) the "health agencies" major and minor; (2) the (non-profit) hospitals; (3) the Red Cross Chapter; (4) the "other social agencies"; (5) pre-existing fundraising bodies for any of these. If it is now clear what organizations are usually held to be fit subjects for unification with reference to fundraising,[10] we are ready to discuss what parts of agency finances are or may be involved.

*Moneys involved.* If we assume that an agency, as defined, is not-for-profit and is neither (apart from momentary fluctuations) amassing reserves nor going into debt, then in general its annual income and its annual financial outgo must be the same. The second of these sums is commonly referred to as its "total budget" or, more exactly, as its "total operational budget." It is *not* this figure, but only a part of this figure that is, or might be, the object of unified fundraising.

It is usual to talk in fundraising circles of the agency's "deficit" as being the legitimate concern of the central fundraising organization. The "deficit," in this context, means the agency's total money outgo less its total money income.[11] But if the notion of "total budget" takes in too much to be relevant for federated fundraising, the "deficit" takes in too little. The "deficit" is the total outgo less the total income; and the total income may, and frequently does, itself include "gifts"—gifts which may well be thought of as part of that sum which is to be "unified."[12] The notion of deficit takes in too little, then, because part of what otherwise would be the gap between outgo and income may already be gift-income, not yet unified, but certainly subject to consideration for unification.

If an agency budget could be broken up in the way shown in Tables LXXX and LXXXI, it would be easy to see to what money the notion of united fundraising is potentially relevant. The first "budget" shown (Table LXXX) represents things as they now are, i.e., "deficit financing." (The hypothetical illustration is not intended to resemble any particular agency, nor are the figures suggested intended to resemble particular realities; nevertheless, the considerations involved are realistic.) It shows (by an asterisk) three kinds of gifts that are, unquestionably, subject to possible unification. It also separates clearly the problem of subsidizing production[13] of a service from the problem of subsidizing the selling of it.[14] The first "budget" shows, in the bottom right-hand corner, the amount that would have to be raised under these hypothetical circumstances by the central fundraising body: $6,700.

TABLE LXXX

HYPOTHETICAL AGENCY: BUDGET WITH "DEFICIT FINANCING"

| Column | A | B | C | D | E | F |
|---|---|---|---|---|---|---|
| | | | | Shortage (—) or Surplus (+) | | |
| Service | Cost of service | Market value of service | Returns from consumers | Due to accepted production loss (or inefficiency) or gain (B—A) | Due to accepted sale loss or gain (C—B) | Total (C—A) |
| Swimming instruction | $10,000 | $12,000 | $6,000 | $+2,000 | $—6,000 | $— 4,000 |
| Camp | 25,000 | 20,000 | 12,000 | —5,000 | —8,000 | —13,000 |
| Counselling | 4,000 | 4,000 | 800 | 0 | —3,200 | — 3,200 |
| Cookie sale | 15,000 | 16,000 | 25,000 | +1,000 | +9,000* | +10,000 |
| Businessmen's Club | 2,000 | 3,000 | 5,000 | +1,000 | +2,000* | + 3,000 |
| Gifts from members | 0 | 0 | 500 | 0 | + 500* | + 500 |
| TOTAL | $+56,000 | +55,000 | +49,300 | —1,000 | —5,700 | $— 6,700ᵃ |

*Gift or concealed gift.
ᵃDeficit to be financed by central fundraising body under present system.

The second "budget" (Table LXXXI) shows the same set of circumstances, but with *all giving* (as defined above and in note 12) now centralized in a unified fundraising body. The changes entailed are clearly marked: they involve chiefly the disappearance of the starred items (the gifts and concealed gifts) from column E of Budget I, and the consequent alteration of the sum to be raised by the central fundraising unit from $6,700 to $18,200. Against this increase ($11,500) may be set: the elimination of the gift element ($9,000) of the cookie sale, the elimination of the gift element ($2,000) from the operation of the "businessmen's club," and the total elimination of the "gifts from members" ($500).

The money area of actual "unification" (for all the agencies to be unified) lies, in common practice, somewhere between this first deficit-financing budget and the second which eliminates all direct gifts to agencies and centralizes all the giving involved. Total unification of giving, as far as money is concerned, means a budget of Type II. We shall need a new term to refer to the new figure that *would be* the deficit if all other giving were really cut off (e.g., the figure in the bottom right-hand corner of Budget II): for want of a better term, we shall call these sums, for the several agencies concerned, the "*donanda*."[15] The sum of such sums, i.e., the money that would have to be raised by a fully unified organization, might be called the gross "donandum." But more has to be settled for any unification plan than just the total sum to be involved. What aspects of the enterprise are to be made conjoint?

TABLE LXXXI

HYPOTHETICAL AGENCY: BUDGET WITH UNIFIED GIVING
(Dollar amounts as in Table LXXX)

| | | | | | | |
|---|---|---|---|---|---|---|
| Swimming instruction | $10,000 | $12,000 | $ 6,000 | $+2,000 | $—6,000 | $— 4,000 |
| Camp | 25,000 | 20,000 | 12,000 | —5,000 | —8,000 | —13,000 |
| Counselling | 4,000 | 4,000 | 800 | 0 | —3,200 | — 3,200 |
| Cookie sale | 15,000 | 16,000 | 16,000[b] | 1,000 | 0[b] | 1,000[b] |
| Businessmen's Club | 2,000 | 3,000 | 3,000[b] | 1,000 | 0[b] | 1,000[b] |
| Gifts from members | 0 | 0 | 0[b] | 0 | 0[b] | 0[b] |
| TOTAL | $56,000 | $55,000 | $37,800[b] | $—1,000 | $—17,200[b] | $—18,200[bc] |

[b]Differs from Budget I above.
[c]Shortage to be financed by fully unified fund.

It is obvious from the remainder of this book, if it was not obvious before, that fundraising is a bundle of activities rather than one activity. To specify these activities in detail at this point would be in effect prematurely to summarize the book. Without any pretence at completeness, therefore, but rather to serve as a reminder of the complexities involved, the reader is referred to the tabular line-up of "unifiable fundraising activities" on page 356. An attempt (not wholly successful) has been made to arrange them in a rough hierarchy such that no one is likely to consider unifying activities lower on the page before (or without) unifying those higher on the page.[16] As many or as few of these as desired might be brought together under a joint organization. And virtually as much freedom to combine in various ways exists in reference to who is to be confronted with a "united" demand.

Independently, then, of the answers to any of the foregoing questions, the question as to what part of the donor-aggregate is to be brought under a unified scheme must be resolved. It is possible to think of application to the whole donor-aggregate. It is also possible to think of application only to the corporate gifts. Quite commonly, the application is thought of in con-

### UNIFIABLE FUNDRAISING ACTIVITIES

I  Market-creating   A  Public relations, publicity, propaganda
                     B  "Product packaging"
                     C  Power or influence mobilization

II  Tool forging     A  Solicitor recruitment
                     B  Solicitor training
                     C  "Cultivation"

III  Operation       A  Solicitation (Pledges)
                        1. (a) Corporately organized sector
                           (b) Non-corporately organized sector
                        2. (a) Corporation gifts
                           (b) Other
                     B  Collection (Money)
                     C  Record-keeping
                     D  Research

IV  Control          A  Policing of market (Solicitation Control)
                        (External Control)
                     B  Policing of demand (Budget Control)
                     C  Allocation and adjustment
                     D  "Standard" setting

V  General           A  Provision, control and use of symbols, etc.
                     B  Maintenance of campaign pattern and control of change in
                        pattern

nection with the entire corporately organized sector (and many of the arguments that "support" United Fund are based only on experience with the corporate sector). Some think in terms of a controlled sector (the corporately organized) and a deliberately chosen competitive one (the entire remainder of the donor-aggregate). The object of this last combination is to minimize "bother" for the business community, while simultaneously giving it a probe into "public opinion" by giving it a chance to see and be guided according to how the general public responds to the various appeals. Many people argue that not only does such a set-up unify only those who wish to be unified, but that it tends to "keep the agencies on their toes," and permits the businessmen some check on the popular acceptance of their own judgments and behavior in this sphere.

It ought to be clear, if it was not earlier, that the varieties of possible schemes of unified fundraising are very large indeed: any combination of agencies can be unified for fundraising, with respect to any portion of their donanda, and therein for any number of fundraising activities, and with respect to all or any portion of the donors. It is from this rich field of possibilities—what agencies, what part of the gross donandum, which fundraising activities, which givers—that the fundraising unification plan for any community should be picked, if an apt fit is to be made to local desires and possibilities.[17]

Instead of posing the problem of unification in terms of more or less, and more or less of what—i.e., in terms of the foregoing considerations—it is commonly raised as an all-or-nothing matter, a black-or-white, "United Fund" or no "United Fund" choice, in which "he who is not with us is against us and he who gathereth not with us scattereth abroad." The question as to how much unification of what, for what, is desired or required, is thus generally lost to sight in a clamorous joining of issues around a favorite and particular solution—"United Fund." What, then, is a United Fund?

### The Favorite Case: The United Fund

A United Fund is simply a unified fundraising body that combines at least some of the fundraising activities, for at least some of the donandum, for at least the Red Cross or a major health agency and more than one other social agency, with respect to at least some appreciable segment of the donor-aggregate. While this abstract definition covers everything that is required for a unified fundraising organization to qualify as a United Fund,[18] and while a few United Funds have risen fullblown from the foam without benefit of a pre-existing Chest,[19] in the concrete situation the question as to whether or not to have a "United Fund" strips down essentially into the question of whether or not somehow[20] to unite (for the operation of fundraising) existing Chest facilities with those of the Red Cross and/or one or more of the "major" health agencies.[21]

A United Fund is thus, in practice, some integration for fundraising of a Chest portion with a Red Cross portion and/or a major health agency portion. Charts 47 and 48 indicate some of the possibilities of combination with respect to number of agencies and proportion of donandum. All but two of the twelve possibilities in Chart 47, and all but four of the sixty types of federation in the second would be called "United Funds." The existing Indianapolis unified fundraising organization is type 2..1..0. on Chart 47, or probably, type 21.12.00 on Chart 48, i.e., it is a United Fund that has many social agencies; a low portion of their donandum is raised; the Red Cross is not represented at all; and there is only one major health agency, although it gets a large portion of its donandum from the Chest.

The definition of a United Fund, it appears, is a matter of historic accident. It is purely a series of historical accidents, for instance, that certain agencies were swept together for fundraising purposes into an "organization" that came to be called generically a "Community Chest" (or some similar title) in one epoch; that others[22] were swept in, mostly later, without raising any problems of principle or name-changing; and that in the present era the inclusion or otherwise of one, some, or all of six nameable agencies is held to be a critical issue for local MOPS fundraising, which requires a battle on principle, and, if a new unit results, a change of name. Probably too the drawing of battle-lines in such rigid terms is largely a matter of historic accident also.[23]

The protagonists of the "United Fund" (thus defined) allege certain advantages for it, though it is difficult to distinguish (designedly so, we believe) in the welter of debate what they believe to be the *peculiar* advantages of the United Fund, as against some other form of unification. "We *need* a United Fund because . . ." the argument invariably runs; and we have already made clear, we hope, that this ought to mean: "*If and only if* we have a United Fund can the following objectives be achieved" (see chapter 8). Similarly, the opponents of a United Fund put forth a set of arguments which deserve critical examination.

Perhaps the best brief collection of pro arguments appears in a pamphlet[24] put out by the United Community Funds and Councils of America, under the heading "Federation Makes Sense. . . ." Although not explicitly tied to the term "United Fund," but rather to the more ambiguous "United Community Campaigns" (which means either a United Fund or a Community Chest), the arguments are approximately the same as those employed as specially or exclusively applicable to a United Fund. We are quoting the argument in full, having taken the liberty only of numbering the parts for convenience of later reference. It runs as follows:

A united campaign benefits everyone in the community . . . the contributor, the participating agencies, the volunteer workers, the people who use the services.

I. It benefits the contributor
   A. eliminates annoyance of many separate appeals throughout the year
   B. helps the contributor give systematically and intelligently to an all-around program of service
   C. assures that the money contributed will go where it is most needed
   D. assures the giver that he is giving for approved and efficiently administered services
   E. assures that the money is not going into high overhead and campaign expenses. (Chests and United Funds averaged 2.8% year-round administration and 4.1% campaign expense last year.)

II. It benefits the participating agencies
   A. reduces cost of fundraising—more of each dollar raised goes for services
   B. frees agency staff and volunteers from the necessity of soliciting money, enabling them to devote full-time to service programs
   C. assures fair distribution of funds through annual budget reviews
   D. spreads the interest of givers to a broader view of the whole community's needs, rather than those of a "pet charity" only
   E. helps awaken citizens to a sharing of responsibility as volunteer workers
   F. federation produces stability—the movement has weathered two hot wars, a deep depression and a cold war, emerging stronger than ever from each. From 1929 to 1935 the percentage reduction in federated campaign results was lower than any other major economic index.

III. It benefits volunteer workers
   A. saves time and energy of volunteers, enabling them to concentrate on one major effort instead of many campaigns
   B. provides an opportunity for men and women in the community to take an active part in planning for community welfare and allows them to help determine budgets, policies, fund-distribution and service programs.

IV.  It benefits people who use community services
  A.  assures that efficiently administered and professionally sound agencies are available to offer services when and where they are needed
  B.  eliminates duplication of service and improves standards of existing service agencies
  C.  brings new agencies into being to provide unmet needs
  D.  provides co-ordinated system of information so that persons needing help can be directed to the proper agency quickly.

The arguments seem worth examining one at a time, as a preliminary step to the more general questions brought under review in the latter part of the chapter.

I A *Elimination of the annoyance of multiple appeals.* A United Fund eliminates only *some portion* of this "annoyance,"[25] since no United Fund includes all or even nearly all appeals. Other forms of unification, e.g., "in-plant federation,"[26] could and do achieve as much or more (for those instituting them).

I B *Induction of systematic, intelligent giving to all-around program.* If the words "helps the contributor give systematically" mean the institution of payroll deduction, this is indeed "systematic." But payroll deduction is a mode of collection and not a necessary consequence of the presence or absence of a United Fund, i.e., it applies equally well in theory, and equally often in practice, to in-plant federation.

The meaning of "helps the contributor give . . . intelligently" is also unclear. If it is to be inferred that the giver has more or better information under the non-competitive United Fund appeal than he has under the present welter of competing appeals, we have seen no evidence for the contention, and, on the basis of Chest history, grave reason to doubt the assertion. The words, "all-round program of service," suggest a kind of planning under the United Fund which would yield results different from those of the separate activities before union. We doubt that such effective "planning" occurs; and, indeed, we doubt if the now unfederated agencies could be brought even half-willingly into a United Fund if they thought their programs *would be* seriously affected.

I C *Fit of money-distribution to need.* We have seen no evidence that the money "will go where it is most needed." Indeed, we have met no one willing to say in advance, and in the abstract or the concrete, where it *is* "most needed." What seems to occur under most federations, at best, is a freezing of the disequalities or accidents of money- and power-distribution that happen to obtain at the time that federation takes place. The claim that a United Fund can allocate funds to all agencies on a more equitable, rational, and useful basis is thus somewhat dubious.

It is felt by many people that a United Fund—because it includes so large a proportion of the agencies—is able to allocate funds in terms of the over-all "needs" of the community. Since the budgeting review of all activities is then in the hands of a single group, it is argued that the distribution of funds can be made to stimulate programs that "should be" expanded and to curtail programs that are "less valuable" to the community. This view presupposes that the budget review group has a general plan against which to evaluate all agency programs, and that the review group is sufficiently familiar with the work of the agencies to be able to make the evaluation.[27] The possibility of such well-founded planning seems remote even now; familiarity may turn out to be even more difficult to secure with a larger number of agencies than it evidently is at present.

I D *Giving restricted to approved and efficient services.* Of course, the United Fund must "assure the giver" that it "approves" the agencies it campaigns for, but this is mere tautology. Only the value of that assurance —as against the present state of affairs, or some other proposed state—is worth disputing. As for "efficiently administered services," this claim too is perhaps credible: but if the implication is "more efficiently administered than before United Fund"—and *that* would be the relevant argument—we have seen no evidence for such a contention.

I E *Economy in campaign and administrative expense.* This is perhaps the most cogent and credible argument, so far. The evidence for a relative saving in campaign costs seems weighty. (Similar results would, doubtless, obtain also in other fields, for example, if the dairies of a given city were persuaded or forced to use a single delivery system.) But the actual saving as measured by the percentages distributed to the agencies is relatively trivial: of the order of 2 per cent in favor of the United Funds.[28]

II A *Economy in fundraising.* The argument and the comment thereon are those of I E.

II B *The freeing of laymen and staff from fundraising for "service" duties.* As far as agency staff is concerned the point must be conceded, i.e., unification leads to specialization. But many will regard this as a mixed blessing, arguing that it is the very contact with laymen made necessary by annual fundraising that keeps staff "realistic" and the agency "on its toes." The complementary belief is that agencies in a federation tend to become "dependent" and "unrealistic." (Some agencies, like some Orders of nuns, regard direct "begging" as, additionally, of intrinsic worth.) We do not regard this counter-argument as a very weighty one in this context.

As far as volunteers are concerned we have no evidence, direct or indirect, that there is a total net saving in volunteer time. To evaluate the claim of the United Funds that "calls on business for volunteer workers are reduced" would require comparison of man-hours used by non-United Fund campaigns with those of United Fund campaigns. This report has frequently suggested that we find no reasonable way to estimate more than very roughly the number of volunteer workers used in a campaign and, consequently, the number of volunteer man-hours used. In any case, one cannot add volunteer hours indiscriminately, since even from an economic viewpoint, they have different costs. It is quite likely that a United Fund would be as costly in terms of money value of donated time as any present set-up; indeed it might well take more of the time of top-echelon leadership. What appears to be the case, however, is that an individual is called upon to serve in fewer campaigns annually or in the course of his career, where there is a United Fund; but this is certainly no evidence that the number of people involved or the total man-hours expended or the cost to the business community of these is less in a United Fund campaign than in the non-United Fund campaign.

Similarly inconclusive is the selling point of a United Fund that firms and organizations benefit from its single annual campaign in a diminution of costs of the campaign to the firm or organization. Neither we nor those who advance the argument have, of course, any way to measure the costs to the firm or organization either with a United Fund or without. Moreover, there are many ways to reduce campaign costs to a firm, and none of these ways is exclusive to the United Fund form of organization.

II C *Assurance of "fair" fund distribution by budget review.* This is a central argument, and one very difficult to credit. The present distribution of money between the Chests and the "Independents" is in terms of public "appeal," the proposed one is in terms of "budgeting"; but this would almost inevitably be a decision by a small group on the basis of habit, presented "argument," and such "facts" as can be obtained, without, presumably, any over-all plan or thought-out philosophy in terms of which aptness can be evaluated or "fairness" assessed—at least, so one might safely predict out of the very nature of the structure and the parallel behavior in the Chests themselves. Such budgeting—not definably different from budgeting as presently practised in the Chest—is more like the political process of log-rolling than a judicial process in equity or an administrative decision. One would have to add, moreover, that unlike the Congressional arrangements, there is no assurance in Chest practice that at least all interests are represented on some agreed basis (as they are on a territorial one in politics). Thus not even the secondary good of an *orderly* adjustment of competing interests (which is not to be confused, of course, with "fairness") can be systematically provided by traditional or foreseeable budgeting procedures in the Chest or in the larger fund.

II D *Decrease of agency-mindedness; increase in community-minded- ness.* We have no evidence, and considerable reason to doubt, that the interests of givers, once removed from their "pet charity," are re-attached with anything like the same meaning, warmth, intensity or satisfaction to the "whole community's needs." (There is, of course, no argument as yet that this is a desirable or preferable state of affairs. Would one argue in like fashion about families or churches—or the "community" itself as against the state?) There is, moreover, reason to think that a United Fund— like a Chest, only on a greater scale—by the very fact of "merging" or "con- founding" agencies in one appeal, and thereby reducing their visibility while promoting the feeling that the federation "supervises all that" (assessment of merit, control of performance)—actually relieves the citizen of his prior feeling of responsibility and leaves him somewhat apathetic. The process is similar to the increase in political apathy in the face of bureaucracy and "big government."

II E *Stimulation of volunteers to more responsibility.* It is difficult to understand what this claim means. If claim II B were sustained—diminished *use* of volunteers in fundraising—how could this increased "awakening" of volunteers to responsibility be explained?

II F *Achievement of economic stability for philanthropy.* This claim is also hard to interpret and evaluate. Naturally enough, generally—and especially in Indianapolis—philanthropy augments with crisis. But the same could be said of Red Cross and other notably unfederated causes. The claim seems irrelevant to the United Fund issue.

III A *Time-saving for volunteers.* Repeats, essentially, part of II B. We have no evidence whatever to suggest that there is or would be a net saving in time for volunteers in general—or, especially, for "top top leaders."

III B *Increase in active involvement of laymen.* If merger allowed *more* people to take part in the activities listed, the tendency would run counter to the experience in business, and to the argument that there is economy in volunteer time. In any case, the numbers participating in budgeting, etc., stand in no known relation to the efficiency or adequacy of the process.

IV A *Assurance of "availability" of sound, apt agencies.* This argument is a hodgepodge of I C, I D, etc. It is difficult to see, for instance, in what sense the incorporation in a United Fund of the Red Cross Chapter (in Indianapolis, or most places) would make the Chapter any more "efficiently administered and professionally sound" or better enable it to "offer services when and where they are needed." The same question could be asked about any other presently well-run organization still outside the Chest.

IV B *Elimination of duplication of service and improvement of agency "standards."* From the historic record, the evidence does not seem strong that federation for fundraising "eliminates duplication of service" or "improves standards." Preservation of professional standards now rests largely with professional associations and national groupings of agencies. What a United Fund could do in this respect regarding Red Cross or the major health agencies is difficult indeed to guess for the future and a matter of no evidence, as far as we know, for the past.

IV C *Fathering new agencies to meet "unmet needs."* We do not know how the facts stand on this claim. We have already (in chapter 8) decried the whole confounding discussion in terms of "needs." But, this apart, we have no evidence that fundraising federations give birth to new agencies, or facilitate citizens' wishes in this respect, and we are not convinced that a fundraising federation is a proper or desired locus for such activities. In

Indianapolis, new agencies tend to be born out of the needs to develop "program" of such "young" organizations as Junior League or Junior Chamber of Commerce. Once the experimental or pioneer stage is over, these programs may be passed over into the regular structure of the social agencies—thus posing a new problem for the fundraisers. These "free" organizations seem a likelier source of innovation than does the federation.

IV D *Provision of appropriate information and referral service.* This "co-ordinated system of information" has been notoriously wanting in the existing Indianapolis federation, and the direction of people "to the proper agency quickly" is not something for which it or any other Indianapolis service is famous. A common referral bureau for all agencies might or might not improve matters, but it is obviously independent of the United Fund issue. There seems to be confusion at this point between fundraising for existing "services" and provision of new "services"—such as rational referral —that could be provided by almost any body better than by the fundraisers.

What is perhaps most interesting about all these arguments, taken together, is not the lack of evidence to support them or their tendentiousness, but the assertion they would seem to imply that to be justified *a United Fund would have to function as the argument says it does.* This view may give a better clue as to what might sensibly be done than would any further abstract dispute over the issue itself.

Although we have seen no summary as concise as the foregoing of the views of the opponents of United Funds, we have abstracted from articles and books on the subject the following sixteen points which, we believe, include many of the objections to United Funds and many of the arguments for maintaining "independent" fundraising:[29]

(1) Independent fundraising protects the free enterprise system.
(2) Independent fundraising preserves freedom of choice and action in philanthropy.
(3) Independent appeals "are our best hope of conquering mankind's leading diseases."[30]
(4) Independent appeals raise more money for their causes than unified campaigns raise for these causes.
(5) "The united appeal does not provide anything like enough money to support the minimal research necessary."[31]
(6) Independent appeals bring to the public an educational message which is lost in unification.
(7) Independent campaigns "emphasize one principal selling point at a time"[32] and are, thereby, more effective.
(8) Independent appeals reach more people than do united campaigns.
(9) "Designation" in United Funds "is not in effect a reality."[33]
(10) "After the initial enthusiasm that always accompanies a new idea has worn off, the giving to a United Fund tends to level off and frequently actually to decrease."[34]
(11) Budget control by United Funds restricts the growth of young agencies.

(12) Although some persons have undoubtedly been overworked in a number of campaigns, there are numbers of willing workers who have never been asked to participate in fundraising campaigns.

(13) United Funds cannot include all appeals. Further, they are unable to raise all of the deficit even for the agencies included.

(14) Some, at least, of the national health agencies have already united several causes in one appeal.

(15) United Funds foster the control of "private" philanthropy by "professionals" (both fundraisers and social workers) to the detriment of lay control.

(16) Even if all the claims of the supporters of united campaigns are valid, there are other means—perhaps more certain—of attaining the same ends.

These arguments against United Fund fare not much better, under scrutiny, than the arguments for it.

(1) It is difficult to know what is meant when it is alleged that independent fundraising "protects" the free enterprise system. That it is in the system, no one doubts. But so are merger and amalgamation, chosen or forced. And so are trade associations for self-policing. And so are large units of production. "United Fund" resembles these. Only as these verge on monopoly is the system threatened, and each case is therefore evaluated on its merits: *is* it substantially in restraint of trade? The question, therefore, is whether a United Fund—or whatever kind or degree of unification is proposed—is substantially a monopoly, and would sensibly and undesirably restrict the operation of the voluntary agency trade. The closer the United Fund comes to what its proponents allege for it—"it unites all drives"—the more open to this risk it no doubt does become.

(2) The second argument is essentially that further unification would substantially restrict the freedom of donors. This is almost true by definition. Under the United Fund the donor has practically no control over the distribution of his gift. His only choice, for all practical purposes, is whether or not to support MOPS fundraising organizations.[35] And often the donor is not permitted to make the choice—under the present system of solicitation of firms and their employees, the possibility of refusal to contribute is very small, and under United Fund is likely to be less. To refuse to participate in a United Fund campaign would expose an organization or an individual even more sharply than is the case at present to the possibility of economic and social sanctions. Some firms are almost literally forced to contribute, simply because the solicitor who requests the firm's contribution represents a good customer. Even when a firm is "friendly" to the Fund, and for the same reason, the amount "requested" and contributed is often "all the traffic will bear."[36] The individual finds it even more difficult to resist. In many firms, not only management and the union but fellow workers almost or altogether "insist" on the employee contributing. It requires a very strong dislike of the United Fund (or of the principles involved) for an individual to withstand such pressure—unless

he is secure both financially and socially (a rare combination in America).[37] But even when the donor is permitted to make the choice, or when, despite efforts to circumvent the possibility of choice, a donor asserts his right of choice, it is not an easy one to make. For there are few, if any, federations which do not include *some* agencies to which almost any person wants to be responsive. There is almost never a black-and-white situation in which the donor can say the federation is all bad or all good. Consequently, the decision must be made on complicated grounds indeed, and when so much annoyance, if not abuse, can be avoided by contributing, the scales are often tipped by the latter consideration.

Yet there may be some compensation for restriction of freedom. The important question—as we shall see later—is whether unification gives the donor in exchange for his diminished freedom some augmented control that he wishes to have. This is a crucial question, and we shall have to re-examine it towards the end of this chapter.

Unified fundraising also restricts to some degree the liberty of action of the agencies—as long, at least, as they can be kept from "fringing off." Again, the critical question is whether there are any compensatory gains to set against this loss—for the agencies themselves, for the donors, for the society generally or for all of these. This also must be reserved for later discussion.

(3) Whether or not independent fundraising appeals are the "best" hope of conquering disease is anyone's guess, at this time. Certainly, historically, the methods of controlling disease have often been pioneered and developed through programs sponsored by bodies other than the "private agencies." For example, control of yellow fever was first attained by the army and the true vaccine for this disease was developed under a grant from the Rockefeller Foundation. In relation to some diseases— mental diseases most notably—the private contribution to research into them or for the care of victims is so trifling as to be infinitesimal.

(4) To support the claim that independent appeals "raise more money for their causes" than United Funds do or would raise for the same causes, every arguer has his favorite case evidence.[38] Typical of these case arguments are the following, put forward by the American Heart Association:

Omaha—received $10,000 in 1952, $16,368 in 1953 and 1954 from United Fund. In 1955, conducted own drive raising $42,900.
Columbus, O.—received $58,000 in 1954 from federated fund. In 1955, denied increase, conducted own drive for about $80,000.
Buffalo, N.Y.—"Offered $54,500 (same as 1954) but needing $90,000, Heart withdrew from United Fund. In 3-hour house-to-house Heart Sunday collection, receipts totaled over $145,000."[39]

In each of these cases, it clearly appears that the Heart Association received more than it would have from the United Fund. But the most that can be said on the basis of these cases is that, in at least some cities, an independent appeal raised more money for the cause than did the United Fund previously. One cannot go on from such selected cases to say that in general independent appeals do better than unified appeals. (Neither, as will appear later, can the contrary be asserted, on the basis of any systematic evidence.)

(5) The charge that "the united appeal" does not provide money enough for "minimal research"[40] (for the health agencies) is too vague to permit serious treatment. The only relevant question would be: "Does it do better or worse in this respect?" But this is essentially the question of the last paragraph.

(6) The argument for the connection between fundraising and the "education" of the public, in general, and the giver, in particular, is hard to evaluate. Certainly, that there is a connection is one of the strongest contentions of the most ardent "anti-unifiers." As usual, direct evidence is lacking. Although two studies[41] have been made which present evidence somewhat related to this problem, neither was seeking information bearing directly on it. What material is available[42] suggests that there is a slightly greater knowledge about the program of the health agencies among people who have contributed to the campaign than among those who have not. This finding might be interpreted either as meaning that those who "know" tend to give, or that those who give tend to "know." There is an interesting body of evidence—in relation, at least, to one health appeal—against the latter view.

However, whether or not the independent appeals bring an educational message to the public via the campaign is probably no longer an either-or matter, since it has become fairly common practice for the health agencies included in United Funds to carry on "educational" campaigns during the period when they had formerly solicited for funds. Thus the educational value of an independent campaign is not wholly lost under unification. On the contrary, some say, the agency is thus able to concentrate on the educational program without the distraction of the money campaign which might actually divert attention from the "advertising"—although many fundraisers believe that the money-message and the knowledge-message reinforce each other where they are presented together. There seems to be no evidence as to whether joint or separate presentation of "education" and "appeal" is more effective.

(7) The argument as to the ability of the "independents" to make one point at a time boils down to saying that United Funds have to publicize too many activities together to make the combined appeal very effective. It is frequently suggested that this is bad advertising practice; good practice, it is said, "follows the Ford Motor Company formula" of concentrating in each particular year on one out of innumerable possible "features." We have seen in connection with the existing Chests some of this too-many-eggs-in-one-basket effect, and hence the argument does hold and would

carry even greater weight for a United Fund. If, however, the United Fund *does* get the money, then this boils down merely to the previous argument that United Fund succeeds financially but fails "educationally" (Argument 6). If the United Fund does *not* get the money, this is Argument 4 again. We shall return to this question of what money the United Funds do get, later.

(8) We have seen no evidence for the argument so strongly maintained by proponents of independent campaigns that more people were "reached" by independent fundraising than were reached afterwards in a united appeal[43] but neither were we able to discover any data which showed the contrary.

(9) The contention that "designation"—the naming of a particular agency to receive one's benefices—is not an effective reality in United Fund is incontrovertible. Neither, for that matter, is designation an effective reality for Chests.[44] But this simply restates Argument 2—some further freedom is lost—and again we should not so much question the fact of that loss as ask whether there are commensurate gains.

(10) There is little evidence to support or controvert the view that United Funds usually "level off" after a short interval of enthusiasm. Certainly, some United Funds have had decreases in giving in second, third, and fourth campaigns—and some have not raised as much in their first appeals as did the separate campaigns in the previous year. As of November 1956, the United Funds which were not new were reporting no greater gains compared with their previous year than were the ordinary Community Chests.[45] On the other hand, some United Funds have shown regular increases from their first campaigns, for example, Detroit. We shall examine such systematic evidence as there is later in the chapter.

(11) We do not know whether or not "budget control by United Funds restricts the growth of young agencies." We do not think anyone else knows.[46] And we do not know which view, favorable or unfavorable, would be taken, by laymen or professionals, if the restriction were a fact. Whatever may be the truth in reference to United Funds must also have been substantially true for the Chests, and no existing independent would encourage the growth of a "young agency" which it believed to trench upon its own field. The point is worth making, however, that the wider the "union," the more important it is to make special provision for innovation and invention if sclerosis is to be avoided.

(12) We have discussed some of the ramifications of this problem of over-utilizing the drive-happy few earlier in this chapter and in chapter 11. Although it is probably true that there are large numbers of people who would work in fundraising campaigns if asked (one of the Indianapolis health agencies has systematic evidence that there were great numbers of volunteers willing to help with fundraising who had never before been asked to serve by anyone), the problem is not so simple as merely locating

these persons. The crucial issue is whether the persons who complain most about the recurring and frequent requests for their time would be relieved of these requests if new persons were recruited into the campaigns. In all probability the same demands would still be made on the time of the "top top leaders," even though every fundraising group were surfeited with volunteers. It is doubtful that many "large" campaigns could operate successfully lacking active élite support; on the other hand, "small" campaigns[47] might not need it so direly. If this is true—and there are some small campaigns in Indianapolis which succeed without substantially involving the top echelon of leadership—then the inference to be drawn is that unified fundraising requires *more* active participation (and not mere tacit approval by lack of opposition) of the top top leadership: the larger the amount to be raised, the greater the need for more of the time and energy of more "top top leaders."

(13) Hardly anyone advocating United Fund believes that all appeals would be included in it, and it is certainly true that many unified fund-raising organizations do not meet the total deficit of member agencies. Undoubtedly this sometimes occurs because of failure to raise sufficient funds. But many of the unified organizations never were intended to meet the total deficit of the member agencies. Some are designed to meet only a portion of the deficit, for example, the Chicago Community Fund. These facts thus only become a charge against United Fund for those who believe that it is the proper function of a United Fund (or Community Chest) to meet the entire deficit of all member agencies. (Actually, one school of thought holds that it is better to force the agencies to meet part of their deficit by raising a portion of the funds themselves; their ability to do so is said to demonstrate continued public acceptance and support of the agency.) The only serious charge is that many proponents of United Fund put about the belief that United Fund will meet all deficits of all agencies, although a quite other plan is intended.

What the argument does point to is the absence of a clear policy that would make explicit why it is preferable—if it is—to take more agencies into the present federation before the point has been reached where some reasoned fraction of the donanda of the already incorporated agencies is being raised.

(14) This argument seems to assert virtually that some of the existing health agencies are already themselves federations. Although the claim is certainly reasonable (e.g., Heart Association and Cerebral Palsy), it is hard to see why this should be a reason for opposing further unification. One might ask, "If this much unification has been workable, why not more?" This is *a fortiori* a reasonable rejoinder when we remember that the Chest —as pointed out earlier—may in many cases already include one or more sub-federations.

(15) Tied in with this argument as to greater control by the professionals

is the question whether it is desirable or undesirable. And, as with most of our previous discussions about these arguments, there is no evidence available to help us make an evaluation.

It is probably a realistic statement of the situation to say that professionals have acquired more power in fundraising over the past twenty or thirty years, and that the power of the professionals in some matters increases *pari passu* with the size of the drive. But the important consideration here is the kind of power they have gained. It appears that the professionals have increased control over the distribution of funds. But there does not seem to have been generally any appreciable increase in control of fundraising by professionals, at least in Indianapolis. Our observations of campaigns there suggest that any increased control which the professional might have is limited to a great extent to the basic procedures in the solicitation, i.e., the professional seems to determine what pattern of solicitation will be used (for example, unit accounts *versus*, say, advanced gifts). But the organization of the campaign divisions seems to be predominantly still in the province of the lay leaders, and each lay leader imposes something of his own organizational scheme on the campaign in which he is working.[48] We would have to concur, however, in the view that increasing size has a bearing on the continuation of lay potency; indeed, even at present levels of unification, this problem may be as important as any that faces the Chest.

(16) The question of alternative and perhaps better means to achieve the desired effects is, we believe, the most crucial of any raised by either side in the argument. We feel that it is of such importance as to merit an entire section in this chapter. Consequently, we defer that discussion.

But before discussing these alternatives, we should perhaps abandon abstract argument to look at what little evidence is available for evaluating United Funds themselves, as they currently operate.

We were unable to find any data which were consistently reported for the majority of United Funds with regard to any important question. One might almost say that there is "no evidence," only a selection of information which is suggestive, but since this is the best there is, this is what must be brought under scrutiny. The principal source of information is the annual report *Experience in United Funds*, issued by the United Community Funds and Councils of America.[49] On their first question—How Many United Funds are There?—despite the foregoing strictures, the evidence is probably sufficiently reliable.[50] There are some 821 (according to the booklet) or 824 (according to the 1956 *Directory*). Thus some 42 per cent of all campaigns are "United" (as, of course, Indianapolis is) in the sense that they include at least one of the Big Six.

Not only is this so, but it is also true that the larger the campaign, the more likely it is to be United (*partly* as a consequence of the fact that the more United it is, the larger it is likely to be). Table LXXXII illustrates this tendency. Again, the segment of all federations that are United Funds has been growing faster than the non-United segment, as Table LXXXIII shows. It is thus clear that—whether sound or unsound—there is a trend towards inclusion of one or more of the Big Six. To what extent, and how many?

TABLE LXXXII

TYPE OF FUND BY SIZE OF FUND, 1956

| Campaign size | Percentage | |
|---|---|---|
| | United Fund | Other |
| Under $50,000 | 39.5% | 60.5% |
| $ 50,000 to $199,999 | 40.7 | 59.3 |
| $200,000 to $999,999 | 58.9 | 41.1 |
| $1 million or over | 62.7 | 37.3 |
| All sizes | 42.3% | 57.7% |

TABLE LXXXIII

NUMBER AND INCREASE IN NUMBER OF UNITED FUNDS, 1953-6

| Year | Number of all campaigns in United States | Number | | Interval | Growth of United Funds in number | Growth of other than United Fund in number | Growth in number of both |
|---|---|---|---|---|---|---|---|
| | | United Fund | Not United Fund | | | | |
| 1953 | 1,501 | 343 | 1,158 | — | | | |
| 1954 | 1,627 | 545 | 1,082 | 1953-54 | 59% | −7% | 8% |
| 1955 | 1,792 | 689 | 1,103 | 1954-55 | 26 | 2 | 10 |
| 1956 | 1,873 | 824 | 1,049 | 1955-56 | 20 | −5 | 5 |
| | | | | 1953-56 | 140% | −9% | 25% |

TABLE LXXXIV

TYPE OF APPEAL INCLUDED:
PERCENTAGE OF ALL CAMPAIGNS OF SPECIFIED SIZES, 1956[a]

| Campaign size | Appeal included—Percentage of all campaigns | | | | | |
|---|---|---|---|---|---|---|
| | Cancer | Heart | Red Cross | Crippled Children | Polio | TB |
| Under $100,000 | 20.9% | 22.8% | 24.5% | 5.7% | 5.3% | 2.2% |
| $100,000—199,999 | 23.2 | 16.9 | 31.6 | 6.8 | 4.5 | 3.4 |
| $200,000—499,999 | 27.5 | 29.8 | 48.9 | 9.2 | 3.1 | 5.3 |
| $500,000—999,999 | 34.7 | 34.7 | 59.2 | 14.3 | 4.1 | 0.0 |
| $1,000,000—2,499,999 | 34.9 | 39.5 | 55.8 | 11.6 | 2.3 | 4.7 |
| $2,500,000 and up | 37.5 | 37.5 | 58.3 | 0.0 | 8.3 | 4.2 |
| All sizes | 22.4% | 23.6% | 28.8% | 6.3% | 5.1% | 2.6% |

[a]Computed from Directory and from 1956 Experience in United Funds, Table 3. Data here are for United States and Canada.

Table LXXXIV indicates for five campaign sizes what proportion of each includes each of the Big Six in 1956. The table is clearly divisible into a segment of relative success in getting the appeal "in"—Cancer, Heart, and Red Cross—and a segment of relative failure, consisting of Crippled Children, Polio, and TB. Moreover, the tendency of the largest campaigns to have a greater attractive (or coercive) power over each of the Big Six is rather regularly visible throughout the table.

This tendency is also visible if we take for each campaign size the "proportion of all theoretically possible inclusions." By the "theoretically possible inclusions" we mean six times the number of campaigns, i.e., we are assessing here as if every campaign had in its area every one of the Big Six which it "could" include. The results then appear as in Table LXXXV.

TABLE LXXXV

ACHIEVED NUMBER OF BIG SIX INCLUSIONS AS PROPORTION OF NUMBER
THEORETICALLY POSSIBLE (1956) BY CAMPAIGN SIZE

| Campaign size | Actual number of inclusions of Big Six | Theoretical maximum number of inclusions | Inclusiveness ratio[a] |
|---|---|---|---|
| Under $100,000 | 1,236 | 9,090 | 13.6% |
| $100,000–199,999 | 153 | 1,062 | 14.4 |
| $200,000–499,999 | 162 | 786 | 20.6 |
| $500,000–999,999 | 72 | 294 | 24.5 |
| $1,000,000–2,499,999 | 64 | 258 | 24.8 |
| $2,500,000 and up | 35 | 144 | 24.3 |
| All sizes | 1,722 | 11,634 | 14.8% |

[a]Actual divided by theoretically possible inclusions.

A conservative estimate, then, of how much the total potential of "unitedness" has been reached would be about 15 per cent; and it is clear that even the largest campaigns ($1 million and over) have gone less than a fourth of the way.

But even this may be an exaggeration if "unitedness" means inclusion *by consent*. Here, once again, ignorance dogs us, because—excluding Red Cross, which is never included without its own consent—we do not know in 49.5 per cent of the cases whether even the minimum of consent (i.e., at least agreeing to accept the money) was had. If we take as the test of "unitedness," as we reasonably may, known inclusion by consent, then the over-all figure falls to 1,253 known inclusions for the whole country (about 45 per cent of them, Red Cross) or a "known consented inclusiveness ratio" of 10.8 per cent. The corresponding figure for the Big Five health agencies—i.e., excluding Red Cross—is 7.2 per cent. This seems something less than the landslide towards "unitedness" which is the carefully fostered popular image of what is happening.[51]

The next key question is probably the one in reference to *new* United Funds: "Do they raise as much as the individual agencies raised previously in their separate appeals?" On the basis of the published data we have to say that we simply do not know. The published tables for 1955 and 1956 refer respectively to 60 per cent and 73 per cent of the United Funds of each year, and little or no reliance can, therefore, be placed in their claims about gains, since it is altogether likely that the fraction not reporting is the "lower" tail of the distribution.[52] Certainly nothing we know permits us to credit the following widely touted claim: "The 'average' United Fund raises about 20 per cent more in its first campaign than all participating agencies raised the previous year in their separate appeals."[53] On the published evidence, no one knows how much "an average new United Fund" raises in its first year more than its components raised in independence—but it is probably more of the order of 10 per cent than the 20 per cent suggested.[54]

The next important question is, according to the Community Chest, and Councils, "Do United Fund allocations to agencies show increases over a period of years?" Again, we cannot evaluate the evidence, chiefly because we do not even know, in this case, what proportion of the experience it purports to report. The published table reports on only three of the Big Six. For the period 1953 to 1956, it reports on 77 United Funds that included Cancer, 61 that included Heart, and 79 that included Red Cross. For the first two, we do not know what proportion of the experience this is; for Red Cross, we only know that in 1953 there were 128 chapters included in United Funds in the Directory, and that therefore the table probably reports only 60 to 70 per cent of the experience. If so, we feel no reasonable inference can be drawn from it.[55]

Another favorite question is "Do United Funds continue to be successful over a period of years?" which means (excluding the new ones[56]), what was their percentage gain over the previous year, and how does this compare with percentage gain over previous years in non-United Funds. The picture from 1953 to 1957 is drawn in Table LXXXVI. On the basis of this table—one of the few where the information (except for 1957) is relatively complete—it is very difficult to see in what sense the United Fund (with or without Red Cross) shows an appreciably better average record of gain. Indeed, for the first four years, where the data are relatively complete, the non-United Funds show better gains in two years, and the United Funds in the other two. The thesis that there are greater annual percentage gains for United Funds—as compared with non-United ones—is thus gravely to be doubted.

Still another favorite question has to do with multiplicity of appeals: "Do some national agencies participating in United Funds also conduct separate appeals?" Again our ignorance is almost boundless: we have reports for only three of the Big Six—Red Cross, Heart, and Cancer—and

TABLE LXXXVI

Campaign Results for United Funds and Non-United Funds
(Excluding new United Funds each Year)
1953-7[a]

| Campaign year | Non-United Funds | Percentage of previous year | | |
|---|---|---|---|---|
| | | United Funds | | |
| | | Without Red Cross | With Red Cross | With or without Red Cross |
| 1953 | 104.9% | 104.8% | 103.8% | 104.3% |
| 1954 | 105.5 | 103.8 | 105.7 | 105.1 |
| 1955 | 101.6 | 100.9 | 102.5 | 102.1 |
| 1956 | 106.8 | 110.3 | 110.0 | 110.0 |
| 1957 | 110.6 | 109.3 | 107.7 | 107.8 |
| P[b] | 132.8% | 132.3% | 133.2% | 132.7% |

[a]1957 only so far as reported by September 27, 1956.

[b]The figure P does not represent exactly the gain over the period, or the "average" of the gains; it represents their product, i.e., what would be the final "principal" that would result from $1 invested in 1952 and paying in each year the interest-rate (rate of increase) shown. This must be a close approximation to the figure we want but cannot have.

Sources: 1953 to 1955, *1956 Experience in United Funds,* Table 10, p. 6; 1956, *1956 Directory, op. cit.;* 1957 *Campaign Facts and Figures,* no. 3, showing results up to September 27, 1956. The data for the last column of the table are all taken from the Directories.

these report on only 51 per cent, 28 per cent, and 31 per cent of the known cases in which they are included in the United Fund. If we go back to the total number of campaigns (1,939 in all) each of which might, at a maximum, "eliminate" six appeals, we have as before 11,634 possible "eliminations" (see Table LXXXV). Of these, 516 are known to have taken place: the "known elimination ratio" (the degree to which the job of elimination is known to be done) is therefore about 4.4 per cent. Again, no landslide.

The best question has been saved to the last: "How does the organization of a United Fund affect corporate and employee giving and the number of contributors?" Sadly, no one has the remotest idea. The available report[57] deals with 36, 15, and 10 cities respectively out of the 161 new United Funds of 1956. Such data have no meaningful standing: they cannot even be said to be suggestive, since almost inevitably those doing best report most gladly.

We may ask one more question, though we cannot fully answer it, partly because few cities report, and partly because some items we would like to separate are lumped together. The question is "What about allocations to agencies?" Table LXXXVII presents the data, and shows a 1.3 per cent to 1.9 per cent differential in the percentage United Funds are able to allocate to the agencies as compared with non-United Funds. Even if we assume that there are enough cities here to make these figures reliable, it would seem that the United Fund effects at most a 1 or 2 per cent economy over the Chest.[58]

Table LXXXVI may be insufficiently specific for some purposes: we may wish to ask how agencies severally fared under unification, rather than how all of them fare together. The United Community Funds and Councils of America listed the "median per capita" appropriations made by 129 United Funds including Red Cross, and by 128 Community Chests,[59] to specific agencies.[60] Chests made greater median per capita appropriations than did United Funds to sixteen agencies;[61] United Funds made greater median per capita appropriations than did Chests to five agencies[62]

TABLE LXXXVII

DISTRIBUTION OF TOTAL ALLOCATIONS FOR 1956,[a] 278 CITIES

| | Number of cities | Chests United Funds and Councils[b] | Shrinkage | Allocation to agencies |
|---|---|---|---|---|
| United Funds including Red Cross | 129 | 9.5% | 4.3% | 86.2% |
| United Funds not including Red Cross | 21 | 11.0 | 3.4 | 85.6 |
| Community Chests | 128 | 12.8 | 2.9 | 84.3 |

[a]Allocations for reserves and contingency funds are not included.

[b]Includes campaign, year-round administration, Community Welfare Councils, Social Service Exchange, and other common services such as Volunteer Service Bureaus, Information and Referral Centers, etc.

SOURCE: *Budgeting for 1956*, Bulletin 187 (New York: U.C.F. & C.A., no date), p. 14, Table 9.

(besides those to which *by definition* only it could contribute: Cancer, Crippled Children, Heart, and Red Cross); and Chest and United Funds appropriated about equal median percapitas to four agencies.[63] If we eliminate the national appeals, the number that fare better in a Chest is fourteen; the number that fare better in the United Fund is four; and the number of indifferents is four also.[64] This suggests, moreover, that Chests are—taking the median, as well we may, as the most representative figure— contributing more per capita to the *local* agencies than are the United Funds.

The systematic evidence on the leading questions is now pretty well exhausted and on these main issues we are left nowhere—or at least in grave doubt. Where there are enough cases to generalize safely we can reach two conclusions: (*a*) United Funds are popular and becoming more popular, but the task of incorporating the Big Six is only well begun (about 15 per cent done, or less), and (*b*) the evidence shows no significant differences in growth rates (as judged by average annual increase in take) over a number of years as between United Funds and non-United

Funds. The questions asked certainly suggest what needs to be known to make sensible decisions, but until some systematic, reliable reporting of results is obtained, few firm conclusions about United Funds can justifiably be drawn; indeed on most points it is difficult if not impossible to make reasonably safe and intelligent guesses.

## Alternative Forms of More Unified Fundraising

During the long discussion of the "United Fund"—necessitated because of the popular way of posing the issue—we have had to exclude from attention not only the question of unified *giving* (to which we must come later), but also other ways of unifying soliciting than what is known as "United Fund." To the other possibilities we must now briefly turn.[65]

### (1) *Joint solicitation without other unification*

One proposal that we report, only because it was forcibly put to us as a way to economize without creating a fundraising monolith, simply consists in "joint solicitation" of all donors by one common soliciting team, acting, however, on behalf of all the appeals severally.

The present "independents" and the present "Chest" would continue, it was suggested, otherwise pretty well as they are. There would be no common budgeting or goal-setting where it does not now exist. What would be "unified," then, would be only the time of the campaign and a limited number of the "bundle of activities" involved in fundraising (spelled out in the list on p. 356). More particularly, the following items from that list might be unified, leaving all others independent:

1. Some small common part of public relations, publicity, and propaganda (Item I A);
2. The whole of solicitor recruitment and training (Items II A and II B);
3. The whole of solicitation itself (Item III A).

As the scheme was put to us, the solicitor would merely present separate pledge cards for each organization participating in the campaign (or perhaps a single pledge card with a blank in which to insert the amount pledged to each organization). For example, he might hand to the prospective donor a card for the Red Cross, then one for the Chest, next one for Mental Health, then Cerebral Palsy, then Tuberculosis, then Multiple Sclerosis, etc., giving the donor an "opportunity" to pledge an amount to each. This system, it is claimed, has one advantage over present methods: the volunteers making the solicitation would, in one "contact," complete the approved solicitation for an entire year. Each call would undoubtedly require more time to complete than a solicitation for a single campaign; but, since all appeals would be made in this one contact, it would probably represent considerably less time than the total of calls for a number of organizations. Thus, any volunteer would be called upon to serve in only one campaign a year; and the donor's freedom would at least be maintained, and probably increased,[66] i.e., he would have or could have almost the same freedom as under No Federation[67] to select those agencies he wished to support and to refuse to give to any others (especially to those which he might feel to be unworthy, or already well enough supported). Impractical or not, the scheme evidently reflects an attempt to search for what might be called "limited unification." Other attempts to achieve the same objective boil down, essentially, to schemes for *multiple* community-wide federations for soliciting.

### (2) *Multiple community-wide federations for soliciting*

There are several possibilities here. One would federate *closely related agencies.* This type of federation (of which there would be several in each community) would depend for its organizing principle on the stated function of the agencies. The types of functions which could serve as criteria for inclusion might be those commonly in use in Chests and Councils today. On one scheme, agencies might be organized for fund-raising into four separate groups whose main functions would be Health, Education, Recreation, or Welfare.[68] Another organizing principle might be in terms of people served—Children, Youth, Families, or "General."[69] Or, a system similar to that adopted by the National Information Bureau[70] might be used—e.g., Youth, Veterans', General and Specialized Welfare, Negro Welfare, Human and Race Relations, etc. Each such federation would tend to be relatively small in number of agencies, though not necessarily in number of dollars raised.

The use of some such organizational scheme, if it were to federate agencies in a way conformable with people's wishes to discriminate,[71] would have some of the advantages (and disadvantages) of No Federation and, at the same time, would provide some of the advantages (and disadvantages) of more federation. Although the donor would not be able to make his pledge to a specific agency, he could, if he so desired, select particular areas of philanthropic concern for support. For example, although he would be unable to select the Boy Scouts as a specific recipient, he would be able to choose "Youth Services," in preference, say, to "Family Services." Thus, the donor's range of selectivity is less than it is with some existing schemes, but increased immeasurably over what it is with monolithic unification.

Federations of this type would also provide some reduction in campaign costs compared with the costs under No Federation, because of reduction in unit cost of raising each dollar, assuming that the federation would raise a larger sum than the individual agencies.[72] And this scheme provides—at least to some extent—for "expert" allocation of resources. For *within* each federation, persons with presumably more information, understanding, and interest than would be available either under defederation or total unification, would be allocating the resources of the federation to agencies with which they were relatively "intimately" acquainted.[73] Thus a series of federations of closely related agencies might well provide the donor with some degree of control over the distribution of his money and, at the same time, permit a sensible amount of "expert" guidance in the allocation of all funds within the area of function of each group of agencies.

An attempt to solve the same problem in much the same manner, but with a different basis for organization, would arrange the soliciting agencies essentially into two great federations for fundraising: one for the "service" agencies and one for the "health" agencies.

*Service Federations*, i.e., federations of social service agencies for raising local operating funds, are quite common in the United States today: many of the smaller Community Chests could serve as models. The typical federation of this type consists of a "merger," for fundraising purposes only, of a number of agencies, whose funds, acquired from the federation, are used almost exclusively for local operating expenses.[74] With this type of federation, it is true, the donor has lost a great deal of his power of choice between agencies: he may now support all members of the federation or support none. This does not mean, however, that he has no alternatives. Perhaps not all local agencies would belong to such a federation; but even if they did, there would still be available for the support of the donor the numerous "national agencies" which are excluded from the federation.

A "service federation" makes it possible to make allocations to agencies in terms of an over-all community "plan." Since most, if not all, local operating budgets would come under review by such a federation, distribution of funds could be made so that programs deemed vital, or useful to "the community," would be stimulated, while programs which seemed to the budgeters of less importance could be reduced or eliminated. (Such planning is possible, but, as we have seen earlier in this chapter, in practice is seldom attained.) "Community planning" of this kind is, of course, largely independent of the wishes of the donor *qua* donor.

There are few models of *Health Federations*[75] but, apart from the "field" covered, this type would in most respects be like a Service Federation. Perhaps the name "Health Federation" is too narrow since the organization might well include such agencies as the Red Cross[76]—as well as Mental Health. But the main basis for inclusion in the federation would be that the allocation to the agencies would include substantial sums for distribution to the state and/or national organizations with which the local agency is affiliated, i.e., for non-local use. For the most part, it so happens, agencies which follow this practice call themselves or are called "Health Agencies." Most of them are of relatively recent origin, for example, Polio, Heart, Crippled Children, Cerebral Palsy, Multiple Sclerosis, Mental Health, though there are also some older agencies, for example, Red Cross and Tuberculosis.[77]

It is difficult to believe that the "Health Agencies" would unify with one another for fundraising any more gladly than they would unify with the "Social Agencies" in a United Fund.[78] But we are thinking here less of the desire of the agencies, and more of how the donor does classify the appeals, and how some freedom may still be preserved for him while the disorder he evidently finds so distasteful might be reduced. If a community had only a Service and a Health Federation, the MOPS campaigns would be reduced to two a year.[79] Such campaigns might be held respectively in the fall and in the spring, thus ensuring a tapping of the community purse on more than one occasion annually,[80] and yet not so frequently, perhaps, as to produce resentment against "an excessive number of requests."[81]

With these two federations only, the donor's area of choice would be rather closely limited. He might choose to support either the Service Federation or the Health Federation, or to give to both of these, or to exclude MOPS fundraising organizations altogether as objects of his philanthropy. Though he would to this extent be circumscribed in his giving, some advantages in reduction of campaign costs and in number of campaigns would obviously be obtained.[82]

### (3) Federation for solicitation of commerce and industry

Such a federation—a "partial" Chest or United Fund, in the sense that, for the Industrial and Commercial sector, it does what a Chest or United Fund does—could coexist indifferently with either. A federation of this type might well be patterned after the Chicago Community Fund,[82] soliciting the larger businesses and/or their employees, and leaving the remaining businesses and the general public wide open to solicitation by the agencies. Agencies participating in such a federation are barred only from soliciting those firms and individuals designated by the federation as having contributed to its campaign.

Like other federations, this type offers little, if any, protection to the donors who are organized under it. Quite naturally, the orientation is away from the interests of the donors and towards those of the agencies. Its main advantage lies in eliminating some part of the "multiplicity of appeals" as far as the larger business establishments are concerned.[83] Another advantage alleged is that the federation, by concentrating on the larger donors, is able to do for the agencies a better job of fundraising on this segment of the donor-aggregate than the agencies would be able to do separately. Thus, while the donor would have little protection, many of the advantages of efficiency which may accrue through federation would, it is said, be obtained.

### (4) Total federation of soliciting

This scheme, unlike the foregoing, is not a plan "short of" United Fund, but goes beyond it.[84] Total Federation, as an idea,[85] is merely a logical extension of United Fund. The whole range of MOPS fundraising organizations would, it is said, have their campaigns merged into one gigantic campaign. Such a scheme appears to be improbable of accomplishment in a system of private philanthropy. Yet, as fundraising efforts approach a "perfect" private taxation system,[86] fewer and fewer checks and balances are left in the system to prevent such a development.

With the advent of Total Federation, sought or unsought, there would remain, one suspects, only one major difference between private and public philanthropy: the administration of public philanthropy—at least nominally —is under the control of the voter as donor-taxpayer, while the administration of private philanthropy would under Total Federation be largely under the control of a small élite group. Thus, the difference between Total Federation and a government-operated plan is essentially very nearly that between taxation with representation (Public Philanthropy) and taxation without representation (Totally Federated Private Philanthropy).

Perhaps we should not overstate the resemblance, because even Total Federation would not be able to impose *legal* sanctions. But the choice left to the donor would be to give to all MOPS fundraising organizations or to none. This leaves little room for choice; and if, as one would suspect, the pressures available to the federation would virtually force participation as the fundraising system became more inclusive, then the donor's choice would be even more nominal than it now is—or, even, than it would be under United Fund. There would be small option as to whether or not to give: probably every donor would find it expedient to contribute if he wanted to work and live at all comfortably in the community.

Whether or not Total Federation would be more efficient than other federated fundraising is difficult to guess. Such a monopoly might very well finally result in less efficient operation. Since there would be little or no stimulus and example from other fundraising efforts, it is not likely that the super-federation would be able to develop and maintain the most efficient operation.[87]

## UNIFICATION AMONG DONORS

It is time to turn from our preoccupation with unification among solicitors to a discussion of unification among donors. Such a unification, the emergence out of a hapless donor-aggregate of a vital donor community, may be viewed either as an *alternative* to the proposed federation among solicitors or as an *accompaniment* to organization on one side of organization on the other. On the first view, if the donors were self-organized to give through an instrument of their own creation and choosing, the question of whether there was to be one major beneficiary or a series of independent ones would become very secondary. On the second view, the organization of one set of interests—those of the receivers—calls for the organization of the other set of interests—those of the givers—to permit appropriate checks, to ensure adequate balance, and to secure negotiation between parties of approximately equal powers and capacities for self-defence.[88]

Not that the idea of *some* unification among donors is merely an untried idea, or by any means wholly new. One most popular form, In-Plant Federation, we have already met in this chapter, and while solicitors see it very often as a mere prelude to United Fund, donors may well see it as an alternative or counterweight: an organization, at the plant level, of themselves as donors to deal together with the solicitors, unified or divided.

### Plant Level: In-Plant Federation

The term "in-plant federation"[89] has been used in a great variety of ways, and one of the most difficult problems in public discussion of the subject is to distinguish clearly between the essential fact of a plant-level donors' organization, the form of the solicitation, and the many techniques which can be used to implement the program. "In-plant federation" means simply that within an organization—for example, a firm, an agency, or a government office—only one general solicitation is conducted among the employees for the support of any, and all, charitable activities to which the organization subscribes,[90] and that decisions as to the distribution of the results are made by all the donors or some of them at plant level.

Many people regard what is merely one of the possible techniques of collecting money as an essential feature of In-Plant Federation. "Payroll deduction" is commonly an accompaniment, but is not a necessary feature of In-Plant Federation, which can be operated with any one of a number of collection techniques. There are advantages with payroll deduction—it tends to result in larger pledges[91] and undoubtedly facilitates their collection—but there is usually a high total cost of collection to the employer.

Similarly no particular protocol of distribution is inherent in In-Plant Federation. Although some method for distributing the funds collected must be developed by any organization using In-Plant Federation, there is no set pattern which is essential to it as a form of organization. The method of allocating the funds to agencies (or unified fundraising organizations) has little, if any, effect on the operation of In-Plant Federation—except that the wishes of all the contributors must presumably be satisfied, to a greater or less extent, depending on the degree of donor control in each plant. Some of the possible ways of allocating funds are: designation by each donor; allocation by a management committee; allocation by an employee committee; allocation by a committee which has both management and employee representatives; allocation by a labor union committee. Any of these methods permits changes to be made with regard to the appeals supported, or the proportion given to each appeal, whenever the situation is felt to warrant such changes. Sometimes, by fiat of management or as a result of committee decision, a relatively fixed or permanent formula for allocating funds to specified agencies is employed. Under yet other arrangements the rule is to allocate in proportion to each appeal's changing annual goal.[92] Such methods tend to be less adaptable to changing situations than do those which employ committees to make the decisions on changes in the amount allocated and on appeals to be included.

The distinction to be held in mind is between a form and level of organization among donors, on one hand, and whatever solicitation program and distribution scheme they may decide upon, on the other.[93] The essential part of In-Plant Federation is the unification *in the plant* of the giving: each In-Plant Federation represents at that level a *union of givers*, able to dictate how many campaigns a year they will permit themselves to be exposed to (within their plant), how communication in reference to these will be carried on, and how the resultant take is to be distributed between potential recipients. In so far as this is a collective decision at plant level, there may be some loss of freedom to the individual worker (though many could contract out of or "slow down" any arrangement they thought too arbitrary or onerous). But whatever freedom is lost here to the individual donor is reserved to the plant-level group of donors, who are at least better able to act in concert to utilize that freedom than is any atomized general public or unorganized donor-aggregate.

### Sector Level: Industrial and Commercial Donors' Association

It need not, however, be taken for granted that donor unification must be restricted to plant level. Just as there is no visible obstacle to a partial United Fund for the Commercial and Industrial sector, so also there is no visible reason why this key segment of the donorate might not also organize itself into a donor sub-community, with benefit to solicitors and donors alike. It is important, of course, to distinguish clearly between the idea here presented and the scheme described in the earlier section on the unification of solicitation, i.e., between federations formed by the Industrial and Commercial donors themselves to give, and to regulate and rationalize their own giving, and federations formed by groups of agencies to get money from Industrial and Commercial donors.

The former, which we are now discussing, is simply an alliance for association of such Industrial and Commercial donors as care to join with a view to: (1) giving money; (2) concerting policy; (3) rationalizing their joint behavior; (4) protecting themselves against intimidation, fraud, or exploitation; and (5) in general, giving effect to their common philanthropic wishes by counterpoising to the giant fundraising organization at least one unit of comparable size which could deal with it on equal terms and preserve some independence.

The funds of such an Association, derived from the pledges of firms and/or their employees, would then be disbursed to any and all agencies approved by the donor-group itself, in approved proportions and ways, and subject to approved checks. The association would not only provide defence against a multiplicity of campaigns, but could also make the decision for its constituent businesses and businessmen—or else advise them—as to what philanthropies to support and in what proportions. It might very well operate a trust fund ("banking") for the philanthropy of businesses and their employees—something that seems to be required, in the interests of the solicitors, to balance out the year-to-year fluctuations in available take.

In combination with In-Plant Federation, an Industrial and Commercial Donors' Association could, it would seem, very adequately supply for businesses the same advantages as would United Fund, and also offer advantages[94] which it is difficult to see how a United Fund could provide.

Such a form of organization would also provide an unusual solicitation situation for all agencies—"independents," members of local federations, or national organizations alike. All non-members of the federation would be open to solicitation by each and every agency—at least within limitations which may be self-imposed. But while all agencies which hope to be beneficiaries of the Association of Industrial and Commercial Donors would necessarily have to present their case for funds to it, much of the now necessary effort of solicitation would be eliminated. This situation would, one might well believe, provide some protection of the major donors and, at the same time, permit the agencies a considerable amount of freedom of action. But again there is no evident reason why organization of donors should be restricted to the sector level as long as soliciting is organized at the community-wide level.

### Community Level: General Donors' Association

The interests of donors could probably best be protected by the formation of an organization which had this as its sole function. This may seem obvious; yet, as far as we were able to learn, no such organization is now in existence.[95]

Donors—particularly major donors—appear (as far as our study has exposed us to them) to want neither to be parsimonious nor wasteful in their allocation of funds, but to ensure by their gifts the intelligent planning of voluntary services, so that these may go forward and develop sensibly, and on a scale that improves with the disposable resources of the community and with the enlarging aspirations of people for a tolerably good life for all. The protection of the interests of donors is therefore not opposed to the protection of the interests of professional fundraisers or of the agencies or the agencies' clients. No donor we encountered wished merely to cut gifts or punish fundraisers or hobble agencies. Their concerns were with the sense or lack of it in the tangled mass of philanthropically supported enterprises, with the sense and common honesty (or the lack of them) in the appeals and—our phrase, not theirs—the gift-load distribution. What they seemed to be asking, put positively, was the same kind of commonsense oversight of results, and control of input and outgo, that characterizes an ordinarily well-run business. What they wanted—as the study itself shows, as well as presumes—was information that would permit them to adjust their practices of giving and the government of giving so that they could confidently give more or less, as seemed appropriate. They did not ask or expect to be given an argument that would justify diminished involvement, monetary or personal.

If there is to be anything like such sensible planning—or indeed, if there is to be something that moves towards that goal rather than away from it— the donors must be in a position which permits them continuous access to accurate and relevant information. Beyond this, they must be in a position which permits them, once they have the information, to exert an appropriate degree of continuous control.

Neither such information nor such control, we infer from what we have observed, now comes, or is likely to come, out of the existing Chest-Council-Agency set-up. The information customarily procured and presented by these organizations does not appear to be of a kind which adequately protects the donors' interest. Nor does it appear that any minor reform of the structure would make this possible or likely. It seems about as reason-able to look to the Chest or Council for representation or protection of the donor or the public interest in these matters as it would be to look to a public utility for the protection of the public interest in rate cases. If the utility accountant and public relations men are doing a good job, the utility normally appears to have a good case for higher rates. For this reason, courts or public utility commissions or other bodies—independent of the utilities concerned—are provided where the facts and the arguments can be brought into public review, often under the safeguard of sworn testi-mony, and with an advocate to plead the public interest against that of the utility concerned. It would appear to be idle to try to "solve" the problem of public interest by adding staff to the utility which would better enable it to "prove" its case, or to try to decide the issues by some process ("budget-ing") which merely allocated among the many departments of the utility the proportion of the total take each was "entitled" to.

If the case is clear in reference to a public utility, traditionally it has been less clear in the field of fundraising, or the work supported thereby. And there is now no body corresponding to the public utility commission before which the interests of the donor might be heard—or, alternatively, by which the interests of the donor might be represented. The lack of such a body may be due to the seemingly widespread illusion that either the Chest or the Council, or both, provides a service of this nature. As far as we can tell, neither group provides an independent audit or anything that approximates it, nor is either group able to protect the general public interest or that of the donors.

The illusion that the Chest or the Council provides such a check seems to stem from the belief that the governing bodies of these institutions are made up of "representative laymen" and that these laymen will serve to protect the interests of either the public or the donors or both. Whether or not they are representative is irrelevant to what follows,[96] since it is also an illusion that protection of the donors' interest could be provided by a Chest or Council, even if it did have a "representative" body of laymen to govern it. The illusion, in turn, rests on a misconception of the role and behavior of the laymen in such an agency. Observation indicates that no matter what the interest with which the layman first comes to such an organization, in a relatively short time he is no longer the watchdog or champion of that interest, but has instead become the champion or protagonist of the organization itself.[97] There need be no conscious break or shift in allegiance. It is simply that as the layman becomes involved (after he has asked the first few searching questions), he tends shortly to take for fact that which the organization puts out as fact, and his capacity to judge issues (on behalf of the interest he originally intended to represent or protect) diminishes rapidly towards ineffectiveness. Indeed, in several cases that have come under our direct view, the layman has become so enthused in a partisan sense that he has shown himself willing to manipulate, to mislead, and to deceive the very interest-group of which he himself is a member—the group of major donors and, more particularly, the businessmen in his own line of business. Such enthusiasm may, no doubt, be commendable, but it is pressing human nature too far to look to it for any check or brake on the already sufficient enthusiasms of the professional fundraisers.

There are additional reasons why it seems idle to look to the Chest or Council to fulfil the function of protecting donors. The situation in each case deserves separate examination.

The Chest, it seems, cannot act as the protector of the donor interest since the donor-community, if there is one (or the donor-aggregate, if there is not) is a source of potential "resistance" to the work of the Chest and the Chest must, therefore, devise suitable devices for overcoming such resistance. The test of the adequacy of those devices from the viewpoint of the Chest is the test of success: are they able, in practice, to get the money out of the donors or the potential donors? Thus, the Chest's function of obtaining all the funds it is able to get from the donors is hardly compatible with protection of their interest.[98]

Placing the protection of donors with the Health and Welfare Council would serve principally to compound confusion, and, very likely, to make the present situation considerably worse. Even when the inflated claims that Councils make have been dismissed, it is perhaps difficult to appreciate how special, how narrowly circumscribed are their interests, and how partisan is the role that they do and perhaps must play.

It is true that Councils no longer generally represent purely the interests of the social agencies in quite the same way that many did until recently. They were then quite explicitly called "Councils of Social Agencies." In some ways that organization of the Council—clearly in terms of the interests of the professionals and social agencies—may have been better, since at least it was then clear what the Council *did* represent. In any case, a Council now tends to be at the best a representative of the "Welfare Community," i.e., all those operators and their associated and convinced laymen who share a particular, and perhaps not very widely held, view of what would be to the community's interest and benefit.[99] But under the new dispensation a Council still has its own particular agenda. Having ceased to be a sort of co-operative or holding company for the agencies—to which at least competing interests could then be successfully opposed—it is often driven to seek power on its own account, and sometimes at the expense of its own agencies, in order, so far as possible, to get the role of "planning" wholly into its own hands.[100]

What has been said above for Chest laymen is true with even greater force, perhaps, for Council laymen, judging by the claims, written or spoken, to which they have lent themselves. They seem even less able to see the picture except in the special perspective that their Council position provides.

For the Chest or Council to assume the role of donor-protector would confuse issues for the donors still further. To have the appearance of independence without its reality seems worse than to have the frank appearance of partisanship. A lobbyist may be no great threat; but a lobbyist cast as a judge represents some public danger. Any person who is to make any searching inquiry into the validity of agency claims or the relative merits or values of their arguments or performances must know in whose interest he is inquiring and to whom he is responsible.

In the course of this study, its staff has been, as already pointed out, struck with the amount of statistical juggling that goes on, and more particularly with the emergence of a new type of professional armed with pseudo-rational standards and formulae (such as those for giving) and often clad in a mantle of pseudo-research. Indeed, as we said earlier, in one community we examined which had a most "successful" Chest, the "research" wing of that Chest comes very close to being a successful espionage system directed against the donor who is reluctant to accept outside guidance as to his giving or giving procedures. The admitted sole object of this research department, which is regarded as a model by its local sponsors and national admirers, is to find the weak point in a business organization at which pressure can most effectively be brought to bear. The object of the pressure is, of course, to get a management decision to give at a given level reversed in favor of a larger gift. Against this kind of professional, it seems to us, the business community is more defenceless and helpless than it was against the more old-fashioned type of openly partisan fund-seeker.

To the degree that the foregoing argument holds, it would seem that the first step worthy of consideration would be the creation of a suitably serviced donors' association, independent of the Chest and Council.[101]

A General Donors' Association would presumably have as its main function the evaluation of all appeals to which its members are subject.

It might, at least, provide an advisory service on philanthropy to its members. The merits of each appeal would be examined both as to the size of the goal and as to the use to which the funds would be put. The association's staff, probably no more than an executive and secretary initially,[102] would analyse and report upon the load-distribution. But, more important, perhaps, than any of these advice-and-analysis functions—though it rests upon them—would be the provision of a means for donors of various kinds to meet, discuss in an atmosphere free of propaganda their "rights" and their "obligations," and see to the recognition of the one upon the discharge of the other.

What is suggested essentially here, then, is a system of analysis and planning by, and bargaining or honest negotiation between, separate research and action bodies, each of which is partisan to the interests which it represents: the Federation would have its own research and planning activities devoted solely to the function of raising the money; the Council would have its own research and planning activities devoted solely to the integration and development (whether it be expansion or contraction) of agency programs; and the Association would have its own research and planning activities devoted solely to evaluating appeals in order to protect all donors.

While there *might* be some increase in cost in setting up the third organization—and we do not believe this to be so—certainly in the long run, the donors' association would produce substantial savings for the donors —not only because it would provide a shield against the multitudes of appeals, but also because it would assist in the introduction of the rationality that all appear to desire into a field which presently lives on a substantial diet of fiction, folklore, and myth.

### UNIFICATION INDEPENDENTLY OF SOLICITORS AND OF DONORS

Perhaps—as already suggested—the answer that will prove most apt in the years to come is not an answer in terms of "either . . . or" but of "both . . . and." Perhaps it is not a matter of choice between unifying and strengthening solicitors and unifying and strengthening donors.

The degree of integration or unification on the fundraising side may well call for—in the best interest of all—a corresponding degree of integration on the fund-giving side. It may well be that to United Fund there should be counterpoised United Donors.

### UNIFICATION AND CONTROL

No matter what form or forms of unification are attempted or put into effect, there will always remain problems of control. These need now to be directly addressed. Essentially, again, they may be viewed as dual problems—problems in the control of *asking* and problems in the control of *giving*. We propose to deal with these in that order.

## Control of Giving

The very idea of "controlling" giving—either in the sense of preventing foolish giving or in the sense of compelling wise donation—is repugnant to those sentiments that lie at the very core of voluntary organization. The right to be foolish is perhaps as precious a right as can well be conceived, and it is in fact in the name of preventing foolishness that so many more obvious rights have, historically, so often been subverted.

We are perhaps mistaken, then, in speaking of "controlling" giving, when the best that can be hoped is that it should be free but *informed*. If this view is taken, then the problem is one of information for the donor; this whole study is an essay in just that, and all the suggestions in the preceding sections regarding organization of donors and the encouragement of a donor-community are ways in which, we think, such informing of the donor may be institutionalized and made effective. The essential point of it all—and it needs, surely, no further pressing—is that if the donor is to be informed (rather than confused, conformed, and led about) he will either have to look to some relatively neutral source for his information (instead of to a party at interest) or to count upon an instrument of his own choosing, a Donors' Association, to protect him against the instruments of the solicitors' choosing, with their quite natural but by no means neutral designs upon his income.

## Control of Asking

We may pass to the problem of controlling "asking." This also has some difficult constitutional and ethical aspects, but we find ourselves forced to discuss it at greater length, if only because it is such a widespread practice and one not so evidently repugnant to traditional freedoms. We have also left the discussion of endorsement of legitimate causes and the control of "charity rackets" until now because these activities can be, and often are, carried on outside the fundraising system itself, and there is much to recommend this separation. Endorsement and control present a large number of problems but we shall deal with only a few.[103]

A number of different methods have been used in trying to safeguard the field of philanthropy from the more blatant rackets and the more excessively expensive fundraising efforts. These methods are essentially of two kinds: Police Controls and Educational Controls.

By "police control" we do not mean control by the police; we mean, analogically, effective control by the use of actual or potential power under law. There are many methods which rely on some form of legal sanction for the control of solicitation for charity and other "good works." Laws enacted by twenty states and numerous cities present a diverse array of method of administration: in Iowa and Pennsylvania, the Secretary of State has jurisdiction over the administration of the law; the Department of Welfare acts in New York State; while in Ohio it is the Attorney-General who is given authority.

Indianapolis, itself, serves well as an example of police control of solicitation. The constituent Act[104] in Indianapolis is dated 1942, but it supersedes earlier "legislation" of 1934, as its title shows. Visibly, Indianapolis has long been committed to the desire to exert in this area a police power, and has long had legislation purporting to permit it to do so.[105] Under the ordinance, all charity solicitation (except some religious solicitation) must be licensed by the Charities Solicitation Commission before the solicitation can be made. The Commission is charged with the responsibility of determining that the organization meets the requirements of the ordinance before issuing a licence. The major requirements are that the solicitation should cost no more than a reasonable amount (no more than 25 per cent of the amount raised in most cases), that the soliciting organization have adequate accounting and auditing procedures, and that the money raised will be used for charitable purposes.

It is difficult to evaluate the effectiveness of police control of solicitation in Indianapolis. From the number of appeals which have seemed to be in violation of the ordinance and yet have gone unpunished, it would appear that the ordinance is not very strictly enforced. On June 28, 1955, the *Indianapolis News* printed the following article under the headline "Law vs. the Law," "Police Fight License to Solicit Funds":

> The city's Charity Solicitation Commission and the Fraternal Order of Police couldn't agree today on whether the order should have a license to solicit funds.
> As far as the commission is concerned, the FOP is breaking the law.
> But Detective Sgt. Cecil London, FOP president, snorted defiance.
> "The commission has no business telling us we need a license. We don't think we should. We never have, and we don't intend to. It's no soap," he said.
> The commission, headed by Mrs. John Burkhart, says FOP must get a charity solicitation license since its members are selling tickets for the fifth annual Police Athletic League circus July 9 and 10. Circus profits benefit the PAL clubs for boys sponsored by FOP to curb juvenile delinquency.
> A city ordinance . . . is designed to regulate solicitations for charitable and other purposes.
> "We're not after charity for anybody. We're not a charity organization," London stoutly maintained. "We never have had to take out a license and we've never had any trouble!"
> His boss, Chief of Police John Ambuhl, backed him up. In Ambuhl's opinion, the FOP has violated no law. Ambuhl is a member of the six-man commission. And he's also a member of the FOP.
> The city's legal department is puzzling over the dispute.

Other organizations which have been denied licences have gone ahead with their solicitation without any punitive action being taken by the Commission.[106]

Beyond the question of whether such legislation is momentarily effective, is the long-term question of whether it is constitutional at all under United States law. We cannot enter here into a detailed argument on a legal question upon which, evidently, even competent constitutional lawyers have different opinions. But there is a grave doubt as to constitutionality, and it is worth stating where the doubt lies.

No one doubts that the legislation in question is grounded in the undisputed inherent police powers of the City, nor is it seriously doubted that those powers include the power to enact ordinances for the protection of health, life, and property[107]—or the protection of the financial safety of the public.[108] The doubt is not here, nor is it related to a possible question as to whether the ordinance is legally binding upon non-residents, or as to the legality of the provisions that might appear to limit the uses to which the United States mail may be put. The serious doubt is as to whether the statute could be sustained under the Fourteenth Amendment (". . . No State shall make or enforce any law which shall abridge the privileges or immunities of citizens of the United States, nor shall any State deprive any person of life, liberty or property without due process of law . . ."), more particularly since this declaration is held to embrace the liberties guaranteed under the First Amendment. The latter liberties include those of free speech and freedom of religion, and these liberties are clearly touched upon in the Ordinance, at least in so far as the Commission may be required to determine—without regard to "due process"—what is a religious cause, and whether or not the organization is run by people of good character and in a businesslike manner. The power of the Commission to deny a licence, in its discretion, if it finds against the good character of the charitable organization and its members, might therefore seem to place a prior restraint upon the right of every person, under the Constitution, to solicit contributions for a worthy charitable purpose, provided he acts in good faith and honestly applies them to that purpose.

Many ordinances of this type in other cities are also suspect as to their constitutionality according to persons interested in solicitation control. But despite the mentioned weaknesses—in effectiveness and, probably, legality—such ordinances, in practice, probably serve to put some check on grossly fraudulent solicitations. On a short-run pragmatic view, this might serve to recommend them. But even a devotee of the method would surely have to concede that, since such laws are difficult to enforce, even if constitutional, it would appear that police control of solicitation does not provide, by itself, a sufficiently good method of controlling solicitations. We may therefore properly look for an alternative or supplement.

This may be found in "educational control," by which we mean all of those methods which use information services as the main weapon against rackets, poorly administered agencies, agencies duplicating functions of other agencies, and solicitation techniques which are wasteful. The Subscriptions Investigating Committee of the Chicago Association of Commerce and Industry[110] and the Contributors Information Bureau of the Welfare and Health Council of New York City provide excellent examples of educational control, and of the kinds of organizations to which these informational services are often attached.[111]

The statements about fundraising organizations used by these groups are normally confined simply to indications that they "approve" or "do not approve" the campaign,[112] since there is considerable danger of becoming subject to legal action in saying anything very specific for or against a fundraising organization. Sometimes, a list of approved organizations is published, and the subscribers or members of the service have the opportunity of receiving confidential reports about organizations which are not approved. Other services do not publish any lists, but simply make available to the subscriber, information about any fundraising organization—whether approved or not.

Approval is usually dependent on the fundraising organization's meeting a stated set of criteria. Among the usual criteria are requirements that: (a) the organization should be a not-for-profit social or "civic" agency; (b) the accounts should be audited annually by a public accountant; (c) the organization should maintain a sufficient and competent staff which conducts the program according to "recognized standards of work"; (d) the agency should meet a "recognized need"; (e) there should be an active, responsible board which meets regularly (often also it is required that the board not be paid by the agency); (f) there should be participation by the agency in appropriate co-ordinating programs; and (g) "ethical" methods of fundraising should be used.[113]

Organizations which attempt to educate the public to be careful about the causes to which they contribute have been associated historically with three types of parent organizations. Some have been sponsored by Chambers of Commerce (as in Chicago), others by a Health and Welfare Council or its equivalent (as in New York City) and still others by a Better Business Bureau or its equivalent (as in many small towns and cities).

The methods of control by Chambers of Commerce seem to be related to the size of the city in which the control is attempted. Some large city Chambers have investigating committees (sometimes with secret membership) which report at regular intervals to Chamber members. In some places, a permit must be secured from the Chamber before its members will contribute to an organization.[114] The Better Business Bureau method is quite similar. The national Bureau exchanges information with its local affiliates and maintains a file of over 150,000 names of individuals and organizations. It handles more than 10,000 inquiries a year.

But none of these educational programs seems wholly satisfactory. Undoubtedly many members of these services refer to the information about each organization to which they contemplate contributing, but, since the demand for more and better regulation seems nearly universal, apparently the programs are too limited with regard to the number of people they reach, or too many subscribers are ignoring the recommendations.

Although both types of solicitation control—police and educational—have been used for local situations, neither appears, then, to be sufficiently effective. Perhaps they are ineffective because the problem has not been taken seriously enough. Perhaps it has not been made structurally and organizationally clear that the responsibility for protecting the donors—if they are to be protected—lies with the donors: it cannot ethically be devolved upon the fundraisers, or effectively fobbed off, as a side-issue, upon Chambers of Commerce or Better Business Bureaus. A Donors' Association—besides its other indicated functions—might well locate this responsibility where it belongs, i.e., with the group who stand most to benefit if all goes well, and who will likely be blamed anyway if all does not. Such an association could hardly perform its main tasks without explicitly approving "sound" agencies and organizations and, at least by implication, disapproving of "unworthy" solicitations. It would not keep all unworthy causes from raising money—any more than do any of the present methods—but it would certainly reduce the opportunities for the unscrupulous to "turn a fast buck"; and it would be particularly effective in closing the door to further exploitation of the larger donors, which is of considerable consequence not only for those donors but for all other donors, and—viewing them together—for all solicitors as well.

## Unification and Freedom

We have discussed a number of possible approaches to fundraising and the problems it raises in modern America. What we have tried to do is to indicate the kinds of checks and balances which might well have to be built into the system if it is not to become even more monolithic and monopolistic.[115]

Among the possibilities we have discussed, we have tried to find some which are adaptable to many situations. A Donors' Association would be useful in almost any fundraising situation, but it does *not* become essential until agency federations grow big and powerful enough to ignore very largely the interest of the donors. In-Plant Federation, although often considered as primarily a soliciting device applicable in any type of fundraising situation, may more usefully be viewed in terms of donor organization, and, therefore, offers a clear alternative to any further fundraising unification, if mature consideration should indicate that, with more solicitor "unification," the losses would outweigh the benefits.

What seems to be the key problem is the devising of a system which makes explicit the difference in interest of the parties to fundraising. Almost any combination of the possibilities which we have mentioned—and, no doubt, others which we have not discussed—might provide a useful, workable philanthropic endeavour, so long as the interests of donors, fundraisers, and agencies are simultaneously advanced, in so far as they are common, and protected where clash of interest occurs. This might be done either in an integrated structure, or, more probably, by the establishment of three separate organizations, each of which has the advance and protection of one of these interests as its major or sole purpose. The problem is only obscured when it is stated as a problem in freedom *or* control: what the parties to the transaction seem most evidently to want is controls in one field which will increase their freedom in matters deemed more important.

The preservation of some considerable freedom in philanthropy becomes a consideration of overwhelming import, not only because, in general, in the modern world, freedom is becoming increasingly difficult to preserve and so increasingly valuable in the face of universal, large-scale bureaucratization, but also because, in particular, and in this area, the very sense of the enterprise and the core of its claim is that it does provide an arena for voluntary and dedicated behavior. If the enterprise becomes organized on so large a scale that it can (because of its power) or must (because of its needs) secure conformity by constraint and coercion, then the "voluntary" element may well become so attenuated that a principal ground for the loyalty required for its defence is radically undercut. And if, at the same time that the soliciting enterprise becomes so organized, the giving enterprise becomes either increasingly divided or increasingly organized by the solicitors in common cause, then another motive in the supporting layman—the sense of his own potency and effectiveness—may be so weakened that he can only be impressed into service as an impotent and profitless servant. Neither of these consequences—already both visible as clouds upon the horizon—seems to be consonant with the general philosophy of North American society, or in particular, with the expressed philosophies underlying social work in general and community organization, in particular.[116]

But if these end-results, undesired by any so far as we know, are to be avoided, then thought must be taken to build in appropriate institutional means to prevent them, or, more positively, to secure something else. That "something else" to be sought is, perhaps, at this stage in the history of philanthropy, the precipitation of a community of free givers: "free" because they are informed and left with meaningful choices, and "a community" because the ground for consensus has been cleared and the machinery provided for reaching and remaking it out of their own strength, knowledge, wisdom, and wit.[117]

# V. CONCLUSION

# 14. Summary

THE OBJECT of the study, as given to Community Surveys, Inc. both by its own Board of Directors and the Board of Directors of the Indianapolis Community Chest, was to seek for answers to the persistent question: "What's wrong with our Chest?" The evidence that something was "wrong" was held to lie in the Chest's obvious incapacity to attract or retain "top top leadership" and its persistent financial "failure," i.e., its incapacity to meet or beat the "goals" it set for itself from year to year.

It seemed to us that in order to answer this question we would have to dig deep for more than superficial answers. We would have to try to understand something of the history of philanthropy in America (of which the Chest's history is only a part); something of the peculiar life of Indiana and Indianapolis (of which fundraising is only a part); something of the interplay of these two developments, i.e., of the history of philanthropy in Indianapolis. With this for background, we would have to examine what the objectives or aims of the Indianapolis Chest seemed to be—not only as stated on paper, but as shown in the speech and in the action of the Chest's professional staff and intimate lay supporters.

Before evaluating the Chest any further it seemed necessary to set up something more than arbitrary standards of judgment. The local community believed the Chest to be "failing" in the arbitrary sense that it frequently failed to meet its goal. But for all we knew, and all anybody in Indianapolis or elsewhere knew, this failure might have represented nothing more than an error of judgment in setting the goal too high. Moreover, "failure," if it is to be made a spur to greater effort, must mean failure-in-relation-to-opportunity. We had therefore, we felt, to find a way of judging the "potential" of a given city; only in relation to that potential could it meaningfully be said that a given Chest was "succeeding" or "failing" to do what might reasonably be expected, i.e., to do what other Chests in like circumstances were doing.

In the same way that we had to define standards for financial "success" we had to try to define standards for "social success": the human side of the operation that makes the financial one possible.

We would then be in a position, we hoped, to state what are some of the major problems of mass fundraising, and what are the facts-of-life in

Indianapolis—first on the money side, and then on the human side. Only with these tasks done, did we feel it right to ask what might be done in Indianapolis, either with the present Chest structure or under some substantial further unification—a more "United Fund."

## PHILANTHROPY IN AMERICA

The whole of American history itself is but a day, historically, and yet it is within that day that the whole of "modern history" lies. In the short span from Plymouth Rock to the Geneva Conference or the Suez crisis, America appears serially as a discovery, a string of settlements, a group of colonies, a nation, and, finally, a Colossus, bestriding the modern world and pouring out upon it an endless stream of invention, social and technical. It is this that is—if anything is—peculiarly "the American way."

Paralleling this meteoric rise—from the wilderness to the traffic-jam in ten generations—has been the fact of change as virtually the only changeless fact of life. Every social institution, every habit of life for the individual, taste and fashion, manners and morals, culture, even, and personality type— all these form, reform, and are transformed with such dizzying rapidity that one is hard put to it to find those principles of continuity which give the story its distinctive character as *American* history.

Within this tumbling flow of events—and partly in response to other changes and partly in terms of its own intrinsic logic—American philanthropy changes, until the enterprise of today is barely recognizable as the offspring of yesterday. It is only in the context of this rapid and radical change, that the confusion of thought and the emotional distress of those who seek brotherly bread and find an otherly stone in the field of philanthropy are properly to be appreciated.

Even within this brief period, philanthropy has itself undergone a number of revolutions. Its major source of income is rapidly becoming the corporation instead of the individual. "Planned" routines of giving—payroll deduction and the year-round campaign—succeed impulse giving; and the beneficiary becomes ever more remote in space and vividness from the donor. The religious mandate to "charity" becomes the civic duty to "bear your fair share," and the problem for the private conscience—"Let not thy right hand know . . ."—becomes a matter of published performance and group "standards." The collection plate or the beggar's extended hand—or its written equivalent, the "subscription list"—is succeeded by a virtual private tax with social penalties not only for the miserly who do not give at all but for the non-conformist who wish to give otherwise or to some other cause. An industry—fundraising—and a profession—the fundraiser—are developed and elaborated to pressure and persuade, to organize giving and mould opinion, to wage a "campaign," regular, relentless, and, as far as possible, irresistible. Preoccupation shifts from the mere relief of disaster and the remedy of dramatic distress to a vaguer, more open-ended program calculated to better or improve life generally—a program that is in principle without stint or limit. The beneficiaries are no longer the unfortunate few, the "needy": "Everybody benefits," it is said, "everybody gives." The fund-seeking agencies multiply, the techniques elaborate and become standardized (the "fund-raising breakfast," for instance) or differentiate and become the hour's passing novelty (the "Telethon" or the "Marines' March," for examples). The pressures increase, the arguments begin to contradict each other, and the layman begins to ask "What's it all about?" and "Where will it all end?"

The sense that "there is a problem" seems universal, judging by the amount of informal discussion and of propaganda literature, pro and con. The sense of how acute the problem is varies from place to place. What makes the problem problematic is partly a result of all this change and growth, partly a matter of local outlook, local ways of life and thought, local habits and traditions and history.

## INDIANA

Indiana is said to be "the heart of America"; Indianapolis prides itself on being "the nation's crossroads." Whatever Indiana is, it is not "everywhere"; it is something special—if only because it thinks of itself as such. What it is, is caught in a word, "Hoosier," and the word evokes an image. The image is not clearly specified and defined—such figures ("John Bull," "Uncle Sam") rarely are—but the word rallies loyalties and regulates behavior. For everything, there is a "Hoosier way," and there is no question that that way is best. It is not only a way: it is *the* way—the way that America ought to follow, indeed had best follow if it is to remain genuinely American and true to its glorious tradition.

That is what the Hoosier way is, as the vocal Hoosier sees it: not a variant of the American way, but its essence, its epitome. "Independence" is its key word: the individual, "independent" of other individuals; the business, "independent" of government; the state government, "independent" of that most subversive of influences, "federal aid." The philanthropic program that really catches at the Hoosier heart because its method embodies "individualism" has as its motto a phrase that sums up the Hoosier hope: "Self Help."

For similar reasons, the word second to "independent" in the Hoosier vocabulary of virtues is "native" or "home-grown." The same belief, fundamentally, that speaks for "independence"—the faith in the strength and virtue of local resources: individual, social, and material—speaks for the native son, or, where this is impossible, for the Hoosier by adoption. If local strength is sufficient, why import "outsiders"—or outside ideas or advice or patterns. The resultant distrust of the "expert," of the plan, of high-flown or abstract ideas has the virtues of its vices: it keeps feet on the ground even if, sometimes, that hobbles movement. Be the field medicine or mental health, welfare or architecture, city planning or psychiatry, the distrust seems evenly high.

This desired pattern of freedom from the expert and from planning is, however, only intermittently achieved. For some reason—the rate of social change, the complexity of the matters to be adjusted to, the fact that today's productive habits are tomorrow's adaptive shackles—the settled ways do not produce the desired results. The hospitals deteriorate, the leadership divides, the old families fall into apathy or isolate themselves or become isolated, the welfare community fragments. Crisis reigns. With the advent of crisis, the need for the advice or intervention of the expert temporarily abates the distrust. He is called in, deliberation takes place, a plan is agreed. Something eventuates, but not what was expected. Inquiry is often not permitted to probe deep enough or to ask the right questions. Or the plan finally adopted is only some part of an original whole plan, and meaningless without reference to the whole—just as a set of steps is meaningless without the house behind it. Or the expert is retained for a just-not-sufficient time: just as he has found his feet and is prepared to act for change his welcome is worn out and he goes—or is sent. The situation is "under control" again, but the next crisis is already bred and moving to its maturity.

This intermittency of exposure to "experts" carries also another consequence. The need to make quick decisions in crisis, given the lack of extended contact (even if it were conflict) with the very competent advisers, makes for some haphazardness in the selection of those finally chosen. It is hard to evaluate the worth of specialist advice without constant practice in the hearing and judging of it. So one sees good advice repudiated, and the most fantastic and arrant nonsense accepted. Suspicion and gullibility go hand in hand. The pseudo-expert who is "reassuring," who gives the impression that great goals can be achieved at low costs and with little disturbance, the man who is "positive," who questions little and criticizes less, has immeasurably the best chance of survival.

Even where the competent specialist or "expert" survives, this is by no means assurance that he and the layman will be able to join their competence to secure the effect both desire. The self-sufficiency ideology makes it difficult for the layman to believe that he will have to work hard, intellectually, and perhaps emotionally, to ensure that he can really "follow"; the "expert," especially if, as with some social workers, he is a doctrinaire nondirectivist, will not realize that, in this situation, he must "lead" or perish— but not lead too much or too far.

The third word in the Hoosier lexicon is "practical." The dislike for what is "theoretical," or what appears theoretical, is as cordial as the dislike for the abstract or high-flown. "Practical" means "what works," especially in the short run—and often, consequently, only for the short run. This tendency or bent militates both against standing sufficiently far off to see particulars in their general bearing, and against historical perspective (although Hoosiers love history) or the long look ahead.

When we ask what, as a consequence, Hoosiers are "against"—and they express oppositions more strongly than protagonisms—we sense that they are against the urban, the secular, the specialized, the centralized, the big, the planned, and the continuous. Such strands in the culture affect both the content and the style—and hence the problems—of doing philanthropic business.

## Philanthropy in Indianapolis

The early history of Indianapolis philanthropy is full of color, full of interesting people, full of benign concern, full of inventiveness and the previously encountered talent for spontaneity and freshness of approach. So much is this the case, that the Hoosier capital has not only frequently shown the nation the way but, by the very excellence for their day of its institutions, tended to attract unintended objects for its beneficence. As long as a century ago we find the "attracted pauper"—the dependent drawn hither because the relief of dependency was to be expected—becoming a problem for discussion.

A quarter of a century later, Indianapolis still seems well abreast of the nation philanthropically, sometimes even in the van. The Charity Organization Society and the Indianapolis Benevolent Society—the combined Chest-and-Council and the principal relief agency of their day—come into existence early, operate amicably, and, if the record is to be trusted, effectively and economically. The city's "top top names" appear in the record and the bearers of those names are evidently themselves engaged—or represented by a member of the family—in the operation.

It is only as the city begins to expand and the problems multiply, as the agencies become more complex and the beneficiaries more remote from the benefactors, that the first indications of serious problems appear. As an 1886 report puts it: "County, neighborhood and village charity will not do for cities. . . ." But for another generation thereafter, local resources are to prove pretty well adequate for local problems. It is really not until small city ways are shown inadequate to big city days that the problems become at all acute. The movement to a stage when the Indianapolis agencies proliferate, grow, specialize, and make increasing appeals for time and money evidently parallels the process in most cities of comparable size. When the period of integration, reunification, federation, is reached, the previously accepted ways of acting and organizing seem no longer adequate, and the new ways, hard to learn.

Yet they continue, since these problems first become evidently pressing in the second decade of the twentieth century, and the Great War of 1914-1918 pulls together in crisis the men and resources to effect at least a temporary solution—in much the same way as, a quarter-century later, the second Great

War was to pull the nation out of a depression to which also it had found no solution.

The First World War marked a period of reprieve for the problem of federation or integration, but it was also the birth period for some local agencies (most notably the Red Cross) and the expansion period for others. These were later to provide new or augmented problems for those who wished to see greater order in fundraising or operation, even at the cost of some freedom. The very success of Indianapolis in these crisis enterprises was in itself to make later problems more acute and later failures more distasteful.

What may be called the period of federation—ushered in about 1920—begins locally in failure and continues in defeat. The Chest begins with so colossal a misjudgment of its potentialities or so decisive a campaign defeat as to secure only a $313,000 take upon a million-dollar goal. At this period, the "top top leadership" is still represented—it has neither been self-withdrawn in despair nor "rotated off the Boards" on principle. But its presence, if necessary to victory, is clearly not sufficient. The record of defeat is to be unbroken up to the Second World War with the exception of four odd years, two of them representing a crisis: the onset of the Great Depression. Again there is to be in the decade last past (1945-1955) but a single "victory"—in the year of the "Korean Incident."

So persistent a discrepancy between intent and achievement argues either some lack of judgment in selecting and declaring the former, or some ineptitude or obstacle in reaching the latter. Which of these is the case we can only learn from subsequent analysis.

But not only is there a failure of finance—if failure it be—there are also signs of strain of a different order in the welfare community. For the whole period and for all the agencies, to fasten upon these years the label "strife-torn" would be to exaggerate; but hostility and recrimination are often severe enough and affect enough persons or agencies, to be audible outside the city, in the relevant professional circles, and to put against its name a question mark as a desirable place to work. Though in some quarters they continue excellent, in others lay-professional relations grow tense and distant enough to make the felt "meeting of minds" on both sides thin and doubtful, and the typical lay-professional relationships, correct, cold, distant, and, to both sides, puzzling or problematic.

It is against this historic background that the contemporary scene may best be viewed. The beginning-point for securing such a view may well be to ask what the Chest is; and the best way to get at that definition initially may be to infer what it is from what "it" says and does. Fundamental in its self-definition are those statements or acts that define *purposes*, and to these we may now turn.

From here on, moreover, we are interested no longer in all philanthropy, but in mass, operational, periodic, secular fundraising, "MOPS fundraising" as we call it—the dominant modern form.

## Aims and Purposes of the Chest

The Chest is, of course, on one view a group of people. Groups of people, depending on how they are organized or how much "spontaneous" agreement there is, may speak as one man or, clamorously, with the tongues of many. The effect may be one of unison, chorus—or Babel.

The Chest is not so organized that, regardless of latent disagreement, it can speak with one voice, as in a dictatorship or similar "authoritarian structure." If there is no achieved agreement on ends, it cannot be made to appear that there is by the structural device of permitting only one man to "speak for" the organization. Differences in statements of ends are, therefore, to be expected, even if there were "agreement on essentials"—as in any good democracy. But, as the sequel will show, it is precisely with respect to essentials that the expressions regarding what the Chest is or should be differ most; and the differences are not stylistic variants in defining a common core of wish or expectation, but deep divisions within and between men as to "what it is all about." These divisions do have immediate and visible consequences: we see policy being pressed in inconsistent directions, incompatible action taken and inconsistent public statements made by different persons with, in general, a great deal of interpersonal wear and tear and strain. And, within men, we see conflict, disillusionment, anger, cynicism, disappointment, or apathy. Hence, these theoretical issues have practical consequences.

The latent issues are of many kinds, but the principal ones, and those most charged emotionally, revolve around several distinct questions. One of these—perhaps the most fundamental—is whether the Chest ought fundamentally to conceive of itself in relation to the community as an occupying army, levying what it needs while provoking as little rebellion as possible, or whether it ought to conceive itself more on the model of an instrumentality of local desire, registering rather than manipulating public opinion, expressing local forces rather than molding them. This fundamental question can be seen behind others now to be asked.

(1) *Is the paramount objective of the Chest* (or ought it to be) *the extraction of money from the public or the organizing of that public into a community,* united in virtue of its shared endeavor to provide for certain health and welfare activities? Should an increase in the take from those already giving be the main aim of campaign policy, or should an increase in "participation" in the giving of money—"broadening the base"—be the principal focus of concern?

(2) *Is the Chest primarily* (or ought it to be) *an organization of "the best people"* (or the "fortunate") to provide for the needy or "less fortunate"—*or is it "an organization of all the people"* doing things for one another? Should control vest in a small number of people who can act decisively and powerfully for the Chest, or should it be spread in such a manner that, even

though immediate effectiveness is diminished, all sizeable segments of the community are represented, and, in some sense, participant?

(3) *Is the Chest* (or ought it to be) *an organization that embodies in its statements and its relations a substantial degree of honesty and plain dealing, or is it sufficient to have the semblance of so doing?* Should the Chest strive towards "full, frank and free disclosure," or towards whatever permissible dishonesty is involved in the conception of "most effective selling"? Is "education" or "propaganda" the model for communication? Who is to tell the truth, in respect to what, and to whom?

(4) *Is the Chest giving* (or ought it to give) *primary emphasis to long-run considerations or to short-term advantage?* Is the "land" (the giving public) to be "cultivated" for its long-term yield or "mined" for its maximum short-run return?

(5) *Is the Chest striving* (or ought it to strive) *to preserve the voluntary element in giving, or should it exert the maximum pressure in order to secure maximum immediate returns?* This question applies both to money-getting and service-getting (recruiting and retention of solicitors). As an organization of givers of money and services, is it an army of volunteers or an army of conscripts?

(6) *Is the Chest* (or ought it to be) *primarily an organization for channelling charity or an organization for implementing mutual service?* Is it, put plainly, the money arm of a special recourse for the unusually "needy," or is it the money arm for a set of routine or regular "services for all"?

It is not being suggested here that these oppositions can be entirely resolved, nor, certainly, that black-or-white solutions are practically possible —or, even, ethically desirable. All that is being pointed to is great and widespread present disagreement about fundamental aims and procedures, accompanied by the dislocations between people and within them that one would expect, and without explicit recognition of what is troubling people or, therefore, any machinery for resolving conflict or compounding difference in working compromise. If the resultant emotional tone can be caught in one word, that word would be "irritation." Sometimes running high, sometimes low—mostly like a low-grade fever without obvious focal infection—irritation now with this, now with that aspect of Chest operation characterizes much interview material.

## How to Assess a Chest's Financial Performance

It is time to turn from ideals to money, from that about which men are disagreed to what all would consider one indispensable requirement of successful Chest operation. Yet even when attention is restricted to a Chest's money-raising capacity, there is by no means any widespread agreement as to how its financial success or lack thereof is to be assessed. Some people wish to assess a Chest by the proportion of the local "need" it meets; some by its capacity to achieve its self-set goal; some by the share of the national income (or of the income of all Chests combined) that it gets; some by its capacity to show, in its annual take, substantial, consistent increase; some by its capacity to make giving rational, or by the degree of achieved equity between givers; some by performance in terms of total take or take per capita. Without prejudice to other forms of analysis, we elected to study performance-in-relation-to-opportunity, sensing that the question our sponsors really asked amounted to "How well is our Chest doing in relation to what it could do?" i.e., in relation to its "market."

Since there was no established way of assessing a Chest area's potential, we had to attempt to devise one. We listened to everyone available and likely to have an informed opinion as to what does and does not affect a Chest's per capita take. We tested these and other factors (some thirty-odd) to see whether, in general, they seemed to affect Chest performance. By trial and error (i.e., by statistical testing) we established five factors that together accounted for nearly three-fourths (74 per cent) of all the variation between the percapitas of various Chests, and in that sense permitted us to define "opportunity" for any given Chest, and, therefore, to compare its known performance with its assessed opportunity. The five factors, listed in order of statistical importance, are: (1) the *region* in which the Chest is located; (2) the *population*-size of the city or Chest area; (3) the *productivity* of the area, as measured by an index of business and manufacturing activity; (4) the *population composition* as measured by the percentage non-white; (5) the *tendency to save* as measured by E-bond purchases.

For each of the 41 relevant cities in the region of Indianapolis (the North Central region) we were thus able to compute the percapita to be expected for the year nearest to that of the last census, given each city's own characteristics.

Judged by that standard, in that year (1951), Indianapolis would be expected to raise $3.07 percapita as against $2.54 actually raised. The resultant deficit from average expectation was about $290,000. Using the growth of total Chest take (all Chests) around the country to bring that estimate more up to date, on average expectation, Indianapolis should have raised $2.4 million (as against the $1.56 million actually raised) in 1954—and $2.5 to $2.6 million (as against the $2.03 million raised) in the campaign of 1955 for funds for 1956.

The factors examined and then dismissed as having no further explanatory value (for example, how well "competitive" fundraising bodies such as the Red Cross or churches, are doing) are as important for many purposes of discussion as is the establishment of the above way of estimating opportunity itself. Space, however, will not permit us to review them here.

In any case, we now have, for each relevant Chest in the area, a measure of expected performance, a measure of actual performance, and the difference or deviation between these. We refer to this difference (expected minus actual performance) as the degree of "disappointingness" for each Chest.

We made a considerable effort to see if we could in any way account for disappointingness (as thus defined) in Chest performance. Having, as we thought, looked at enough city characteristics to make further research in that direction unpromising, we speculated that perhaps we might find in Chest behavior itself some condition that made for disappointingness.

## Disappointingness

### Disequality

We had early in our analysis of "gift-lists" of many kinds been struck with the fact that, when plotted on ordinary graph paper, gift by gift, in order of size, the lists—no matter what campaign they referred to, or whether the amounts plotted were the gifts of individuals or the gifts of corporations (out of their own coffers) computed on a per employee (or per capita basis) —looked very much alike in their shape (or "distribution"). They all looked more or less like what in cattle-branding parlance would be called a "lazy J." The reason for the family resemblance is that all (or nearly all) consist of (a) a small number of large gifts differing very sizeably from one another, together with (b) a large number of small gifts differing from each other by relatively little. The amount of "disequality" in such lists seemed to us to be one factor that might have a bearing on the level of giving—particularly since we had heard of leading donors in Indianapolis saying that they would give no more because they felt they were "already out too far ahead of the parade."

There were considerable technical problems in getting satisfactory measures of "disequality"—and we finally had to accept certain crude indexes in reference to at least two instances: (a) the disequality between the share of the total campaign take to come directly out of corporation funds and the "non-corporate share," and (b) the probable disequality in different cities for the whole gift-list. Only for one feature of the campaign—the "standards" developed for giving by executives—were we able to use more refined and exact measures of disequality.

Indeed, for the first measure we used simply the percentage of the total take contributed in corporate gifts. We called this the "index of corporate dependency," a measure of dependency purely on the decisions of a handful of men in a handful of companies or firms. For the second measure, we used the percentage of the total Chest take contributed by the ten leading givers. We called this an "index of concentration," but we might well have called it an "index of dependency on leading donors." For the third measure—the disequality in the standard for executive giving (and in actual executive giving)—we used a refined tool similar to a measure of "progressiveness" in income-tax matters. ("Progressiveness" is not here used in the layman's laudatory sense, but in the scientist's neutral one: it means only the degree to which the principle of the higher-the-income-the-higher-the-tax-rate is embodied in the tax structure, or, here, in the gift structure.) We have called this measure an "index of progressiveness"; but if equity is defined for executives, as it widely is for wage workers and corporations, as a flat rate on income, we could with consistency have spoken of this as a measure of "disequity" or an "index of inequity."

We lack sufficient data to give conclusive answers, but, properly comparing comparable cities, all the evidence we have points in the same direction:
1. The greater the degree of corporate dependency, the greater the disappointingness of the general Chest performance per capita.
2. The greater the degree of leading-donor dependency, the greater the disappointingness of the general Chest performance per capita.
3. The greater the degree of inequity in the standard for and in the actual executive giving, both the lower the level of executive generosity and the greater the disappointingness of the general Chest performance per capita.

These propositions seem particularly cogent in view of the high rating Indianapolis has on all three measures, and in view of the widespread tendency of Chests in difficulty to make increasing demands upon leading givers in order to "improve" their situation. This principle of leaning heavily upon one's friends—"the [exploit] your buddy system," as Army terminology has it—seems, in general, not to lead towards the desired effect, i.e., towards a general rise in the percapita actually raised closer to the percapita statistically to be expected. The findings are also, perhaps, particularly cogent for executives, since to them, and them only, is the "progressive" principle widely applied and only for them is it recommended, and since the "progressiveness" implied in all such standards reviewed by us is far greater even than that of the federal income tax.

This analysis forces the bringing under review of the whole system of "standards"—particularly since they are intended to represent (or rather to epitomize) the principal product, in our judgment, that the Chest has to sell: the rationalization of giving, or, at least, of approved canons or norms of giving.

This complex topic cannot be fully entered into here, but the principal problems may be stated. The first problem is the setting of rational or sense-making standards; the second is the securing on a sufficient scale of their adoption. These problems may be separated, but in practice the sense the standards make may depend to a large degree on the goodness of the negotiating procedure used to secure their adoption, and success in securing adoption may depend on the sense they make.

The first problem of "standards" (total goal having, presumably, been set on other grounds) begins in the division of the goal between the corporate gift and the personal gift, i.e., in the determination of the proportions of the gift to be taken, respectively, out of corporate and individual income. No rational principle of division in this respect can be suggested by us, although it may well be that no decision of greater importance to subsequent campaign policy and success has to be made. One possible method of arriving at a division, not necessarily rational but acceptable, would be by negotiation, within a donors' association, between representatives of corporations (and ownership, generally) on one side and representatives of the employed population (whether "employees," "executives" or "professional" people) on the other. An alternative method of making the division is implicit in the "Shell formula," by which essentially whatever giving behavior is evidenced in one year by the "personal sector" is "matched" by the corporations collectively in the subsequent year (and then sub-divided between them on the basis of employment). This solution at one and the same time makes individuals (rather than corporations) the decision-makers, and disposes of the problem of negotiating what is to be the corporate share. It also dispenses with the whole series of difficult situations connected with "trade groups." (It should be noted, perhaps, that the "Shell formula" can be still further generalized: the suggested fifty-fifty split is only one of innumerable possible solutions.)

If the corporate standard is not automatically decided—as it *is* in the case of the Shell formula—the next problem is to determine what may be called the "logic of assessment": Is the "standard" to be based on presumed utilization by the firm's employees of the services supported by the Chest, or is it to be based on the firm's income? Present practice is largely to demand from each firm whichever is the greater of a "tax" on employment or a "tax" on income. A "middle ground" is frequently sought by using numbers of employees as the basis for standard-setting on the argument that it is at once an index of likely utilization and of relative profit or income in a homogeneous "trade group." The method has several weaknesses, the greatest of which is, perhaps, that a radically different standard is applied to all trade groups where the income-per-employee is relatively high—the banks, for instance. A second serious weakness is that the method provides no rational basis for allocating to the different trade groups each one's share of the "tax," so that a major task of rationalizing giving is left largely untouched and an unknown factor of inequity attends the setting of all subordinate standards. (It could also be questioned whether, indeed, employment *is* a satisfactory measure of net income or profitability.)

In any case, in a very popular version of this hodgepodge "system" of corporate standards, the situation is further complicated by a gimmick not usually made explicit: that no firm may, as a consequence of applying the standard, be encouraged or "permitted" to reduce its total corporate gift, regardless of changes in employment. Thus, a firm whose employment is falling is victimized—in terms of the logic of the standard itself, which defines equity as equal per-employee corporate giving.

Turning from the corporate to the non-corporate sector, the problem of setting standards becomes one in allocating "fair shares" of the non-corporate goal to all relevant individuals. As usual, two mutually contradictory principles are employed: virtually everyone is to be solicited at his place of work for a gift for his entire family, and virtually everyone is to be solicited at home for a contribution in the name of the same family. Neglecting the problems connected with the simultaneous employment of these two mutually contradictory principles, and attending to place-of-work solicitation only, the problem boils down to allocating the non-corporate goal among workers. For reasons which may have a great deal to do with relative vulnerability or accessibility to pressure, the field of income-earning individuals is usually subdivided for standard-setting into "professionals," "employees," and "executives." Whatever case may be made for organizing soliciting units on this basis, none has been made in our hearing that justifies different standards on the basis of this particular division—although, in practice, this is the way standards *are* set. To employees, the going standards seek to apply a "flat rate tax" on income; to executives, a higher and much more sharply "progressive tax" on income.

Before much credibility can be attached to the rationality of personal giving standards it would seem that reasonable answers must be provided for the following questions:

(*a*) Is there any warrant for dividing up the field of personal givers occupationally—or indeed in any other way except by income earned—for purposes of standard-setting?

(*b*) If not, is there to be an "exemption" level (like tax-exemption) below which no gift is to be "expected" (i.e., campaigned for) although, of course, one can be accepted if made?

(*c*) Regardless of whether there is to be such a level or not, for the whole population to be "standardized," should there be different rates of progressiveness in different income-bands (as is the case at present)?

(*d*) If not, how "progressive" is the bite of the standard to be—from zero progressiveness (a flat rate) to the kind of progressiveness implicit in the Columbus (Ohio) standard where the rate, in dollars per thousand, is set by the number of thousands of dollars in the income, i.e., where the rule is, in effect, "to determine your fair-share gift, take your income (in thousands) and multiply it by itself." One critical point, even if there is to be progressiveness, might be whether or not to set the progressiveness higher than the income tax progressiveness (as it is for executives at present) or equal to it or lower?

(*e*) Should the standards be based upon gross income or upon net? Or, to achieve what is said to be intended, should they not be based upon:

$$\frac{\text{True cost of gift to giver}}{\text{Income left after gift and tax}} \; ?$$

(Here, "true cost of gift to giver" means his actual gift less the amount by which giving reduces his tax bill; and "income left after gift and tax" means his gross income, less his income tax, less his gift and plus the tax rebate he gets from making the gift.)

(*f*) Once all the foregoing questions are decided, at what level must the "tax" be set to bring in the return required by the non-corporate goal?

Answers to these questions are not technically difficult, but, together, the questions suggest other searching queries related to social policy and inter-personal and inter-group ethics (albeit on a "small" scale). If the "standards" are to represent nothing more than "what the traffic will bear," many will ask what is the advantage of having a federated fundraising agency at all; if they are to represent more than this, some attention seems to be required to their fundamental purpose, rationale, and consistency.

### The Chest and Other Philanthropies

One tempting line of explanation for Chest "failure" is to account for it in terms of someone else's success. If it is possible to assume that there is at any one time, say in any given year, a relatively fixed pool of philanthropic dollars, then the success of one organization must obviously be purchased at the expense of another, and failure in one organization may be due to "favoritism" in the community in the partialling out of the available limited pool of dollars. The reason, we were told, for Chest failure in Indianapolis might very well be the fact of disproportionate Red Cross success; or, alternatively or as well, it might be due to the fact that a pious community, supporting its churches on a generous scale, has little money left over for its major secular philanthropy, the Chest.

The first question to be posed then is whether, in fact, giving behavior suggests the notion of a fixed philanthropic dollar pool for shares of which various philanthropies compete, or whether, on the contrary, the behavior suggests that "giving one dollar loosens up another," so that the philanthropies reinforce one another rather than compete.

A first examination of the relevant data for our carefully drawn sample of cities suggests that, whatever else may be true, it is *not* generally the case that the better one philanthropy does, the worse is the fate of the other. Religious giving per member in two major denominations, Red Cross giving per capita, and Chest giving per capita are all positively related to each other: the higher the one, the higher the others.

A more sophisticated examination suggests, however, that this positive relation is ascribable to the common situation—the city characteristics, especially the population—in each set of philanthropies. After allowance is made for the relevant city characteristics, the variations city by city between the philanthropies seem to be independent, i.e., after allowing for the common situation of philanthropies in the same city, one would most safely assume that what one philanthropy can do is *not* affected, in general, by what the others are doing—they neither compete with nor reinforce one another.

While, therefore, the success of the Indianapolis Red Cross is quite notable (its success being assessed, like that of the Chest, in relation to "opportunity") the failure of the Chest cannot be ascribed to this cause, unless Indianapolis differs in some unknown way from the generality of cities examined. Neither can the failure be explained by atypical "success" in religious fundraising—partly because secular giving and religious giving do not seem to be competitively related, and partly because there is no notable success in religious giving in Indianapolis, as far as our data for the two religious denominations for the forty-one cities will permit us to judge.

Even where a particular campaign had sought an unusual and sizeable sum of money—the Indianapolis Hospital campaign's recent $12 million, for example—we were able to find no evidence that this reduced the level of giving to other seekers of funds, though there may have been a delay in getting the sums expected. Actually the impact on MOPS fundraising of this once-in-a-lifetime, large-scale fundraising may have been the reverse: it may have served to "raise the sights," if only because large numbers of people argue, fallaciously or not, "If we could do that, we must be able to do this," and begin to act accordingly. Since—if there are enough such people—they are both subject and object of their own prediction there is some tendency for the phenomenon of self-justifying expectation to occur.

In examining the "sources" of the funds of Red Cross, Hospital Association, and Chest for possible clues as to reasons for the continuing quiet success of one, the one-shot dramatic success of the other, and the continuing failure of the third, one of the matters we examined was the amount of corporate dependency in each campaign. All that the evidence suggests, on this score, is that within a city, the larger the campaign, the larger the corporate dependence: for the Hospital, Chest, and Red Cross the respective percentages (for 1952-53) are 49, 46, and 39—or, if Foundation gifts are included with those of firms in an "impersonal sector," 60, 55 and 42 per cent. (This finding *within* a city is not to be confused with the earlier finding *between* cities that the higher the corporate dependency the more disappointing the Chest.) Since the two successful campaigns have the highest and lowest corporate dependency, this dependency presumably does not by itself account for failure and success locally—though the possibility is not excluded that the Indianapolis Chest's corporate dependency is too high (or too low) for maximum success.

As far as the form of organization for solicitation is concerned—the degree to which solicitation is organized through firms rather than otherwise—the organizations resemble one another sufficiently (81, 80 and 83 per cent "firm-organized," respectively) that no conclusion can be drawn on this score, either, as to reasons for success.

If we combine these two forms of analysis, and treat only the firm-organized sector (over 80 per cent of each campaign anyway), all we find is that *within this sector* again, the larger the campaign the greater the corporate dependency (61, 57, and 47 per cent of the sector total respectively) and the lower the corresponding dependency on employees (39, 43, and 53 per cent.

Dependency on the ten leading gifts is similarly distributed by campaign size: Hospital 28 per cent, Chest 23 per cent, Red Cross 12 per cent. Again this does not vitiate the contention that, as between Chests, the greater the lead-giver dependency, the greater the disappointingness. The same effect as for ten leading gifts is achieved in comparing the percentage proceeds from the hundred leading firm gifts: they account respectively for 36, 34 and 25 per cent of the campaign totals. The same is true, as between Chest and Red Cross, if the percentage raised by the top fifth of the leading firm givers of each is compared.

One recent trend that differentiates the Red Cross and the Community Chest—it may have little bearing on success as such, but certainly has a bearing on "spreading the base"—is that the Chest has tended to increase its corporate and employee take per employee (from giving firms, 1951-5) in about the same proportions, while the Red Cross has reduced its per-employee take from firms and increased its per employee take from employees. These results may or may not be related to the fact that the Chest raises a greater proportion of its take from very large firms (5,000 or more employees) than does the Red Cross, and the Red Cross receives a larger proportion from very small ones (less than 100 employees). It is in the very large firms only that the employee pledges run highest; except for these very largest firms (and except for a few recent Chest years) it appears that the larger the firm the smaller the employee gift per employee to the Chest. (This is probably, largely, an effect of differential participation rather than differential giving among those who do give.)

To an astounding degree (the correlation is of the order of .985) the Red Cross and Community Chest obtain almost identical proportions of their take (among the firms pledging) from each of the industry groups such as "Automotive," "Banks," and "Manufacturing" (over a three- and four-year period respectively). There is therefore no ground here for relative success or failure. Nor do these proportions tend to change from year to year. The impression created is that, as between philanthropies, or from year to year for each philanthropy, the proportion of the take to be expected from any industry group changes very little, i.e., it is as though industry groups in

Indianapolis had fixed relative "giving potentials" or yield limits. What holds true for each of these industry groups, moreover, holds true even when the employee giving in each and the firm giving in each are separately analysed. Over each industry group, both firm decisions and employee decisions (taken together or separately) result in about the same proportionate contribution to the Red Cross and to the Chest for each of the years examined (1951-5).

The most striking change currently going on in the Chest, perhaps, and not paralleled in the Red Cross, is the Chest's increasing dependency upon "ICO"—the Industrial and Commercial Organizations. The proportion rises from 66 per cent in 1950 to 76 per cent in 1955. What this means appears far more striking if the increase is related to increase in the Chest take: it means that something between 64 per cent (1951-2) and 93 per cent (1954-5) of any increase in take comes from this single sector. Over the six-year period, 96.4 per cent of the Chest's increase comes from ICO, i.e., for all practical purposes it is the sole source of "growth." Within this sector, the firm's share (the corporate gift) represents an almost unvarying 60 per cent. Campaign policy—which one year "emphasizes" employee giving and another year "goes after firm gifts"—does not appear to affect these proportions appreciably.

Many of these ratios may be very enduring: a study published in 1930, covering the years from 1923 to 1928 and many cities, shows that corporations contributed between 42 and 45 per cent of the total take; our figures, for Indianapolis for 1950-5, show firms contributing between 40 and 45 per cent of the total take. Even within such a category as "Manufacturing," the proportions contributed by its constituent trade groups seem relatively invariant from year to year. As far apart as six years (1950 and 1955) and as between seventeen sub-groups in Manufacturing, the correlation between the amounts contributed is .92.

On the basis of the evidence so far, it is difficult to believe that the discrepancy between Red Cross and Hospital success on one side, and Chest disappointingness or failure on the other, rests primarily on anything so simple as differential access to different sources of funds—although the increasing Chest dependency on ICO and the decreasing Red Cross dependence on the firm gift within ICO may be suggestive.

It is time to turn back now, from matters financial to matters social, from money to the persons who make money.

### STANDARDS FOR SOCIAL SUCCESS

If arriving at suitable financial standards represents, as it does, a complex problem for technical reasons, arriving at suitable social standards represents an even more difficult social and ethical problem—partly for the reasons indicated in connection with the discussion of conflicting aims and purposes.

Social evaluation of the Chest appears to be made locally, usually by different persons, from at least four different perspectives:

(1) The perspective of those who regard the welfare sector as primarily a problem in *social control*, i.e., a problem in "reducing the multiplicity of drives," in eliminating "charity rackets," in introducing or increasing wisdom and reason in planning and operating the agencies, or maintaining or increasing the interest of "the best people" so that the enterprise may be "properly" run.

(2) The perspective of those who regard the Chest (if successful) primarily as another *civic asset*, both in the sense that it brings together in a common cause those who are otherwise divided—different social classes, ethnic groups, the two sexes, management and labor—and in the sense that it adds to the city's renown or repute, and therefore to its power to attract industrial or cultural enterprise.

(3) The perspective of those interested in *the "goodness" of the people* of a community. Many of these tend to believe either that vigorous "giving" is a good in itself, or an index of some other virtue or virtues. Others believe that the by-products of "campaigning"—the "connections" and "friendships" formed, the business "contacts" so established or customers thus turned up, the practice of "stewardship" associated with the use of one's selling talents and the handling of trust funds—all these are either goods themselves, or productive of better people, or people better related to each other.

(4) The perspective of those who view the Chest's success primarily in terms of the rate of "growth" (measured by money expenditure or otherwise) it permits the local welfare community. The "agency-centered" among these—clearly the vast majority of laymen and many also of the professionals—tend to equate this test with the rate of "growth" it permits "their" agency.

Judged variously by various people in the community—and the list omits thousands who "Don't know . . . What is it? . . . Don't care"—the Indianapolis Chest comes off variously ill or well, according to which yardstick is held up against it and who does the sighting.

### Social Control

On the first score—social control—no one will deny that the Chest has "reduced the multiplicity of drives," i.e., that there are fewer drives than there otherwise would be (though *not* fewer drives than there were before the Chest came into existence). But many feel—some, uncritically, on the score that if a little medicine is good, a lot must be better—that more reduction of the multiplicity is required, and that, indeed, no rest is justified until "all" are included in "one big campaign." Later, when the new United Funds are again outflanked, as the Chests are, by new fundraising inventions, further incorporation of the competitors will have to take place. We shall have to return to these problems of unification.

As for "charity rackets," such control as there is seems to depend very little on the "success" of the Chest, though its very existence to some minor extent discourages the overly enterprising. There is, besides, a Better Business Bureau and a Charities Solicitation Commission, which also exert some counteraction to the more patently piratical endeavors.

As far as introducing wisdom and reason into agency planning and operation is concerned, this is still before the community as a promise rather than observable as an ongoing process: observation of the procedure of "budgeting" by the Chest is the best diagnostic of the strength and nature of the actual control exerted, and our observations did not seem to show that the first was great or the other apt by even fairly ordinary standards of "planning."

With regard to "maintaining and increasing the interest of the best people"—probably the heart of the matter—for a variety of reasons, some intrinsic to Indianapolis and some probably characteristic of the whole Chest movement, the local Chest seems to be in process of becoming a purely middle-class enterprise and ceasing, therewith, to be even an upper-class concern. This loss of concern, together with the loss of upper-class example and the upper-class techniques of securing large effects (via influence or esteem) with small efforts, accounts for many of the observed difficulties and demoralized and demoralizing behavior. What is even more devastating is that the middle leadership cannot reconcile itself to this loss and "take hold" on its own (and perhaps achieve success); nor does it appear able to "bring back" the "top top leadership," to which, in many cases, it no longer even has free access. A continually disappointed expectation seems to paralyse resolution in either direction, or, more accurately perhaps, to make for feeble efforts, first in the one direction, then in the other.

### Civic Asset

That the Chest cannot perform one of its functions as a civic asset—that of adding to the community's cross-country repute—while it is failing financially is not only obvious, but one of the few considerations that seems to touch at all deeply many major donors, regardless of their "agency-mindedness," their views on United Fund, or their social status. All, for this purpose at least, would prefer a successful Chest—if the price were not too high.

As to the other civic-asset function—the healing over of basic divisions in the community in the face of common need or for the sake of joint and transcending interest—the Indianapolis situation is peculiar. Some divisions which exist in other communities are not here as breaches to be bridged: there are no sizeable groups of foreign-born to be assimilated, or large religious minorities to be caught up, for this purpose at least, in a common fellowship. As for the significant divisions that do exist, these seem to be too "hot"—given the present composition of the welfare community leadership—for the Chest to be able to address them with seriousness: the split between upper and middle classes already referred to; the cleavage within the upper-middle class between the old local leadership, mostly a birth élite, and the new imported leaders of the national corporations, mostly an élite of mobility; the division of interest (on some scores, at least) between management of business and management of labor; Negro-white relations. These divisions and the sources of incapacity to cope with them are related in circular fashion to one another.

### The Goodness of the People

Those who view the Chest as making people "better" by virtue of "vigorous giving" or "experience in stewardship" tend to be somewhat more unhappy about the Indianapolis situation than do those who merely expect that it will knit up the fabric of the business community by providing occasions to meet "friends," make "contacts," discover "prospects," or develop or exercise leadership or influence. Even the latter, however, tend, in so far as such experiences are limited by the Indianapolis social structure, to be disappointed in the result, even though the Chest does afford a great deal of opportunity for just these things.

### The "Welfare" of the Welfare Community

Though complaints are sufficiently numerous within the Welfare Community, lay and professional, as to the sad effect of the Chest's failure on agency expansion, these complaints differ markedly in tone and intent from the complaints of those who are only in the Welfare Community as leading donors or donor leaders. Both wish to see the Chest succeed, but one group measures success largely by the amount of "expansion" permitted, and the other by the rationality, control, economy, "elimination of waste, duplication and overlap" that success could enable. These no doubt legitimate and complementary sets of aims are rarely, if ever, brought together because of the divisions of leadership already referred to. The proper point of juncture is indicated by the remark of at least one leading donor (repeated by many others in other terms) that only if he could have the assurances of control, economy, "sense," etc., would his corporation substantially increase its level of giving, i.e., make expansion possible. The efforts of the would-be "expanders" to expand anyway by using more irresistible stratagems, in many cases make the would-be "controllers" feel an increased sense of alienation between the donor and solicitor "communities." The fear increases that "the sky is the limit" or that "Why, there's no end to it . . ." and fund unification which was first desired on the ground of economy comes to be desired as a ground for seizing or reclaiming power in order just to set limits. If unification is effected on the latter ground (and in the atmosphere necessarily attending such a *putsch*) it is doubtful if the other "unifying" effects of a successful community MOPS fundraising enterprise can be had at all, or, at least, for many years thereafter.

It is perhaps in order to turn now from the general criteria for social success for the Chest to some aspects of the campaign itself: the problems of methods and manning.

## METHODS AND MANNING

### The General Problems

The "cast of characters" relevant for MOPS fundraising includes—in different relations, as the organization, like an army, expands for campaign or contracts to recuperate—the *general public*, the leaders of and followers in the *Welfare Community*, the lay and professional *"campaign leadership,"* the leading donors and donor leaders and others in the *"donor-aggregate,"* and some, presumably, *ultimate beneficiaries* of the entire operation. The appropriate relating of their roles to one another, and the issue of these roles in a meaningful and satisfying "play" is, in one sense, the whole problem of methods and manning.

Opinion as to the proper role of "the general public" is, as has been indicated earlier, somewhat divided: it ranges all the way from the opinion that they are functionally and in relation to the fundraiser like "natural resources" to the miner or farmer, to the view that they are the primary target of "education" and the proper object of "community organization." Whichever view is taken, or whatever uneasy blend of the two, is likely to affect other problems of manning, since the orientation adopted is likely to attract some leaders and repel others, perhaps dividing the leadership along class lines.

The Welfare Community—more especially the major agencies and the Health and Welfare Council and their surrounding clouds of laymen, plus the personnel of the parallel public agencies—is not only the principal proximate beneficiary of MOPS fundraising, but the reason for the fundraising and the only public witness to the "need." The relation of the Welfare Community, but particularly of its leadership, to the donor leadership is of immense consequence for the general air of confidence or distrust that permeates the whole, and seeps out to the public in general—and, much more important, to the leading donors who "can afford money but cannot afford to be out on a limb."

The problems connected with the "campaign leadership" include not only the relations of this body to other bodies mentioned, but, within the group, delicate problems of relating professionals to laymen, and again, within the group of laymen, similar delicacies in relating the "elder statesmen" to the "young campaigners."

Special again to the donor-aggregate—additional, that is, to the problem of relating it to the others—are the twin problems of organizing out of this mere aggregate a "donor community," and finding the right relation between leading donors (people who give a lot of money, with or without "involvement") and donor leaders (people deeply involved in leading donors to give, whether or not they give large sums themselves). The first problem is connected with one we spoke of earlier—the negotiation of consensus, which is what (the process, not the result) constitutes a community. The second problem brings up questions of "representation," particularly the difficult question whether mere weight of "interest" is the basic qualification for representation, or mere weight of money. The first view drives towards "Whosoever will may come"; the second, towards a substantial identity of donor leadership with leading donorship, and perhaps an approximation to "One dollar, one vote."

The "ultimate beneficiaries" are also two: the direct consumers of agency services, and those who benefit by such consumption, e.g., employers, if it is true that their workers thus get better recreation (or other "services") and if it is true that they are more profitable workers as a consequence.

Within this complex context, the primary problem of the MOPS fundraiser is to ensure that the "right" person asks "everyone" in "the community" for the "right" sum at the right time—and often enough successfully to secure the "right" total. Each of these terms has its problems, but not all need detain us here.

The question of who is the "right" person to do the asking is itself bound up with the conflict between keeping the enterprise volunteer and keeping it effective. To the degree that it is sought to maximize "voluntariness," solicitors tend to be matched to solicitees in terms of social status; to the degree that it is desired to overbear "resistance" and "get the money anyhow," the instruction goes out to "get his boss to *tell* him." "*Bosses* talking to *bosses*, that's what makes the campaign" is the way one seasoned campaigner has it. But whichever policy is attempted—and it probably makes a great deal of difference—for the small numbers that give the bulk of the money and for "the others," the vast mass that gives the smaller portion of the take, the situation is largely one of strangers talking to strangers. Solicitor and donor are related as salesman to customer, and the rules of "buyer beware" and "sell what you can" not only seem to apply, but to raise less disturbing questions than when the same methods are applied—as they are—by the in-group momentarily involved in the campaign to the rest of the in-group momentarily not so involved.

Once these fundamental problems have been settled, comes the task of organizing the campaign year appropriately. Though the campaign falls into four phases, closely related to each other—post campaign (post-mortem and reflection), pre-campaign planning, pre-campaign organizing (and, sometimes, soliciting), and the drive itself—the tendency is more and more under official cover of "an annual drive" to conduct a "year-round campaign". in which cultivation and resolicitation are never actively discontinued.

A MOPS fundraising organization has other pressing and perennial long-term problems. These have to do with the provision of the right *reward-system*, the right *social structure*, the right amount and kind of continuity. "Right," in this context, means "effective." The people who are required to make this provision are the "elected" "representatives" who are presumably to act for both the voting membership of the permanent organization (every giver!) *and* the special interest group or segment of the community from which each is actually chosen and whose interests he is also supposed to "guard." Regardless of their source of origin in and nominal mandate to "represent" any one of these subsidiary interest-groups, members tend, via assimilation or involvement, to come finally to represent either the going "line" of the permanent organization or what they take to be (by guess or trial-and-error, since they do not have access) the thought and wish of "the best people." So situated—and with each member still feeling perhaps also responsible in some degree to his original interest-group—the elected group does not feel and cannot be clearly answerable to any one source of authority. The result, almost unavoidably in terms of self-protection, is the diffusion of authority and responsibility among the governing group, with all the risks that attend such a practice—particularly that what is everybody's business is finally found to be nobody's. On the other hand, this masterless role leaves room for many alternatives, since some part of the public must be pleased by almost any outcome, and hence the situation gives opportunity for creative decision—or would do so if the other ingredients necessary thereto, such as clear purpose and accurate information, were present to permit it.

## Rewards

Leaders so situated, nevertheless, "must"—and evidently sometimes can—provide for motive, machinery, and ballast. It is their necessity to provide—if it is to be provided at all—a reward-system that will not only satisfy the current campaigner, but will make him "want to" sign on again, and thus aid in the maintenance of the structure and the preservation of the continuities. The reward-system must be capable at a minimum of providing a pleasant experience of shared labor at campaign time. Beyond this, if it is to attract and retain otherwise busy men, it must minister to the feeling of personal worth, and to pride in the product which is the result of joint effort. Successful performance within the philanthropic community must be linked with recognition in the social and economic structure outside it—and vice versa. Consequently, a stable structure inside the philanthropic community is required (corresponding roughly to the one in the larger community) and a stable set of sense-making expectations and realities of promotion must be maintained to induce the needed people to make a career, rather than a series of episodes of their philanthropic lives. Finally, these subsidiary rewards, sufficient for many, must somehow be caught up in a purpose and a set of symbols felt to transcend limited individual purpose—if some of "the best people" are to be attracted at all or retained, once attracted.

The ability so to organize men in a voluntary association depends upon a subtle blend of "rule" (organizing power, mobilizing fear, exerting control) and "government" (using influence, awarding prestige, according esteem, mobilizing fellowship or love, educing voluntary proper behaviour). The alternative to such successful blending is diminished or diminishingly effective manpower, increasingly impossible tasks for the would-be governors, and an increasing reliance out of necessity on "rule" rather than government. And so round again circularly.

### Structure

If the key campaign relation is solicitor-donor, the key relation in the permanent organization is leader-follower. This relation, where it is successful and where an attractive "ladder of promotion" is provided, subsists between "elder statesmen" (who largely govern, but also rule) and "young campaigners" (who transmit the campaign purpose, through the rank and file, out to the general population). Given soundness in this key relationship, it can be used to create appropriate relations between the community's social structure on one side and—separately—the campaign structure and the permanent organization structure, on the other. If the social class organization of a community can be represented in a series of layers, then something like what is indicated by the following diagram seems to be required for continuing success in the relations between it and the campaign and permanent organization.

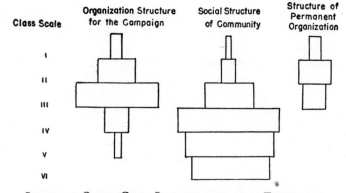

SCHEME OF SOCIAL CLASS STRUCTURE FOR MOPS FUNDRAISING
RELATED TO SOCIAL CLASS STRUCTURE OF COMMUNITY

*Continuity*

The primary problem that both affects and is affected by the reward-system and the social structure is that of providing for continuity. Reward cannot be effective or structure secure in the absence of the feeling that "we are going to be in business for a long time to come"—and essentially as we are. The key word is "essentially," for continuity in essential matters is not the enemy but the host of spontaneity and innovation in the unessential but important. If the moral order is secure, invention can be afforded and variation indulged or encouraged.

Continuity requires the yearly winning of new adherents; the screening, preening, care, and comfort of those already had; continuous training, encouragement to self-study, the providing of ground for the feeling of steady self-improvement; and the gradual deepening in meaning and spreading in extent of what it is that is valued and shared by virtue of common membership in the inner circles of the organization.

Having thus posed the problems, we may again turn back to the Indianapolis picture.

## METHODS AND MANNING: INDIANAPOLIS

In the sense that no one seriously proposes abandoning the Chest altogether or dissolving it into its component units—although there is talk of substituting a United Fund for it or of containing it in a United Fund—in this sense, at least, the Chest may be said to have minimal acceptance already. Its problem is to develop more than such minimal acceptance—something more like what the Red Cross Chapter won in World War I, regained in the Second World War, and has maintained since. Perhaps comparison between the two will be illuminating.

The most striking contrast in the planning and organization of the two campaigns is in the clear, fixed ranks and the established methods and traditions of campaigning in the Red Cross (with consequent highly "visible" promotion) and the more obscure levels in the Chest hierarchy and the constant improvisation of campaign pattern. The first pattern leads to the comfortable feeling of tradition, to clarity about status at any one time, to inter-year comparability; and such clarity, in turn, makes for the establishment of clear norms of performance and the feeling of belonging to the historic company of those who have gone before. The consequences for the reward-system, for the continuous adaptation of the structure, and for the preservation of the continuities are, in the Red Cross, what one would thus expect them to be: good. Even given the Red Cross campaign situation of a "three-party system"—the paid outside professionals, the Red Cross Chapter's own professionals, and the laymen—the stable relations from year to year provide sharp contrast with the Chest situation of continuous change of pattern. The latter results in relations so muddied that no one knows from year to year what are the proper protocols for even the most basic relations, for example, those between the lay campaign manager and the professional staff and sub-staff.

We cannot tell by direct comparison whether, with reference to the whole soliciting apparatus, the Chest is undermanned (per $100,000 raised) or the Red Cross overgenerously provided for. Certainly the latter uses more people per dollar raised—but this may be characteristic of smaller campaigns anyway.

This basic difference in sheer size of campaign—making necessary a demand for "dollars per capita" by the Chest and only for "pennies per capita" by all other agencies—accounts also for some aspects of the success of the Red Cross and others. Statistical evidence suggests that Red Cross Chapters generally do not, because of their size, "press" significantly upon community resources. They can consequently demand fewer sacrifices, take a more *laissez-faire* attitude to giving standards, make fewer excessive claims to rationality, and hence, without making fewer friends, certainly make fewer enemies. The Chest is driven back upon rationality as its motif; and if this cannot be both achieved and linked to satisfying emotional and appropriate social experience, the ice is very thin on one side and the other.

The relation of the goal (the money sum sought) to the appeal (the communicated ground upon which it is sought) is also better achieved in the Red Cross. This is hardly because the Chest supports a greater hodge-podge of "services" than does the Red Cross: either could qualify, in this respect, as a sort of department store or bazaar. The difference lies in the fact that the Red Cross has been able—and the Chest has not—to discover the unity in its diversity (essentially service-in-crisis), and to communicate it in words and set it forth in a highly meaningful symbol: the red (for love and compassion) cross (for service and sacrifice). Indeed, in the public eye, government services apart, the Red Cross has almost a monopoly in the handling of disaster; and this view of it makes it clearly indispensable and a legitimate claimant on every purse. Moreover, since there is no paucity of disaster, almost any year's Red Cross campaign has vivid reinforcement for its "necessity" from the news columns. Since, particularly, Hoosiers seem to have a preference for dealing dramatically with crisis rather than quietly with routine, this fact, combined with the others, gives the Red Cross appeal a decisive edge.

Another considerable difference between the two organizations—and again one that probably operates to the advantage of the Red Cross as far as successful results are concerned—has to do with the relative emphasis on "continuity" on the Board in the Red Cross and the correlative emphasis on "rotation" off the Board in the Chest. Comparing Red Cross experience over forty years with Chest experience for the last decade, the average number of Board membership-years served was just over twelve in the case of the Red Cross, just over three for the Chest. (The comparison must not be taken too literally because of the different bases—no one can serve twelve years in a decade!—but the figures are symbolic of a real difference.) Beyond this literal continuity, the Red Cross seems to have more roles that can be taken by ex-Board members, without derogation to their dignity, than does the Chest, and hence what discontinuities there are, tend to be bridged by continued service in the one case and not in the other.

There is also some further difference in the convincingness with which each organization can point to the goodness of its "budgeting" procedure as evidence of its good faith. Not only does the Chest have all the log-rolling problems of a federation to contend with (as well as the normal difficulties of budgeting anything), but its procedure has not always been orderly, nor often early enough to implicate the campaign chairman. More-over, it does not budget independently but shares control with another body—the Health and Welfare Council. While, therefore, the Red Cross can say of its budget "Why, it's been gone over, inch by inch, by Mr.——," the Chest Campaign Manager may make direct claims, "I know every penny is needed," and still not be believed by anyone who has been through "the procedure" or knows about it from one who has. In the case of the Red Cross the person (not committee) mentioned will be someone of unquestionably top-drawer social status or of unblemished business repute —which comment brings us to the whole question of social status.

It is a commonplace now, surely, of everyday discourse as well as socio-logical thought, that a process of mutual social rating and ranking goes on in every American community, a process which results in a social order in which everyone or every category of persons has a place. These "places" are connected not only with people's "opinions" (though, in a sense, those are the fundamental facts) but with such other visible indices as behavior, style of life, place of residence, magnitude and source of income, etc. Taking our cues, here, from sharp class-evaluative comments made by the persons we interviewed and observed, and checking or supplementing these by objective data, we "rated" the leadership of the philanthropic and welfare community (to reflect community judgment, not our own). This was done along a seven-point scale of what we came to call "Estimated Social Status" (ESS). Where we had insufficient information to decide whether a given leader belonged in the very top class ("1"—the "upper upper") or the next lower ("2"—the "lower upper"), we arbitrarily split the difference and assigned him an ESS rating of "1.5." This is a rough method indeed— but sufficiently exact, we believe, for our purpose here.

Applying these scales to the some 548 persons central to the campaign organization of the Chest and the Red Cross, we found:

(a) Both organizations have personnel coming from the "top tops" (ESS 1 and 1.5) down to the level of "the little fellow" (ESS 5)—but no further.

(*b*) Both organizations have in their central group (elder statesmen plus young campaigners) a somewhat similar distribution by status; although if the three top categories are merged (ESS 1 to ESS 3) the Red Cross has an edge.

(*c*) With respect to "elder statesmen," the Chest drew more of such people from the top two categories (ESS 1 and 2) than did the Red Cross: 38 per cent as against 26 per cent. What is striking, however, and accounts perhaps for the charge of the Chest lacking "top leadership," is that its total group of elder statesmen is a much smaller fraction of its inner campaign organization than is true for the Red Cross (25 per cent in one case; 11 per cent in the other).

(*d*) One difference between the two campaigns consisted in the use by the Red Cross in its higher campaign echelons of what it calls "the ladies" and the relative neglect at these levels by the Chest of what it calls "the women."

(*e*) Another observable difference was the utilization by the Red Cross of its active "elder statesmen" either at the high levels or in "special" roles; the Chest in order to man its soliciting divisions had to use about a third of its "elder statesmen" down with the "young campaigners" in soliciting activity.

Further difficulties with the problem of social status for the Chest are illustrated by the trouble it has in securing a campaign chairman. For a variety of reasons that again reinforce one another—such as the fact of previous "failure" making it hard to get the right man, which makes it hard to avoid further failure—the Campaign General Chairman is selected only late, and usually only after "many" (seventeen, we were told in one year) have refused. The likelihood of getting a marginal man or a merely mobile one is very great, the probability of getting a "top top" man, small, as the following ratings for the last ten chairmen indicate.

| Estimated Social Status | | Number of chairmen |
|:---:|:---:|:---:|
| 1 | | 0 |
| 1.5 | | 0 |
| 2 | | 2 |
| 2.5 | | 4 |
| 3 | | 4 |
| AVERAGE RATING 2.6 | TOTAL | 10 |

An earlier decade would have shown a higher average ESS for General Chairmen of the Chest campaign, but since the end of World War II the trend in the social status of General Chairmen seems to have been down.

Perhaps the differences between the three organizations, as far as social status is concerned, come most visibly to the fore in diagramming the

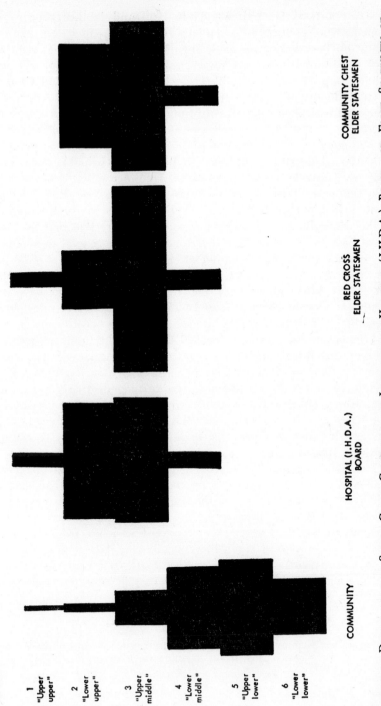

Social Class

1 "Upper upper"

2 "Lower upper"

3 "Upper middle"

4 "Lower middle"

5 "Upper lower"

6 "Lower lower"

COMMUNITY

HOSPITAL (I.H.D.A.) BOARD

RED CROSS ELDER STATESMEN

COMMUNITY CHEST ELDER STATESMEN

PERCENTAGE DISTRIBUTION BY SOCIAL CLASS: COMMUNITY OF INDIANAPOLIS, HOSPITAL (I.H.D.A.) BOARD, AND ELDER STATESMEN OF RED CROSS CHAPTER AND COMMUNITY CHEST relative proportions from each ESS to be found in the group of elder statesmen. The picture is essentially that represented on page 423. The most obvious differences are in the disproportionately large representation of both upper classes ("upper upper" and "lower upper") in the Hospital group as compared with either the Chest or the Red Cross; and the virtual identity of "upper uppers" in the Hospital and Red Cross groups, as compared with their total absence from the Chest. Such differences make a difference.

But the mere social composition of Board or elder statesmen group does not tell the whole story: an "army in being" is a valuable asset, but, in combat, an "army in action" is essential. How active is the Chest Board?

Over the past eleven years the percentage of Chest Board members who attended less than half of each year's meetings has varied from 39 to 57 of the whole Board; the average is 49 per cent—so that roughly half the Board is "not there" more than half the time. The general trend through the decade is towards increasing non-attendance.

Mere average attendance is not sufficient, of course, for effective participation. Many key matters requiring statesmanlike decision have to be taken up and developed in at least two or three successive meetings. But the percentage of the Board that attends any two consecutive meetings in a year varies, over the decade, from 33.3 down to 21.6; and the percentage who attend any three varies from 21.6 to 10.3. If the latter is taken as the criterion for minimum effectiveness in governing, then less than a fifth of the members of the Board are able to provide effective government so defined. Moreover, by this test, things were no better in the prewar years; i.e., the Chest, so far as we know, by this test has never had even effective government by such leadership as it did have. In general—i.e., for every year except 1955—the higher the social status of the Board member the lower his attendance was likely to be. Sixty-two per cent of the membership of higher social status (ESS 2 or higher) were less than half-time attenders; 38 per cent of the membership of lower social status (ESS 2.5 or lower) were in that attendance (or, rather, non-attendance) category.

The abdication or exclusion of the "top top leadership" from the Indianapolis Chest seems total—it is not there at all. The abdication of the top of the next layer is virtual—they are on the Board, but very often they are simply "not with it."

## WHAT MIGHT BE DONE: THE PRESENT CHEST

The questions that now arise touch chiefly upon the alternatives open to the Chest, i.e., upon the essential question "What Might Be Done." Among the proposals as to what "might be done," none has received more widespread "discussion" than the suggestion that "we have a 'United Fund.'" This suggestion, regarded as a simple decision, easily drawing people into a "for" or "agin'" party, has actually bound up with it so many complexities and contingencies that it is better to discuss it as a separate issue—doubly so since, whether or not a "United Fund" is wise (or possible) probably depends on some alterations in the present Chest. For this reason, we discuss some of the alternatives open without "further unification," and then the problems connected with further unification itself.

What might be done without altering the pattern of constituent agencies of the present Chest is to bring under review, and realign where desired, its Internal Relations, both formal and informal; and to review, and change where required, those External Relations upon which its manpower problems, the communication of its message, and its ability to keep in touch with what it is itself doing, all depend. We discuss these in order.

The *formal staff relations* of the Chest, at the time we knew it, were such as would have caused grave difficulty to any concern, regardless of how easy its task otherwise. Virtually all formal control of all major phases of Chest function lay, undelegated, in the overworked hands of the General Manager. The basic design was that of the star. Communication among persons at peripheral points had to take place through him or by informal circumventing of the formal channels—or not at all. One simple reorganization plan suggested in the text would cut from nine to five the persons reporting directly to him; a better plan would cut the nine to two assistants: one for the operation and promotion functions, one for research and control. Alternatives may suggest themselves upon further reflection.

Despite—or because of—the "tightness" of the formal organization, the various Campaign Associates, the Labor Relations Secretary, and the Public Relations Director seem driven to operate in so loose a relation to one another that the effect is sometimes a little like that of Stephen Leacock's horseman, riding off in all directions at once. The Labor Relations Secretary, particularly, seems to constitute a virtually independent entity, unrelated to Board policy or administrative direction. Research, even of a relatively pedestrian, self-informing kind, is notable for its absence. All these matters could, one might think, quite easily be brought under scrutiny and almost any change or reform would be an improvement.

In the *formal relations of professional staff to lay leaders* the most subjectively distressing and objectively confounding perennial problem is the ever-unsettled question of the relation between the lay General Chairman of the campaign and the professional General Manager of the Chest. When even well-intentioned sub-staff say that they "cannot tell who's boss around here," action is contradictory, and morale, low. A permanent resolution either way would be less wasteful and destructive of good human relations than any amount of "flexibility" in adjusting to the annual unknown, the character of the Campaign Chairman, and attendant "misunderstanding."

In one very profound sense, however, these confusions and ineptitudes of the *formal* staff-staff and lay-professional relations are the consequence rather than the cause of problematic *informal* human relations, not only in the Chest but, pervasively, in the Welfare Community. There is, on the professional side, generally, a widespread uneasiness, an insecurity with reference to tenure and "appreciation" (that is, informed judgment, not sentimental approval), a feeling of not being fully wanted or understood, that makes for ineffective work and poor formal relations as well. In many quarters outside the city, and in more professional circles than social work ones, one may hear Indianapolis discussed as a "risky" place to work, a "challenge" to go to (like a visit to headhunters, perhaps), or a place "where you don't stick your neck out if you value it." The amount of discussion of *what,* if you are a professional, you can afford to tell "your" laymen, and how (tactfully, gradually, insidiously) is notable. Such problems obtain everywhere, but not everywhere so acutely. Before one can consider what might be done, it is necessary to ask what else in the situation in Indanapolis—other than the split leadership, the distrust of the expert, the preference for crisis-remedy over routine-maintenance—what else in Indianapolis contributes to this uneasiness of relation, and the mutual dissatisfactions that accompany it.

One relationship that had not been explored up to this point drove itself in upon us with increasing force: the relation between the "public" (or government) and "private" (or non-government) sectors of the Welfare Community. It is obvious that, to a great degree, the latter takes its program from the former: what the task of the Welfare Community "is" amounts almost by definition to what isn't done by government, or private persons acting singly, or business. What may be obvious for activities may not be so obvious for relationships, but it is true that if insecurity and resentment and poor conditions generally pervade one sector of the Welfare Community, they will have consequences in the other—partly because tasks will be ill or not at all performed in the worse sector, but chiefly because the same professions serve both fields, and people in one sector "identify" with their likes in the other. Sympathies follow professional bounds more nearly than the dividing lines between public and private.

Two facts brought together may shed some further light. First, the very essence of a profession is its felt power to determine in large degree its own form and fate, to avoid or defeat "interference," particularly politically grounded interference. But, second, the very heart and essence of Hoosier life seems to be "politics," and its attendant shifts, manoeuvres, patronage-necessities, and preoccupations. One result of this Hoosier preference—a preference the Chest cannot, by itself, expect to alter—is a virtually continuous insecurity of professional personnel in the public sector, particularly of senior or more competent personnel. There appear to be long-standing difficulties in recruiting the best professionals, and even greater difficulties in retaining the best of those recruited. The resultant weaknesses are weaknesses not of the public sector alone, but of the professional bodies that serve both; and the distrusts and uncertainties get communicated back and forth across the public-private line.

Abstractly, it might be possible to hedge against the insecurities by building up adequate "paternal" (in the best sense) relations between laymen and professionals, and adequate "fraternal" relations among the professionals. But the problems of the fragmented lay leadership, to which we have so often pointed earlier, make difficult the establishment of good enough "fathering" or sponsoring relationships, so that we are again brought back to the problem of securing enough good "top top leadership." The establishment of suitable fraternal relations between professionals has also been hampered historically by the local high distrust (actual or not, but widely believed in) of anything resembling a Union—even an effective professional association, if the professionals are employed professionals, as against, say, lawyers or doctors in private practice. Nothing short of direct encouragement of the professionals by outstanding lay leaders is likely to move the professionals so to proceed, though their lack of means for legitimate mutual protection and support is frequently deplored.

Any hope of securing the "return"—perhaps even the first effective advent —of the "top top leadership" must depend on something more, we suspect, than an appeal to them to do the job which legitimizes their title—to lead. If there is to be such a return, we believe, there must be changes in the Chest—and if there are to be changes of this order in the Chest, there must be such a return. This implies that the changes and the return are interdependent, i.e., there would have to be negotiation between the parties leading to the taking of simultaneous action—if it is to occur.

But if the ground of that negotiation is to be more than sentiment, it must be in terms of *interest*. And the interest of the "top top leadership" in the quality of the Chest seems never to have been made sufficiently clear. That interest of the "top top leadership" is probably only well served in a community where the Chest operates well; and a Chest only operates well, in any community, probably, if it has "top top leadership."

Where it does operate well, the principal particular service it affords the business community—and especially the top levels of ownership and management—is the provision of an essentially free testing- and training-ground for executive personnel. In a sense it does for manpower what the Aberdeen Proving Grounds does for weapons: it "proves" the goodness of personnel (as against matériel) in a test free of danger to the operating personnel of the organization that is to benefit. In a community where the relations between the power-structure and the Chest are "right," promising executives are given what amounts to a trial run or shakedown cruise, in the Welfare Community—in terms of which their capacity to "perform right" may be judged before they are, as it were, commissioned or promoted. But they will be the likelier to perform right as the "top top leadership" is itself close to the Welfare Community—to symbolize importance, to provide

example, and to observe effort; if it is not present to observe, there is no
one of consequence to the middle-range leaders to assess whether or not
they have performed right. "Succeed" then comes to be substituted for
"perform right"—and "succeed" means getting the money by almost any
stratagem (which is *not* what "upper uppers" means by "right" performance). Getting the money by almost any stratagem seems, at the moment,
not too far from the tone and temper of recent Chest campaigns.

We have already insensibly been led into the discussion of the Chest's
*external relations.* Perhaps enough has already been said about the place
of the "top top leadership" in this field, except for one additional observation. The problem of distributing leadership from various levels in the
community over the various levels of the Welfare Community is one that
cannot—even in theory—be solved by the Chest alone. And while—in theory
—it might be solved by all the agencies acting together, they are simply
not likely to act so together. So we find ourselves driven to the view that
the leadership will have to organize itself, perhaps in a Donors' Association,
in order both to protect itself and to ensure some sensible and economical
distribution of its resources over the positions where it is needed—if such a
sensible fit is to be had at all, or even approximated.

Having made the point that the adequate performance of middle-range
leadership rests largely on the presence of "top top leadership" and of a
proper and properly supervised promotion-system within the philanthropic
field itself, we may ask what other conditions are necessary to the adequate
care and feeding of lay leaders, especially at these intermediate levels. We
have reason, from our interview material, to think that a stable system of
expectations with reference to procedures and rituals (as well as extrinsic
rewards and promotions) and a wholehearted conviction as to the worthiness of the cause and its methods are additional necessities for this group
upon whom really falls the heaviest burden of actual work in their avocational (as well, probably, as in their vocational) life. But such stable
expectations and the conservation and adequate symbolizing of higher or
transcendent purposes require the presence not only of "top top" laymen
but of staff of an equal caliber, i.e., staff as competent in their realm as the
laymen are in theirs, and consequently as assured and secure in their own
place and role.

Conviction in leaders and staff can be firmer and the external relations
of the Chest therefore more satisfactory only if its "message" is clear. And
before the Chest can clarify its message, it must resolve the value-conflicts
spoken of earlier. And before it can tackle these, it must decide whether in
its fundamental nature it is (or is to be) an alien body living off the
community like an occupying army, or a pacific power or instrumentality
to mobilize free consent and give effect to community wish. If the decision
is in the latter direction, the process by which the basic value-problems
may be reached at and continuingly resolved or appropriately compromised

is known to any skilled discussion leader, or indeed to any capable executive.

Similarly, the problem of "standards"—which is the epitome or symbol of what the Chest has to sell: rationality in giving, or equity in the distribution of the gift-load—is both technical and social. The technical side has already been sufficiently developed. The social problem here—as with the value-questions—is so to institute and maintain a process of discussion among significant donors that the issues involved are clear to them, and the con-sensus reached makes sense technically and is binding morally. Such pro-cedures are not "easy," but again they are not beyond available competence.

In nearly every respect, the Chest is where it is because it does not know where it is; yet it cannot know where it is without adequate resources for informing itself. Such resources for self-location and self-observation require some provision for research facilities, and some willingness not to subvert those facilities by using them only upon lines of inquiry that promise to "turn a fast buck," or make money quickly and in the short run.

## UNIFIED FUNDRAISING

The problems dealt with in the few preceding sections would seem to be problems for the Chest whether or not there is any further fundraising unification: and, moreover, some attempts to deal with them would probably prove, in practice, to precede necessarily any voluntary achievement of any further unification. Assuming them to be dealt with, it is time to turn to the problem of unification itself.

The magic word in Chest circles today—not everywhere, but widely—is "United Fund." It appears to be widely believed that the question is capable of a yes-or-no answer, and that the "yes" answer carries with it the near-certain promise of more money, fewer campaigns, less expenditure of executive manpower, and greater rationality in fund-distribution. Such an argument is worth examining.

Simple as it may seem, the subject is actually a very complex one. It is important to indicate first, perhaps, that "United Fund" is only one parti-cular answer to the general problem of fund unification. The general problem requires answers to at least four major questions:

(1) What "agencies" are to be "unified"?
(2) With respect to what portion of their monies?
(3) And in regard to which fundraising activities?
(4) And for what body of donors?

A United Fund presents an answer to the first question—all the agencies now in the Chest, plus any or all of (a) the Red Cross, and (b) the five major "health agencies"—but on all other points it is mute. It does *not* have to be—as many people believe it does—a unification for all of the agencies, of all fundraising activities, for all classes of donors, for all monies other than those "earned," in order to qualify as a United Fund.

The arguments for and against the United Fund seem to us, when abstractly presented, hardly worth examination, though that is just what, in the preceding chapter, we have given them. To each one—pro and con —there is a rejoinder that is to the judicially minded equally plausible or convincing. The net effect of the appeal to argument may well be nil. What then of the appeal to experience?

Unfortunately, the experience is so ill reported that very little can be said in the general case. The principal source of general information is the United Community Funds and Councils of America, and there can hardly be any doubt that this organization is on the pro side. The trouble with the evidence is not the research agency's preference or bias but simply the fact that it evidently does not have enough evidence to make a case one way or the other, on most important points.

A few things seem clear: there are more and more United Funds each year, and their number is increasing faster than the total number of Chests (other than United Fund). In general, also, the larger the campaign, the likelier it is to be a United Fund; 40 per cent of the "small" (under $200,000) campaigns are such; and 60 per cent of the "large" ($200,000 and over). The "very large" ($1 million and over) were 62.7 per cent (42 of them out of 67) United Funds of some kind.

It is also clear that these 42 largest United Funds nearly all include the Red Cross (90 per cent); and more than half include Heart (62 per cent) and Cancer (57 per cent). On the average, each includes 3.4 of the Big Six; or, to put it another way, if "fully united" means including all the Big Six, these largest United Funds show 56 per cent "unitedness." Putting the two statements together one might say that of the largest ($1 million and over) campaigns about two in three have some "unitedness," and, on the average, the "unitedness" of the "united" ones is 56 per cent; the whole group of largest campaigns has thus gone 35 per cent of the way towards unitedness.

If, however, being "united" means consent on the part of the included Big Six—at least, consent to accept the money once raised—we hardly know, apart from Red Cross, where we stand. For the others, in anywhere from 25 per cent of the local cases (Heart) to 47 per cent (Polio) we simply do not know whether they have been united in this sense into the United Funds that "include" them. If known consent to inclusion is the measure, then the 1,873 United States campaigns of all kinds have 1,253 known consented inclusions (out of a theoretically possible 11,238), i.e., by this measure the whole movement has gone some 11 per cent of the way towards "unitedness." Similarly the 821 funds that claim to be "united" have gone 25 per cent of the way, at least.

On a number of key questions we have insufficient information. The arguments as to how much more the new United Funds raise (in their first year of operation) when compared with the results of independent fund-raising by their constituents (in their last year of independence) rest on figures which omit 40 per cent of the cases in the 1955 argument and 27 per cent in the 1956 argument. If success and willingness to report it are related, little reliance can be placed in such figures, and we must say we do not know how well the United Funds do in this vital respect.

Similarly, with the vital question of how the Big Six fare under unification. The data are reported for only three of the Big Six, and for two of these—Cancer and Heart—we do not know what proportion of the cases is reported at all. For the third, Red Cross, which on the average got 2 per cent more each year in the 1953-6 interval, even this alleged gain rests on reports from only 79 of about 128 United Funds that had Red Cross in them in 1953.

We do not even know for 49 per cent of the cases (Red Cross), 72 per cent of the cases (Heart), and 69 per cent of the cases (Cancer) whether or not, even in the United Fund territory, they conducted as well a separate campaign. For the other Big Three, the published data tell us nothing.

For similar reasons, the contentions regarding increases for new United Funds in number-of-subscribers-by-size-of-gift and average employee gift, and employee participation must be regarded, to say the least, as unconvincing. The arguments rest on 22, 9 and 6 per cent of the cases!

There is thus no convincing evidence that new United Funds raise in their first year substantially more than their independent constituents did in their last; no convincing evidence of how the Big Six fare under United Fund in terms of increase in allocations; insufficient evidence that United Fund actually reduces substantially the appeals even of the organizations it "unites"; and inadequate evidence to suggest that it raises (even when new) the participation or gift-level of employees.

As measured by average annual gain over each previous year, the 1952-6 evidence is equivocal as to whether the average annual gain in United Funds is greater than the average annual gain in Community Chests without the Big Six. Such evidence as there is seems to favor slightly the non-United Funds.

Unless the mere fact that "more and more people are doing it" (i.e., that a fashion exists, or has been manufactured) is taken as convincing, it seems difficult to support the United Fund argument on any criterion of "success." The reported knowledge is simply insufficient.

If we are thus driven away from the "general experience" as decisive either way, we are thrown back partly on social philosophy, partly on an attempt to make guesses, not in general, but for the Indianapolis situation.

From the viewpoint of social policy, the problem appears as a problem in freedom and control: whose freedom with respect to what is it proposed to limit or abrogate for the sake of control over what by whom? The United Fund answer seems to be that some sizeable part of the freedom of all the Big Six to get what they can by their own methods in their own way is to be abrogated—and, necessarily, therewith, the freedom of the donor to give in proportions he "chooses" to a large variety of respectable causes. These limitations upon freedom are ostensibly to be borne for the sake of greater control over "multiplicity of campaigns," over "being bothered," over manpower utilization, over money-raising ("success"), over money-alloca- tion ("budgeting") and gift-load distribution ("standards"). But we have little or no evidence that any of the gains in control that supposedly justify the sacrifice in freedom, actually occur. The evidence on the first three is doubtful; and the evidence for better budgeting or more sensible load- distribution is virtually nil. The classic position in democratic social philo- sophy has been that the evidence for greater and more valuable control should be overwhelming before a case for the sacrifice of a freedom can be said to be made out, and it is difficult to reconcile this position with a recommendation to sacrifice certain freedoms for doubtful gains. This view may have peculiar weight in Indiana, where, as described, even such centralization in other matters as has been easily accepted in other regions is viewed with grave misgiving, if not outright hostility.

The question of unification also has peculiar weight because United Fund is not the only alternative open in order to achieve or attempt the purposes described. "In-Plant Federation" implies for those organizations that choose it, the possibility of limiting, within the corporately organized sector, all campaigns to as few or as many per annum as each plant chooses; it also permits participation in allocation decisions of hundreds of plant committees, and, in the election of those committees, of thousands of workers. Some loss of freedom is entailed—but significantly less; and, cor- respondingly, control is more diffuse and there is less of it.

If a case could be made out for the desirability of more control than this, at least the argument for In-Plant Federation as an alternative would be shaken. The necessary argument for greater control rests essentially on two grounds: one has to do with leadership, the other with planning. The argu- ment as to leadership is essentially that, attracted or compelled by the magnitude of the enterprise and the possibility of really effective control, "top top leadership," previously alienated from the Chest, can be brought to "return" or "come in" to a United Fund. The argument as to planning is that only under a United Fund can there be adequate planning of local services via budgetary control.

Both arguments seem incontrovertible. We cannot predict what would happen in Indianapolis—though, if access could be had to the "top top leadership" at all, this would be a simple matter for discovery by negotia- tion. But, in general, the return (or new adherence) of "top top leadership" to a United Fund is, we suspect, the primary cause of success where there is success.

As to planning, one would have to examine its wisdom and its possibility. We are unconvinced, on the basis of what we have seen, that the wisdom exists in any small body of professionals or laymen to develop a plan for the community's social services with a result demonstrably or credibly better than what has grown up substantially on the basis of how donors happened to distribute their money. But this is a judgment—and an arguable one—and the whole question of "wisdom" may be waived. What is much harder to believe in than wisdom, is the bare possibility of such planning under United Fund. No United Fund as far as we know has a binding contract to retain for any long period any one of the Big Six against its wish. This implies that none of these could have its budget substantially cut, or be long refused the kinds of gains others were getting. "Planning" is therefore limited either to freezing the present budgetary relationships, or to adjusting them to vary according to a committee guess as to what the traffic will bear, i.e., what would happen if a disaffected member "fringed off." In the latter case, the committee would be guessing as to what would happen if the committee did not exist, and planning to do what would happen anyway without a plan! The possibility of planning thus seems remote, and if the hope of it is what brings the leaders back, the possibility of their subsequent disappointment and consequent defection (or redefection) would have to be considered.

A middle solution that sacrifices less freedom and demands less control is at least available, as already stated, in the shape of In-Plant Federation. If to this were added a Donors' Association, or a Donors' Consultative Service for those who cared to bind themselves to a common policy or to develop their several policies at least in consultation with each other, it would seem that the degree of control and the desired necessary sacrifices of freedom could be continuously adjusted in terms of the donors' desires to affiliate or disaffiliate, avail themselves or not, of the service. This double solution suggests, for the donors, a maximum of such control as they really wish to secure at the price of such sacrifices of freedom as they really wish to make, i.e., it suggests a genuinely voluntary association. The philanthropies themselves retain their independence and reserve their freedom of action—except that, in so far as they have common interests, the very existence of a Donors' Association would tend to encourage them to co-operate with respect to these, i.e., would tend to call out a limited-purpose voluntary association of voluntary associations.

Two such looser, interest-separated enterprises may, in general, but most particularly in the climate of Indianapolis, have much to recommend them over the alternative interest-confounded and monolithic United Fund. Whether or not this is the case is a matter for exploration and discovery. What is vital is that a suitable fit for Indianapolis be found which will permit desired and possible controls with the minimum sacrifice of valued and still defensible freedoms. Discovering what that fit is, is a problem for "Community Organization" in the best sense of that term: a problem, that is, in facilitating for free, intelligent, and respect-worthy men the process of discovering the facts and possibilities and values involved, with a view to reaching free, intelligent, and respect-worthy decisions.

# 15. Epilogue

EVERYONE—perhaps especially the social scientist—is entitled to permit himself a degree of naïveté. Everyone—perhaps especially the social scientist—may allow himself some afterthoughts, although "afterthoughts" may not be the best term for reflections that early, late, and last forced themselves again and again upon us, but that had to be put out of mind temporarily until the study, as defined, was completed. The study is now completed. The afterthoughts concern our "location" of the problem and our address to it as represented in this report.

Implicitly, in accepting the problem given us by citizens of Indianapolis—"What's wrong with our Chest, and how can we do better?"—we assumed that a sufficiently large or powerful group of people were sufficiently motivated by a desire to see the Chest succeed, that it would only be necessary and surely sufficient to identify for them those technical and social obstacles that seemed to stand between them and clear policy, between them and well-planned action, between them and concert about ends and means, between them and "success"—or at least the means to "success." We therefore "located" our problem in terms of providing basic facts about philanthropy; tools of analysis; logical clarification; and sociological insight with reference to what goes on in the Chest and outside.

This "location" make sense *if* the problem really fits our assumption. Useful as it may be, however, for other purposes, it makes little sense if the problem lies at another level.

Perhaps it does lie at another level—instead, or as well. If it lies at another level *instead,* some large part of the report may be irrelevant. If it lies at another level *as well,* the report can be but a prologue or preface to something else. But what do we mean when we ask whether "the problem lies at another level"?

We mean something that is a commonplace of social research, as well as a commonplace of experience: that "manifest" and "latent," "evident" and "concealed," "ostensible" and "actual" motives, charters, purposes, problems are rarely in human affairs the same, for any individual or any group. If the principal reward of belonging to a certain kind of bridge-club is really the attendant gossip, and the principal function of the cards is to give the ladies something graceful to do with their hands, then, a club of this type which is not operating satisfactorily will be better served by the advice of a Louella Parsons or a Westbrook Pegler than that of an Ely Culbertson or Easley Blackwood. If two children are "quarrelling about nothing" because they enjoy quarrelling, or thus avert boredom, or test one another's verbal and, presently, physical powers, then a well-meaning parent or teacher who shows them that "there is really no issue," right as he may be, is really spoiling the game.

Our concern is lest we have, unwittingly, acted the role of that kind of parent or teacher. Why?

We have been so often and so forcibly struck—as we have reported—with the confusion of thought, the seeming disorder of procedure, the maladaptation of means to ends, the sudden tacks and turns of policy—like the behaviour of children "arbitrarily" dropping one game for another—within an organization governed primarily by top-notch business people, and the contrast between this and the vocational life of the businessman has been so sharp, that we have been driven to ask at least two more reflective questions. The first question is: "Is this contrast accidental, and if not, what purpose does it serve?" The second is: "*Can* such an organization be otherwise operated?"

The question of whether or not the contrast is accidental could only be answered with great certainty either by deeper psychological analysis of the motivation and sources of satisfactions of individual businessmen, or by a more situational analysis that would examine for correlations[1] between the vocational and avocational lives of the persons concerned, especially their welfare and philanthropic careers. This we have not been able to do in any systematic way.

What we have then is a set of general contrasts which serve to suggest that, at least for many of the businessmen involved, participation in philanthropy or welfare serves as a kind of *relief* to their everyday occupations in much the same manner as play serves as a relief from work. The work situation of a modern executive calls for an unusual amount of attention to detail, foresight, tolerance of the "human factor," self-control, team-centered (or whatever is the opposite of egocentric) behavior, moderation in tone and exactitude in expression, conservatism in making claims, restraint in "playing politics" within the organization and forbearance in particular from log-rolling. The key word may not be "constraint"—though it is that for many—but it certainly is not "abandon."

In contrast with this, perhaps slightly overdrawn, "monastic" picture,[2] participation in philanthropy or the welfare agencies allows room for such gifts of innovation, invention, freewheeling imagination, ingenuity for politics in general and log-rolling in particular as a man may have, together with some very considerable latitude in the making of claims, the elaboration of "plans" without any proximate check on their success or responsibility for their failure, and, in general, generous allowance for spontaneity, color, romance and even, upon occasion, some permissible clowning.

The contrast is too marked, too good a fit to what would be required if the avocational life in this respect were designed for the relief of the vocational, to permit us to regard the contrast as purely coincidental. We must note that philanthropy as part of the avocational life *does* furnish relief. We may ask further if it *must*, i.e., if indeed it could not be operated at all—or only with less "success"—if it failed to provide contrast with the serious workaday world. From the persistence of the behaviour in any one place, and from its prevalence in many or most places—indeed from its revival again and again where it has been allowed to die[3]—we are driven to the view that the avocation of philanthropic government must provide some substantial contrast to the serious, closely calculated vocation of business life. Perhaps it would be a mistake to conclude, however, that the philanthropic enterprise must provide *mere* relief from the boredoms, restraints, and close-calculated behaviors of business life. Indeed, were this the case, the prospects for "improvement" of the enterprise, in so far at least as its ostensible purpose is concerned, would be very dim.

It may be that the "ideally successful" Chest or other MOPS fundraising enterprise would provide an area in which the close application of serious, thoughtful, and businesslike procedures would have a place, and the provision of imaginative play, of ritual and other necessary but "non-rational" satisfactions would also be cared for.

If this is so—and it seems likely—then the question of order and priority must be settled. Perhaps that Chest would succeed best and longest which, having given and continuously giving careful attention to the reasonableness and congruence of its aims, to the rationality and equity of its demands, to the sense and businesslikeness of its procedures, to the efficiency of its operations and the decency and humaneness of its interpersonal relations, *then* turned to the provision of space and means for play, romance, spontaneity and freedom in appropriate places and within and about its otherwise carefully founded enterprise. In the culture of America "duty comes before pleasure," and it is doubtful if most people can play with real playfulness unless they know that their work is done. It may be, similarly, that in an organization known to have done its "work," participants will feel that some play is a due reward, and does not raise a spectre "Are we just kidding one another?"; and it may be that the spectators of such an organization will feel that the play represents the perfect symbol of men recreating themselves, having worked well for the common weal.

Whatever the solution, we must add to what we have said that the finding of the right order and balance between work and play that would join effectiveness and satisfaction to seemliness and spontaneity is one continuing discovery to be made, and remade, by the would-be "successful" fundraising organization—or indeed, perhaps, any human association, voluntary or non-voluntary.

# CHARTS

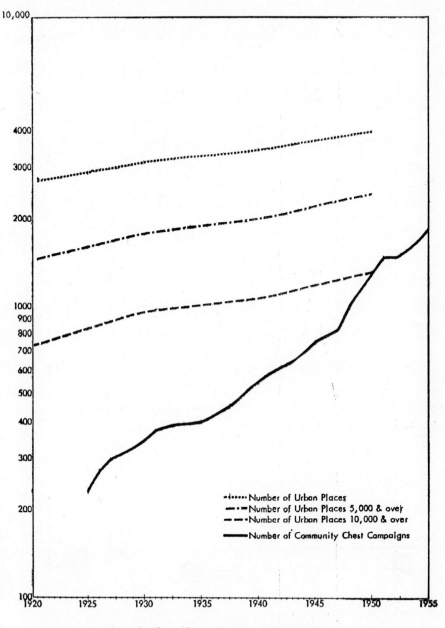

CHART 1. Number of urban places (U.S.A., 1920–1950) and number of
Community Chest campaigns (1920-1955).

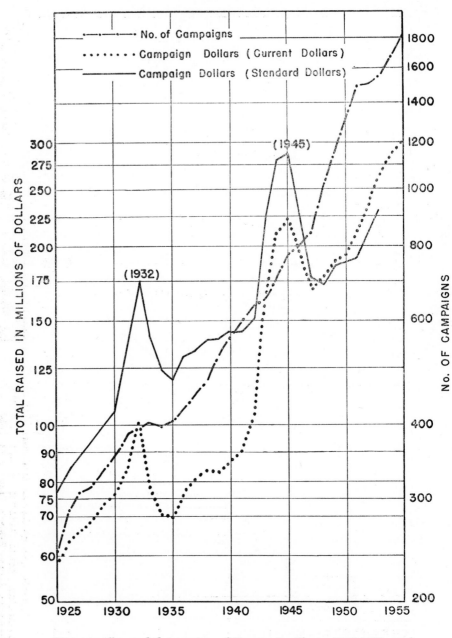

CHART 2. All recorded campaigns of Community Chests, 1925-1955: total number and total take.

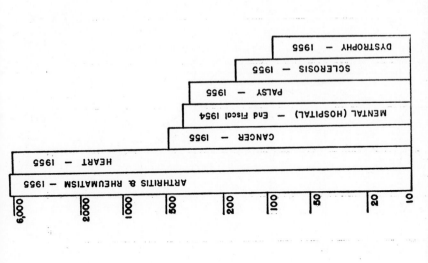

CHART 4. Estimated prevalence rates (cases per 100,000 population) for selected diseases. Source: United States Department of Health, Education and Welfare, National Office of Vital Statistics, April, 1956.

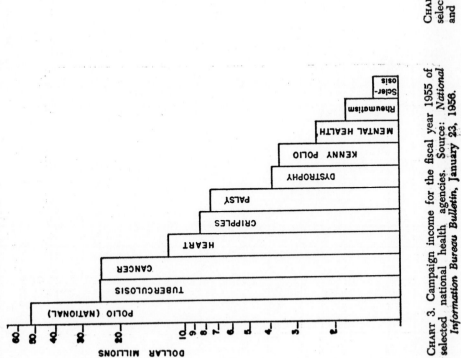

CHART 3. Campaign income for the fiscal year 1955 of selected national health agencies. Source: *National Information Bureau Bulletin*, January 23, 1956.

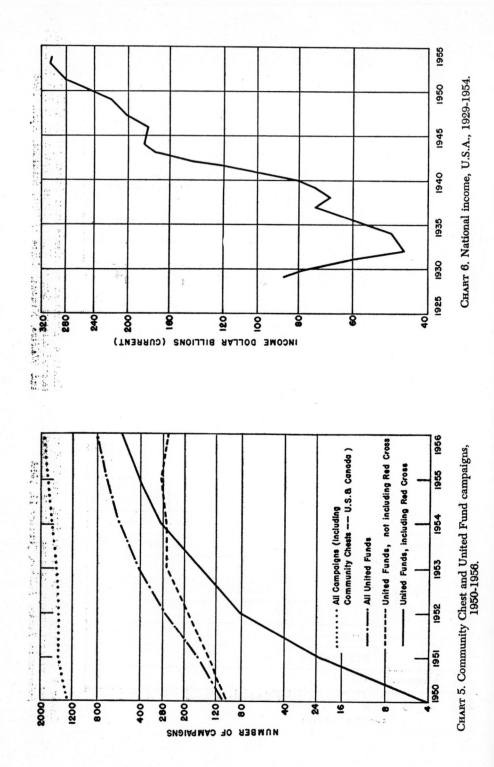

CHART 6. National income, U.S.A., 1929-1954.

CHART 5. Community Chest and United Fund campaigns, 1950-1956.

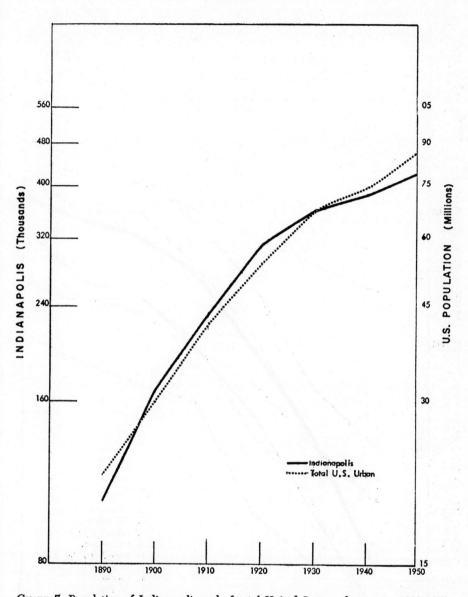

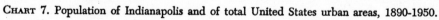

CHART 7. Population of Indianapolis and of total United States urban areas, 1890-1950.

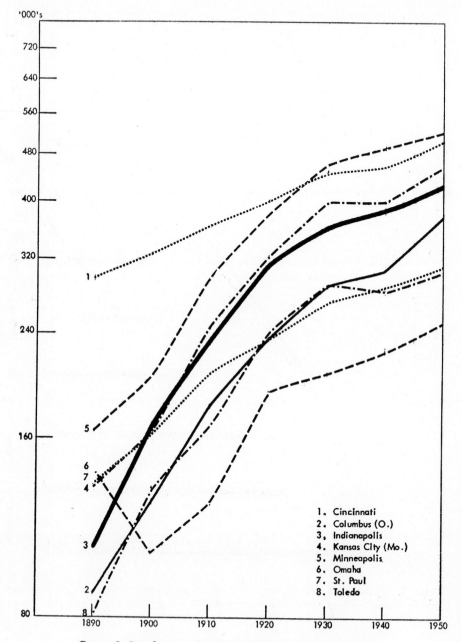

'000's

720

640

560

480

400

320

240

160

80

1. Cincinnati
2. Columbus (O.)
3. Indianapolis
4. Kansas City (Mo.)
5. Minneapolis
6. Omaha
7. St. Paul
8. Toledo

1890   1900   1910   1920   1930   1940   1950

CHART 8. Populations of eight Midwestern cities, 1890-1950.

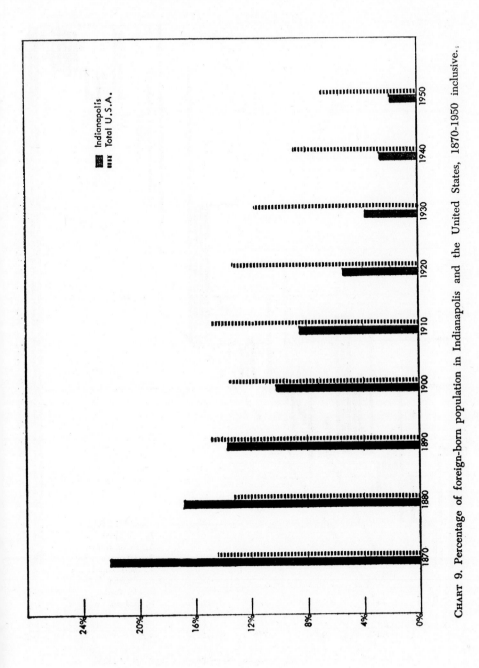

CHART 9. Percentage of foreign-born population in Indianapolis and the United States, 1870-1950 inclusive.

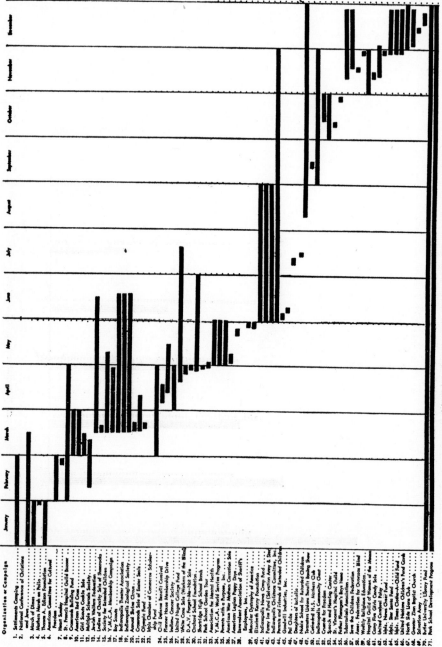

CHART 10. Some of the opportunities to give in Indianapolis during 1955.

$'000's

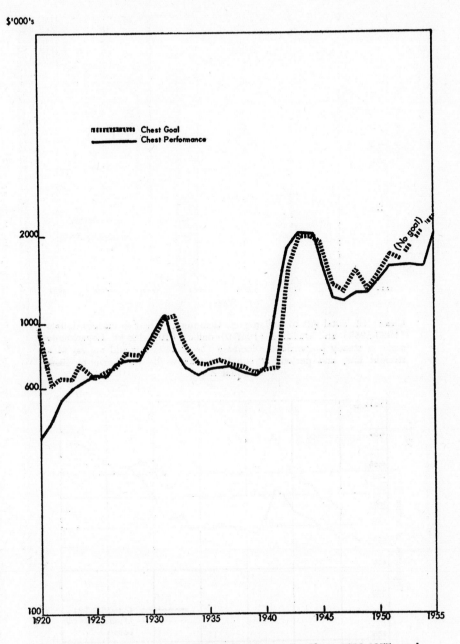

CHART 11. Campaigns of the Indianapolis Community Chest, 1920-1955: goal and amount raised.

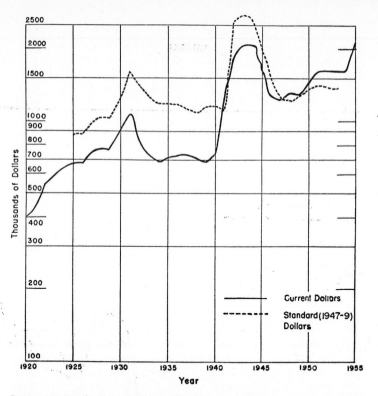

CHART 12. Total gift to Indianapolis Community Chest in current dollars (1920-1955) and standard (1947-9) dollars (1925-1954). Logarithmic scale: a steady proportionate increase (or decrease) would appear as a straight line, and periods of equal increase would be shown by lines of equal slope.

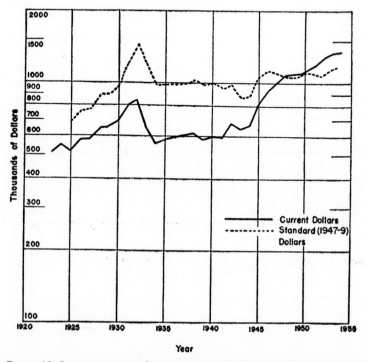

CHART 13. Payments to member agencies of the Indianapolis Community Chest, 1924-1954.

CHART 14. National income, U.S.A. (1929–1954), and take of all Chests combined (1925-1955): the "one-mill tax."

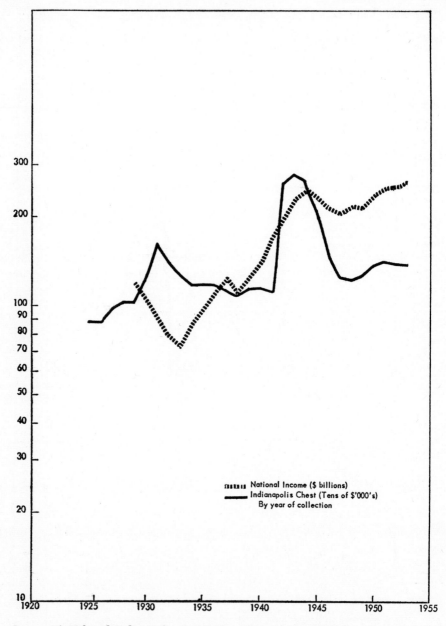

CHART 15. Take of Indianapolis Community Chest (1925-1953) shown in relation to national income, U.S.A. (1929–1953), in standard (1947–9) dollars.

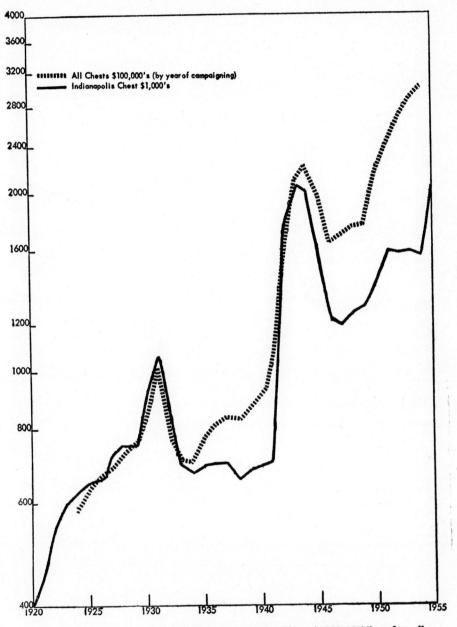

CHART 16. Total gifts to Indianapolis Community Chest (1920-1955) and to all
Chests combined (1924-1954).

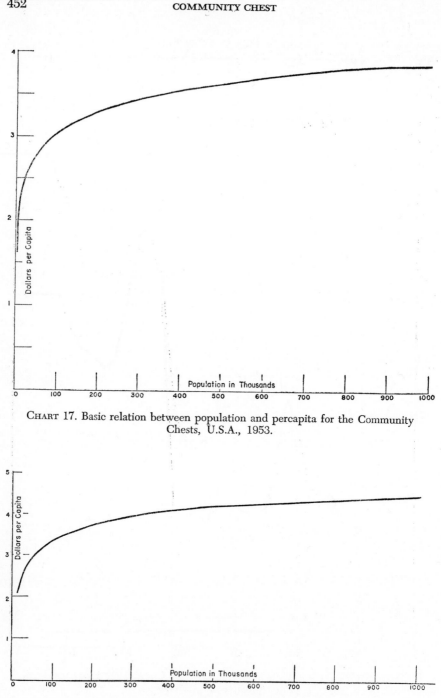

CHART 17. Basic relation between population and percapita for the Community Chests, U.S.A., 1953.

CHART 18. Basic relation between population and percapita for the Community Chests, North Central region, U.S.A., 1953.

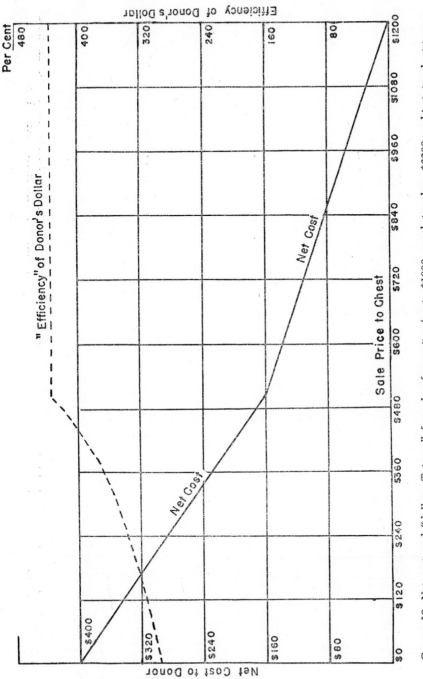

CHART 19. Net cost and "dollar efficiency" for sale of security (cost, $1000; market value, $2200; subject to short-term Capital Gains Tax, owner in 60 per cent tax bracket) to the Community Chest at various prices.

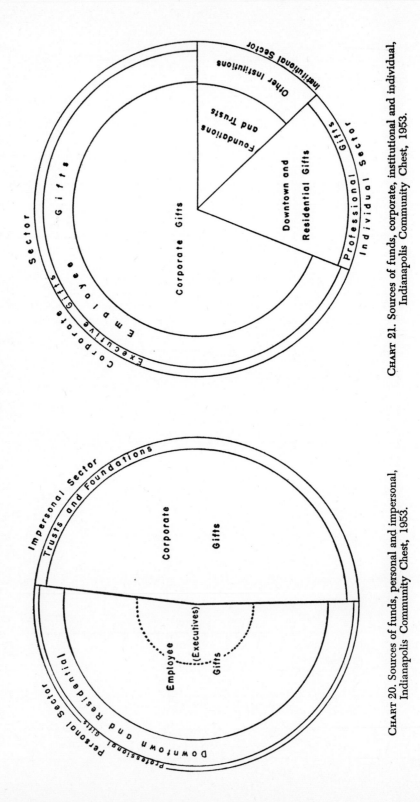

CHART 21. Sources of funds, corporate, institutional and individual, Indianapolis Community Chest, 1953.

CHART 20. Sources of funds, personal and impersonal, Indianapolis Community Chest, 1953.

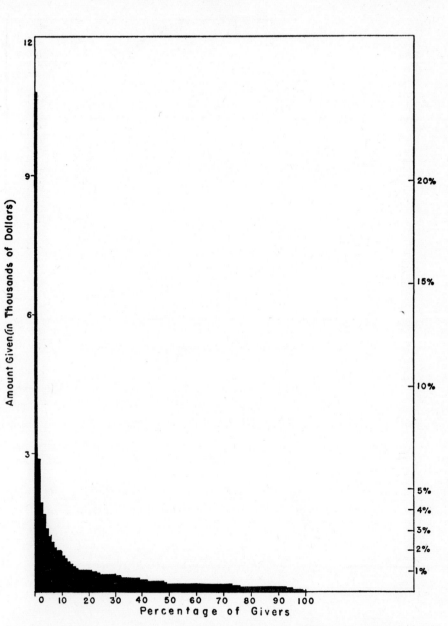

CHART 22. Amount of gift and percentage of total (*N*=1831), contributed by each 1 per cent of executive givers, Indianapolis Community Chest, 1953.

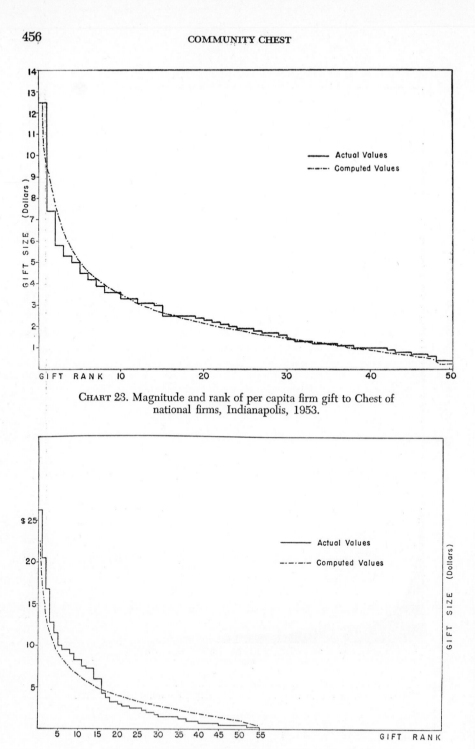

CHART 23. Magnitude and rank of per capita firm gift to Chest of national firms, Indianapolis, 1953.

CHART 24. Magnitude and rank of per capita gifts to Chest of 55 largest home firms, Indianapolis, 1953.

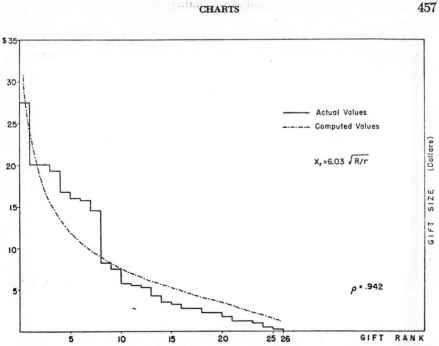

CHART 25. Magnitude and rank of per capita firm gifts to Chest, insurance, Indianapolis, 1953.

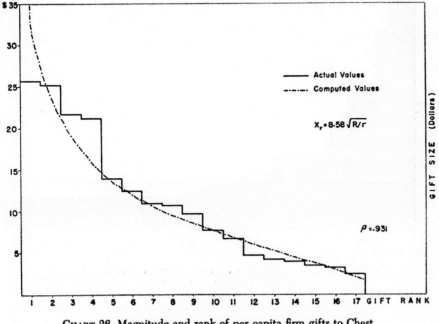

CHART 26. Magnitude and rank of per capita firm gifts to Chest, banks, Indianapolis, 1953.

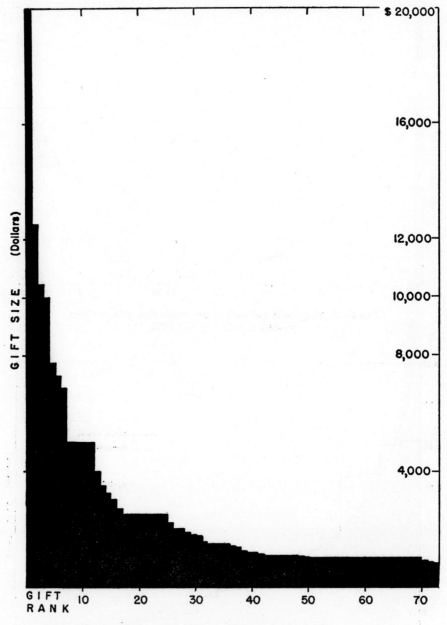

CHART 27. Magnitude and rank, top eighty pledges to Indianapolis Jewish
Welfare Federation, 1954-1955.

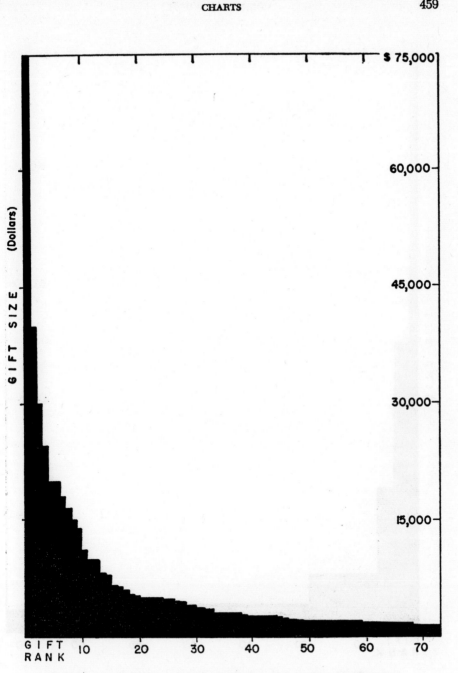

CHART 28. Magnitude and rank, eighty largest firm gifts, Indianapolis
Community Chest, 1953.

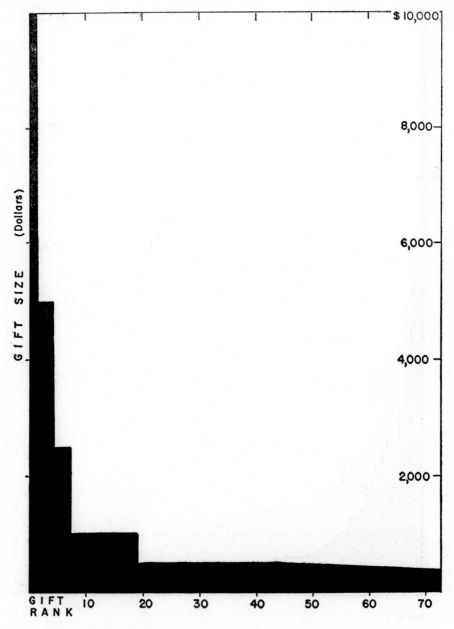

CHART 29. Magnitude and rank, first eighty suggested gifts in a $100,000 campaign, professional fundraiser's model (1,493 gifts).

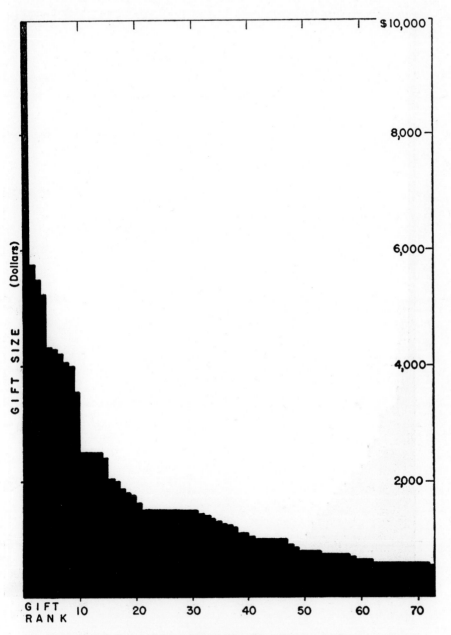

CHART 30. Magnitude and rank, eighty largest firm gifts to the Community Chest, Jacksonville, Florida, 1951.

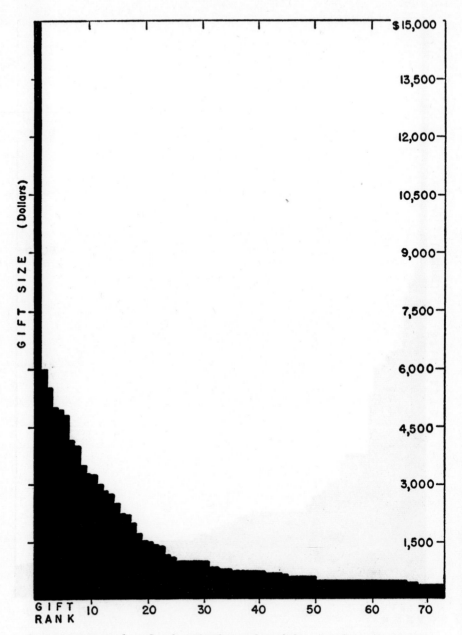

CHART 31. Magnitude and rank, eighty largest firm pledges to Indianapolis Chapter, American Red Cross, 1953.

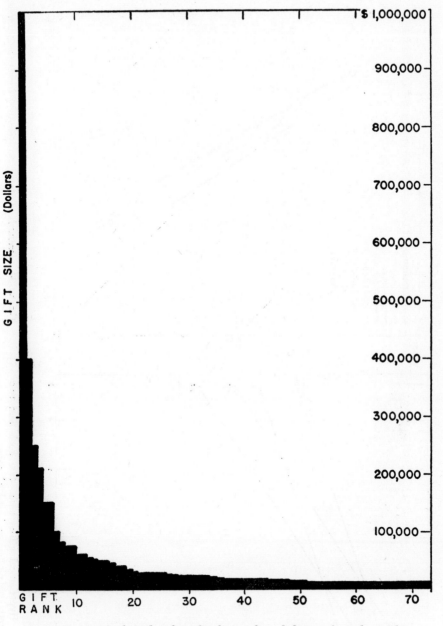

CHART 32. Magnitude and rank, eighty largest firm pledges to the Indianapolis
Hospital Development Association, 1952-3.

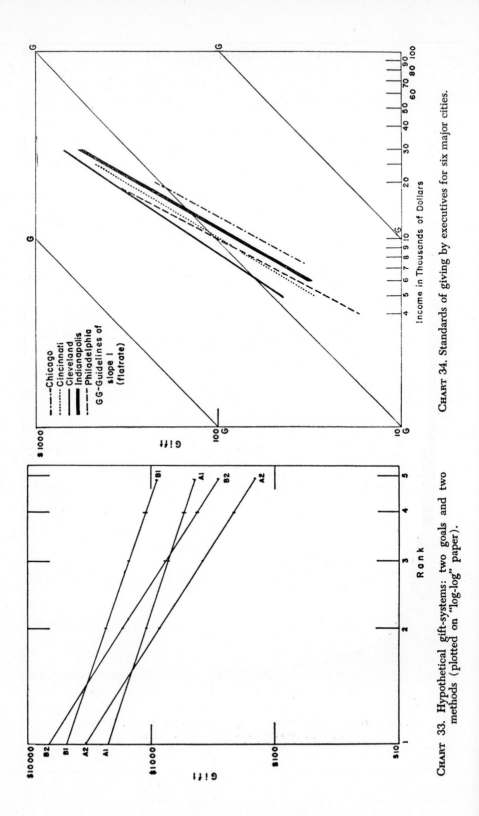

CHART 34. Standards of giving by executives for six major cities.

CHART 33. Hypothetical gift-systems: two goals and two methods (plotted on "log-log" paper).

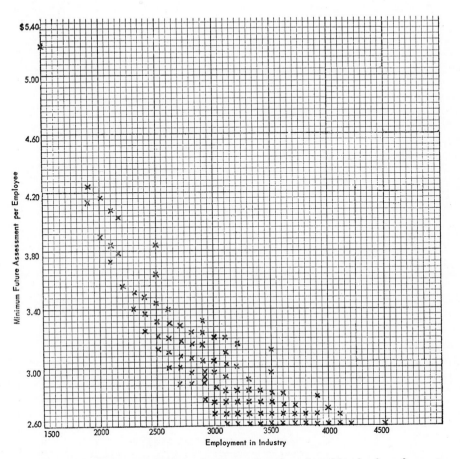

CHART 35. Variation in per-employee "assessment" under selected levels of employment in an industry (hypothetical firms and industry).

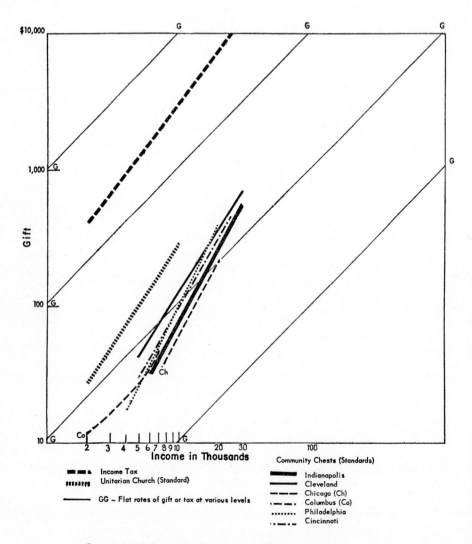

CHART 36. Gift standards and income tax, for six major cities.

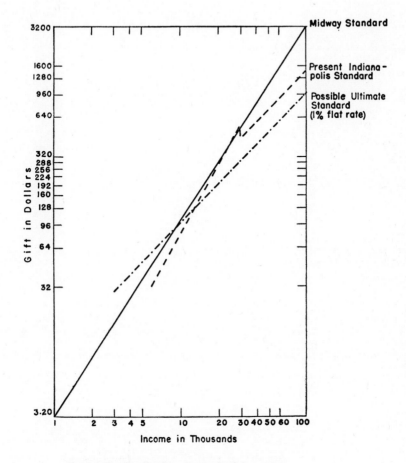

CHART 37. The "midway" standard for giving.

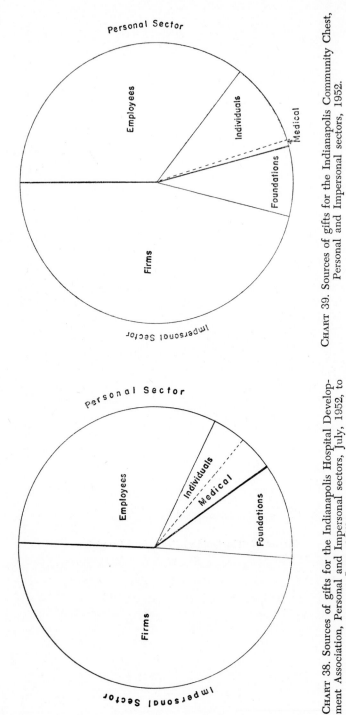

Personal Sector

Employees

Individuals

Medical

Foundations

Firms

Impersonal Sector

CHART 39. Sources of gifts for the Indianapolis Community Chest, Personal and Impersonal sectors, 1952.

Personal Sector

Employees

Individuals

Medical

Foundations

Firms

Impersonal Sector

CHART 38. Sources of gifts for the Indianapolis Hospital Development Association, Personal and Impersonal sectors, July, 1952, to June, 1953.

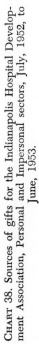

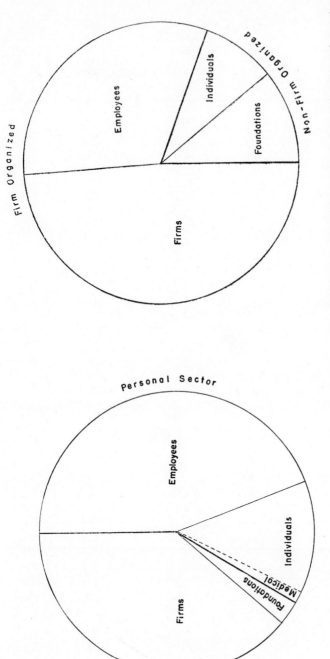

CHART 41. Sources of gifts for the Indianapolis Hospital Development Association, Firm Organized and Non-Firm Organized sectors, July, 1952, to June, 1953.

CHART 40. Sources of gifts for the Indianapolis Chapter, American Red Cross, Personal and Impersonal sectors, 1952.

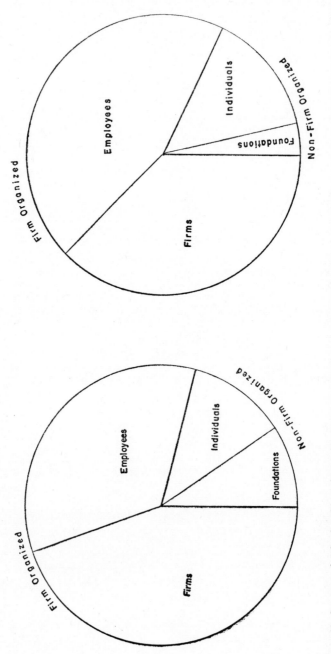

CHART 42. Sources of gifts for the Indianapolis Community Chest, Firm Organized and Non-Firm Organized sectors, 1952.

CHART 43. Sources of gifts for the Indianapolis Chapter, American Red Cross, Firm Organized and Non-Firm Organized sectors, 1953.

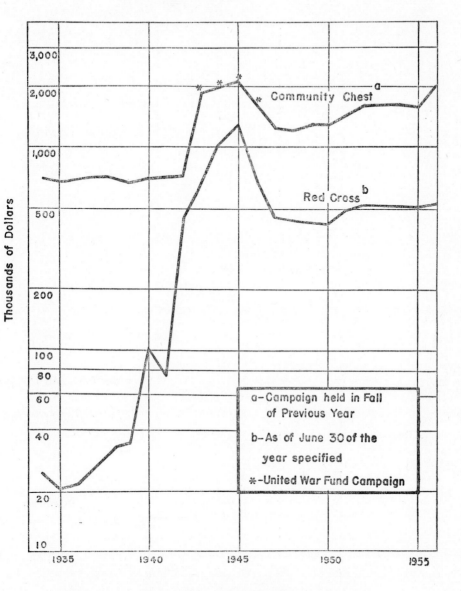

CHART 44. Amounts raised by Community Chest and Red Cross
in Indianapolis, 1934-1956.

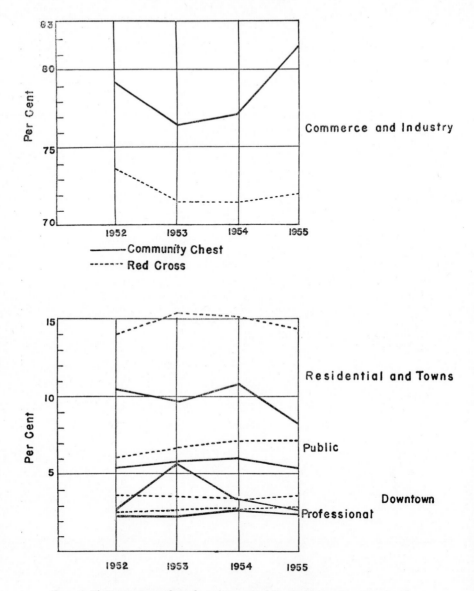

CHART 45. Percentage of total amount raised by divisions, Community Chest and Red Cross, Indianapolis, 1952-1955.

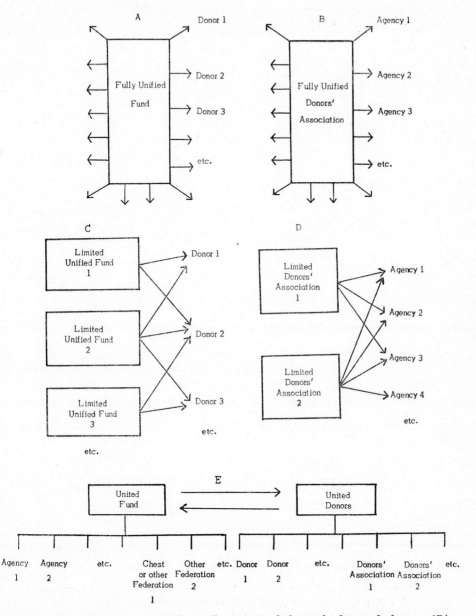

CHART 46. Possibilities of "unification": (A) Unified Fund, disunited donors; (B) Unified donors, disunited solicitors; (C) Partial unification of funds; (D) Partial unification of donors; (E) United Fund and United Donors.

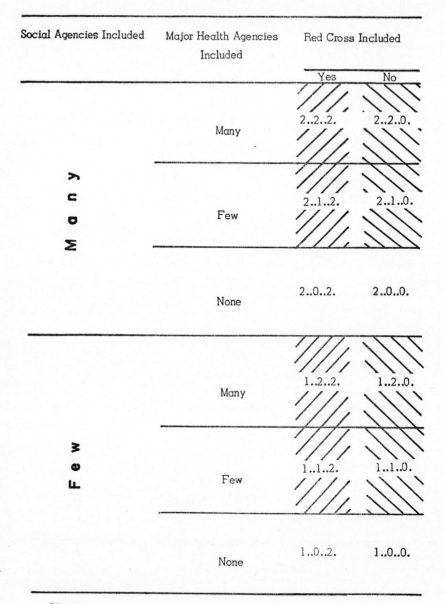

Social Agencies Included   Major Health Agencies   Red Cross Included
                                Included

                                                    Yes          No

**Many**

Many                        2..2..2.      2..2..0.

                  Few       2..1..2.      2..1..0.

                  None      2..0..2.      2..0..0.

**Few**

                  Many      1..2..2.      1..2..0.

                  Few       1..1..2.      1..1..0.

                  None      1..0..2.      1..0..0.

(Numbers in cells are type-numbers for classification purposes.)
(Shaded areas :United Fund *with* Red Cross ////////: *without* \\\\\\\\\)

CHART 47. Major types: Community Chests and United Funds.

| "Social Agencies" | | Major "Health Agencies" Added | | Red Cross | | |
| --- | --- | --- | --- | --- | --- | --- |
| | | | | Included | | Excluded |
| Number Included | Proportion of Donandum Financed | Number Included | Proportion of Donandum Financed | Red Cross Donandum | | |
| | | | | High | Low | Nil |
| MANY | HIGH | Many | High | 22.22.22 | 22.22.21 | 22.22.00 |
| | | | Low | 22.21.22 | 22.21.21 | 22.21.00 |
| | | Few | High | 22.12.22 | 22.12.21 | 22.12.00 |
| | | | Low | 22.11.22 | 22.11.21 | 22.11.00 |
| | | None | Nil | 22.00.22 | 22.00.21 | 22.00.00 |
| | LOW | Many | High | 21.22.22 | 21.22.21 | 21.22.00 |
| | | | Low | 21.21.22 | 21.21.21 | 21.21.00 |
| | | Few | High | 21.12.22 | 21.12.21 | 21.12.00 |
| | | | Low | 21.11.22 | 21.11.21 | 21.11.00 |
| | | None | Nil | 21.00.22 | 21.00.21 | 21.00.00 |
| FEW | HIGH | Many | High | 12.22.22 | 12.22.21 | 12.22.00 |
| | | | Low | 12.21.22 | 12.21.21 | 12.21.00 |
| | | Few | High | 12.12.22 | 12.12.21 | 12.12.00 |
| | | | Low | 12.11.22 | 12.11.21 | 12.11.00 |
| | | None | Nil | 12.00.22 | 12.00.21 | 12.00.00 |
| | LOW | Many | High | 11.22.22 | 11.22.21 | 11.22.00 |
| | | | Low | 11.21.22 | 11.21.21 | 11.21.00 |
| | | Few | High | 11.12.22 | 11.12.21 | 11.12.00 |
| | | | Low | 11.11.22 | 11.11.21 | 11.11.00 |
| | | None | Nil | 11.00.22 | 11.00.21 | 11.00.00 |

(Numbers in cells are type numbers for classification purposes.)

(Shaded Areas: ///// United Fund *with* Red Cross: \\\\\ United Fund *without* Red Cross.)

CHART 48. Types and subtypes: Community Chests and United Funds.

# NOTES

# Notes

## CHAPTER 1

1. In one year, 1954, just before the study began, the Chest held a campaign without a publicly stated objective, in order precisely to avoid the risk of being stigmatized as failing. Of course, there were expectations even here, but they were vague and various, so that different persons at the same time or the same person at different times could claim that *that* campaign was really "quite a success when you take everything into account" or was "just as poor as last year's."

2. The "scatter" of reaction was immense. Many, almost immediately, "appreciated the difficulties" and stood solid for a program of research that took some account of the complexities. Others "went along," but were "disappointed" in the face of the seeming impossibility of getting "fast, definite, practical answers—that's what we need!" Among these latter, some expressed this convinced-against-their-better-judgment feeling by calling periodically for truncation of the agreed program, i.e., by asking for pronouncements on policy before data to illuminate them were available; others expressed the same feeling by "going along" verbally, but simultaneously treating the study as irrelevant, by fighting actively while the study was under way for decision in terms of their views on those matters the study had been set up (at their request) to examine. (One sponsor is said to have stated, in his attempt to secure action his way, that the study would have no bearing on a problem which was actually central to its purpose.)

3. Even so, the problems of defining and redefining the meaning of research were by no means at an end. By a curious transposition of terms, common perhaps generally in North America, the words "theoretical" and "practical," used respectively for blame and praise, were employed with reference to research in almost the precise opposite of their dictionary meanings. A "practical" study in this vocabulary is one that takes as a going theory all the untested beliefs and untried and unexamined premises or assumptions that may well be and usually are the source of the difficulties under review; hence a "practical" study, on this view, is one that (because of its faulty theory) is commonly doomed to practical futility. A "theoretical" study, on the contrary, is one that brings just these vital points under review and therefore permits some possibility of finding practical remedies. But by definition—to those so oriented—"theoretical" means impractical (or irrelevant) rather than ultra-practical. The difficulty of communication on this point never ceased to plague the study, even in relation to some of those who agreed that the study did deal with the very "practical" problems they had raised in ways that, for the first time, made some order and sense of them.

4. Sometimes there is no precise "sum demanded," but what is asked for is any amount within a set range, which is referred to as a "standard."

5. Indeed the only study which we encountered that sheds light on the relation between gift and motive suggests that the "higher" the motive claimed, the lower the average gift. See Federation of Jewish Philanthropies of New York, *Report of the Committee to Study Fund-Raising Procedures and Practices* (1954). (Interpretation, ours.)

6. Cutting across and complicating these normal difficulties were others of a more abnormal sort. For most of our period of observation the Chest was in, or conceived itself to be in, a state of crisis. The feeling of crisis put a premium on secrecy of negotiation and made for a feeling of such delicacy in the issues that even the sponsors of the study saw fit to exclude the researchers from the scene of negotiation at some points that would have been most illuminating because they were most critical. Such

procedure merely made it difficult to get information, which then came second-hand from more sources than one, instead of directly and by observation.

7. For the criteria of relevance, see chapter 6.

8. "Concentrated" is the word since we had and used other data at points, e.g., church giving (in two Protestant denominations), giving to the Jewish Welfare Federation locally, etc. Church giving is a matter of member—as against mass—fundraising; and the Jewish Welfare Federation offers an instance of something in between, i.e., a constituency, thinking of itself as something less closely bound than a church congregation, but more closely related in interest and fate than any general public.

9. "Contrasted," because the hospital campaign is non-periodical and not primarily "operational." In practice it may turn out also to be periodic, i.e., there are suggestions that new solicitation will have to be engaged in at periodic intervals; but the campaign under study here was presented and thought of as a "once-in-a-lifetime" operation.

10. Mary T. Haugh, M.A. (Research Assistant and Co-Author); Nora Congdon Jenkins, Ph.D. (Research Assistant and Co-Author); Robert Wallace Jones, Jr., M.A. (Research Associate and Co-Author); Buford H. Junker, Ph.D. (Study Director and Co-Author); Irving Miller, B.S. (Statistician); Donald M. Salzman, M.A. (Field Director, Redevelopment Study); John R. Seeley (Executive Director, Co-Author and Editor); Mrs. John Sherbun (Secretary); and Mrs. Donald F. West, A.B. (General Secretary). Miss Haugh was chiefly responsible for chapter 2; Mrs. Jenkins, for chapter 4 and many of the underlying "sub-studies"; Mr. Jones, for a great deal of the field-work, wholly for chapter 9 and largely for chapter 13; Mr. Junker for field-work, field-work supervision, and chapters 3, 7, 10, and 11; Mr. Miller for all statistical supervision and several sub-studies; Mrs. Sherbun and Mrs. West for the immense task of physical production; and Mr. Salzman for the collection of some basic data.

11. The English Foundation Building, erected in 1953, was provided for in the will of William E. English; occupancy was limited to organizations which were "voluntary, not tax supported, agencies . . . fully organized Indianapolis groups." The building is operated by the William E. English Foundation, which was incorporated to carry out specific provisions of Mr. English's will.

12. Participation was minimized, but not omitted. At one minimum level we ate with our "objects of observation," and—at some risk to digestion—observed, listened, and noted as we ate. At a nearer-maximum level, one staff member, at least, took part himself in at least one campaign.

13. Paid staffs, we interviewed almost exhaustively, certainly exhaustingly, and mostly to the point of diminishing returns and repetition of content. (In the text, we refer to all these paid staff people as "professionals," even though we know that social workers would prefer to reserve the term for those with special training.)

14. These sub-studies represent probes into the data. Some of them are quoted in this report. Some, it is hoped, will be published in suitable technical journals, hereafter.

15. Some, whom obligation would incline the authors to list here, must remain unlisted because naming them would be equivalent to divulging particular sources of information.

16. Harry T. Ice, President, 1952; William J. Stout, President, 1953, 1954; Gerald R. Redding, President, 1955, Vice-President, 1953, 1954; Mrs. Boyd I. Miller, Vice-President, 1952; Clark S. Wheeler, Vice-President, 1955; Willis B. Conner, Jr., Treasurer, 1952, 1953, 1954, 1955; Philip Adler, Jr., Secretary, 1952, 1953, 1954; Mrs. Perry W. Lesh, Secretary, 1955; Lionel Artis (1954, 1955)*; R. Norman Baxter; Hon. Phillip L. Bayt; George A. Bischoff; Robert L. Brokenburr (1952, 1953); Harry O. Dougherty; George A. Kuhn; Howard S. Morse; Dr. Cleon A. Nafe; Hon. Saul I. Rabb; Dr. M. O. Ross; William L. Schloss (1953, 1954, 1955); Mrs. Harold B. West; and Evans Woollen, Jr. (*Dates in parentheses appear after the names of those who were on the Board for less than the four years.)

17. Lilly Endowment, Inc., Indianapolis Foundation, Indianapolis Community Chest, and Baxter Foundation. L. S. Ayres & Co. generously lent office furniture.

18. Mr. William H. Book, Executive Vice-President of the Indianapolis Chamber of Commerce, and Mr. Carl Dortch, Assistant General Manager and Director of the Bureau of Governmental Research, were most helpful.

19. Community Chest: General Manager from the initiation of our study to April 1, 1956, Mr. Michael F. McCaffrey; succeeded, thereafter, by Mr. Richard H. Fague.

20. Indianapolis Hospital Development Association: Mr. Jack S. Killen, Executive Secretary.

21. The American Red Cross, Indianapolis Chapter: Mr. Virgil Sheppard, Executive Director.


## CHAPTER 2

1. Ernest Victor Hollis, *Philanthropic Foundations and Higher Education* (New York: Columbia University Press, 1938), pp. 3, vii.

2. From a speech by Mary E. Richmond before the Civic Club in Philadelphia; quoted in *Churches and Social Welfare*, vol. II, *The Changing Scene* (National Council of the Churches of Christ in the U.S.A., 1955), p. 34.

3. Wayne McMillen, "Financing Social Work," *Social Work Year Book, 1954* (New York: American Association of Social Workers), p. 218.

4. George B. Mangold, *Organization for Social Welfare* (New York: Macmillan, 1934), p. 49, quoted in *Churches and Social Welfare*, vol. II, *The Changing Scene*, p. 24.

5. Edward C. Jenkins, *Philanthropy in America* (New York: Association Press, 1950), pp. 13-14.

6. His bequest is still being used for the Mullanphy Travelers Aid of St. Louis.

7. The American Red Cross was chartered by Congress in 1905.

8. Cecil Clare North, *The Community and Social Welfare* (New York: McGraw-Hill, 1931), p. 111, quoted in *Churches and Social Welfare*, vol. II, *The Changing Scene*, p. 25.

9. Private initiative in settlement houses was often followed by government action. In 1894, Jane Addams at Hull House opened a small playground. Four years later, the Chicago City Council appropriated funds for playgrounds for the first time.

10. Jenkins, *Philanthropy in America*, p. 105.

11. *Yesterday and Today with Community Chests* (New York: Community Chests and Councils, Inc., 1937), p. 9.

12. Even before the destruction of the Second Temple in the year 70 A.D., accepted methods of collecting and distributing funds for philanthropy were in existence. Two types of collections have persisted to our day—the *Kuppah*, the weekly money collection for the poor (the equivalent of today's weekly payroll deduction for the Community Chest), and the *Tamhui*, the weekly collection of goods in kind. For a more detailed history, see "Jewish Philanthropy" by Mordecai M. Kaplan, in *Intelligent Philanthropy* (Chicago: University of Chicago Press, 1930), pp. 52-89.

13. The Jewish Welfare Federation of Indianapolis was organized in 1904.

14. Quoted in Pierce Williams and Frederick E. Croxton, *Corporation Contributions to Organized Community Welfare Services* (New York: National Bureau of Economic Research, Inc., 1930), p. 52.

15. F. Emerson Andrews, *Philanthropic Foundations* (New York: Russell Sage Foundation, 1956), p. 11.

16. The United Negro College Fund is the newest development in this field; it provides an organized way for corporations, the new "giants of philanthropy," to contribute to the maintenance of private institutions of higher education for Negroes.

17. Until quite recently the American Cancer Society has relied on independent financing for its support, but in some cities its local chapters are members of fund-raising federations. (This is the case in Indianapolis.)

18. *Yesterday and Today with Community Chests*, p. 11.

19. *Ibid.*, p. 10.

20. Fundraising history is full of examples illustrating the principle found in this case, namely, the adaptation to philanthropic use of a device that social and technological advance has made available in non-philanthropic activities. The "pledge" is apparently derived from the ideas of signing a promise to pay and signing a declaration of adherence (as to a church).

21. *Yesterday and Today with Community Chests*, p. 12.

22. It is important to remember that five bond issues (the four Liberty Loans and the Victory Loan) were also oversubscribed in this same period.

23. Costs of campaigns conducted by members of the American Association of Fund Raising Counsel vary from 3 per cent in campaigns of one million dollars or more to 17 per cent in smaller campaigns down to $50,000 according to testimony by Dr. Arnaud C. Marts, president of the Association (*Chicago Daily Tribune*, June 11, 1955), before a New York legislative committee in December, 1953.

24. John Price Jones, *The American Giver: A Review of American Generosity* (New York: Inter-River Press, 1954), p. 15.

25. Willford Isbell King, *Trends in Philanthropy* (New York: National Bureau of Economic Research, Inc., 1928), p. 78.

26. *Yesterday and Today with Community Chests*, p. 17.

27. Up to this time, the federal government had been responsible for social services for a few groups, such as Indians, seamen, and veterans. While there was little actual welfare service, the government was active in research (fact-finding) and some (limited) administration. The Office of Education was established in 1867, and the Bureau of Labor in 1884. The 1909 White House Conference on the Care of Dependent Children led to the establishment of the Children's Bureau in 1912.

28. *Yesterday and Today with Community Chests*, p. 15.

29. *Ibid.*, p. 15

30. Jones, *The American Giver*, p. 21.

31. Of course, many small businesses exist in the United States, but the trend at this time seems to be towards big business under a modified capitalist system. Even "small business" in the federal definition today includes enterprises of considerable size.

32. An example of this department's activities well exemplifies the American philosophy regarding voluntary agencies. The Salk polio vaccine (1955) was developed under a grant from the National Foundation for Infantile Paralysis, *but* its administration and distribution are under the Department of Health, Education and Welfare.

33. This enlargement of the area of responsibility of government has proceeded apace here, as in other Western nations, despite the access to power of a government that "believes in" decentralization and the devolution of functions onto lower level bodies. The logics or logistics of large-scale social organization seem to render differences in political belief or social philosophy trivial, as far as the actual trend to centralization is concerned.

34. Russell H. Kurtz, "Veterans Administration," *Social Work Year Book, 1954*, p. 215.

35. Earlier there had been tried a few test lawsuits, some of which upheld the right of corporations to contribute to hospitals and recreation agencies in communities where their employees needed the facilities. Texas was the first state (1917) to enact legislation affecting corporate gifts, but in a rather negative way: ". . . nothing in this Article shall inhibit corporations from contributing to any bona fide organization . . . organized for purely religious, charitable or eleemosynary activities. . . ." New York (1918), Illinois (1919), and Ohio (1920) enacted permissive laws. By 1935, Congress had enacted a law authorizing corporations to deduct from their taxable income up to 5 per cent of their income for gifts to eligible charitable organizations.

36. Such permissible deductions are 20 per cent of income for individuals (plus an additional 10 per cent or a total of 30 per cent, if the last 10 per cent is for religious or educational groups) and 5 per cent for corporations.

37. Andrews, *Philanthropic Foundations*, p. 29.

38. F. Emerson Andrews, *Philanthropic Giving* (New York: Russell Sage Foundation, 1950), p. 14.

39. David Riesman, *Individualism Reconsidered* (Glencoe, Ill.: Free Press, 1954), pp. 226-7.

40. Hearings before the Select (Cox) Committee (1952), and the Special (Reece) Committee (1954).

41. *Final Report of the Select Committee to Investigate Foundations and Other Organizations*, Eighty-second Congress, Second Session, House Report No. 2514 (Wash-

ington: Government Printing Office, 1953), p. 9 (quoted in Andrews, *Philanthropic Foundations*, p. 344).

42. The Indianapolis Foundation was established in 1924, and is among the larger ones of the United States.

43. Quoted from a speech by Dr. Frank Sparks at the Third National Solicitations Conference, Cleveland, Ohio, March 24, 1956.

44. F. Emerson Andrews, in *Corporation Giving* (Philadelphia: Russell Sage Foundation, 1952), p. 71, says the corporation welfare $1 for 1950 was allocated as follows: Welfare agencies, 44.3¢; Hospitals, 14.8¢; Health agencies, 11.8¢; Education, 21.2¢; Religious agencies, 4.1¢; Unallocated, 3.8¢.

45. Fund drives for the operation of hospitals are included in local Community Chest campaigns.

46. "Telethons" for health appeals are a phenomenon of this decade. The first ones on a national basis aroused widespread interest and support. Top entertainment people were represented throughout the program—usually one of sixteen to twenty hours' duration. The first local telethons were also successful, but as the novelty wore off and the calibre of the entertainment was lowered, receipts fell off. In the entertainment world, it seems that certain performers are now specializing in telethons, and they travel around and appear locally throughout the country.

The Letter Carriers' March for Muscular Dystrophy was a collection taken up by postmen on their regular mail routes, but during the evening hours. The Mothers' March for Polio is an annual appeal made on January 31, the birthday of President Franklin D. Roosevelt, instrumental in founding the National Foundation for Infantile Paralysis. The Marching Marines, one of the newer ideas, consisted of two groups of Hoosier Marine Corps Reserves, one group starting at Richmond, the other at Terre Haute, marching to Indianapolis, taking one step forward for every dime contributed to the Polio Fund. The Fire Fighters' March is another of these gimmicks used to raise funds for the health agencies. The appropriateness of this use of public servants is now being widely and seriously questioned; in the case of policemen, particularly, the risks are both obvious and grave.

47. Prevalence rates for the communicable diseases were not available to us—hence not all desirable comparisons between Charts 3 and 4 can be made.

48. See, again, Charts 1 and 2. Between 1920 and 1950 urban places generally were increasing in number at the rate of 1.3 per cent per annum; urban places of 10,000 or over, at 2 per cent per annum; but Community Chest campaigns, at about 7 per cent per annum!

49. "To determine and control its budget and goal. To conduct a roll-call for members and funds in the month designated by the Board of Governors. To conduct emergency campaigns in disaster, war or other unforeseen need when authorized by the Board of Governors. To issue a membership card to each person from whose contribution the Red Cross received $1 or more." *New York Times*, April 6, 1955.

50. Campaigns which included one or more of the "Big Six" appeals (Cancer, Crippled Children, Heart, Polio, Red Cross, Tuberculosis).

51. *Community* (United Community Funds and Councils of America, Inc.), vol. 31, no. 8, April, 1956, p. 162.

52. For other discussion of the possible roles of a Donors' Association, see chapters 13 and 14.

53. *Wall Street Journal*, Tuesday, May 10, 1955.

54. As mentioned earlier, the United Community Funds and Chests raised $299,443,972. The National Red Cross raised $93,190,000.

55. John Price Jones Company, Inc., *Philanthropic Digest*, vol. II, no. 1, January 3, 1956.

56. *Time* (September 24, 1956) devoted its cover to "Philanthropist Rockefeller" and in its pages offered a general discussion of philanthropy, especially the Foundations. The reported "philosophy" sounds very thin and shows remarkably little evolution.

57. Charity Solicitation Commission of Indianapolis; eff. October 24, 1942. See General Ordinance No. 71-1942.

58. See chapter 13 for discussion of the legality of such ordinances.

59. Participants in the Conference have been: representatives of commerce and industry; retail merchants; national, state and local Chambers of Commerce and Better Business Bureaus; Community Chests; United Funds; Foundations; health, welfare and education groups; and public officials. See *Proceedings of the Second National Conference on Solicitations, March 24-25, 1955* (Cleveland: National Conference on Solicitations, Inc., 1955); and *Proceedings of the Third National Conference on Solicitations.*

60. For further discussion on this point, see chapter 13.

61. Matthew 19:21; Leviticus 27:30.

62. Perhaps this is a cause (as well as an effect) of the optimism—the optimism in relation to matters material—so often noted as an American characteristic.

63. American scales seem generally to run only to positive terms. "Substandard," "seconds" are not common terminology. Best, better, and good, pretty well exhaust the usable range. One scale in use—the approved one for olives—runs: Supercolossal, Colossal, Jumbo, Giant, Mammoth, Extra Large, Large, Medium, Small, Midget and Peewee (Midget and Peewee are not for general sale!).

64. "Very nearly" because hardly anything that is bought and sold merely supplies "need" in its basic biological sense. What is edible food and potable water depends—within some wide limits set by the human stomach—on a *social* definition of what is good, and what may be consumed without social and psychological harm. Thus a bombed-out population may be starving for meat in the midst of a relatively plentiful supply, if the supply happens to be in the form of horse, cat, or rat, and if these are not socially suitable foods.

65. For this term, its use to mean the apt adaptation of means to ends, and its logical opposition to and presumed threat in reality to what he calls "substantive rationality," see Karl Mannheim, *Ideology and Utopia* (New York: Harcourt, Brace, 1940). For an opposite view of the effects (i.e., the prediction that the one kind of "rationalization" would evoke the other) see Thorstein Veblen.

66. Except in the short run, the invention of specialized machinery does not change the picture. Machinery-making becomes a business itself requiring more differentiation and specialization. And the perfecting of machines to make machines simply takes us up another level of abstraction. The same is true of "automation," no matter how far carried.

67. Some of these "devices" are mechanical inventions: the bookkeeping machine, the counter-sorter, the direct-line teletype; some are social inventions: the management committee, the (endless) "conferences," the "briefing-session" or, latest, staff "brainstorming."

68. Curiously, there is a vast amount of exaggeration in these images. The typical businessman of today does not deal only in hard goods and measurable production-processes. He has many problems in his business similar to those of the social worker, and he frequently knows about them, accepts some unavoidable indeterminacies, and deals with them by rules of thumb essentially similar to those of the "professional," i.e., the person with formal training in one of the "helping" professions or fields. But the self-image he brings to the agency Board table and feels he is expected to defend there, is the image of himself as the hardheaded (if not hardboiled) man of action and captain of industry, i.e., the image to be defended is an image of the businessman of the last generation. By a still more curious transposition the businessman—that same businessman—that the professional imagines himself to be dealing with is modelled on an image a generation or two older yet, certainly pre-Depression and perhaps pre-World War I. Similarly the businessman's image of the professional is largely colored by the picture created by the social worker of the twenties, if not by one of the "Charities and Corrections" era. These dated masks on one side and images on the other make for not a little of the currently observed strain.

69. "May the best man win," "Root, hog, or die," "Winner take all," "Competition is the life of trade," "Everything has its price"—the whole compendium of free, private, individualistic, competitive lore.

70. Symphony music (to some extent), "character building" (outside private and proprietary camps and schools), adult education (on any large scale), etc.

71. It should be noted, perhaps, that the Preamble to the United States Constitution

cites as one of the objects of the order to be ordained and established that it is to "promote the general welfare." No one, even among those most opposed to the extension of the functions of government into the field of social welfare, seems to quarrel with the intent of the Constitution; the quarrel, if there is one, is over the relative emphasis on each of the two words "general" and "welfare." Those who believe that the *general* welfare is best secured under minimum and most general rules which in effect define conditions under which "nearly everybody benefits" look one way; those who feel that the general *welfare* is but a name for the sum of particular welfares each to be relatively specifically planned and provided for, look another. Many people, evidently, find themselves somewhere in between: tolerant of something more detailed (less general) than very general laws, fearful of a luxuriant growth of very specific ones (as nurturing bureaucracy and a "government of men instead of government of laws"). For further reference to "the general welfare," see Constitution, Article 1, Section 8 (Powers of Congress) which defines this as one of the obligations to provide for which taxes may be "laid and collected."

72. The practical implications are immense. The complementarists "cannot understand why in a time of high prosperity we should have increasing Chest goals." Their basic view of how the systems should operate is something like Model A. The people who

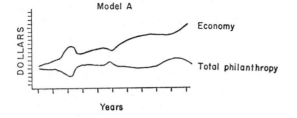

think of philanthropy as a demonstration of surplus potentiality think that the system should operate more like Model B.

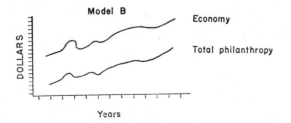

In the absence of any resolution between these views, no one can quite decide whether (equating Chest demands with taxes) a high-prosperity-high-tax policy makes sense (a sort of Keynesian philanthropy) or a high-prosperity-low-tax policy or, perhaps (via the Foundation as a mechanism) a principle of virtually constant tax.

What tends to happen, by pursuit of the path of least resistance is the establishment essentially of the relationship of Model B; although a glance at Chart 14 serves to suggest a period before the mid-thirties when the relation was more like Model A, and a period thereafter when the relation was more like B.

73. Socialism, communism (state capitalism), fascism, the "welfare state"—whatever these terms may designate exactly—certainly represent, in this context, competing political-economic-social systems. This is not to suggest, of course, that the "American system" has no common elements with any of these.

74. For some, "New Deal" or "Fair Deal"; for others, the "Welfare State"; for others, variously, "creeping socialism," "centralism," "everything done by the government," "government interference," etc.

75. What is feared is a non-revolutionary system—if Russell Davenport is right in characterizing what exists in America as the system of "permanent revolution." On this view, these revolutionary businessmen are protecting their right to preserve their revolution perennial. See *U.S.A., the Permanent Revolution* by the Editors of *Fortune* in collaboration with Russell W. Davenport (New York: Prentice-Hall, 1951).

76. Still minorities numerically, perhaps, but no longer minor in power or general esteem.

77. Whatever is negotiated into the wage-structure or the "fringe benefits" need not be (and cannot be for the groups affected) a matter either of government program or of philanthropy-supported "need satisfaction."

78. Who is to get "credit" for workers' gifts: firm or union, or both?

79. It should not be thought that "better" canons have been worked out when it is a sacred institution that is involved in the fundraising. Indeed, one of the more blatantly Machiavellian of the fundraising manuals we studied was intended primarily for churches. The recommendations for a fundraising breakfast seem peculiarly illuminating. After emphasizing the importance of the minister's presence (to give the right spiritual tone) it suggests that the fundraiser, a few principal donors, and the minister enter into a conspiracy to the following effect: that these principal donors be encouraged early in the breakfast to make a false declaration of what they intend to give (i.e., that they pledge a lesser sum) and that subsequently (after the oratory) they declare themselves (falsely) to have "changed their mind" and then "increase" their pledge. This is said to have a very good effect in encouraging other donors really to increase their intended gifts, i.e., it is recommended as a *successful* deceit, and, for all we know, it may well be. See Edwin S. Newman and Leo J. Margolin, *Fundraising Made Easy*, (New York: Oceana Publications, 1954), especially chapter V, for "successful" techniques.

80. See, for example, *Redevelopment: Some Human Gains and Losses* (Indianapolis: Community Surveys, Inc., 1956).

81. It may be, however, that the shift in the center of gravity of American giving to *literal* giving abroad on a gigantic scale, deals adequately with the problems posed by the disappearance of "foreigners" to give to at home. We are not suggesting that this is the motive for foreign aid—but it might be the effect and reward.

82. See A. C. Spectorsky, *The Exurbanites* (Philadelphia: Lippincott, 1955). See also, perhaps, John R. Seeley, R. Alexander Sim, and Elizabeth W. Loosley, *Crestwood Heights* (Toronto: University of Toronto Press, 1956).

83. Instruments, not actualities. The endemic snarling of traffic, characteristic of most United States cities, makes the potential high speed of the vehicle largely irrelevant: a high-powered car may be a matter of pride, but no notable producer—in the city—of efficiency of movement.

84. For a vital distinction between what in human affairs can be *solved*, and what must be left merely to be *resolved*—or the guilt on non-resolution *absolved*—see T. V. Smith, "Solve, Resolve, and Absolve," *The Social Welfare Forum, 1955* (published for the National Conference of Social Work by Columbia University Press, 1955).

85. If in addition to having the theme of solution of a problem, the cause has something to do with children (preferably small children) and health (preferably physical health) the popular appeal is almost irresistible—regardless of other merit.

86. Many small gifts, from many small givers, easily obtained are what we mean by "popular money." The "March of Dimes" is an ideal type. See David L. Sills, *The National Foundation: Its Volunteer and Public Support*, vol. I of three volumes (prepared for the National Foundation for Infantile Paralysis, by the Bureau of Applied Social Research, Columbia University, August, 1954).

87. We are not by any means criticizing biological research, or preoccupation with health (or, rather, disease). We are only pointing out that (a) popular appeal (in the present state of technology) leads to a distribution of the philanthropic dollar which is quite different from the distribution to be expected under planning by experts, and that (b) the effect is to drive the technology still further in the direction it was going, regardless of desirability, i.e., into further rapid development in the fields where greatest knowledge already exists and fewer and less urgent problems lie.

It is chiefly upon this ground—if any—that the argument against restoring competition between appeals might be made, i.e., on the ground that laymen are not (and cannot be) in any position to judge the merits of the causes put before them. This would seem also to argue for fund unification ("United Fund") *if* this would make for more rational or dispassionate planning. The usual basis for uniting—the relative power and bargaining position and budget of the unifying organizations—of course, makes such an assumption dubious, i.e., there *is* reason to doubt that the unification "deal" does anything more than freeze the current irrational distribution (the distribution, that is, that unification is intended to improve). (See chapter 13, re further "unification.") It is also upon this ground that a case can be made out for the grouping together organizationally of even the health appeals, in the hope that at least between them some order might be introduced. As someone was reported to have brightly observed, in any case "All the best diseases have already been organized." Someone else has suggested putting period to the multiplication (if not order into the multiplicity) by organizing a "Society for the Unorganized Diseases."

88. Compare the quiet and quaint announcement for an earlier disaster: "Lady ——— has opened a subscription at ——— House for such as are desirous of alleviating the present distress," with the mobilization of power and opinion in a modern "supplementary disaster campaign."

89. The Wells Organizations raise funds for churches only.

90. Here, as with similar claims, we must not be too literal. It is difficult to doubt, however, that there has been considerable extension in the range of social class of those who consume the supported "services." Actually, in Marion County, as in so many places, competent opinion admits there is no unduplicated count of persons served and no reasonable estimate has been made. This does not prevent the tossing around of astronomical figures and percentages during the Chest campaign.

91. The most remarkable comment we heard reiterated in the highest places with the greatest frequency (in reference to the study here being reported) was to the effect that "No one [who matters] would read 500 pages about *that*," i.e., no governor of a $2,000,000 or more a year enterprise (equivalent to the care of a $40,000,000 machine) would read 500 or more pages in order to understand the situation with which he himself had expressed acute dissatisfaction and because of which he had permitted the expenditure of the very sizeable time and money cost of this study.

CHAPTER 3

1. *The World Almanac and Book of Facts for 1956,* Harry Hansen, editor (New York World-Telegram and The Sun, 125 Barclay Street, New York 15, N.Y.), pp. 179-180.

2. Robert S. Lynd and Helen Merrell Lynd, *Middletown* (New York: Harcourt, Brace and Co., 1929) and *Middletown in Transition* (New York: Harcourt, Brace and Co., 1937).

3. John Bartlow Martin, *Indiana: An Interpretation* (New York: Alfred Knopf, 1947) and Heath Bowman, *Hoosier* (Indianapolis: Bobbs-Merrill Co., 1941).

4. Bowman, *Indiana,* p. 275.

5. Two exceptions may have been: (1) the problem of the Juvenile Court in Indianapolis in the late 1930's, when a local committee made a study and issued a "bombshell" report to secure reforms; and (2) the problem of a serious lack of hospital facilities in the Indianapolis area, recognized in 1950, studied by outside experts, and acted upon in the nationally publicized fund drive for $12,000,000 conducted by the Indianapolis Hospital Development Association. There are doubtless many other examples, but Indiana and its constituent communities seem mostly to have had specific problems of merely local interest, dealt with locally.

Indianans might point out to the social scientists that the study of "average" or "healthy" communities is, or ought to be, just as important to science as probing into pathological conditions. Indiana is full of opportunities to capture samples of the

"American way of life" that have disappeared, or may never have existed elsewhere in the nation—but then, perhaps, so are Kentucky, Ohio, Illinois, and other states where more, or at least better known, local community studies have been made.

6. The renascence of the Ku Klux Klan in the 1920's is an obvious example. The fear and awe commanded by the American Legion have at times been less than worthy of respect. Radical organizations like the Silver Shirts, the White Circle, etc., have had their day in Indiana; but the search for examples reminds one that many other communities also have had "crackpot" periods in their pasts. Perhaps after a century or so, Indiana will be able to remember its excesses as Massachusetts can now regard its Salem witchcraft trials.

7. John Bartlow Martin, *Indiana.*

8. *Ibid.,* p. 42.

9. Like George Ade, who is supposed to have said, "Many good men come from Indiana; the better they are, the quicker they come." *Ibid.,* p. 109.

10. *Ibid.* Martin also says, quoting George Leighton, a journalist, that in all their work, "The idea is always the same: the semi-acid tongued, horse-trading, prosperous, rather generous character." The same character shows up in Tarkington's *The Man from Home,* according to Martin: "in . . . Daniel Voorhees Pike of Kokomo who was turned loose among the corrupt Europeans on the Riviera . . . and with his wise cracks and home spun virtues confounded continental evil [is the] same hard-to-beat Hoosier."

11. A slight variation of the theme, "Once a Hoosier, always a Hoosier," is contained in the following excerpt from a regular column in an Indianapolis newspaper ("Ringside in Hoosierland," by Wayne Guthrie, *Indianapolis News,* July 30, 1956):

> "Mrs. Lewis Young, Parma Heights, O., offers proof that you can take a person out of Indiana but you can't take Indiana out of a person.
>
> "She said that one doesn't have to be a native Hoosier or even a 'lifer' on Hoosier soil to get the thrill that comes each year with the approach of the 500-mile Speedway race.
>
> " 'I've lived in and out of Indiana my 27 years but even when in the state of Washington we had newspapers mailed to us on race day,' she added.
>
> " 'When we lived in Syracuse, N.Y., I sat glued to the radio for snatches of news of the race and kept a pencil sheet of runnings, pit stops, etc. Now here in Ohio my family and I are quite happy to receive the entire running and it is easier to keep up with this great event.' "

It is perhaps significant that the "typical Hoosier" of John Gunther's *Inside U.S.A.* is, in fact, a New Englander.

12. The Indianapolis newspapers may refer to a resident of East Chicago (Indiana) or Gary or any place "in the Calumet area" as "Hoosier," but there seems to be less use of the label by people "up North." "Chicagoland" includes some sizable part of Indiana's people.

13. Occasionally the newspapers will label someone an "ex-Hoosier," and the context then commonly indicates that an expatriate is being rejected as not a true or "loyal Hoosier."

14. Missionary work of the sort referred to is exemplified in publicity given to (*a*) Flanner House and the "self-help" program (for example, in *Reader's Digest,* November, 1955, in the article "Cleo Blackburn's Grand Design") and (*b*) the Indianapolis Hospital Development Association campaign (for example, *Saturday Evening Post,* issue of March 22, 1952, the article entitled "They Don't Want Uncle's Money") as well as the continuing follow-up work done by the general chairman of that campaign in making speeches elsewhere to tell how Indianapolis is building hospitals without federal aid.

15. This view is emphatically repudiated by many Hoosiers and just as emphatically asserted by many "newcomers" of more years' residence than any of the authors had. The former say—perhaps justly—that the interaction between natives and newcomers has varied from time to time, and is largely a matter of the "personality" of each newcomer. Undoubtedly, such variation occurs, and undoubtedly personal differences play a part: perhaps we should only say that in the period we observed, and in other periods

reported to us (extending back about four decades), Hoosiers appeared to newcomers as friendly but distant, and that relatively separate systems of social interaction arose for the natives and for the newcomers.

16. Such minority profanity may, for example, be heard among Negroes in Chicago: one Negro may call another, "You black nigger!" or another describe certain behavior as "just plain niggerish!" Neither, of course, would tolerate such language from a white man.

17. Similarly, the term "Naptown" (for Indianapolis) is a way of avoiding a long word, "Indianapolis"; but it is also a way of referring to a large city in a deprecatory manner. Is "Hoosier" sometimes used with this intent?

18. John Bartlow Martin, *Indiana*, p. vii.

19. Perhaps this is because, in the capital city, both the natives and those newcomers we listened to found it politic to remember that their setting is indeed "Hoosierland"; or perhaps their use of the term is on occasion defensive and apologetic, or even at times a reflection of a feeling of superiority to still more rural parts of the state.

20. *The Indianapolis Story of Progress, 1946-1954* (Indianapolis Chamber of Commerce, 1955), p. 2.

21. In the *World Almanac*, 1956, pp. 637-9. That is, Indiana has no direct tax on retail purchases, and the Gross Income Tax is considered to be in lieu of such; obviously it is not equivalent in its effect to a progressive tax on incomes.

22. Along with the radial plan, a grid system of main and side streets was provided within the "Mile Square." The grid system, which characterizes all American cities affected by the thinking behind the Northwest Ordinance of 1787, has never become completely dominant in the street arrangement of Indianapolis, partly because the terrain is cut by the White River and a number of creeks and "runs," and partly because the railroads radiate out from "the first Union Station in America" (1857) located south of the Circle. The railroads, with embankments for long stretches, have been paralleled in a few directions by extensions of the radial streets beginning in the center of town and becoming highways outward bound. As the civil city expanded by annexations, the problems of imposing a grid system across radial lines (rails and highways) and meandering streams increased, with the result that in 1955 there were too few cross-town and north-south through streets for a city nearly 60 square miles in area. Some of the earlier annexations (before World War II) were of areas which each had a small factory, the dwellings of its employees, and perhaps a church, school, store, and other services making up a small, almost autonomous village. Such an area usually had a street layout suitable for the planning of the factory in relation to its railroad siding, water supply, etc., and this did not fit easily into an expansion of a uniform grid system, even if Indianapolis had brought one along with it in its growth.

The economies of street, sidewalk, and alley construction, sewerage, water mains, gas and electric utilities, etc., are considerable when a consistent grid system is adhered to, compared with the costs of linking up a great variety of patterns; they appear not only in connection with the immediate exploitation and enjoyment of the newly annexed territory but more importantly in connection with the ultimate problem of providing "main drags," across the city and north-south, to carry the heavy burden of modern traffic. When the latter problem is faced, the difficulties of "thinking big" about providing throughways, with a tradition-bound paucity of resources, become evident. The proposed national highway program, judging from preliminary road maps published in the daily press, will make Indianapolis even more of a "Cross-roads" for east-west and north-south traffic, and so it is very likely that the dilemmas that have beset street-planners in Indianapolis for decades will be increased.

Perhaps we are unduly pessimistic about how this new and potentially enormous problem will be handled in Indianapolis. Another view is given by the Indianapolis Chamber of Commerce, in its August, 1956, *News Briefs*.

23. See *Redevelopment: Some Human Gains and Losses* (Indianapolis: Community Surveys, Inc., 1956).

24. See chapter 11 for a summary of the Hospital campaign, which is also analysed in chapter 9.

25. In the expressions of the Hoosier reluctance to plan and to trust the expert two views get mixed up: (1) the notion that the future is not knowable (which, if true,

makes planning impossible), and (2) the small town thinking that it is desirable to "save" money by not spending it *now*. Actually this second view might, under certain conditions, turn out to be good economics: the people now here can save and wait until they get more people (and more industrial taxpayers) to come in, attracted by low tax rates; then, all can be invited to bear the costs which have, actually, been foreseen, at least by the oldest settlers.

26. Consistent with this recognition of the omnicompetence of Everyman, but also recognizing his need for protection from "expertise," the preceding section, Section 20, reads: "Plain wording.—Every act and joint resolution shall be plainly worded, avoiding, as far as practicable, the use of technical terms."

27. John Bartlow Martin, *Indiana*, pp. 38-9.

28. Indiana, General Assembly, Acts, 1931.

29. A good deal of litigation, of course, preceded and followed the actions of 1931. The Supreme Court's establishment of rules and regulations and of the Board of Law Examiners had been authorized by the legislature of 1931, but it was not really until 1935 that the new system of requiring bar examinations was firmly established. (It had been easier to regulate the licensing of bartenders, we were told, and at least to require that a licensed bartender know how to mix a drink.)

See *Burns Annotated Indiana Statutes, 1955*, Cumulative Pocket Supplement, vol. 2 Part 2, 4-3605 (p. 99) for the following: "Admission to practice law—Restraint against unauthorized practice—Jurisdiction of Supreme Court—The supreme court of this state shall have exclusive jurisdiction to admit attorneys to practice law in all courts of the state and exclusive jurisdiction to issue restraining orders and injunctions in all cases involving the unauthorized practice of the law under such rules and regulations as it may prescribe." (Indiana, General Assembly, Acts, 1931, ch. 64, sec. 1, p. 150; 1951, ch. 143, sec. 1, p. 382.)

30. *In re Todd*, 208 Ind. 168, 193 N.E. 865.

31. *Burns Indiana Statutes 1955 Replacement Volume*, vol. 1, p. 150.

32. Quoted from *Indiana Reports*, vol. 208, p. 172. Evidently *In re Todd* was a case and a decision significant for easing the process of amending the Indiana Constitution of 1851, at least in terms of small bits like Section 21, Article 7. The process still requires passage of an act to submit the change to the voters after two biennial sessions of the General Assembly have passed it in exactly the same wording. The Act of 1931 referred to must therefore have passed the legislature in 1929, a good three years or more before the amendment was put to the voters in 1932. Indiana is, of course, far from being alone among the Midwestern states still struggling with a Constitution written in and adapted to a pioneer setting.

33. To use the term associated with the famous sociologist, Professor (now Emeritus) William Fielding Ogburn, of the University of Chicago. See *Social Change* (New York: Viking Press, 1922).

34. According to the *Indianapolis Star* (March 24, 1955) the Yard Parks organization, then in its seventh year, had been formed "by aroused civic leaders after John Gunther called Indianapolis 'the dirtiest city in the United States' in one of his books." According to the *Star* (March 19, 1955), in the column "As the Day Begins," "We felt that Gunther did us less than justice"; and the writer goes on to say, in the old Hoosier spirit, that even if New York City is worse, "Let's assert our civic pride and make Indianapolis the best-groomed city in the land, bar none. With a little effort, it could be."

35. *The Leisure of a People: Report of a Recreation Survey of Indianapolis*, conducted under the auspices of the Council of Social Agencies and financed by the Indianapolis Foundation (printed by Clarence E. Crippin & Son, Inc., 1929), p. 240.

36. *Ibid.*, pp. 113-115, wherein it is also recounted how planners from elsewhere, especially Olmsted and Kessler, from 1895 to World War I worked hard with local leaders to accomplish much of what the city enjoys in 1956.

37. Scarcely a day will pass in Indianapolis when an attentive reader of the local newspapers will not encounter samples of this. The proposed civic auditorium was in the news off and on all through 1955-6, and, we were told, it is one of the oldest topics of controversy lying around, barring perhaps the dilapidated County building and the proposed "City-County Building" which is sometimes mentioned as possibly accom-

modating a civic auditorium too. The following excerpts from the *Indianapolis Star* for August 24 and 25, 1956, illustrate the Hoosier attitudes both about spending money and about trusting the expert:

### "COUNTY COUNCIL LIKELY TO DENY FUNDS FOR AUDITORIUM SURVEY

"A majority of Marion County Council members indicated yesterday they will vote today to reject a request for $2,000 to finance a new survey on the proposed civic auditorium.

"The request for funds to match the $2,000 voted for the survey by the City Council, was presented to the county board yesterday by Henry W. Manz, manager of the Indianapolis–Marion County Building Authority.

"The survey, to be conducted by the International Association of Auditorium Managers, would consider the size, site and business potential for the proposed auditorium.

"Manz said that if action is taken soon, the block bounded by Pennsylvania, Delaware, North and Michigan streets might be obtained as a site. The property is now owned by Indiana University.

"Major dissenter was Councilman A. C. Crandall, who declared: 'It seems to me we can get the job done without hiring a $4,000 consultant. This going to a specialist stuff is overdone.'

"Councilman I. W. Cotton favored the plan.

"Most other council members appeared lukewarm to the project. Council President R. N. Mannon ended the discussion by telling Manz: 'Come back in a few months. Let's give it some more thought.'

"Calvin Hamilton, executive director of the Metropolitan Plan Commission asked the council to approve an increased budget which would provide a $98,935 budget for employee salaries, including a $500 raise for himself.

"Hamilton now receives $10,000 a year.

"He also asked for funds to hire six more employees."

### "COUNTY COUNCIL OK's $2,000 FOR AUDITORIUM SURVEY

"In an abrupt about-face, the Marion County Council voted yesterday to appropriate $2,000 to the Indianapolis–Marion County Building Authority to finance the cost of a survey for a civic auditorium.

"The final vote, hailed as a 'good step forward' by Henry W. Manz, building authority manager, came after a declaration Thursday by several council members that they would oppose the appropriation.

"The change in vote by four members came about largely through the efforts of Councilman I. W. Cotton who convinced them that an earlier request by Manz for $100,000 as the county's share in advance architect's fees 'has nothing to do with this $2,000.'

"The four dissenters, A. C. Crandall, Mrs. Josephine K. Bickett, Nelson Swift, and Frank J. Billeter, switched their vote, but only with the understanding that 'we turn down the $100,000.'

" 'Let's not have short memories,' Crandall said.

"The authority's proposed 1957 budget, which includes the $100,000 request, will come up for final action Sept. 4.

"Manz said the survey team, the International Association of Auditorium Managers, would 'do whatever they can under whatever circumstances prevail.'

"Manz had told the council that the team felt a better survey would be made if architects were under contract and it could work with them.

"The consultants will be paid $4,000 to be shared equally by the city and county.

"The City Council already has appropriated its $2,000 share."

38. *The Tattler*, published by the Citizens Committee of Greater Indianapolis, 4355 Clarendon Road, Indianapolis 8, Indiana, vol. II, no. 2, July, 1956, p. 2.

39. Variously represented in American beliefs and practices regarding "Equal opportunity for all"; "There are really no classes here anyway: any man can rise to the top if he has what it takes," etc.

40. No city so large has yet been given a thoroughgoing study by social scientists.

41. *The Newcomers Key to Indianapolis,* copyright 1947 by R. Earl Briggs (Indianapolis: Newcomers "Key to Our City" Service, 1947), p. 14.

42. See chapter 11 (especially the appendix: Estimated Social Status) for a more complete discussion of social status in the context which makes it important to this study, that of mass fundraising. See also chapters 12 and 13 for implications.

43. Geographical mobility—actual change of residence and not merely travel—is so common in American experience, and there is currently perhaps such a high rate of moving about, that the reader should have no difficulty with the notion that there is something very close to a general American "social class system"—even if no social scientists have yet made the systematic comparisons of the thousands of communities that would be needed to establish what is universal in it and what merely local variant.

44. There were fairly miniscule "tough" districts in the oldest part of town.

45. In part, the Marion County road system facilitates the achievement of privacy or even virtual isolation, if desired. Many county roads end in either a *cul-de-sac* or a small settlement, and others escape discontinuity only by elaborate jogs around sections of land, or take meandering routes along creeks and runs.

46. A kind of "chain reaction" from this is apparent in the dilemma of the Community Chest, discussion of which is reserved to later chapters.

47. Natalie Rogoff, *Recent Trends in Occupational Mobility* (Glencoe, Illinois: The Free Press, 1953), p. 46.

48. W. Lloyd Warner and James C. Abegglen, *Occupational Mobility in American Business and Industry, 1928–1952* (Minneapolis: University of Minnesota Press, 1955). Data excerpted from "Appendix Table 17—Distribution by State of Residence of 1928 Business Leaders and by State of Present Business of 1952 Business Leaders," and the computed "Percentage Gain or Loss" added by us (in the last column). The whole analysis in the next six text pages follows Warner and Abegglen in form, and uses re-computations of their data. We are deeply indebted to them on both scores although they are not responsible for our analysis.

49. The nation's proportion of foreign-born was lower than that of Indianapolis in 1870 and 1880, but has been higher ever since. For details, see chapter 4.

50. We might also call it a "fault" in the Hoosier version of the American social class system (a "fault" by analogy to the geological term, and *not* with regard to ethics or morality).

51. We might also call it a "fault" in the etiquette and structure of the initiation system.

52. That is, as explained in chapters 10 and 11, the Red Cross bridges the cleavages between "top top leaders" and those lower in status, and also overcomes the cleavages between new and old residents, by supplying a framework within which urbanity and cosmopolitan etiquette may thrive.

53. Like the "American Dilemma" of Gunnar Myrdal, the Hoosier dilemma entails "wanting to have it both ways."

54. The Chest in 1955-6 and before, and possibly a United Fund if one is established in the future—and if the present social system persists.


CHAPTER 4

1. The population of Indianapolis had reached 100,000 before 1890. In the 1890 census, Indianapolis ranked 26th in size among the cities of the United States; in 1950, it ranked 23rd. Table A, p. 493, and Charts 7, 8 show population data for Indianapolis and comparative data for the United States.

2. By the Rev. Oscar C. McCulloch, a prominent figure in philanthropy in Indianapolis in the 1870's and 1880's; see below in this chapter.

3. We have relied largely for the general early history of Indianapolis on Jacob Piatt Dunn, *Greater Indianapolis: The History, the Institutions, and the People of a City of Homes* (Chicago: Lewis Publishing Co., 1910).

4. Otto F. Walls, "A History of Social Welfare in Indiana," *Indiana Magazine of History,* vol. 45, no. 4 (December 1949), pp. 383-400.

## TABLE A

POPULATION OF INDIANAPOLIS, TOTAL URBAN AND TOTAL U.S. POPULATION FROM 1820 TO 1950, INCLUSIVE; AND PERCENTAGE INCREASE FROM ONE DECADE TO THE NEXT

| Year | Population of Indianapolis[a] | Percentage increase for decade | U.S. urban areas[b] | Percentage increase | Population of U.S.[b] | % Increase over preceding census |
|---|---|---|---|---|---|---|
| 1820 | — | — | 693,255 | — | 9,638,453 | 33.1% |
| 1825 | 762 | — | — | — | — | — |
| 1827 | 1,066 | — | — | — | — | — |
| 1830 | — | — | 1,127,247 | 62.6% | 12,866,020 | 33.5 |
| 1835 | 1,683 | — | — | — | — | — |
| 1840 | 2,692 | — | 1,845,055 | 63.7 | 17,069,453 | 32.7 |
| 1847 | 6,000 | — | — | — | — | — |
| 1850 | 8,091 | 200.6% | 3,543,716 | 92.1 | 23,191,876 | 35.9 |
| 1860 | 18,611 | 130.0 | 6,216,518 | 75.4 | 31,443,321 | 35.6 |
| 1870 | 48,244 | 159.2 | 9,902,361 | 59.3 | 39,818,449 | 26.0 |
| 1880 | 75,056 | 55.6 | 14,129,735 | 42.7 | 50,155,783 | 26.0 |
| 1890 | 105,436 | 40.5 | 22,106,265 | 56.5 | 62,947,714 | 25.5 |
| 1900 | 169,164 | 60.4 | 30,159,921 | 36.4 | 75,994,575 | 20.7 |
| 1910 | 233,650 | 38.1 | 41,998,932 | 39.3 | 91,972,266 | 21.0 |
| 1920 | 314,194 | 34.5 | 54,157,973 | 29.0 | 105,710,620 | 14.9 |
| 1930 | 364,161 | 15.9 | 68,954,823 | 27.3 | 122,775,046 | 16.1 |
| 1940 | 386,972 | 6.3 | 74,423,702 | 7.9 | 131,669,275 | 7.2 |
| 1950 | 427,173 | 10.4 | 88,927,464 | 19.5 | 150,697,361 | 14.5 |

[a]Indianapolis population before 1840 from J. P. Dunn, *Greater Indianapolis*; 1840-1880, inclusive, Bureau of the Census, *Population Bulletin*, First Series, "Indiana: Number and Distribution of Inhabitants"; 1890-1950, Bureau of the Census, *Statistical Abstract of the United States, 1954*.

[b]*Statistical Abstract*, 1954.

5. For the limited sense in which Indianapolis is "planned," see, however, the earlier discussion in chapter 3.

6. Dunn, *Greater Indianapolis*, pp. 8, 9.

7. Quite a contrast to the present connotation of "deadly"!

8. Dunn, *Greater Indianapolis*, p. 54.

9. *The Organized Charities of Indianapolis*, published by the Charity Organization Society (no date, but apparently published shortly after 1910).

10. Some of the "fish stories" are rather astonishing; for example, young Amos Hanway (later a preacher) reported in the 1820's about his catch in the vicinity of Indianapolis: "The biggest salmon I ever caught weighed sixteen pounds. I once caught a pike that measured four feet and two inches; at another time a gar-fish that measured over three feet, and a blue catfish that weighed sixteen and a quarter pounds." (Dunn, *Greater Indianapolis*, p. 67.)

11. *Western Censor and Emigrants' Guide* ("agin the government"), first published on March 7, 1823. Indianapolis had had a newspaper from the beginning; before the town was organized, a justice of the peace had been appointed, on January 9, 1821, and the first number of the *Gazette*, a weekly paper, appeared on January 28, 1821.

12. Dunn, *Greater Indianapolis*, p. 72.

13. *Ibid.*, p. 73.

14. *Ibid.*, p. 80.

15. *Ibid.*, p. 79. There were exceptions (e.g., "preachers of the gospel") and additions (e.g., landowners and storekeepers).

16. *Ibid.*, p. 99.

17. "The Central Canal was designed to be a waterway connecting the Wabash and

Erie Canal with Evansville by way of Indianapolis. The only part ever put into actual operation was the seven miles through Indianapolis to Broad Ripple. Excavation of the canal began in 1837, and was accompanied by an influx of large numbers of laborers who encamped in that part of the town west of the canal line, adding to the blighted conditions already in existence in the west and northwest part of the donation [the four sections of land allocated by Congress to the State for a capital]." Albert E. Dickens, *The Growth and Structure of Real Property Uses in Indianapolis,* Indiana Business Study no. 17 (School of Business, Indiana University, May 1939).

18. In 1840, the official census figure was, however, only 2,662.

19. Family Service Association, *Handbook for Members* (Indianapolis, 1952), p. 20. Note that we have already in the Benevolent Society, then, a "secular" philanthropic organization.

20. Note the contrast with today's "principle of rotation"—for which see chapters 3, 10, and 11.

21. Again, note the contrast with today's multiplicity of specialists and consultants in the successor organization.

22. John M. Butler, "The New Charity," *Indianapolis Charities Yearbook: 1885-95;* Part I, "Ten Minute Talks on Phases of Charity Delivered at the Fiftieth Annual Public Meeting of the Indianapolis Benevolent Society at Tomlinson Hall, Sunday evening, November 28, 1886."

There appears to be some difference of opinion concerning the presence of "paupers" in Indianapolis. In 1822, "paupers" were sufficiently numerous that legal provision was made to render them exempt from paying the "head tax"; in 1835, according to this report, there was no "pauper class" in Indianapolis. Of course, it is recognized that both of these statements could be true, although it is doubtful whether there was any intent in either case to draw a distinction between "paupers" and "pauper class": it seems more likely that the later reporter was seeing, in retrospect, that to which he could point with pride—the "good old days"—as Hoosiers tend to do today.

23. *The Organized Charities,* p. 4. This "relief" function has almost disappeared from the program of the Family Service Association of today, in Indianapolis, as elsewhere; the Great Depression saw its transfer to government.

24. In 1857, a committee including James Blake (City Commissioner 1861-4), Calvin Fletcher, J. M. Ray, Alfred Harrison, and S. T. Brown, "among the foremost of the city," was appointed to call on businessmen of the city for relief contributions. (*Ibid.,* p. 4.)

25. For further details concerning the foreign-born population of Indianapolis, see Table B below and Chart 9. Germans were one of the immigrant groups of this period. "They were part of the famous group of '48'ers who settled in various parts of the

TABLE B

PERCENTAGE OF FOREIGN-BORN RESIDENTS OF INDIANAPOLIS AND
PERCENTAGE OF FOREIGN-BORN IN THE TOTAL U.S. POPULATION
FROM 1870 TO 1950, INCLUSIVE

| Year | Foreign-born residents of Indianapolis as percentage of Indianapolis population | Foreign-born residents of U.S.A. as percentage of its population |
|------|------|------|
| 1870 | 22.1% | 14.4% |
| 1880 | 16.8 | 13.3 |
| 1890 | 13.7 | 14.8 |
| 1900 | 10.2 | 13.6 |
| 1910 | 8.5 | 14.7 |
| 1920 | 5.4 | 13.2 |
| 1930 | 3.8 | 11.6 |
| 1940 | 2.7 | 8.8 |
| 1950 | 2.0[a] | 6.9 |

[a]Estimated.

country, having come here as rebels against the religious intolerance, political cruelties and taxation hardships of the Old Country. They, too, have put their mark upon the life of Indianapolis in a number of ways, especially in the realms of music, art, and physical culture." *Leisure of a People* (Indianapolis: Council of Social Agencies and Clarence E. Crippin, 1929), p. 21.

26. Mary Sinclair, M.A., "A History of the Auxiliary to the Children's Bureau of the Indianapolis Orphan Asylum, 1932-50" (unpublished thesis, Indiana University, 1951).

27. *Ibid.*

28. *Ibid.*, p. 4. Again this account offers some interesting parallels with the present day. See chapters 10, 11, and 12.

29. Gertrude Taggart, "Philosophy Changing in Care of Children," *Public Welfare in Indiana*, vol. 54, no. 7 (July, 1944), p. 11.

30. Record-keeping even then was not, evidently, very exact.

31. The attitude towards children—especially orphans and destitute or "poor idle" ones—in the last half of the nineteenth century is illustrated by a practice beginning in the 1850's which "concerned dependent children of New York City who were crowded into stock cars and shipped west by the New York Charities Aid Association. Advance contact was usually made with responsible citizens at stations along the railroad line. The children would be herded like cattle on an auction block while citizens gathered to select those they were willing to take into their homes. Children . . . were quickly taken by middle western farmers, which shows how valuable children were to the frontier rural economy." Between 1853 and 1864, 1,326 of these children were placed in Indiana—the largest number placed in any one state; during the next ten years 1,484 children were placed in Indiana. (Walls, "Social Welfare in Indiana.") Further evidence of the prevalent attitude towards children is seen in the stated object at the founding of the Charities Aid Society: "to provide work, food, and homes for these needy children." (*Ibid.*)

32. The beginnings of the national Y.M.C.A. are mentioned in chapter 2.

33. See later in this chapter for other developments in 1907.

34. *The Organized Charities*, p. 27.

35. "*You've Asked the Questions—Here are the Answers*," a Community Chest pamphlet (no date, but evidently 1938 or 1939).

36. The *Indianapolis Telephone Directory* of August 1956 lists an additional branch: the Inter-Collegiate Branch at Butler University. One, the Senate Avenue Branch, is, however, primarily for Negro men and boys.

37. *Directory of Community Resources* (Health and Welfare Council of Indianapolis and Marion County, 1955).

38. Robert S. Lynd and Helen Merrell Lynd, *Middletown* (New York: Harcourt, Brace and Co., 1929), p. 459.

39. *The Organized Charities*, p. 5. The north European—especially German—immigrants were arriving in rather large numbers at this time, though these are improbably the "foreign" paupers referred to.

Hoosier provincialism may be evidenced in this attitude towards "foreigners" and especially poor foreigners. In any case, the recommendation could readily be endorsed by the present-day Charities Solicitation Commission.

40. *Ibid.*

41. Mildred Pauline Beard *et al.*, "The Needs of, and Services Available to the Aged in Indianapolis and Marion County as Indicated by a Study of Selected Voluntary Agencies in Indianapolis" (unpublished M.A. thesis, Indiana University, 1955), p. 17.

42. *Ibid.*

43. The early 1860's, the war years, were times of extreme hardship for many. The cost of living in the northern states increased 75 per cent in fifteen months, and was still soaring nine months later; real estate was selling at exhorbitant prices and business in general was booming. Indianapolis acquired some 30 factories and packing houses. "With the exception of Chicago and Cincinnati, Indianapolis [in 1879] was the largest meat packing center in the world." *Indianapolis News*, November 5, 1927.

Soldier's pay in 1862 was $9.00 per month after "depreciation." "Think of what penury it meant to thousands of families whose breadwinners earned so little, or perhaps were cut off entirely"; Dunn, *Greater Indianapolis*, p. 232.

44. "From 314 families relieved in 1870, the number of such families steadily and rapidly increased until by 1879 there were 3,000 (perhaps 15,000 persons) in a total population of 75,000 who were more or less dependent. It was the old familiar story of parasites seeking the easiest means of sustenance. Not only did the willing mendicants of our city flock to this public crib but 'paupers from all over the State were shipped in by thrifty township trustees, or came here because Indianapolis was such a benevolent city!' Among these home dependents were numerous related families so bound together by inter-marriage that the whole mass clung together in a 'pauper ganglion.' " (*The Organized Charities*, p. 6.) The latest discovery of one of the most talked-of books in social work in the last few years—Bradley Buell's *Community Planning for Human Services* (New York: Columbia, 1952)—rediscovers this relatedness between "persons with problems"—and between problems of various kinds.

45. At least a half dozen other cities in the United States had Charity Organization societies at this time. Rev. S. H. Gurteen of the Buffalo, New York, Charity Organization Society, who was the speaker for the annual meeting of the Indianapolis Benevolent Society in 1879, gave inspiration and suggestions on "Methods of Organization in Charitable Relief," which influenced the organization of the group in Indianapolis.

46. *The Organized Charities*, p. 7.

47. Thurman B. Rice, "The Beginnings of Organized Charity in Indianapolis," *Monthly Bulletin*, Indiana State Board of Health, vol. LV, no. 9 (September, 1952), p. 210. The expressed hope sounds like today's Chest charter, and tomorrow's United Fund dream.

48. Beard, "Needs of . . . Aged in Indianapolis." This Order is unique in that the nuns themselves must beg; they are not permitted to accept large trusts or steady incomes. The Congregation was still active in Indianapolis in 1956.

49. *Indianapolis Star*, October 10, 1948. The girls were sheltered until they could return to their own homes; or else foster homes were found for them. The program at the Convent included: . . . classes, including four years of accredited high school courses, . . . cooking, canning, home decoration, sewing, weaving, commercial sewing on a variety of electric sewing machines and even—a highly popular part of the curriculum—"manners according to Emily Post." The Community Fund contributed $250 a month (in 1948) to the school, and the various counties from which the girls came paid 75¢ a day for their food; for other income, the home depends on "charity."

50. *Indianapolis News*, October 16, 1926.

51. The Training School for Nurses was later taken over by the city.

52. Mrs. Benjamin Harrison presided over one of the booths at a Mission fair; and James Whitcomb Riley contributed verses for the *Flower Mission Record*.

53. *Indianapolis News*, October 16, 1926. The Eleanor Home, the first children's hospital in Indianapolis, was maintained until the City Hospital provided a unit for the care of children.

54. *Ibid.*

55. Butler, "The New Charity."

56. The 1901-2 report of the Society's activities (quoted in the *Indianapolis Times*, September 2, 1951) reads:

"One of the forward steps of the Society has been that of clearing our streets of many beggars.

"Occasionally now, a blind or crippled beggar or musician is seen on our streets, but not often, and when seen, if reported to the police or to the Charity Organization Society, he is ordered from the streets or arrested.

"All of them are first offered an opportunity to work or to learn a trade whereby they can earn a living, but so far not one has accepted the professional aid. They nearly all drink and live in the foulest homes.

"A very great obstacle in the way of complete reform in this line is the promiscuous giving, not only to the beggar, but to the mission and lodging-house that entertains the tramp without a good equivalent in work. Where any mission or society advertises [to] feed, lodge and clothe men who beg for a living, it should be declared a public nuisance and its business closed up."

57. *Indianapolis News*, April 3, 1931.

58. Reprinted in *Indianapolis Star*, May 10, 1940.

59. It is difficult to ascertain a termination date for the Wood Yard at the Friendly Inn—as for so many organizations and activities. However, about 1930, the Wood Yard was revived at the Wheeler Mission. Logs were supplied from a thirty-acre grove owned by the mission; they were felled and hauled by an experienced crew but were cut into furnace and fire-place lengths by transients. A man in need, coming to the agency, "is given the use of a shower, his meals free the first day and his first night's lodging free. After that, he is asked to work at least one hour at wood cutting or some other task for each meal and one hour for each night's lodging. . . . Men from other cities are given temporary care and then advised to return to their home communities where their own respective welfare agencies will assume the responsibility of their care." *Indianapolis Star*, January 24, 1932. This is, perhaps, another example of the citizens of Indianapolis not caring to care for "foreigners"—the basic Elizabethan Poor Laws orientation.

60. Wallace Warrack, "Fifty Years Ago: Notes from the Minutes of the Indianapolis Benevolent Society," *Indiana Bulletin of Charities and Correction*, no. 179 (February, 1930), pp. 35-8. Some new moves of the welfare community tend now in the opposite direction (i.e., virtually to prevent savings): see *Redevelopment: Some Human Gains and Losses* (Indianapolis: Community Surveys, Inc., 1956).

61. By 1930, the Dime Savings and Loan Association had become the Dime Savings Department of the Family Welfare Society; it was liquidated in 1935 because, according to Family Service Association notes, it was "expensive and burdensome."

62. In 1954, Alpha Home was operating on about $14,000 per year, obtained from the Community Chest, gifts, endowments, fees from residents ($45.40 per month), and proceeds from dinners and teas.

63. Established as the result of recommendations made by the Charity Organization Society, the Board of Children's Guardians "rescues little children from abodes of vice and crime, and places them where the appeal of the child for the protection and tenderness of a father and a mother, and the brooding of a home are not unheeded." "Reports of Societies, 1892-93," *Indianapolis Charities Yearbook: 1885-95*.

64. Dunn, *Greater Indianapolis*, p. 606.

65. Family Service Association, *Handbook for Members*, pp. 23-4.

66. Dunn, *Greater Indianapolis*, p. 623.

67. If the historic statement is true, great progress has been made in establishing slums since. See Community Surveys, *Redevelopment*.

68. A description of the beginnings of the Summer Mission in 1890 relates: An open pavilion on what is now the campus of Butler University "was screened and cleaned; additional cottages were built on the high ground overlooking the canal and the river to the west. Transportation was afforded by the streetcar line to Fairview Park. Free passes for mothers and their children were granted, and in this way thousands of children got care, food, medical attention and such other aids to health as could be afforded on such a slender basis. A number of physicians served the institution without compensation." Rice, "Beginnings of Organized Charity in Indianapolis," p. 210. The "Health Hints" distributed by the mission still appear up to date as of this writing.

69. See *Indianapolis News*, April 22, 1932. The Wheeler City Rescue Mission has had a notable history of varying activities. From its beginning (in 1893) the Mission has been closely affiliated with the churches of the city. In 1929, it moved into what was regarded at that time as "one of the finest mission buildings in America," and was a member of the International Union of Gospel Missions "which admits only missions of high standing with local indorsement of the churches, and business men." Self-help activities, including the Wood Yard of the Friendly Inn, were on the program, as well as (in 1955) emergency care, relief, medical aid, and religious services for families and for transient men.

70. See *Indianapolis News*, May 20, 1942. The Volunteers of America now operate the Theodora Home for the emergency care of girls, mothers, and children; sponsor the Sunset Club for older women; and provide relief, counsel, and religious services for many types of "needy" people. In 1942, the Volunteers extended their work on

an "inter-agency" basis: any recognized public or private agency might requisition the available stocks of the organization—clothes, furniture, bedding, etc.

71. The choice of those included for mention or analysis, at this point of the chapter and others, is not based on an evaluation of worth or accomplishments, religious affiliation or source of support (except that tax-supported institutions are generally omitted), leaders or clientele; but rather on priority, availability of descriptive materials, and such subjective characteristics as uniqueness of some phase of their program or its value in illustrating some phase of philanthropy.

72. *Leisure of a People*, p. 391. In 1955, the organized program at Flanner House offered threefold services to the Negroes of Indianapolis: self-help services; vocational aid (including training); and social services (including adult and youth activities, day nursery, and family counselling).

73. Through co-operative effort, good homes within their means are being built by higher class Negroes. See Community Surveys, *Redevelopment*, for some implications.

74. See their leaflet, *The New Frontier* (no date, no publisher).

75. One might infer from this some things as to the state of the city water supply and sanitary system.

76. McCulloch Club Settlement, Baptist Christian Center, the American Settlement, and perhaps others.

77. Dunn, *Greater Indianapolis*, p. 432. It is a nice question whether the multiplicity of campaigns complained of today, as if it were a novelty, is really new or more multiplex, particularly in relation to resources.

78. The Legal Aid Bureau was established in 1912. At least twice since that date the Indianapolis Bar Association has set up an organization to give free legal advice to the needy: in 1930, a committee of young attorneys was to take over this responsibility; in 1941, the Legal Aid Society was formed. As usual, it is difficult to discover what became of these earlier enterprises. There seems to be a tendency for agencies that do not survive to be "sunk without a trace."

79. The Christmas Clearing House—another "repeat"—was reactivated as the Christmas Clearing Bureau in 1954.

80. "Community Chest—Pre-History: Report of Allied Charities Committee, 1911," unpublished report.

81. What exactly is meant in practice by such co-ordination would require another research to define or describe, and another book to report.

82. This service is maintained by the Council and used by some agencies and opposed by others; its utility is questioned by many—including some staff members of the Council, and some non-local professionals in the field. See, for example, Morton Teicher, "Let's Abolish the Social Service Exchange," *Social Work Journal* (January, 1952), pp. 8 *et seq.*

83. *Historical Highlights of the Indianapolis Chapter of the American National Red Cross, published in commemoration of its 40th anniversary, July 19, 1916-1956.*

84. In 1920 (the nearest census year), the population was slightly less than one-third of 1 per cent (.30 per cent) of the total population of the United States, i.e., the quota was just about proportioned to the population. If, however, the "prospects" for Red Cross donations were urban people, Indianapolis's quota on a population basis should have been $580,000; if the prospects were really urban folk in centers of 25,000 (or more) population, Indianapolis's quota should have been $832,000.

85. Marie Cecile and Anselm Chomel, *A Red Cross Chapter at Work* (Indianapolis: Hollenbeck Press, 1920), p. 53; p. 54; p. 54—a telegram from the National Secretary of the War Council; p. 77.

86. See chapter 3 for reasons for success. See also chapters 11 and 12.

87. "All the people divided into two parts—those who joined the army or the navy and those who joined the Red Cross." M. C. and A. Chomel, *Red Cross Chapter*, p. 63.

88. *Ibid.*, p. 58.

89. *Ibid.*, p. 60.

90. "Officers and directors of the Indianapolis Chamber of Commerce, the Indianapolis Board of Trade, the Indianapolis Merchants' Association, the Indianapolis Clearing House Association, the Indianapolis Real Estate Board, the Rotary Club, the Optimists Club, the Kiwanis Club and men holding responsible positions in the Community and

in organized labor" (*Community Chest Records*: "Chest History: 1918-1921"). The weight, in the movement, of the business community is clear without further comment; the actual involvement of labor (until much later) has been questioned. (See chapter 12.)

91. *Articles of Incorporation* of the War Chest Board, April 29, 1918. Among the officers were many names familiar in Indianapolis: Lilly, Ayres, Huesmann, Fletcher, Vonnegut, to name a few. Mr. William Fortune was elected president, and Mr. C. B. Sommers was the first campaign chairman.

92. This is the number according to the Press. It represented approximately 32 per cent of the population of Indianapolis (1920 census); in 1950, approximately 35 per cent of the population contributed to the Community Chest.

93. *Community Chest Records*: "History of War Chest Board: 1918-1922."

94. *Ibid.* Similar comment is still heard today.

95. This situation was also to repeat itself in the next generation.

96. The social service agencies were not represented at the organization meeting of the War Chest, and they seemed to be given little part in the preliminary planning for implementing the "principles"; perhaps this did something to awaken a strong feeling of resentment among them against the policies of the War Chest Board.

97. The First War Fund Board: William Fortune, President; *L. C. Huesmann*, Vice President; Stoughton A. Fletcher, Treasurer; Myron Green, Secretary; Aquilla Jones; J. K. Lilly; *J. W. Lilly*; *W. J. Mooney*; *Edgar A. Perkins*; Frank D. Stalnaker; C. B. Sommers. First Indianapolis Community Fund Board: *L. S. Huesmann*, Chairman; Fred Hoke, Vice Chairman; Frederick Ayres, Treasurer; Rt. Rev. Francis Gavisk; Mrs. George C. Hitt; Edward A. Kahn; *J. W. Lilly*; *W. J. Mooney*; *Edgar A. Perkins*; Mrs. Frank D. Stalnaker; Franklin Vonnegut. (*Community Chest Records*: "Minutes of the Community Fund, 1920.") Italics have been added to indicate the overlap.

98. "Indianapolis Community Fund 1920-1923: Notes on Early History of the Fund," Notes on Minutes of July 27, 1920 meeting (typed report). Subsequent history was to indicate the desirability of *obscuring* interests rather than making them plainly identifiable. The Chest certainly ceased to speak of itself as a tool or instrument of the agencies, and the Council of Social Agencies changed its name (and make-up) to the Health and Welfare Council. The concern was not only with appearances: it seemed strategic in both cases actually to make the bodies "representative" of more interests than those of the agencies. This was not, to any sensible extent, possible; and the upshot is usually a genuine desire to make these bodies broadly based together with a claim that they already are—which in turn militates against their becoming so. The possibility of a return to frank representation of agency or inter-agency interest by these bodies is well worth entertaining and is discussed in chapter 12.

99. How this goal was decided upon is itself an interesting piece of history. If the record is to be credited, the sum about to be agreed upon was $750,000; at this point a "top top leader" in the business community suggested that if they were going to go after that kind of money, they "might as well" go after a million, and the decision was made on that basis. "In discussing the amount of the goal for the campaign, Mr. —— expressed his opinion that one million dollars would be just as popular as seven hundred fifty thousand dollars, and would answer the requirements better, as most givers would subscribe in proportion to their previous gifts to the War Chest" (Minutes of November 1, 1920, meeting of Community Chest).

100. Minutes of April 5, 1921, meeting of Indianapolis Community Chest.

101. We shall later make the point that "top top leadership" is *necessary* to Chest success, usually, but often not *sufficient*; i.e., other factors are also involved.

102. Indianapolis Community Fund, *25th Anniversary Report* (no date, probably 1945).

103. *Community Chest Records*: "Indianapolis Community Fund 1920-1923." Like so many early statements, these still pretty well represent current aspirations rather than past achievements.

104. Even though the War Chest Board voted in 1918 an appropriation of $100,000 to provide for Red Cross memberships of War Chest subscribers, it "sanctioned" an "enrollment campaign" in deference to the desire of national officers of the American Red Cross. (M. C. and A. Chomel, *Red Cross Chapter*, p. 87.)

105. *Community Chest Records*: "Indianapolis Community Fund 1920-1923." We shall later (see chapters 12 and 13) raise a question as to whether or not this was a major error.

106. Indianapolis Community Fund and Council of Social Agencies, *Constitution and By-Laws* (1924), p. 6.

107. *Community Chest Records*: "What is Your Council?" This same argument in almost identical words is now being made for a United Fund (see chapter 13), even though the Chests never achieved anything like the stated objective.

108. Indianapolis Community Fund and Council of Social Agencies, *Constitution*, pp. 26-8.

109. *Ibid.*, pp. 16-17.

110. *Community Chest Records*: "Chest History: Annual Meeting of Community Fund, February 23, 1925."

111. *Community Chest Records*: "Chest History: Community Fund Annual Dinner, February, 1926."

112. *Community Chest Records*: "Chest History: Annual Dinner of Community Fund, February 8, 1927." One never knows from such statements whether the leaders really believe they are succeeding or failing: there is a taboo, generally, on mentioning failure in public—so that when it *is* mentioned, it shocks public opinion which has been led to believe in continuous victory.

113. *The Leisure of a People.* The Church Federation was "surveying" recreational needs and facilities (this was followed in 1929 by a comprehensive "recreation survey" sponsored by the Council of Social Agencies, financed by the Indianapolis Foundation, and directed by a representative of the Playground and Recreation Association of America, and published as *The Leisure of a People*). The Council of Social Agencies in co-operation with the National Probation Association was studying the problem of probation in the local courts of criminal jurisdiction (this study also was made possible by a grant from the Indianapolis Foundation). Public interest in the handling of the crime situation was said to be intense.

114. The proportion of the income of the Community Fund which was spent for "character-building" had been slowly increasing, and that spent for "relief" decreasing; by 1932 the proportions for each had changed radically. Below are the percentages spent for various types of services in selected years (selected on the basis of availability of data):

| | 1924 | 1925 | 1926 | 1932 | 1940 | 1941 |
|---|---|---|---|---|---|---|
| Character-building | 25% | 33% | 36% | | 37% | 39% |
| Families—relief and reconstruction | 35 | 33 | 32 | 64 | 38 | 37 |
| Homes for children | 15 | 14 | 13 | | 16 | 16 |
| Health | 11 | 10 | 9 | 6 | 5 | 5 |
| Disabled soldiers | 3 | 3 | 4 | | | |
| Delinquency | | 4 | 4 | 1 | | |
| Homes for the aged | 2 | 3 | 3 | 6 | 1 | 1 |
| Camps | | | | | 2 | 2 |
| Settlements | 8 | | | | | |
| "Relief activities of other agencies" | | | | 6 | | |
| "Community Welfare" | | | | 17 | | |

The accuracy of the data in the above table cannot be vouched for since (*a*) the lack of dates on publications of the Community Fund make exact dates a matter of conjecture; (*b*) no explanation was found as to the basis for determining the agencies —or activities—to be included in each category; and (*c*) the categories varied from year to year (it could even be that an agency classified, for example, as "Settlements" one year might be "Character-building" another). When "Campaign expenses," "Administration," and "Joint service to agencies" were included in the tabulations, the percentages were re-computed omitting them in order to make the data as comparable as possible. (These data were collected from pamphlets and/or campaign literature published by the Community Fund, and from newspaper clippings.)

115. "Families—relief," "Health," "Homes for the aged," and "Relief activities of other agencies" were all classified as "Relief." See *How 70,230 Citizens Saved a City,* pamphlet presumably published by the Indianapolis Community Fund about 1932 (no date or publisher is listed).

116. National Youth Administration—created by executive order (1935) ". . . in order that young people caught in the depression might have their chance in school, their turn as apprentices and their opportunity for jobs. . . ."

Works Progress Administration—a federal agency, established in 1935, to provide work for the unemployed by granting funds to the states for the creation of public projects.

Civilian Conservation Corps—an agency established by the United States government to provide employment and vocational training for youthful unemployed citizens through the performance of useful work in connection with the conservation and development of the natural resources of the country.

National Recovery Administration—the general title covering the various agencies [PWA, FERA, WPA, etc.] and administrative officers whose function, according to the National Industrial Recovery Act, was the rehabilitation of the unemployed by means of various work projects or by the administration of direct relief.

Descriptions of WPA, CCC and NRA are from *Webster's Twentieth Century Dictionary of the English Language,* unabridged (New York: Publishers Guild, Inc., 1940).

117. *Indianapolis Star,* December 25, 1931.

118. P. 2.

119. We had also, however, been told that the Red Cross and the Community Chest severed relations, as far as fundraising was concerned, because (*a*) the Red Cross was not getting enough money, and (*b*) the Chest asked it to withdraw. Both impressions are widespread. Of course, "The record showeth not. . . ."

120. "Red Cross—Community Fund Relations"—agreement dated January 13, 1933, published in *The Biggest Dollar in the World,* a pamphlet issued by the Red Cross for their November 11-30, 1933, campaign. Curiously, "The Biggest Bargain in the World" was the theme of the Chest's 1954 Annual Meeting.

121. See note 114 for further detail.

122. *These are the Facts,* a pamphlet published by the United War Fund (1942 or 1943—no date given).

123. *Ibid.*

124. The general classifications, as described in the budget, were:

| | |
|---|---|
| For Our Men in Service | 17.3% |
| For Our Allies | 11.8 |
| Reserve Emergency Fund | 11.1 |
| For Our Home Front: | |
|     Civilian Defense Council | .4 |
|     Indianapolis Community Fund | 44.0 |
|     Home Front Planning and Coordination | 2.7 |
| Allowance for Shrinkage and Collection Losses | 10.0 |
| Administration and Fundraising | 2.7 |
| TOTAL | 100.0% |

The $706,000 allocated "For Our Home Front" compares perhaps favorably with the $701,445 raised the previous year (in 1941) by the Indianapolis Community Fund.

125. "The new name was selected because it better described the purpose of the agency and it conformed to the national pattern developed by agency members of the Family Service Association of America." Family Service Association, *Handbook for Members,* p. 26.

126. *Ibid.* A Community Surveys, Inc., study shows a rank correlation of −.68 between Family Service Association case-rates and median incomes in Indianapolis census tracts; i.e., economic status probably accounts now for only about 46 per cent of the variation in case-rates by census tracts. See Community Surveys, Inc., Study 1.

127. Perhaps even before then—such data are difficult to come by.

128. Red Cross collections for 1937 Ohio–Mississippi Valley flood disaster (*Indianapolis Star*, June 19, 1937):

| City | Amount | Population° | Percapita° |
|------|--------|-------------|------------|
| Washington | $299,746 | 663,091 | $0.45 |
| INDIANAPOLIS | 257,347 | 386,972 | .67 |
| Rochester, N.Y. | 164,607 | 324,975 | .51 |
| Minneapolis | 161,607 | 492,370 | .33 |
| Columbus, O. | 155,984 | 306,087 | .51 |
| Newark, N.J. | 126,782 | 429,760 | .30 |
| New Orleans | 115,638 | 494,537 | .23 |
| Kansas City, Mo. | 108,076 | 399,178 | .27 |
| Toledo, O. | 102,313 | 282,349 | .36 |
| Seattle, Wash. | 101,790 | 368,302 | .28 |
| Atlanta, Ga. | 99,756 | 302,288 | .33 |
| Worcester, Mass. | 74,781 | 193,694 | .39 |
| Louisville, Ky. | 73,065 | 319,077 | .23 |

°Population figures (1940 Census) and percapitas were not included in the newspaper article.

129. *Be Proud of Your Gift,* a pamphlet published by the Indianapolis Community Fund in 1938, gives the following "late reports from other cities in regard to their *per capita* rate of giving to all private social work, both Fund and non-Fund":

| | |
|---|---|
| Providence, R.I. | $4.00 |
| Richmond, Va. | 3.97 |
| Minneapolis, Minn. | 3.87 |
| Worcester, Mass. | 3.01 |
| | |
| AVERAGE | 2.62 |
| | |
| Buffalo, N.Y. | 2.21 |
| Dayton, O. | 2.12 |
| New Orleans, La. | 2.00 |
| INDIANAPOLIS | 1.89 |
| Galveston, Tex. | 1.43 |
| Kansas City, Kans. | 1.30 |

130. The number of cities in this comparison is so small that any inference we might make from these figures alone would be unreliable. However, the evidence is only being used to corroborate better-founded findings, and hence does add plausibility.

131. Beard, "Needs of . . . Aged in Indianapolis."

132. United States Department of Labor, Children's Bureau, *The Community Welfare Picture, 1940.*

133. Community Surveys, Inc. "guestimate"—there being no adequate record, and no better-founded opinion.

134. *For a Better City: Annual Report of the Indianapolis Foundation for the year 1954.*

135. From annual reports of Lilly Endowment, Inc.

136. The essence of the scheme is the Marathon or "endurance test" aspect. See R. K. Merton, M. Fiske and A. Curtis, *Mass Persuasion* (New York: Harper, 1946).

137. One is not to infer that the other 39 agencies receiving funds from the Community Chest in 1955 derive *all* of their support from the Chest: membership dues; income from endowments; special projects; "service" charges; gifts from Foundations, "friends," and other restricted groups, as well as possibly general campaigns of which we were not aware, furnish a suggestive list of other sources of income concerning which we do not have information.

## CHAPTER 5

1. What the area to be organized is, will vary with (1) the strength and ambition of the Chest, (2) the concentration of population (which will decide whether or not it is economical to "incorporate" or "annex" surrounding territory), (3) the proximity of other Chests (which will raise jurisdictional, or boundary, or territorial problems) and, perhaps, to some degree, (4) the area actually "served" by the agencies the Chest supports.

2. Many Chests argue that the proper basis on which to decide the "Chest citizenship" of a given person is not where he lives but where he makes his livelihood, i.e., works. Others would argue that the relevant criterion would be the source of support of the agencies to which he turns for service (or would have to turn to for service if he needed it). Obviously, these three criteria for "citizenship" overlap but do not wholly coincide, and become thus matters for negotiation—or continuing dispute or warfare—between neighboring Chests. In the dispute, it is not unlikely that growing use by the Chest of the corporation as a unit-of-collection will ensure that place-of-work will determine point-of-collection. Where this works "injustice," Chests will probably negotiate agreement as to redistribution of part of their take to remedy inequities—or, as they are doing in some places, drive for greater geographic "unification" so as to eliminate the problem. The result tends to be a regional Chest whose area of domination geographically includes all the people who would be included by any of the three criteria: place of work, place of residence, source of social service. A case in point is the Bay area around San Francisco.

3. As will appear later, the ambiguous statement that the Chest needs "mass support" confuses at times the thinking even of its own core group. If "mass support" refers to money, the statement may well be accurate; if "mass support" means moral support, it is very dubious.

4. This all refers, of course, to the community structure. The skill of the staff is also quite a factor. See chapters 10 and 11.

5. The diagram only portrays the "order of intimacy": it is not drawn to exact scale nor does it show all the complexities of campaign organization as reported in chapters 10 and 11. The numbers in each cell are "informed guesses" (for the Chest) since no one—curiously—has even approximately reliable counts for any but the two innermost squares.

6. For the counterpoising of brotherhood and otherhood as alternative attitudes, see Benjamin Nelson, *Idea of Usury* (Oxford University Press, 1950).

7. The exact meaning of and relation between these terms should be made clear. If $N$ (number) is the total population being talked about, $S$ (sum) is the total gift, $D$ the number of donors, $Pa$ participation, $G_D$ gift per donor and $G_{PC}$ the per capita gift, then:

$$Pa = \frac{D}{N}$$ i.e., "participation" is the number of contributors divided by the whole population in question (or all the possible contributors);

$$G_D = \frac{S}{D}$$ i.e., the gift per donor is the sum received divided by the number of givers;

and

$$G_{PC} = \frac{S}{N}$$ i.e., the gift per capita is the sum received divided by the whole population (or all the possible contributors).

It should be obvious that these are not three "independent" measures; if two are known, the third can be easily computed, i.e.,

$$Pa = \frac{G_{PC}}{G_D}$$ i.e., the participation *is* the ratio of the per capita to the per donor gift;

and

$$G_D = \frac{G_{PC}}{Pa}$$ i.e., the gift per donor *is* the percapita divided by participation;

and

$$G_{PC} = Pa \times G_D$$ i.e., the percapita is the product of participation and gift per donor.

It was curious, given these relations, to find, in the course of the study, the same person often worrying *separately* about all three measures.

8. This opinion is supported by the view that the main Chest function—morally ultimate if not most important, in practice—is "Community education": "We want people to understand what we are doing."

9. This measure indicates a public relations or community organization view i.e., that the main product of Chest operation is a favorably oriented mass of individuals —in a sense organized into a community *in virtue of* their common liking for the Community Chest.

10. It is clearly visible from note 7, that since $N$ (the population) is, from the fundraiser's viewpoint, fixed, the only way to increase $Pa$ (participation) is to increase the number of donors. This might be done by asking potential donors for less; certainly, a policy of "refusing gifts below a certain amount" militates against increasing $Pa$. Similarly, the only way to increase $G_{PC}$ (the percapita) is to increase the total take, which might be achieved by concentrating pressure on fewer donors, thus perhaps eventually reducing participation. Those who wanted "higher gifts per donor" could have them either by increasing percapitas or decreasing participation. Concentrating effort on a few large givers would tend to do both!

11. The nature of the supposed relationship is usually not made clear, although an exact statement of what is "supposed" would be most important for policy, i.e., for deciding where to put the most effort. (The question has the same importance for the fundraiser as the question of how much fertilizer may be applied before diminishing returns set in, has for the farmer.)

Community Surveys Study 91 sets up the problem and indicates a definite and, at least clear, model answer. It brings together and makes use of three arguments frequently heard, but never confronted, let alone integrated: (1) that the probability of getting a new gift depends on the proportion of both givers and non-givers, so that it would be at a maximum when for every fifty non-givers ("prospects") there were fifty givers ("salesmen"); (2) that the probability of getting a gift depends on the social pressure of the number of givers in relation to the number of non-givers, so that the greater the percentage of givers, the easier it is to get more; and (3) that as the easiest prospects are picked off, "selling" gets tougher and tougher, so that the more one has the less one is likely to get.

The model in the study suggests a way in which these three likely tendencies may combine to produce a situation in which the probability of getting another gift falls off after about 67 per cent participation is reached. If the model is valid, and if increased participation is aimed at, and if the energy that can be put into getting it is not unlimited, this suggests clearly that the energy ought to go first into firms that have not yet reached 67 per cent (actually two-thirds) participation.

To test the model would require a carefully devised study. The point is that it is at least *clear*, that it points to a policy, and that those who recommend another should indicate their assumptions and reasoning with equal clarity. (It is also, perhaps, no coincidence that many fundraisers believe, on an intuitive basis, that increasing participation gets tough after the 70 per cent point has been reached.)

12. Both laymen and professionals among the percapita-minded tend to view the proportion of non-givers as a datum that has to be adjusted to, i.e., that calls for resignation more than (misplaced) effort.

13. There is something also in the occupation of the Chest or agency executive that urges him strongly in the same direction: this is his power-situation vis-à-vis his governing board, invariably more representative ideologically of élite large donors (or potential donors) than of mass small donors (or potential donors). If his organization has mass-participation, he may feel that he can speak for the unrepresented interest, and, therefore, in an important sense, act as a counterweight to his Board and (since he has many masters) as a relatively free agent. He may prefer this position either because he "likes to" be relatively free, or because he thinks it "wrong" that he should be so wholly and indefensibly responsible to a segment of the community.

14. Note that those who favor the emphasis on percapita also feel that they derive their mandate from "democracy." The participation-minded tend to emphasize the "all the people" and "balance of power" elements; the percapita-minded emphasize "equality," or rather "equalization" in something of the sense of the Bureau of Internal

Revenue: much is to be expected of those who receive much, little of those who receive little, nothing, perhaps, of those who receive least.

15. American readers may need to be warned against assuming that the authors mean "good" and "bad" respectively when they use the terms "democratic" and "aristocratic," or that they write with tongue in cheek when they speak of "the best people." Such identifications would represent an ideology without scientific warrant.

16. The "aristocratic" view can maintain that the Chest *is* (and ought to be) an élite organization because, as subsequent analysis will show, it is that to a large extent already. The "democratic" view is generally only a view of what "ought to be" (no Chest known to the authors is anything like what this hope would have it) although some people (see next note) are able to believe that a large measure of "democracy" exists.

17. The word "represents" is, of course, itself full of ambiguities, and its very vagueness serves to cover over real differences of opinion and to prevent any attempt to solve or resolve the problems involved. Within this fog or atmosphere of clouded meaning, many who dearly value the "democratic" aim (in the sense defined) are able to believe that the Chest (like the Health and Welfare Council) is democratic because it is "representative." The evidence adduced for its representativeness varies: (1) the fact that there is no organized opposition to it serves for some as proof that it must be "broadly representative," i.e., conformed to widespread wish; (2) that so many contribute money is taken by others as indicative of the same "fact," despite gnawing knowledge as to how contributions are really secured and what they really mean; (3) that "labor" is "represented" on Chest Board and staff (i.e., that persons who are related to labor union management so appear) is taken by others as significant of "all points of view being represented," as is also some "representation" of major minorities, e.g., Negroes, Roman Catholics, Jews. A—rather thin—comfort to yet others lies in the belief that, in any case, the best people somehow "represent" the interest of the not-best (i.e., speak for the best interests of all, if only all knew where their best interests lay) much as good parents "represent" the true interests of their children. Finally, many (and this is even more characteristic of Council than of Chest argument) console themselves that people participate "pretty well in terms of how interested they are" and that therefore the system is democratic since it is "open to all." To believe in the last argument a whole body of knowledge about the when and where of meetings, and the differential facilities of various people to attend them—all well-known facts to both laymen and professionals—must be held temporarily out of awareness.

18. Indeed, there is much evidence that a United Fund (where it is effective) is precisely an expression of the desire to concentrate power for maximum effect rather than to disperse it for maximum "representativeness." See chapter 13.

19. The enlargement of the governing body with a simultaneous concentration of real power in smaller committees thereof has characterized many "democracies," and not been thought *of itself* destructive of democratic intent. Whether or not it is subversive of intent would turn partly on the system of making up such committees, partly on the system of reporting from the committees, and largely on the effective degree of control over the parts by the whole. The Indianapolis Chest does not have any stated system (such as "Seniority" in the United States Senate) for allocation to committees or choice of committee chairmen, nor is there any evident desire for—or, perhaps, possibility of—reporting to the major body in such a way as to make clear the debate as well as the conclusion.

20. It is, probably, pure supposition that "the public" would not be glad to feel that the organization was in atypical hands. On the other hand, in so far as the Chest approximates a taxing body, perhaps there is warrant for the emphasis on the second version in the traditional American theme "No taxation without representation." The Chest is not, of course, alone in this dual and contradictory message. The Health and Welfare Council tries even harder to have itself defined as "best" and also as "typical," i.e., average.

21. The amount of expected or accepted misrepresentation may be less, for instance, in a university catalogue than a garden seed brochure, though both may seek to cast their product in the best light permissible. Similarly, a salesman of second-hand autos will be expected to be more "generous" in his allowances to himself for "approximation" in description than would the salesman, say, of an ethical drug house.

22. It should be noted, throughout, that the point being made is sociological, not ethical; we are not directly concerned here with what is right or wrong, good or bad, but with what people think or feel in these matters in so far as it affects social organization or behavior.

23. See, for example, Robert and Helen Lynd, *Middletown* (New York: Harcourt Brace and Co., 1929), p. 304.

24. Provided the interests of "his" agency are not involved!

25. This might be thought a natural-enough difference between in-group and out-group behavior. But the same would be true if he were addressing the same in-group in the two different roles on two different occasions.

26. By no means all. See below; and see also chapters 11, 12, 13.

27. See chapters 12 and 14.

28. Perhaps, most obviously, when an organization has been "failing" even though it has been predominantly in the "best" hands.

29. Indeed, on the limited evidence we have, we should be driven to guess that the ethics of exploit are at present becoming dominant over those of stewardship. The future lies most probably with the smart young operators—at least, for the next decade, at a guess.

30. That this crisis mentality is rather American, somewhat Midwestern, and very Hoosier will be evident from earlier chapters. What seems to compound it, and raise it almost to the level of a ruling principle in Indianapolis, is the relative newness of the Chest as a movement or institution (already alluded to) and the fact of near-continuous "failure." The fact of "failure" seems to lead around in a vicious spiral to more improvisation, novelty, and crisis-oriented action, which militates further against success; and so the spiral continues. We shall have to return to this crisis mentality and its effects again and again.

31. Perhaps the word "voluntary" is ambiguous. In its widest meaning, a voluntary act is an act performed because the actor positively wants to perform that act. In its narrowest meaning a "voluntary" act *could* mean an act which the actor was unwilling to face the consequences of not doing, e.g., paying taxes. Probably no human act is wholly voluntary in the first sense or wholly free of a voluntary element in the second. But this difficulty with words does not obscure, for most people, a vital distinction between acts where choice is fraught with little or no penalty and those where penalties run pretty high; most people are able to distinguish between volunteering for military service and being conscripted. The distinction may be represented graphically thus.

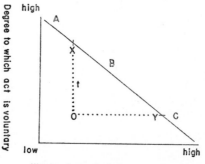

Segment *A* may be thought of as one where "taste" rules: freedom is high and penalties relatively trivial. Segment *B* may be thought of as the area of "propriety": penalties for infractions increase, effective freedom diminishes. Segment *C* may be thought of as the area of "legality," where weighty sanctions increase rapidly and freedom to commit certain kinds of acts (e.g., speeding, tax-fraud, murder) is very thin and tenuous.

Points *X* and *Y* at the boundaries of segment *B* are critical points. The more a voluntary organization is able to mobilize social pressure, the closer its operation falls to point $Y$; the more the same organization is able by clever public relations to secure acceptance of its voluntary character the more the public image of it will fall near point $X$. The greater the discrepancy between fact and representation, the greater the risk of alienating and demoralizing at least some people. Many people seem to desire the efficiency and control of point $Y$ actualities with the "good public relations" value of a point $X$ image. (Some would even wish the image to fall in segment $A$; and a few believe that this is actually the case.) The level of tension in the organization ($t$) may be proportioned to the distance $O$ $X$.

32. It is perhaps not to be wondered at that a general scheme of this kind should succeed (on the whole) over long periods of time in America. It is in the American dream that "this is a free country"; it follows that "we are free men"; the implication is that, if I am to retain my own self-respect I must think of myself as largely free. Some coercion cannot in reality be escaped, wherever concerted action is to be had. Dream meets reality; the outcome is a widespread desire to pretend there is more freedom in any situation than can actually be found there. In this sense the individual person's need for self-respect converges with the organization's need for a respectable image to nourish and preserve, and the two together perpetuate a substantial degree of illusion. It is probably only when the gap is too great that moral problems arise for individuals and social problems (difficulty in concerting action or manufacturing "enthusiasm") for the group.

33. Palatability is not necessarily excluded. The elements in the American culture that approve the ethics of exploit, do not bar enjoyment, direct or vicarious, of "putting one over." In fact, for some, this adds a fillip of enjoyment to what would otherwise, perhaps, be a rather dull routine. See chapter 15.

34. For the source of this second distinction see Marie Jahoda, "Psychological Issues in Civil Liberties," *American Psychologist*, vol. 11, no. 5, pp. 234-40.

35. This is an actual policy-suggestion, not an imagined or possible one.

36. One senior executive of one large business, at least, objected effectively both to the minimum-gift rule (no sum below a certain amount accepted) as contravening the principle of "the widow's mite," and to executives even knowing (let alone reviewing!) the gifts of their employees, on the ground that "What a man does in things like this is between him and his conscience." He also objected to executive-led pep meetings; he was willing only to pass on to the employees the Chest's literature together with a statement that his organization did support and approve the campaign. Of a recent campaign that edged towards Type IV pressure he said: "They did more to promote communism than anyone else in Indianapolis this year," by which he meant essentially that what he felt was a violation of freedom and privacy could only disaffect those who supported free enterprise precisely because their support was conditioned on the system's capacity to preserve these freedoms.

37. This situation has arisen for the several agencies for many reasons, but among others because it was felt that two functions would, in effect, permit two kinds of appeals to two different kinds of potential donors vulnerable to two different types of persuasion: "altruism" and mere "extended self-interest." That, in practice, in a day of very audible publicity it would be difficult to keep the two audiences distinct and the two messages separate was not generally foreseen; neither, perhaps, was it seen clearly enough that there was a tendency for these messages to "interfere," i.e., to cancel one another out, rather than reinforce one another, for many auditors.

38. What was said of the agencies in the preceding note is also largely true of any Chest taken as a whole.

39. Indeed the question as to which is the cause in situations of mutual influence like this (and perhaps, quite generally, in the social sciences) is an idle or unfruitful one. As John Dewey pointed out, long ago, one should select, define, and treat as "cause" that element in the situation (or those elements) that can most easily and effectively be got at and altered in the direction consistent with one's purpose.

40. These deserve, but cannot have, a chapter of their own; however, the following three illustrations may suffice:

(a) *Evaluating Chest performance by percapita in comparison with "other cities."*

In the absence of any accepted theory of what is a basis for fair comparison (or what makes one city fairly comparable with another) that list tends to be selected which favors the argument of the moment. This means, in general, that no secure evaluation of performance can be had, and that demonstration of "how we are doing" depends on who selects the list in which "we" are made to appear.

(b) *Evaluating Chest performance by percentage performance* in comparison with other cities. Neglecting the previous question of comparability (i.e., even assuming that the cities compared are properly comparable), we find the following strange but characteristic form of analysis. Let us assume, for simplicity, that city A is being compared with cities B and C (or their average) and that the data are like this:

| Source of gift | City | | | Average of B and C |
| --- | --- | --- | --- | --- |
| | A | B | C | |
| Corporations | 57% | 52% | 56% | 55% |
| Employees | 37% | 33% | 36% | 35% |
| Other | 6% | 15% | 8% | 10% |
| Total | 100% | 100% | 100% | 100% |

A typical report will conclude that "city A is 'doing well' in respect to Corporate and Employee giving, but needs to put more effort into getting 'more' from Other Sources." The fact that by this test it follows necessarily for any city that it cannot be "doing well" in all categories seems to be overlooked by those who make and those who accept the argument. The fact, too, that as cities B and C are successively surveyed by this method, and the "weakness" of each is discovered, and each is encouraged to do better in that respect, a system is suggested in which (a) each city has (by sheer logic) a weakness to correct, and (b) in practice, each city must increase its "take," thus altering the averages, and thus creating the condition for a new round of effort, is also not appreciated.

(c) *Equity in standard-setting.* In one notoriously successful city we encountered the following argument:

(i) The Chest does "better" when standards are known and equitable.
(ii) We have therefore developed this standard.
(iii) We have to agree, on our own showing, that it may (and sometimes will) increase inequity (by our own definition).
(iv) This will not harm the Chest because no one yet knows of the inequity.


CHAPTER VI

1. There is, of course, no unanimity *within* each group, nor—often—consistency within individuals.

2. This may seem less of a difficulty to the non-scientist than it does to the scientist. The scientist knows that one cannot, in general, "simultaneously maximize two functions," and that there is no solution at all (because the question is meaningless) to such a problem, for example, as "How shall we get the most money while doing the least social damage?" He will state, and rightly, that the problem cannot be *solved*. The non-scientist, the "practical man," also knows something: that he must get some money and must not do more than a certain amount of social damage. And he also knows that he has *resolved* such problems by compromise before, and indeed does so every day.

What is really happening in the non-scientist's practical and perhaps wise decision is that he has a largely unconscious "price-system" somewhere in his mind which enables him somewhat "intuitively" to assess, for the given problem, how much extra money justifies how much social damage. He can, therefore, in practice, make decisions from moment to moment because he can intuitively convert all values into one value, just as he can convert goods of many kinds and services into money values to make business decisions. He, therefore, in our earlier terminology, only has to "maximize one function"—which is frequently, but not always, a "soluble" problem. But as long as his implicit price-system is unknown to him (it may be "felt" but he cannot state it) or as long as it is private knowledge (unlike market prices which are public knowledge), it is impossible to develop a policy of principle, or for anyone—say a consultant—to tell him what the "best" solution is. (A "bad" consultant would substitute his own private price-system to provide such a solution, and there is no warrant for thinking that this would be an improvement; a "good" consultant would get these unconscious price-systems into consciousness, and the private ones out into public statement and discussion, so that policy could be set—instead of dealing with every issue, crisis-wise, as a "special case." Indeed, this procedure in any such organization as the Chest should be a principal function of the staff: the provision of aid in the making and remaking of rational consensus. It is a time-taking, perhaps, but not technically difficult, procedure.)

3. Our curiosity has been much stimulated in the course of this research by the observation that, in the fundraising organizations governed and ruled largely by business-men, there is very little thinking in terms to which one would expect them to be habituated: costs and returns. Because they are so preoccupied with "goals" and "ideals," the inescapable fact that there are no free goods, and that an increase in one good invariably implies a decrease in another (e.g., an increase in percapita *may* imply a reduction for someone in freedom as to whether to give, or merely, for the solicitors, in leisure) seems to escape the attention of these businessmen. This kind of thinking may be implicit in the ascription by some businessmen to some social workers or fundraisers of the title "social dreamers," but it is not possible to say that this way of thought characterizes the professional in this field any more than it does the laymen who are involved. Indeed, as often as not, the contrary would seem to be the case.

Considerable gain in theoretical clarity and firmness of action might well accrue from an increase in lively, hard-headed realism of the business kind. The notion that ideals are not best served by realistic thinking—which view may underlie this strange situation—will not, of course, stand examination.

4. Or, sometimes, the same person on different occasions.

5. There are others we heard of that seemed minor adaptations of those discussed; and there are, doubtless, some we did not hear of.

6. "Contenders" because the problems of notes 2 and 3 apply with equal force here. Among the possible measures of financial success, one must either select one, or, if several are adopted, make explicit what the relations among them are—or accept the confusion and irresolution of "Looking at it that way . . .; but, looking at it this way. . . ."

7. This is only a suggested measure; no Chest known to us uses it, though many talk about it and nearly all use it centrally in their propaganda.

8. If the child set his own task—as the Chest sets its campaign aim—this would, of course, be a different measure—"Proportion of goal achieved" (Type III B).

9. The truth of the proposition (it is a very dubious one) is not being examined here. What is being pointed to is the frequency with which a proposition in social engineering—"If you want X, Y is required"—is hidden behind a statement of "needs."

10. The statements are frequently fallacious in two senses. In the first, the alleged connection may not be true at all; for example, more recreation may not reduce delin-quency rates. But even if it does, this is not what the statement asserts: when we say "more recreation is 'needed' to combat delinquency" we should mean *if and only if* more recreation is provided will delinquency be reduced. If an increased police force or better lighting would also reduce delinquency, then—even assuming we all wish to reduce it and pay the price—all we know is that more recreation *or* more police *or* better lighting (*or* something else) is "needed."

11. It must be admitted that the distinction between relieving distress and creating happiness is no more clear-cut than the difference between an honest man and a thief —and is just as important, even though the most honest may be a little larcenous and the most larcenous occasionally, or in some matters, honest. It must be also admitted that what is distress and what is happiness are relative to time and place, so that some may be distressed simply because they do not have as much as (or enough more than) others. But at any one time it is not any more difficult to agree on what are the more obvious and acute distresses, than it is to decide on what constitutes "clear

and present danger" in connection with incitement to riot. The relief of these is one thing; other "program" is another. A very respectable argument can be made to the effect that as public policy concerns itself with both (instead of with the first only) the door to authoritarian policy is opened and a threat to a free or "open" society is posed. (See Karl R. Popper, *The Open Society and Its Enemies*, Princeton: Princeton University Press, 1950.) It is an easy extension to say that as Chests (or other MOPS operations) approximate private taxation systems, the problem becomes more acute, since there is lacking widespread public knowledge of decisions, public participation in elections, or the habit of changing the entire government when people are disappointed with program. Chests, as pointed out in chapter 5, usually collect for "charity" (relief of distress) and "community service" (contribution to happiness) programs. The wisdom of this juncture might be well worth reviewing.

12. Literally infinity because happiness is—almost by definition—that of which one cannot have too much, i.e., the demand for which is infinite.

13. Here is suggested, then, another measure of Chest "success": the ratio of the "take" to community income. This is almost exactly measure VII C, i.e.,

$$\frac{\text{Amount raised per household}}{\text{Income per family}}.$$

If "households" and "families" are approximately equal in number (and if the few "unrelated individuals" are neglected), this is necessarily about the same ratio as:

$$\frac{\text{Chest take}}{\text{Community (personal) income}}.$$

14. A frequently heard statement in a recent Chest campaign was to the effect that the goal reflected the summed needs of the agencies after their budgets had been carefully pruned by cautious businessmen, i.e., after "wants" had been cut to "needs." Without questioning, for the moment, the actuality or (if actual) the nature of this "budget review," it can be seen, from the foregoing, that the argument is still specious: the goal represented the sum of those portions of the agencies' *wants* that some particular group of businessmen had thought warranted, allowable, or, perhaps, possible.

15. For a more exact definition, see chapter 13.

16. How these decisions are made in practice is a part of the story of agency government that is of considerable interest in its own right.

17. We might suggest—without high hope—that *wherever* the term is used in this field, the reader or listener should regard it at least as a danger signal.

18. The inter-Chest reporting organization—the United Community Funds and Councils of America—classifies cities by amount raised in the campaign previous to the one being reported. Thus, for example, a "Type III city," is one which in the year before the one being reported raised $50,000-$99,999.

19. The crudity is perhaps all too obvious. A "Class VII" ($1 to $2.5 million) city could change from a "poor" Chest to a "good" one in terms of performance without altering its *rank* among the thirty or forty cities classified with it, i.e., a radical improvement might not show up on the measure at all.

20. Some arbitrariness cannot be avoided; but it is obvious that, by the measure proposed, a slight shift in classification boundaries (e.g., if Class III were redefined as $50,000 to $90,000 instead of $50,000 to $99,999) would move a given Chest (raising, say, about $95,000) from near a top rank to near a bottom one—without any change in its performance.

21. This comes close to saying that the basis for measuring the achievement of City X is the previous achievement of City X. This may be appropriate enough in sports—"handicapping"—or in motivating children in school to "compete each with himself instead of one another," but it is unusual in the adult world where the effectiveness or efficiency of a performance is to be evaluated.

22. The analogy (cf. note 21) would be the measurement in a race of, say, the speed of a given car as compared with other cars having the same capacity for speed (i.e., horsepower and other relevant factors).

23. Indeed, so obviously did this seem a satisfactory measure to many that when, in the initial stages of this study, we questioned whether the Indianapolis Chest

(which has rarely "made goal") was indeed "failing" (in relation to its opportunities) many felt that we were questioning the self-evident. One layman indeed likened the question to a quibble as to whether the tablecloth before him was "white or cream" (in a context where the point was that it wasn't, say, black or red).

24. Studies 29, 31, 32, 33, 39, 45, 46, 64, 65, 66 and 70. These and all other "substudies" are on file at Community Services, Inc., Indianapolis; and at the universities of Toronto and Chicago, Indiana University, and the Library of Congress.

25. Study 70.

26. Study 39. The Welfare Index is taken from Robert C. Angell's "The Moral Integration of American Cities" in the *American Journal of Sociology*, vol. LVII, no. 1 (July, 1951), pp. 76-81. It incorporates three measures:

$$I \text{ (a measure of ``Success'')} \quad = \quad \frac{\text{Amount raised by Chest}}{\text{Chest goal}}$$

$$J \text{ (a measure of ``Participation'')} \quad = \quad \frac{\text{Number of pledgers}}{\text{Number of families}}$$

$$L \text{ (a measure of ``Sacrifice'')} \quad = \quad \frac{\text{Amount raised by Chest}}{\text{Area retail sales}}$$

Study 39 contends that $J$ and $L$, separately or jointly, correlate at least as well with certain city characteristics as does any combination that also has $I$ in it.

27. Nevertheless, because we feel sure that this measure will continue to be used, we report briefly in the appendix to this chapter selected propositions from the studies completed on this basis. Those with serious interests may wish to consult the studies, which develop some further highly suggestive leads.

28. Few Chests in setting goal fail to take account of what (they think) can be done—as well as what "needs to be" done. This is what is meant in this connection by "being realistic" or "knowing what *can* and *can't* be done in this town" or "knowing what you can get away with." Goals, therefore, generally reflect partly estimates—good or bad—of local opportunity.

29. For the problem involved in the simultaneous use of several measures—unless some rational way of combining them or converting them into one measure is known —see notes 2, 3 and 6 of this chapter.

30. Mrs. Esther M. Moore, Director, Department of Research and Statistics, United Community Funds and Councils of America, in a letter to Community Surveys, Inc., commenting upon some of our studies, October 8, 1954.

31. It might be assumed, for instance, that the rising demand would bring into the market a new class of buyers who might pay on a fee basis the costs of increased services—or more than these costs (i.e., part of the existing costs). We do not wish to imply that this is a warranted assumption, but we have no evidence that is not.

32. It must not be overlooked that some not inconsiderable part of the budget of virtually every agency goes precisely towards efforts to make the "demand" rise, i.e., into what, when approved by an agency Board is called "selling" or "good public relations," and when payment or fund-raising time comes is regarded as the undesirable cause of a constantly mounting bill. Very often, as the preoccupation, even of the same person, shifts from "how it looks" to "what it costs" the same act of agency self-promotion looks, now shining silver, now very dull metal indeed.

33. We also cannot, of course, make either of the alternative assumptions, i.e., that Indianapolis has increased or decreased in importance. It is perhaps a significant comment on many aspects of social control in Indianapolis that: (*a*) no agency or research body had any data or valid indexes that would permit one to estimate growth in income from year to year, and that (*b*) each organization that was asked—eight or more in all—"thought" that at least one of the others had such data. (Perhaps the situation is the same in many other cities.)

34. We say "ideally," because in practice (*a*) the solicitation area is generally ill defined, (*b*) the population, even where the territory is defined, is rarely known with any accuracy for more than a few (censal) years, and (*c*) a temptation exists to use different populations for the denominator (e.g., now that of the "central city,"

now that of the "Standard Metropolitan Area") according to passing desire to imply (before campaign) "Look how badly we have been doing" or (after campaign) "Look how well we just did." Some Chests solve the whole problem by using the same population as the basis from the date of one publication of a census to the next!

35. Folklore already had it that, the larger the center, the larger the percapita to be expected—only nobody knew how much larger.

36. See C. Arnold Anderson, "Community Chest Campaigns as an Index of Community Integration," *Social Forces*, vol. 33, no. 1, pp. 76-81. For a summary and discussion of this study, see also C.S.I. Study 54. For the use of an index based partly on number of families, see Robert C. Angell, "The Moral Integration of American Cities," *American Journal of Sociology*; and for discussion and further analysis of Angell's studies see note 26 to this chapter, and C.S.I. Studies 28, 32, 38, 39, 40, 82 and 89.

37. The point is—if not already sufficiently clear—that the "mean" income is

$$\frac{\text{Total community income}}{\text{Number of families}}.$$

If therefore we have as the measure:

$$\frac{\text{Chest gift per family}}{\text{Community income per family}},$$

this is the same as

$$\frac{\text{Chest gift}}{\text{Community income}}.$$

But, if the published figure is the "median" income (the middle income in a series arranged in order of size) then multiplying this figure by the number of families will not give the community income, will always give a figure less than the community income, and will "distort" the index differently in different cities, depending on how incomes are distributed in each.

38. See, for example, "Survey of Buying Power," *Sales Management*, vol. 70, no. 10 (May 10, 1953).

39. "Some subscribers, particularly research men and other technicians, may be left dissatisfied with the above description of how SALES MANAGEMENT makes its annual estimates of income. The editors regret that they cannot take them through each step and process. To SALES MANAGEMENT the formula and techniques used in making these estimates for the annual 'Survey of Buying Power' are an important and valuable 'stock in trade.'" "Survey of Buying Power," *Sales Management*, May 10, 1953, p. 28.

40. From the fundraiser's viewpoint, because the tendency is for him to measure his own success, and for those "involved" with him to measure his success, by how much he can raise. His "floor" is what is "needed" or "reasonably to be expected"— but he has no "ceiling." From a more general viewpoint—that of the whole society or of a detached observer—he may be doing as "badly" when he raises more than is "reasonably expectable" as when he raises less. If, for example, $5 per capita is a reasonable expectation, it may be as damaging to raise $6 per capita as to raise $4. We do not say this is so. We merely say that only the fundraiser and his entourage may unquestioningly take the view in this situation that "anything over $5 per capita is good, and the more the merrier." It should be noted, that, in our own analysis, we have not departed from this fundraiser's view—simply because we had no warrant for an alternative position. Our stand here is, therefore, still open to question.

41. By "theory" we mean here, as in any other science, a body of connected hypotheses that have undergone the gruelling test of confrontation with facts, to test credibility, and confrontation with logic, to test consistency. At any given moment, the body of theory is what is most credible about the science. We explain this here, only because for many of our informants certainly, and for some of our readers very probably, "theory" is often taken to mean mere opinion separate from facts, dubious, and relatively irrelevant to action. The truth is that theory is central to action, that, in acting, every sane person is proceeding upon a theory; if he believes otherwise, he is merely unaware of what theory or theories he *is* acting upon, and unwilling or unable

to bring them under critical review. The choice is not between "theory" and "action" (or "practicality") but between action founded on naïve or uncriticized theory, and action founded upon matured or tested theory.

42. See, for example, Robert C. Angell, "Moral Integration of American Cities," and C. Arnold Anderson, "Community Chest Campaigns."

43. It may be clear that such a process of testing is virtually infinite, unless the true causes of the behavior under examination are few and the researcher is lucky enough to hit upon these causes early. If one were trying to account for inter-city differences, say, in the volume of bank clearings or the total expenditure on drugs, one might soon hope to find a few leading city characteristics that accounted for some of the variation. After the first steps it usually becomes harder to find characteristics that —independently of the first few—account for much more of the variation. In practice— in such complex matters—one hardly ever hopes or expects to account for all the variation. Where one stops is a matter of purpose, time, and sheer economic exhaustion.

44. Nearly all of them are.

45. Note that this decision turns on what the problem is: if the examination were to discover the reasons for variation in the effects of a medicinal (e.g., the Salk vaccine) which sometimes might prove fatal, most doctors would gladly accept the "expense" of taking a very large number of variables into account for the sake of a relatively very small gain in accuracy. Our present case is not like this.

46. If we are trying to explain differences in the sale of heavy baseball bats—to take a silly, but perhaps clarifying illustration—and if we have already established that sales vary with the sex and age distribution in each city, it will add very little to our knowledge if a researcher tells us that sales vary also with the distribution of voices, sales going down as voices go up (alto and soprano) and sales going up as voices go down (bass and baritone). The reason this adds little to the explanation is obvious: the age-sex variables and the voice-variable are not "independent." The first tells us that only young men (mostly) buy heavy baseball bats; the voice analysis tells us about the same thing. It might be added that the terms "independence" and "[absence of] correlation" have specific (but not identical) meanings in statistical theory. In the discussion, we are using the terms in their colloquial sense, that is, as if they were synonymous and meant "absence of statistically detectable relationship."

47. See especially (but not exclusively) Studies 28, 32, 40, 41, 47, 53, 54, 57, 58, 63, 68, 70, 78, 79, 81, 82, 84, 85, 86, 87, 88, 89, 90, 91, 93, 94, 95, and 96. For availability of these studies see note 25 of this chapter.

48. See particularly Studies 28 and 32.

49. By "the South" is meant the states defined by the Census as "West South Central," "East South Central," and "South Atlantic," i.e., Texas, Oklahoma, Arkansas, and Louisiana; Mississippi, Alabama, Tennessee, and Kentucky; Florida, Georgia, the Carolinas, the Virginias, Maryland, and Delaware.

50. If the point seems trivial, let us recall that Indianapolis tended to compare itself, where the Chest was concerned, with southern cities when it wished to feel good and with northeastern cities when it wished to feel bad. Perhaps local people felt that its sobriquet, "the most northern of southern cities," entitled it to this Janus-like look.

51. See especially Study 29 on regionality and differential "failure" rates; and Study 53, for differences in the relation between gift and population (of Chest area) for several regions.

52. The decision was made in order to provide ourselves with ready access to census facts, and to provide others with ready comparison with materials based on the same geographic units. We later learned that the United Community Funds and Councils of America had a somewhat different, private, regional scheme of its own, which we were urged to use instead. We reviewed but did not revise our decision, since it seemed preferable for general consumption to employ the more widely used and generally recognized system. For regions and their definition, see, e.g., United States Department of Commerce, Bureau of the Census, *County and City Data Book* (Washington, D.C., 1952), p. viii.

53. For details and exact statements see Study 53.

54. *Ibid.*

55. $C = 1.27 \log P -\$2.99$, where $C$ is the percapita to be expected and $P$ is the population of the place.

56. In statistical terms, $r = .612$; $r^2 = .3745$ ($N = 190$). Throughout, when we speak of what is "explained" or "accounted for," we mean the term to be taken in the above *statistical* sense.

In strict statistical terms, "accounted for," "explained," and similar terms used in this context refer only to the square of some coefficient of correlation, i.e., causation is not necessarily implied by the statistical analysis per se. However, we felt free to use these terms more colloquially since, in our judgment, most relationships discussed in the text suggest some causal ties or underlying common causes.

57. We have already referred (chapter 5) to the rather freewheeling way in which local Chests tend to estimate and report "their" populations. Since the most recent accurate population data were from the 1950 Census, and since the only data for most of the other variables that might bear on giving to the Chest were in this source, most of the balance of this analysis is built around Chest performances for the campaigns conducted during 1950, or the "1951 campaigns."

58. For definition, see Census, *County and City Data Book*.

59. See Study 57.

60. See Studies 57 and 58.

61. St. Louis and Cleveland were included even though their populations were over 1,000,000; it was felt that they might be too large, but Cleveland, we felt, had to be included because of frequent comparisons with Indianapolis, and St. Louis because it was of the same order of magnitude as Cleveland. Other adjustments had to be made: for example, Cedar Rapids and Waterloo have solicitation populations under 100,000. Some Chests in areas having more than one major Chest were dropped. Details are given in Study 57.

62. See Study 68.

63. Technically: $R_{1.2345} = .86$; $R^2_{1.2345} = .74$ ($N = 41$).

64. Actually, logarithm of population: variable I A, Table XII.

65. An index of business volume per capita; variable II B, Table XII.

66. Variable IV A, Table XII.

67. Actually, E-bond sales per capita; variable II C, Table XII.

68. Technically, the "betas" which give an indication of relative importance are:

| | | |
|---|---|---|
| $\beta_2$ Population size (log of) | .665 |
| $\beta_4$ Productivity | .282 |
| $\beta_6$ Population composition | −.218 |
| $\beta_3$ Savings | .208 |

It will be noted that the last two are about equal in importance.

69. In most references in the text, "population" has been used for "log population" where, in the context, the distinction makes no difference.

70. "Effect" in the sense of effect on statistical expectation; *not* necessarily in terms of social cause.

71. All reproduced from Study 68.

72. Computed on the usual "compound interest" basis.

73. A statistical expectation of what the variables indicate "should" happen on the average—not the authors' estimate of what *will* happen, which depends on a number of unforeseeable changes (see chapters 12 and 13) and which would, given the local situation, have to be *much* more conservative. As of date of publication, the Chest had raised over $2.4 million in the 1957 campaign.

73a. If these figures seem astronomical by present local standards, it should be recalled that the formation of a "United Fund" to secure them is not logically excluded by the reasoning employed. Indeed, the reasoning presupposes that many cities like Indianapolis (in outward or obvious characteristics), having already formed United Funds, have boosted their total and the national total at least by the amount previously raised by organizations they incorporated to become "United." (The difference between the two predicted figures turns on which of the two percentage rates of increase in the text is thought safer for prediction.)

74. Such an interpretation, while, in our opinion, very much in the right direction, perhaps goes too far for at least three reasons:

(a) It may be that the character and philosophy of the general manager, the kinds of tricks and gimmicks employed, and so on, are themselves so standardized that a city of a given size tends to select these characteristics of personnel and elements of behavior in a given way. We do not (on the basis of informal observation) believe this to be so. But, *if* it were so, then we would have to admit that the 74 per cent of variation already accounted for on the basis of four city characteristics, was actually a *joint* effect of these city characteristics and the Chest characteristics involved.

(b) We cannot, by the methods employed, be so specific as the 74 per cent–26 per cent relation suggests for any year but the one examined, or for another region, or for a different size-range of cities. The determining effect of city characteristics may be greater than we suppose even for the year examined, and it may be that the residual portion in which the "voluntary" behavior of the Chest has any effect is diminishing from year to year.

(c) We have no way of estimating what would be the effects of some new invention in fundraising, an invention that might alter the relations between what might be called the city-determined and the Chest-determinable portions of the variation in giving.

75. Or if anybody else could with reasonable satisfaction to the affected parties.

76. Money is, of course, *necessary*; it is not always *sufficient*.

77. Anything wholly dependent on the previously employed city characteristics would add nothing, of course, to our power of explanation. See note 50.

78. Again, all additional "items" should be checked to make sure they are not themselves (wholly or overly) dependent on the "explaining characteristics" already used.

79. In Study 28, where it was found significant in its own right (particularly outside the South, and particularly with reference to in-migration). It also shows up as significant in Study 54 (C.S.I. analysis of an article by C. Arnold Anderson, "Community Chest Campaigns") as one of only two characteristics found by the author to be significant. The relation with percapita is, of course, negative: the greater the migration the lower the percapita. This factor was reviewed in Study 68 for its significance in context.

80. See Studies 58 and 68. Population growth was measured in both absolute and relative terms.

81. $r = .64$. See Studies 54 and 68 ($N = 41$).

82. See chapter 9 and also Studies 19 and 20. At that time, in Indianapolis (a) the larger the industrial firm, the larger, on the average, the corporate gift ($\rho = .71$), but (b) the larger the industrial firm also, the smaller the corporate gift per employee ($\rho = -.43$). Here $\rho$ is the rank-order correlation, and $N = 181$.

83. See Study 21.

84. See Studies 8 and 25. The test we employed was one we took to be inferable from the work of Zipf. See G. K. Zipf, *Human Behavior and the Principle of Least Effort* (Cambridge, Mass.: Addison-Wesley Press, 1949). We tested for conformity of the distribution to the simple harmonic series: $r\,S_r = K$, where $S_r$ is the size of the $r$th firm in a ranked list, $r$ is its rank, and $K$ is a suitable constant. For the data of Study 25, the correlation between theory and actuality is very close: $\rho' = .977$. ($N$ is 181, and $\rho'$ refers to the root of the squared deviations divided by the root of the original variance.)

85. Latitude and temperature (variables VI B and C), which were tested for peculiar reasons, do have an effect, regardless of region, and independent of one another, but the chain of causal relations is too tenuous and speculative to be worth commenting upon here.

86. See especially Studies 28, 32, 82, and 89.

87. Both, as defined in Angell's study, "Moral Integration of American Cities."

88. See Angell; also C.S.I. Study 28. For the whole country, omitting the South, $r = -.32$. ($N$ is 28, and the resultant $r$ is thus below the 5 per cent level of confidence. However, since the 1950 data showed the same direction of relationship, the inference that crime rate and welfare index are negatively correlated seems warranted.)

89. Third highest in a list of twenty-eight (non-Southern) cities of population 100,000 or greater.

90. The statistical significance, not the meaning. The latter still puzzles us, since a

high crime rate may be an expression of so many factors—particularly when, as here, the index gives great weight to the more extreme forms of violent crime, i.e., murder and non-negligent homicide.

91. See Study 89.

92. $r = .569$. ($N = 41$. This is significant beyond the .01 level by a two-tailed test.)

93. It might readily contribute another 3 or 4 percentage points, however, thus lowering the unexplained variance to 22 or 21 per cent.

94. See Studies 84, 85, 94, and 95.

95. See Studies 78, 79, 81, 82, 88, 90, and 93.

96. See Study 93.

97. $r_{12} = .350$, $r_{13} = .414$, $r_{14} = .392$; $r_{23} = .406$ where $X_1$ is the per capita gift to the Chest, $X_2$ is the per member gift in one Protestant denomination, $X_3$ is the similar gift in the other, and $X_4$ the gift to both. ($N = 38$, and these correlations are all significant at the .05 level by a two-tailed test.)

98. "Religious" and "secular," of course, only in terms of the beneficiary institution, and not in terms of motivation; many people may give to the Chest on religious grounds, and many may give to the church out of the most secular motives.

99. For 1950 and 1951 respectively, $r = .55$, and $r = .50$. ($N = 41$; these correlations are beyond the .01 confidence level by a two-tailed test.)

100. $\rho = .07$. ($N = 39$; $\rho$ is the coefficient of rank correlation; and for this $N$, this $\rho$ does not differ significantly from zero.)

101. See Study 94. $r = .37$. ($N = 41$; $.05 > P > .01$, by a two-tailed test.)

102. See Study 94.

103. See Study 79. $r = .53$. ($N = 41$; $P < .01$ by a two-tailed test.) It will be recalled that the Chest dependence on population alone was indicated by $r = .74$.

104. See Study 93. Two correlations are sufficiently large, however ($\rho = -.255$ and $-.256$), to suggest quite strongly negative (rather than positive) relationships with percentage non-white and migration. ($\rho$ is the rank-order correlation coefficient; $N$ is 39; and $P \approx .057$ by a one-tailed test.)

105. These are of the order of "dimes per capita," varying (in 1951, for the North Central cities) from about 9¢ to 29¢, i.e., from about one to three dimes. (See Study 93.) It is interesting—and perhaps important—to note, however, that the variation in Chest, Red Cross, and TB percapitas *is* proportionate to size of percapita and that the coefficient of variation is therefore virtually identical for all three. Thus (in an obvious notation):

$$V_{CC} = 27.6 \text{ per cent}$$
$$V_{RC} = 25.4$$
$$V_{TB} = 29.8$$

106. See Studies 70 and 90.

107. Nevertheless—and this needs emphasis—what residual relationship there is (for the Red Cross and Chest deviations) is *positive*, i.e., on this evidence it is harder to believe in a competitive theory of fundraising than in a somewhat tenuously operating co-operative or mutual-aid one.

108. See Study 86. The correlations between number of clergymen per capita on one side and Chest percapita and Church permember, on the other, are respectively: $r = -.462$ and $r = -.262$. Both are significant, the former at the .01 level, the latter at the .05, by a one-tailed test ($N = 41$). The former is also significant at the .01 level by a two-tailed test.

109. If this view should be valid, it is important to know where Indianapolis stands: eighteenth highest in the list of 41 cities in number of clergymen per capita. If Chest percapita were predicted from this characteristic alone, Indianapolis in 1950 was doing about as well as expectable (within 7¢).

110. One might expect this relation on the simple ground that the salaries of many social workers would enter into Chest agency budgets, and therefore into agency deficits, and therefore into Chest goal, and therefore into Chest take.

111. One can hardly escape the suggestion, however, that number of "religious workers" and number of "social workers" per capita measures urbanism, while number of clergymen per capita measures ruralism (see discussion in text). One cannot, however, write off—we believe—the high number of clergymen in some cities to a prevalence

of Negro "store front" churches, since the correlation between number of clergymen and percentage non-white is negative ($\rho = -.212$). The correlation of population with number of clergymen per capita is also negative, and quite significant ($\rho = -.522$). For religious and social workers respectively, the correlations are as follows (see Study 97):

RANK-ORDER CORRELATIONS

| Population variable | Type of worker | |
|---|---|---|
| | Religious | Social |
| Size | .346* | .297* |
| Composition | .005 | —.043 |

*Significant by a one-tailed test.

112. But not necessarily more heavily than all of them together—though this may also be true.

113. See Studies 33 and 70. See also appendix to this chapter.

114. The difference in this respect between U.F. and O.E.F. is *not* statistically significant ($.70 > P > .50$). The difference between O.E.F. and O.C.C. *is* ($.01 > P > .001$). The new vocabulary (1955 and on) lumps what were formerly discriminated as "Other Extended Federation" and "United Funds" into one "United Fund" category, and then reseparates them into "United Funds with Red Cross" and "United Funds without Red Cross"—which certainly clarifies the distinction that the United Community Funds and Councils of America wishes to make.

115. See Study 54. Using a similar measure, number of pledges divided by number of households in solicitation area, C. Arnold Anderson (in "Community Chest Campaigns") finds that it is one of two variables out of nine he tested (the other, as previously reported, was migration), which is significantly related to his criterion measures. His rejected seven are: (*a*) Average effective buying income per family; (*b*) Percentage of households with less than $1,500 income; (*c*) Percentage of households with $5,000 or more income; (*d*) Percentage of Chest take in $100-or-more donations; (*e*) Percentage of Chest take in $25-or-less donations; (*f*) Percentage of pledges that were $25 or more; and (*g*) Pledges of $10 to $24.99 as percentage of all pledges under $25. In re-analysing Anderson's own data, C.S.I. could not agree that all of these could be dismissed as non-significant (see Study 54).

116. See Studies 82 and 89.

117. We suspect, however, that participation is important for theory. It correlates highly ($r = .58; N = 38$) with E-bond sales per capita, which was, we were told, at the time of purchase referred to, largely another measure of efficient organization plus worker willingness to "go along with" management-backed schemes.

118. Data for three cities are not obtainable.

119. This 78 per cent is, however, not nearly as good as the results of a recent study that the Chest permitted a local, commercial research body to do for them in the shape of a "public opinion poll." That research (summer of 1956) yielded the striking percentage "Yes" shown below to the following question: "Did you, or any member of your household, give to the Community Chest last year?"

| | Type of neighborhood | | | | |
|---|---|---|---|---|---|
| | A | B | C | D | Total |
| Percentage Yes | 95.1% | 97.4% | 93.3% | 70.0% | 92.5% |

The neighborhoods range, by the researchers' definition, from "better" (A) to "worse" (D), but except among the very poor, this seems to leave the Chest, participation-wise, all dressed up with no place—or few places—to go. (See "Public Opinion Survey—1956," Indianapolis Community Chest, Inc., Walker Research Service, Indianapolis.)

120. Study 47.

121. $r = .74$ ($N = 25; P < .01$ by a two-tailed test).

122. $r = .76$ ($N = 15$, because United Funds excluded; $P < .01$ by a two-tailed test).

123. Even so, of course, this would mean that a city of a given size ought to expend a given amount to secure an appropriate percapita. This—in 1954—Indianapolis was not doing. It was spending 18.7¢ per capita, second lowest in a list of 25 cities whose expenditure ranged from 12.9¢ to 47.9¢; i.e., (1) given its population, Indianapolis was spending far less than its expected amount for Administration and Campaign per capita, but (2) given its expenditure for these per capita, it was getting more gift per capita than was reasonably to be expected.

124. The correlations are, respectively, $r = .20$ and $r = .43$. The sample is so small (eight cases) that these figures do not have statistical significance, and are reported only as easy ways to summarize tendency. They merely suggest that the burden of proving the safety of a stringently penny-pinching policy in this respect ought to be on the proponents of "economy" in this matter—assuming, of course, sensible expenditure as the alternative.

125. Indeed, if we take Chest income and outgo, the regulative principle would seem to be "from each [donor] according to his capacity; to each [beneficiary] according to his need," as an ancillary or corrective within a free enterprise economy. It should be noted, perhaps, that every social system seems to have such corrective or countervailing practices and institutions.

126. For example, per employee, per hotel room, per dollar of deposits, etc. The justification for this shift will be examined in chapter 8.

127. These ideas will be more fully treated in chapter 8. The crudeness of the measures we are driven to use is purely a function of the crudeness of form in which Chest data are reported. Economists and others have developed quite refined measures, which would give considerable precision to the analysis, but such measures cannot readily be applied to gross data. See, for example, H. T. Davis's adaptation of Pareto's Law of Income, *The Analysis of Economic Time Series* (Principia Press, Inc., 1941); G. K. Zipf, *Human Behavior and the Principle of Least Effort* (1949); Community Surveys, Mathematical Memo 3.

128. For details, and qualifications, see Study 87, and chapter 8.

129. The rank-order correlation between concentration and disappointing performance is: $\rho = -.32$. This is significant: $P \approx .04$, by a one-tailed test ($N = 31$).

## CHAPTER 7

1. See chapter 6 for comparisons of cities—especially for references to studies which assume that Chest performance is a measure of something else, such as the "moral integration" of cities. Also see later in this chapter for further discussion of this inversion of the question at issue.

2. See chapter 2 for discussion of "endorsements" and other attempts to control charity rackets. See chapter 4 for a summary of the Indianapolis experience. The daily press and articles in periodicals supply ample evidence of the existence of such frauds and of the difficulties of suppressing them. A recent example was reported in *Time* magazine, July 16, 1956, in connection with the disappearance of Jesus de Galindez who had acted as "the official Basque representative and fund-raiser in the U.S." Galindez, registered as a foreign agent with the United States Department of Justice, had been appointed by Jose de Aguirre, "first and only President of the Basque republic," who heads the Paris "government" of that short-lived autonomous state abolished by Franco. The *Time* story concludes, "One striking fact stood out in the flurry of news about Galindez' fund raising: in the generous U.S. it is entirely possible for an obscure exile to pass the hat for the nonrecognized government of a nonexistent country—and take in a cool million."

3. Such activity usually takes place in collaboration with a Health and Welfare Council. If the latter brings into significant association most of those interested, so much the better.

4. *Yesterday and Today with Community Chests* (New York: Community Chests and Councils, Inc., 1937), p. 9.

5. I.e., in so far as they lacked a co-ordinated program and were unable either to command universal support or to promise immunity from other solicitations.

6. They are now (1956) being organized to a greater extent by the new Council.

7. Some thought of Community Surveys, Inc., as performing some of these independent functions.

8. See chapters 10 and 11, especially the Appendix, "Estimated Social Status."

9. Since the whole society now dispenses the alms called "primary income maintenance" and pays for them out of public taxation.

10. The Chest becomes a "limited purpose organization"—in fact, a special corporation for fundraising which divides responsibility for budgeting and allocations with the Council.

11. The Red Cross and the "health agencies" are most prominent among the organizations that also engage in community-wide fundraising by means of "drives," and a "division of labor" in campaign work as well as in philanthropic giving appears in these connections also. One of the most interesting aspects of the division of labor is illustrated by the manner in which a "health drive," making a very emotional appeal on a Telethon, can find so many functions for persons of low social status—persons who would otherwise never darken the door of a Chest or Red Cross campaign headquarters.

12. See chapters 9, 10, and 11.

13. See chapter 10 for the problems of human organization in MOPS fundraising, and chapter 11 for detailed comparisons of the Indianapolis Chest with other organizations. See also chapter 12 for the problems of non-top leadership.

14. In chapter 3 we noted that, in Hoosier culture, one of the major themes seems to be deserving of the title, "The Principle of Variance." In its applications, by extension from the field of real estate activity, "variance" seems to be the correct word to describe the Hoosier demand for, and tolerance of, freedom of the individual to exploit his opportunities to the utmost. The Hoosier's "good man" seems to be one who *is* "a character": a shrewd but simple trader ("Of course, I'm just a country boy") who knows in his secret heart that he can outdo any "city slicker" on earth; one who is wary of all strangers but warmly claims those who become Hoosiers by adoption; and one who is a natural-born missionary to the heathen so unfortunate as to be residents of other territories. Such a man applauds conformity to *local* controls; but he also likes to see someone resist "pressure" to comply with the "fair share" giving standards set forth in a Chest campaign because, even if it is locally organized, it includes some "foreign" elements, such as the use of some of the money to support national and state voluntary programs for health, welfare, and informal education.

15. *Yesterday and Today with Community Chests*, p. 42.

16. See discussion in chapter 6, and references there to Robert C. Angell and C. Arnold Anderson.

17. See chapters 9 and 11, especially, for details about the Indianapolis Chest's financial and social history.

18. The reputation gained locally may become known elsewhere also, and help a man's career. See especially Aileen D. Ross, "Philanthropic Activity and the Business Career" in *Social Forces*, vol. 32, no. 3 (March, 1954), pp. 274-280. Dr. Ross describes how philanthropic activity (especially participation in fundraising) influences the career of the businessman in various ways; she also points out that it is a substantial activity of *successful* businessmen, and not only facilitates business careers but also enters substantially into the public relations programs of modern corporations. Her data are for a city where the Chest has not been a notable financial "success" in recent years, but this seems to have little to do with this aspect of the federation's social significance.

19. For various "over-dependencies" and their consequences, see chapter 6.

20. The personnel of campaign leadership changes through the years, of course, so "new" people are continually moving into a position to do to others what has been and will be done to them. The pattern here is reminiscent of fraternity hazing.

21. Attempts to "measure morale" in military organizations and business firms have at least shown important differences in *esprit de corps* from one comparable unit to another, and have also pointed to the fact that no simple set of management "gimmicks" produces the result desired from all units, even though the organizations are "alike" on an organization chart. Inter-city comparisons would be enormously difficult to make, if one tried to take account of the underlying social structures and processes in each.

In the present study we have not attempted a morale survey even in Indianapolis, and we have had only glimpses of the situations in a few other places. The reason we suggest that "high" morale might be developed in a situation approaching "minimal voluntarism" (and maximum "pressure"), so far as federated fundraising campaigns are concerned, is that in such matters the *context* is what really counts: it may be that in a one-industry city with a United Fund and a favorable set of relations between aggressive managements and union leaders, the relative absence of "voluntarism" in employee giving would actually maintain, or at least not undermine, morale. In a city with diversified industrial pursuits, and particularly one with the Hoosier tradition such as that in Indianapolis (or one like it), more "voluntarism" is required; or perhaps one should say, the situation is not favorable to the very great increase in "pressure" that would be required to seek more participation at higher levels of giving if, suddenly, greatly increased sums are sought to be raised by the federation. Giving and other phases of philanthropic activity are so much matters of habitual action that massive changes come slowly. In Indianapolis, it does not at present look as if either the managements are able to co-ordinate with each other, or as if the unions are strongly enough organized, that any very great increase in "pressure" and decrease in "voluntarism" could be accomplished in any short period of time. This discussion might become more "academic" if the Indianapolis Chest campaigns in 1956, 1957 and 1958 build steadily upon the remarkable one of 1955, and begin to "succeed" financially as well as socially. So far as we could see in 1955, especially, the prospects were not bright.

22. More fully discussed in chapters 10 and 11.

23. We did not gather the biographies of most of these persons, but are aware from a few cases that a great variety of "philanthropic careers" exists, with persons engaging for different periods in their lives in fundraising or fund-spending or both. In Indianapolis, there has been a tendency, perhaps recent, to limit the fundraising period to a few years in the middle, rather than the later, stages of a man's business career, and in some cases this means that men are "used up," if not "browned off," before middle age!

24. An agency capable of going it alone, or one whose directors believe they could "do better outside the Chest," might well be openly critical of the fundraisers, but agencies in a weaker position apparently go on and do the best they can with whatever they are given.

25. The failure of attempts in 1950, and again in 1955, to establish a United Fund in Indianapolis is another symptom of this lack of desire to enlarge the federation, perhaps because its capacity for "growth" might well be enhanced and something closer to a levy of the national "one-mill tax" would indeed have to be made.

CHAPTER 8

1. Or differential "opportunity to give," in a favorite formulation. This distribution of gift-load is not to be confused with distributing the money to recipients; it only concerns the burden on the giver.

2. Disposable income means what is left after all prior obligations, legal or other, have been met.

3. Policy-making is further complicated for the fundraisers by the divisions, uncertainties, and shifts and twists of thinking among the donors. A fundraiser may take it for granted that in any appeal: (*a*) not all donors can be expected to respond, (*b*) among those who do respond, not all will meet any agreed standard, (*c*) hence any "standard" must (in a sense) disingenuously claim to be applicable to all, although the only real reason for setting it as high as it is in practice set, is the certain knowledge that not all will apply it. Here, as elsewhere, in a sort of circular response—like boys building up in successive steps to a fight—one dubiously honest "defence" on one side calls out a protective defence in deceit on the other, which calls for more counter-protection, and so on. The problem is how to structure the situation so as to truncate the process. The only alternative is to accept the distrusts engendered as part of the "costs of doing business."

4. This is a degree of fundraising unification nowhere approximated in practice, and seldom (though sometimes) dreamt or spoken of.

5. What advantages such a scheme would have, otherwise, over the present situation or over the transfer of these united activities to the citizens in their united political capacity (i.e., to government) must be left for discussion elsewhere. For some problems of unification, see chapter 13.

6. For how unusually modest this would be, see the description of actualities later in the chapter.

7. I.e., the higher the income the higher the rate.

8. Obviously also, it does not matter—as far as internal contradiction is concerned—whether they all agree on a fixed level of progressiveness, instead. If they do, and if effective exposure to their claims is a function of income, as it seems to be, then the final result will be much more "progressive" than any *one* of them intends or believes equitable.

9. I.e., towards the inclusion of all giving to organizations, "religious," "educational," "health" and "welfare," to name but a few major recipients.

10. It is important to emphasize that we are speaking here of actual giving—not of mere organization for giving, important as that is. Individuals—"employees" or "executives"—may be organized through the corporation or similar unit, but from the present viewpoint this is *individual giving corporately organized*. The corporate or Foundation gift, or the gift of any other fictive person, is the alternative source of income.

11. In the 1955 campaign of the Indianapolis Community Chest, under the direction of the General Chairman (a banker) material was circulated demonstrating ways of "stretching" the gift dollar, i.e., of tax avoidance (not to be confused with tax evasion). Under some circumstances (e.g., the gift of rapidly appreciated stock) a gift to the Community Chest could result also in a profit to the donor. Table A referring to a person "in the 60% tax bracket" and dealing with a stock subject to short-term Capital Gains tax, having a cost of $1000 and a present market value of $2200—sold to the Chest at "cost"—should make this happy situation clear.

TABLE A

| Situation if stock sold on open market | | Situation if stock sold to Community Chest for $1000 | | | |
| --- | --- | --- | --- | --- | --- |
| | | For donor | | For Chest | |
| Proceeds of sale: | $2200 | Proceeds of sale: | $1000 | Proceeds of sale: | $2200 |
| | | Exemption for gift | | Cost: | 1000 |
| Short-term C.G. tax: | 720 | to charity: | 720 | | |
| (60% of $1200 gain) | | (60% of $1200) | | | |
| Net return | $1480 | Net return | $1720 | Net proceeds | $1200 |

Profit to donor by gift: $ 240
Gain to Chest: $1200

Immediate loss to U.S. tax fund: $1440

*In general*, if $M_c$ is the market cost, $M_v$ the present market value, and S the selling price to the Chest (S $\not< M_c$); ($M_v \not< M_c$):

The Chest gain is: $M_v -$ S

The donor's profit is: $.2 M_v - .6 M_c + .4$ S

Total cost to tax fund: $1.2 M_v - .6 M_c - .6$ S

or 60 per cent of (twice the market value, less cost, less selling price).

If the stock is sold to the Chest at cost ($M_c$), as in the illustration, then:

Chest gain is: $M_v - M_c$

Donor's profit is: $.2 (M_v - M_c)$

Cost to tax fund is: $1.2 (M_v - M_c)$.

But $M_v - M_c$ is the value of the stock less its cost, i.e., the amount by which the stock has appreciated.

| | |
|---|---|
| The Chest therefore gets, net: | The amount of the appreciation |
| The donor profits, net: | ⅘ the amount of the appreciation |
| The tax fund loses: | 1⅘ times the amount of the appreciation. |

There is no limit to this loss by the tax fund, presumably, until the point is reached where 60 per cent of the appreciation is equal to the donor's total allowable exemption for gifts to charity.

If the taxpayer in question were in a higher bracket than 60 per cent, his profit would be correspondingly increased. If $r$ (which runs as high as 91 per cent) is the tax rate on the highest portion of his income, and if the gift is made from income within this bracket, the situation if the security is sold to the Chest is as follows:

| | |
|---|---|
| Net proceeds to stockholder if stock sold on open market: | $.4\,M_v + .6\,M_c$ |
| Net proceeds to stockholder if stock sold at cost to Chest: | $rM_v + (1 - r)\,M_c$ |
| Additional profit to stockholder by selling at cost to Chest: | $(r - .4)\,(M_v - M_c)$ |
| Gain to Chest: | $M_v - M_c$ |
| Loss to U.S. tax fund: | $(r + .6)\,(M_v - M_c).$ |

To put the matter very simply, if the taxpayer were in an 80 or 90 per cent tax bracket, by selling his security to the Chest at cost:

(a) He would retain 80 or 90 per cent respectively of the appreciation in the stock (instead of 40 per cent of it);

(b) The Chest would get the full value of the appreciation, and

(c) The cost to the tax fund would be 140 or 150 per cent respectively of the appreciation.

Even if we assume that in the absence of a Chest, such functions as it supports would have to be carried on by government, and that identical costs would have to be paid out of taxes, it is clear that there is a still further loss to the tax fund, i.e., the difference between the Chest's gain (100 per cent of appreciation) and the tax fund's loss (140 to 150 per cent of appreciation in the illustration), i.e., 40 to 50 per cent of the appreciation in the stock. In general terms the additional tax loss is the additional stockholder's profit of: $(r - .4)\,(M_v - M_c)$.

The whole argument may seem farfetched, but it is so only in so far as it is difficult to find people who (a) have sizeable holdings of stock that (b) has appreciated radically in the "short-term gain interval," and (c) who are under constraint to sell it immediately anyway. If the last condition does not apply—i.e., if it could be held beyond this interval—the whole argument falls. (It should be noted that it is the fundraiser's argument that is farfetched—not our argument upon it, which merely spells out consequences.)

Under more likely circumstances—say a corporation subject to 52 per cent corporate tax on profits, and prior to that a 25 per cent capital gains tax on gains on capital holdings—the corporation might sell securities to the Chest at any price from market selling price (no benefit to Chest) down to nothing (a "gift") with the following results. Let us suppose a security of market value $1200, bought at $500, and sold to the Chest at the various prices of Table B.

Table B will bear careful examination. If the donor corporation wishes to maximize the "efficiency" of its dollar—see next to last line of table—it will sell the security to the Chest at any price at or above cost and below (no matter how little) market value. There is, however, no advantage for it as far as "efficiency" is concerned in selling to the Chest above cost as compared with selling at cost. Nor—if it wishes the Chest to get a fixed amount out of it, say $700—does it matter from anybody's viewpoint

## TABLE B

| Item | (Gift) $0 | Sale Price to Chest | | | | | |
|---|---|---|---|---|---|---|---|
| | | $200 | $400 | $500 | $600 | $900 | $1200[a] |
| Market value | $1200 | $1200 | $1200 | $1200 | $1200 | $1200 | $1200 |
| Less Capital Gains tax if sold on market | 175 | 175 | 175 | 175 | 175 | 175 | 175 |
| Net market value of security | $1025 | $1025 | $1025 | $1025 | $1025 | $1025 | $1025 |
| Less deduction on corporation tax for charity gift | 624 | 520 | 416 | 364 | 312 | 156 | 0 |
| Cost to donor so far | $ 401 | $ 505 | $ 609 | $ 661 | $ 713 | $ 869 | $1025 |
| Less return from sale | 0 | 200 | 400 | 500 | 600 | 900 | 1200 |
| Cost (−) or gain (+) | −$ 401 | −$ 305 | −$ 209 | −$ 161 | −$ 113 | +$ 31 | +$ 175 |
| Plus Capital Gains tax payable | 0 | 0 | 0 | 0 | 25 | 100 | 175 |
| Total cost to donor[b] | $ 401 | $ 305 | $ 209 | $ 161 | $ 138 | $ 69 | $ 0 |
| Total gain to Chest | $1200 | $1000 | $ 800 | $ 700 | $ 600 | $ 300 | $ 0 |
| "Efficiency" of donor's dollar[b][c] | 297% | 328% | 383% | 435% | 435% | 435% | N.A. |
| Total cost to tax fund | $ 799 | $ 695 | $ 591 | $ 539 | $ 462 | $ 231 | $ 0 |

[a]Equivalent to retaining stock and selling it on open market.
[b]A visual impression may be gained from Chart 19.
[c]Gain to Chest as a percentage of cost to donor.

## TABLE C

| Item | Sale at or below cost | Sale at or above cost |
|---|---|---|
| Market value | $M_v$ | $M_v$ |
| Less Capital Gains tax ordinarily payable | $.25\ (M_v - M_c)$ | $.25\ (M_v - M_c)$ |
| Value after tax | $.75\ M_v + .25\ M_c$ | $.75\ M_v + .25\ M_c$ |
| Less deduction for charity gift | $.52\ M_v - .52\ S$ | $.52\ M_v - .52\ S$ |
| Cost so far | $.23\ M_v + .25\ M_c - 48\ S$ | $.23\ M_v + .25\ M_c - 48\ S$ |
| Capital Gains tax actually to be paid | 0 | $.25\ (S - M_c)$ |
| Net cost to donor | $.23\ M_v + .25\ M_c - 48\ S$ | $.23\ (M_v - S)$ |
| Chest gain | $M_v - S$ | $M_v - S$ |
| Efficiency of giving dollar | $\dfrac{M_v - S}{.23\ M_v + .25\ M_c - 48\ S}$ | 435% (for all values of S from cost up to total market value) |

whether it sells one such security at its cost $500, or two such securities, if it has them, at $850 each. (Profit to Chest, $700; cost to donor, $161 in either case.)

In general terms, using the notation of the previous example, the relations of Table C apply. Chart 19 presents the situation in graphic form.

12. Even here it is difficult to say who "really" pays this portion. If there were no taxes but corporate taxes, and if we assume a constant level of tax-recovered government expenditure (i.e., that the government does not cut expenditures by the tax on $1 because that dollar is "given" to charity) then, in the first instance, this must act to raise the corporate tax-rate for everybody, and hence to make the "non-contributing" firms into forced contributors. This is the probable general effect, and at this point we *do* have the reality, and not only the semblance, of a tax on corporations for "voluntary" services. But some corporations can pass on all or most of such a tax to their consumers or customers, and some cannot; the same is true for the portion they "actually pay," i.e., the original net cost of their gift. Hence whether or not all or part is paid by the generality of consumers (a really forced tax) or by the stockholders (in some sense, at least, a gift volunteered by "their" agents, i.e., management) cannot be told with any certainty, and depends largely on the nature of each firm's market. All of this argument, incidentally, applies to the Corporation Tax itself: no one, as far as we know, knows who actually pays what part of it nor with what effect on the economy, e.g., on savings tendency, reserve formation, profit level, output, etc.

13. Defined, for the purpose of this discussion, as a percentage:

$$100 \times \frac{\text{Total corporate gift}}{\text{Total gift}}.$$

14. As defined in chapter 6.

15. The evidence is admittedly weak. We were forced (by lack of earlier data that included Indianapolis) to compare 1954 and 1955 "dependence" with 1951 "disappointingness." This would tend obviously to attenuate any existing relations, so that the relation may be stronger than the statistics suggest. Moreover we had data for only 19 of our 41 cities for 1954 and 16 of them for 1955. Even so, the correlations between corporate dependency and disappointingness were as follows:

$$1954: \quad r = .28,$$
$$1955: \quad r = .23.$$

These correlations are not by themselves reliable, but taken together with the evidence in chapter 6 they suggest a relation between dependence and disappointingness (even though the two correlations are not independent).

The marked dependency of Indianapolis in its 1955 (for 1956) campaign may therefore be cause for re-examination of policy—although Indianapolis has "always" been a high-dependency city. (See chapter 9.)

16. On the basis of other general evidence in this chapter, and in view of some known complaints about the "exploitation of the already generous giver."

17. One corporation's policy might not be worth examining except that (*a*) it is one of the largest and most influential of United States corporations, and (*b*) its definition was avidly seized upon by many fundraisers (as being "better" than they now get) and by many donors (as being "at least definite") regardless of the implications for social policy.

18. I.e., there were six out of seven cases in the predicted direction. The sample is small, but the probability of such a showing by chance is about .023.

19. Not at all a necessary assumption: indeed, no less open to question than the wisdom of a corporation tax as against, say, personal income and/or excise taxes only.

20. A not very likely assumption: see note 12. If the opposite assumption is made (i.e., that in most cases, and for all practical purposes, the cost of the "gift" is passed on to the consumer as a cost-of-doing-business element in the price he pays) then it is difficult to see why the corporations should not between them take on the entire burden, sharing it between them on a dollar volume basis, and hence in effect saddling everyone with the equivalent of a use-tax or sales-tax, i.e., a tax on all expenditures (rather than on income). This scheme has, probably, as much (and as little) to recommend it as has any general sales tax. If gifts from corporations dealing in essential commodities (water,

milk, bread, etc.) were refused we should have the equivalent of a "luxury tax"—which may commend itself better in a Puritan culture.

21. Fixed, that is, in any one year. From year to year one might, on the basis of experience so far, expect increasing percentage demands.

22. Indeed, in the 1956 Indianapolis Chest campaign, firms were invited to contribute 1½ per cent of their "pre-tax net," on the ground, never too well clarified, that some select firms out of a group in Cleveland that was already specially selected for study (by virtue of voluntary co-operation) had at some time contributed 1½ per cent. (Actually, they had contributed more nearly 1¼ per cent, but in view of the double selection factor, and the consequent known bias in the sample, and the careful screening of this bias from the Indianapolis audience, the honest error of ¼ of 1 per cent seems trivial.) In any case, since several other standards were set before the same businessmen, and since they were at no point instructed as to which it was desired they apply, a defect in any one of the standards may have had little effect on the gifts.

23. This also would not be wholly satisfactory, even if available. It is not at all clear that allocations to reserves, provision for reinvestment or the retirement of bonded debt, do not constitute claims prior to "giving," i.e., it might readily be argued that these are competitive necessities for each firm. If to any substantial degree they are, this leaves little but the dividend fund to make gift payments out of. There would be much to be said—if the corporate gift is really intended to come out of stockholders' pockets—for keying the standard to the stockholders' dividends-received plus capital-gains-made figure.

24. The "interested party" would have to assume that the firm was giving not far above standard. This might, incidentally, discourage firms from giving above the standard lest they be thought to have greater incomes than they actually had. Of course, if they wished to appear to be doing just this, one might see interesting covert rate-busting of the standard!

25. Or, where it violates common sense too plainly, some more sensible, but equally arbitrary, assumption.

26. For the kind of competitiveness it is desired to engender and that, evidently, it is believed easy and profitable to exploit, the "theme" of the 1956 (for 1957) campaign of the Indianapolis Community Chest may furnish a suitable example. For the Commerce and Industry division, within a more general "Red Man" (i.e., American Indian) theme, the slogan developed was "Scalp Chief Red Feather," successful scalping to be rewarded by recognition and the presentation of a statuette "like an Oscar." "Chief Red Feather" is the donor in the trade group with the highest percapita last year; "scalping" is the excelling of that percapita by a different firm.

If the suggested theme and activity should really "take," and if enthusiasm and excitement should sweep aside, as is clearly hoped, previous preoccupations with reasonableness and equity, it might well be that the goal announced ($2.4 million, as compared with last year's achieved $2.03 million) could be substantially exceeded. Protecting against such a contingency, however, is the announcement of an additional or alternative "challenge goal" of $3 million—the sum said to be required really to permit the agencies to plan soundly for the future.

27. Though this is by no means all that is said for it. Actually, the yardstick within one industry of equal-profits-per-employee requires a whole host of further unlikely assumptions. Firms above and below "optimum size" for that industry at that moment, in terms of man-to-machine ratio, are likely to have lower profit-rates. If those with such ratios above and below are assessed equal per-employee "taxes," this would seem to penalize the large inefficient firm and thereby favor the small inefficient one. Why this should be thought desirable is not clear.

28. See, for example, Robert K. Merton and Paul F. Lazarsfeld, eds., *Continuities in Social Research* (Glencoe, Ill.: Free Press, 1950), pp. 40-105.

29. We do *not* know, of course, that such reference groups would not classify adequately by capacity-to-pay-per-unit. We also do not know whether if thus "properly" classified (by criteria felt to be socially relevant) many or most companies might not feel that obligation-to-pay was paramount and the equalization of capacity trivial —just as executives at comparable social (rather than economic) levels may feel they have to afford houses or cars of a given standard of reputability.

30. Trade groups (industry groups) as, for example, defined in the *Corporate Yardstick Primer*, published by Community Chests and Councils of America, Inc. (no date).

31. One would probably have to assume only (*a*) equal availability of service to all, (*b*) equal suitability of service to all, (*c*) equal risk for all of being in need of the services in question. Assumption (*a*) is probably reasonable, although the geographic factor is quite important, and allegations do arise that employees of firms in the outer urban shell—where new large firms tend to locate—are, in effect, discriminated against in service. (For the effect of distance—and other factors—on utilization of agencies, see Community Surveys, Inc., Studies 1, 18, 56 and 60 on the caseload of the Family Service Association by rate, type of problem, income, housing conditions, and *distance* from the agency. Study 1 suggests that half the variation in utilization is probably ascribable to distance, independent of income.) Assumption (*b*) is probably valid within each trade group; i.e., firms might be expected to have similar proportions of people in different social class levels—which is, likely, the central consideration in assessing suitability of services. Assumption (*c*) is more dubious: larger or more generous or profitable or monopolistic firms, themselves providing many services which are identical with or alternative to "voluntary association" services (e.g., recreation programs, regular X-rays, counselling services), may well be considered to be already paying directly for some part of what would otherwise have to be provided through "voluntary agency" channels. To the degree that this is so, they do not provide bodies of employees with equal-risk-of-exposure. This objection cannot—in the short run—be taken count of, but it may serve to drive home the point made earlier: that the only relevant, meaningful unit of analysis in this field is the sum of all the giver's "voluntary" (i.e., non-tax, non-commercial) payments (other than for private consumption), and not his "gift" to any one philanthropy.

32. See chapter 6 for the general tendency to address to different donors different messages—regardless of consistency or compatibility—in the hope that what one does not "buy" the other will.

33. A sort of tax-for-the-right-to-do-business.

34. Two or three cities are attempting to solve the problem of equity between or among trade groups in other ways but not, so far, with notable success. This is said to be the "next area to require attention."

35. A better measure might be some composite of (weighted) time and other deposits, since these are really different units. A still better measure might be earnings, where, as in most cases, these *are* matters of public knowledge. The most striking suggestion to come to our notice for a unit-of-accountability is that "morticians" be evaluated on a dollars per interment basis. (See report of "3rd Annual Workshop for Campaign Researchers and Statisticians," Detroit, February 6, 1956, p. 5.) This may sound a little ghoulish, but is probably entirely logical.

36. We are excluding from discussion, for the moment, a separate category for "professionals."

37. Several considerations are bound up with each alternative: (*a*) place of collection, (*b*) unit for organizing sentiment and action, (*c*) channels of communication and control, e.g., the corporately organized group involves the addition of one or two more units of consent and one or two more links in communication—corporate management and union management, (*d*) self-conception appealed to: worker or citizen or neighbor, and (*e*) sector of life invaded: public and work life or private and home life.

38. See Study 43.

39. Perhaps in the Chest movement only. Opinion in the Red Cross is fairly solid that it is desirable to retain residential solicitation because it contributes a sizeable fraction of campaign take; makes for good public relations; makes good use of their volunteers, especially "the ladies"; and continues the tradition of the original *membership* campaign, or "Roll Call." See chapter 10, note 30.

40. We have a distinctly contrary impression both from informal communication with neighbors and from the opinion of fundraisers.

41. This is very dubious. It is extremely costly, relatively, in literature used and wasted, in the staff needed to organize time and effort, and in division of purpose and type of appeal between two different classes of consumers. It requires about 5,000

solicitors (ladies) to raise about $25 apiece. The remaining 94 per cent of the campaign take is raised by about 10,000 to 15,000 face-to-face solicitors who raise on the average about $125 to $190 apiece.

42. This is also questionable. As pointed out in chapter 11, "the women" in the Chest are not given comparable status with the men, regardless of their social standing. (This, of course, works the other way, also: because of the standing they will have in the Chest, women of higher social standing may be happier to serve elsewhere.) In any case, the (woman) chairman of the Residential section, with incomparably the greatest army under direct command (5,000) is ranked far lower in the hierarchy than many with far smaller personnel responsibilities. This is a potent source of tension rather than goodwill.

43. This is dubious too. Even though some small fish may be caught in this second net, it offers an opportunity for many to escape altogether by playing the "I'm sure he gave at work; I think she gave at home" game. We have no exact figures, but have reason to think this a practice fairly widely employed, often even an error made in good faith.

44. This can hardly be doubted. But it is another example of trying to have things both ways. Employers are to be encouraged to give in proportion to number-of-employees-and-their families (some "standards" use a family-size multiplier), employees are to be encouraged to give to their limit on behalf of their families, but "any woman can find a few dollars around the house, or in the teapot, or take it out of the house-keeping money."

45. At any rate, no one has yet dreamed up a "standard" for such duplicate or dual giving.

46. Currently, commonly $6,000 per annum (though $4,000 has been used).

47. A salesman, a foreman, and a junior member of a management team, as well as the highest paid or most socially prominent president of the largest corporation, may thus, despite their various identifications and loyalties, be lumped together—as against all other "personal" givers.

48. The same considerations regarding reference groups apply here as in the earlier discussion in this chapter regarding corporations.

49. In Indianapolis, for "special reasons" there is a dual division to be discussed below, but represented pictorially as in the accompanying diagram, i.e., a flat rate up to $6,000, a steeply progressive rate thence up to $30,000, and again a flat rate, beyond that point. See Study 73.

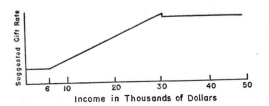

The "special reasons" were urged on the campaign's general chairman, by one senior campaign leader and prominent executive. He urged that the table of standards be "cut off" (i.e., terminated) at the $20,000 or $30,000 income level on two grounds: that those with larger incomes could figure it out for themselves—"extend it," and anyway "Let's don't scare them off." The upshot was the curious anomaly reported: a suggested flat rate above $30,000 and below $6,000.

50. The hope is, of course, that by bringing it under deliberate review here it may cease to be so naïvely natural, and become more an expression of chosen policy.

51. Indeed, in many cases it is most misleading, just as average income statistics are misleading—and for the same reasons. A millionaire and his two servants may have incomes of $1,000,000, $3000, and $2600 respectively, but it is misleading (even if true) to say that the average income on his estate is $335,200 per occupant! In reporting executives' gifts, for instance, the Chest knowingly engages in this sort of prevarication with statistics "because it looks better that way."

52. This is called "rank ordering" the list, and the numbers assigned to the gifts are called "ranks"; 1 for the leading gift, 2 for the next largest, etc.

53. The median is the middle gift of a ranked series. It is a more informative descriptive measure, where inequalities are marked, than is the "average" because it is less influenced by extreme values. In the illustration of note 51, $3,000 is a better description of the typical income than is $335,200.

54. Or "skew" or lack of symmetry. When data are not symmetrical, the average and the median will differ, usually the more so, the greater the asymmetry.

55. Actually, of course, a "reverse" or "lazy" J.

56. It does matter to some extent: not to the J shape, as such, but to the regularity or evenness of the curve.

57. This is most remarkable, because it is widely believed that giving behavior is far different where there is a "constituency"—which the Jewish Welfare Federation approximates—from what it is where there is merely a "public"—which the Community Chest approximates.

58. Much of the confusion in discussion of fundraising, we suspect, stems not from a conflict in policy (though that too occurs) but from lack of precision as to terms and their meanings and the general lack of adequate conceptual tools.

59. The imaginary illustration is quite realistic in this respect. Many gift lists we examined had about the amount of disequality in the illustration.

60. I.e., the ordinal numbers of the gifts when they are arranged in order of size, largest first. Thus the first gift has rank "1," the next largest "2," and so on. See note 52.

61. The formula has been adjusted to reflect those elements of a campaign that appear important to us: total, disequality, and dependency. The derivation of the formulae involved is as follows:

$$G_R = a' \ R^b c$$

where

$G_R$ is the $R$th gift,

$b$ is the slope of a (least squares) regression line on log-log paper,

$c$ is $\dfrac{1}{\Sigma R^b}$,

$a'$ is $a\Sigma R^b$,

and $a$ is the constant in $G_R = aR^b$.

In general $a'$ will approximate the goal or total, $c$ the concentration on the leading giver alone, $b$ a generalized measure of disequality (of ratios), albeit heavily influenced by the effect of the bigger gifts. The last qualification seems to us an advantage, since, if there is a feeling of victimization, it is likely to exist among the larger givers and in reference to these proportionately large disequalities.

62. Higher, regardless of sign, i.e., $-2$ is "higher" than $-1$.

63. "Profitably," that is, in the sense of this section—that we are trying to clarify or refine some intuitive notions for later, more exact, use. Whether rank analysis by itself has utility is a matter for further research.

64. A similar method can be used in order to compare different standards of giving one with another. See below in this chapter.

65. We have no means at present of furnishing guidance as to what disequality "should be" tolerated. If the tools suggested—or similar or radically improved ones— were systematically used, some empirical sense for tolerable levels would develop as experience cumulated. This all assumes that we must treat crude disequality as itself a primary problem. If circumstances permit a breakthrough to considerations of equity instead (i.e., to a consideration of equality or disequality in relation to capacity or obligation) the whole analysis in terms of ranked crude gifts may be abandoned in favor of analysis like that suggested in the next section for gift-in-relation-to-income.

66. Note that only two of these determinations are really independent, i.e., when two have been chosen the third is determined automatically.

67. If the scheme seems "impractical," it is only because no known Community Chest would really permit (if it could avoid it), let alone encourage, a leading giver to reduce his gift. But it is not possible (in this case) to get the increase sought,

*and* to lower disequality according to plan, without permitting this reduction. This problem will reappear later in the chapter.

68. A matter perhaps for negotiation. See note 65.

69. Or some other measure of disequality, if it should turn out to be more useful for analysis in such homogeneous groups; e.g., if in very homogeneous groups the distribution should turn out to be something other than generalized harmonic curves.

*If* the noted disequalities were completely functions of disequalities in income, then groups homogeneous as to income would *not* show this characteristic J-distribution. We have no reason to think, however, that disequalities in income are the only factors that produce the noted systematic disequalities in gifts.

70. Note that if we are going to translate measures of disequality into measures of inequity we must assume equal obligation as well as equal capacity. This assumption may well be questioned. An individual who gives generously to other organizations may be only debatably under equal obligation to give to "his" Chest; a firm that maintains expensive "fringe benefits" such that its employees are differentially less likely to use Chest agencies may also only debatably be said to be under equal obligation. But the assumption *is* freely made by Chest people: indeed to the point where non-conformity in giving is widely regarded and freely talked about with rancor as avoidance or evasion of an obvious obligation. The similarity of the terms to those of the tax authorities is probably no accident.

71. For a list so short, the illustration in terms of formulae may be unconvincing, because we can pretty well see what we want to see "by inspection." But the illustration is only meant to illustrate. In practice, we should be dealing with very long lists and large groups, and some "boiling down" to a descriptive formula would be essential before we could see very much.

72. It is to be noted that we have now abandoned analysis by mere rank of gift and are analysing the gifts by the giver's income.

73. I.e., if $G = a\ I'c$, i.e., if the exponent of $I'$ is 1.

74. Let the reader again be reminded that one Chest *recommends,* and others in their recommendations approximate, schemes A 1 and B 1, *as far as disequality or inequity is concerned.* See section in this chapter on Standards.

75. If accuracy is measured by the correlation between actual gifts and formula-predicted ones, these correlations run mostly between .90 and .99, mostly nearer the latter. See Studies 22, 23, 24 and 36. We are aware of the risks in applying correlation formulae to data so radically non-normal, but the measures here merely confirm what the eye grasps—a most remarkably close fit.

76. Really two independent components: level and disequality. The first has been further split into two to make clearly visible separately the "scope" of the campaign, and the degree of dependence on a leading (or "standard") giver.

77. Partly because of the difficulty and labor involved in developing the fundamental tools listed above, chiefly because appropriate and reliable data were not available.

78. We have treated the ratio of the corporate to the non-corporate gift as a "disequality" which, of course, it is. It is not, however, of quite the same kind as the other disequalities referred to, i.e., it deals with two categories rather than with disequalities or inequities in "giving units." The total corporate gift would represent the decision of a giving unit if and only if the corporate donors were organized to act in concert.

79. The needed information is not available for many cities, nor, often, complete for those that do report—some failing to report one set of items, some another. Such "reporting" makes routine accounting—let alone research—difficult, and serves to call into question the relation of the Chests to their national organization, generally. This problem will have to be touched upon again in chapter 12.

80. All but two cities for which the data were available in the case of the "index of concentration" (31 cities of our 41) and all but three cities for which data were available (29 cities) in the case of the "index of disequality." This dropping of "inconvenient" cases comes close to special argument, except that (*a*) two of the cities had turned up as atypical on a number of other measures and (*b*) all other evidence converges in the one direction. The excepted cities are worth noting, however, and the reasons for their exceptionality are worth exploration in a further study. In any

case, the reader has been adequately warned. See Study 87, and Mathematical Memos 3 and 4.

81. The two measures are not, of course, independent. If they were, we should be talking of two things instead of two ways of getting at one thing. Freed of the common influence of place size, the correlation ($N = 29$) between the two measures is .43.

82. See also chapter 6.

83. I.e., it points to an underlying negative relationship between the deviation itself and the index. By a one-tailed test, $.05 > P > .025$.

84. By either a one or two-tailed test, $P < .01$.

85. For a study of actual giving by executives in Indianapolis, see Study 13. It—and the analysis in other studies—points to remarkably low levels of giving and great "progressiveness." The median gift of a (probably favorably biased) sample of 1831 Indianapolis executives turned out to be $10, for executives whose salaries ranged from $6,000 to $100,000 (with a median of $7,700). The over-all average gift-rate among executives in the sample in 1953 was just over one-fourth of 1 per cent of income.

86. Boston has to be excepted because its Chest—without any indication to its donors that the reference is to another city—simply reprints the Cleveland standards on the pledge-cards as a guide to giving (i.e., Boston's standards here have no known relation to Boston's behavior).

Indianapolis has to be excepted because it openly used an average of other cities. It did so because it felt the standards based on the behavior of even the most generous fifth of its executive givers were shockingly low, in relation to Chest ambitions. (The median gift of the "most generous fifth" was $48, and of the "second most generous fifth," $20.) So Indianapolis's standards do bear a known (but unsystematic) relation to its behavior, i.e., they are well above it. They also bear a known relation to behavior in other cities (the average of *their* best fifth). For details of giving by Indianapolis executives, see Study 13; for the discrepancy between actual and standard, see Study 77. (On the average, the standard would yield three to four times the average actual gift.)

87. We tested this hypothesis of identical slopes on the Indianapolis data taken as a whole, and on the top fifth and second fifth. The respective $b$'s are 1.92, 1.92, and 1.93.

88. In order to standardize or render generosity measures comparable we had to compute the original log-log regression equations, as follows:

| Executive giving plan | Formula | |
|---|---|---|
| | $b$ | $a$ |
| Chicago | $\log G = 1.98 \log I$ | $-6.14$ |
| Cincinnati | $\log G = 1.72 \log I$ | $-4.89$ |
| Cleveland | $\log G = 1.54 \log I$ | $-4.04$ |
| Indianapolis | $\log G = 1.78 \log I$ | $-5.22$ |
| Lowell, Mass. | $\log G = 1.83 \log I$ | $-5.26$ |
| Milwaukee | $\log G = 1.80 \log I$ | $-5.29$ |
| Philadelphia | $\log G = 1.94 \log I$ | $-5.76$ |

The negative correspondence between progressiveness (as measured by $b$) and the coefficient $a$ is almost perfect ($\rho = .964$), indicating that the lines representing the various standards pass virtually through a common point (see note 89).

The force of the foregoing argument is weakened when it is recalled that the $a$'s in the standardized equation are affected by the actual salary levels (or points) selected to standardize upon—in just the same way as "standardized death-rates" depend for their value on the "standard population selected." The weakening is less serious than may appear, however, since the salary intervals actually used in the various schemes are very similar. To argue seriously against the seeming evidence as computed (and impression) it would have to be shown that some conceivably useful series of salary intervals for a "standard" of this kind did, in fact, substantially attenuate (or reverse) the negative relation found.

Progressiveness is satisfactorily indicated by the $b$'s. To obtain a satisfactory measure of over-all level of giving or "generosity" is, however, more difficult, since the $a$'s are not, as already pointed out, independent of the $b$'s.

We resorted to an essentially arbitrary solution, as follows, but one which makes sense (this does not indicate the actual computational steps, to which there were valid short-cuts, but our reasoning): (1) the formulae of the several cities may differ merely because different salary intervals were set forth in the standards; (2) in order to eliminate this source of difference, the formulae were used to compute their *implied* gifts for the salary intervals actually employed in the Indianapolis standards; (3) the geometric mean of these computed gifts was obtained and divided (in every case) by the geometric mean of the salary intervals in the Indianapolis standards; (4) the equation was then completed as if each city used only the Indianapolis salary intervals. The result was a "standardized form" in which every city had the same geometric mean salary. Accordingly in the formulae of Table XXVIII the first figure is the geometric mean giving rate (i.e., gift divided by salary) implied by the particular city's original formula (but standardized upon the Indianapolis salary intervals). The $b$'s remain the same as in the original formulae. The figure in parentheses is the geometric mean of the Indianapolis salaries—and hence the same in each formula. The exponent of this figure is $(1 - b)$—specific for each city—and is needed to complete the "standard form." See Mathematical Memo 2 for details.

89. Using the expressions only as summary measures or mnemonic aids, and without attributing statistical significance, we may say that, as between these $a$'s and $b$'s, $\rho = -.43$, $r = -.51$. In general $a$, in the original equations of note 88, appears empirically related to $b$, so that approximately $a = 2 - 4b$. We have therefore a general standard for all standards, such that $\log G = b \log I - (4b - 2)$. *To the degree that this relation holds, progressiveness can be regarded as the sole determinant of the gift structure.* Since the probable limits for $b$ are 1 and 2, this amounts to saying that all likely standard schemes fall between $G = .01\ I$, where $I$ is the income (a 1 per cent flat-rate tax) and $G = (I')^2$ where $I'$ is the income in thousands (i.e., the Columbus scheme).

These all give an equivalent gift at the $10,000 income level, but the Columbus-type scheme, of course, is far more onerous above this (e.g., at $25,000, the first scheme suggests a $250 gift, the second a $625 one).

Midway between these two extremes would be their geometric mean, i.e.,

$$G = \sqrt{\frac{I}{100}\left(\frac{I}{1000}\right)^2} = \frac{I^{1.5}}{10^4}.$$

This, of course, yields also a $100 (1 per cent) gift at the $10,000 income level, but a $395 at the $25,000 one. The index, it should be noted, is close to Cleveland's 1.54. The equivalent formula in standardized form is $G = .0120\ I^{1.5}\ (\$14,450)^{-.5}$, i.e., it falls at about Cincinnati's scale of generosity and Cleveland's scale of progressiveness.

While the $a$'s and the $b$'s of Table XXVIII are not independent of each other (in the sense that for a given $b$ and salary schedule, the $a$'s are determined) it is true, as pointed out in note 88, that the $b$'s were determined from the standards for the individual cities and superimposed on the Indianapolis salary schedule. There is accordingly no *a priori* reason to expect any particular relationship (or indeed, any) between these $a$'s and $b$'s.

90. Correlation on four cases is worthless except as a descriptive summary or mnemonic aid in reference to the table; but for this purpose, it can be said that for these four cases the correlation between disequality and disappointingness is .72.

91. This would probably be true *a fortiori* if due allowance were made for the proper "weights" (relative frequencies) for each salary interval. A slightly higher yield from the very numerous lower-income executives would more than compensate for a slightly lower one from the few higher-income ones.

92. We shall not deal at any length here with giving in the professions because (*a*) the money amount involved is small; (*b*) in any case, we have heard no convincing reasoning that would make us believe there was any logically defensible cause to apply any special standard to professionals, i.e., that they should be treated differently in setting standards from any other recipients of a personal income. The argument that the profession itself is the best unit of organization and the most effective instrument of pressure is not being questioned; but that does not logically imply different principles of standard-setting.

93. If direct access to post-tax earnings can be had for most firms, there is only waste, as far as the setting of standards is concerned, in classifying them by trade groups (if, also, capacity to pay—i.e., earnings—is the basis for the standard). Under these circumstances, there is strong reason from the viewpoint of simplicity for treating all alike as far as the standards are concerned (like "employees," regardless of industry or employment, if a flat-rate is aimed at) or all alike in any one income category (like "executives," regardless of industry, if a progressive rate is aimed at). The notion that earnings figures cannot be secured or estimated closely is not to be too lightly accepted as a datum. It may well be that what a firm would—understandably—not reveal to a Chest staff and Board, or to the public generally, it might be willing to reveal to an independent research body or a committee of laymen independent of the Chest. Regardless of this, and with still less "risk of revelation," if the basic idea of a minimum percentage of post-tax net were widely accepted, firms needing secrecy might agree—without revealing anything—to give "at least the agreed percentage of post-tax net." No one could then infer any earnings figure from the gift. This would, of course, in these cases, permit no check. But the effectiveness of the check may be questioned anyway; and the widespread suspicion that without a check businessmen may not act honorably in such matters needs questioning also. If a few firms should falsely gain repute by being credited with a standard-or-better gift it would probably be of no great consequence; that many would attempt to do so is not lightly to be credited.

94. If capacity to pay is *not* the decisive criterion, the whole discussion shifts. For if desire or propensity to pay, or obligation to pay because of location or utilization of services is decisive, then either the basis of organizing groups should be different (see earlier discussion re "reference groups"), or again no necessity to standardize by groups arises.

95. See *Corporation Yardstick Primer*, p. 1. It should be particularly noted that from an ethical and logical viewpoint standards should be dealt with from the top down, and not, as is being done, from the bottom up. If, for instance, the division into corporate and non-corporate shares is "unfair," then every subsequent allocation (e.g., to trade groups or persons) merely increases the equality in sharing injustice. Similarly, if the trade-group total is unjust, measures to get equitable sharing of the total by individual firms imply the even distribution of inequity. It is by no means demonstrable that this is even a relative gain in equity.

96. The month of the 1956 biennial national conference of the Community Chests and Councils of America. See relevant Community Surveys field reports (February 11, 1956) and attached documents and exhibits.

97. Where the corporation has extended operations over several regions of the country, these differences might be quite considerable. And since they might readily be related also to the relative operating costs of Chest agencies, there is reason to think percapita should, in equity, be adjusted accordingly.

98. It would serve in particular to diminish the now growing volume of complaint by some "liberal" trade groups that they are carrying—as a group—more than their fair share.

99. To render this concrete, suppose that there are about 600,000 people in Marion County; and suppose that 200,000 employees (persons working for some corporate entity entitled to give "gifts") represent 200,000 families; and suppose further (as is being alleged in the current campaign) that the average annual income per family is of the order of $6,000. If each *family* contributed 1¼ mills per dollar of income—i.e., ⅛ of 1 per cent, in contrast to the ⅕ to ³⁄₁₀ of 1 per cent now being asked of "employees," besides what is asked, in residential solicitation, of their wives—the Corporation gift in the following year and the Personal gift in the year in question would total $3,000,000

(the "challenge goal" for the Chest for the fall of 1956 campaign) with the Corporation share being just half. (Some small allowance would have to be made under such a scheme for that number of employees not employed by units entitled to give as units, e.g., government organizations. But actually this would be more than offset, likely, by the duplication in the corporate gift involved where more than one person per family was employed in any corporation.)

100. See *Corporation Yardstick Primer*.

101. The plan is fully presented and discussed in Study 55, from which only parts have been reproduced here.

102. Note particularly that "below average" and "above average" do *not* mean in this peculiar usage those who gave less and more respectively than the general average for their trade group.

103. It should be recalled that it is the introduction of equity as between per-employee gifts that is the ostensible aim of the scheme!

104. By our terms—not the Cleveland ones.

105. See *Corporation Yardstick Primer*.

106. A classic expression of this point of view was put forward by one prominent Chest research man at the C.C.C. Conference (February, 1956) previously alluded to. He felt that "the liberal givers must be kept in the leadership since high tide raises the level of all ships." His city, of course, uses the Cleveland Plan.

107. The manager of a Chest in a city also using the Cleveland plan was asked whether he saw the incompatibility in (1) the argument for equity that the plan employs and (2) the obvious consequence (shown in a plainly printed example) that a firm whose employment fell off would be victimized by an extortionate percapita. He said he did. Being next asked how such a duplex argument could be put to and accepted by businessmen, he laughed confidentially and said, "But *they* don't know that [that it is an inconsistent argument and an unfair practice if the logic of the standard holds at all]." He appears to be right—since no protest from business has yet appeared —so that the standard may well hold as long as gullibility is endemic and prosperity universal. A Community Surveys researcher put it most gently: ". . . all standards are arbitrary . . . but . . . firms appeared to accept the standards gracefully. The firm leaders apparently get the feeling that 'rationality' is being introduced into giving." Perhaps he took the view of a character in a Louis Auchinloss story: "It was impossible, he decided irritably, to exaggerate the gullibility of the commercially successful"; see *The Edification of Marianne* (New York: New American Library, 1955), p. 135. For another treatment in fiction of fundraising, especially professional fundraising, see John O'Hara, *Hope of Heaven* (New York: Bantam Books, 1956).

108. *Not*—as in the Cleveland scheme—the same total gift if employment falls off.

109. For a more detailed discussion of standards for giving by executives, see Study 73. For other information on this giving, see also Studies 13, 30, 36, 71, 75, 76 and 77.

110. Using the same notation as previously, the equation for the tax scheme is:

$$T = a\ I^{1.30} \ \text{(where } T \text{ is the tax).}$$

The formula for the church scheme is

$$C = a\ I^{1.45} \quad \text{(where } C \text{ is the per-member standard of the church).}$$

The formulae for the Chests vary:

from $G = a\ I^{1.45}$
to $G = a\ I^{2.00}$ (where $G$ is the Chest Gift demanded),

i.e., to the point where the gift asked is some fraction of a man's income *squared* ($a$ refers to the scale or level, and $I$ to income).

111. As we suggested might be done in the case of the corporation.

112. This may not be quite obvious. Given income $I$, and (neglecting deductions) a tax rate $r_T$, and a gift standard $r_G$, we have the following:

Net cost of gift:

$$I\ r_G\ (1 - r_T)$$

Net income after tax, gift, and exemption for gift:

$$I\,(\,1 - r_T - r_G + r_T\,r_G\,)$$

Net giving ratio:

$$\frac{r_G(1-r_T)}{1-r_T-r_G+r_Tr_G}$$

But this is greater than $r_G$, i.e.,

$$\frac{r_G(1-r_T)}{1-r_T-r_G+r_Tr_G} > r_G$$

i.e.,

$$1-r_T > 1-r_T-r_G+r_Tr_G$$

i.e.,

$$0 > r_Tr_G-r_G$$

i.e.,

$$0 > r_G(r_T-1);$$

but $r_G$ is positive, and since $r_T$ cannot be as great as 1, unless the tax is "total," $(r_T - 1)$ is negative, and therefore the expression on the right is less than zero; and therefore the net giving ratio is even higher than the gift-rate.

113. The greater progressiveness is also susceptible of proof. If $I_1$ is the higher income and $r_{T1}$ the greater tax rate and $r_{G1}$ the greater gift rate; then it is required to prove that the higher giving ratio divided by its gift rate is greater than the lower giving ratio divided by its gift rate, i.e., that

$$\frac{1-r_{T1}}{1-r_{T1}-r_{G1}+r_{T1}r_{G1}} > \frac{1-r_{T2}}{1-r_{T2}-r_{G2}+r_{T2}r_{G2}}$$

i.e., that

$$\frac{1-r_{T1}-r_{G1}+r_{T1}r_{G1}}{1-r_{T1}} < \frac{1-r_{T2}-r_{G2}+r_{T2}r_{G2}}{1-r_{T2}}$$

i.e., that

$$1-\frac{r_{G1}-r_{T1}r_{G1}}{1-r_{T1}} < 1-\frac{r_{G2}-r_{T2}r_{G2}}{1-r_{T2}}$$

i.e., that

$$\frac{r_{G1}(1-r_{T1})}{1-r_{T1}} > \frac{r_{G2}(1-r_{T2})}{1-r_{T2}}$$

i.e., that

$$r_{G1} > r_{G2}.$$

But $r_{G1} > r_{G2}$ by definition. Therefore, the net results are even more progressive than the crude.

114. And since it also seems unlikely that such standards could now gain currency in the face of union opposition to be expected.

115. Midway between the extremes of note 89.

116. From what we have seen, we would guess that in most cities where there is marked success in using standards, it is due rather to the process of standard-setting than to the standards employed (since the present ones seem to us to make little sense), and we are reluctant to concur with the view of some fundraisers that success has accrued really because something has been "put over."

117. For more detailed discussion, see chapter 12.

## CHAPTER 9

1. The answer amounted to saying that among the comparable forty-one cities of our sample, Indianapolis was the thirty-eighth best (i.e., almost the poorest)—as measured by deviation from expected gift per capita. (Incidentally, Milwaukee, which was described during the 1955 Community Chest campaign as being average for cities the size of Indianapolis, is also in the bottom sixth of the list of forty-one cities.) By the same token, the Red Cross of Indianapolis stood third or fourth highest on its list (depending on which year is chosen). On its giving to churches, Indianapolis, by the tests we used, is in the middle—twentieth of the forty-one.

2. Important, also, in the selection, were the co-operation and interest shown by the Boards and executives of these two organizations—not that any organization proved uncooperative or reluctant. We also made use of data supplied by the Jewish Welfare Association, the Tuberculosis Association, and others. All were most cordial and helpful.

3. Measured by amount raised—about one-half to twelve million dollars.

4. Divisions are arbitrary groupings of donors for the purposes of solicitation and reporting. They are somewhat related to the geographic location of the persons or organizations to be solicited, but this basis of grouping is cross-cut by the type of solicitation to be made.

5. However, just such comparison is often made by all hands, since unfortunately, the similarity of names for campaign divisions among the several organizations tempts one to do so. It will be seen later that, even within the same organization, two consecutive campaigns will often not report the same sources of gifts in the same divisions.

6. Not all gifts are recorded by the fundraising organizations as separate entries. Many "acts of giving" are grouped—both in place of work and in residential solicitations. This failure to record separate "acts of giving" limits analysis by preventing examination of the total distribution of gifts. As a result, one is limited to "best guesses" as to the breadth of support for these organizations. As a first approximation one might estimate that 20,000 separate records of gifts to the Chest would have been involved for each year analysed; about 15,000 each year for the Red Cross; and at least 5,000 for the one campaign of the Hospital Association. But even this, because of the "lumping" referred to, would not have given us what we wanted.

7. Included, for the respective organizations, for 1953-5, are firms employing 15 or more persons and firms employing 10 or more persons. Prior to 1953, this Division in the Chest included only those firms employing 25 or more persons.

8. However, this was no small task. The detailed study of money-raising was limited to certain years on the arbitrary bases of convenience, accessibility, and comparability. Even this meant that some ten thousand separate entries in the records had to be collected, put in analysable form and then, of course, analysed. When a number of characteristics of the firms were added for comparative purposes, the task which, at first, seemed so straightforward and "simple," became considerably more difficult and time-consuming.

9. What we did was to classify money-results from various categories of the Hospital campaign which to some extent are comparable with similar categories constructed for Chest and Red Cross. Particular attention was paid to classifying the gifts of those firms and their employees which were in Industrial and Commercial Organizations. Even so, we were unable to obtain complete comparability. We resorted to a grouping device which resulted in "Firm" and "Employee" gifts for the Hospital campaign. These include, not only the firm and employee gifts of ICO, but also those of any firm or employee group so reported. Certainly, this leads to inconsistencies in comparison, but we saw no way, within our resources, to do better.

10. The "state of the data" is really quite amazing. There are unnumbered examples in our files of published material which, upon examination, proves to be highly inaccurate. Even when a particular datum is traced to the original record, inconsistencies are often found. This is particularly true of the records of the Chest, though there are a few examples in the Red Cross documents. No problem of this type arose in the Hospital records. A special form of this type of problem comes from inaccuracy of addition. One case from the files of the Community Chest is typical. In a list of three

numbers and the total, the sum of the three did not equal the total. We traced this error through three different documents and all three differed from each other in reporting supposedly the same amounts. Even when we found the original record, there was an error in addition—not, however, the same error which we had set out to correct.

11. The best example is General Motors which has, at least, six separate operations in Indianapolis. The gift by General Motors has been regarded as coming from the firm, but it has always been assigned to the Allison Division of G.M.

12. The Hospital campaign raises a somewhat different problem. It was a single campaign that ran from November, 1950, through December, 1953. If one considers that the pledges to that campaign were paid off as late as 1956, the problem of comparison with annual campaigns becomes increasingly difficult. Again we have made the best of a practical problem that has no neat solution. Since most of the Hospital pledges were obtained in the year from July, 1952, through June, 1953, the campaigns for the Chest in 1952 and for the Red Cross in 1953 were chosen for most comparisons. However, where additional information is obtained by comparison with other years, the data for these years have been presented.

13. Usually teams of five to ten solicitors, to whom are assigned persons or organizations to be solicited, frequently on a geographic basis, but often on the basis of "potential." See chapter 10.

14. The decision is, of course, made by individuals, even here, but they are now acting in their formal role and for the organization.

15. I.e., its employees other than executives. For the source, meaning, and utility of the distinction, see chapter 8.

16. We did this, not because the gifts of Foundations and other organizations are very similar to those of individuals, but simply because they are still less similar to "Firm Organized Giving."

17. In chapter 11, we shall see that even the social status of the persons directing solicitation of these different groupings of donors is different.

18. Parts of the total "donor-aggregate" to which we shall refer later.

19. We wished to include giving by attorneys, and thus analyse most of the giving from the professions. However, it would have been an almost impossible task to isolate giving by attorneys in the Hospital campaign.

20. Not that many other donors are not subject to both kinds of pressure and obligation; they are, but not to the same degree.

21. It is hard to make clear how close these three campaigns are in the percentage raised in the Firm Organized sector. The Red Cross, for instance, would require only a slight shift in gifts received to put its percentage at almost exactly 80 per cent. If the gift of only one donor of a particular size (and there are about 25 to 30 such donors) were withheld or reduced, the Red Cross would be even closer to the percentages for the Hospital and Chest. (On at least one occasion, a reduction in size of gift even greater than that suggested has occurred.)

22. One might guess that, in general, within a city, the larger the campaign, the greater the dependence on contributions from management sources; and, the smaller the campaign, the greater the dependence on labor sources. The point should not be pushed too far, however, since "Firm" is not completely equatable with management, nor "Employee," with labor: the Employee gift, in this context, includes that of the "executives," i.e., management.

23. See chapters 6 and 8.

24. We are considering only single donors. Thus, a number of gifts by employees, as a group, would be larger when lumped together (as they are for reporting) than some of the gifts counted, but they were excluded as being from a number of donors. The ten leading gifts are, it turns out, all contributed by Firms or Foundations.

25. Note that this includes the entire Hospital campaign, while previously we have been discussing only one year.

26. The choice of the number 100 (leading firm gifts) is arbitrary. However, it has some basis in custom, since the United Community Chests and Councils of America has for many years used the one hundred leading corporate gifts as one basis for comparing Chests.

27. This relationship is even more pronounced if we add to the 100 Leading Firm

Gifts any of the 10 Leading Gifts that are not already included; i.e., the larger gifts of Foundations. The percentages are then: Hospital, 43.8; Chest, 41.2; Red Cross, 26.6.

28. Because the Chest, in 1952, reported very few firms employing less than 25 persons in a way that would make this comparison possible, it was necessary to limit the analysis to firms employing 25 or more persons. We would have preferred to examine the top 20 per cent of all givers, but a list of all givers is not available.

29. We were unable, in the time available, to compile the necessary list for the Hospital campaign.

30. It is perhaps notable, given the relative sizes of the campaigns, that the Chest received Firm gifts from 470 firms employing 25 or more persons, while the Red Cross received 583 such gifts. In this sense, the Red Cross seems to have been even more successful in "broadening the base"—a favorite preoccupation of the Chest.

31. This view, by the way, is supported to some extent by the statements of many professional fundraisers, both local and national. The professionals, when evaluating the possibilities of raising a specific amount of money, often approach the problem by estimating how much must be raised from large contributions, and they increase the percentage to be got from the top few when the amount to be raised is larger. It must be remembered we are only talking now of comparisons *within* cities. As *between* cities, we showed, in chapter 6, that for Community Chests in 31 of the 41 North Central cities there is a slight negative correlation between rank order of percentage of total amount contributed by the ten leading givers and rank order of amount raised. Thus, *within* cities, perhaps, the larger the campaign total the greater the dependency on leading givers; and, *between* cities, the larger this dependency, the lower the total.

32. To the nearest $1,000.

33. To the nearest $1,000. Figure supplied by the Indianapolis Hospital Development Association from audited reports. We will use this figure as the "Total Pledge Received" by the Hospital campaign, even though later adjustments have changed that figure.

34. Actually, solicitation continued after this date, particularly among employee groups, to compensate for losses on pledges resulting from persons leaving a place of employment, and from other causes. Many companies for a long time solicited new employees so that at least the original total pledge of the employees of such a company would be met.

35. This is the total of net receipts from contributions to the 1953 campaign as of December 31, 1953, the closing date of the Red Cross for contributions from the campaigns for that year. Any collections on pledges for the 1953 campaign received after January 1, 1954, are credited in their records to the 1954 campaign.

36. This is the total of net receipts from contributions to the 1952 campaign as of December 31, 1954, the closing date of the Community Chest for contributions from the 1952 campaign. The Community Chest continues to credit to the campaign in which the pledge is made payments received up to two years after the year in which the pledge was made.

37. Here we mean July, 1952, the beginning of the year we are comparing.

38. By the time all the collections for 1954 are recorded, the decrease will be somewhat smaller. It is possible, though not probable, that the final result will show a very small increase.

39. The test used is the same as the one applied to tosses of a coin, if we equate increases with heads and decreases with tails. The whole series looks like a series of tosses from a coin so "loaded" as to turn up heads (increase) 5/7 of the time and tails (decrease) 2/7 of the time. If we now take the three campaigns after the Hospital campaign, one appropriate question is how often would one expect to get at least two tails in tossing such a coint three (the number of these campaigns) times. The answer is that one would expect to get such an outcome by mere chance about one-fifth of the time ($p = .198$), i.e., quite often.

An alternative way to look at the matter would be this: given the fact of two failures in seven years, what is the probability that *by mere chance* both of them would fall in two of the last three campaigns. The answer, then, is a seventh of the time ($p = .143$).

40. Treating the percentages as "scores," and the four years before the Hospital campaign as one category, and the three following years as another, we get the following results by analysis of variance:

| Source of variation | Variation | df | Estimated variance | F | P |
|---|---|---|---|---|---|
| Between | 61.54 | 1 | 61.54 | 5.78 | >.05 |
| Within | 53.27 | 5 | 10.65 | — | — |
| TOTAL | 114.81 | 6 | | | |

41. The corresponding data for the two four-year periods are as follows:

| Source of variation | Variation | df | Estimated variance | F | P |
|---|---|---|---|---|---|
| Between | 4.06 | 1 | 4.06 | — | — |
| Within | 713.36 | 6 | 118.89 | — | — |
| TOTAL | 717.42 | 7 | | | |

42. The campaigns for 1951, 1952, and 1953 were carried on in the atmosphere of the Korean War. Although many persons appraise the war—or, by official definition, "police action"—as having increased giving to Red Cross, we were unable to test that effect, if any.

43. For the Red Cross, the data read:

| Source of variation | Variation | df | Estimated variance | F | P |
|---|---|---|---|---|---|
| Between | 30.03 | 1 | 30.03 | — | — |
| Within | 710.57 | 6 | 118.43 | — | — |
| TOTAL | 740.60 | 7 | | | |

44. Computed from the formula:

$$r = 100\left(\sqrt[n]{\frac{P_j}{P_i}} - 1\right)$$

where $r$ is the average annual percentage increase; $P_j$ is the amount raised in the last year; $P_i$ is the amount raised in the first year; and $n$ is the number of years compared, i.e., the number of years for which we used data, less one.

45. Although there were no specific goals in 1953 and 1954, the Chest's campaign staff had set a goal to be attained over a three-year period.

46. There are two major reasons for dropping the Hospital campaign from further comparison. First, since it was a single campaign for capital funds, the problems faced and methods used are somewhat different from those faced and used by annual campaigns for operating funds. Second, it would have been an almost insuperable task to put the Hospital data in a form comparable (for detail) with Red Cross and Chest.

47. Although separate campaigns were held in 1933, the Red Cross received part of its support from the Chest, so that independent comparison was not feasible for 1933.

48. The campaigns held in the fall of 1942, 1943, 1944, and 1945 were called "United War Fund" campaigns, but for convenience we refer to these still as "Chest" campaigns.

49. The "campaign for 1945" was held in the fall of 1944. Throughout this report the phrase "campaign *for*" refers to the campaign which took place in the fall of the year preceding the specified year. When we say "campaign *in*," we mean the campaign in the fall of the year specified. Community Chests have the long-established custom of presenting data in the form "campaign for," and we have generally followed this accepted practice.

50. If we use "standard dollars," however (adjusted to the 1947-9 average) the Chest actually dropped back after the war to the level it had attained in 1932. The Chest was still well above the 1942 level, however.

51. For a similar association of events in the First World War, see chapter 4.

52. It may be asked what is the fundamental relation in Indianapolis between the Chest total each year and the Red Cross total. Many forms of relation were tested, but the following seems to supply the simplest description for the fourteen-year interval. If (to remove irrelevant year-to-year fluctuations) the 14 campaign totals are converted to 12 "three-year moving averages," the relation between them is linear and (if C is the Chest total and R is the Red Cross total) is expressed by:

$$C = \$907,000 + 1.005 \ R,$$

i.e., the Chest total is generally a plain $900,000 greater than the Red Cross total. (The fit is very close: $r = .90$, which even for twelve items is "significant.")

53. Although there have been minor changes within some of the divisions and between some of the divisions, these have been so small as to be of no significance to our analysis.

54. This was a different system again from that used in some earlier reports.

55. We were able to break the amount reported for this division into parts. These parts were added to the amounts for various divisions in order to make the data comparable with Red Cross data. The divisions to which these parts were added were those in which they previously had been solicited and in which they since have been solicited.

56. In addition to the differences in reporting gifts, explained in the footnotes to Table XLIV, there appear to be a number of accidental differences resulting from a variety of causes which make comparison of divisional reports for the two organizations very difficult. Some of the causes, to mention but a few, are: lack of information that firms exist or are large enough (in number of employees) to be included in the proper division; a tendency for gifts to be made through a division other than the one in which the gift was solicited because of close ties (usually family) to a solicitor working in the campaign; and sheer error.

57. The major change was in Downtown; the changes in Public and Residential had no effect on our comparison.

58. E.g., for 1955, Division A (except for Professional) was combined with Commerce and Industry for our comparison. Real Estate and Neighborhood Business were combined with Residential, and the three equated with Residential-and-Towns. Public was unchanged, as were Downtown and Professional divisions. There were also a number of minor changes which were ignored in the comparison, since they had little effect on the analysis. The result is not totally satisfactory for comparative purposes, but is better than previous comparisons, and as refined as our resources permit or our objective justifies.

59. But the results of the Downtown division for the Chest in 1953 are not as reliable as the results in this division in the other three years. It seems likely that the much larger percentage raised in 1953 in Downtown division resulted more from changes in the reporting system than from increased giving by the donors in the division.

60. Since the Chest has such a large volume from Commerce-and-Industry, only a very slight change in that division produces relatively large changes in the other four. Thus, in 1953, because Commerce-and-Industry had a small decrease, Downtown had a very large increase as percentage of total amount raised. The strong effect in the Chest of changes in Commerce-and-Industry perhaps accounts for the more erratic behavior of the curves for the other divisions for the Chest.

61. Unit Account solicitation involves, simply, the solicitation of the gift of a firm, the gift of its employees, and the gift of its executives as a single operation. Thus the gifts that are Firm Organized are treated as a "unit," both for soliciting and for reporting. In practice, there are many modifications made, so that one seldom finds Unit Account solicitation in its pure form. The 1955 Chest campaign employed a highly modified Unit Accounts plan. Fortunately, the Chest records for the firms included in Unit Accounts were available so that comparison could be carried back through 1950.

62. As would be expected, there were some differences between Red Cross and Chest unit accounts because of the difference in the basis for inclusion. However, we

found that neither organization rigidly adhered to the criterion for inclusion—the exact number of employees. The Red Cross and Chest both included firms employing very few people—sometimes as few as one. Further, some firms which did have a large enough number of employees were not included by one or the other of the organizations in unit accounts. It was necessary, then, to find the giving records of some ICO firms in other records of the Chest and Red Cross. We were not always successful in the search and this results in some error. The amount of error is very small, though we are unable to estimate its magnitude with any reliability. The error resulting from failure to find records is, however, almost certainly less than 1 per cent of the total amount raised in ICO.

63. Put another way, it could be said that the Firm pledges per employee to the Chest are nearly four times as large as the corresponding pledges to the Red Cross (five and a half times as large in 1955); and the Employee pledges per employee to the Chest are about two and one half to three times as large as the corresponding pledges to the Red Cross. The relative sizes of the budgets of the two organizations in this period were between about three to one and four to one.

64. There are many measures of size—mostly economic—other than number of employees. As examples, amount of sales, gross profit, net profit, and pre-tax net income, have all been used as measures of "size" of firms. However, data for these measures were not readily available for a large enough number of firms, so we were driven to define size of firm by number of employees, which was the customary practice in philanthropy anyway.

65. We were unable to obtain more accurate figures for the number of employees of each firm without the use of slow and expensive methods which probably would not have produced *significantly* more accurate data. However, we did not make any thorough-going tests to determine the accuracy, or lack of accuracy in these figures. We did check some reported figures with the classifications in the *Blue Book* published by the Indianapolis Chamber of Commerce, and found that only one firm in the one hundred checked reported to the Chest a number of employees which would be in a different classification.

The reported number of employees of many firms is nevertheless generally slightly inflated. Since the figure was given to the Chest as part of a request for solicitation supplies, in many cases there was a tendency to overstate the number of employees to ensure getting a sufficient amount of material to carry out the solicitation satisfactorily.

66. The rank correlations (between size of firm and gift per employee), which for such small samples are merely suggestive, are as follows:

| Year | Firm gift[a] | | Employee gift[a] | |
|------|----------------|-----------|----------------|-----------|
| | Community Chest | Red Cross | Community Chest | Red Cross |
| 1951 | −.8 | — | −.9 | — |
| 1952 | −.3 | −.8 | −.7 | −1.0 |
| 1953 | +.2 | −.8 | +.3 | −1.0 |
| 1954 | +.8 | −.6 | +.7 | − .5 |
| 1955 | +.7 | −.6 | +.7 | − .1 |

[a]Omitting firms employing 5000 or more.

67. There are a number of probable reasons for this which are discussed in chapter 11. Perhaps also, however, such large firms may have employees of higher average income (or median income) from whom, therefore, more might reasonably be expected.

68. One might ask whether the number of employees involved in each group is large enough to make the conclusion drawn here reliable. The answer is "Yes." Table L in the text shows the number of employees in each size group. The employees in the group "5000 & over" account for about one-fifth of the total number of employees in all firms employing 25 or more persons.

69. One explanation of the apparently changing pattern may be that the Chest in 1953 and 1954 was endeavoring to increase Employee giving. In attempting to increase Employee giving, the campaigners may have concentrated their efforts on the larger firms. Thus success in increasing Employee gifts among these firms would change the

pattern in the way described. However, Employee pledging per employee actually declined in 1953, and showed a moderate increase in 1954. Hence, the change in pattern *cannot* with assurance be interpreted as showing success in the campaign effort. At best, the campaign effort *may be* responsible for the change in pattern—as far as the data presented in Table LI B go.

70. We used a modified form of the Standard Industrial Classification prepared by the then Community Chests and Councils of America, Inc., for classifying firms by industry. We adopted this classification simply because it was already in use by the Chest. See *Corporate Yardstick Primer* (New York: Community Chests and Councils of America, Inc., no date).

71. A more detailed breakdown of industry groups will be discussed later in this chapter, and the classifications will be termed "minor industrial groups."

72. As a mnemonic aid as to how closely these percentages fit—and not as a measure of statistical significance—we could say that $r = .99$, $N = 15$.

73. This is probably related to the inclusion in the Red Cross campaign of a large number of small firms, few of which are manufacturers and many of which are retail establishments, and to the previously mentioned differential dependency of the Chest on large gifts from large firms.

74. Obviously, different industry groups have very great differences in number of employees. For example, on the average, manufacturing operations use greater numbers of employees per firm than do retail operations (not including suppliers, etc.).

75. If we are thinking of the proportionate change in one industry group in relation to itself, there are some greater differences (for example, in Hotels and Utilities), but in percentage difference of total gift, the greatest is in Manufacturing.

76. The consistency found might be due to the fact that a few very large pledges comprise so great a proportion of the total amount pledged as to preclude the possibility of much variation in the proportions. Or it might be due to relatively fixed relations for assets or income or employment as between such large groups, together with a tendency for the group as a whole to give in appropriate proportions, regardless of the variability of giving in individual units or firms. If the latter is the case, we have self-established, "natural" standards actually in operation, at least for these large groups. On the other hand we may be viewing nothing more than the effects of habit or custom or established and self-justifying expectations.

77. It would, of course, have made no difference to this comparison if we had, instead, used standard dollars.

78. Since the war, the Indianapolis Chest has been getting considerably less than this one cent per dollar.

79. This finding may have relatively little value in estimating probable income from a particular campaign for the Chest, but it might possibly be useful for estimating the probable income of the Chest over a period of years. There is a tendency in crisis periods for all Chests to receive more, and therefore for the Indianapolis Chest to receive somewhat more than this proportion (0.001 per cent) of the national income; but the tendency to receive somewhat less than the proportion in non-crisis periods may more than counterbalance the increase in crisis periods.

80. It might be thought that the increase from 1952 to 1953 resulted from the change in the basis for including firms in ICO. As a close approximation to the effect of including firms employing less than 25 persons, we eliminated the pledging of those firms for all six years (prior to the change in criterion for inclusion, the Chest had included firms employing less than 25 persons). Amounts pledged in ICO for firms employing 25 or more persons as percentages of total amount pledged in the campaign for the six years then are:

| 1950 | 65.4% | 1952 | 67.1% | 1954 | 68.7% |
| 1951 | 67.2 | 1953 | 68.9 | 1955 | 73.4 |

Thus, the pattern is almost the same as when we used the pledges of all firms in ICO. The net effect of including (since 1953) additional firms employing less than 25 persons seems to be to increase the amount raised in ICO, as a percentage of total amount raised in the campaign, by one to two percentage points.

81. However, in the 1953 campaign, when the Chest was emphasizing Employee giving, Firm pledges per employee were below the 1952 level. And, strikingly,

Employee pledging per employee in the campaign for 1953 drops, although in 1954 the loss is more than recovered. But the largest increase in Employee pledging per employee occurs in the same year as the largest increase in Firm pledging per employee (1955, the year of emphasis on firm giving). One is tempted to generalize these findings and suggest that increases and decreases in Firm pledges per employee produce similar changes in Employee pledges per employee. Of course, one could equally well state the causal relation the other way; i.e., changes in Employee pledges per employee produce changes in Firm pledges per employee. All one can say safely is that they seem to change together.

82. Actually, as a preliminary step, we computed the correlation using all firms that gave in either year; i.e., including firms which pledged nothing in one year but which made a pledge in the other year. For this group, the inter-year correlation, $r = .65$ ($N > 1500$). This meant that we excluded from the analysis 560 firms which made *no* Firm pledge in either year; 134 firms which made a Firm pledge in 1954, but none in 1955; and another 154 firms which made a Firm pledge in 1955, but none in 1954. The 560 firms making no Firm pledge in either year are slightly more than one-third of all firms solicited in ICO. (Incidentally, the net gain in number of firms making Firm pledges in 1955 over 1954 is only 20, suggesting that a special effort in the Chest campaign to obtain pledges from previous non-givers was not especially fruitful.)

PERCENTAGE OF TOTAL CONTRIBUTIONS TO COMMUNITY CHESTS FROM ALL SOURCES THAT WERE CONTRIBUTIONS FROM CORPORATIONS FOR THIRTY CITIES IN NORTH CENTRAL REGION, 1923-8 (see notes 85, 86)

| City | 1928 | 1927 | 1926 | 1925 | 1924 | 1923 |
|------|------|------|------|------|------|------|
| Canton, O. | 34.2% | 34.9% | 36.7% | 36.8% | 38.0% | 38.0% |
| Cincinnati, O. | 28.7 | 28.3 | 23.4 | 28.0 | 30.2 | 29.2 |
| Cleveland, O. | 22.6 | 28.7 | 24.2 | 24.0 | 24.5 | — |
| Columbus, O. | 34.0 | 32.5 | 30.3 | 29.5 | 29.1 | — |
| Dayton, O. | 24.4 | 26.0 | 28.4 | 24.6 | 23.2 | 22.1 |
| Duluth, Minn. | 27.1 | 31.0 | 30.9 | 24.0 | 25.2 | — |
| Flint, Mich. | 24.2 | 21.7 | 27.1 | 28.7 | 23.6 | — |
| Fort Wayne, Ind. | 23.3 | 21.1 | 17.1 | 21.3 | — | — |
| Grand Rapids, Mich. | 32.4 | 33.7 | 33.2 | 31.5 | 33.4 | 32.0 |
| Indianapolis, Ind. | 42.1 | 44.5 | 43.0 | 42.9 | 43.5 | 41.5 |
| Kansas City, Kans. | 7.5 | 7.6 | 7.2 | 6.2 | 5.8 | 6.3 |
| Kansas City, Mo. | 30.2 | 29.6 | 32.2 | 29.0 | 28.4 | — |
| Kalamazoo, Mich. | 26.3 | 31.3 | 30.2 | — | — | — |
| Lansing, Mich. | 37.4 | 36.7 | 37.2 | 32.3 | 33.4 | 32.1 |
| Lincoln, Nebr. | 25.5 | 29.0 | 26.0 | 25.4 | 20.7 | 16.7 |
| Madison, Wis. | 19.2 | 17.7 | — | — | — | — |
| Milwaukee, Wis. | 30.5 | 30.2 | 30.4 | 30.7 | 31.5 | 30.7 |
| Minneapolis, Minn. | 31.9 | 31.6 | 30.8 | 30.7 | 30.9 | 35.6 |
| Omaha, Nebr. | 25.8 | 26.1 | 26.4 | 23.6 | 16.1 | — |
| Saginaw, Mich. | 28.4 | 32.7 | 26.1 | 32.2 | 29.4 | 28.4 |
| St. Louis, Mo. | 19.4 | 20.6 | — | — | — | — |
| St. Paul, Minn. | 37.9 | 37.4 | 36.7 | 36.8 | 39.0 | 40.5 |
| Sioux City, Iowa | 37.0 | 38.9 | 37.3 | 34.7 | 40.3 | 46.3 |
| Springfield, Ill. | 25.0 | 25.5 | 22.9 | 22.5 | — | — |
| Springfield, O. | 32.9 | 33.5 | 34.0 | 33.2 | 32.5 | — |
| South Bend, Ind. | 24.3 | 23.1 | 20.0 | 19.6 | 17.7 | 16.5 |
| Terre Haute, Ind. | 26.3 | 26.5 | 25.8 | 25.5 | 21.7 | — |
| Toledo, O. | 29.6 | 30.0 | 28.9 | 29.0 | 27.6 | 27.7 |
| Wichita, Kans. | 24.2 | 24.1 | 24.7 | 23.6 | 21.8 | 21.4 |
| Youngstown, O. | 34.0 | 31.5 | 32.2 | 28.4 | 31.2 | 36.1 |
| National average | 22.5 | 23.1 | 22.3 | 21.9 | 21.8 | 21.4 |

83. $r = .75$; $N = 708$; $r^2 = .56$, i.e., over half the variation in the second year is accounted for by that of the first.

84. The regression equation for all firms giving in both years is $Y = \$1.51 + 1.12\,X$, $Y$ being the per employee Firm gift in the later year, and $X$ in the earlier. If we include firms that gave in either year (i.e., exclude only those who gave in neither) we get $Y = \$1.93 + 1.04\,X$. The first of these two equations suggests that on the average the larger per-employee increases came from the previously smaller per-employee givers— which is clearly in line with the Chest's intent.

85. Pierce Williams and Frederick E. Croxton, *Corporation Contributions to Organized Welfare Services* (New York: National Bureau of Economic Research, 1930); excerpts from Appendix Table I, pp. 247 ff. are given in the table on p. 542.

86. Some concern has been expressed in Indianapolis that the percentage contributed by Firms is so much greater than the national average. Although we are unable to say just how far above the national average Indianapolis is at present, we can bring some evidence to bear from the 1920's. The table on p. 542 shows the percentage of total contributions made by corporations for 30 of the 41 cities we used in inter-city comparison, and the national average for all cities used in the Williams and Croxton study. Indianapolis then ranked highest among the 30 cities in all years except 1923 (when it ranked second). In all years, the Indianapolis percentage was almost double that of the national average. Thus it would seem that historically Indianapolis has relied on "corporation/firm" giving to a much greater extent than have most other cities. It is unfortunate that we have insufficient data to determine what the percentages were during the intervening years, since such information would tell us whether the pattern of large proportions of the total being contributed by "corporation/firm" is a consistent one.

87. As a descriptive summary or mnemonic aid only, for the 1950 and 1955 percentages, $r = .97$.

PROPORTION OF EMPLOYEES IN MANUFACTURING FOR 17 MINOR INDUSTRY GROUPS, COMMUNITY CHEST, 1950-5 (see note 88)

| Minor industry groups | 1950 | 1951 | 1952 | 1953 | 1954 | 1955 |
|---|---|---|---|---|---|---|
| TOTAL | 100.0% | 100.0% | 100.0% | 100.0% | 100.0% | 100.0% |
| A | 16.6 | 24.1 | 25.6 | 21.2 | 22.7 | 22.5 |
| B | 8.5 | 8.6 | 8.9 | 7.7 | 8.2 | 7.4 |
| C | 2.7 | 2.5 | 2.4 | 2.5 | 2.7 | 2.5 |
| D | 4.3 | 3.8 | 4.1 | 4.5 | 4.9 | 5.0 |
| E | 11.1 | 10.0 | 9.4 | 10.7 | 9.9 | 9.5 |
| F | 3.3 | 2.8 | 2.9 | 2.6 | 2.8 | 2.8 |
| G | 6.7 | 6.0 | 5.1 | 5.6 | 5.1 | 5.9 |
| H | 24.5 | 22.9 | 21.7 | 25.4 | 22.8 | 23.3 |
| I | 14.1 | 10.8 | 11.5 | 11.4 | 11.9 | 12.4 |
| J | 2.5 | 2.1 | 1.8 | 1.2 | 1.2 | 1.2 |
| K | 1.3 | 1.2 | 1.2 | 1.2 | 1.2 | 1.2 |
| L | 0.4 | 0.4 | 0.2 | 0.5 | 0.6 | 0.5 |
| M | 1.1 | 1.2 | 1.1 | 1.2 | 1.3 | 1.3 |
| N | 2.1 | 2.6 | 3.1 | 3.3 | 3.4 | 3.2 |
| O | 0.0 | 0.0 | 0.0 | 0.0 | 0.0 | 0.1 |
| P | 0.2 | 0.4 | 0.4 | 0.3 | 0.4 | 0.4 |
| Q | 0.6 | 0.6 | 0.6 | 0.7 | 0.9 | 0.8 |

88. The table on p. 543 shows the proportion of employees in each minor industry group for Manufacturing.

89. Again, only for descriptive or mnemonic purposes, as between 1950 and 1955, $r = .57$. The over-all pattern suggests cumulating small year-to-year changes, because between any two years' figures the correlations are much higher.

90. During the 1955 campaign, one of the standards for giving suggested by the Chest was a 50 per cent increase to bring giving to the level of the increased goal. (Such an increase would actually have produced an amount somewhat greater than the goal.) However, from Table LXII of the text it can be seen that this increase was not achieved (at least for per-employee gifts) in Manufacturing. The increase for Manufacturing as a whole was 28 per cent, and only two of the minor industry groups equalled or exceeded the suggested 50 per cent increase, while two showed decreases from 1954. The actual increase in amount pledged in Manufacturing from 1954 to 1955 is 35 per cent, which is still well below the suggested standard. The difference between the 28 per cent increase in per-employee pledges and the 35 per cent increase in amount pledged results from an increase in number of employees during the same period.

91. Data tabulated and computed but not published, for reasons of economy.

92. Moreover, we had reservations about the accuracy of the sources of our information as to presence or absence of a union in particular firms. Several firms which we were informed had no union, have since come to our attention as being organized.

Our mistrust of the data stems also from a rather interesting development in the course of the study. The Labor Relations Secretary of the Chest stated that he "could not" make available to us his records (which he claimed had been given him in confidence and could not be revealed even to Chest personnel) and also suggested that it would be unwise, if not futile, to contact the two large union federations. We had an impression of little or no control over his action by the Chest's Manager or the Chest's Board. (We discuss this situation more fully in chapter 12.) We did not subsequently seek the information from any union organization, partly for this reason, and partly also because the preliminary examination of the data seemed to indicate that further analysis would not be fruitful.

CHAPTER 10

1. Any human organization—in business or government, and in war or peace—is "effective" in so far as it reaches its goals. It is "efficient" in so far as it reaches its goals and at the same time provides appropriate human satisfactions in work well done. See *The Functions of the Executive* by Chester I. Barnard, President of the New Jersey Bell Telephone Company (Cambridge, Mass.: Harvard University Press, 1946), pp. 19-21.

2. For problems regarding the definition by any Chest of what its area "really is," see chapters 5 and 6.

3. So far as social status in the community is bound up with rank in campaign organizations, etc., social classes are discussed in chapter 11, and again in chapter 14.

4. See chapter 5. See also Murray G. Ross, *Community Organization, Theory and Principles* (New York: Harper & Brothers, 1955), pp. 3-5 ff. for a full discussion of "the theory underlying community planning services for human welfare and the principles involved in the understanding and use of the community organization process." We are especially indebted to Professor Ross for his development of the concept, the "Welfare Community."

5. Although some of these individuals participated in fundraising in 1955, none in this list limited his participation to fundraising.

6. Professor Ross points out that Welfare or Recreation or Adult Education Councils are or represent "functional communities" which sometimes "fail to identify their true nature, and confuse themselves with the geographic community," and that when such associations "think of themselves as councils of the geographic community" they "fail to distinguish their functions clearly." The latter are, he says (pp. 40-1): "(1) to create the 'welfare community,' i.e., to bring into significant association those persons who are

part of the social organization of the welfare community; (2) to make plans to meet the general needs of the welfare community and the welfare needs of the geographic community; and (3) to win support of the geographic community for its welfare plans." A "functional community" is thus, he says, like a "minority group" within the "geographic community," where its task is the advancement of a specialized program felt to be useful and desirable for all. He gives a warning (pp. 43-4) about the "chaos" which results when a Welfare Council is confused as to whether it is working within its "functional community" or is engaged in community organization in the larger geographic community: "It is, for example, impossible to work with all the people in either community, and it is therefore essential to identify the major subgroups or subcultures in the community in which one is working. A welfare council confused about whether it is engaged in community organization in a geographic community or in a functional community will have no way of identifying clearly its subgroups, and the cooperative welfare organization it should be building will be handicapped by seeking (often in vain) to involve many subgroups from the geographic community who will have little interest, desire, or need to be intimately involved in the welfare community."

7. Composed of the General Chairman and the eight chairmen of the soliciting divisions.

8. A whole set of problems in the human organization of any fundraising campaign revolves around the Layman-Professional relation; where these arise in our discussion, the professionals will be clearly distinguished from the other Campaign Directors.

9. Kansas City, with its United Fund, is somewhere between Type II and Type I. It is not a one-industry town. Many of its Leading Donors, acting together as merchants, manufacturers, bankers, lawyers, etc. in a fairly extensive collaboration, also acted as Donor Leaders in instituting the United Fund and in continuing to support it.

10. Even where "employees" are protected, executives may not be. So far, the principal methods accepted to achieve protection seem to be: (1) forbidding any fundraising organization to have full information regarding employee giving (individual names and amounts pledged or cash contributed); (2) excluding some or even all drives from in-plant solicitation; (3) combining certain drives into an in-plant federation —with or without payroll contributions or deductions (as in withholding from the payroll for income tax purposes) and usually with employee or union participation with management in selecting drives for such a "combined appeal."

Since the third method tends to raise larger amounts of money from the employees, especially if the fundraisers manage to "sell the payroll contributions plan," the protection feature of this solution must be shown to rest upon the wisdom of the particular selection of drives put together in the firm's "combined appeal," as well as upon some control of pressure, now transferred from the mass media plus management to the in-group of fellow-workers plus management.

11. For problems of finding and keeping leaders, see chapter 3. For problems of their employ, see chapters 11, 12, and 14.

12. The union also represents an interest in resisting undue "pressure from the bosses," and in recent years unions have sought and won increasing participation (and due credit) in MOPS campaigns.

13. And, if recognized, whether or not it is approved.

14. For the conditions under which incentives and rewards can occur, see chapter 12.

15. Such study is only possible, of course, if the records are accurate, and kept on a comparable basis from year to year. This is not by any means always the case.

16. See Community Surveys, Inc., Study 10.

17. A constituency is a small group of people who are bound by their membership in a moral order that minimizes the possibility that any one of them has financial resources or views or attitudes unknown to others in the group. In that kind of situation, the fundraisers (usually amateurs, but leaders) commonly set up a "Rating Committee"—or its equivalent—which can come very close to estimating in each case what the individual's gift should be, in terms of his ability to pay. Acceptance of or desire for continued membership in the constituency amounts to acquiescence in this operation of the moral order. The smaller the constituency, the more likely it is that the dollar amount that can be raised is predictable. Moreover the group can reach

consensus face-to-face, and no fundraising effort doubtful of success need even be tried.

18. As applied in Indianapolis to the city and county taken together, and as used elsewhere for similar geographic or economic unities.

19. See, however, chapter 8 on appropriateness of groupings.

20. Various documents gave us the "Plans" or "Tentative Time Schedules" for campaigns in San Francisco (UBAC); the general scheme of the Chest in Montreal; and similar kinds of information for other cities. The campaign of the Indianapolis Hospital Development Association was not a "periodic" but a "once-in-a-lifetime" affair, at least in the eyes of the contributors; and it was also a building fund campaign, not to be confused with one for operating funds in which a group of voluntary hospitals might seek funds each year. But as shown in chapter 9, the general pattern of the Hospital campaign was similar to that of the Community Chest, both in technical design or pattern of results and in human organization. In respect to the latter, the Hospital campaign extended over a much longer period of time and at its peak involved many more people.

21. The Hospital campaign had a similar chronology of events, but began with Period 2—officially in October, 1950, when fundraising for the Hospital Survey and for campaign expenses began—continued through Periods 3 and 4 until the Final Report meeting in December, 1953. Since then, it has continued activities similar to those in Period 1 for any annual community-wide campaign.

22. Some leaders are designated as having peculiarly vital and secret information; they are needed in the campaign precisely because of their access to otherwise carefully protected "inside dope." Their role may or may not include revelation of what they know. If it does not, they can "help" by advising in the light of their knowledge of the secret, or by giving to the committee they belong to an air of "knowingness"—since everyone knows they know what there is to know.

23. This was noticeable in the 1955 Red Cross campaign, and was attributed by informants to continuity of leadership and planning over the past decade; it coincided also with stability and clarity in the relations between lay leaders and professionals. See chapters 12 and 14.

24. How the Indianapolis Chest has operated in this vicious circle and how the Red Cross Chapter has so far avoided it, are discussed in chapter 11. A dilemma of such proportions cannot be met by an easy executive decision, but raises a problem of administration of the highest order of difficulty and subtlety in a society that wishes to be free and believes that effective voluntary organizations of this kind are instrumental in keeping it so. "What might be done" in such a dilemma is discussed in chapters 12 and 13.

25. This leg-work—together with the "handling of materials"—is really the "dirty work" of the Chest campaign, and tends to be relegated, here as elsewhere, to lower-status personnel. For some reason—perhaps connected with its "mission" and symbolism —the Red Cross has managed to keep its similar "dirty work" sufficiently "glorified" that higher status personnel (but not, of course, the highest) can engage in it without loss of dignity: indeed, perhaps, as in Christian feet-washing, with some ritual gain. (For our sense of the importance of how "dirty work" is handled in any profession or human organization, we are indebted to Professor Everett C. Hughes.)

26. A leader should not do his team's work. If he and they are "good," he should not *have* to. But he *should be able* to. And the only test of ability is demonstration in breakdown. So breakdown is not wholly an evil; it has the sweet uses of all adversity.

27. The very nature of the campaign—here, as militarily—makes for urgency and emergency. Rapid and accurate communication, here as there, is so vital as to be capable of deciding the outcome.

28. Publication in newspapers and elsewhere of gifts in a current campaign can be controlled from campaign headquarters, commonly, as in a recent Indianapolis campaign, by releasing names and amounts only in cases where the donors have given specific permission. But a campaign organization's records, at the top level, may show the individual or firm "history of giving" for some years past, and such information must be carefully guarded. Hence, down the line, the solicitor receives names and amounts of past and expected gifts only concerning the few "prospects" that have been assigned to him.

29. Despite this seeming lag from expectation, the campaign in question went "over the top," and on time by the final meeting.

30. Prior to World War II, the Red Cross conducted its "Annual Roll Call" or drive for "Members and Funds" in November, between Armistice Day and Thanksgiving. In Indianapolis, the Chapter had been a member agency of the Community Fund since 1921, but in 1933 began its own separate campaign. This was primarily a residential canvass carried on by women, and not designed, like the modern Red Cross campaign, to solicit large-scale corporations and in fact all business firms for firm gifts, executive gifts, and employee gifts. In Indianapolis, the growth of the Red Cross campaign in dollar volume to its present half million size began with World War II. From 1921 to 1939 the local Chapter raised (or received from the Community Fund) between $20,000 and $35,000 each year; in 1940, the amount it raised for itself was about $100,000; and in 1941-42, over $440,000, which included $92,000 raised in the last Autumn "Roll Call" this Chapter conducted, in 1941. The annual Autumn "Roll Call" was abandoned when President Roosevelt in 1942 directed that the Red Cross campaign be deferred until March, 1943, in order not to conflict with the United War Fund appeals in the autumn. For fourteen years, therefore, the local Red Cross campaign has been held in March. Beginning in 1943, it has raised about $400,000 to $650,000 each peace year—and in the two War years, 1944 and 1945, over $1,000,000 each year. In 1952, the Chapter established its present level of fundraising of slightly over a half million dollars each year, and the sub-goal for the modern equivalent of the residential "Roll Call" now accounts for only about 10 per cent of the total, although the sentimental and public relations importance of the Residential division is never forgotten in the design of the campaign. Times have changed in another respect, too: what the Red Cross now raises is about 20 per cent of the total raised by the Chest and Red Cross combined, and this represents a considerably larger proportion of such a combination than the sum the Red Cross received in the 1920's when it was a member agency of the Community Fund—or even in the 1930's.

31. Directors of such voluntary organizations are often selected, by the "nominating" process, so that together they may be said to "represent a cross-section of the community"; hence some persons are included because it is felt they represent, severally, important ethnic or religious groups, organized labor, large civic enterprises, leading donors, significant parts of the Welfare Community, etc.

32. In the Red Cross or the Chest charters and traditions they can nearly always find what they need to give their administrative actions appropriate secular and even sacred sanctions. But even more than this, the Directors bring to their leadership positions various religious convictions, beliefs about good citizenship, and other products of family training and educational experience, so that each can make an individual contribution that is pretty certain to be "in the main stream" of contemporary American thought about such voluntary associations, the "main stream" being itself a product of just such pooling of heterogeneous elements. Like most School Boards, these Boards of voluntary associations are usually composed of civic leaders and persons of high status in the business and social worlds who are likely to give expression to conservative rather than radical views, and who are unlikely to do anything which would alienate the influential, "the best people," or even "the public." Such established organizations as these are almost never seriously challenged: the YMCA after World War I was subjected to an extraordinary amount of criticism but has clearly survived it. For the last point see M. G. Ross, *The Y.M.C.A. in Canada* (Toronto: Ryerson, 1951) pp. 291-294, and the parallel history of the Y.M.C.A. in the United States by Dr. C. Howard Hopkins.

33. See chapter 15 for this problem in a different context.

34. Here and elsewhere in this study we find it necessary to distinguish between "rule" and "government" because, while both modes of acting have been observed in administrators at work in Indianapolis mass fundraising organizations, and while both have important contributions to make to the organizations' well-being, voluntary associations seem to require a particular blend that is different from that familiar in business organizations, military organizations, and various forms of national states. It may be suggested that, in the continuum below, as we move from left to right, the need for "government" as against mere "rule" increases:

| Army | Elementary school | | Voluntary association |
|------|-------------------|---|----------------------|
| Dictatorship | Democratic state | Business | Play-group (supervised) |

In this range from "much rule, little government" to "little rule, much government" the following are variously blended:

| *Rule* | *Government* |
|--------|--------------|
| Involves power | Involves influence, prestige, esteem |
| Relies largely on fear and associated emotions | Relies largely on love and associated emotions |
| Utilizes punishments | Utilizes rewards |
| Mobilizes "negative" emotions | Mobilizes "positive" emotions |
| Political and administrative controls are dominant | Social controls are dominant, both internalized ones ("self-control") and "group pressure to conform" |
| Rites and ceremonies *demonstrate* power | Rites and ceremonies *create* (express and maintain) solidarity |

35. For the actual, present interpersonal situation in this respect, see chapters 11, 12, and 14.

36. See chapters 11, 12, and 14.

37. What might be done in such an impasse is discussed in chapters 12 and 13.

38. This comes very close to an older saying that "the unexamined life is not worth leading"—and for the same reason: purpose is discovered and rediscovered in the process of examination and re-examination. A study such as this is intended to be an institutionalized form of just such "examination," for just that purpose—to discover or rediscover meaning.

39. It is not being asserted that this is their sole motive. Quite the contrary. We met, in the course of the study, executives who hid intrinsically human motives under the bushel of "it's good business," for fear lest their light so shine before men that they be thought unbusinesslike.

40. For suggestive material regarding executives' behavior, and the modern corporation's expectations that its executives will include participation in civic enterprises in their career lines, see, for example, "Absentee-Owned Corporations and Community Power Structures," by R. J. Pellegrin and C. H. Coates in the *American Journal of Sociology*, LXI, 5 (March, 1956), pp. 413-419. See also Aileen D. Ross, "Philanthropic Activity and the Business Career," *Social Forces*, XXXII (March, 1954), pp. 274-280: ". . . there is a decided relationship between the rise of a man to the top executive positions in charitable campaigns, and his rise in the business hierarchy"; ". . . it is very difficult for a man to avoid canvassing [soliciting] once he is well started in his business career"; ". . . a career in philanthropy is dependent *on* the business career, for a man must be high up in the business world before he is in a position of sufficient influence to take over the top philanthropic positions," and so on.

See also Everett C. Hughes, "The Institutional Office and the Person," *American Journal of Sociology*, XLIII (Nov., 1937), p. 411, quoted in Aileen Ross: "The interlocking of the directorships of educational, charitable and other philanthropic agencies is due . . . to the very fact that they are philanthropic. Philanthropy, as we know it, implies economic success; it comes late in a career. It may come only in the second generation of success. But when it does come, it is quite as much a matter of assuming certain prerogatives and responsibilities in the control of philanthropic institutions as of giving money. The prerogatives and responsibilities form part of the successful man's conception of himself, and part of the world's expectation of him."

Much of this seems to be untrue of Indianapolis. It describes a situation in which the Donor Leaders are also Leading Donors and have achieved collaboration in an "inner circle." In "Wellsville" (Aileen Ross's pseudonym for "her" community) the Protestant minority apparently found it easier to secularize the Chest and bring it completely within the realm of the business community. In Indianapolis it looks as though *secularization* is resisted, perhaps more by those in the Welfare Community

Leadership than by the Donor Leaders; but anyway the situation seems quite different, and certainly not yet so institutionalized as to be easily taken for granted.

41. That a representative "cross-section" appears is, of course, not the case. But the illusion seems to be common enough.

42. A United Fund, if it is proposed *only* as a new effort to accomplish the original negative Purpose, would be a federation whose Appeal would lack not only emotionality, but also the rationality attaching to a positive Purpose such as that which suffused the original Chest movement with enthusiasm in the 1920's.

43. See chapter 15.

CHAPTER 11

1. Variously found, as described in chapter 10, in the "Donor-Aggregate," the "Welfare Community," and among the "Ultimate Beneficiaries," etc.

2. Notably in May-June, 1950, and during 1955-6.

3. The Hospital campaign in Indianapolis is in a somewhat different category. Few other cities, probably, got into such straits for lack of building voluntary or other hospitals during the years 1931 to 1950. Perhaps no other city met quite such a crisis—or needed so desperately to get going on such a large-scale building fund campaign in so short a time; we cannot, therefore, compare the Hospital campaign directly with any other in terms of "acceptance." It is commonly said that it was an overwhelming "success," and it almost certainly rated something better than minimal acceptance.

4. With these and other comparisons we shall lay the foundations for chapters 12 and 13: "What Might be Done."

5. It was evident, at these meetings, that behind MOPS fundraising for a *federation* like the Chest (or a United Fund), there is much more than the business community's view of federation as a "good thing" simply because "it reduces the multiplicity of appeals." For one thing, there is considerable variation amongst the federated agencies in their dependence upon Chest allocations: some could not, probably, survive without such funds; others can and do supplement these funds with "outside" gifts and also income from fees, etc.; and a few could so easily raise very large sums if they conducted separate campaigns that they are in a peculiarly strong bargaining position within the federation. Thus, both because of their evident popularity and the need to keep them in the "one big campaign" (lest, with separate drives, they weaken the case for "united giving"), the federation's leaders work to keep these few in the fold. On the other hand, the promoters of these few want both to get as much money as possible through the more efficient "single campaign" and to maintain freedom to add adherents who can "help out," so that, in future negotiations with the federation, they can "lead from strength" and make a threat to withdraw a safe one—since they are "popular" members to include in the "Appeal." The 1955 Chest campaign included one of the major "health drives," and it is significant that negotiations regarding the allocation to be made to it were *not* subject to "hearings," such as the Review Groups conducted for the regular member agencies. Instead, the Cancer Society negotiated directly with the Executive Committee of the Chest's Board of Directors. Thus, a federation such as the Chest is actually held together by a most complex weaving of official and informal social relations, which requires the time and effort of many persons all through the year.

A problem not easily solved is how to publicize these negotiations, hearings, and other interactions, many of them being informal, or how to make them known in any manner which will secure widespread "participation" and "consent." Some issues might be very divisive, if available for more public debate; and, at the very least, their exposure would work against the ideal of unity which the federation is intended to represent and put into effect. Another difficulty is that much of the information is confidential, and some of it is quite personal and private; moreover, only the main results are of sufficient public interest to be printed in the local newspapers. The whole process never receives full publicity, for these reasons; and the problem of the permanent organization of a federation changes from one of how to secure participation and consent to one of how to build and maintain "public confidence," regardless. (See chapter 6 for the desire for widespread participation, and chapters 12 and 14 for some problems of its insufficiency.)

6. The pattern happens, also, to be "military" in its general structure and in some of the titles of rank used. (The latter are, curiously, most evident in the soliciting divisions largely "manned" by women, and this may reflect the emancipation movement of World War I and before.)

7. No such test of the effectiveness of the innovation of the Chest luncheons held in the summer of 1955 is possible, for example, since it was thought necessary that "everybody" in a list of 1,600 firm executives should be invited to attend. In a later section of this chapter, we present conclusions that can be drawn from analysis of attendance or non-attendance as related to increased giving in 1955 over 1954.

8. This is, perhaps, the major feature of MOPS fundraising which keeps its professionals in business—but also in possession of "more of an art than a science."

9. The following tabulation shows that the Chest campaign used fewer campaign *leaders* per $100,000 raised and more campaign *workers* per $100,000 raised, than did the Red Cross; the Chest campaign also had fewer campaign leaders per 100 workers than did the Red Cross.

|  | Chest ( $2,000,000) | Red Cross ( $500,000) |
|---|---|---|
| Leaders per $100,000 raised | 18 | 37 |
| Led per $100,000 raised | 1,250 | 1,000 |
| Ratio of leaders to led | 1.44% | 3.70% |

10. The "clan wail" of fundraisers is normally, "We could always use more workers"; and when "volunteers" let them down, professionals themselves may do some soliciting. But the latter practice is frowned upon, as in violation of the spirit and even the legitimacy of voluntary fundraising and as a very serious threat to the definition of the professional's correct role.

11. But for what full unification means, and would require and would still leave problematic, see chapter 13.

12. There is reason to believe that a United Fund would require more manpower, even proportionately, than the present manpower of the Chest and Red Cross combined.

13. As stated elsewhere (chapters 6 and 9), however, inter-city comparisons of Chest results suggest that the greater the dependence of such a "dollars per capita" campaign upon very large "leading gifts," the lower its per capita results tend to be, in comparison with what city size and other city characteristics would lead one to expect.

14. "Must," that is, if such large sums are to be sought at all by similar methods. Alternatives are: (1) public taxation to support some or all such causes, or (2) change in tax laws to encourage more individual philanthropists. The present system, finding that voluntary giving does not produce "enough," tends to develop in the direction of a pattern of "private taxation." See chapter 3 on "pressures."

15. Certainly, in the present climate of fundraising, *emotionality* has been emphasized by the pennies per capita campaigns, particularly those "health drives" having a handicapped child as the central figure in their appeals. In view of this, all other reasons apart, a dollars per capita campaign is almost driven to make *rationality* its central theme, although this is not to say that it can or should avoid basic human sentiments in shaping its appeal.

16. Such improved records are needed not only to satisfy a general historian's desire for information as to exactly "where" an institution was, decade by decade to the present, but also to satisfy a practical administrator's need to know "where we have been," "where we are" and, hence, "where we are headed."

17. The contrast between "crisis" and "routine" as a matter of difference in point of view between a patient and a doctor, for example, has been developed by Professor Everett C. Hughes, of the University of Chicago, in his studies of occupations and professions. An organization like a hospital is designed to cope with crises in a routine way—and so is a fire department and a Red Cross chapter.

18. What would be a "non-local contribution," or how state and national bodies are to be supported, on this view, is something less than clear.

19. For example, we were told that the local Chapter does not own property, not even the new Annex added to the Chapter House in 1955.

20. The number of the non-local agencies would be increased if the "health drives"—in addition to the Cancer Society, now in the Chest "Appeal"—that might be incorporated in a more complete United Fund were to be added.

21. This analogy to "federation" seems preferable to comparing the Red Cross with a single agency, like a member agency of the Community Chest, since a single agency is likely to have a more specialized, more stabilized, and less heterogeneous program, which continues year after year. Presumably the Red Cross Chapter must keep itself in continuous readiness to change its distribution of personnel or its allocations of money as between its services, according to disaster needs as they arise, and in terms of slower changes in public demand too.

22. By-Laws, Indianapolis Community Chest, Inc., March 23, 1950 (mimeographed). Article V, Section 4.

23. *Ibid.*, Article V, Section 3. Until 1950, the Community Chest and the Council of Social Agencies were administered together, and it may be that this furnishes the reason why, in some businessmen's minds, the Chest and "social dreamers" are still closely associated, even though the (partial) separation occurred more than five years ago.

24. In many successful Chest cities such service is very eagerly sought, to the point where a person not invited will feel "excluded."

25. "Informal" because no mere change of By-Laws will achieve the results desired. And at this point the community-wide federation becomes involved with the total social structure of the local community. In so far as the latter remains fragmented and its communication channels "discontinuous" in parts of the power structure, the administrators of the federation face a very difficult task. Not only is there considerable doubt that a fundraising federation today can do the job of "community organization" and civic uplift that the early proponents of the Community Chest movement believed in, but in the Indianapolis case, there may be some other task of metropolitan improvement that the people and the leaders will feel to be more urgent and exciting. If the federation were to develop patterns for greater neighborhood participation in fundraising, along with greater neighborhood participation by persons drawn into the Welfare Community by the Health and Welfare Council and its member agencies, there is a possibility that people in Indianapolis would take to a "community organization" movement, with some by-products in the realm of metropolitan improvement and civic pride. But the tendency of large-scale federation is to neglect Residential solicitation in order to make sure of getting the bulk of the funds from firms and through in-plant federations. What makes a federation a financial success may not make it a success by social standards, if one of the latter standards is an increased "sense of belonging" to a "community."

26. A variety of solutions to this problem doubtless exists, and the budgeting process need not be unified with the goal-setting task. In one successful Chest (Cleveland) "what *should* be raised" is primarily determined in a budgeting process in which the agencies' demands are reviewed and summed up, the total is transmitted to the fundraising organization, which independently makes a kind of businessman's estimate of "what *can* be raised"; and the goal thus set is given to the campaign leadership as "the job to be done."

In another Chest city, a special Goal Committee considers both what "should" and what "can" be raised, and the goal recommended is then passed on to the Chest Board for approval. In that case, even though the different points of view (of donors, agencies as beneficiaries, fundraisers, etc.) are considered, the Goal Committee's work is only one step in a complex but orderly year-round procedure that connects budgeting with goal-setting, but at certain points clearly distinguishes the interests represented by each participant, and otherwise provides for the reduction of confusion.

27. This introduces some slight inaccuracy, since there are caste lines as well as class lines, but the cases involved were so rare as not substantially to affect our analysis.

28. For a complete exposition of these methods and a bibliography on social class stratification, see Warner, Meeker, and Eells, *Social Class in America: A Manual of Procedure for the Measurement of Social Status* (Chicago: Science Research Associates, Inc., 1949).

29. In the 1955 campaigns the composition of these levels, which we call "Elder

Statesmen" and "Young Campaigners," was as follows:

RED CROSS, 1955 CAMPAIGN

*Elder Statesmen*

Board of Directors
41 persons

29 men and 12 women. (*None* of these served directly in the campaign's soliciting divisions; but four, two men and two women, participated as Young Campaigners by virtue of membership in the Public Information Committee; and one, the Chapter Chairman, also served *ex officio* on the Campaign Executive Committee.) Total unduplicated names: 41 persons; 29 men and 12 women.

Chapter Fund
Committee
14 persons

10 men and 4 women. (Of these, 12 are also Board members, 1 is a former Board member, and 1 is the last year's General Chairman, a volunteer for some years past in this case, who serves as Committee Chairman.) Total unduplicated names: 2 persons; 2 men, no women.

Audit Committee

(Members not listed. Chairman is Chapter Treasurer and member of Board.) Total unduplicated names: 0

*Elder Statesmen*: Total unduplicated names: 43 persons; 31 men and 12 women.

*Young Campaigners*

Public Information
Committee
14 persons

9 men and 5 women. (Of these, 2 men and 2 women are also on the Board of Directors.) Total unduplicated names: 10 persons; 7 men and 3 women.

Campaign Executive
Committee
13 persons

10 men and 3 women. (The General Chairman of the Campaign and the chairmen of the eight soliciting divisions, plus the Chapter Chairman and chairmen of the three other committees listed.) Total unduplicated names: 9 persons; 7 men and 2 women.

| Soliciting divisions | Persons listed[a] | Men | Women | Total unduplicated names[b] | Men | Women |
|---|---|---|---|---|---|---|
| General Chairman | 1 | 1 | 0 | 0 | 0 | 0 |
| Industrial | 13 | 13 | 0 | 12 | 12 | 0 |
| Commercial | 13 | 13 | 0 | 12 | 12 | 0 |
| Public | 10 | 10 | 0 | 9 | 9 | 0 |
| Government & Education | 16 | 13 | 3 | 15 | 12 | 3 |
| Professional | 3 | 1 | 2 | 2 | 0 | 2 |
| Downtown | 26 | 26 | 0 | 25 | 25 | 0 |
| Residential | 34 | 2 | 32 | 33 | 2 | 31 |
| Towns | 16 | 1 | 15 | 15 | 1 | 14 |
| TOTAL | 132[a] | 80 | 52 | 123[b] | 73 | 50 |

[a]Includes Group Chairman and Co-chairmen of soliciting committees in Industrial, Commercial, Public, Government and Education, and Professional divisions; Majors and Captains in Downtown division; Colonels and Majors in Residential divisions; and Chairmen and Co-Chairmen in Towns division.

[b]Excludes the General Chairman and the chairmen of the eight divisions, who are counted as members of the Campaign Executive Committee.

TOTAL

*Young Campaigners*: Total unduplicated names: 142 persons; 87 men and 55 women.

*Elder Statesmen and Young Campaigners*: Total unduplicated names: 185 persons; 118 men and 67 women.

COMMUNITY CHEST, 1955 CAMPAIGN

*Elder Statesmen*

Board of Directors
42 persons

40 men and 2 women. (Fifteen of the men also served in Young Campaigner positions in the campaign; 13 of them in leadership posts in the soliciting divisions—1 as General Chairman, 10 in Division A, and 1 each in C & I and Public divisions; and 2 of them served on Committees—1 in Labor Relations, 1 in Public Relations.)

*Elder Statesmen*: Total unduplicated names: 42 persons; 40 men and 2 women.

*Young Campaigners*

Labor Relations
Committee
4 persons

4 men, no women. (One man was also on Board of Directors.) Total unduplicated names: 3 persons; 3 men and no women.

Public Relations
Committee
19 persons

19 men, no women. (One man was also on Board of Directors. All represented various media; none held leadership positions in soliciting divisions.) Total unduplicated names: 18 persons; 18 men and no women.

| Soliciting divisions | Persons listed | Men | Women | Total unduplicated names[a] | Men | Women |
|---|---|---|---|---|---|---|
| General Chairman and Co-chairman | 2 | 2 | 0 | 1 | 1 | 0 |
| Division A | 39 | 39 | 0 | 29 | 29 | 0 |
| Commerce & Industry | 43 | 43 | 0 | 42 | 42 | 0 |
| Public | 30 | 27 | 3 | 29 | 26 | 3 |
| Metropolitan | 199 | 130 | 69 | 199 | 130 | 69 |
| TOTAL | 313 | 241 | 72 | 300 | 228 | 72 |

[a]Of the total "Persons listed" (313), 13 men from the Board of Directors (i.e., counted as Elder Statesmen) also served in soliciting divisions: 10 in Division A; 1 in C & I; 1 in Public; and 1 was the Campaign General Chairman.

TOTAL

*Young Campaigners*: Total unduplicated names: 321 persons; 249 men and 72 women.

*Elder Statesmen and Young Campaigners*: Total unduplicated names: 363 persons; 289 men and 74 women.

30. For the Community Chest, $\chi^2 = 7.18$, $.01 > P > .001$. For the Red Cross, $\chi^2 = 1.42$, $P > .20$. (Data from Table LXVIII in the text.)

31. In 1949 the goal was lowered to a sum only $23,000 more than the amount raised in 1948, so that a "success" was registered when only about $2,600 over goal was pledged. If this was intended as an experiment to break the Chest's "losing streak," it evidently did not succeed beyond its own limits.

If there are two major popular attitudes about campaign goals, they seem to be (a) that the goal should be "realistic"—that is, actually represent the total accepted as "needed" and as obtainable, and (b) that the goal should be reached or surpassed often enough to identify the campaign with "success." But the Indianapolis Chest, ever since 1920, when only $400,000 was raised towards a goal of one million dollars, has fairly consistently said to the public, in effect, "The needs are so great that the goal is X dollars more than we raised last year when we also failed to raise enough." In view of the tremendous popular appeal of "success" in making goals or "breaking the record," especially in this community, it is very puzzling to note that the Chest, in all but one of the past ten years, has persevered, counter to popular feelings, and has instead stressed "meeting the needs" when this so frequently results in what is commonly evaluated as "failure." In a world where "nothing succeeds like success" and where the business leaders, who are essential in the leadership and manning of the campaign, are hardly ever fond of associating with "failure," it may be that the Chest's quite consistent policy of failing has had a great deal to do with its difficulties in recruiting and training "top leadership," both in its regular year-round government and in its campaign organization.

Obviously the goal to be sought need not be and is not wholly determined by the agencies' "needs"—with or without adequate "budgeting." We have noted that while the Chest in the 1930's was apparently allocating enough to match the agencies' total operating expenses, in the 1950's the amount allocated had become about half or less of the agencies' expenses. The agencies include a number which can and do raise funds "outside" in the form of contributions (apart from fees and other "earned income"). In other cities where this is the case, and notably in the case of the Chicago Community Fund, the federation makes this clearly part of its policy: a spokesman for the Chicago Fund said, in part, "The Community Fund meets only a portion of the needs of the agencies . . . up to about 50%. We say that raising money is essential to agency vitality and as a proof of its worth. The agencies will raise about $20 million for 1956 and the Fund will raise about $9 million." In the Chicago case, the Fund has the "franchise" to solicit corporations for firm gifts and employee contributions, and the agencies must seek funds elsewhere. The Fund's budgeting process permits pre-campaign reviews and enters directly into setting the goal. The result is that federated fundraising becomes more of the kind of "game" that businessmen like to play: it does not require them to become deeply involved in "causes" themselves—instead, it frees them to conduct bits of "free enterprise" in other fund drives closer to each man's own particular interests. Such an arrangement offers practical ways of clearly linking the business community, nowadays the source of the greater portion of philanthropic funds, whether raised through federation or not, with the Welfare Community—and on terms that may be more satisfactory to both in the long run than appears to be the present state of affairs in Indianapolis, at least among those who feel that the Chest or a United Fund should attempt to do the entire job of fundraising.

32. Even the outstanding 1957 campaign, which had raised over $2.28 million by the end of the campaign, had set its goal at $2.4 million (and a "challenge goal" at $3 million) and hence was not able to announce victory on Victory Night (late 1956). Happily, it was later (early in 1957) able to do so.

33. See study 29. In 1953, 59 per cent of all Chests in the United States "failed."

34. The Welfare Community Leaders in 1955 included about 1800 persons, as described in chapter 10. Of the total of 363 persons in positions of leadership in the Chest campaign, 113 (31.1 per cent) also appeared in our Welfare Leadership list, chiefly as Board members of agencies other than the Chest. Of the total of 185 in the Red Cross campaign leadership, 63 (35.6 per cent) also appeared in our Welfare Leadership file. Paid workers in social agencies, especially executives, were included in that file, but only three were active in the Chest's campaign leadership, and only one in the Red Cross.

35. Names were listed in the *Indianapolis Times* for September 21, 1955.

36. As of 1955, 2 of these were active only on the Red Cross Board of Directors; 6 appeared in our file only because they were wives of men who were on boards of other welfare agencies; and the remaining 23 persons (8.0 per cent of the 284 honored

OVERLAP WITHIN LEADERSHIP POOL ($N$ PERSONS) BETWEEN RED CROSS AND COMMUNITY CHEST

| | Red Cross leaders | | |
|---|---|---|---|
| Chest leaders | Yes | No | Total |
| Yes | 21 | 342 | 363 |
| No | 164 | ($N - 527$) | $N - 363$ |
| TOTAL | 185 | $N - 185$ | $N$ |

volunteers) were the only ones of this group who had diversified interests in the Welfare Community.

37. No woman participated in both campaigns—at least at the level of leadership described earlier for the Elder Statesmen and the Young Campaigners. The husband of one lady in the Red Cross Elder Statesman group was himself a Young Campaigner in the Chest drive, but this kind of duplication is apparently rare.

38. The statistically wary may convince themselves by inserting various trial figures in the "unknown" cell of the fourfold table on p. 554. Only as $N$ approaches 5,000 does $\chi^2$ become of such magnitude that $P < .05$.

39. We here define "participation ratio" as the percentage in the leadership divided by the percentage in the population.

40. Sixty persons, or 11.4 per cent, of the total campaign leadership list are "unknown"—that is, information to "rate" them was either inadequate or not available—and most of them are probably in the lower-middle class, with a few in the upper-middle. The nature of campaign leadership participation rules out the likelihood that any are lower class, and it is highly unlikely that the "unknown" include any upper class persons. The chances are, therefore, that if all in the leadership list had been successfully identified and "rated," the distribution would be even more heavily middle and upper class than that shown in the summary Table LXXII.

41. For the distinction between the "birth élite" and the "mobile élite" see Warner and Abegglen, *Big Business Leaders in America* (New York: Harper and Brothers, 1955). Family heads in top business positions in firms founded by their fathers are called "birth élite." Those who have climbed to such positions from the lower ranks in this or any other community are called "mobile élite."

42. Indianapolis Medical Society, *Bulletin*, March, 1952.

43. The Indiana State Hospital and Health Center Plan of 1950 had defined the hospitals' service area as "consisting primarily of Marion County" together with certain specified portions of Boone, Hamilton, Hancock, Hendricks, Johnson, Morgan, and Shelby counties.

44. At Methodist Hospital, Norways Foundation Hospital, St. Francis Hospital, and certain private patient facilities at Indiana University Medical Center (Robert Long Hospital and the Coleman Hospital). See *A Climate That Counts*, brochure distributed by IHDA, Autumn, 1952.

45. Of the 43 Red Cross Elder Statesmen, 27.9 per cent were women; and of the 42 Chest Board members, only two or 4.7 per cent were women; the 98 IHDA Board members included 7 women, or 7.1 per cent. The proportion of women seems to be related to campaign design, especially to the fact that the larger the campaign the more attention is paid to solicitation of corporations and of individuals corporately organized; but obviously, even so, the Chest has fewer women in high positions than one would expect.

46. In 1955 the Chest Board reached something of a low point in number of meetings (only 7, compared with an eleven-year average of 10.7), and six of the meetings were held in the first six months of the year—that is, before the "aggressive" and comparatively successful campaign of 1955. But even so, the last meeting was attended by only 13 out of the 42 persons on the roster. The record for 1955 is briefly summarized in the following:

| Date: | Jan. 27 | Feb. 25 | Mar. 31 | Apr. 28 | May 26 | June 17 | Nov. 10 | Average |
|---|---|---|---|---|---|---|---|---|
| No. present | 22 | 21 | 19 | 19 | 20 | 21 | 13 | 19.3 |
| Percentage present | 52% | 50% | 45% | 45% | 48% | 50% | 31% | 46% |

It may be that the Chest Board reached a low in morale in 1955, as well; but we did not observe its meetings in any other years, and hence can only guess.

47. Hence, Division A, as described in chapter 9, was set up.

48. In its brief five-page form, the Plan did not mention "standards" for firm gifts by trade or industry classifications, although staff studies of past records had been going forward, and this became one of the many features of the "aggressive" campaign that actually developed. For the related problems, see chapters 6 and 8.

49. His efforts were so intensive and unremitting that the whole professional staff combined was barely able to cope with his single-handed output of query and

instruction. Never had one man in so short a time made such impact on so many—at least in local Chest history.

50. This statement was made before the Chest Board authorized the Executive Committee and the campaign leaders to declare the Goal of $2.3 million. The speaker had just heard it might be $2 million, or about $500,000 over the amount raised in 1954. But his figure of "half a million" and his comment applied equally well to the difference between the 1955 Goal eventually set and the hoped-for sum of $1.8 million in the 1954 campaign which had declared no formal Goal.

51. The position in his company of each person was determined by reference to the 1955 City Directory. This source leaves much to be desired in fullness of coverage. If spelling of names is a criterion, then the accuracy of occupational status is also suspect. However, this was the only easily available source and, for the purposes of this analysis, seems sufficiently accurate.

52. Forty-five persons of the other 154 who attended the luncheons came as agency representatives. Of the remaining 109 persons present at the luncheons, 30 held 49 Chest or agency Board memberships; and the wives of five of these also were Board members.

53. Of course, many of those who could not be classified as Welfare Community Leaders may be highly interested in the work of the Chest and its agencies. For example, some may have been Boy Scout Masters, Girl Scout Leaders, members of Kirschbaum Center, etc. We were unable to test for such relations; nevertheless, the 80 per cent who are not leaders should not be regarded as having no interest in the Welfare Community.

54. We here include Firm, Executive, and Employee pledges as the Total pledge. Analysis of Firm pledge alone would have been difficult since some firms report the Firm pledge with Employee pledge; and other firms report Employee pledge with Executive pledge.

55. Accounted for by different numbers of employees in 1954 and 1955 and in the two groups.

56. By analysis of variance.

57. Defined here as "above or below the average (arithmetic mean) total pledge in 1954."

58. To simplify the problem (in time) we took a sample of 100 of the 1,600 firms according to the following scheme, but otherwise at random.

NUMBERS IN SAMPLE

|  | Generosity in 1954 | |
| --- | --- | --- |
| Attendance | Below average[a] | Above average[b] |
| Attenders | 25 | 25 |
| Non-attenders | 25 | 25 |

[a]Less than $1150.
[b]More than $1150.

59. The analysis gave the following results:

TABLE A

ANALYSIS OF GENEROSITY AND ATTENDANCE
AS FACTORS IN THE PERCENTAGE INCREASE IN AMOUNT PLEDGED

| Source of variation | Variation | Degrees of freedom | Mean square | F |
| --- | --- | --- | --- | --- |
| Error | 1,100,369.84 | 96 | 11,462.19 | — |
| Attendance | .06 | 1 | .06 | — |
| Generosity | 5,859.90 | 1 | 5,859.90 | — |
| Interaction | 2,161.31 | 1 | 2,161.31 | — |

TABLE B

ANALYSIS OF GENEROSITY AND ATTENDANCE
AS FACTORS IN THE PERCENTAGE INCREASE IN PER-EMPLOYEE PLEDGES

| Source of variation | Variation | Degrees of freedom | Mean square | F |
|---|---|---|---|---|
| Error | 1,203,503.60 | 96 | 12,662.12 | — |
| Attendance | 3,945.10 | 1 | 3,945.10 | — |
| Generosity | 8,087.40 | 1 | 8,087.40 | — |
| Interaction | 27.77 | 1 | 27.77 | — |

TABLE C

ANALYSIS OF GENEROSITY AND ATTENDANCE
AS FACTORS IN THE DOLLAR INCREASE IN AMOUNT PLEDGED

| Source of variation | Variation | Degrees of freedom | Mean square | F | P |
|---|---|---|---|---|---|
| Error | 1,215,053,841 | 96 | 12,656,811 | — | — |
| Attendance | 19,987,158 | 1 | 19,987,158 | 1.5792 | .05 |
| Generosity | 138,135,360 | 1 | 138,135,360 | 10.9139 | .01 |
| Interaction | 14,692,656 | 1 | 14,692,656 | 1.1608 | .05 |

60. Significant at the 1 per cent level.

61. We do not believe this is an insurmountable problem—it has been handled in situations even more delicate than that of the Chest.


CHAPTER 12

1. This remark, however warranted as of the date of writing, might no longer be so by the date of publication, since the Chest continued to change after we ceased to study it. This warning might well be extended to much else of what we report. Such studies as this cannot avoid their own historic limits.

2. In both cases, of course, there is "feedback," and national policy "responds to" some "averaging" of local votes or vetoes; but this should not be allowed to obscure the main point.

3. It will, of course, be obvious that whatever is done to improve "the Chest as it is" will have a bearing one way or the other on the prospects of a wider federation. We do not know which way this would weigh because "improvement" would, for many, remove present obstacles to wider federation ("You can't merge a successful concern in a failing one") but for many others, the same improvement would remove the pressure for any further federation at all ("We need a United Fund here to get us out of the rut").

4. Throughout, however, we have followed lay terminology and referred to the paid workers, trained or not, as "professionals."

5. See later in this chapter, and also chapter 14. See also chapters 10 and 11 regarding "rule and government."

6. It should be especially recalled here that what is said is believed to be true up to the point where our interviewing ceased, i.e., April 1, 1956. Allowance may have to be made for changes occurring since that date. See also note 1.

7. This description does not include volunteer or volunteered personnel. The diagram is based upon findings in a number of interviews, and direct and extended observations by our staff, mainly the latter.

8. To some extent, an informal communications network which has some co-ordinating function did develop around one of the Campaign Associates. But these activities are

without formal sanction, explicit or implicit, and this limits their effectiveness. Any decision made at this informal level suffers from three major weaknesses: (1) it can be, and often is, superseded by a decision at the formal level; (2) action depends on "voluntary" agreement by the participants and, as often happens, individuals change their views and attitudes with little, if any, communication of these changes to their confrères, i.e., there is no feedback; and (3) "negotiating" time for such "voluntary" agreements is excessive and expensive.

9. The Chest often throws its entire work force into "crash" operations which, in the light of later developments, turn out to be not nearly so important of accomplishment as they seemed at the time. Of course, in setting up a campaign, situations do develop which require diversion of all available manpower, but, it seems to us, this occurs more frequently than is necessary or useful. It seems almost to become the traditional way of working—what one might call a "routine of crisis" or a "crisis routine."

10. The two Campaign Associates spend considerable time outside the office in "cultivation" work. The lack of secretaries makes it very difficult to arrange appointments or change the time of appointments with the persons being "cultivated." Hence some persons outside the Chest feel that the Chest is careless in its dealings with them. This tends to carry over into a view that the entire Chest operation is inefficient.

11. On one occasion, a particular campaign news release was sent out without the knowledge of the Campaign Associate most directly concerned. The release was in error and resulted in considerable additional work by the Associate to smooth over the rather difficult situation which developed. On another occasion, we were told, the lack of co-ordination between a Campaign Associate and the Labor Relations Secretary resulted in one very large company refusing to carry on an employee solicitation. Such breakdowns seem to be numerous, rather than unusual, and occur most frequently in situations of unusual importance.

12. His statement of his duties (besides the nominal ones) says "they are to train union members to be aware of the Community Chest agencies and their services, and to operate a referral service to agencies for union members"—which duplicates, it would seem, the referral service of the Health and Welfare Council.

13. Even when the stated view of the national federation towards a particular proposal is favorable, the Labor Relations Secretary has refused to carry out a Chest program because of "local conditions." Questioning about the "local conditions" produces coy answers such as, "You fellows wouldn't know about that."

14. The Chest Board has union representatives as members. We were told that the Labor Relations Secretary, feeling that he had not received an adequate salary increase, brought two union people (not Board members) with him to negotiate an additional increase with the General Manager. The General Manager knew nothing of the "grievance" until the appearance of this unusually constituted "Grievance Committee."

15. The "Schools Program" exemplifies the lack of planning and the crisis nature of the operation. Although a schools program has been in operation for almost an entire year, the Chest still has not decided any of the basic principles on which the program is to be founded. The purposes of the program have been variously stated as "to educate the children" and "to increase giving." Yet "educate" *for what*, and "increase giving" *when* and *by whom* are not mentioned or much thought about. The Chest, then, has not decided even the most basic question as to whether to emphasize, in this area, long-run or short-run considerations. The question of whether the program is to educate the children in the whole area of private (and perhaps, public) philanthropy, or only make converts to the Chest program has not been considered, as far as we know. After all, it is not clear that a program emphasizing the Chest to the exclusion of other "good works" would be more beneficial to the Chest than would a program designed to enlighten the student as to the problems of philanthropy. Indeed, if the Chest has a good "case" at all, this view can hardly be admitted. (We are describing a situation which existed prior to January, 1956. Since that time, some members of the Chest staff have shown awareness of the problem but there is still, as of the date of writing, in late 1956, no established policy.)

16. Most frequently the references are to parallels with selling soap, refrigerators, or soft drinks.

17. Though one must admit that present-day advertising in the United States tends to emphasize the intangible benefits of tangible products, for example, the social status

to be derived from drinking Pepsi Cola or smoking L & M's (not to mention other ways of becoming a "man of distinction").

18. The creation of "Division A" from a part of Commerce and Industry division and the Professional division is typical. And only three years earlier, the Unit Accounts method of solicitation had superseded "Advanced Gifts." Thus, two thoroughgoing changes occurred within three years. In the same period a number of firms (about 50) were shifted in and out of the Unit Accounts.

The Metropolitan division was also a new unit in the 1955 campaign, and was composed of a number of formerly separate divisions. Even within Residential (a subdivision of Metropolitan) several changes (though relatively minor) were made, which contributed to a feeling of lack of continuity, for example, the method of attaching contributions to pledge cards, the use of stop cards, etc. One solicitor, a woman, was heard to complain, "They change it [the method of solicitation] every year." Another solicitor commented, "It would be a lot easier if we did things the same way as last time."

The examples used do not imply criticism (or, for that matter, lack of criticism) of the specific changes, but rather are used as indications of how much and in what ways the campaigns differ from year to year.

19. It seems improbable that a single individual would be able to handle all three functions alone, but this might be done with a scheme such as:

Service Functions
|

Research                    Budgeting                    Administration
                                                         and Personnel

or some variation of this.

It should be pointed out that since January, 1956, the Chest has combined Budgeting with Administration but has not included Personnel in the new arrangement. Nor has a complete program been established.

20. Moreover the data which U.C.F. & C. have to use are highly suspect if the records of the Indianapolis Chest (or indeed any other "data" we had occasion to check) are any criterion.

21. Not that "evaluations" are not made. Many people will talk about the "success" or "effectiveness" of a technique or program or gimmick, but this is always an intuitive evaluation—often correct, but probably just as often incorrect. At least, those we have examined were as often demonstrated to be wrong guesses as right ones.

22. Perhaps the first task facing a research director would be the installation of a records system with sufficient accuracy and flexibility to make research feasible (though there have been some recent improvements in this system).

23. This is not to say that research could not be carried on for the Chest's agencies (or, for that matter, anyone) but the research program should be as independent as possible. (However, it is hard to foresee when within the next five to ten years a Chest research staff would have time available for anything but its own research.)

24. As we have shown in chapters 8, 9, and 11, it is all too easy to stop short of important findings in examination of data. For example, had we stopped examination of per capita gifts after finding Indianapolis about in the middle for the forty-one cities, we would have been unable to develop the significant relations found for the deviations of percapita (chapters 6 and 9). In the case of campaign luncheons, the initial material looked as though attendance had been significant for pledging, but when only one other possibility was examined, it became clear that attendance was not significant (see chapter 11).

25. The Chest is not the only organization in which Type II situations have developed. They have happened even in the Indianapolis Red Cross campaign, but rarely. The difference is that in a Chest stigmatized as a "failure" the type is all too likely to appear too frequently.

26. The figure has been slightly altered to protect the informant.

27. The truth or untruth of the rumor is not quite such a matter of indifference operationally. The rumor does not need to be true to be effective. But, if true, then actualities will periodically reinforce it, and will speed circulation and renew feeling.

28. Indeed, not even the rumors assert such global charges. If there is at the

moment no crisis, they take the form of "Generally . . ." or "Mostly . . . ." Such qualification does not usually need to be made explicit. If we say, ordinarily, that a politician is "dishonest" we do not mean invariably and to all people; we mean "frequently enough to be notable."

29. Some of it—but by no means all—precipitated by our presence and our inquiry.

30. We should except the legal profession from this statement, since none of our evidence bears on it, and it was not discussed in our hearing, nor did newspaper reports make evident periodic conflicts as in the other professions. (For "cultural lag" in many other particulars, see chapter 3.)

31. On the importance of this distinction for the teacher, see Seeley, Sim, and Loosley, *Crestwood Heights* (Toronto: University of Toronto Press, 1956, pp. 258–9).

32. "At the most fundamental level," that is, in terms of present-day circumstances. One could inquire more fundamentally, but not for our purpose very profitably, perhaps, into the historic events and attitudes that became embodied in the law and the practice.

33. Rare in our experience, at least. Not only did most of those we talked to note and approve, but those we met who were concerned with or active in extending the bounds of the "merit system" talked as if they were in a minority, and mostly expressed limited ambitions in this direction, at that.

34. In one division of state government it looked for a while as though the game of ten little Indians were being played among the professionals concerned—except that the scores ran higher.

35. Again, this is not to say that there are no top-notch professionals in the public sector, or that patronage is everywhere king. No such sweeping assertions can be made. But anyone who has lived through even one election to see the pre-changeover scurrying for posts of safety, or job-offers to cover contingencies, or "explorations as to what's being offered" elsewhere will appreciate the tendency being pointed to. Even where the "merit system" obtains, its coverage at the top, where job-satisfaction must be paramount and power real, is nominal; a man who cannot be fired can be frozen into impotence, and hence—if he has self-respect—driven to "resignation."

36. Where strong paternal relations obtain without strong fraternal ones, the paternalized, more dependent than ever, feeling weaker may show timidity or, if bold, destructiveness. Where strong fraternal relations obtain without strong paternal ones, difficulties will arise in the relation of the agency to the community.

37. We know that "paternalism" is virtually a "dirty word" now, but this is surely because it is commonly used to refer to the essentially dependency-promoting activities of an authoritarian father. No such meaning is necessarily inherent in the term, and certainly none such is intended here.

38. Some teachers' unions, for instance, are sufficiently powerful—e.g., in Ontario—that "unjustified dismissals" or arbitrarily abrogated agreements are there a matter almost entirely of past history. The idea of a profession with a "union" is not a contradiction in terms; indeed the one is almost indispensable to the meaning of the other. (Cf. the bar associations and medical associations as cases in point.) The alternative to an effective union in this sphere would seem to be not "no union" but "no profession."

39. Both in the logical and moral sense of that term.

40. And, as we have observed, even when successful, curiously relegated back to limbo after the crisis has been met.

41. It is not, of course, to be assumed that the paternal-filial relation described implies some personal "strength" in the layman that is lacking in the "professional." We have seen no evidence of such differential distribution of strength. What is differentially distributed is power, and it is the place of the agency in the social structure—not the personal characteristics of laymen as against professionals—that calls for such quasi-paternal forms of behavior. And the choice actually made by any individual as to which part of the social structure to work in is bound up with far more considerations than personal strength or weakness.

42. We are not "casting doubt on our own witnesses" or aspersing our informants on this particular. We mean simply that we had no access to contemporary records bearing on the point, and so we had to rely wholly on the memory now of witnesses then.

43. The meaning of this representation—as of the Negro or Jewish or other minority representation—is not clear. It seems to be chiefly symbolic: an accolade, a gesture of

deference towards a group of growing importance. No one supposes—though the contrary pretense is often made—that these representatives actually "speak for" their minorities, or are intended so to do. Indeed, in the case of "labor," despite intensive investigation, we were unable to discover whether there was a "labor view" here to express, and, if so, what it was. In this and similar situations, there is, in fact, a conflict between the representative principle supposed and the natural behavior of the minority in question. The minority in having a "representative" elected to such a body is being allowed an opportunity to validate its new "respectability," and in order to do this it must play down its "difference from the rest of the community"; the representative principle, on the contrary, calls for action in terms of that difference. Under these circumstances a type of "representative" tends to arise who is unrepresentative in the sense that he is unlike his minority and like the majority; this makes for the much-desired "smooth" human relations, but for poor communication and uneven policy. For a comparable situation in the "politics of staying out of power" see *Crestwood Heights*, pp. 286, 287; 468.

44. This relatively recent conflict (1948-51) filled the newspapers with acrimonious debate. The ostensible issue was whether or not public relief records should be opened to public inspection. On the issue, the professional fraternity took the client-protective view and answered a resounding "No"; the newspapers took the taxpayer-protective view and answered a thundering "Yes." The outcome of the long-drawn battle was an unequivocal "Yes."

45. "The candle" to the professional is in this case more than his professional or personal interest. Here, as frequently elsewhere, he acts with divided heart because he genuinely fears to divide the Welfare Community and perhaps disserve his "clients" (via cut budgets) even in the short run and even for an ultimate long-term gain. Older professions face similar ethical issues (e.g., how much a patient's comfort may be sacrificed for scientific gain now and more comfort for more patients later) but have worked out accepted ways of resolving an issue where they cannot solve a problem.

46. Or seem to be. The claim is made. The genuine hope is that events will sometime justify the claim. But, with or without justification, the definition must stand for strategic reasons.

47. Councils are not, of course, alone in seeking to obscure such conflicts by "transcending" them. (See, e.g., Saul Alinsky, *Reveille for Radicals*, Chicago: University of Chicago Press, 1946.) This is not only a possible policy but one, under some circumstances, eminently workable and, perhaps, much to be preferred. The "under some circumstances," however, presupposes some common, meaningful "higher" value among the otherwise conflicting participants: for example, patriotism in war, the desire for self and mutual preservation under disaster conditions. What seems to make the Council procedure pragmatically dubious—as well as pretentious, perhaps—is the evident absence of any such transcendent widely shared value in reference to local welfare matters. For a discussion and definition of the problem, see M. G. Ross, *Community Organization, Theory and Principles* (New York: Harper & Brothers, 1955).

48. During the life of the research project, the Council achieved two most notable "gains." It began to function as the staff (advisory) arm of the Chest, so that it was in a preferred position to affect the fate of any agency via its Chest budget; and it also achieved a role as adviser to the principal local Foundation on all matters affecting local giving, so that it also had a quasi-judicial function in reference to sources of funds for the agencies, alternative to the Chest. The last achievement carried more weight and power than is immediately evident: since many other donors do, and still more are believed to, "follow the lead" of the Foundation in question, this particular control would be quite decisive. (That the agencies may exaggerate the amount of such control means only that they feel just as much "overpowered"—and act on that assumption in relation to the Council—as though the power were as great as they think it.)

49. One of the fears that is sure to arise among the laymen in considering the issue posed is that it will lead to requests for "still more money." While the problems we have been considering are not chiefly financial, this demand for higher salaries is sure to arise. As usual, such demands are based upon two different motives: the common and "rational" desire (which is the heartbeat of the free enterprise system) to get as much as possible of what there is to get; and the "irrational" motive to use money, in the face of insecurity, as a symbol of or substitute for security in one's job and social

relations. The emergence of adequate human relations in the welfare community would tend to diminish motivation of the second kind, but to give a means for the expression of legitimate ambitions of the first kind. This issue (of "proper" returns for labor) would then have to be met on its own merits, but would, in any case, be limited by the state of the national market for the services in question. The tendency would be for Indianapolis salary-scales then to approximate the rates in the national market. The belief that such an approximation can long be delayed is probably illusory in any case: we have made no systematic study of social-work salaries and turnover or mobility in Indianapolis, but there is reason to believe that in some fields it acts as a "training ground" for the better workers and the higher officers, so that the expense of apprenticeship, but not its benefits, tends to accrue to the local Welfare Community's costs.

50. We do not mean to imply what we do not know: that the benefits, narrowly or economically viewed, exceed the costs, though this may well be the case. We are only asserting that there *are* some substantial benefits to be taken into account in assessing costs.

51. Low-cost, in the burden that falls on any one corporation; low-cost, since the losses, if any, resulting from errors of judgment are charged off to the whole donor-aggregate; low-cost, since a great deal of the money involved would otherwise go into tax-payments. (This last is only an economy from the viewpoint of any one taxpayer, and not from that of all of them taken together.)

52. It is not a matter of getting good training or none, but of getting training or, literally, "counter-training." We have observed what is virtually training in practices that no well-run business would tolerate, i.e., "counter-training" for business utility.

53. Failing such close supervision, any such tests may provide positively misleading results at high cost, i.e., results that would more often produce error with the test than were previously provided without the test (and its cost).

54. The absence of close supervision will suggest to many that, in the eyes of "higher authority," either the enterprise is unimportant or that it does not make fair discrimination possible, and hence is not worth the effort.

55. Some national enterprises do indeed charge all such costs to their Personnel Department budgets, and expect and require personnel benefits and returns.

56. This tendency to provide on a just-not-sufficient basis was observed in many areas of behavior in Indianapolis—in giving, in planning, in providing time for meetings, in doing the necessary "homework," etc.—but we did not feel it sufficiently distinctive to Indianapolis to give it a place in chapter 3. Sudden death is in many situations, needless to say, preferable to slow starvation.

57. The reason for thinking this condition perhaps sufficient is that the "top top leadership" is precisely that group whose power, whose command over "loyalties," and whose ability to demand repayment of previous "favors" (or prepayment of future ones) is a maximum. Their very presence is therefore not merely an asset to the agency but bespeaks the command of other manpower assets. Moreover, in a great degree, their special skill lies in maximizing conforming behavior while minimizing coercion—or, at least, overt coercion—to secure it. But this is exactly what the agency wants or needs—maximum conformity with at least the air of willingness. (See chapter 5.)

58. By this we mean so many persons available at each defined rank.

59. This is also the problem of many an *actual* unfortunate personnel manager.

60. Some things can be done better by non-élite persons, since every skill is also a training against something (i.e., a handicap) and every status implies that there are some acts not consonant with retention of that status (i.e., a restraint).

61. This would ensure at least a good distribution between the "common arms" on one side and the agencies themselves, on the other; it would not ensure any best distribution between the several agencies in terms of *their* importance.

62. It is this inability to get together on matters vital to the successful operation of the "common arms" that helps to make us doubtful as to the virtues of further unification (see chapter 13). It is also the absence of any effective organization to exert pressure on behalf of donors for such rational utilization of what they have to give that helps make us sympathetic to the idea of a donors' association (see below in text; also chapters 13 and 14).

63. And yet, of course, nearly every emergence of a "higher" unit of government requires just this: the emergence of the United States required, for instance, the abro-

gation of the treaty-making and entry-barring powers of the several states. In effect, in major matters the care and keeping of the states *is* in the hands of the federal government. In the present state of things in welfare, the agencies seem able neither to relinquish sufficient powers to a common "government" (the Chest-and-Council or some such body) nor to operate satisfactorily the present semi-confederacy.

64. Where there is enough of a good for all (e.g., air) few people care who gets how much. Distribution problems become acute with scarcity.

65. See David L. Sills, *The National Foundation.* It was often remarked in Indianapolis in this connection that the leadership group was so limited that the same people had to be asked—by the same agency and by other agencies—to perform in the same roles over and over again. At the same time, a study by the Indiana Heart Foundation (Marion County Committee) indicated a vast pool of untapped leadership, volunteers willing to work who had "never before been asked to do anything." Both sets of impressions are probably correct: there is a vast pool of unused lower-level leadership and rank and file, and there is so tremendous an overuse of the limited amount of top talent *available* that the tendency is to see virtually the same group of faces assembled around a number of Board tables, or in any major fundraising inside committee. (The key word is "available": there is also a very large segment of the highest social status group not used by and evidently not available to the philanthropic enterprises. See chapter 11.)

66. What can be done by these methods should not, however, be underestimated. When the limited pool of executives lent to the Chest in the campaign period to flesh out its normally skeleton staff is used at one point for stuffing envelopes and at another for running errands and similar office-boy routines something other than maximum efficiency in utilization of resources is surely being achieved. Although the outward result is the same, the procedure should not be confused with the practice of some religious Orders in assigning menial tasks to highly placed personnel for the sake of inducing humility or educing a suitable expression of it. It is doubtful in the first place that this is the spiritual outcome for these "loaned executives," and in any case it is obvious from the other campaign efforts that humility in the soliciting organization is precisely what is not being aimed at.

67. The reader should, perhaps, be fairly and explicitly warned that the same possibility attaches to the argument of this chapter and other chapters, wherever value-problems are involved. The sole differential assets of the writers are relative detachment from the issues immediately involved and whatever has accrued to them by way of wisdom, knowledge, or caution from the study of other institutions, in Indianapolis and elsewhere.

68. And the logic by which it or some other body would have to proceed on a more grandiose scale if further unification (United Fund or some other form) were to take place.

69. And, *a fortiori,* the logic on which a more ambitious unification would have to be founded.

70. The problem of achieving disinterestedness (*in this sense*) may also further reinforce the logic behind the proposal of a donors' association. It is probably practically impossible and perhaps morally unreasonable not to expect an agency to issue propaganda, limited chiefly and sometimes only by what it can get away with or what "the traffic will bear." It is probably equally impossible practically and unreasonable morally to expect donors of time or money to make sensible or apt decisions on the issues when surrounded by the clamor of the propaganda, frequently party to the making of it, and *unrepresented and undefended in their capacity as donors* and (with others) community policy-makers.

71. It should simultaneously be recognized that all practical collective decisions have the same character to a large extent, including more particularly the public law. The difference between a good law and a bad one, or a wise one and an unwise one, may depend on the degree to which experience and expert knowledge are permitted to inform but not decide the enactive process. But judgment is inescapable, and democratic theory does argue that wide consensus in important matters (rather than the expert decision) produces the best decision, not always and at every point, but simply over-all and in the long run. This view, and the preferences founded upon it, the authors obviously share.

72. The situation is caught by the German proverb "Wer A sagt, muss B sagen": Who says A, must also say B. It also suggests Lenin's saying that Communism is not a train that permits you to get on and off wherever you please. No matter how dissimilar in other respects, the same may be true for the organization of the private sector of the Welfare Community.

73. Actually what is meant is some further fund unification. Technically, Indianapolis already has a United Fund. (See chapter 13.)

74. For some suggestive material see William Foote Whyte (ed.), *Industry and Society* (New York: McGraw Hill, 1946); F. J. Roethlisberger and William J. Dickson, *Management and the Worker* (Cambridge, Mass.: Harvard University Press, 1943), F. J. Roethlisberger, *The Human Problems of an Industrial Civilization* (New York: Macmillan, 1933); Elliott Jaques, *The Changing Culture of a Factory* (London: Tavistock Publications Ltd., 1951).

75. Cf. Aileen Ross, *Social Forces*, XXXII (March, 1954), and Robert Blishen, unpublished M.A. thesis, McGill University.

76. Doubtless in the course of a campaign every motive from love to hate, from desire to over-conform to desire to over-distinguish oneself, operates usefully (to the MOPS fundraiser) in someone. As suggested in chapter 1, we cannot hope to examine questions of idiosyncratic motivation here. But for additional material on "rewards," see chapters 10 and 11.

77. David L. Sills, *The National Foundation*, vol. IV, pp. 41-51.

78. See Aileen Ross, *op. cit.*, Robert R. Blishen, *op. cit.*, and Roland J. Pellegrin and Charles H. Coates, *American Journal of Sociology*, LXI (March, 1956).

79. *Certainty* of reward is by no means necessary, but only belief in the possibility— and occasional confirmation—as the successful operation of the American economic system amply demonstrates. For detailed illustrative confirmation of this view, see Ely Chinoy, *Automobile Workers and the American Dream* (New York: Doubleday, 1955). Psychologists now believe that what they call intermittent or "irregular reinforcement" works even better in evoking effort among rats also.

80. This does not apply only to middle-range and lower leadership, which stands to gain in occupational and social status. Even top leadership must somehow occasionally "revalidate" status by act. (See *Crestwood Heights*, chapter 10.)

81. Even though the overlap in personnel may be considerable, as everyone well knows, the social upper crust and the centers of power are not constituted by the same persons, i.e., we have two *related* systems here, not one.

82. Consciously making "traditions" is no novelty in America. Cf. the history of the new Air Force Academy which had "traditions" before the building materials were settled or the training staff shaken down.

83. Sadly, we cannot go beyond this impression, to say that no Chest succeeds without this condition or that all suceed with it.

84. Changes, not necessarily by way of adding, subtracting, or substituting personnel itself, but in the skills evidenced and the procedures employed.

85. "Smooth," not in the sense of eliminating friction—the Dale Carnegie dream-world's smoothness—but in the sense of eliminating non-productive friction, i.e., of so utilizing unavoidable (and desirable) differences and tensions as to benefit the different parties to the enterprise. Actually identity would be as fatal as totality of difference. Professionals utterly like "their" laymen would be of no help to them in doing precisely what those laymen want done but cannot do by themselves.

86. We do not know whether there was or was not frequently in Indianapolis a better choice of a professional at the time of selection. What we have noted about the widespread "distrust of the expert" (chapter 3), what little we know about comparative salary levels, what we have observed and reported about conditions of tenure and stability, and what has been observed of those who leave Indianapolis by choice or need, would incline us (if we had to guess) to believe that Indianapolis frequently chooses and still more frequently keeps personnel of something considerably less than the highest caliber available. (It is not, of course, to be inferred from this observation that any particular professional who has endured in Indianapolis is, *prima facie*, other than of the highest caliber.)

87. It was possible for a campaign chairman at an assignment meeting to respond to the name of one of the town's leading citizens (probably among the highest status

1/20 of 1 per cent) by asking "Who's *he?*" (not in derision but in ignorance). It was possible for a committee of top-middle leaders to believe that they had easy access for advice to "top top leadership" and to discover too late that no such access was possible.

Similar errors occur on the professional side even to the point of confounding people of similar surname but vastly different social status. In fact, the preoccupation of the professional with power and influence as a means to securing giving conformity is as notable as what looks like his trained incapacity to orient himself correctly with reference to it. For most, the whole sociological literature of the last twenty years on this subject might as well not exist, and the techniques for orientation (see e.g., *Social Class in America*) might as well lie undiscovered. A great part, probably, of this selective inattention stems from the preoccupation with the practical as against the theoretical—which, as we have previously indicated, is at the root of so much practical difficulty.

88. The exceptions are frequent enough to make it worth our drawing attention to another common type-situation where, relying on his capacity for double-talk and the layman's inability to analyse and check, the professional manifests an assurance in selecting the facts to be put at the layman's disposal and in manipulating the sentiments of individuals and the decisions of groups. There is some reason to think that this type of situation is emerging towards ascendancy. (Cf. chapter 5.)

88a. And, incidentally, also that part of the message by which the manpower is itself, in part, recruited and sustained.

89. The Chest claims, of course, not only to be the harbinger of order in fundraising, but, through its agencies, the indispensable element in the preservation of social order too. The following quotation from a campaign chairman in a letter to solicitors illustrates: "About the only reason we don't have gangs running wild here is that the Red Feather Agencies which work with youth groups are doing a superhuman job."

90. Or—in many cases—empirical research as to what is workable, or what are the relations among efforts and results. The division into problems of value and problems of means is, of course, in classic form. Cf. Max Weber's use of *Wertrationalität* and *Zweckrationalität* as tools of analysis. The heuristic utility of the distinction is not diminished by the recognition (cf., for example, John Dewey) that what are ends and what are means depend on moment-to-moment orientation, and are, in any case, by no means independent definititions. By values, in this context, we mean what he meant, i.e., ends-in-view. Cf. John Dewey, *Human Nature and Conduct* (New York: Henry Holt, 1922).

91. The same would be true for much other MOPS fundraising, and perhaps non-MOPS fundraising as well. Certainly it is not the distinction between operational and capital campaigns, nor the distinction between periodic and non-periodic ones, that makes any difference in these respects.

92. Assuming, perhaps precariously, that there is a "community," and that one can meaningfully postulate some convergent or common "will" among its members. The one is, of course, true to the degree that the other is, i.e., these are two ways of saying the same thing.

93. It may well be a coincidence, but surely it is a striking one, that the vocabulary of so much fundraising is the vocabulary of war. Military ranks characterize some fund-raising organizations. All, or nearly all, "campaign." All have an "objective" and "objectives." They "go over the top." They have "victory" dinners; or they talk of "defeat." Some have zero hour, and the equivalent of D-day or V-day. Much talk is of "generals," "corporals" and "rank and file." Phrases such as "ably led," "suitably captained," etc., occur. "Strategy" and "tactics" are discussed.

The vocabulary of politics (which overlaps that of war) and the vocabulary of sport and of selling sometimes predominate, but the abiding definitions sound bellicose. Perhaps half bellicosity, half boyish play at Red Indians is one of the 1956 campaign slogans of the Chest, "Scalp Chief Red Feather."

94. "Blanketing the community" with propaganda (called, of course, "education" or "information") via massive use of the newspapers, radio, TV, streetcar cards, posters, dodgers, throwaways, pamphlets, bulletin board notices, word-of-mouth communication and the much desired (in Indianapolis) billboard on Monument Circle, is the under-standably looked-for consummation of months of "public-relations work" in what is now defined as an all-year-round campaign. The defined end is that "no one can fail to hear our message," i.e., essentially to develop a captive audience.

95. Also a term from the military vocabulary, though adopted as well by that type of "selling" which equally bases its thinking on the warlike model.

96. As reported to us in one city: "If you don't get the right decision [to conform fully to Chest-set 'standards'] you see who you've got on the Board that might work on whoever won't go along [the Chief executive of the Corporation]. If there's nobody there, you check over their accountants and attorneys. Or, if you can't get anything that way a lot of these men [Board members] are in other businesses or they [the attorneys, accountants, etc.] have partners and you may be able to get to them. We keep all that on a card like this [showing card] and we try to keep it up to date and keep adding."

97. Perhaps the principal variation in use is seasonal: before the campaign the excited, gleeful vocabulary of manoeuvre and outmanoeuvre; during the campaign the jubilant lingo of victory and the bitter vocabulary of defeat ("those s.o.b.'s!" "that bastard . . ."); between old campaign's end and new campaign's beginning the earnest talk of education, community organization, etc.

98. We have in mind, for instance, that a more open and exact definition would regulate expectations sufficiently to reduce shock and conflict within persons (lay and professional) and the early "burning out" of motivation and the extension of cynicism. It can hardly be overemphasized that for many laymen their entry into the ranks of the Chest (or those of a similar organization) rests upon the hope and expectation that here—precisely in contrast to their occupational lives—aims and methods may be nearer to their "ideals." (For "ideals" we may substitute, as someone has said, "what their mothers told them the world was like as against what the neighbors say it is.") Similarly, many of the professionals entered the field in the hope that (like the profession of medicine, say) it would furnish a way for the expression of ideals without making undue financial self-sacrifice a necessity. Both of these groups exhibit the signs of moral shock, and its repercussions, as they learn what is actually involved. Such "learning" goes forward, again, in all professions and institutions, but older ones tend to have clearer definitions and initial expectations, and have long since worked out a set of procedures for producing such disillusionment as is necessary, and for explaining and containing it without destructive effects on the learner or the institution.

99. So that it corresponds pretty well with present behavior, with only clarity of thought and aptness of organization added.

100. Widely and openly defined, if strategy permits—but at least clearly defined for the highest echelons of command.

101. "Open covenants openly arrived at" may be as difficult a principle (in the absolute) in philanthropy as it is in diplomacy. But the very degree to which this is so probably defines the actual latent enmities or, at least, conflicts of interest and oppositions of force.

102. Note that, there as here, "normal" relations do not mean relations of unadulterated amity either; they mean relations in which, given an attenuation of belligerency, the parties deal *more* openly with each other and deal *more* in terms of the common ground or joint interest they have than in terms of the contested ground or competitive or conflicting interest.

103. This also would have to be done gradually, partly for appearance' sake, partly so as not to dislocate the organization in transition. There might even still be a place for some of these as a deceptive screen, but not, of course, in effective policy-making positions.

104. We do not know at this point whether these alleged economies are real or spurious. See chapter 13.

105. The procedures indicated do not sound like and are not much like a "campaign." They imply negotiation and the meeting of minds rather than fighting and the putting down of opposition or the "putting over"—as it is so frequently called—of a "message."

106. Note that this step would be avoided altogether (as a matter for negotiation or individual decision) upon the general adoption by the corporations of the "Shell formula." The Shell formula makes the corporate gift: the firm's employment multiplied by the area's average family size, multiplied by last year's Chest take per family. What it implies, if generalized, is that individuals make the decisions as to gifts and corporations match their gifts in the following year. In thus locating the pace-setting with individuals, the formula removes from management to a sensible degree the onus of

planning the city's "voluntary" enterprises as well, and potentially removes from management most blame or credit for the result. The individual donor resumes a freedom—and a responsibility.

107. Unless this is "automatically" settled as described in note 106, or otherwise.

108. This view of course rouses the fear of "being a sucker" and "letting someone get away with something." This is not necessary; a tax would prevent it.

109. About 98.5 per cent in 1955.

110. For the weaknesses of our data, the necessity for recomputing the figures we were given, etc., see chapter 9.

111. As the "research director" of the Chest of another large city, said (of any question or datum): "If it won't make money for us, we're not interested." The trouble is not with his laudable singleness of aim, but with the narrowness and datedness of his conception of what will make money. As usual, these people believe they are modelling themselves on the businessman, and they are—the businessman of sixty years or more ago.

112. One often finds the same blindness in army combat officers who maintain contempt for the paperwork necessary to keep a combat unit functioning. The overtones of such expressions as "flying a desk in Washington" express what is meant. Such attitudes in the combat team may be readily understandable; if they persist at command level, combat may snarl into immobility and impotence. The Chest's problem is similar.

113. This over-emphasis characterizes not only the Chest, but many agency Boards, perhaps because this is one point where laymen feel "at home." The result often is increased "efficiency" in doing what may be of no importance to anyone.

114. We take as "first order facts" the accounts, representing the pledges. Simp'e sums of these or averages are the "second order facts" we are talking about. Comparisons among such averages or trend lines based on the performance of different years would be, in this vocabulary, "third order facts." Such higher order material is, in the Chest circles we have penetrated, even more dubious.

115. A "problem" in so far as the lack of secure factual foundations is reflected in generalized insecurity about the Chest and many agencies in many laymen.

116. Some Chests employ such personnel for such purposes, and also for other functions, such as keeping track of announced industrial promotions to facilitate "cultivation" and "public relations." They tend to call these people "Research Directors." This titling is, we think, to be deplored as misleading both to Leading Donors and to Donor Leaders.

117. They suspect it does, and we have no contrary evidence. But there exists no evidence of the kind that would justify a business decision of parallel scale, e.g., the selection of a brand name or advertising theme.

118. Even so, there is room to be concerned lest, with the addition of market research, united fundraising may still further weaken and overwhelm the non-united donors. This concern furnishes another reason for considering seriously a Donors' Association.

119. Dreams—practical dreams—may go beyond this point. Since many large donors express themselves as being unhappy because "there is no training to tell you anything about [wise] giving," and since, obviously, there is no systematic or adequate training for fundraisers, and since, further, there is no common ground of fact and ethic between would-be giver and would-be taker, the desirability of an eventual Philanthropic Training Institute (for both givers and takers) located in some suitable university, might well be considered. If the Training Institute came into existence only some years after the Research Institute, so that (a) there was a reliable body of significant information around which to build teaching, and (b) whatever "teaching" there was would be suffused or imbued with the research outlook, there would be a fair chance that finally the tone of negotiation and the attitude of inquiry might come to substitute for the actualities of "attack" and "defence" in the field of philanthropy itself. A large part of the necessity of this report itself stems from the lack of cleared common ground between fund-giver and fund-taker. We have reason to think that some large fund-givers are already seeking some such solution for themselves as is here suggested. (We are not overlooking the fact that some faint approximation to what we here call for already exists, for example, in the course in "Educational Promotion and Fundraising" at Teachers College, Columbia University. What we are suggesting requires, we believe, a much broader and deeper approach to the whole problem, and one that involves future donors as well as fundraisers in a common enterprise in research and their own education in this field.)

## CHAPTER 13

1. The phrase "duplication, overlap and waste"—applied indifferently to fundraising activities themselves, or to the activities of the agencies thus supported—was so often employed in our hearing, nearly always with all three terms specified, that we were almost driven to abbreviate this to "d.o.w. complaint."

2. Indeed it is difficult not to believe that this is already the case as the lone donor confronts the Chest, and, *a fortiori*, the tendency as unification proceeds at the present rate.

3. The difference cannot be overemphasized. The ideal type of unified fundraising looks like A of Chart 46: a monolithic recipient confronts donors as single, divided, isolated, and weak as possible. The ideal type of unified giving looks like diagram B: a monolithic giving body faces out upon single, divided, isolated, and competitive agencies. Nobody wants quite these ideal types, but these are the "poles" towards which discussion tends to be drawn, while the weight of the present effort is to move affairs, as far as feasible, toward A.

When we speak of "middle ground" we shall mean either something less than a monolithic structure on either side (as in diagrams C and D) or a similar degree of unification in both (as in E).

4. When analysis of the current talk reveals no clear definition of the meaning of an "agency," no agreement as to which agencies are to be held in mind, no clear image of what kinds of funds are to be involved, and vagueness about which functions are to be communized, the reason for the discussion becomes obvious.

5. It is customary to say that Chests and similar MOPS fundraising confederacies raise money for "social agencies" or for "social service agencies," or some such term. But this is defining the ill-defined by the worse-defined. After consulting encyclopedias, social work texts, social work yearbooks, and the constitutions of the agencies themselves, and after consulting and discussing with social workers at great length, we have been unable to find a definition of a social agency that seems sufficiently broad to apply to those organizations now so called and also sufficiently narrow to exclude closely related enterprises. We may have succeeded no better at a definition, but at least we have attempted to define the little-known by the better-known, instead of the worse-known.

6. For definitions of "sales" and "gifts," see below, note 12.

7. A social agency supporting itself wholly out of "sales" might be suspect, but would still, presumably, be a social agency. During the life of this project, one social worker set himself up in "private practice"—just like a physician. A formal association of such free private enterprise social workers, paying themselves salaries but otherwise only covering costs, would fall within the agency area as we have defined it, but not in the area of potential fundraising unification.

8. If a "United Fund" including the present Chest were to be organized in Indianapolis on the basis most commonly discussed now, we should have, for instance:

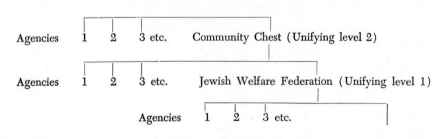

"United Fund" (Unifying level 3)

Agencies    1    2    3 etc.    Community Chest (Unifying level 2)

Agencies    1    2    3 etc.    Jewish Welfare Federation (Unifying level 1)

Agencies    1    2    3 etc.

At a later date there might be demand for a union of United Funds!

9. Indeed, so strongly does this seem to be the case in Kansas City, Mo., that Com-

munity Studies, Inc., a most powerful research and planning body, reports it has given up recommending that *any* agency be abolished, and has concluded that the best that can be done is to find new functions for old agencies, if existing functions make little social planning sense. See William D. Bryant in *Human Development Bulletin*, Sixth Annual Symposium (Chicago: Human Development Student Organization, Committee on Human Development, 1955), p. 20. Bryant also quotes Professor E. C. Hughes: ". . . social agencies never die they just change function."

We also are thus driven to discuss the problem of unified fundraising apart from the question of organic federation or reorganization of agencies, although this question of federation is a logically prior question, i.e., it would make more administrative sense to ask, first "What functions should be federated or reorganized in what agencies?" and only then, "How shall the fundraising needs of *these* 'agencies' be jointly or severally organized?"

10. Again, if this exercise in definition seems pedantic, may we remind the reader that we have listened to heated discussion for and against United Fund where one man (a most eminent citizen and protagonist) thought it meant an agency to take care of *all* forms of giving (down to the little "office pool" for a departing secretary) and another that it meant nothing more than "getting the Red Cross to come in with the Chest."

To take a concrete instance, we listened at great length to an enthusiastic, not to say passionate defence of the United Fund idea by one of the city's leading citizens. Not only did he defend the idea, but assured us "It's coming. The businessmen of this community won't stand for anything else." And he proposed to lead the fight for "it." Then in a revealing final comment, he said "We [his business] are going to put it in next year." We inquired what this meant, and it turned out to mean that his organization was adopting "in-plant federation." (See discussion below in text and description in note 26.) When we then asked, after pointing out the difference in meanings, which of the two he really wanted and thought others wanted, he said in so many words "in-plant federation." The idea that his organization would not be able to pick and choose beneficiaries made him indignant. Certainly he didn't want anybody—a United Fund—telling him what share of the organization's gift should go to what philanthropies. "You want to keep that [freedom of choice among charities]. What we care about is one campaign—just the one campaign [in his business]."

Small wonder that the virtues and vices of the scheme seemed different to each—and to the others around the table who had other unexplicit definitions.

11. This assumes, of course, that expenditure is greater than income; otherwise the agency has a "surplus."

12. Even the term "gift" is not clear, and this lack of definiteness, too, adds its quota to the confusion, since again some money transactions that are thought of by some as part of the activity to be brought under control are thought of by others as falling clearly outside the area. *In this context*, the term opposite to "gift" is "sale": the ideal "gift" is one where money passes from the donor and nothing passes to him in exchange; the ideal "sale" is one where money passes from the donor and full market value in something he normally wants (in the everyday sense of that term) passes to him in exchange. Instances can be found all the way between the two extremes. A Girl Scout Cookie Sale is a typical mixed case: if it is true for a given sale of these cookies that they represent nearly full market value in something normally wanted (in that quantity and at that time) by the "buyer," they represent a "sale"; if, however, they represent a little less than market value, and if they are bought "indulgently" ("We *could* use some") rather than out of want, by this much there is a gift element in the transaction. The mailed Christmas and Easter Seal "Sales" on which some organizations depend, represent "gifts" in so far as the value of the "merchandise" falls well below the "voluntary" purchase price. The "license number key tags" are of the same character in this respect. "Raffles" and "lotteries" or "drawings" (for charity purposes) are hard to classify because no one knows the fair market value of a "chance," i.e., even in an open market there would be a discrepancy (the entrepreneur's profit and overhead) between the price and the true statistical or equity value of a chance. Since there is no regular open market in these things, one cannot tell whether charity lotteries simply appropriate for charity the entrepreneurial profit, or whether there is an additional gift element involved.

What is at issue may be illustrated in the following diagram, which shows on one axis the "money cost" to a donor, and on the other axis the market value received (assuming, again, of course, that he "wants" the item received). The line OS, at every point of which cost and value are equal is the line of "sale." The line OG, at every point of which (except O) there is a cost with no return value is the line of pure "gift." Any other line in the area OGS is a mixed case: part "gift," part "sale," e.g., the line AB might represent the Girl Scout Cookie Sale; or, to take another example, membership in the Businessmen's Club of a Y.M.C.A. where the fee at that level carries both the true costs and some part of the costs of program for others.

The area between all such lines as AB and the line of "sale" represents in every case the area of gift that must be thought of as the subject of potential unification.

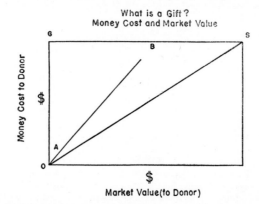

What is a Gift?
Money Cost and Market Value

Market Value(to Donor)

13. By "subsidizing production" is meant payment for the difference between market value and cost, where the cost is higher than market value. The "camp" item in the hypothetical budget is of this kind: the cost is known to exceed the commercial value, but the "loss" involved has perhaps been accepted for non-commercial reasons.

14. By "subsidizing selling" is meant payment for the difference between sale-price and market value where sale-price is set below market value.

15. On the analogy of agenda—the things to be done—the donanda are the things (or sums) to be given.

16. This is not wholly so (and hence we do not have a true "scale") since among the actual suggestions put to us, at least one recommended only the unification of the solicitor army, i.e. any one solicitor would solicit in one interview for all the relevant agencies one after the other. He would ask, for example, for the Chest Gift, then the Red Cross Gift, then the T.B. Association Gift; and so on (not necessarily in that order, of course).

17. Of a somewhat different nature from the *locally* organized United Fund (which we have just discussed) is what might be referred to as a *nationally* organized United Fund. During World War II, the United States used a system very similar to this. In that period, practically all fund drives (with some outstanding exceptions) were combined into a single campaign with state-wide quotas set by a national planning group. These state quotas were broken into county and city quotas. The quota of each geographic unit included local "needs" as well as state and national "needs." For further discussion of such schemes, see Harold J. Seymour, *Design for Giving* (New York: Harper, 1947).

Many of the top leaders (both locally and nationally) were drawn into active sponsorship of and participation in the War Fund Drive. This suggests that a national United Fund might well succeed in attracting to itself the top leadership, unless, of course, the War Fund participation of the leaders stemmed only from patriotic "motivations."

Under such a federation, the donor has still less control of the distribution of his gift and feebler protection of his interest than with total local federation. With a national United Fund, the major decisions are made outside the local community, by a still more remote group.

We have found no way of determining how efficient such an operation would be. Nor can we say whether it could be "successful" at all in a non-crisis situation.

18. On the basis of official definition alone, a situation could arise in which a United Fund would be a great deal less of a unified fundraising organization than are many Chests.

19. We could now define a "Chest"! It is simply a unified fundraising organization that for at least some fundraising activities, and some part of the donandum and donor-aggregate supplies joint facilities for some social agencies, but not for the Red Cross or any major health agency.

20. "Somehow," because the mere designation "United Fund" leaves the question of organizational structure wide open. Any of the following would be a "United Fund":

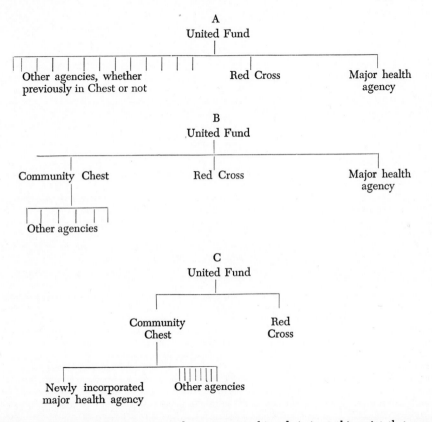

Since in most cases form A cannot be or is not achieved, it is at this point that some agency executives (and others) feel that a distinction between "second-class citizens" and "first-class citizens" is being set up in terms of those respectively on lower and upper tiers of the diagram. These are not, of course, "paper distinctions": an agency which in reality is in a position corresponding to one level of the chart *is* actually in a very different position as to power, bargaining and money-getting from an agency at another level.

21. This simplest definition is evidently frequently not what the layman understands. The "man in the street"—as far as we have encountered him—evidently thinks "United Fund" means he will only be asked for a money gift once a year by one organization, for all charitable purposes (except church).

But no more than one United Fund out of those raising $500,000 or more (for 1956) includes all the Bix Six health agencies, with acceptance of the funds agreed to by the local organization of the national organization. (And it is not clear that the one possible actually does so. See *1956 Experience in United Funds,* Tables 3 and 4, p. 3.) Where the United Fund is sufficiently powerful in the community, the federation may raise money to be used for the work of a particular agency, and then if the agency refuses the money—as happens frequently—the federation spends the money for the type of work for which the agency would have used the funds. Where the federation does not wield enough strength in the community to make the claim that it is raising funds for the support of the work of agencies which refuse to join, such agencies have claimed success in separate campaigns. (One of the problems in analysis of United Funds stems from the reporting procedure by which the fund reports an appeal as "included" in the fund, whether or not the local affiliate of the national organization has agreed to participate.)

Moreover, no United Fund, in our knowledge, tries to include the multitude of mail campaigns. Most of these originate outside the area in which the federation operates and, under the present legal structure, there is little, if anything, that the federation can do to prevent mail solicitation—except by way of an "educational" program against contributing to such solicitations. Of course, beyond these campaigns, there are all kinds of appeals which the individual faces each year, and which could hardly be included in any probable United Fund. (It may be, of course, that the claim of a "single" campaign a year is merely a publicity or propaganda device. United Fund policy-makers may very well regard the problem of "total inclusiveness" as academic and one with which they will never have to deal, i.e., they may not care whether there are MOPS campaigns other than the United Fund.) Consequently, even if the United Fund should succeed in federating all local agencies, there are few funds which, presently, can rightly claim, even for the major appeals, that the goal of "Put All Your Begs in One Ask-it" has been met. It is certainly true that the number of MOPS fundraising campaigns has been reduced in communities—such as Detroit—where the United Fund is strong. Unfortunately, it is too early to determine if the United Funds will be able, over a period of time, to hold down the number of campaigns either by including new agencies or by training the public to shun such "independent" appeals. This is a problem for which Community Chests—actually the United Funds of their day—never succeeded in finding an adequate solution. The development of the "health" drives posed this problem for the Chests, and the methods of trying to cope with it are too numerous to mention. Nor were the Chests ever able, as far as we know, to include all local MOPS campaigns. How United Funds can handle the problem—after the initial enthusiasm has worn off—is obviously a moot question.

Actually, in Indianapolis, the intense discussion around whether or not to have a United Fund reflects an older vocabulary. By the 1956 definition of United Community Funds and Councils of America, Inc., Indianapolis already has a United Fund, i.e., its unified fundraising organization includes one "major" health agency, the Marion County Cancer Society (a unit of the American Cancer Society, Indiana Division). The only possible further United Fund question is therefore whether to "unify" Red Cross, and/or more of the "big five" health agencies and/or, perhaps, some other agencies. The commonest expression of the desired program, there, is the serial incorporation (or co-corporation) *for fundraising* in that order of (*a*) Red Cross, (*b*) as many other major health agencies as possible, and (*c*) other major agencies. It is widely believed that the accession of (*a*) would make (*b*) more susceptible, and the access of (*b*) or any part of it would render (*c*) more tractable.

22. E.g., Boy Scouts, Girl Scouts, Y.M.C.A., Y.W.C.A., Salvation Army and other "more national than local" agencies.

23. Perhaps it is not quite all historic accident. When tempers are cool and reasonableness is felt likely to have its day, problems tend to be posed in manageable terms of quantity or amount and degree; when a battle is to be organized (or a pseudo-battle), when tempers run high, when propaganda is to be made, the issues tend to be posed in black-white terms. The public side of war and politics are examples (on the private side, of course, negotiation and calculation in more reasonable terms goes on, and even the public "unconditional surrender" means something else behind the scenes). For the use of warlike thinking and military and war terms in connection with MOPS fundraising generally, see chapters 12 and 14.

24. *Federation Facts Book, 1956 United Community Campaigns* (New York: United Community Funds and Councils of America, 1956), pp. 7 and 8.

25. The disadvantages of "a multiplicity of campaigns" are obvious, and are widely protested. Some of the most frequently heard complaints from businessmen are, "There are too many campaigns," "They use too many of our men as volunteers," and "It costs us too much to solicit our employees for all of them." A workable solution to this problem therefore seems worth exploring. Other federations can help alleviate the condition, but, unless they approximate total federation, businesses are still subjected to numerous appeals. Not so many complainants seem to see that the more campaigns are "combined," the more choice among beneficiaries is reduced. This may not be so important to the donor. What should be equally obvious—that the greater the combination the harder it is to refuse altogether, and indeed the harder it is to refuse the precise amount asked—is also not so frequently spoken of, although "worries" in this direction are expressed. The relative rarity of expressed fear on this score may be because so many of our laymen informants have been or are deeply implicated on the fundraising side, and fewer deal with the problem of giving for their own corporation or professional group or peers.

26. "In-plant federation" is a species of unified fundraising in which only a part of the donor-aggregate (the corporately organized sector) is the object of a unified solicitation for part of the donandum for, usually, more agencies than are included in a Chest. What happens essentially is that each plant so federated has a single campaign for the "causes" of its own choice, and then divides up the proceeds between these causes in proportions of its own choosing. For further discussion, see last section of this chapter.

27. The United Fund budget review group in many cases does not review in detail the agency budgets (though Kansas City seems to be an exception). Rather, the United Fund may make allocations to federations of local agencies—e.g., Community Chest—and, indeed, many a major agency will affiliate with the United Fund only on the basis of no review of its budget being permitted. Thus, the budget is often in terms of broad areas of service rather than in terms of program. This would seem to vitiate the claim being discussed, since the effect of such a budgeting procedure is simply to put broad limits to all programs (if limits can be set at all), or to groups of programs, while the actual planning remains at the same level of control as prior to the United Fund.

28. *Budgeting for 1956* (New York: U.C.F. & C.A., no date), Chart A, p. 1. The evidence is, however, even here, by no means unequivocal. Many costs of any federated —or non-federated—campaign never appear in the financial statement of the fundraising organization, and may never be estimated. For example, "sponsored luncheons," for which the sponsors pay the cost, never show in the records of fundraising organizations as a dollar contribution and a dollar expenditure. Similarly, many materials are contributed which, had they been bought by the organization, would have been properly recorded as fundraising expenses.

Of a somewhat different nature are the costs to firms of the time of volunteer workers and the costs of carrying out employee solicitation. We know of no reliable estimate of the cost to firms of volunteer workers' time, but the hours must be enormous, relative to paid staff time. One large firm in Indianapolis estimates the cost to the firm of soliciting its workers at about one-third of the amount contributed by the workers (the firm stated the cost as a dollar amount and we computed the ratio).

We have by no means covered all such costs. At any rate, they are large—probably larger altogether than the total amounts reported as "expense." These qualifications to discussion of "campaign and administrative expense" should be borne in mind, since the ratio of "hidden" to reported expense may well be the factor which accounts for "reduced" cost of fundraising by United Funds.

29. Although some of the points are not direct quotations, the paraphrasing has preserved—to a great extent—the words and phrases of the sources.

30. Bruce Barton, "Independent Action and Thought Hailed by Bruce Barton," *The Heart Fund Story* (New York: American Heart Association, no date).

31. Irvin H. Page, "Federal Control is Foreseen if Voluntary Programs Fail," *ibid.*

32. Robert Keith Leavitt, *Common Sense about Fund Raising* (New York, 1949).

33. Rome A. Betts, "Will Giving be Regimented? Or Shall We Retain Free Choice?" *The Heart Fund Story*.

34. *Ibid*.

35. Even if he should be a member of the budgeting group (whether in Chest or United Fund) he has little power to control the specific appropriations—and, as a "disburser" of funds, his duties are defined as representing the interests of the whole community. He must, then, subjugate his interests as a donor to his responsibilities as a representative of the community, a task so patently difficult that it creates great strain and confusion in the budgeting process.

36. Even in the present Chest, heady dreams are dreamed and stirring stories told. One current dream is that of getting persons friendly to the Chest elected to the Boards of Directors of recalcitrant corporations, i.e., in effect, of *capturing the corporations for the Chest*. But this may not be all dream: persons, who have a right to know, allege enthusiastically that this *was* done in the last campaign, and that this really points the way. We must admit that before the boldness of this scheme the previously employed petty pressures pale.

37. For the young executive of a firm to refuse to contribute, or even to pledge less than his "fair share," is often tantamout to economic, and possibly, social suicide. We have heard prominent executives publicly assert and defend the procedure they use. One said in essence that his multi-million dollar corporation would not fire a man for contributing less than his fair share, but a senior executive would call him in, and tell him what he, personally, thought of him—in no uncertain terms. Another senior executive of a very large Indianapolis corporation told us with relish how a worker who failed to contribute his "fair share" would be faced with successive "interviews" by three committees: the last—the final recourse—a two-man committee representing the labor union and the higher ranks of management. Management, in many firms, views the "attitudes of personnel towards community responsibility" as a key measure of the employee's ability "to fit into our way of doing things." And "community responsibility" is here defined by company (usually management) policy. Nor is the pressure limited to economic sanctions. Friends often express attitudes which make it difficult to resist contributing at the "fair share" level. "Fair share" here means simply the "standards" which the local Chest or United Fund management has agreed upon, i.e., the quasi-tax rates set.

Of course, this discussion is applicable, to a lesser degree, to any federation, but in the United Fund situation, the resources of the whole community are usually so well mobilized as to make it nearly impossible to escape these pressures.

38. Not that case study is not useful for some purposes; but in examining arguments of this type, all parties can find some cases to support their mutually contradictory conclusions.

39. *The Heart Fund Story*. Interestingly enough, the third example, Buffalo, N.Y., raises another problem. How can an organization justify raising 50 per cent more than it "needs"? Unless the rather large amount is applied to reduce the goal in succeeding campaigns, this becomes a fairly serious question. Can an organization spend 50 per cent more than its "needs" effectively? And, if it can, does this then raise the level of "need" so that in the future it is 50 per cent higher?

40. The relation of these "health agencies" to research may deserve examination in its own right, though we have no space for detailed treatment here. Whether or not it is wise to make the provision of research money, and therewith the development of various fields of research, dependent to any sensible degree on public opinion could be a matter of very lively debate.

But, in any case, the health agencies today provide probably only a relatively small proportion of the research funds currently being allocated from all sources—including government, foundations, university funds, grants from individuals, etc.—for research on diseases. (Research in poliomyelitis may be an exception.) And it is hard to see how this situation could be changed appreciably. Moreover, unless the health organizations should change the way in which funds are distributed, there can hardly be a large increase in the amount available for research. Many health agencies distribute funds collected at the local level as follows: 40 per cent local, 20 per cent state and 40 per cent national. Consequently, if, as in the case of the Heart Association, the policy is to use one-half of the amount received by the national organization for research, for every extra $1 to be spent in research, five more dollars would have to be added to what was raised in the locality.

41. Survey Research Center, *The American Public Discuss Cancer and the American Cancer Society Campaign* (Ann Arbor: University of Michigan, 1948) and *The National Foundation.* The latter supports the point made at the end of the paragraph.

42. Since the data are contained in a number of tables in each study and since, in any event, the results are so inconclusive for this problem, we have not included the specific material.

43. The only comparison we were able to find (for a number of cities) was between the number of United Fund contributors and the number of contributors to the last separate Community Chest campaign. This clearly shows nothing as far as the number of persons reached by the independent campaigns is concerned. *1956 Experience in United Funds* (New York: Community Chests and Councils of America, Inc., no date).

44. This contention cannot be made too clear, since the "power of designation" is an illusion carefully fostered by most Chests and believed in by most citizens. The sole effect of a given contributor's "designating" on the back of his pledge-card which agency is to get his money, is to complicate the bookkeeping. "His" dollars go to that agency all right, but a corresponding number of somebody else's are taken away and redistributed according to the prearranged budget, so that every agency gets with designation what it would have got without designation. "Designation" is thus a delusion for most and a snare for some.

45. *Campaign Facts and Figures,* no. 8 (New York: United Community Funds and Councils of America, November 8, 1956) p. 1:

| Type of Organization | Number | 1957 amount raised as percentage of | |
| --- | --- | --- | --- |
| | | 1957 goal | 1956 amount raised |
| Community Chests (excluding United Fund) | 63 | 101.0% | 106.9% |
| All United Funds (other than first year)[a] | 67 | 99.2 | 106.3 |
| United Funds with Red Cross (not first year) | 56 | 99.0 | 106.2 |
| United Funds without Red Cross (not first year) | 11 | 100.0 | 107.0 |

[a]Computed by C.S.I.

It should be recognized that the evidence for 1957 was at the time of writing by no means all in.

46. However, at least one staunch supporter of the United Fund movement has expressed doubt about the ability of United Funds to handle the problem of new agencies. In a speech at the 12th Annual Public Relations Clinic sponsored by Community Chests and Councils of America, Inc., Mr. James Turrentine, Assistant to the President, in charge of Public Relations, Pitney-Bowes, Inc., suggested that a United Fund "is inflexible to new causes." And continuing with a related problem, he asked, "Do we freeze the individual agency and only permit growth as the funds grow?" He answered his question with the "hope" that the United Fund would permit differential growth among the agencies. But he also indicated that there is considerable doubt that the Polio Foundation would have received sufficient funds to carry on its program had the local chapters been members of United Funds.

47. "Large" and "small" are relative terms and we would be hard put to define them. Perhaps the distinction here is between "pennies per capita" campaigns and "dollars per capita" campaigns. For a city the size of Indianapolis the top figure

attainable—without the active intervention on behalf of the campaign by a sizeable group of "generals"—we would guess to be about $100,000 or 20¢ per capita.

48. The lay leader's control is subject to certain limitations also. For example, he is to some extent bound by the organization of preceding campaigns. And, too, there are probably some limits to what the traffic will bear, i.e., he must keep his campaign within limits tolerated by the donors—more particularly, the leading donors.

49. *1955 Experience in United Funds and Extended Federation Campaigns* (New York: Community Chests and Councils of America, Inc., no date) and *1956 Experience in United Funds.* Each bit of material presented here is drawn from differing numbers of United Funds in almost every instance. Consequently, great care must be exercised in comparing one piece of information with another. One example may serve to indicate how careful one must be in using this information. Such a simple report as the "Number of United Funds [including Red Cross] known to Community Chests and Councils, by Year" will do. These different figures are supposed to refer to the same situation.

NUMBER OF UNITED FUNDS INCLUDING RED CROSS KNOWN TO COMMUNITY CHESTS AND COUNCILS, BY YEAR, 1950-6

| Year | Reported in 1955 | Reported in 1956 |
|------|------------------|------------------|
| 1950 | 2 | 4 |
| 1951 | 12 | 23 |
| 1952 | 61 | 83 |
| 1953 | 127 | 156 |
| 1954 | 280 | 297 |
| 1955 | 383 | 412 |

The figures do not agree for any one of the six years reported. Yet the information recorded above is obviously the easiest of access and verification that might be sought concerning United Funds. Without, by implication, criticizing U.C.F. & C.A. or its staff, we cannot help feeling uneasy about the reliability of the associated data. Working under conditions of limited co-operation—if it can be called co-operation—from the member organizations, the national organization cannot hope to produce material which is consistent throughout. However, it would have been useful to all users of the more recent publication (*1956 Experience in United Funds*) if some explanation had been given as to the reasons for the differences between the two reports.

50. Most of the following evidence is based on *1956 Experience in United Funds.*

51. Put on another basis—i.e., comparing the number of "known consents" with the number of chapters (or equivalent local units) of each of the Big Six—we get *their* percentage "united." The percentages are of the following order: Cancer, 8 to 9; Crippled Children, 5 to 6; Heart, 12 to 13; Polio, less than 1; Red Cross, 15 to 16; T.B., less than 1; Big Six, taken together, about 8; Big Five—i.e., omitting Red Cross—about 5. (We cannot give exact percentages because the number of chapters continually changes.)

52. Not in order that the claims may be further credited, but merely to put in evidence the kind of claim made in general discussion, we are summarizing the 1955 and 1956 tables on p. 577, top. To make our point clear, if the forty-nine non-reporting cities in 1955 were all among the least successful, then the median gain for all new United Funds that year would be nearer 8 per cent than the 20 per cent reported. The same would be true *a fortiori* for 1956, if the same assumption is made about non-reporting cities.

53. *1956 Experience in United Funds,* p. 3.

54. Again assuming that the non-reporters are at the bottom of the distribution.

RESULTS OF FIRST YEAR OF UNITED FUND CAMPAIGNS COMPARED WITH TOTAL RAISED BY
ALL UNITED FUND AGENCIES IN THEIR LAST INDEPENDENT CAMPAIGNS

|  | Percentage increase | |
|---|---|---|
|  | Reported in 1955[a] (74 cities) | Reported in 1956[b] (117 cities) |
| First quartile[c] | 33.9% | 34.0% |
| Median | 20.0 | 19.6 |
| Third quartile[c] | 10.9 | 10.9 |

[a]From Table 6, *1955 Experience in United Funds and Extended Federation Campaigns.*
[b]From Table 6, *1956 Experience in United Funds.*
[c]The "first quartile" includes the 25 per cent most successful cities (of those reporting); the "third quartile" the 25 per cent least successful; the percentages reported are thus, for 1955, the increase-rates (roughly) for the 56th, 37th, and 18th most successful of the 74 reporting from a total of 123.

55. Again, not for credit, but for information as to the proponents' point of departure, we quote two tables (Table 7 from *1956 Experience,* Table 10 from *1955 Experience*):

TRENDS IN ALLOCATIONS FROM UNITED FUNDS TO SELECTED AGENCIES,* 1953-6

| Agency | Number of cities reporting | 1953 Receipts from United Funds | 1956 Allocations from United Funds | Percentage increase |
|---|---|---|---|---|
| Cancer | 77 | $1,875,013 | $ 2,494,787 | +33.1% |
| Heart | 61 | 765,930 | 1,070,097 | +39.7 |
| Red Cross | 79 | 9,663,555 | 10,247,946 | + 6.0 |

*Includes all cities which reported this information for both years.

PERCENTAGE INCREASE IN APPROPRIATIONS TO SELECTED APPEALS,* 1954-5

| Appeal | Number of cities reporting | Percentage increase 1954-5 |
|---|---|---|
| Cancer | 140 | 7.7% |
| Heart | 112 | 9.2 |
| Red Cross | 83 | —0.8 |

*Includes all cities which reported information for both years.

If the figures are at all reliable, the Red Cross average annual gain (from 1953 to 1956) of 2 per cent, and its 1954-5 loss of 0.8 per cent, are worth noting in view of what is taken as the primary issue for United Fund in Indianapolis: inclusion of the Red Cross as the "first step."
56. The new ones have to be excluded because of the practice of comparing their new take with what their Chest alone raised the previous year.
57. See Tables 13 and 14, *1956 Experience,* p. 7.
58. The proper comparison would, of course, be for new United Funds and between them and their previous constituents. As to how this comparison would result, we have no knowledge.
59. Note that United Funds not including Red Cross—the Indianapolis situation—were not included.

60. *Budgeting for 1956,* Table 6, p. 7.

61. Community Chests appropriated a larger median percapita than did the United Funds to the following agencies: Arthritis and Rheumatism, Boys' Clubs, Boy Scouts, Combined family and children's agencies, Day nurseries, Girls' Clubs, Girl Scouts, Hospitals and clinics (except mental), Jewish family and children's services, Mental Health Association, Mental health clinics, Non-sectarian children's agencies, Nursing services, Salvation Army, Settlements and Community Centers, YMCA.

62. Camp Fire Girls, Children's institutions, Cerebral Palsy, Jewish Community Centers, Non-sectarian family agencies.

63. Catholic Charities, Legal Aid Society, Travelers' Aid, YWCA.

64. *Budgeting for 1956,* Chart D, p. 6 and Table 8, p. 12. However, the *mean* per capita appropriations of United Funds appear to be somewhat higher than for Chests—but we have warned about the distorting effects of distributions like these on the mean before. Median percapita is a more meaningful figure.

65. We are knowingly excluding from attention, as impractical or unlikely, the possibility of "no federation" or "defederation" of existing combines, although even after eighty years of federated fundraising in America, some donors—we do not know what proportion—feel that the best form of fundraising is for each agency to raise on its own behalf the funds necessary to its operation. The ideal form of fundraising, for these people, is a free enterprise system in which competition operates "to weed out those agencies which do not meet with public approval and to stimulate those agencies which are popular enough to raise sufficient funds to permit expansion of program." Thus, for some donors, No Federation provides better checks, in the form of judgments by individual donors, on the efficiency of operation and the worthiness of the cause espoused by an agency. This is anathema to many professional fundraisers and some amateurs. They argue, and probably rightly so, that the cost of raising funds for agencies on an individual basis increases greatly as the number of separate campaigns increases. (There is reason to think that percentage cost of fundraising is generally a function of the size of the campaign, relative costs falling as dollar volume rises. This is not quite the same thing as saying that costs fall as number of campaigns fall, but the effect is similar.) It is also argued that the amount of "volunteer effort" required for a "multiplicity of campaigns" is increased. This argument is dubious, as has been indicated in the text. Another argument against defederation is based upon the view that the general public is not able to judge the value of or need for agencies any better than it can judge any other highly technical matter. The same fundraisers, however, claim to derive their general mandate, and their estimate of what should be each major agency's share, from "popular support."

One advantage to the donor of reduced or eliminated federation has to do with designation. It is not now possible for a donor to make his pledge to a specific agency or to exclude any agency from benefiting from his pledge. To give the illusion of some such freedom, almost every federated fundraising scheme permits a form of "designation"—the donor may state which agencies he wishes to share in his pledge and how much of the pledge each agency is to receive. These designations are, as far as we know, always "honored," but, under the budgeting procedures in use, this designation is effectively a fiction (as pointed out in note 44). Since the agencies are "deficit financed," the federation is committed to meeting the deficits of all the agencies—at least, so far as it is able to do so. Consequently, the net effect of designation is nil.

With No Federation, the donor not only has an effective privilege of "designating," but the very nature of the fundraising forces him to "designate." Many people in the Welfare Community see this as a grievous fault in non-federated appeals. In their view, the average donor simply hasn't the time, and if he did have the time, doesn't have the skills or information, to evaluate the worthiness of an appeal. Hence, it is said, federated fundraising provides a safeguard against rackets and against the continuation of agencies which have lost their function, or have no value to the community, and at the same time ensures support for the unpopular but "worthy" cause. Federated fundraising, they feel, provides "expert" control over the allocation of the "scarce commodity," the philanthropic dollar. (We shall look more closely at this view later in the discussion.)

Actually, it is possible to combine the "competitive" and the merger principle, if this is desired, by confronting one group of donors with a combined appeal and another group with a competitive one (as in Chicago). The corporate givers alone, or the givers in the whole corporately organized sector (including "employees") may be appealed to only as from a "United Fund" *in that sector,* while the "general public" is left as a "free competitive market" for all agencies to appeal to independently. The corporations (or the corporately organized sector) could then either follow public opinion in distribution by giving similarly, or compensate for its errors by giving in opposite proportions. Those who believe *Vox populi, vox Dei* will wish it to proceed in the first manner; those who believe that (in these respects) "The Public, Sir, is a great Beast" will wish it to proceed in the second. But the flexibility is possible, and the choices are there.

66. Such a solicitation program might raise all kinds of problems as far as the publicity of each organization is concerned. Further, the solicitor could hardly be used as "salesman" for each of the causes since he would be trying to sell too many items at once to make his sales talk very effective. Perhaps, however, there would be no more difficulty selling each agency with joint solicitation than with United Fund.

67. See note 65.

68. Not that we endorse such separation as meaningful, but that the agencies frequently so classify themselves and virtually teach the public so to think about and feel toward them.

69. Many "Directories of Services Available" produced by Health and Welfare Councils (or their equivalents) so attempt to classify the otherwise chaotic-seeming welter of agencies.

70. For details, see chapter 2, Appendix.

71. For some such wishes—for example, to discriminate in favor of males versus females, the young against the old, the unbroken against the broken, the middle class in preference to the lowest—see chapter 5.

72. It is *not* clear that any saving in volunteer or volunteered manpower—either in numbers or in time—would accrue. The federated campaign may require as much use of manpower as did the separate campaigns—or even more. But there probably is a tendency for a federation to use a large number of persons for a short period of time, while the separate campaigns may very well use a small number of people—often even the same people in each campaign—for a relatively long period of time. But this consequence, if the view is well founded, follows in *any* form of federation discussed in the text.

73. This would tend to ensure relatively effective operation of the agencies with regard both to efficiency and to provision of service.

74. Such funds as are sent outside the local community are almost entirely for the payment of dues to a national organization to which the local agencies are affiliated. The national organizations of this type provide primarily advisory service and a "clearing house" function; they do not carry on extensive programs apart from the program of the local organization.

75. Champaign-Urbana, Illinois, has such a federation.

76. Much, though not all Red Cross program is concerned with health. The main emphasis appears to be on the biological, as against the psychological or social, if one may be permitted such distinctions.

77. For the relevance of the agency's "age," see note 78.

78. Indeed, we have been told that, if it comes to forced unification, the *old* and established health agencies would rather unite with *old* and established social agencies than with *young* and, to them brash, health agencies.

79. There would, no doubt, be campaigns by organizations which refused to join the appropriate federation, as well as by organizations excluded from the federation. These probably would not have sufficient support to carry on a mass campaign, however. Additionally, there would continue, whether locally desired or not, the numerous mail appeals from organizations which lack local affiliates—barring the passage of effective (and constitutional) legislation prohibiting such solicitations.

80. It is said by many professional fundraisers that somewhat larger sums can be

raised if people are asked to contribute several times instead of once a year. This seems more probable in the case of persons who do not make pledges which are paid in instalments—either through payroll deduction or individually.

81. The numerous complaints we heard in the course of the study about the "excessive number of campaigns," appeared to be confined largely to executives and other managerial personnel of companies, and to the owners of smaller businesses. It is difficult to say how much resentment really is engendered by a "multiplicity of campaigns." Certainly the complaints we heard were made by persons of some importance to the MOPS fundraising organizations in Indianapolis; even though their number may be small, these persons have considerably more power and influence than mere number would indicate. We shall take another look at this problem later in this chapter.

82. It should also be possible in such a scheme to go some way towards meeting one objection of some people to many of the health drives; i.e., that many health drives (compared with one another) receive funds that are disproportionate to the incidence of the disease or diseases in which they are interested, or to some other criterion of "need."

Incidence (sometimes prevalence) is thus often used as a criterion of "need" of the agency. But the "need" of the organization is also related to other things such as relative cost of research (e.g., large research centers or many scattered investigators), cost of prevention, cost of cure and/or care in individual cases, problems of diagnosis, cost of "educational" publicity (to stimulate the public and "needle" the doctors). Mere incidence or prevalence has no known relation to "need"—or, indeed, by itself, to any sort of *planning* wisdom.

But it might not be too much to hope that, if once the health agencies were brought together into one federation, they would exert some vigilance and police powers over one another. At least, it would bring those with a common preoccupation with the field of health, and competitive interests within that field, into frequent enough association to reduce, perhaps, in the common interest, the more unabashedly wild of the "all the traffic will bear" performers.

82. Such a form of organization, we were satisfied, seemed to work well in Chicago, and we could see no special circumstances there that would make its adoption elsewhere *prima facie* contraindicated.

83. Presumably, also, it could be expanded to include other classes of donors, if desired—though as it did so it would approach what we have discussed as a United Fund.

84. This, too, might seem like a wild scheme—except for the fact that we discovered a number of laymen, central to present fundraising policy-making, ardent supporters of "the United Fund idea" who thought that just this—total federation—was what a United Fund was designed to bring about.

85. We know of no attempt to organize such a scheme, though we heard such ambitions reported from other cities.

86. As we have seen in chapter 8 and elsewhere, even the fairly weak United Funds and strong Chests operate something like a private taxation system.

87. We have avoided using the term "competition" because it is not at all clear that competition is operative in the philanthropic field. Much has been said about the effects of competition for the philanthropic dollar, but it is highly doubtful that the fundraising organizations have approached anywhere near the limits in terms of dollars available to philanthropy. Hence, they are no more in competition with each other than they are with appliance dealers, taverns, movies, etc.

88. It will not do, we think, to say that the "ultimate interest of the solicitors and the donors is the same—a good community." Of course it is. So is the ultimate interest of labor and management the same—a good economy; but few would be willing on this ground to suggest that wage-rates be set by a mixed committee on which no one represented anything, or that one should "watch out for" the interests of the other. The economy in the American political system seems to fare best when both sets of interests, well organized and clear-headed about their common stake *and* their several separate stakes, bargain in good faith. It is true that the common interest must "ultimately" contain the self-interest; but, meanwhile, it must not be permitted to override it.

If there is some virtue in blurring, with regard to donor-solicitor relations, what is kept so clear in management-labor ones, it is difficult to discover what that virtue is.

89. We use this term in deference to custom and to simplify communication. It is something of a misnomer since In-Plant Federation is not a "federation" (a combination of agencies) but a combined appeal—often forced on one or more of the agencies included in the combined appeal—within a "giving unit" and essentially under its own control.

90. This does not necessarily imply that all employees of the organization are protected from all other solicitations. This *may* be one of the features of In-Plant Federation, but it is certainly not a necessary feature. It is quite possible that an employee would ask other employees of his acquaintance to support his "favorite good work," but this would be on a private basis and would lack the formal sanction of the organization. Further, it would not be permitted as a general solicitation of the organization.

91. This is true for reasons analogical to those in other fields where the dollar volume has been increased by the institution of instalment credit. "Payroll deduction" similarly permits a more generous disposal of income not yet earned—and it increases charitable payments just as it increases the purchase of government bonds.

92. As such schemes became general, such a formula could easily put a premium on some pretty wild goal-setting.

93. In-Plant Federation may or may not include the pledge of the organization in whose plant the federation operates—almost always a firm. While the pledge of the organization—the "firm gift"—is often made a part of the In-Plant Federation total, it is not essential that this be so, and the solicitation of employees only could be, and often is, handled on the In-Plant Federation basis.

94. There is no limit on the kinds of appeals to which it could be responsive, for example.

95. AID—Associated In-Group Donors—in Los Angeles, functions as a somewhat broader form of In-Plant Federation, and is very similar to the Chicago Community Fund, though AID *is* a donor group rather than an agency group.

96. For previous discussion of the representativeness of the laymen, see chapter 11.

97. If this does not happen, he may be said to be not quite "loyal" or, in social work parlance, "not sufficiently involved." See again discussion in chapter 11.

98. Even so, the donor is not completely defenceless. But his sole refuge, very nearly, is gentle sabotage, i.e., giving just-not-sufficient sums as a way of expressing simultaneously his sympathy and his protest. Under these circumstances, Chest (or similar MOPS fundraising) affairs tend to be poorly conducted, and this in turn both permits the would-be private taxation system to be avoided and gives fresh occasion for the expression of dissatisfaction.

99. See M. G. Ross, *Community Organization,* for some of the distinctions involved.

100. Locally, we have yet to see the damage that this will do to the agencies severally, although we are beginning to see signs of it; some agency executives are already alarmed, particularly about the drawing into the Council's orbit of those laymen on whom the agencies traditionally rely for aid and guidance.

101. Although the establishment of a donors' protective league appears to us a necessary step, it may not be sufficient in itself to remedy the situation which exists presently in Indianapolis. Actually, such an association can only protect the donor; it cannot make the agencies or fundraisers function well, though it may stop them in certain respects from operating badly.

102. Probably no more than an executive and a secretary, initially. Of course, if membership warrants, the organization might grow much larger (i.e., if real economies result—increases in satisfaction per dollar expended).

103. Many of the problems which we will not discuss are situational in nature, i.e., apply only to particular types of endorsement and control.

104. City of Indianapolis, Indiana, General Ordinance No. 71-1942 (effective October 24, 1942), *Creating a* CHARITY SOLICITATIONS COMMISSION *and Providing for the Licensing and Regulation of Charity and Similar Solicitations in the City of Indianapolis* repeals and supersedes General Ordinance No. 13, 1934.

105. In other cities, the movement to control—mostly via "selective endorsement" or

its equivalent—goes further back, indeed to the 1920's or earlier. This movement in Chicago, we are told, was closely connected with the founding of the Chicago School of Civics and Philanthropy, which preceded the present famous School of Social Service Administration of the University of Chicago. The movement and its unforeseen consequences actually began as a "Subscriptions Investigating Department," which in turn grew out of a request made by Chicago's Mayor and social agencies to the Association of Commerce.

It is curious that problems similar to those of today led, through a Chamber of Commerce, to the founding of a school for professionals, and that out of the consequent growth of professionalism new problems arise for the layman, and new solutions have to be sought. Perhaps the moral is that "solutions" are intrinsically transient, and that each generation must re-solve the problems of the preceding generation, only now in new terms relevant for its day.

106. Even the Chest campaign in 1955 may have been in violation of the ordinance. Paragraph (q) of Section 4 of the ordinance forbids issuing a licence to organizations which use methods which are misleading to those solicited as to the manner in which the funds are distributed.

Several campaign leaders and speakers for the Chest stated that the funds were to be distributed to "fifty Red Feather Agencies," yet there were at that time by staff count and recount fewer than forty agencies included in the Indianapolis Community Chest. The literature more carefully spoke of "fifty Red Feather Services," but the term was designed for ambiguity and in verbal communication "services" was translated into "agencies"—with the intended effect.

107. 130 Ind. 149 and 211 Ind. 621.

108. 204 Ind. 79.

109. An interesting case for the United Fund plus Charities Regulation proponents is *American Cancer Society* v. *City of Dayton* (1953) 114 N.E. (2d) 219. Dayton had attempted to deny the plaintiff the right to solicit funds independently since the Community Fund had made an allocation to the American Cancer Society. The Ohio Supreme Court found for the plaintiff, holding unconstitutional those provisions of the city ordinance which empowered the licensing commission to deny a licence if it found that another charity drive had covered this same subject.

110. The work of the Subscriptions Investigating Committee is part of the work of the Division of Health, Welfare and Education of the Chicago Association of Commerce and Industry.

111. Another organization of importance is the National Information Bureau which supplies information to subscribers on what is happening in the control of solicitation. But this is a national service, and our main concern here is with the local problem of control and approval.

112. Some such organizations, even more cautious, will not go so far as to "approve" or fail to approve. They will simply list those organizations that other approved organizations approve—and leave the client to infer, as well he may in his own terms, that all others are suspect or disapproved.

113. Fundraising techniques currently disapproved of include such things as telephone appeals by paid solicitors on a commission basis; sending unrequested merchandise, tickets, etc., on a "remit or return" basis; entertainments where the agency receives a disproportionately low percentage of the gross income; and general appeals in which the cost is greater than 25 per cent (an arbitrary figure) of the total amount raised.

114. The Chamber of Commerce functions, then, like a donors' organization for the industrial and commercial donors. The objection to such an organization, if any, is that in the present state of complexity such a function needs more special attention, knowledge, and skill than the more or less casual attachment to a Chamber of Commerce would, frequently, make possible. The question, moreover, of whether a Chamber of Commerce is "politically" wise to accept such an additional responsibility needs careful examination before a positive answer can lightly be returned.

115. Such a monopoly would be ripe for government intervention and control, particularly so if an economic crisis such as the Depression developed which would require support beyond the resources of private philanthropy.

116. See M. G. Ross, *Community Organization.*

117. The last word is hereby given in rejoinder to some of the views expressed in this chapter. The statement that follows represents the considered judgment—after reading the chapter—of some thoughtful Indianapolis laymen, long interested and deeply involved in the leadership both of the Chest and the movement for a United Fund.

"The authors recommend 'In-Plant Federated Campaigns' and a 'Donors' Association' in lieu of a 'United Fund.' In our opinion, a logical analysis of the facts presented in this book does not appear to support this conclusion.

"The United Fund would receive contributions from firms, their employees and foundations. It would constitute one annual solicitation for all local charitable, character building and health agencies plus national health programs. Techniques would be employed similar to those used in In-Plant Federated Campaigns such as one employee campaign a year with a payroll deduction plan except that (1) the United Fund and its affiliated organizations would assume the responsibility for studying agency budgets and allocating funds, and (2) the United Fund would recommend uniform standards of giving by contributors.

"In-Plant Federated Campaigns permit each company or employee group to make its own allocations to various charitable agencies. It is illogical to assume that employees in hundreds of plants could intelligently budget these contributions without adequate knowledge of the needs of these agencies.

"It takes days of study of agency budgets and the interviewing of key representatives of agencies to budget intelligently the community's charitable gifts. The criticism of this program has been that the members of the budget committee each have personal interests in various agencies. This is correct and if they had no such interest in one or more agencies, they would not be qualified to compare and review the budgets of many agencies. However, this is no factor in controlling allocations to any agency because only one or two members of a budget committee, which would constitute less than 10 per cent of the membership of the budget committee, would have any personal interest in any agency whose budget would be under consideration.

"The authors also contend that the amounts allocated each year under this method are too greatly influenced by the amount of allocations in the prior year. It appears essential that annual allocations be influenced by amounts allocated in prior years so that there can be some continuity of operations of the various agencies who are members of the Community Chest or United Fund. No trained staff or continuous program could otherwise be developed. It is the budget committee's responsibility to control trends in the amount of budgets and the general programs to which the funds are allocated so that the services of the various agencies may continuously be improved and made more effective.

"Therefore it appears, based upon the above analysis, that the most intelligent method of budgeting is that made by a budget committee of a United Fund after a careful and intelligent analysis of the needs of these community and health agencies.

"A Donors' Association is nothing more than a Community Chest or a United Fund under a different name because the personnel who would comprise the budget committee of a Donors' Association would basically be the same as that of a budget committee of a United Fund or a Community Chest in as much as people from the same leadership group would occupy positions on all of these committees.

"If the members of a Donors' Association were so far removed from the agencies as to have no personal interest in any of them, they could not budget intelligently.

"It appears that a United Fund will raise more charitable funds in a community for the following reasons:

"1. It attracts more outstanding business and community leadership because it is a new and successful program that enables this group to present more effectively the donor's viewpoint to the recipients of the community's charitable contributions.

"2. It creates a new enthusiasm in such community leaders because of their desire to reduce the expense and the number of annual charitable solicitations.

"3. It raises more money, or a comparable sum of money, than was raised previously by the same agencies in many large cities.

"4. The percentage cost of fund raising is reduced because of the economies that result in one large campaign compared to the costs of multiple campaigns.

"5. In addition, less aggregate manpower is needed on an annual basis because of the reduced number of charitable campaigns.

"6. Further, the payroll deduction contribution plan at the employee level of giving can be more readily sold under the United Fund than under any other plan because of the greater cooperation of employers, employees and community leaders."

## CHAPTER 15

1. Negative correlations, of course, since what is striking is contrast.

2. Becoming increasingly "monastic" we suggest as bureaucracies grow in size—except where suitable countermeasures in the form of countenanced sabotage are introduced and accepted. For the uses of sabotage see T. Veblen, *The Engineers and the Price-System.*

3. Indianapolis is one case in point, at least with reference to the campaign. Following a period of relatively quiet, sober, hoopla-free campaigning, it has now returned to a period in which solicitors, playing at Indians, are encouraged to "scalp Chief Red Feather" with the Indian motif (not the scalping terminology) carried throughout this section of the campaign.

# INDEX

# Index

# Acknowledgments

GRATEFUL ACKNOWLEDGMENT is made to the following institutions, organizations, publishers, and journals for permission to quote from books or articles published by them: American Heart Association, *The Heart Fund Story;* *American Journal of Sociology* (published by University of Chicago Press), "The Institutional Office and the Person," by Everett C. Hughes, November, 1937; American Red Cross, Indianapolis Chapter, various printed and multigraphed documents; Barnard College, an essay by David Riesman published in *Individualism Reconsidered* (Free Press, 1954); Bobbs-Merrill Company, Inc., *Hoosier,* by Heath Bowman (1941); Citizens Committee of Greater Indianapolis, *The Tattler,* issue of July, 1956; Columbia University Press, *Philanthropic Foundations and Higher Education,* by Ernest Victor Hollis (1938); Free Press, *Recent Trends in Occupational Mobility,* by Natalie Rogoff (1953); Harcourt, Brace and Company, Inc., *Middletown,* by Robert S. and Helen Merrell Lynd (1929); Harper & Brothers, *Community Organization, Theory and Principles,* by Murray G. Ross (1955); Indiana University, Division of Social Service, unpublished Master's theses by Mary Sinclair and by Mildred Pauline Beard *et al.;* Indianapolis Chamber of Commerce, *The Indianapolis Story of Progress, 1946-1954;* Indianapolis Community Chest, various printed and multigraphed documents; Alfred A. Knopf, Incorporated, *Indiana: An Interpretation,* by John Bartlow Martin (1947); McGraw-Hill Book Company, Inc., *The Community and Social Welfare,* by Cecil Clare North; Macmillan Company, *Organization for Social Welfare,* by George B. Mangold (1934); National Bureau of Economic Research Incorporated, *Corporation Contributions to Organized Community Welfare Services,* by Pierce Williams and Frederick E. Croxton (1930); National Council of the Churches of Christ in the United States of America, *Churches and Social Welfare,* volume II, *The Changing Scene* (1955); *New York Times,* issue of April 6, 1955; Russell Sage Foundation, *Philanthropic Foundations,* by F. Emerson Andrews (1956); *Social Forces* (published by University of North Carolina Press), "Philanthropic Activity and the Business Career," by Aileen D. Ross, March, 1954; *Time,* "The Hat Passer," issue of July 16, 1956; *World Almanac and Book of Facts for 1956,* edited by Harry Hansen; United Community Funds and Councils of America, Incorporated, various publications (Mrs. Esther M. Moore, Director of the Department of Research and Statistics of this organization, kindly gave us permission to quote from her letter of October 8, 1954, to Community Surveys, Inc.).